HANDBOOK ON COMPUTER LEARNING AND INTELLIGENCE

Volume 2: Deep Learning, Intelligent Control and Evolutionary Computation

HANDBOOK ON COMPUTER LEARNING AND INTELLIGENCE

Volume 2: Deep Learning, Intelligent Control and Evolutionary Computation

Editor

Plamen Parvanov Angelov

Lancaster University, UK

NEW JERSEY · LONDON · SINGAPORE · BEIJING · SHANGHAI · HONG KONG · TAIPEI · CHENNAI · TOKYO

Published by

World Scientific Publishing Co. Pte. Ltd.

5 Toh Tuck Link, Singapore 596224

USA office: 27 Warren Street, Suite 401-402, Hackensack, NJ 07601

UK office: 57 Shelton Street, Covent Garden, London WC2H 9HE

Library of Congress Cataloging-in-Publication Data
Names: Angelov, Plamen P., editor.
Title: Handbook on computer learning and intelligence / editor,
    Plamen Parvanov Angelov, Lancaster University, UK.
Other titles: Handbook on computational intelligence.
Description: New Jersey : World Scientific, [2022] | Includes bibliographical references and index. |
    Contents: Volume 1. Explainable AI and supervised learning --
    Volume 2. Deep learning, intelligent control and evolutionary computation.
Identifiers: LCCN 2021052472 | ISBN 9789811245145 (set) | ISBN 9789811246043 (v. 1 ; hardcover) |
    ISBN 9789811246074 (v. 2 ; hardcover) | ISBN 9789811247323 (set ; ebook for institutions) |
    ISBN 9789811247330 (set ; ebook for individuals)
Subjects: LCSH: Expert systems (Computer science)--Handbooks, manuals, etc. |
    Neural networks (Computer science)--Handbooks, manuals, etc. | Systems engineering--
    Data processing--Handbooks, manuals, etc. | Intelligent control systems--Handbooks, manuals, etc. |
    Computational intelligence--Handbooks, manuals, etc.
Classification: LCC QA76.76.E95 H3556 2022 | DDC 006.3/3--dc23/eng/20211105
LC record available at https://lccn.loc.gov/2021052472

British Library Cataloguing-in-Publication Data
A catalogue record for this book is available from the British Library.

For any available supplementary material, please visit
https://www.worldscientific.com/worldscibooks/10.1142/12498#t=suppl

Desk Editors: Nandha Kumar/Amanda Yun

Typeset by Stallion Press
Email: enquiries@stallionpress.com

Printed in Singapore

Preface

The Handbook aims to be a one-stop-shop for the various aspects of the broad research area of *Computer learning and Intelligence*. It is organized in two volumes and five parts as follows:

Volume 1 includes two parts:

     Part 1   Explainable AI

     Part II Supervised Learning

Volume 2 has three parts:

     Part III Deep Learning

     Part IV Intelligent Control

     Part V   Evolutionary Computation

The Handbook has twenty-six chapters in total, which detail the theory, methodology and applications of *Computer Learning and Intelligence*. These individual contributions are authored by some of the leading experts in the respective areas and often are co-authored by a small team of associates. They offer a cocktail of individual contributions that span the spectrum of the key topics as outlined in the titles of the five parts. In total, over 67 authors from over 20 different countries contributed to this carefully crafted final product. This collaborative effort brought together leading researchers and scientists form USA, Canada, Wales, Northern Ireland, England, Japan, Sweden, Italy, Spain, Austria, Slovenia, Romania, Singapore, New Zealand, Brazil, Russia, India, Mexico, Hong Kong, China, Pakistan and Qatar.

The scope of the Handbook covers the most important aspects of the topic of *Computer Learning and Intelligence*.

Preparing, compiling and editing this Handbook was an enjoyable and inspirational experience.

I hope you will also enjoy reading it, will find answers to your questions and will use this book in your everyday work.

Plamen Parvanov Angelov
Lancaster, UK
3 June 2022

About the Editor

 **Professor Plamen Parvanov Angelov** holds a Personal Chair in Intelligent Systems and is Director of Research at the School of Computing and Communications at Lancaster University, UK. He obtained his PhD in 1993 and DSc (Doctor of Sciences) degree in 2015 when he also become Fellow of IEEE. Prof. Angelov is the founding Director of the Lancaster Intelligent, Robotic and Autonomous systems (LIRA) Research Centre which brings together over 60 faculty/academics across fifteen different departments of Lancaster University. Prof. Angelov is a Fellow of the European Laboratory for Learning and Intelligent Systems (ELLIS) and of the Institution of Engineering and Technology (IET) as well as a Governor-at-large of the International Neural Networks Society (INNS) for a third consecutive three-year term following two consecutive terms holding the elected role of Vice President. In the last decade, Prof. Angelov is also Governor-at-large of the Systems, Man and Cybernetics Society of the IEEE. Prof. Angelov founded two research groups (the Intelligent Systems Research group in 2010 and the Data Science group at 2014) and was a founding member of the Data Science Institute and of the CyberSecurity Academic Centre of Excellence at Lancaster.

Prof. Angelov has published over 370 publications in leading journals and peer-reviewed conference proceedings, 3 granted US patents, 3 research monographs (by Wiley, 2012 and Springer, 2002 and 2018) cited over 12300 times with an h-index of 58 (according to Google Scholar). He has an active research portfolio in the area of computer learning and intelligence, and internationally recognized results into online and evolving learning and algorithms. More recently, his research is focused on explainable deep learning as well as anthropomorphic and empirical computer learning.

Prof. Angelov leads numerous projects (including several multimillion ones) funded by UK research councils, EU, industry, European Space Agency, etc. His research was recognized by the 2020 Dennis Gabor Award for "outstanding contributions to engineering applications of neural networks", *The Engineer Innovation and Technology 2008 Special Award'* and *'For outstanding Services'* (2013) by IEEE and INNS. He is also the founding co-Editor-in-Chief of Springer's journal on *Evolving Systems* and Associate Editor of several leading international journals, including *IEEE Transactions on Cybernetics, IEEE Transactions on Fuzzy Systems, IEEE Transactions on AI*, etc. He gave over 30 dozen keynote/plenary talks at high profile conferences. Prof. Angelov was General Co-Chair of a number of high-profile IEEE conferences and is the founding Chair of the Technical Committee on Evolving Intelligent Systems, Systems, Man and Cybernetics Society of the IEEE. He is also co-chairing the working group (WG) on a new standard on Explainable AI created by his initiative within the Standards Committee of the Computational Intelligent Society of the IEEE which he chaired from 2010–2012. Prof. Angelov is the founding co-Director of one of the funded programs by ELLIS on Human-centered machine learning. He was a member of the International Program Committee of over 100 international conferences (primarily IEEE conferences).

Acknowledgments

The Editor would like to acknowledge the unwavering support and love of his wife Rositsa, his children (Mariela and Lachezar) as well as of his mother, Lilyana.

Contents

Handbook on Computer Learning and Intelligence

Introduction by the Editor

You are holding in your hand the second edition of the handbook that was published six years ago as *Handbook on Computational Intelligence*. The research field has evolved so much during the last five years that we decided to not only update the content with new chapters but also change the title of the handbook. At the same time, the core chapters (15 out of 26) have been written and significantly updated by the same authors. The structure of the book is also largely the same, though some parts evolved to cover new phenomena better. For example, the part Deep Learning evolved from the artificial neural networks, and the part Explainable AI evolved from fuzzy logic. The new title, *Computer Learning and Intelligence*, better reflects the new state-of-the-art in the area that spans machine learning and artificial intelligence (AI), but is more application and engineering oriented rather than being theoretically abstract or statistics oriented like many other texts that also use these terms.

The term *computer learning* is used instead of the common term *machine learning* deliberately. Not only does it link with the term *computational intelligence* but it also reflects more accurately the nature of learning algorithms that are of interest. These are implemented on computing devices spanning from the Cloud to the Edge, covering personal and networked computers and other computerized tools. The term *machine* is more often used in a mechanical and mechatronic context as a physical device contrasting the (still) electronic nature of the computers. In addition, the term *machine learning*, the genesis of which stems from the research area of AI, is now used almost as a synonym for *statistical learning*. In fact, *learning* is much more than function approximation, parameter learning, and number fitting. An important element of learning is reasoning, knowledge representation, expression and handling (storage, organization, retrieval), as well as decision-making and cognition. Statistical learning is quite successful today, but it seems to oversimplify some of these aspects. In this handbook, we aim to provide all perspectives, and therefore, we combine computer learning with intelligence.

Talking about intelligence, we mentioned *computational intelligence*, which was the subject of the first edition of the handbook. As is well known, this term itself came around toward the end of the last century and covers areas of research that are inspired and that "borrow"/"mimic" such forms of natural intelligence as the human brain (artificial neural networks), human reasoning (fuzzy logic and systems), and natural evolution (evolutionary systems). Intelligence is also at the core of the widely used term AI. The very idea of developing systems, devices, algorithms, and techniques that possess characteristics of *intelligence* and are computational (not just conceptual) dates back to the middle of the 20th century or even earlier, but only now it is becoming truly widespread, moving from the labs to the real-life applications.

In this handbook, while not claiming to provide an exhaustive picture of this dynamic and fast-developing area, we provide some key directions and examples written in self-contained chapters, which are, however, organized in parts on topics such as:

- Explainable AI
- Supervising Learning
- Deep Learning
- Intelligent Control
- Evolutionary Computation

The primary goal of *Computer Learning and Intelligence* is to provide efficient computational solutions to the existing open problems from theoretical and application points of view with regard to the understanding, representation, modeling, visualization, reasoning, decision, prediction, classification, analysis, and control of physical objects, environmental or social phenomena, etc., to which the traditional methods, techniques, and theories (primarily so-called first principles based, deterministic, or probabilistic, often expressed as differential equations, regression, and Bayesian models, and stemming from mass and energy balance) cannot provide a valid or useful/practical solution.

Another specific feature of *Computer Learning and Intelligence* is that it offers solutions that bear characteristics of *intelligence*, which is usually attributed to humans only. This has to be considered broadly rather than literally, as is the area of AI. This is, perhaps, clearer with fuzzy logic, where systems can make decisions very much like humans do. This is in a stark contrast to the deterministic-type expert systems or probabilistic associative rules. One can argue that artificial neural networks, including deep learning, process the data in a manner that is similar to what the human brain does. For evolutionary computation, the argument is that the population of candidate solutions "evolves" toward the optimum in a manner similar to the way species or living organisms evolve in nature.

The handbook is composed of 2 volumes and 5 parts, which contain 26 chapters. Eleven of these chapters are new in comparison to the first edition, while the other 15 chapters are substantially improved and revised. More specifically,

Volume 1 includes Part I (Explainable AI) and Part II (Supervised Learning).

Volume 2 includes Part III (Deep Learning), Part IV (Intelligent Control), and Part V (Evolutionary Computation).

In Part I the readers can find six chapters on explainable AI, including:

- *Explainable AI and Computational Intelligence: Past and Present*

  This new chapter provides a historical perspective of explainable AI. It is written by Dr. Mojtaba Yeganejou and Prof. Scott Dick from the University of Alberta, Canada.

- *Fundamentals of Fuzzy Sets Theory*

  This chapter is a thoroughly revised version of the chapter with the same title from the first edition of the handbook. It provides a step-by-step introduction to the theory of fuzzy sets, which itself is anchored in the theory of reasoning and is one of the most prominent and well-developed forms of explainable AI (the others being decision trees and symbolic AI). It is written by one of the leading experts in this area, former president of the International Fuzzy Systems Association (IFSA), Prof. Fernando Gomide from UNICAMP, Campinas, Brazil.

- *Granular Computing*

  This chapter is also a thoroughly revised version from the first edition of the handbook and is written by two of the pioneers in this area, Profs. Witold Pedrycz from the University of Alberta, Canada, and Andrzej Bargiela. Granular computing became a cornerstone of the area of explainable AI, and this chapter offers a thorough review of the problems and solutions that granular computing offers.

- *Evolving Fuzzy and Neuro-Fuzzy Systems: Fundamentals, Stability, Explainability, Useability, and Applications*

  Since its introduction around the turn of the century by Profs. Plamen Angelov and Nikola Kasabov, the area of evolving fuzzy and neuro-fuzzy systems has been constantly developing as a form of explainable AI and machine learning. This thoroughly revised chapter, in comparison to the version in the first edition, offers a review of the problems and some of the solutions. It is authored by one of the leading experts in this area, Dr. Edwin Lughofer from Johannes Kepler University Linz, Austria.

- *Incremental Fuzzy Machine Learning for Online Classification of Emotions in Games from EEG Data Streams*

This new chapter is authored by Prof. Daniel Leite and Drs. Volnei Frigeri Jr and Rodrigo Medeiros from Adolfo Ibáñez University, Chile, and the Federal University of Minas Gerais, Brazil. It offers one specific approach to a form of explainable AI and its application to games and EEG data stream processing.

- *Causal Reasoning*

  This new chapter is authored by Drs. Ramin Ramezani and Wenhao Zhang and Prof. Arash Naeim). It describes the very important topic of causality in AI.

Part II consists of six chapters, which cover the area of supervised learning:

- *Fuzzy Classifiers*

  This is a thoroughly revised and refreshed chapter that was also a part of the first edition of the handbook. It covers the area of fuzzy rule-based classifiers, which combine explainable AI and intelligence, more generally, as well as the area of machine or computer learning. It is written by Prof. Hamid Bouchachia from Bournemouth University, UK.

- *Kernel Models and Support Vector Machines*

  This chapter offers a very skillful review of one of the hottest topics in research and applications related to supervised computer learning. It is written by Drs. Denis Kolev, Mikhail Suvorov, and Dmitry Kangin and is a thorough revision of the version that was included in the first edition of the handbook.

- *Evolving Connectionist Systems for Adaptive Learning and Knowledge Discovery: From Neuro-Fuzzy to Spiking, Neurogenetic, and Quantum Inspired: A Review of Principles and Applications*

  This chapter offers a review of one of the cornerstones of computer learning and intelligence, namely the evolving connectionist systems, and is written by the pioneer in this area, Prof. Nikola Kasabov from the Auckland University of Technology, New Zealand.

- *Supervised Learning Using Spiking Neural Networks*

  This is a new chapter written by Drs. Abeegithan Jeyasothy from the Nanyang Technological University, Singapore; Shirin Dora from the University of Ulster, Northern Ireland, UK; Sundaram Suresh from the Indian Institute of Science; and Prof. Narasimhan Sundararajan, who recently retired from the Nanyang Technological University, Singapore. It covers the topic of supervised computer learning of a particular type of artificial neural networks that holds a lot of promise—spiking neural networks.

- *Fault Detection and Diagnosis based on LSTM Neural Network Applied to a Level Control Pilot Plant*

This is a thoroughly revised and updated chapter in comparison to the version in the first edition of the handbook. It covers an area of high industrial interest and now includes long short-term memory type of neural networks and is authored by Drs. Emerson V. de Oliveira, Yuri Thomas Nunes, and Malison Ribeira Santos and Prof. Luiz Affonso Guedez from the Federal University of Rio Grande du Nord, Natal, Brazil.

- *Conversational Agents: Theory and Applications*

  This is a new chapter that combines intelligence with supervised computer learning. It is authored by Prof. Mattias Wahde and Dr. Marco Virgolin from the Chalmers University, Sweden.

The second volume consist of three parts. The first of these, part III, is devoted to deep learning and consists of five chapters, four of which are new and specially written for the second edition of the handbook:

- *Deep Learning and Its Adversarial Robustness: A Brief Introduction*

  This new chapter, written by Drs. Fu Wang, Chi Zhang, PeiPei Xu, and Wenjie Ruan from Exeter University, UK, provides a brief introduction to the hot topic of deep learning to understand its robustness under adversarial perturbations.

- *Deep Learning for Graph-Structured Data*

  This new chapter written by leading experts in the area of deep learning, Drs. Luca Pasa and Nicolò Navarin and Prof. Alessandro Sperduti, describes methods that are specifically tailored to graph-structured data.

- *A Critical Appraisal on Deep Neural Networks: Bridge the Gap from Deep Learning to Neuroscience via XAI*

  This new chapter, written by Anna-Sophia Bartle from the University of Tubingen, Germany; Ziping Jiang from Lancaster University, UK; Richard Jiang from Lancaster University UK, Ahmed Bouridane from Northumbria University, UK, and Somaya Almaadeed from Qatar University, provides a critical analysis of the deep learning techniques trying to bridge the divide between neuroscience and explainable AI

- *Ensemble Learning*

  This is a thoroughly revised chapter written by the same authors as in the first edition (Dr. Yong Liu and Prof. Qiangfu Zhao) and covers the area of ensemble learning.

- *A Multistream Deep Rule-Based Ensemble System for Aerial Image Scene Classification*

  This is a new chapter contributed by Dr. Xiaowei Gu from the University of Aberystwyth in Wales, UK, and by Prof. Plamen Angelov. It provides an explainable-by-design form of deep learning, which can also take the form of linguistic rule base and is applied to aerial image scene classification.

Part IV consists of four chapters covering the topic of intelligent control:

- *Fuzzy Model-Based Control: Predictive and Adaptive Approach*

  This chapter is a thorough revision of the chapter form the first edition of the handbook and is co-authored by Prof. Igor Škrjanc and Dr. Sašo Blažič from Ljubljana University, Slovenia.

- *Reinforcement Learning with Applications in Automation Control and Game Theory*

  This chapter written by renowned world leaders in this area, Dr. Kyriakos G. Vamvoudakis from the Georgia Institute of Technology, Prof. Frank L. Lewis from the University of Texas, and Dr. Draguna Vrabie from the Pacific Northwest National Laboratory in the USA. In this thoroughly revised and updated chapter in comparison to the version in the first edition, the authors describe reinforcement learning that is being applied not only to systems control but also to game theory.

- *Nature-Inspired Optimal Tuning of Fuzzy Controllers*

  This chapter is also a thorough revision from the first edition by the same authors, Prof. Radu-Emil Precup and Dr. Radu-Codrut David, both from the Politehnica University of Timisoara, Romania.

- *Indirect Self-Evolving Fuzzy Control Approaches and Their Applications*

  This is a new chapter and is written by Drs. Zhao-Xu Yang and Hai-Jun Rong from Xian Jiaotong University, China.

Finally, Part V includes five chapters on evolutionary computation:

- *Evolutionary Computation: History View and Basic Concepts*

  This is a thoroughly revised chapter from the first edition of the handbook, which sets the scene with a historical and philosophical introduction of the topic. It is written by one of the leading scientists in this area, Dr. Carlos A. Coello-Coello from CINVESTAV, Mexico, and co-authored by Carlos Segura from the Centre of Research in Mathematics, Mexico, and Gara Miranda from the University of La Laguna, Tenerife, Spain.

- *An Empirical Study of Algorithmic Bias*

  This chapter is written by the same author as in the first edition, Prof. Dipankar Dasgupta from the University of Memphis, USA, and co-authored by his associate Dr. Sanjib Sen, but it offers a new topic: an empirical study of algorithmic bias.

- *Collective Intelligence: A Comprehensive Review of Metaheuristic Algorithms Inspired by Animals*

  This chapter is a thoroughly revised version of the chapter by the same author, Dr. Fevrier Valdez from the Institute of Technology, Tijuana, Mexico, who contributed to the first edition.

- *Fuzzy Dynamic Parameter Adaptation for Gray Wolf Optimization of Modular Granular Neural Networks Applied to Human Recognition Using the Iris Biometric Measure*

  This chapter is a thoroughly revised version of the chapters contributed by the authors to the first edition of the handbook. It is written by the leading experts in the area of fuzzy systems, Drs. Patricia Melin and Daniela Sanchez and Prof. Oscar Castillo from the Tijuana Institute of Technology, Mexico.

- *Evaluating Inter-task Similarity for Multifactorial Evolutionary Algorithm from Different Perspectives*

  The last chapter of this part of the second volume and of the handbook is new and is contributed by Lei Zhou and Drs. Liang Feng from Chongqing University, China, and Min Jiang from Xiamen University, China, and Prof. Kay Chen Tan from City University of Hong Kong.

In conclusion, this handbook is a thoroughly revised and updated second edition and is composed with care, aiming to cover all main aspects and recent trends in the *computer learning and intelligence* area of research and offering solid background knowledge as well as end-point applications. It is designed to be a one-stop shop for interested readers, but by no means aims to completely replace all other sources in this dynamically evolving area of research.

Enjoy reading it.

Plamen Parvanov Angelov
Editor of the Handbook
Lancaster, UK
3 June 2022

Part III

Deep Learning

https://doi.org/10.1142/9789811247323_0013

Chapter 13

Deep Learning and Its Adversarial Robustness: A Brief Introduction

Fu Wang, Chi Zhang, Peipei Xu, and Wenjie Ruan

College of Engineering, Mathematics and Physical Sciences
University of Exeter, UK

Deep learning, one of the most remarkable techniques in computational intelligence, has become increasingly popular and powerful in recent years. In this chapter, we, first of all, revisit the history of deep learning and then introduce two typical deep learning models including convolutional neural networks (CNNs) and recurrent neural networks (RNNs). After that, we present how the deep learning models are trained and introduce currently popular deep learning libraries and frameworks. Then we focus primarily on a newly emerged research direction in deep learning—adversarial robustness. Finally, we show some applications and point out some challenges of deep learning. This chapter cannot exhaustively cover every aspect of deep learning. Instead, it gives a short introduction to deep learning and its adversarial robustness, and provides a taste of what deep learning is, how to train a neural network, and why deep learning is vulnerable to adversarial attacks, and how to evaluate its robustness.

13.1. Introduction

As a branch of computational intelligence, deep learning or deep neural networks (DNNs) have achieved great success in many applications such as image analysis [1], speech recognition [2], and text understanding [3]. Deep learning has demonstrated superior capability in approximating and reducing large, complex datasets into highly accurate predictive and transformational outputs [4].

The origin of deep learning can be traced back to 1943, when Walter Pitts and Warren McCulloch built a mathematical model, the M-P model, to mimic the biological neural networks inside the human brain [5]. The M-P model is the earliest and most basic unit of artificial neural networks. It is an over-simplification of the biological brain yet successfully simulates the fundamental function of a real neuron cell in our brain [5]. As shown in Figure 13.1, a neuron receives signals from other neurons and compares the sum of inputs with a threshold. The output of this neuron is then calculated based on a defined activation function.

In 1958, Frank Rosenblatt proposed the perceptron, one of the simple artificial neural networks [6]. Figure 13.2 shows the structure of a perceptron. A single-layer perceptron has a very limited learning capacity, which cannot even solve a XOR problem [7]. But a multilayer perceptron exhibits a better learning performance by stacking multiple hidden layers, as shown in Figure 13.2(b). Such a structure is still commonly seen in modern deep neural networks with a new name, i.e., fully connected layer, since the neurons in each layer connect every neuron in the next layer. Kunihiko Fukushima, known as the inventor of convolutional neural networks, proposed a type of neural network, called neocognitron [8]. It enables the model to easily learn the visual patterns by adopting a hierarchical and multilayered structure.

In the development of deep learning, there were several technical breakthroughs that significantly boosted its advances [9]. The first notable breakthrough was the backpropagation (BP) algorithm which is now a standard method for training neural networks, that computes the gradient of the loss function for weights in the network by the chain rule. The invention of BP can be traced back to 1970, when Seppo Linnainmaa presented a FORTRAN code for backpropagation in his master's thesis [10]. In 1985, the concept of BP was for the first time applied in neural networks [11]. Later on, Yann LeCun demonstrated the first practical BP applied in handwritten zip code recognition [12].

Another significant breakthrough in deep learning is the development of graphics processing units (GPUs), which has improved the computational speed

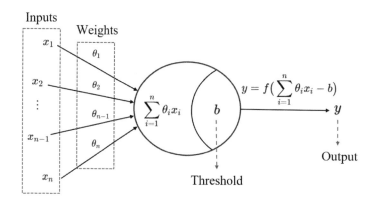

Figure 13.1:   An M-P model.

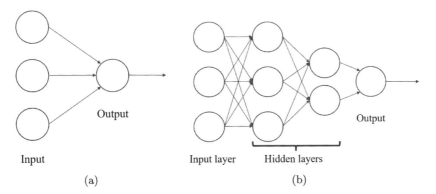

Figure 13.2:   Illustrations of a single-layer perceptron and a three-layer perceptron.

by thousands of times since 1999 [13]. Deep learning has also revealed a continuously improved performance when more data are used for training. For this reason, Fei-Fei Li launched ImageNet in 2009 [1], which is an open-source database containing more than 14 million labeled images. With the computational power of GPUs and the well-maintained database ImageNet, deep learning started to demonstrate a surprisingly remarkable performance on many challenging tasks [4]. A notable example is AlexNet [14], which has won several international image competitions and demonstrated a significant improvement in the best performance in multiple image databases [14]. Since then, deep learning has become one of the most important realms in computational intelligence. A more comprehensive introduction to the development of deep learning can be seen in [15–17].

13.2. Structures of Deep Learning

In this section, we first detail the activation functions that are widely applied in deep neural networks. Then, we introduce two typical deep learning structures—convolutional neural networks and recurrent neural networks.

13.2.1. *Activation Functions*

Activation function is the most important component in deep neural networks, empowering models with a superior capacity to learn nonlinear and complex representations. Typical activation functions used in deep neural networks include Sigmoid, Hyperbolic Tangent (Tanh), and Rectified Linear Unit (ReLU).

The Sigmoid activation function was pervasively adopted at the early stage of neural networks and still plays an important role in deep learning models [18].

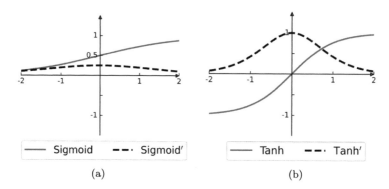

Figure 13.3:   Illustration of the Sigmoid and Tanh activation functions.

Its mathematical form and derivative can be written as

$$f_{\text{sig}}(x) = \frac{1}{1 + e^{-x}},$$

$$\frac{df_{\text{sig}}(x)}{dx} = f_{\text{sig}}(x)\big(1 - f_{\text{sig}}(x)\big).$$

(13.1)

As we can see, the derivation of the Sigmoid function is very easy to compute and its output range lies in (0, 1). As Figure 13.3(a) shows, the output range of Sigmoid is not zero-centered, which might slow down the training progress [18].

The Hyperbolic Tangent activation function, on the other hand, stretches the output range of the Sigmoid function and makes it zero-centered. The Tanh function and its derivative are given by

$$f_{\text{tanh}}(x) = \frac{e^{x} - e^{-x}}{e^{x} + e^{-x}},$$

$$\frac{df_{\text{tanh}}(x)}{dx} = 1 - f_{\text{tanh}}^{2}(x).$$

(13.2)

As Figure 13.3 show, the gradient of Tanh is steeper than that of Sigmoid, so deep neural networks with Tanh activation functions usually converge faster in training than when using Sigmoid activation.

A common disadvantage of Sigmoid and Tanh is that they both suffer from the vanishing gradient issue. That is, after several training epochs, the gradient will be very close to zero, preventing the effective update of the model parameters in backpropagation.

The most popular activation functions adopted by deep learning are Rectified Linear Unit (ReLU) and its variants (visualized in Figure 13.4). ReLU is extremely simple and computational-friendly and can be written as

$$f_{\text{ReLU}}(x) = \max(0, x),$$

$$\frac{df_{\text{ReLU}}(x)}{dx} = \begin{cases} 1, & x \geq 0, \\ 0, & x < 0. \end{cases} \tag{13.3}$$

ReLU follows the biological features of neuron cells, which only fire if the inputs exceed a certain threshold. Note that ReLU is non-differentiable at zero, and all positive inputs have the same non-zero derivative, one, which could prevent the vanishing gradient problem in backpropagation.

The drawback of ReLU activation is known as dead ReLU problem, i.e., some neurons may never activate and only output zero. One way to address this issue is to give a small slope to negative inputs, which leads to parametric ReLU activation, denoted by P-ReLU. Its mathematical form is

$$f_{\text{P-ReLU}}(x) = \max(ax, x),$$

$$\frac{df_{\text{P-ReLU}}(x)}{dx} = \begin{cases} 1, & x \geq 0, \\ a, & x < 0. \end{cases} \tag{13.4}$$

where a is a pre-defined small parameter, e.g., 0.01, or a trainable parameter. Theoretically, P-ReLU inherits ReLU's benefits and does not have the dead ReLU problem. But there is no substantial evidence that P-ReLU is always better than ReLU.

Another variant of ReLU is called Exponential Linear Units (ELU) and its mathematical form is

$$f_{\text{ELU}}(x) = \begin{cases} x, & x \geq 0, \\ a(e^x - 1), & x < 0, \end{cases}$$

$$\frac{df_{\text{ELU}}(x)}{dx} = \begin{cases} 1, & x \geq 0, \\ f_{\text{ELU}}(x) + a, & x < 0. \end{cases} \tag{13.5}$$

Compared to ReLU, ELU can utilize negative inputs and is almost zero-centered. Although empirical studies show that ELU can marginally improve the performance of deep neural networks on classification tasks, it is still unconfirmed whether it can fully surpass ReLU. Figure 13.4 shows the visualization of ReLU, P-ReLU and ELU.

Multiple hidden layers with nonlinear activation functions forge the core idea of deep neural networks. Deep learning utilizes various types of layers to extract features from data automatically. In the next section, we introduce convolutional neural networks, one of the deep learning structures that have achieved human-level performance on many image classification tasks [1].

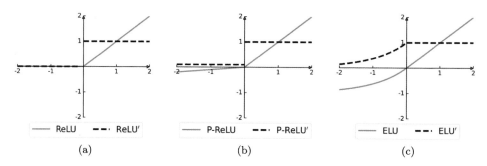

Figure 13.4: Illustration of different ReLU activation functions.

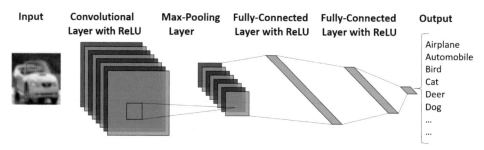

Figure 13.5: An example of convolutional neural network, comprising a convolutional layer with ReLU activation, a max-pooling layer, and two fully-connected layers with ReLU activation.

13.2.2. *Structures of Convolutional Neural Networks*

Convolutional neural networks (CNNs) are widely applied on many computer vision tasks including image classification, semantic segmentation, and object detection [19]. The connectivity patterns between hidden neurons in CNNs were actually inspired by the animal visual cortex [20–22]. Such connections based on shared weights allow CNNs to encode visual patterns and empower the network to succeed in image-focused tasks while reducing the learnable parameters in CNNs.

Typically, three types of layers are widely adopted by CNNs, i.e., convolutional layers, pooling layers, and fully connected layers. Figure 13.5 shows a simple CNN architecture for MNIST classification [23]. There are four basic components in this DNN architecture.

- **Input Layer**: It is the layer that takes in input data such as images.
- **Convolutional Layer**: It is the layer that adopts convolutional kernels to transform the image data into features in different levels. Convolutional layers also utilize activation functions, such as Sigmoid and ReLU, which are used to produce the output of each convolutional kernel.

- **Pooling Layer**: It is the layer that essentially performs a downsampling operation on its input, with an aim to reduce the parameter number in the network. The pooling operation is normally max pooling or average pooling.
- **Fully Connected Layer**: It is the layer that is the same as standard neural networks, with an aim to make the final classification or prediction.

The core idea of CNNs is to utilize a series of layer-by-layer transformations, such as convolution and downsampling, to learn the representations of the input data for various classification or regression tasks. Now we explain the convolutional layer and pooling layer, detailing their structures and operations.

13.2.2.1. *Convolutional layer*

The power of the convolutional layer lies in that it can capture the *spatial* and *temporal* dependencies on the input data (e.g., images) by convolutional kernels. A kernel usually has small dimensions (e.g., 3×3, 5×5) and is applied to convolve the entire input across the spatial dimensionality. As shown in Figure 13.6, the output of a convolutional layer on a single kernel is usually a 2D feature map. Since every convolutional kernel will produce a feature map, all feature maps are finally stacked together to form the full output of the convolutional layer.

There are three key hyper-parameters that decide the convolutional operation, namely, *depth*, *stride*, and *zero-padding*.

- **Depth** describes the 3rd (e.g., for gray images) or 4th dimension (e.g., for RGB images) of the output of the convolutional layer. It essentially measures the number of kernels applied in this convolutional layer. As a result, a small depth can significantly reduce the hidden neuron numbers, which could also compromise the representation learning capability of the neural network.

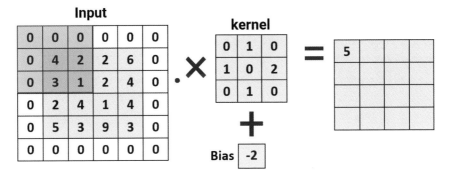

Figure 13.6: An example of convolutional operation: after the zero-padding, the kernel and the receptive field will first of all go through an element-wise multiplication, then be summed up and plus the bias. The kernel will traverse the whole input to produce all the elements in output matrix.

- **Stride** is the size of the step the convolutional kernel moves each time on the input data. A stride size is usually 1, meaning the kernel slides one pixel by one pixel. On increasing the stride size, the kernel slides over the input with a larger interval and thus has less overlap between the receptive fields.
- **Zero-padding** means that zero-value is added to surround the input with zeros, so that the feature map will not shrink. In addition to keeping the spatial sizes constant after convolution, padding also improves the performance by preserving part information of the border.

It is important to understand the hyper-parameters in convolutional layers. To visualize the convolutional operation and the impact of depth, stride, and zero-padding, you could refer to the website https://cs231n.github.io/convolutional-networks/#conv, which provides a detailed explanation and a few useful visualizations.

13.2.2.2. *Pooling layer*

The addition of a pooling layer after the convolutional layer is a common pattern within a convolutional neural network that may be repeated one or more times. The pooling operation involves sliding a two-dimensional filter over each channel of the feature map and summarizing the features lying within the region covered by the filter. Pooling layers can reduce the dimensions of the feature maps. Thus, it reduces the learnable parameter number in the network. The pooling layer also summarizes the features present in a region of the feature map generated by a convolution layer. So, further operations are performed on summarized features instead of precisely positioned features generated by the convolution layer. This makes the model more robust to variations in the position of the features in the input image. Typically, max pooling and average pooling are widely used in CNNs.

- Max pooling is a pooling operation that selects the maximum element from the region of the feature map covered by the filter. Thus, the output after the max-pooling layer would be a feature map containing the most prominent features of the previous feature map.
- Average pooling computes the average of the elements from the region of the feature map covered by the filter. Thus, average pooling gives the average of the features in a patch.

13.2.2.3. *Stacking together*

Finally, we can stack convolutional layers and pooling layers by repeating them multiple times, followed by one or a few fully connected layers. We can build a typical CNN architecture, as shown by Figure 13.5 and 13.7. We can see that,

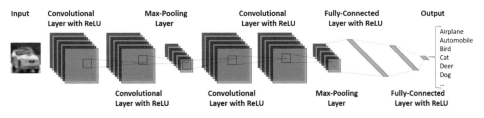

Figure 13.7: An example of complicated convolutional neural network: it contains multiple convolutional layers and max-pooling layers.

compared to a traditional neural network that only contains the fully connected layers, adopting multiple convolutional and pooling layers enables the network to learn complex visual features and further boost the classification performance.

13.2.2.4. *Summary*

We introduced the basic structures of convolutional neural networks in this section. Since AlexNet achieved a huge success in the ImageNet competition, CNNs are predominantly applied in the computer vision area, and significantly improve the state-of-the-art performances on many computer vision tasks. Meanwhile, the development of CNNs has made deep learning models more practical in solving real-world problems. For example, face recognition has been integrated into smartphones to identify their owners and secure sensitive operations, including identity verification and payment. In addition to vision tasks, convolution layers serve as a fundamental building block that can automatically extract local features. So they are essential components in a wide range of deep learning models, such as WaveNet [24] for speech synthesis and TIMAM [25] for text-to-image matching tasks.

13.2.3. *Structures of Recurrent Neural Networks*

Recurrent neural networks (RNNs) refer to neural networks with loops and gates, specifying sequential processing. With further in-depth research on neural networks, scientists found out that although feed-forward neural networks, such as Multilayer Perceptron (MLP) and CNNs, can handle large grades of values well, they are insufficient for processing sequential data. When modeling human neuronal connectivity, scientists observed that human brain neurons are not one-way connected. Instead, they are connected in a dense web, namely a recurrent network. Inspired by such observations, the notion of RNNs was first built by David Everett Rumelhart in 1986 [11]. In the same year, Michael I. Jordan built a simple RNN structure, a Jordan network, which directly uses the output of the network for feedback [26]. In 1990, Jeffrey L. Elman made an improvement in the structure by feedback of the output of the internal state, i.e., the output of hidden layers [27]. He also trained the network through backpropagation, which generated the RNN model we use today. However, these models face problems such as gradient vanishing and gradient exploding, when the networks and data volumes are large. Such problems were not alleviated until the invention of long short-term memory (LSTM) networks by Hochreiter and Schmidhuber in 1997 [28]. The LSTM structure including gates and loops, allowing for the processing of the entire sequential data, has a wide application in speech recognition, natural language procession, etc. Based on the LSTM model, Kyunghyun Cho et al. developed gated recurrent units (GRU) [29], which bear resemblance to simplified LSTM units. There are also other RNN techniques, such as bi-directional RNNs, which show a good performances when combined with LSTM or GRU. In this section, we introduce the basic structure of RNNs, analyze their working principles by unrolling the loop, and illustrate the unique structure of LSTM and GRU. We also demonstrate the specific applications of RNNs based on its structures and discuss the challenges of this technique.

13.2.3.1. *Vanilla RNN and unfolding*

Let's start by introducing a vanilla RNN, which has only one input node x, one hidden unit h, and one output node o, with only one loop. As shown in Figure 13.8, where the weights are listed besides the connection, we initialize the hidden state at the very beginning ($t = 0$) to 0 and implement no bias. Given an input sequence $x = 0.5, 1, -1, -2$ at time steps 1 to 4, the values of the hidden units and outputs are as shown in the table in Figure 13.8.

Assuming that the input sequence of a RNN is $x = x_1, \ldots, x_n$, then the output of the RNN is $o = o_1, \ldots, o_n$, with a hidden state $h = h_0, \ldots, h_n$, we present a

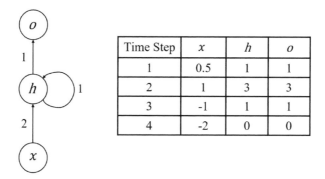

Time Step	x	h	o
1	0.5	1	1
2	1	3	3
3	-1	1	1
4	-2	0	0

Figure 13.8:   Simple structure of RNN with three layers and ReLU activation.

more general form of RNN as follows:

$$h_t = \delta(U x_t + W h_{t-1} + b_h),$$
$$o_t = \phi(V h_t + b_y),$$

(13.6)

where $1 < i < n$, and δ and ϕ are the activation functions in nodes h and o.

Nowadays, most of the analyses of RNNs tend to open the loop structure through an unfolding process. A RNN with a fixed input length can be transformed into an equivalent feed-forward network, which not only provides a more straightforward observation but also makes techniques designed for feed-forward networks suitable for RNNs. Figure 13.9 illustrates how a simple RNN unit is transformed into a feed-forward model. This equivalent feed-forward model shares the parameters with the original RNN, while the number of layers increases to the input sequence length. However, for RNNs only with the loop structure, the information at the very beginning may have little influence on the final output when the sequence is too long. That is when the long short-term memory (LSTM) structure takes place, which is proposed to address such problems and performs well when processing long sequential data.

13.2.3.2. *Long short-term memory*

Unlike standard RNNs only with loops, the LSTM network has its own specific structure LSTM cell. In the LSTM unit shown in Figure 13.10, the data flow is controlled by an input gate i_t, an output gate o_t, and a forget gate f_t. These gates regulate not only the input and output information between cells but also the cell states themselves. They are realized by the combination of linear transformation and activation functions, such as Sigmoid δ and Tanh.

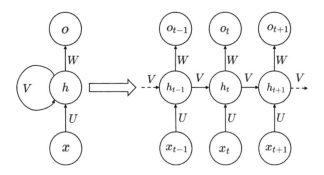

Figure 13.9: Transforming a vanilla RNN into a feed-forward model.

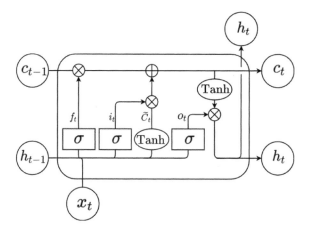

Figure 13.10: An LSTM unit.

The mathematical form of an LSTM unit can be formulated as

$$f_t = \delta(W_f x_t + U_f h_{t-1} + b_f),$$
$$i_t = \delta(W_i x_t + U_i h_{t-1} + b_i),$$
$$o_t = \delta(W_o x_t + U_o h_{t-1} + b_o),$$
$$\widetilde{c}_t = \tanh(W_c x_t + U c h_{t-1} + b_c),$$
$$c_t = f_t \circ c_{t-1} + i_t \circ \widetilde{c}_t,$$
$$h_t = o_t \circ \tanh(c_t),$$

(13.7)

where x, h, c, and t represent input, hidden state, cell state, and time point, respectively. Both W and U indicate the weight matrix. The forget gate f_t transforms input x_t and hidden state h_{t-1}. It selects useful information in c_{t-1} and abandons the rest. The input gate i_t controls what values should be added to the cell state, and the vector $\widetilde{c}_t$ provides all the possible values for addition. i_t and $\widetilde{c}_t$ work together to update the cell state. When we have the new cell state c_t, we use tanh to scale its value to the range -1 to 1. The output gate o_t function plays the role of a filter, which selects the information from the scaled cell state and passes it to the hidden state h_t that will soon be output.

Given the specific cell and gate structure, we do not need to moderate the whole sequence of information. Through the selecting and forgetting procedure, we can moderate only a part of the data, which improves the accuracy and efficiency of processing long sequence data. There are also different variants of LSTM. For example, LSTM with peephole connections, where gates can directly access cell state information, was quite popular. In the next part, we discuss a simplified version of LSTM, i.e., the gated recurrent unit, which is more commonly used at present.

13.2.3.3. *Gated recurrent unit*

Compared with LSTM, the gated recurrent unit (GRU) contains only two gates, i.e., the update gate and the reset gate, where the output gate is omitted. This structure was first presented by Kyunghyun Cho et al. in 2014 to deal with the gradient vanishing problem when processing long sequential data via fewer gates. The structure of GRU is shown in Figure 13.11. Unlike LSTM with the cell state, GRU has only hidden state h_t for transmission between units and output delivery. Therefore, a GRU, has fewer parameters to learn during the training process and shows better performances on smaller datasets. Equation (13.8) presents the mathematical form of GRU, in which x_t represents the input data. Both W and U are weight matrices and b indicates the bias matrix. To generate the gate z_t, we first make a linear transformation of both input x_t and hidden state h_{t-1} from the last time point, and then apply a nonlinear transformation by the sigmoid function. The resulting value z_t helps decide which data to pass to next time steps. The reset gate r_t has a structure similar to that of update gate, only with different weight W_r, U_r and bias b_r parameters. The reset gate selects useful information from the hidden state h_{t-1} at the last time point and forgets the irrelevant information. Combined with a linear transformation and tanh activation, it delivers the candidate hidden state $\widetilde{h}_t$, which may also be referred to as current memory content, where useful information from the past is kept. The last step is to update the hidden state and gives out h_t. We use update gate z_t to take element-wise products with both h_{t-1} and $\widetilde{h}_t$ and deliver the new hidden state h_t, which can be written as

$$
\begin{aligned}
z_t &= \delta(W_z x_t + U_z h_{t-1} + b_z), \\
r_t &= \delta(W_r x_t + U_r h_{t-1} + b_r), \\
\widetilde{h}_t &= \tanh(W_h x_t + U_h(r_t \circ h_{t-1}) + b_h), \\
h_t &= (1 - z_t) \circ h_{t-1} + z_t \circ \widetilde{h}_t.
\end{aligned}
\tag{13.8}
$$

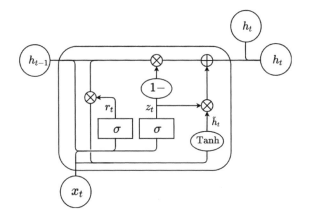

Figure 13.11: A gated recurrent unit.

The GRU model is quite popular in polyphonic music modeling, speech signal modeling, handwriting recognition, etc. Because of the relatively few parameters, it is more efficient in the training process than LSTM, especially when dealing with smaller datasets. However, it still shows limitations in machine translation and language recognition scenarios and may not wholly outperform LSTM.

13.2.3.4. *Application in natural language processing*

Unlike CNNs that commonly appear in computer vision tasks, the specific loop structures and memory function of RNNs lead to their different application scenarios. The previous input of RNNs influences the current input and output. Therefore, RNNs are widely used in processing sequential data and solving temporal problems, where many natural language processing (NLP) tasks fall into this area, e.g., machine translation, named-entity recognition, sentiment analysis, etc. Bengio et al. [30] made the first attempt at applying deep learning in NLP tasks in 2003, and Collobert et al. demonstrated that multiple-layer neural networks may be a better solution compared to traditional statistical NLP features. While the real revolution started with word embedding in 2013, the word2vec toolbox [31] showed that pre-trained word vectors can improve model performance on most downstream tasks. At that time, word embedding could not handle polysemy of human language properly, until Peters et al. [3] proposed a deep contextualized word representation, also known as embedding from language language models (ELMO), which provides an elegant solution to the polysemous problems. Note that ELMO uses BiLSTM, or bidirectional LSTM, as the feature extractor [32]. Right now, it has been demonstrated by many studies that the ability of the Transformer to extract features is far stronger than of the LSTM. ELMO and Transformer had a profound impact on subsequent research and inspired a large number of studies, such as GPT [33] and BERT [34].

13.2.3.5. *Summary*

In this section, we first introduce the basic concept of recurrent neural networks and the working principle of vanilla RNNs and then present two representative models, LSTM and GRU, which are capable of handling long sequential data. Moreover, the gate structure allows modifying only small parts of the data during long sequential data processing, avoiding the gradient vanishing situation. Apart from these two variants, there are still various models of RNN for different application scenarios, such as the bidirectional RNN, deep RNN, continuous-time recurrent neural network, and so on. Although classic RNNs are no longer the best option in NLP, various structures of RNN still enable its used in a wide range of sequence processing applications.

13.3. Training Deep Learning Models

A great number of parameters enable the fantastic representation capability of deep neural networks, but the difficulty of training neural networks grows exponentially with their scale. In this section, we briefly discuss the development of training methods and tricks.

13.3.1. *Gradient Descent and Backpropagation*

From an optimization perspective, training a network f_θ is normally formulated as a minimization problem,

$$\min_\theta L(\theta), \tag{13.9}$$

where we wish to minimize the empirical risk that is given by the expectation of a given loss function over all examples that draw i.i.d. from a distribution $\mathcal{D}$, which can be written as

$$L_\mathcal{D}(\theta) = \mathbb{E}_{(x,y)\sim\mathcal{D}}\ell\left(f_\theta(x), y\right). \tag{13.10}$$

However, in practice, we can only access a finite training set $S = \{(x_i, y_i)\}_{i=1}^n$, so the corresponding empirical risk or training loss is written as

$$L_S(\theta) = \frac{1}{n}\sum_{i=1}^n \ell\left(f_\theta(x_i), y_i\right). \tag{13.11}$$

Assume that ℓ is continuous and differentiable. The landscape of the value of ℓ is just like a mountain area that exists in a high-dimensional space, where dimension depends on the number of parameters in the trained model. Our task can be viewed as searching the lowest valley inside mountains. Imagine that we start at a random location in the mountains. All we can do is to look locally and climb down the hill step by step until we reach a local minimum point. This iterative process is achieved by gradient descent (GD), which can be written as

$$\theta^{k+1} = \theta^k - \eta^k \nabla L_S(\theta^k), \tag{13.12}$$

where $\nabla L_S(\theta)$ is the gradient of θ and shows the direction to climb down, and η^i is the step size, which is also known as the learning rate. When we use GD to train a deep learning model, the gradient of weights $\nabla L_S(\theta)$ is computed from the last layer to the first layer via the chain rule. Therefore, the model's weights are also reversely updated layer by layer, and this process is known as backpropagation. As one of the landmark findings in supervised learning, backpropagation is a foundation of deep learning.

13.3.2. *Stochastic Gradient Descent and Mini-Batching*

Note that in GD, we only conduct backpropagation after the model sees the whole training set, which is feasible yet not efficient. In other words, GD heads to the steepest direction at each step, while we only need to climb down in roughly the right direction. Following this intuitives, stochastic gradient descent (SGD) takes the gradient of the loss for each single training example as an estimation of the actual gradient and conducts gradient descent via backpropagation based on the stochastic estimation, as shown in Figure 13.12(b). By doing so, SGD directly speeds up GD from two perspectives. First, there might be repeated examples in the training set. For instance, we can copy an example ten times to build a training set and train a model on it, where GD is ten times slower than SGD. Besides, even though there are no redundant examples in the training set, SGD does not require the trained model to go over all examples and updates weights much more frequently. Although the stochastic estimation of the actual gradient introduces random noise into gradient descent, the training actually benefits from the noise. At the early training stage, the model has barely learned any information from the training set. Therefore, the noise is relatively small, and an SGD step is basically as good as a GD step. Furthermore, the noise in SGD steps can prevent convergence to a bad local minimum point in the rest stages. On the downside, SGD updates weights for every example, and sometimes the training effect from two extremely different examples may even cancel out. Hence, it takes more steps for SGD to converge at an ideal point than GD and cannot make the best use of parallel computation brought by the advanced graph process unit (GPU). A promising way to address these drawbacks is by calculating the estimation over a subset B of the training set, namely mini-batch. An intuitive way to partition the training set into mini-batches is to randomly shuffle the training set S and divide it into several parts as uniformly as possible. Let $S = \{B_1, B_2, \ldots, B_m\}$ represent the partition result. For any $B_j \in S$, the corresponding loss is written as

$$L_B(\theta) = \frac{1}{|B_j|} \sum_{i=1}^{|B_j|} \ell\left(f_\theta\left(x_i\right), y_i\right), \qquad (13.13)$$

where $|\cdot|$ returns the size of the input batch, namely batch size. Although the estimation is calculated on multiple examples, the time consumption is usually similar to a regular SGD step when employing a GPU with enough memory. By doing so, the frequency of backpropagation has been significantly reduced, and the training effect from any two mini-batches can hardly cancel each other out. Figure 13.12 shows the differences of GD, SGD and SGD with mini-batching.

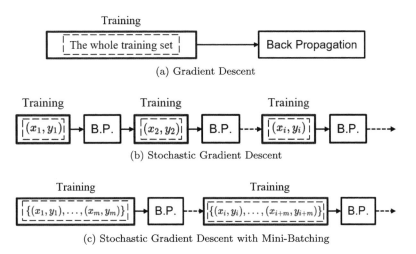

(a) Gradient Descent

(b) Stochastic Gradient Descent

(c) Stochastic Gradient Descent with Mini-Batching

Figure 13.12: An illustration of the pipelines of GD, SGD, and SGD with mini-batching.

13.3.3. *Momentum and Adaptive Methods*

Although SGD with mini-batching outperforms regular SGD when training deep learning models under most scenarios, adding a momentum item can make it even better. The idea of this improvement is similar to the concept of momentum in physics. If SGD is a man trying to climb down a hill step by step, SGD with momentum can be imagined as a ball rolling in the same area. One mathematical form of momentum can be written as

$$p^0 = 0,$$
$$p^{k+1} = \beta p^k + \nabla L(\theta^k), \quad 0 \leq \beta \leq 1, \tag{13.14}$$
$$\theta^{k+1} = \theta^k - \eta^k p^{k+1}.$$

The momentum item can be viewed as a weighted average of current gradient and the momentum item from the previous step, where β is the weight factor. If we unroll (13.14) at any specific step, it can be seen that the gradient items of previous steps have accumulated at the current momentum item, where the old gradient term decays exponentially according to β, and the later gradient has a larger impact at present. This exponential decay is known as the exponential moving average, which we will see again later. Goh [35] provided a vivid visualization about the impact of momentum, where SGD with momentum makes modest moves at each step and finds a better solution than SGD eventually. The insight behind the improvement is that the historical gradient information can smooth the noise in SGD steps and dampen the oscillations.

Except for momentum, another intuitive way to enhance SGD is by adding adaptivity into the training process. In the above methods, we assume that all parameters in the trained model are updated via a global learning rate, while adaptive methods aim to adjust the learning rate for each parameter automatically during training. The earliest attempt in this research direction is the adaptive gradient (AdaGrad) method. AdaGrad starts training with SGD at a global learning rate. For a specific parameter, AdaGrad decreases the corresponding learning rate according to the parameter's gradient value that is calculated via backpropagation. The update process can be written as

$$s^0 = 0,$$
$$s^{k+1} = s^k + \nabla L(\theta^k)^2,$$
$$\theta^{k+1} = \theta^k - \frac{\eta^k}{\sqrt{s^{k+1}} + \epsilon} \nabla L(\theta^k), \tag{13.15}$$

where ϵ is added to avoid dividing zero. The learning rate of a specific parameter will be enlarged if the corresponding item in s^{k+1} is smaller than 1, otherwise it will be shrunk. Note that in AdaGrad, all previous gradient information is treated equally, so most parameters' learning rates decrease during training due to the accumulation of historical gradient. One problem with this adapting strategy is that the training effect of AdaGrad at the later training stage can hardly be maintained because of the small learning rates. The root mean square propagation (RMSProp) method addresses this by taking a weighted average of the historical accumulation item and the square of current gradient, which can be formalized as

$$v^0 = 0,$$
$$v^{k+1} = mv^k + (1 - m)\nabla L(\theta^k)^2,$$
$$\theta^{k+1} = \theta^k - \frac{\eta^k}{\sqrt{v^{k+1}} + \epsilon} \nabla L(\theta^k), \tag{13.16}$$

where $m \in [0, 1)$ is introduced to achieve an exponential moving average of past gradients. Compared to AdaGrad, the newer gradient has larger weights in RMSProp, which prevent the learning rate from continuously decreasing over training. The Adam method combines the RMSProp and momentum together and is the most widely used method at present. An Adam step requires calculating the exponential moving average of momentum and the square of past gradient, which are given by

$$v^0 = 0, \quad p^0 = 0,$$
$$p^{k+1} = \beta_1 p^k + (1 - \beta_1)\nabla L(\theta^k),$$
$$v^{k+1} = \beta_2 v^k + (1 - \beta_2)\nabla L(\theta^k)^2. \tag{13.17}$$

Then the parameters is updated via

$$\theta^{k+1} = \theta^k - \eta^k \frac{p^{k+1}}{\sqrt{v^{k+1}} + \epsilon}. \tag{13.18}$$

Although Adam normally performs better than AdaGRrad and RMSProp in practice, it has two momentum parameters that need to be tuned and uses more memory to conduct backpropagation. On the other hand, our understanding of its theory is still poor. From the practical perspective, Adam is necessary for training some networks for NLP tasks, while both SGD with momentum and Adam generally work well on training CNN models. However, using Adam to minimize the training loss may lead to worse generalization errors than SGD, especially in image problems.

13.3.4. *Challenges in Training*

Except for the high demand for computational resources, training deep neural networks is facing overfitting and gradient vanishing. Overfitting is well studied in the machine learning area, which normally occurs when the trained model is too complex or the training set is not large enough. However, in the scope of deep learning, because we do not really understand why deep learning works, there are no methods or mathematical theorems that can tell us how to quantify a specific model's capability and how many parameters and layers a model needs to handle a specific task. But existing studies show that increasing the model's size in a proper way is the best most likely way to increase the model's performance. Therefore, neural network's complexity keeps growing. In the previous section, we describe how neural networks are trained in supervised learning by default. Under this scenarios, we need a great amount of labeled data to train our models. However, generating such data is heavily dependent on human participation, which is much slower than the evolution of neural network's architecture. Thus, overfitting becomes an inevitable problem, and all we can do is to mitigate it.

As mentioned in Section 13.2.1 that multiple nesting of Sigmoid and Tanh may make the gradient close to zero and cause the gradient vanishing. Before ReLU came out, Hinton et al. [36] proposed an unsupervised layer-wise training approach, which only trains one layer at a time to avoid gradient vanishing. For a given hidden layer, this method takes the output of the previous layer as input to conduct unsupervised training and repeat the same process on the next layer. After all the layers are pre-trained, it is time for gradient descent to fine-tune the model's weights. In fact, this pre-training with the fine-tuning approach first partitions the model's weights and then finds a local optimal setting for each group. The global training starts in the combination of these pre-trained weights, which makes the training process much more efficient. Due to the advancement of computer hardware, this method is rarely

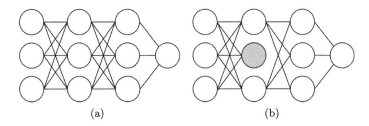

(a)   (b)

Figure 13.13:   Illustration of applying dropout in a multiple-layer perceptron.

used in training small and medium size neural networks now. But this paradigm is still very useful when training very large language models.

Dropout is an interesting approach to prevent overfitting. Suppose we have a multiple-layer perceptron as shown in Figure 13.13(a). Applying dropout during training means that hidden units are randomly discarded with a given probability when performing forward propagation. The discarded unit in Figure 13.13(b) simply outputs zero no matter what its inputs are and remains unchanged at that iteration. Because every hidden unit might be deactivated, dropout introduces random noise into the output of hidden layers. Correspondingly, units in the following layer are forced to find useful patterns and make predictions independently because any specific dimension of their inputs is not reliable. Note that dropout is only applied in the training process, and a sub-model that inherits parameters from the original model is sampled at each training iteration. While at the inference procedure, all these trained sub-models are integrated together to give predictions, which implies the idea of ensemble learning.

Batch normalization is one of the recent milestone works in deep learning that can mitigate both gradient vanishing and overfitting. It applies as the so-called batch normalization layer and plays an important role in improving the training and convergence speed. Neural networks are supposed to learn the distribution of the training data. If the distribution keeps changing, learning will be difficult. Unfortunately, for a specific hidden layer, the distribution of its previous layer's output does change if the activation function is not zero-centered after each weight update. Ioffe et al. [37] used the term *internal covariate shift* to describe this phenomenon.

A straightforward idea to address the internal covariate shift is by normalizing the output of each layer of the neural network. Suppose that we normalize those outputs to 0 mean, 1 variance, which satisfies the normal distribution. However, when the data distribution of each layer is the standard normal distribution, a neural network is completely unable to learn any useful features of the training data. Therefore, it is obviously unreasonable to directly normalize each layer.

To address this, batch normalization introduces two trainable parameters to translate and scale the normalized results to retain information. Generally, the translate and scale parameters are calculated on the training set and directly used to process data at testing. Although we still do not understand why batch normalization is helpful, including it in our neural networks allows training to be more radical. Specifically, batch normalization reduces sensitivity to weight initialization and makes the networks easier to optimize, where we can use larger learning rates to speed up the training process. On the other hand, the translate and scale parameters can be viewed as extra noise because each mini-batch is randomly sampled. Like in dropout and SGD, extra noise enables better generalization and prevents overfitting. However, there might be a difference in the distribution of training data and test data, and the pre-calculated normalization cannot suit the test data perfectly, which leads to inconsistency in the model's performance at training and testing.

As shown in Figure 13.14, batch normalization works on the batch dimension. We can naturally conduct normalization along different dimensions, which motivates layer, instance, and group normalization methods. The first two methods are straightforward, while for group normalization it is relatively hard to get the intuition behind it. Recall that there are many convolution kernels in each layer of a CNN model. The features learned by these kernels are not completely independent. Some of them should have the same distribution and thus can be grouped. In the visual system, there are many physical factors that can cause grouping, such as frequency, shape, brightness, texture, etc. Similarly, in the biological visual system, the responses of neuron cells would also be normalized.

So far, we have only briefly described a few tricks and methods that can make training neural networks easier. Deep learning is a very active field, and there are scores of well-developed methods we have not mentioned. If readers are interested in more, they are advised to further study the existing literature according to specific needs.

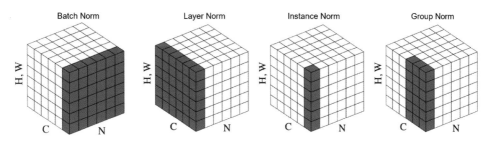

Figure 13.14: Illustration of different types of normalization layers [38]. C, N, and H, W are shorthands for channels, instances in a batch, and spatial location.

13.3.5. *Frameworks*

At the end of this section, we want to give a quick review of deep learning frameworks that greatly boost the development of this area. Although deep learning benefits a lot from advanced GPUs and other hardware, it is not easy for most users and researchers who are not majoring in computer science to make use of such improvements. Deep learning frameworks enable people to implement and customize their neural networks in their projects. Theano is the first framework that focuses on deep learning study. It was developed by Mila, headed by Yoshua Bengio, back in 2008. Caffe is also an early open-source deep learning framework, which was started by Yangqing Jia during his PhD at UC Berkeley. About roughly the same period, Microsoft Research Asia presented a framework called Minerva, which may be the first one that introduced the concept of the computational graph into deep learning implementation. In a computational graph, all components, e.g., input examples, model weights, and even operations, are traded as graph nodes. During the forward propagation, the data flow from the input layer to the output layer, where computation is done at each graph node. Meanwhile, backpropagation can directly utilize the useful intermediate results kept by the computational graph to avoid repeated calculations when updating model weights. Published by Google Brain, TensorFlow further develops the computational graph and is now the most popular framework in the industry. It includes most deep learning algorithm models and is supported by an active open source community. Keras is an advanced framework on top of other frameworks. It provides a unified API to utilize different frameworks and is probably the best option for new programmers. The latest version of TensorFlow also adopts Keras's API to simplify its usage and is now more friendly for beginners. Meanwhile, in the research area, Pytorch is also a popular option. This framework originated from Torch, a Lua-based machine learning library, and was improved by Facebook. Pytorch dynamically builds the corresponding computational graph when performing deep learning tasks, allowing users to customize models and verify their ideas easily. There are many more deep learning frameworks available now, such as MXNet, PaddlePaddle, MegEngine, Mindspore, and so on, which benefit a wide range of users. Meanwhile, it can be seen on GitHub that a growing number of third-party libraries have been developed to enhance these frameworks. Overall, the rapid development of deep learning is inseparable from these open-source frameworks. There is no such thing as the best deep learning frameworks, and we should appreciate those developers, engineers, and scientists who have contributed to such projects.

13.4. The Robustness of Deep Learning

Given the prospect of broad deployment of DNNs in a wide range of applications, it becomes critical that a deep learning model obtain satisfactory yet trustworthy performance. Unfortunately, a large number of recent research studies have demonstrated that deep learning models are actually too fragile or extremely non-robust to be applied in high-stakes applications. Such vulnerability has raised concerns about the safety and trustworthiness of modern deep learning systems, especially those on safety-critical tasks. So, how to enhance the robustness of deep learning models to adversarial attacks is an important topic. Recently, although a significant amount of research has emerged to tackle this challenge [39], it remains an open challenge to researchers in computational intelligence. In this section, we first describe the progress in discovering and understanding such a threat and then introduce how to quantify the deep learning model's robustness via verification techniques. The mainstream defense methods will be summarized at the end of this section.

13.4.1. *Adversarial Threat*

Due to the lack of understanding about the basic properties behind these sophisticated deep learning models, adversarial examples, i.e., a special kind of inputs that are indistinguishable from nature examples but can completely fool the model have become the major security concern.

Adversarial attacks, the procedure that generates adversarial examples, are conceptually similar to the so-called evasion attacks in machine learning [40]. The fact that DNNs are vulnerable to such attacks was first identified by Szegedy et al. back in 2013 [41]. They found that well-trained image classifiers can be misled by trivial perturbations δ generated by maximizing the loss function, which can be formulated as

$$\max_{\delta} \ell(f_\theta(x + \delta), y), \text{ s.t. } \|\delta\| \leq \epsilon,$$

where $\| \cdot \|$ is a pre-defined metric and ϵ is the adversarial budget. Later, Goodfellow et al. proposed the fast gradient sign method (FGSM) [42], which is one of the earliest adversarial attack methods. Along this direction, both basic iterative method [43] and projected gradient descent (PGD) [44] conduct multiple FGSM steps to search strong adversarial examples. PGD also takes advantage of random initialization and re-start, so it performs much better in practice and is adopted by recent works as a robustness testing method. Besides, not only is the most popular adversarial attack at present but it also plays an essential role in adversarial training, a promising defense technique that we will discuss later.

Generally, adversarial attacks can be divided into two types depending on the attacker's goals. Non-targeted attacks want to fool a given classifier to produce wrong predictions, and they do not care about what these predictions exactly are.

In classification tasks, the goal of non-targeted attacks can be described as

$$f_\theta(x + \delta) \neq f_\theta(x), \quad \text{where } f_\theta(x) = y.$$

One step further, targeted attacks aim to manipulate classifiers and make them give a specific prediction, i.e.,

$$f_\theta(x + \delta) = y_t, \quad \text{where } f_\theta(x) = y \text{ and } y \neq y_t.$$

Conducting targeted attacks is more difficult than non-targeted attacks, and they are more threatening for real-world applications. While non-targeted attacks have a higher success rate, they are commonly used to test the robustness of deep learning models under experimental environments.

On the other hand, adversarial attacks are also classified by the ability of the attackers. FGSM and PGD are both white-box attacks, which assume that adversaries can access all information about their victims, especially the gradients of the model during backpropagation. However, conducting black-box attacks is much more difficult and complex than white-box attacks. In this case, the details of deep learning models are hidden from attackers, but they can pretend to be regular users, which can get the model's predictions with respect to input examples. Based on the query results, attackers can either fine-tune a surrogate model to produce transferable adversarial examples or estimate the gradient information to generate malicious perturbation as in white-box scenarios. Because of the inherent high dimensionality of deep learning tasks, attacks usually need thousands of query results to generate one usable adversarial example [45]. The significant amount of queries required by black-box attacks makes them computationally expensive and hard to achieve in real-world tasks. Thus, making full use of the information obtained in the query process to produce efficient adversarial attacks is still an open problem. In addition to the additive perturbation, conducting small spatial transformations such as translation and rotation can also generate adversarial examples [46]. This indicates that l_p norm is not an ideal metric of adversarial threat. Besides, universal adversarial perturbation, i.e., a single perturbation that works on most input examples simultaneously and causes misclassification, is also an interesting and practical technique. Along this direction, we found that combining spatial and additional perturbations can significantly boost the performance of universal adversarial perturbation [47]. Note that adversarial attacks can be easily generalized to a wide range of deep learning tasks beyond classification. As shown in Figure 13.15, our previous work [48] provides an example of how to attack an object detection system via PGD with a limited number of perturbed pixels.

Deep learning models being deceived by adversarial examples under white-box scenarios is almost inevitable at the current state, and existing defense methods can only mitigate the security issues but cannot address them adequately. The existence

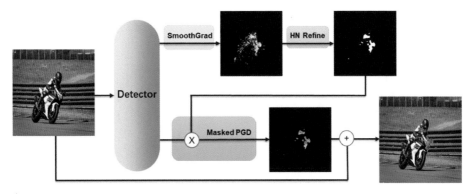

Figure 13.15: Generating an adversarial example toward an object detection system with a limited number of perturbed pixels [48]. Here, SmoothGrad finds the sensitive pixels within an input example, and Half-Neighbor refinement selects the actual perturbed area for PGD attack accordingly.

of adversarial examples demonstrated that small perturbations of the input (normally under l_p metrics) are capable of producing a large distortion at the ending layers [41]. Therefore, in addition to security, enabling adversarial robustness would also help us to better understand the fundamental properties of deep learning and computational intelligence.

13.4.2. *Robustness Verification*

Although DNNs have achieved significant success in many domains, there are serious concerns when applying them to real-world safety-critical systems, such as self-driving cars and medical diagnosis systems. Even though adversarial attacks can evaluate the robustness of DNNs by crafting adversarial examples, these approaches can only falsify robustness claims yet cannot verify them because there is no theoretical guarantee provided on their results. Safety verification can provide the provable guarantee, i.e., when using verification tools to check DNN models, if there is no counterexample (adversarial example), such verification techniques can provide a robustness guarantee. To better explain verification techniques on adversarial robustness, this section explains the relationship between the verification and adversarial threat, then defines verification properties, and further presents various verification techniques.

To verify that the outputs of DNNs are invariant against a small probation, we introduce the maximal safe norm ball for local robustness evaluation, as shown in Figure 13.16. Given a genuine image x_0, we use the l_p norm ball to define the perturbation against the original image, i.e., $\|x - x_0\|_p \leq r$. When the norm ball is small and far away from the decision boundary, DNN gives the invariant output, whereas an intersection with the decision boundary appears on enlarging the norm ball, which means that the perturbation is large enough to change the output.

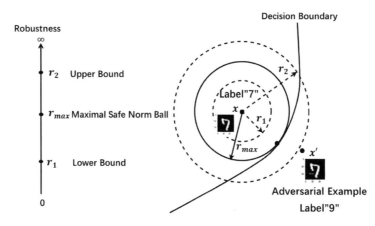

Figure 13.16:   Visualizing the decision boundary and different safety bounds.

In this process, a critical situation exists when the norm ball is tangent to the boundary, generating the maximal safe norm ball r_{max}. No matter what kind of adversarial attacks are used, the model is safe and robust as long as the perturbation is within the range of r_{max}. Otherwise, the model is unsafe because there exists at least one adversarial example. Ideally, we only need to determine the maximal safe radius r_{max} for the robustness analysis. However, in practice, r_{max} is not easy to calculate, we thus estimate the upper bound r_2 and lower bound r_1 of r_{max}, corresponding to the adversarial threat and robustness verification.

13.4.2.1. *Robustness Properties*

Here, we summarize four fundamental definitions that support different kinds of verification techniques.

Definition 1 (Local Robustness Property). Given a neural network $f : \mathbb{R}^n \to \mathbb{R}^m$ and an input x_0, the local robustness of f on x_0 is defined as

$$Robust(f, r) \triangleq \forall \|x - x_0\|_p \leq r, \exists i, j \in \{1, \ldots, m\}, \quad f_i(x) \geq f_j(x). \quad (13.19)$$

For targeted local robustness of f on x_0 and label l, it is defined as

$$Robust_l(f, r) \triangleq \forall \|x - x_0\|_p \leq r, \exists j \in \{1, \ldots, m\}, \quad f_l(x) \geq f_j(x). \quad (13.20)$$

From Definition 1, the local robustness means the decision of a DNN does not change within the region r_{max}. For example, there exists a label l such that, for all inputs x in region r_{max}, and other labels j, the DNN believes that x is more possible to be in class l than in any class j.

To compute the set of outputs with respect to predefined input space, we have the following definition of output reachability.

Definition 2 (Output Reachability Property). Given a neural network f, and an input region $\|x - x_0\|_p \leq r$, the reachable set of f and r is a set $Reach(f, r)$ such that

$$Reach(f, r) \triangleq \{f(x) \mid x \in \|x - x_0\|_p \leq r\}. \tag{13.21}$$

Due to the region r covering a large or infinite number of entities within the input space, there is no realistic algorithm to check their classifications. In addition to the highly nonlinear (or black-box) neural network f, the output reachability problem is highly non-trivial. Based on this, the verification of output reachability is to determine whether all inputs x with distance r can map onto a given output set $\mathcal{Y}$, and whether all outputs in $\mathcal{Y}$ have a corresponding input x within r, that is, check whether the equation $Reach(f, r) = \mathcal{Y}$ is satisfied or not. Normally, the largest or smallest values of a specific dimension of the set $Reach(f, r)$ are much more useful in reachability problem analysis.

Definition 3 (Interval Property). Given a neural network $f : \mathbb{R}^n \to \mathbb{R}^m$, an input x_0, and $\|x - x_0\|_p \leq r$, the interval property of f and r is a convex set $Interval(f, r)$ such that

$$Interval(f, r) \supseteq \{f(x) \mid x \in \|x - x_0\|_p \leq r\}. \tag{13.22}$$

If the set $Interval(f, r)$ is the smallest convex set of points in $\{f(x) \mid x \in \|x - x_0\|_p \leq r\}$, we call this set a convex hull, which means $Interval(f, r)$ is the closest to $\{f(x) \mid x \in \|x - x_0\|_p \leq r\}$.

Unlike output reachability property, the interval property calculates a convex over-approximation of output reachable set. Based on Definition 3, the interval is also seen as an over-approximation of output reachability. Similarly, for f, r and output region $\mathcal{Y}$, we can define the verification of interval property as $\mathcal{Y} \supseteq \{f(x) \mid x \in \|x - x_0\|_p \leq r\}$, which means that all inputs in r are mapped onto $\mathcal{Y}$. The computing process has to check whether the given convex set $\mathcal{Y}$ is an interval satisfying (13.22). Similar to the output reachability property, there exist useful and simple problems, e.g., determining whether a given real number d is a valid upper bound for a specific dimension of $\{f(x) \mid x \in \|x - x_0\|_p \leq r\}$.

Definition 4 (Lipschitzian Property). Given a neural network $f : \mathbb{R}^n \to \mathbb{R}^m$, an input x_0, and $\eta(x_0, l_p, r) = \{x \mid \|x - x_0\|_p \leq r\}$,

$$Lips(f, \eta, l_p) \equiv \sup_{x \in \eta} \frac{|f(x) - f(x_0)|}{\|x - x_0\|_p}. \tag{13.23}$$

Inspired by the Lipschitz optimization [49], $Lips(f, \eta, l_p)$ is a Lipschitzian metric of f, η, and l_p, which is to quantify the changing rate of neural networks within η. Intuitively, the greatest changing rate of this metric is the best Lipschitz constant. Based on the Lipschitzian metric and a real value $d \in \mathbb{R}$, the verification of Lipschitzian property is to find out whether $Lips(f, \eta, l_p) \leq d$. Usually, the value of this metric is not easy to compute, and d is the upper bound for this value.

There are some relationships between the definitions of the above four properties. For example, when the set $Reach(f, r)$ is computed exactly, we can easily evaluate the inclusion of the set in another convex set $Interval(f, r)$. Similarly, based on the Lipschitzian metric $Lips(f, \eta, l_p)$, we can evaluate the interval property and verify this property. Please refer to our papers [39, 50] for more details.

13.4.2.2. *Verification Approaches*

Current verification techniques mainly include constraint solving, search-based approach, optimization, and over-approximation. To make these techniques efficient, one of these categories can also be combined with another category. The most significant aspect of verification techniques is that they can provide a guarantee for the result. Based on the type of guarantee, verification methods can be divided into four categories. They are methods with deterministic guarantee, one-side guarantee, guarantee converging bounds, and statistical guarantee.

Methods with deterministic guarantee state exactly whether a property holds. They transform the verification problem into a set of constraints, further solving them with a constraint solver. As a result, the solvers return a deterministic answer to a query, i.e., either satisfiable or unsatisfiable. Representative solvers used in this area are Boolean satisfiability (SAT) solvers, satisfiability modulo theories (SMT) solvers, linear programming (LP) solvers, and mixed-integer linear programming (MILP) solvers. The SAT method determines if, given a Boolean formula, there exists an assignment to the Boolean variables such that the formula is satisfiable. The prerequisite for the employment is to abstract a network into a set of Boolean combinations, whose example is given in [51]. The SMT method takes one step further and determines the satisfiability of logical formulas with respect to combinations of background theories expressed in classical first-order logic with equality. Classical SMT methods are Reluplex [52] and Planet [53]. The LP method optimizes the linear objective function subject to linear equality or linear inequality constraints. Given the requirement that some of the variables are integral, the LP problem becomes a MILP problem. For instance, a hidden layer

$z_{i+1} = \text{ReLU}(W_i z_i + b_i)$ can be described with the following MILP conditions:

$$W_i z_i + b_i \leq z_{i+1} \leq W_i z_i + b_i + M t_{i+1},$$

$$0 \leq z_{i+1} \leq M(1 - t_{i+1}),$$

where t_{i+1} has value 0 or 1, representing the activated situation, and $M > 0$ is a large constant that can be treated as ∞. The details of the encoding neural network to a MILP problem can be found in [54]. To improve the verification efficiency, extensions are made to the simple MILP method, achieving successful variant methods such as [55] and Sherlock in [56].

Approaches with a one-side guarantee only compute an approximated bound, which can claim the sufficiency of achieving properties. While these methods provide only a bounded estimation with high efficiency, they are applicable for analyzing large models. Some approaches adopt abstract interpretation, using abstract domains, e.g., boxes, zonotopes, and polyhedra, to over-approximate the computation of a set of inputs. Its application has been explored in a few approaches, including AI2 [57] and [58], which can verify interval property but cannot verify reachability property. Because the non-convex property of neural networks partially causes difficulty of verification, methods such as [59] tend to make a convex outer over-approximation of the sets of reachable activation and apply the convex optimization. In the approach ReluVal [60], the interval arithmetic is leveraged to compute rigorous bounds on the DNN outputs, i.e., interval property. The key idea of the interval analysis approach is that given the ranges of operands, an over-estimated range of the output can be computed by using only the lower and upper bounds of the operands. In addition, one-side guarantee approaches also include [61] dealing with output reachability estimation and FastLin/FastLip in [62] using linear approximation for ReLU networks.

Approaches aiming to achieve statistical guarantees on their results usually make claims such as the satisfiability of a property or a value is a lower bound of another value with a certain probability. Typical methods are CLEVER [63] working with Lipschitz property [64], which proposes the robustness estimation to measure the frequency and the severity of adversarial examples. Approaches to compute the converge bounds can be applied on large-scale real world systems and they can work with both output reachability property and interval property. Huang et al. [65] made a layer-to-layer analysis of the network, guaranteeing a misclassification being found if it exists. DeepGame [66] reduces the verification problem to a two-player turn-based game, studying two variants of point-wise robustness.

Unfortunately, these verification algorithms have some weaknesses. Algorithms based on constraint solvers, such as SMT/SAT and MILP/LP, need to encode the entire network layer by layer, limiting them to only work on small-scale or quasi-linear neural networks. Although approaches based on linear approximation, convex optimization, and abstract interpretation can work on nonlinear activation functions, they are essentially a type of over-approximations algorithm, i.e., they generally calculate the lower bound of the maximal safe radius r_{max}. Besides, these algorithms depend on the specific structure of the networks to design different abstract interpretations or linear approximations. Hence, they cannot provide a generic framework for different neural networks.

To circumvent such shortcomings, approaches based on global optimization are developed. DeepGo [50] firstly proves that most neural network layers are Lipschitz continuous and uses Lipschitz optimization to solve the problem. Since the only requirement is Lipschitz continuity, a number of studies have been done to expand this method to various neural network structures. DeepTRE [67] focuses on the Hamming distance, proposing an approach to iteratively generate lower and upper bounds on the network's robustness. The tensor-based approach returns intermediate bounds, allowing for efficient GPU computation. Furthermore, we also proposed a generic framework, DeepQuant [68], to quantify the safety risks on networks based on a Mesh Adaptive Direct Search algorithm.

In summary, the maximal safe radius r_{max} provides the local robustness information of the neural network. The adversarial attacks focus on estimating the upper bound of the radius and searching for adversarial examples outside the upper bound of the safe norm ball, while verification studies the lower bound of r_{max}, ensuring that inputs inside this norm ball are safe. Both analysis methods only concern evaluating existing neural networks. How to further improve the neural network robustness will be discussed in the section on adversarial defense.

13.4.3. *Defense*

While verification aims to provide theoretical guarantees on the robustness and reliability of DNNs, defense methods attempt to enhance such properties from a more practical perspective.

Generally, the defense strategy can be divided into four categories: pre-processing, model enhancement, adversarial training, and certified defenses. Specifically, example pre-processing methods are probably the most straightforward defense. In this strategy, input examples are processed via methods such as median smoothing, bit depth compression, and JPEG compression [69] before feeding them to the deep learning system. Pre-processing can reduce the impact of perturbation and keep enough information within the processed examples for the downstream tasks. Because most kinds of adversarial perturbation are essentially additional noise, pre-processing defenses are highly effective in vision and audio applications. Besides, this pre-processing defense does not require to re-train the protected models and can be deployed directly. Although it might cause a trivial problem if the attackers are aware of the pre-processing procedure, they can correspondingly update the generation of adversarial examples to break or bypass such defense. This means that pre-processing defenses are not reliable in white-box or "gray-box" (attackers have limited knowledge about their target model) environments.

In parallel with pre-processing, model enhancement focuses on deep learning models themselves. The core of this type of method is to improve the robustness by modifying the model architecture, activation functions, and loss functions. A typical defense along this direction is defensive distillation [70], which follows the teacher–student model [71]. Defensive distillation first produces a regular network (teacher) to generate soft labels instead of the one-hot encoding of the true labels (hard labels) to train a student model. This defense had significantly boosted the model's robustness on several benchmarks, but it was soon broken by the C&W attack proposed by Carlini and Wagner [72]. In addition to processing perturbed examples correctly, model enhancement sometimes achieves the defense effect via adversarial detection, i.e., identifying adversarial examples and refusing to give corresponding outputs. Although many model enhancement methods eventually failed [73], this direction is still a valuable and active research direction.

The idea of adversarial training appeared with the FGSM attack [42] and has been significantly generalized by later works [44]. In these pioneering works, adversarial examples were regarded as an augmentation of the original training dataset, and adversarial training required both original examples and adversarial examples to train a robust model. Madry et al. formalized adversarial training as a Min–Max optimization problem:

$$\min_{\theta} \mathbb{E}_{(x,y)\sim\mathcal{D}}\left(\max_{\delta \in B_\epsilon} L(F_\theta(x + \delta))\right). \tag{13.24}$$

Here, in the inner maximization problem, adversarial examples are generated by maximizing the classification loss, while the outer minimization updates model parameters by minimizing the loss on adversarial examples from the inner maximization. Equation (13.24) provides a principled connection between the robustness of neural networks and the adversarial attacks. This indicates that a qualified adversarial attack method could help train robust models. At the current stage, PGD adversarial training is still one of the most effective defenses [73, 74], although there are quite incremental works aiming for improvement. Nevertheless, all these PGD-based adversarial trainings take multiple backpropagations to generate adversarial perturbations, which significantly raises the computational cost. As a result, conducting adversarial training, especially on large-scale networks, is prohibitively time-consuming. On the way to improve its efficiency, recent studies have two interesting findings. On the one hand, Wong et al. [75] demonstrated that high-quality or strong adversarial examples might not be necessary for conducting successful adversarial training. They empirically showed that FGSM with uniform initialization could adversarially train models with considerable robustness more efficiently than PGD adversarial training. On the other hand, YOPO adversarial training [76] simplifies the backpropagation for updating training adversarial examples, i.e., it treats the first layer and others separately during training and generates adversarial examples toward the first layer instead of the whole trained model. This successful attempt suggests that we might need to adversarially train only the first few layers to produce robust deep learning models. Moreover, inspired by recent studies, our work [77] reveals that the connection of the lower bound of Lipschitz constant of a given network and the magnitude of its partial derivative toward adversarial examples. Supported by this theoretical finding, we utilize the gradient's magnitude to quantify the effectiveness of adversarial training and determine the timing to adjust the training procedure. In addition to robustness, adversarial training also benefits the deep learning study in terms of interpretability [78] and data augmentation. Such a technology is getting increasing attention in applications beyond security, such as text-to-image tasks [25, 79] and nature language processing [80]. Therefore, we believe that adversarial training will still be an interesting and promising research topic in the next few years.

The previous defenses are all heuristic strategies and cannot provide theoretical guarantees. Like the defensive distillation method, most defenses are likely to be broken by emerging adversarial attacks. To end such an "arms race", certified defenses aim to theoretically guarantee that the outputs of deep neural networks would not change within a certain disturbance range around inputs. Similar to some verification techniques, certified defenses come out with strong theoretical guarantees. However, they are usually computationally expensive and difficult to be extended on large-scale networks or high-dimensional datasets [50]. A promising method in this direction is randomized smoothing [81], which introduces random noise to smooth the learned feature during training. This technique demonstrates that it is feasible to use randomized perturbation to improve the trained model's robustness concretely. However, it can only work and provide guarantees under the l_2 constraint. Thus, how to generalize it to other threat models is an urgent need of research.

Overall, defending against adversarial attacks is still a work in progress, and we are far from solving this problem. We believe that preventing adversarial threats and interpreting DNNs are two sides of the same coin, and any useful finding on one side would boost our progress on the other side. Although all current defense strategies are not perfect and might only work temporarily, we would gain a better understanding of the fundamental mechanism of deep learning models if we keep digging along this direction.

13.5. Further Reading

After more than 10 years of exploration, deep learning is still a jungle full of secrets and challenges. This chapter only provides a brief yet general introduction, and we are certainly not experts in most sub-areas of this gigantic and fast-developing research topic. So, at the end of this chapter, we provide a simple overview on two emerging deep learning techniques and existing challenges.

13.5.1. *Emerging Deep Learning Models*

One of the most noticeable threads is the generative adversarial networks (GANs) [82]. Beyond learning from data, GAN models can generate new information by utilizing learned features and patterns, which gives birth to many exciting applications. For instance, convolutional neural networks can decouple the semantic content and art style in images and rebuild images with the same semantics but different style [83]. Coloring grayscale images without manual adjustment was a difficult task for computers, which is can be done by a deep learning algorithm called deep colorization [84]. In the audio processing area, Google AI utilized the GAN model to generate high-fidelity raw audio waveforms [85], and the latest deep learning model [86] can even decompose audio into fundamental components, such as loudness, pitch, timbre, and frequency, and manipulate them independently. Various GANs would start new revolutions in a lot of applications, such as Photoshop, one of the popular graphics editors, which includes a neural network-based toolbox to help users advance their arts. Applications such as deepfake and deepnude also raise concern about how to prevent such powerful techniques from being abused.

As we mentioned before, Transformer [32] has greatly boosted the raw performance of DNNs on natural language processing tasks. The most famous deep learning models built upon Transformer are GPT [33] and BERT [34]. The latest version of GPT in 2020, namely GPT-3, is the largest deep neural network, which can generate high-quality text that sometimes cannot be distinguished from that written by a real person. BERT is the most popular method and has been widely used across the NLP industry. One difference between these two models is that GPT has only one direction, while BERT is a bidirectional model. Therefore, BERT usually has a better performance but is incompetent for text generation tasks, which are GPT's specialty. Nowadays, the application of Transformer is no longer limited to the NLP area. Recent studies [87] show that this powerful architecture is capable of vision tasks.

13.5.2. *Challenges*

Despite the exciting new technologies and applications, the difficulties associated with deep learning have not changed significantly.

In addition to adversarial threats and the high demand for computational power, the lack of interpretability is also a big challenge in deep learning. A modern deep neural network usually has billions of weights, intricate architecture, and tons of hyper-parameters such as learning rate, dropout rate, etc. We do not yet fully understand the inner mechanism of these models, especially why and how a deep learning model makes certain decisions. Currently, the training of deep learning models is still largely based on trial and error and lacks a principled way to guide the training. Taking the LeNet-5 model as an example, it has two conventional layers and two fully connected layers [88]. We know that if we train it properly on the MNIST dataset, it can achieve approximately 99% classification accuracy on the test set. However, we cannot know how the accuracy changes without experiments after adding one more conventional layer into the model because we do not have a mathematical tool to formulate the represent capability of deep neural network models. Without such a theoretical guide, designing neural network architectures for a specific task has become a challenging task. This leads us to the neural architecture search (NAS) technology, which aims to find the best network architecture under limited computing resources in an automatic way. However, at the current stage, research on understanding deep learning is still in its infancy.

The lack of labeled data is also a barrier, which significantly limits the applicability of deep learning in some scenarios where only limited data are available. Training a deep learning model to a satisfactory performance usually requires a huge amount of data. For example, ImageNet, the dataset that has significantly accelerated the development of deep learning, contains over 14 million labeled images. While being data-hungry is not a problem for consumer applications where large amounts of data are easily available, copious amounts of labeled training data are rarely available in most industrial applications. So, how to improve the applicability of deep learning models with limited training data is still one of the key challenges today. Emerging techniques such as transfer learning, meta learning, and GANs show some promise with regard to overcoming this challenge.

References

[1] O. Russakovsky, J. Deng, H. Su, et al., Imagenet large scale visual recognition challenge, *Int. J. Comput. Vision*, **115**(3), 211–252 (2015).

[2] D. Amodei, S. Ananthanarayanan, R. Anubhai, J. Bai, E. Battenberg, C. Case, J. Casper, B. Catanzaro, Q. Cheng, G. Chen, et al., Deep speech 2: end-to-end speech recognition in english and mandarin. In *International Conference on Machine Learning*, pp. 173–182. PMLR (2016).

[3] M. E. Peters, M. Neumann, M. Iyyer, et al., Deep contextualized word representations, *arXiv preprint arXiv:1802.05365* (2018).

[4] Y. LeCun, Y. Bengio, and G. Hinton, Deep learning, *Nature*, **521**(7553), 436–444 (2015).

[5] W. S. McCulloch and W. Pitts, A logical calculus of the ideas immanent in nervous activity, *Bull. Math. Biophys.*, **5**(4), 115–133 (1943).

[6] F. Rosenblatt and S. Papert, The perceptron, A perceiving and recognizing automation, Cornell Aeronautical Laboratory Report. pp. 85–460 (1957).

[7] M. Minsky and S. A. Papert, *Perceptrons: An Introduction to Computational Geometry* (MIT Press, 2017).

[8] K. Fukushima, A self-organizing neural network model for a mechanism of pattern recognition unaffected by shift in position, *Biol. Cybern.*, **36**, 193–202 (1980).

[9] T. Gonsalves, The summers and winters of artificial intelligence. In *Advanced Methodologies and Technologies in Artificial Intelligence, Computer Simulation, and Human-Computer Interaction*, pp. 168–179. IGI Global (2019).

[10] S. Linnainmaa, The representation of the cumulative rounding error of an algorithm as a Taylor expansion of the local rounding errors, Master's Thesis (in Finnish), Univ. Helsinki. pp. 6–7 (1970).

[11] D. E. Rumelhart, G. E. Hinton, and R. J. Williams, Learning representations by back-propagating errors, *Nature*, **323**(6088), 533–536 (1986).

[12] Y. LeCun, B. Boser, J. S. Denker, et al., Backpropagation applied to handwritten zip code recognition, *Neural Comput.*, **1**(4), 541–551 (1989).

[13] J. D. Owens, M. Houston, D. Luebke, S. Green, J. E. Stone, and J. C. Phillips, GPU computing, *Proc. IEEE*, **96**(5), 879–899 (2008).

[14] A. Krizhevsky, I. Sutskever, and G. E. Hinton, Imagenet classification with deep convolutional neural networks, *Commun. ACM*, **60**(6), 84–90 (2017).

[15] I. Goodfellow, Y. Bengio, A. Courville, and Y. Bengio, *Deep Learning* (MIT Press Cambridge, 2016).

[16] J. Schmidhuber, Deep learning in neural networks: an overview, *Neural Networks*, **61**, 85–117 (2015).

[17] A. Zhang, Z. C. Lipton, M. Li, and A. J. Smola, *Dive into Deep Learning* (2020). https://d2l.ai.

[18] C. Nwankpa, W. Ijomah, A. Gachagan, and S. Marshall, Activation functions: comparison of trends in practice and research for deep learning, *arXiv preprint arXiv:1811.03378* (2018).

[19] W. Zhang, et al., Shift-invariant pattern recognition neural network and its optical architecture. In *Annual Conference of the Japan Society of Applied Physics* (1988).

[20] D. H. Hubel and T. N. Wiesel, Receptive fields and functional architecture of monkey striate cortex, *J. Physiol.*, **195**(1), 215–243 (1968).

[21] K. Fukushima and S. Miyake, Neocognitron: a self-organizing neural network model for a mechanism of visual pattern recognition. In *Competition and Cooperation in Neural Nets*, pp. 267–285. Springer (1982).

[22] M. Matsugu, K. Mori, Y. Mitari, and Y. Kaneda, Subject independent facial expression recognition with robust face detection using a convolutional neural network, *Neural Networks*, **16**(5–6), 555–559 (2003).

[23] K. O'Shea and R. Nash, An introduction to convolutional neural networks, *arXiv preprint arXiv:1511.08458* (2015).

[24] A. V. D. Oord, S. Dieleman, H. Zen, et al., Wavenet: a generative model for raw audio, *arXiv preprint arXiv:1609.03499* (2016).

[25] N. Sarafianos, X. Xu, and I. A. Kakadiaris, Adversarial representation learning for text-to-image matching. In *International Conference on Computer Vision* (2019).

[26] M. I. Jordan, Serial order: a parallel distributed processing approach. In *Advances in Psychology*, vol. 121, pp. 471–495. Elsevier (1997).

[27] J. L. Elman, Finding structure in time, *Cognit. Sci.*, **14**(2), 179–211 (1990).

[28] S. Hochreiter and J. Schmidhuber, Long short-term memory, *Neural Comput.*, **9**(8), 1735–1780 (1997).

[29] K. Cho, B. van Merrienboer, Ç. Gülçehre, et al., Learning phrase representations using RNN encoder-decoder for statistical machine translation. In *Conference on Empirical Methods in Natural Language Processing* (2014).

[30] Y. Bengio, R. Ducharme, P. Vincent, and C. Jauvin, A neural probabilistic language model, *J. Mach. Learn. Res.*, **3**, 1137–1155 (2003).

[31] T. Mikolov, I. Sutskever, K. Chen, et al., Distributed representations of words and phrases and their compositionality. In *Proceedings of the Advances in Neural Information Processing Systems* (2013).

[32] A. Vaswani, N. Shazeer, N. Parmar, et al., Attention is all you need. In *Proceedings of the Advances in Neural Information Processing Systems* (2017).

[33] A. Radford, K. Narasimhan, T. Salimans, and I. Sutskever, Improving language understanding by generative pre-training (2018).

[34] J. Devlin, M. Chang, K. Lee, and K. Toutanova, BERT: pre-training of deep bidirectional transformers for language understanding. In *North American Chapter of the Association for Computational Linguistics: Human Language Technologies* (2019).

[35] G. Goh, Why momentum really works, *Distill* (2017). doi: 10.23915/distill.00006. URL http://distill.pub/2017/momentum.

[36] G. E. Hinton, S. Osindero, and Y.-W. Teh, A fast learning algorithm for deep belief nets, *Neural Comput.*, **18**(7), 1527–1554 (2006).

[37] S. Ioffe and C. Szegedy, Batch normalization: accelerating deep network training by reducing internal covariate shift, *arXiv preprint arXiv:1502.03167* (2015).

[38] Y. Wu and K. He, Group normalization. In *European Conference on Computer Vision* (2018).

[39] X. Huang, D. Kroening, W. Ruan, et al., A survey of safety and trustworthiness of deep neural networks: verification, testing, adversarial attack and defence, and interpretability, *Comput. Sci. Rev.*, **37**, 100270 (2020).

[40] B. Biggio and F. Roli, Wild patterns: ten years after the rise of adversarial machine learning, *Pattern Recognit.*, **84**, 317–331 (2018).

[41] C. Szegedy, W. Zaremba, I. Sutskever, et al., Intriguing properties of neural networks. In *International Conference on Learning Representations* (2014).

[42] I. J. Goodfellow, J. Shlens, and C. Szegedy, Explaining and harnessing adversarial examples. In *International Conference on Learning Representations* (2015).

[43] A. Kurakin, I. J. Goodfellow, and S. Bengio, Adversarial examples in the physical world. In *International Conference on Learning Representations, Workshop* (2017).

[44] A. Madry, A. Makelov, L. Schmidt, et al., Towards deep learning models resistant to adversarial attacks. In *International Conference on Learning Representations* (2018).

[45] J. Uesato, B. O'Donoghue, P. Kohli, et al., Adversarial risk and the dangers of evaluating against weak attacks. In *International Conference on Machine Learning* (2018).

[46] C. Xiao, J.-Y. Zhu, B. Li, et al., Spatially transformed adversarial examples. In *International Conference on Learning Representations* (2018).

[47] Y. Zhang, W. Ruan, F. Wang, et al., Generalizing universal adversarial attacks beyond additive perturbations. In *IEEE International Conference on Data Mining* (2020).

[48] Y. Zhang, F. Wang, and W. Ruan, Fooling object detectors: adversarial attacks by half-neighbor masks, *arXiv preprint arXiv:2101.00989* (2021).

[49] D. R. Jones, C. D. Perttunen, and B. E. Stuckman, Lipschitzian optimization without the lipschitz constant, *J. Optim. Theory Appl.*, **79**(1), 157–181 (1993).

[50] W. Ruan, X. Huang, and M. Kwiatkowska, Reachability analysis of deep neural networks with provable guarantees. In *International Joint Conference on Artificial Intelligence* (2018).

[51] L. Pulina and A. Tacchella, An abstraction-refinement approach to verification of artificial neural networks. In *International Conference on Computer Aided Verification* (2010).

[52] G. Katz, C. Barrett, D. L. Dill, et al., Reluplex: an efficient SMT solver for verifying deep neural networks. In *International Conference on Computer Aided Verification* (2017).

[53] R. Ehlers, Formal verification of piece-wise linear feed-forward neural networks. In *International Symposium on Automated Technology for Verification and Analysis* (2017).

[54] A. Lomuscio and L. Maganti, An approach to reachability analysis for feed-forward ReLU neural networks, *arXiv preprint arXiv:1706.07351* (2017).

[55] C.-H. Cheng, G. Nührenberg, and H. Ruess, Maximum resilience of artificial neural networks. In *International Symposium on Automated Technology for Verification and Analysis* (2017).

[56] S. Dutta, S. Jha, S. Sanakaranarayanan, et al., Output range analysis for deep neural networks, *arXiv preprint arXiv:1709.09130* (2018).

[57] T. Gehr, M. Mirman, D. Drachsler-Cohen, et al., AI2: safety and robustness certification of neural networks with abstract interpretation. In *IEEE Symposium on Security and Privacy* (2018).

[58] M. Mirman, T. Gehr, and M. Vechev, Differentiable abstract interpretation for provably robust neural networks. In *International Conference on Machine Learning* (2018).

[59] E. Wong and Z. Kolter, Provable defenses against adversarial examples via the convex outer adversarial polytope. In *International Conference on Machine Learning* (2018).

[60] S. Wang, K. Pei, J. Whitehouse, et al., Formal security analysis of neural networks using symbolic intervals. In *USENIX Security Symposium*. USENIX Association (2018).

[61] W. Xiang, H.-D. Tran, and T. T. Johnson, Output reachable set estimation and verification for multi-layer neural networks, *IEEE Trans. Neural Networks Learn. Syst.*, **29**, 5777–5783 (2018).

[62] L. Weng, H. Zhang, H. Chen, et al., Towards fast computation of certified robustness for ReLU networks. In *International Conference on Machine Learning* (2018).

[63] T.-W. Weng, H. Zhang, P.-Y. Chen, et al., Evaluating the robustness of neural networks: an extreme value theory approach, *arXiv preprint arXiv:1801.10578* (2018).

[64] O. Bastani, Y. Ioannou, L. Lampropoulos, et al., Measuring neural net robustness with constraints, *arXiv preprint arXiv:1605.07262* (2016).

[65] X. Huang, M. Kwiatkowska, S. Wang, and M. Wu, Safety verification of deep neural networks. In *International Conference on Computer Aided Verification* (2017).

[66] M. Wu, M. Wicker, W. Ruan, et al., A game-based approximate verification of deep neural networks with provable guarantees, *Theor. Comput. Sci.*, **807**, 298–329 (2020).

[67] W. Ruan, M. Wu, Y. Sun, et al., Global robustness evaluation of deep neural networks with provable guarantees for the Hamming distance. In *International Joint Conference on Artificial Intelligence* (2019).

[68] P. Xu, W. Ruan, and X. Huang, Towards the quantification of safety risks in deep neural networks, *arXiv preprint arXiv:2009.06114* (2020).

[69] R. Shin and D. Song, JPEG-resistant adversarial images. In *Annual Network and Distributed System Security Symposium* (2017).

[70] N. Papernot, P. D. McDaniel, X. Wu, et al., Distillation as a defense to adversarial perturbations against deep neural networks. In *IEEE Symposium on Security and Privacy* (2016).

[71] G. E. Hinton, O. Vinyals, and J. Dean, Distilling the knowledge in a neural network, *arXiv preprint arXiv:1503.02531* (2015).

[72] N. Carlini and D. A. Wagner, Towards evaluating the robustness of neural networks. In *IEEE Symposium on Security and Privacy* (2017).

[73] A. Athalye, N. Carlini, and D. A. Wagner, Obfuscated gradients give a false sense of security: circumventing defenses to adversarial examples. In *International Conference on Machine Learning* (2018).

[74] L. Rice, E. Wong, and J. Z. Kolter, Overfitting in adversarially robust deep learning. In *International Conference on Machine Learning* (2021).

[75] E. Wong, L. Rice, and J. Z. Kolter, Fast is better than free: revisiting adversarial training. In *International Conference on Learning Representations* (2020).

[76] D. Zhang, T. Zhang, Y. Lu, et al., You only propagate once: accelerating adversarial training via maximal principle. In *Proceedings of the Advances in Neural Information Processing Systems* (2019).

[77] F. Wang, Y. Zhang, Y. Zheng, and W. Ruan, Gradient-guided dynamic efficient adversarial training, *arXiv preprint arXiv:2103.03076* (2021).

[78] T. Zhang and Z. Zhu, Interpreting adversarially trained convolutional neural networks. In *International Conference on Machine Learning* (2019).

[79] T. Chen, Y. Liao, C. Chuang, et al., Show, adapt and tell: adversarial training of cross-domain image captioner. In *International Conference on Computer Vision* (2019).

[80] D. Wang, C. Gong, and Q. Liu, Improving neural language modeling via adversarial training. In *International Conference on Machine Learning* (2019).

[81] J. M. Cohen, E. Rosenfeld, and J. Z. Kolter, Certified adversarial robustness via randomized smoothing. In *International Conference on Machine Learning* (2019).

[82] I. Goodfellow, J. Pouget-Abadie, M. Mirza, et al., Generative adversarial nets. In *Proceedings of the Advances in Neural Information Processing Systems* (2014).

[83] L. A. Gatys, A. S. Ecker, and M. Bethge, Image style transfer using convolutional neural networks. In *IEEE Conference on Computer Vision and Pattern Recognition* (2016).

[84] Z. Cheng, Q. Yang, and B. Sheng, Deep colorization. In *International Conference on Computer Aided Verification* (2015).

[85] J. Engel, K. K. Agrawal, S. Chen, et al., Gansynth: adversarial neural audio synthesis, *arXiv preprint arXiv:1902.08710* (2019).

[86] J. Engel, L. Hantrakul, C. Gu, and A. Roberts, DDSP: differentiable digital signal processing, *arXiv preprint arXiv:2001.04643* (2020).

[87] A. Dosovitskiy, L. Beyer, A. Kolesnikov, et al., An image is worth 16 x 16 words: transformers for image recognition at scale. In *International Conference on Learning Representations* (2021).

[88] Y. LeCun, C. Cortes, and C. Burges, MNIST handwritten digit database, *AT&T Labs*, **2** (2010).

Chapter 14

Deep Learning for Graph-Structured Data

Luca Pasa*, Nicolò Navarin[†], and Alessandro Sperduti[‡]

Department of Mathematics, University of Padua
Via Trieste, 63 - 35121 Padova, Italy
*luca.pasa@unipd.it
[†]nicolo.navarin@unipd.it
[‡]alessandro.sperduti@unipd.it

In this chapter, we discuss the application of deep learning techniques to input data that exhibit a graph structure. We consider both the case in which the input is a single, huge graph (e.g., a social network), where we are interested in predicting the properties of single nodes (e.g., users), and the case in which the dataset is composed of many small graphs where we want to predict the properties of whole graphs (e.g., molecule property prediction). We discuss the main components required to define such neural architectures and their alternative definitions in the literature. Finally, we present experimental results comparing the main graph neural networks in the literature.

14.1. Introduction

In this chapter, we consider whether it is possible to define neural network architectures that deal with structured input data. The amount and variety of data generated and stored in modern information processing systems is constantly increasing, as is the use of machine learning (ML) approaches, especially very successful deep learning (DL) solutions, to extract knowledge from them. Traditional ML approaches have been developed assuming data to be encoded into feature vectors; however, many important real-world applications generate data that are naturally represented by more complex structures, such as graphs. Graphs are particularly suited to represent the relations (arcs) between the components (nodes) constituting an entity. For instance, in social network data, single data "points" (i.e., users) are closely inter-related, and not explicitly representing such dependencies would most likely lead to an information loss. Because of this, ML techniques able to directly process structured data have gained more and more attention since the first developments, such as recursive neural networks [1, 2] proposed in the second half of the 1990s. In the last few years, there has been a burst of interest in developing DL models for graph domains, or more in general, for non-Euclidean domains, commonly referred to as *geometric deep learning* [3]. In this chapter, we focus on deep learning for graphs.

14.1.1. *Why Graph Neural Networks?*

The analysis of structured data is not new to the machine learning community. After the first proposals in the field of neural networks [1, 2, 4], in the 2000s, kernel methods for structured data became the dominant approach to dealing with such kinds of data. Kernel methods have been defined for trees [5], graphs, [6–8] and graph with continuous attributes [9, 10]. Kernel methods have been quite successful on the many tasks where small- to medium-sized datasets were available. However, the kernel approach suffers from two main drawbacks:

- lack of scalability to large datasets (with some exceptions);
- scarce ability to deal with real-valued attributes.

For more details on kernel methods for structured data, please refer to the surveys by Giannis et al. [11] or Nils et al. [12]. In the beginning of the 2010s, following the success of deep neural networks in many application domains, in particular of convolutional networks for images [13], the research community started to be interested in the design of deep neural network models for graphs, hoping for a leap in performance, just as it happened in the case of images. The first scientific papers in this research area laid down the basic concepts that are still in use. The core idea is to learn a representation of a node in the graph that is conditioned on the representations of neighboring nodes. While this approach can be easily implemented in trees or DAGs, where the presence of directed arcs allows the updating of the nodes in a reverse topological order, in general graphs the presence of cycles is an obstacle to its implementation. A practical solution that has been identified by earlier researchers [14, 15] consists in using an iterative or multilayer approach, in which each node representation depends on the ones of the neighbors *at the previous iteration or layer*. A few years later, basically the same idea has been derived and implemented, starting from spectral graph theory (see Section 14.4). Having the possibility to learn a representation of a node in a graph is functional to the design of predictors in two main settings, namely prediction of a property of a single node in a (large) graph or of a property of a graph as a whole.

14.1.2. *The Two Main Settings: Node Classification vs. Graph Classification*

There are two main problem settings that can arise when dealing with structured data.

- **Predictions over nodes in a network.** In this setting, the dataset is composed of a single (possibly disconnected) large graph. Each example is a node in the graph, and the learning tasks are defined as predictions over the nodes. An example in this setting is the prediction of properties of a social network user based on his or her connections.
- **Predictions over graphs.** In this case, each example is composed of a whole graph, and the learning tasks are predictions of properties of the whole graphs. An example is the prediction of toxicity in humans of chemical compounds represented by their molecular graph.

Figure 14.1 shows the difference between the two settings. From a technical point of view, both settings require us to define (deep) neural architectures able to learn *graph isomorphic invariant representations* for nodes, which is usually obtained by resorting to a *graph convolution*. However, the second setting requires additional components, as will be discussed in Section 14.7, for learning a graph isomorphic invariant representation for each individual graph.

14.1.3. *Graph Neural Networks Basics*

As mentioned before, the main problem faced by graph neural networks is to compute a *sound* and *meaningful* representation for graph nodes, i.e.,

- it is invariant to the way the graph is represented (e.g., in which order nodes and arcs of a graph are presented);
- it incorporates structural information that is relevant for the prediction task.

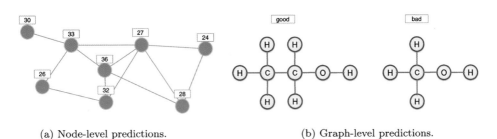

(a) Node-level predictions.　　　　　　　　(b) Graph-level predictions.

Figure 14.1: Examples of tasks on graphs: (a) node regression task, e.g., prediction of the age of users in a social network; (b) graph classification task, e.g., molecule classification. The values inside the boxes are the targets we aim to predict. Note that in (a) there is a target for each node, while in (b) we have a single target per graph.

The first requirement (*soundness*) is justified by the fact that graphs that are *isomorphic* should induce the same function over their nodes. This requirement is so important that even the representations of whole graphs should comply to it; otherwise the same graph represented in different ways may return different predictions, which is of course not desirable. The second requirement (*meaningfulness*) is obvious: learned representations should preserve only the necessary information to best perform the task at hand.

Both requirements can be reasonably satisfied in a neural network by using a convolution operator, defined on graphs, supported by a mechanism of communication (message-passing) between neighboring nodes.

The general idea of graph convolution starts from a parallel between graphs and images. In convolutional networks for images, the hidden representation inherits the shape of the input image (with the exception of pixels close to the border that, if no padding is considered, imply a slight dimension reduction). Let us focus on the first convolutional layer. For each entry in the hidden representation, the convolution layer computes a representation that depends on the corresponding input pixel, and on the neighboring ones (depending on the size of the filter). In practice, we have that each neighboring position has an associated weight. This definition of convolution layer stems from the direct application of the convolution operator.

On graphs, there is not a straightforward corresponding convolution operator. As we will see later, it is possible either to define graph neural networks directly in the graph domain (see Section 14.3), or to resort to the graph spectral domain (see Section 14.4).

14.2. Notation and Definitions

In the following, we use italic letters to refer to variables, bold lowercase letters to refer to vectors, and bold uppercase letters to refer to matrices. The elements of a matrix $\mathbf{A}$ are referred to as a_{ij} (and similarly for vectors). We use uppercase letters to refer to sets or tuples.

In this chapter, we deal with problems and tasks that involve the concept of graph. Let $G = (V, E, \mathbf{X})$ be a graph, where $V = \{v_0, \ldots, v_{n-1}\}$ denotes the set of vertices (or nodes) of the graph, $E \subseteq V \times V$ is the set of edges, and $\mathbf{X} \in \mathbb{R}^{n \times s}$ is a multivariate signal on the graph nodes with the i-th row $\mathbf{x}_i$ representing the attributes of v_i. We define $\mathbf{A} \in \mathbb{R}^{n \times n}$ as the adjacency matrix of the graph, with elements $a_{ij} = 1 \iff (v_i, v_j) \in E$. With $\mathcal{N}(v)$ we denote the set of nodes adjacent to node v.

14.3. Early Models of Graph Neural Network

In this section, we review the early definitions of the graph neural networks that have been proposed in literature. In the following definitions, for the sake of simplicity, we ignore the bias terms. During the reading of this section, it is important to keep in mind that a graph convolution operator can be applied to perform both graph classification and node classification (see Section 14.7). Therefore, while some of them have been applied to graph classification rather than node classification, the basic node relabeling or graph convolution components are the same for both tasks.

The first definition of neural network for structured data, including graphs, has been proposed by Sperduti and Starita in 1997 [2]. The authors propose to use the generalized recursive neuron, a generalization to structures of a recurrent neuron, which is able to build a map from a domain of structures to the set of reals. Using the generalized recursive neurons, the authors show that it is possible to formalize several learning algorithms and models able to deal with structures as generalization of the supervised networks developed for sequences. The core idea is to define a neural architecture that is modeled according to the graph topology. Thanks to weights sharing, the same set of neurons is applied to each vertex in the graph, obtaining a representation in output that is based on the information associated with the vertex and on the representations generated for its neighbors. Although in the paper a learning algorithm based on *recurrent backpropagation* [16, 17] is proposed for general graphs with cycles, no experimental assessment of the algorithm is reported. Later, an approach for general graphs, based on standard backpropagation, has been proposed by Micheli [15] for graph predictions, and by Scarselli et al. [14] for node prediction. Several years later, the approach followed by Micheli was independently (re)proposed in [18] under the name *graph convolution*.

14.3.1. *Recursive Graph Neural Networks*

Scarselli et al. [14] proposed a recursive neural network exploiting the following general form of convolution:

$$\mathbf{h}_v^{t+1} = \sum_{u \in \mathcal{N}(v)} f(\mathbf{h}_u^t, \mathbf{x}_v, \mathbf{x}_u), \qquad (14.1)$$

where $t \geq 0$ is the time of the recurrence, $\mathbf{h}_v^{t+1}$ is the representation of node v at timestep $t + 1$, and f is a neural network whose parameters have to be learned, and are shared among all the vertices. The recurrent system is defined as a contraction mapping, and thus it is guaranteed to converge to a fixed point $\mathbf{h}^\star$. It can be noticed that $\mathbf{h}^\star$ is *sound* since: (i) the terms $f(\mathbf{h}_u^t, \mathbf{x}_v, \mathbf{x}_u)$ do not change with a change in the graph representation; (ii) the terms just mentioned are aggregated by a commutative operator (i.e., sum), and so $\mathbf{h}_v^{t+1}$ ($t \geq 0$) does not depend on the order of presentation of the vertices. This idea has been re-branded later as *neural message passing*, the formal definition of which was proposed by Gilmer et al. [19]

14.3.2. *Feedforward Graph Neural Networks*

In the same year, Micheli [15] proposed the neural network for graphs (NN4G) model. NN4G is based on a graph convolution that is defined as:

$$\mathbf{h}_v^{(1)} = \sigma\left(\bar{\mathbf{W}}^{(1)}\mathbf{x}_v\right), \tag{14.2}$$

$$\mathbf{h}_v^{(i+1)} = \sigma\left(\bar{\mathbf{W}}^{(i+1)}\mathbf{x}_v + \sum_{k=1}^{i}\hat{\mathbf{W}}^{(i+1,k)}\sum_{u\in\mathcal{N}(v)}\mathbf{h}_u^{(k)}\right), \quad i > 0, \tag{14.3}$$

where $1 \leq v \leq n$ is the vertex index, $\hat{\mathbf{W}}^{(l,m)}$ are the weights on the connections from layer m to layer l, $\bar{\mathbf{W}}^{(i+1)}$ are weights transforming the input representations for the $(i+1)$-th layer, and σ is a nonlinear activation function applied element-wise. Note that in this formulation, skip connections are present, to the $(i+1)$-th layer, from layer 1 to layer i. Moreover, *soundness* of $\mathbf{h}_v^{(i+1)}$ for $i \geq 1$ is again guaranteed by the commutativity of the sum over the neighbours (i.e., $\sum_{u\in\mathcal{N}(v)}\mathbf{h}_u^{(k)}$).

14.4. Derivation of Spectral Graph Convolutions

The derivation of the spectral graph convolution operator originates from graph spectral filtering [18]. Let us fix a graph G. Let $x : V \rightarrow \mathbb{R}$ be a signal on the nodes V of the graph G, i.e., a function that associates a real value with each node of V. Since the number of nodes in G is fixed (i.e., n) and the set V can be arbitrarily but consistently ordered[1], we can naturally represent every signal as a vector $\mathbf{x} \in \mathbb{R}^n$, which from now on we will refer to as signal. In order to set up a convolutional network on G, we need the notion of convolution $*_G$ between a signal $\mathbf{x}$ and a filter signal $\mathbf{f}$. However, as we do not have a natural description of translation on graphs, it is not so obvious how to define the convolution directly in the graph domain. This operation is therefore usually defined in the spectral domain of the graph, using an analogy with classical Fourier analysis in which the convolution of two signals is computed as the pointwise product of their Fourier transforms.

For this reason, we start providing the definition of the graph Fourier transform [20]. Let $\mathbf{L}$ be the (normalized) graph Laplacian, defined as

$$\mathbf{L} = \mathbf{I_n} - \mathbf{D}^{-\frac{1}{2}}\mathbf{A}\mathbf{D}^{-\frac{1}{2}}, \tag{14.4}$$

---

[1]The set V is organized in an arbitrary order, for instance, when representing the graph with the corresponding adjacency matrix.

where $\mathbf{I_n}$ is the $n \times n$ identity matrix, and $\mathbf{D}$ is the degree matrix with entries given as

$$
d_{ij} = \begin{cases} \sum_{k=0}^{n-1} a_{ik}, & \text{if } i = j \\ 0, & \text{otherwise} \end{cases}.
\tag{14.5}
$$

Since $\mathbf{L}$ is real, symmetric, and positive semi-definite, we can compute its eigendecomposition as

$$
\mathbf{L} = \mathbf{U}\Lambda\mathbf{U}^\top,
\tag{14.6}
$$

where $\Lambda = \text{diag}(\lambda_0, \ldots, \lambda_{n-1})$ is a diagonal matrix with the ordered eigenvalues of $\mathbf{L}$ as diagonal entries, and the orthonormal matrix $\mathbf{U}$ contains the corresponding eigenvectors $\{\mathbf{u}_0, \ldots, \mathbf{u}_{n-1}\}$ of $\mathbf{L}$ as columns. In many classical settings of Fourier analysis, such as the Euclidean space or the torus, the Fourier transform can be defined in terms of the eigenvalues and eigenvectors of the Laplace operator. In analogy, we consider now the eigenvectors $\{\mathbf{u}_0, \ldots, \mathbf{u}_{n-1}\}$ as the Fourier basis on the graph G, and the eigenvalues $\{\lambda_0, \ldots, \lambda_{n-1}\}$ as the corresponding graph frequencies. In particular, going back to our spatial signal $\mathbf{x}$, we can define its graph Fourier transform as

$$
\hat{\mathbf{x}} = \mathbf{U}^\top\mathbf{x},
\tag{14.7}
$$

and its inverse graph Fourier transform as

$$
\mathbf{x} = \mathbf{U}\hat{\mathbf{x}}.
\tag{14.8}
$$

The entries $\hat{x}_i = \mathbf{x} \cdot \mathbf{u}_i$ are the frequency components or coefficients of the signal $\mathbf{x}$ with respect with the basis function $\mathbf{u}_i$ and associated with the graph frequency λ_i. For this reason, $\hat{\mathbf{x}}$ can also be regarded as a distribution on the spectral domains of the graph, i.e., to each basis function $\mathbf{u}_i$ with frequency λ_i a corresponding coefficient $\hat{x}_i$ is associated.

Using the graph Fourier transform to switch between spatial and spectral domains, we are now ready to define the graph convolution between a filter $\mathbf{f}$ and a signal $\mathbf{x}$ as

$$
\mathbf{f} *_G \mathbf{x} = \mathbf{U}\left(\hat{\mathbf{f}} \odot \hat{\mathbf{x}}\right) = \mathbf{U}\left((\mathbf{U}^\top\mathbf{f}) \odot (\mathbf{U}^\top\mathbf{x})\right),
\tag{14.9}
$$

where $\hat{\mathbf{f}} \odot \hat{\mathbf{x}} = (\hat{f}_0\hat{x}_0, \ldots, \hat{f}_{n-1}\hat{x}_{n-1})$ denotes the component-wise Hadamard product of the two vectors $\hat{\mathbf{x}}$ and $\hat{\mathbf{f}}$.

For graph convolutional networks, it is easier to design the filters $\mathbf{f}$ in the spectral domain as a distribution $\hat{\mathbf{f}}$, and then define the filter $\mathbf{f}$ on the graph as $\mathbf{f} = \mathbf{U}\hat{\mathbf{f}}$.

According to Eq. (14.9), for a given $\hat{\mathbf{f}}$ the application of the convolutional filter $\mathbf{f}$ to a signal $\mathbf{x}$ is given as

$$\mathbf{f} *_G \mathbf{x} = \mathbf{U}\left(\left(\mathbf{U}^\top \mathbf{U}\hat{\mathbf{f}}\right) \odot \left(\mathbf{U}^\top \mathbf{x}\right)\right) = \mathbf{U}\left(\hat{\mathbf{f}} \odot \left(\mathbf{U}^\top \mathbf{x}\right)\right). \tag{14.10}$$

The Hadamard product $\hat{\mathbf{f}} \odot \hat{\mathbf{x}}$ can be formulated in matrix–vector notation as $\hat{\mathbf{f}} \odot \hat{\mathbf{x}} = \hat{\mathbf{F}}\hat{\mathbf{x}}$ by applying the diagonal matrix $\hat{\mathbf{F}} = \text{diag}(\hat{\mathbf{f}})$, given by

$$(\hat{\mathbf{F}})_{ij} = \left(\text{diag}(\hat{\mathbf{f}})\right)_{ij} = \begin{cases} \hat{f}_i & \text{if } i = j \\ 0 & \text{otherwise} \end{cases},$$

to the vector $\hat{\mathbf{x}}$. According to Eq. (14.10), we therefore obtain

$$\mathbf{f} *_G \mathbf{x} = \mathbf{U}\hat{\mathbf{F}}\mathbf{U}^\top \mathbf{x}. \tag{14.11}$$

We can design the diagonal matrix $\hat{\mathbf{F}}$ and, thus, the spectral filter $\mathbf{f}$ in various ways. The simplest way would be to define $\mathbf{f}_\theta$ as a non-parametric filter, i.e., use $\hat{\mathbf{F}}_\theta = \text{diag}(\theta)$, where $\theta = (\theta_0, \ldots, \theta_{n-1})^\top$ is a completely free vector of filter parameters that can be learned by the neural network. However, such a filter grows in size with the data, and it is not well suited for learning.

A simple alternative is to use a polynomial parametrization based on powers of the spectral matrix Λ [21] for the filter, such as,

$$\hat{\mathbf{F}}_\theta = \sum_{i=0}^{k} \theta_i \Lambda^i. \tag{14.12}$$

This filter has $k+1$ parameters $\{\theta_0, \ldots, \theta_k\}$ to learn, and it is spatially k-localized on the graph. One of the main advantages of this filter is that we can formulate it explicitly in the graph domain. Recalling the eigendecomposition $\mathbf{L} = \mathbf{U}\Lambda\mathbf{U}^\top$ of the graph Laplacian, Eqs. (14.11) and (14.12) when combined give

$$\mathbf{f}_\theta *_G \mathbf{x} = \mathbf{U}\hat{\mathbf{F}}_\theta \mathbf{U}^\top \mathbf{x} = \sum_{i=0}^{k} \theta_i \mathbf{U}\Lambda^i \mathbf{U}^\top \mathbf{x}$$

$$= \sum_{i=0}^{k} \theta_i (\mathbf{U}\Lambda\mathbf{U}^\top)^i \mathbf{x} = \sum_{i=0}^{k} \theta_i \mathbf{L}^i \mathbf{x}. \tag{14.13}$$

Note that the computation of the eigendecomposition of the graph Laplacian $\mathbf{L}$ (the cost is of the order $O(n^3)$) is feasible only for relatively small graphs (with some thousands of nodes at most). However, real-world problems involve graphs with hundreds of thousands or even millions of nodes: in these cases, the computation of the eigendecomposition of $\mathbf{L}$ is prohibitive and a filter of the form of Eq. (14.13) has clear advantages compared to a spectral filter given in the form of Eq. (14.11).

Applying the convolution defined in Eq. (14.13) to a multivariate signal $\mathbf{X} \in \mathbb{R}^{n \times s}$ and using m filters, we obtain the following definition for a single graph convolutional layer:

$$\mathbf{H} = \sum_{i=0}^{k} \mathbf{L}^i \mathbf{X} \Theta^{(i)}. \tag{14.14}$$

where $\Theta^{(i)} \in \mathbb{R}^{s \times m}$.

This layer can be directly applied in a single-layer neural network to compute the task predictions, i.e.,

$$\mathbf{Y} = \sigma \left(\sum_{i=0}^{k} \mathbf{L}^i \mathbf{X} \Theta^{(i)} \right), \tag{14.15}$$

where σ is an appropriate activation function for the output task, e.g., the *softmax* for a classification problem with m classes.

14.5. Graph Convolutions in Literature

In this section, we present in detail some of the most widely adopted graph convolutions that have been proposed in the literature.

14.5.1. *Chebyshev Graph Convolution*

The parametrization of the polynomial filter defined in Eq. (14.12) is given in the monomial basis. Alternatively, Defferrard et al. [18] proposed to use Chebyshev polynomials as a polynomial basis. In general, the usage of a Chebyshev basis improves the stability in the case of numerical approximations. By defining the operators

$$T^{(0)}(x) = 1, \ T^{(1)}(x) = x, \ \text{and for } k > 1, \ T^{(k)}(x) = 2x T^{(k-1)}(x) - T^{(k-2)}(x),$$

the filter is defined as

$$\hat{\mathbf{F}}_\theta = \sum_{i=0}^{k} \theta_i T^{(i)}(\tilde{\Lambda}), \tag{14.16}$$

where $\tilde{\Lambda} = \frac{2}{\lambda_{max}} \Lambda - \mathbf{I}_n$ is the diagonal matrix of scaled eigenvectors of the graph Laplacian. The resulting convolution is then:

$$\mathbf{f}_\theta *_G \mathbf{x} = \sum_{i=0}^{k} \theta_i T^{(i)}(\tilde{\mathbf{L}}) \mathbf{x}. \tag{14.17}$$

where $\tilde{\mathbf{L}} = \frac{2}{\lambda_{max}} \mathbf{L} - \mathbf{I}_n$.

14.5.2. *Graph Convolutional Networks*

Kipf et al. [22] proposed to fix order $k = 1$ in Eq. (14.17) to obtain a linear first-order filter for each graph convolutional layer in a neural network. Additionally, they fixed $\theta_0 = \theta_1 = \theta$. They also suggested to stack these simple convolutions to obtain larger receptive fields (i.e., neighbors reachable with an increasing number of hops) in order to improve the discriminatory power of the resulting network. Specifically, the resulting convolution operator is defined as

$$\mathbf{f}_\theta *_G \mathbf{x} = \theta(\mathbf{I_n} + \mathbf{D}^{-\frac{1}{2}}\mathbf{A}\mathbf{D}^{-\frac{1}{2}})\mathbf{x} = \theta(2\mathbf{I_n} - \mathbf{L})\mathbf{x}. \tag{14.18}$$

A renormalization trick to limit the eigenvalues of the resulting matrix is also introduced by the following: $\mathbf{I_n} + \mathbf{D}^{-\frac{1}{2}}\mathbf{A}\mathbf{D}^{-\frac{1}{2}}$ is replaced by $\tilde{\mathbf{D}}^{-\frac{1}{2}}\tilde{\mathbf{A}}\tilde{\mathbf{D}}^{-\frac{1}{2}}$, where $\tilde{\mathbf{A}} = \mathbf{A} + \mathbf{I_n}$ and $d_{ii} = \Sigma_{j=0}^n \tilde{a}_{ij}$. In this way, the spectral filter $\mathbf{f}_\theta$ is built not on the spectral decomposition of the graph Laplacian $\mathbf{L}$ but on the eigendecomposition of the perturbed operator $\tilde{\mathbf{D}}^{-\frac{1}{2}}\tilde{\mathbf{A}}\tilde{\mathbf{D}}^{-\frac{1}{2}}$.

Applying this convolution operator to a multivariate signal $\mathbf{X} \in \mathbb{R}^{n \times s}$ and using m filters, we obtain the following definition for a single graph convolutional layer:

$$\mathbf{H} = \tilde{\mathbf{D}}^{-\frac{1}{2}}\tilde{\mathbf{A}}\tilde{\mathbf{D}}^{-\frac{1}{2}}\mathbf{X}\Theta, \tag{14.19}$$

where $\Theta \in \mathbb{R}^{s \times m}$. This convolutional operation has complexity $O(|E|ms)$. To obtain a Graph Convolutional Network (GCN), several graph convolutional layers are stacked and interleaved by a nonlinear activation function, typically a ReLU.

If $\mathbf{H}^{(0)} = \mathbf{X}$, then, based on single layer convolution in Eq. (14.19), we obtain the following recursive definition for the k-th graph convolutional layer:

$$\mathbf{H}^{(k)} = ReLU(\tilde{\mathbf{D}}^{-\frac{1}{2}}\tilde{\mathbf{A}}\tilde{\mathbf{D}}^{-\frac{1}{2}}\mathbf{H}^{(k-1)}\Theta). \tag{14.20}$$

14.5.3. *GraphConv*

In 2019, Morris et al. [23] investigated GNNs from a theoretical point of view. Specifically, they studied the relationship between GNN and the one-dimensional *Weisfeiler–Lehman graph isomorphism heuristic* (1-WL). 1-WL is an iterative algorithm that computes a graph invariant for labeled graphs, which at each iteration produces a coloring for the nodes of the graph. The output of an iteration depends on the coloring from the previous one. At iteration 0, the algorithm uses as initial coloring the label of the node. The aim of 1-WL is to test whether two graphs $\mathcal{G}$ and $\mathcal{H}$ are isomorphic. After applying the algorithm until convergence on both graphs, if they show different color distributions, the 1-WL test concludes that the graphs are not isomorphic. If the coloring is the same, the graphs may or may not be isomorphic. In fact, this algorithm is not able to distinguish all non-isomorphic graphs (like all graph invariants), but is still a powerful heuristic, which can successfully test isomorphism for a broad class of graphs. A more detailed introduction to 1-WL is reported in Section 14.6. As a result of this theoretical study, Morris et al. [23] defined the *GraphConv* operator inspired by the Weisfeiler–Lehman graph invariant; it is defined as follows:

$$\mathbf{H}^{(i+1)} = \mathbf{H}^{(i)}\bar{\mathbf{W}}^{(i)} + \mathbf{A}\mathbf{H}^{(i)}\hat{\mathbf{W}}^{(i)}, \qquad (14.21)$$

where $\mathbf{H}^0 = \mathbf{X}$, and $\bar{\mathbf{W}}^{(i)}$ and $\hat{\mathbf{W}}^{(i)}$ are two weights matrices. It is interesting to note that this definition of convolution is very similar to NN4G (cf. Eq. (14.3)).

14.5.4. *Graph Convolutions Exploiting Personalized PageRank*

Klicpera et al. [24] proposed a graph convolution by exploiting Personalized PageRank. Let $f(\cdot)$ define a two-layer feedforward neural network. The PPNP layer is defined as

$$\mathbf{H} = \alpha \left(\mathbf{I}_n - (1 - \alpha)\tilde{\mathbf{A}}\right)^{-1} f(\mathbf{X}), \qquad (14.22)$$

where $\tilde{\mathbf{A}} = \mathbf{A} + \mathbf{I}_n$. Such a filter preserves locality due to the properties of Personalized PageRank.

The same paper proposed an approximation, derived by a truncated power iteration, avoiding the expensive computation of the matrix inversion, referred to as APPNP. It is implemented as a multilayer network where the $(l + 1)$-th layer is defined as

$$\mathbf{H}^{(l+1)} = (1 - \alpha)\tilde{\mathbf{S}}\mathbf{H}^{(l)} + \alpha\mathbf{H}^{(0)}, \qquad (14.23)$$

where $\mathbf{H}^{(0)} = f(\mathbf{X})$ and $\tilde{\mathbf{S}}$ is the renormalized adjacency matrix adopted in GCN, i.e., $\tilde{\mathbf{S}} = \tilde{\mathbf{D}}^{-\frac{1}{2}}\tilde{\mathbf{A}}\tilde{\mathbf{D}}^{-\frac{1}{2}}$.

14.5.5. *GCNII*

While the GCN presented in Section 14.5.2 is very popular, one of its main drawbacks is that it is not suited to build deep networks. Actually, the authors proposed to use just two graph convolutional layers. This is a common problem of many graph convolutions, known as the over-smoothing problem [25].

In [26], an extension of GCN was proposed. Authors aimed at the definition of a graph convolution that can be adopted to build truly deep graph neural networks. To pursue this goal, they enhance the original GCN formulation in Eq. (14.20) with *Initial residual* and *Identity mapping* connections (thus the acronym GCNII). The $l + 1$-th layer of GCNII is defined as

$$\mathbf{H}^{(l+1)} = \sigma\left(\left((1 - \alpha_l)\tilde{\mathbf{S}}\mathbf{H}^{(l)} + \alpha_l\mathbf{H}^{(0)}\right)\left((1 - \beta_l)\mathbf{I}_n + \beta_l\mathbf{W}^{(l)}\right)\right), \qquad (14.24)$$

where α and β are hyper-parameters. Authors propose to fix $\alpha_l = 0.1$ or 0.2 for each l, and $\beta_l = \frac{\lambda}{l}$, where λ is a single hyper-parameter to tune.

14.5.6. *Graph Attention Networks*

Graph Attention Networks (GATs) [27] exploit a different convolution operator based on masked self-attention. The attention mechanism was introduced by Bahdanau et al. [28] with the goal of enhancing the performance of the encoder–decoder architecture on neural network-based machine translation tasks. The basic idea behind the proposed attention mechanism is to allow the model to selectively focus on valuable parts of the input, and hence learn the associations between them. In GAT, the attention mechanism is developed by replacing the adjacency matrix in the convolution with a matrix of attention weights

$$\mathbf{H}^{(i+1)} = \sigma(\mathbf{B}^{(i+1)}\mathbf{H}^{(i)}\Theta), \tag{14.25}$$

where $0 \leq i < l$ (the number of layers), $\mathbf{H}^{(0)} = \mathbf{X}$, and the u, v-th element of $\mathbf{B}^{(i+1)}$ is defined as

$$b_{u,v}^{(i+1)} = \frac{\exp(LeakyRELU(\mathbf{w'}^{\top}[\mathbf{Wh}_u^{(i)}||\mathbf{Wh}_v^{(i)}]))}{\sum_{k \in \mathcal{N}(u)} \exp(LeakyRELU(\mathbf{w'}^{\top}[\mathbf{Wh}_u^{(i)}||\mathbf{Wh}_k^{(i)}]))}, \tag{14.26}$$

if $(u, v) \in E$, and 0 otherwise. The vector $\mathbf{w}'$ and the matrix $\mathbf{W}$ are learnable parameters. Authors propose to use multihead attention to stabilize the training. While it may be harder to train, GAT allows to weight differently the neighbors of a node; thus it is a very expressive graph convolution.

14.5.7. *GraphSAGE*

Another interesting proposal for the convolution over the node neighborhood is GraphSage [29], where the aggregation over the neighborhoods is performed by using sum, mean or max-pooling operators, followed by a linear projection in order to update the node representation. In addition to that, the proposed approach exploits a particular neighbor sampling scheme. In fact, the method uniformly samples for each vertex v, a fixed-size set of neighbors $\mathcal{U}(v)$, instead of using the full neighborhood $\mathcal{N}(v)$. Using a fixed-size subset of neighbors allows to maintain the computational footprint of each batch invariant to the actual node degree distribution. Formally, the k-th layer of the GraphSAGE convolution is defined as follows:

$$\mathbf{h}_{\mathcal{U}(v)}^{(k)} = \mathcal{A}^{(k)}(\{\mathbf{h}_u^{(k-1)}, \forall u \in \mathcal{U}(v)\}), \tag{14.27}$$

$$\mathbf{h}_v^{(k)} = \sigma(\mathbf{W}^{(k)}[\mathbf{h}_v^{(k-1)}, \mathbf{h}_{\mathcal{U}(v)}^{(k)}]), \tag{14.28}$$

where $\mathcal{A}^{(k)}$ is the aggregation function used at the k-th layer. In particular, the authors proposed to use different strategies to implement $\mathcal{A}$, such as a mean aggregation function, a pooling aggregator, or even a more complex aggregator based on an LSTM architecture.

14.5.8. *Gated Graph Sequence Neural Networks*

Li et al. [30] extended the recurrent graph neural network proposed by Scarselli et al. in 2009 [14]. They proposed to remove the constraint for the recurrent system to be a contraction mapping, and implemented this idea by adopting recurrent neural networks to define the recurrence. Specifically, the authors adopted the gated recurrent unit (GRU). The recurrent convolution operator is defined as follows:

$$\mathbf{h}_v^{(1)} = [\mathbf{x}_v, \mathbf{0}],$$
$$\mathbf{a}_v^{(t)} = \mathbf{A}_v[\mathbf{h}_v^{(t-1)}, \forall v \in V],$$
$$\mathbf{z}_v^t = \sigma(\mathbf{W}^z \mathbf{a}_v^{(t)} + \mathbf{U}^z \mathbf{h}_v^{(t-1)}),$$
$$\mathbf{r}_v^t = \sigma(\mathbf{W}^r \mathbf{a}_v^{(t)} + \mathbf{U}^r \mathbf{h}_v^{(t-1)}),$$
$$\mathbf{c}_v^t = \tanh(\mathbf{W} \mathbf{a}_v^{(t)} + \mathbf{U}(\mathbf{r}_v^t \odot \mathbf{h}_v^{(t-1)})),$$
$$\mathbf{h}_v^{(t)} = (1 - \mathbf{z}_v^t) \odot \mathbf{h}_v^{(t-1)} + \mathbf{z}_v^t \odot \mathbf{c}_v^t,$$

where $\mathbf{A}_v$ is row v of the adjacency matrix $\mathbf{A}$. Note that the propagation of the node embeddings through the edges is performed by computing $\mathbf{a}_v^{(t)}$, while the other equations describe the GRU unit structure.

14.5.9. *Other Convolutions*

The convolutions presented up to now are the most common and interesting. Moreover, the structure of these operators highlights many elements that the majority of the GCs developed in the last few years have in common. In the literature, many convolutions were developed using some of the discussed operators as a starting point. For instance, DGCNN [31] adopts a graph convolution very similar to GCN [22]. Specifically, it adopts a slightly different propagation scheme for vertices' representations, based on the random-walk graph Laplacian.

A more straightforward approach in defining convolutions on graphs is PATCHY-SAN (PSCN) [32]. This approach is inspired by how convolutions are defined over images. It consists in selecting a fixed number of vertices from each graph and exploiting a canonical ordering on graph vertices. For each vertex, it defines a fixed-size neighborhood, exploiting the same vertex ordering. It requires the vertices of each input graph to be in a canonical ordering, which is as complex as the graph isomorphism problem (no polynomial-time algorithm is known).

The Funnel GCNN (FGCNN) model [33] aims to enhance the gradient propagation using a simple aggregation function and LeakyReLU activation functions. Hinging on the similarity of the adopted graph convolutional operator, that is, the *GraphConv* (see Section 14.5.3), to the Weisfeiler–Lehman (WL) Subtree Kernel [34], it introduces a loss term for the output of each convolutional layer to guide the network to reconstruct the corresponding explicit WL features. Moreover, the number of filters used at each convolutional layer is based on a measure of the WL kernel complexity.

Bianchi et al. [35] developed a convolutional layer based on auto-regressive moving average (ARMA) filters. This particular type of filter, compared to polynomial filters, allows to manage higher order neighborhoods. Moreover, ARMA filters present a flexible frequency response. The resulting nonlinear graph filter enhanced the modeling capability compared to common GNNs that exploit convolutional layers based on polynomial filters.

Recently, geometric graph convolutional networks (Geom-GCN) [36] were proposed. The model exploits a geometric aggregation scheme that is permutation-invariant and consists of three modules: node embedding, structural neighborhood, and bi-level aggregation. For what concerns the node embedding component, the authors proposed to use three different ad-hoc embedding methods to compute node embeddings that preserve specific topology patterns. The structural neighborhood consists in the definition of a neighborhood that is the result of the concatenation of the neighborhood in the graph space and the neighborhood in the latent space. Specifically, the neighborhood of a node v in the latent space is the set of nodes whose distance from v is less than a predefined value. To compute the distance, a particular function is defined over two latent space node representations, and it is based on a similarity measure between nodes in the latent space. The bi-level aggregation exploits two aggregation functions used in defining the graph neural network layer. These two functions guarantee permutation invariance for a graph, and they are able to extract effectively structural information of nodes in neighborhoods.

14.5.10. *Beyond the Message Passing*

Some recent works in the literature exploit the idea of extending graph convolution layers to increase the receptive field size, without increasing the depth of the model. The basic idea underpinning these methods is to consider the case in which the graph convolution can be expressed as a polynomial of the powers of a transformation $\mathcal{T}(\cdot)$ of the adjacency matrix. The models based on this idea are able to simultaneously and directly consider all topological receptive fields up to k-hops, just like the ones that are obtained by a stack of graph convolutional layers of depth k, without incurring the typical limitations related to the complex interactions among the parameters of the GC layers. Formally, the idea is to define a representation as built from the contribution of all topological receptive fields up to k-hops as

$$\mathbf{H} = f(\mathcal{T}(\mathbf{A})^0\mathbf{X}, \mathcal{T}(\mathbf{A})^1\mathbf{X}, \ldots, \mathcal{T}(\mathbf{A})^k\mathbf{X}), \tag{14.29}$$

where $\mathcal{T}(\cdot)$ is a transformation of the adjacency matrix (e.g., the Laplacian matrix), and f is a function that aggregates and transforms the various components obtained from the powers of $\mathcal{T}(\mathbf{A})$, for instance the concatenation, the summation, or even something more complex, such as a multilayer perceptron. The f function can be defined as a parametric function, depending on a set of parameters θ whose values can be estimated from data (e.g., when f involves an MLP). In the following, we discuss some recent works that define instances of this general architectural component.

One of the first methods that exploited this intuition is presented by Atwood and Towsley [37]. In their work, the authors propose two architectures designed to perform node classification and graph classification (we will discuss in depth the distinction between the two tasks in Section 14.7). Specifically, Atwood and Towsley proposed to exploit the power series of the probability transition matrix, multiplied (using the Hadamard product) by the inputs. Moreover, the model developed to perform graph classification exploits the summation as f function. Similarly, the model proposed by Defferrard et al. in 2016 [18] exploits the Chebyshev polynomials and sums the obtained representations over k.

Another interesting approach is that proposed by Tran et al. [38], where the authors consider larger receptive fields compared to standard graph convolutions. They focus on a convolution definition based on the shortest paths, instead of the standard random walks obtained by exponentiation of the adjacency matrix.

Wu et al. introduced a simplification of the graph convolution operator, dubbed Simple Graph Convolution (SGC) [39]. The proposed model is based on the idea that perhaps the nonlinear operator introduced by GCNs is not essential. The authors propose to stack several linear GC operators, since stacking multiple GC layers has an important effect on the location of the learned filters (after k GC layers, the hidden representation of a vertex considers information coming from the vertices up to distance k). Formally, the model is defined as follows: $\mathbf{Y} = softmax(\mathbf{S}^k\mathbf{X}\Theta)$, where $\mathbf{S} = \tilde{\mathbf{D}}^{-\frac{1}{2}}\tilde{\mathbf{A}}\tilde{\mathbf{D}}^{-\frac{1}{2}}$, $\tilde{\mathbf{A}} = \mathbf{A} + \mathbf{I}$, and $\tilde{\mathbf{D}}$ is the degree matrix of $\tilde{\mathbf{A}}$. Notice that, in this case, f selects just the kth power of the diffusion operators. An extension of this work, dubbed Linear Graph Convolution (LGC), was proposed by Navarin et al. [21], where the authors propose to introduce skip connections from each layer to the last one, which is a merge layer implementing the sum operator, followed by a softmax activation $\mathbf{Y} = softmax(\Sigma_{i=0}^k\alpha_i\mathbf{L}^i\mathbf{X}\Theta)$.

Liao et al. in 2019 [40] proposed to construct a deep graph convolutional network, exploiting particular localized polynomial filters based on the Lanczos algorithm, which leverages multiscale information.

In the same year, Chen et al. [41] suggested to replace the neighbor aggregation function by graph-augmented features combining node degree features and multiscale graph-propagated features. Basically, the proposed model concatenates the node degree with the power series of the normalized adjacency matrix. The proposed model aggregates the graph-augmented features of each vertex and projects each of these subsets by using an MLP.

Luan et al. [42] introduced two deep GCNs that rely on Krylov blocks. The first one exploits a GC layer, named snowball, which concatenates multiscale features incrementally, resulting in a densely connected graph network. The architecture stacks several layers, and exploits nonlinear activation functions. The second model, called Truncated Krylov, concatenates multiscale features in each layer. In this model, the topological features from all levels are mixed together. A similar approach is proposed by Rossi et al. [43]. The authors proposed an alternative method, named SIGN, to scale GNNs to very large graphs. This method uses, as a building block, the set of exponentiations of linear diffusion operators. In this building block, every exponentiation of the diffusion operator is linearly projected by a learnable matrix. Moreover, a nonlinear function is applied to the concatenation of the diffusion operators.

Very recently, a model dubbed deep adaptive graph neural network was introduced [44], to learn node representations by adaptively incorporating information from large receptive fields. The model exploits an MLP network for node feature transformation. Then, it constructs a multiscale representation leveraging on the computed node feature transformations and the exponentiation of the adjacency matrix. This representation is obtained by stacking the various adjacency matrix exponentiations (thus obtaining a three-dimensional tensor). Similarly to the GCNs that rely on Krylov blocks [42], also in this case the model projects the obtained multiscale representation using multiplication by a weights matrix, obtaining a representation where the topological features from all levels are mixed together. Moreover, this projection also uses (trainable) retention scores. These scores measure how much information on the corresponding representations derived by different propagation layers should be retained to generate the final representation for each node in order to adaptively balance the information from local and global neighborhoods.

14.5.11. *Relational Data*

In some applications, edges are typed, i.e., edges come with associated labels. This is the case, for instance, with knowledge graphs, where the edges specify the relationship between two concepts. This kind of data is, thus, commonly addressed as relational data.

Graph neural networks can be easily extended to deal with such data [45]. Relational Graph Convolutional Networks are defined for a node v as

$$h_v^{(i+1)} = \sigma \left(\mathbf{W}^{(i)} h_v^{(i)} + \sum_{r \in \mathcal{R}} \sum_{u \in \mathcal{N}_r(v)} \frac{1}{|\mathcal{N}_r(v)|} \mathbf{W}_r'^{(i)} h_u^{(i)} \right), \qquad (14.30)$$

where $\mathcal{R}$ is the set of possible relations, $\mathcal{N}_r(v)$ is the set of neighbors of v that are connected to it via an edge of type r, and $h_v^{(0)} = \mathbf{x}_v$. When the set of possible relations is big, authors suggest to use regularization to constrain $\mathbf{W}_r'^{(i)}$.

Simonovsky and Komodakis [46] proposed a similar approach which was an extension of the model proposed by Duvenaud et al. [47] (see Section 14.3.2) that computes the sum over the neighbors of a vertex by weights conditioned by the edge labels.

14.6. Expressive Power of Graph Neural Networks

When dealing with graphs, the problem of determining whether two graphs are just different representations of the same one is known as the graph isomorphism problem [48], for which there are no known polynomial-time algorithms. This means that, for any graph neural network, there exist infinitely many non-isomorphic graphs that the model cannot distinguish, i.e., that will be mapped to the same representation. This is a central issue for graph neural networks, since the more indistinguishable graphs there are, the more limited is the class of functions the network can represent (i.e., the network can only represent functions that associate the same output to all the graphs that are mapped to the same internal representation).

The expressiveness of graph neural networks has been recently studied [49]. The authors did show that most graph neural networks are at most as powerful as the one-dimensional *Weisfeiler–Lehman* graph invariant (see Section 14.5.3), depending on the adopted neighbor aggregation function. They proved that some GNN variants, such as the GCN described in Section 14.5.2, or graphSAGE described in Section 14.5.7, do not achieve this expressiveness, and proposed the graph isomorphism network (GIN) model, which was proven to be as expressive as the *Weisfeiler–Lehman* test. In GIN, the aggregation over node neighbors is implemented using an MLP; therefore, the resulting GC formulation is the following (where $h_v^{(0)} = \mathbf{x}_v$):

$$h_v^{(k)} = MLP^{(k)}\left((1 + \epsilon^{(k)}) h_v^{(k-1)} + \sum_{u \in \mathcal{N}(v)} h_u^{(k-1)} \right). \qquad (14.31)$$

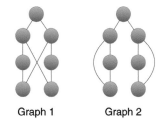

Graph 1   Graph 2

Figure 14.2: Example of two non-isomorphic graphs that cannot be distinguished by the 1-dimensional *Weisfeiler–Lehman* graph invariant test. Note that, in this simple example, all nodes have the same label.

14.6.1. *More Expressive Graph Neural Networks*

While the 1-dimensional *Weisfeiler–Lehman* graph invariant test is a fast and generally effective graph isomorphism test, there are many (even small) pairs of graphs it cannot distinguish. Figure 14.2 reports a pair of graphs that are not isomorphic but that cannot be distinguished by 1-WL test.

One possibility to define more expressive graph neural networks is to inspire their computation to more powerful graph invariants, such as the k-dimensional *Weisfeiler–Lehman* (k-WL) tests, which base the iterative coloring procedure of WL on graphlets of size k. k-WL tests are increasingly powerful for all $k > 2$ ($k = 1$ and $k = 2$ have the same discriminative power).

Some recent works followed this direction. Maron et al. [50] proposed a hierarchy of increasingly expressive graph neural networks, where the k-th order network is as expressive as the k-dim WL. A practical implementation of a network as expressive as the three-dimensional WL is then proposed. The main drawback of the proposed approach is the computational complexity that is quadratic in the number of nodes of the input graphs (even for graphs with sparse connectivity). Moreover, such expressive networks tend to easily overfit the training data.

Morris et al. [51] proposed a more efficient alternative, defining a revisited, local version of the k-WL that exploits the graph sparsity. They proposed a neural network architecture based on such a method and showed that it improves the generalization capability of the network compared to other alternatives in the literature. Again, the main problem of the approach is that to compute the k-order node tuples on which the WL test is based, the computational complexity is $O(n^k)$.

14.7. Prediction Tasks for Graphs

When considering graph-level prediction tasks, the node-level representations computed by the graph convolutional operators need to be aggregated in order to obtain a single (fixed-size) representation of the graph. Thus, one of the main problems to solve in this scenario is how to transform a variable number of node-level representations into a single graph-level one. Formally, a general GNN model for graph classification (or regression) is built according to the equations described in the following. First, d graph convolution layers are stacked

$$\mathbf{H}^{(i)} = \sigma \left(GC(\mathbf{H}^{(i-1)}, G) \right), \tag{14.32}$$

where $\sigma(\cdot)$ is an element-wise nonlinear activation function, $GC(\cdot, \cdot)$ is a graph convolution operator, and $\mathbf{h}_v^{(i)}$ (the v-th row of $\mathbf{H}^{(i)}$) is the representation of node v at the i-th graph convolution layer, $1 \leq i \leq d$, and $\mathbf{h}_v^{(0)} = \mathbf{x}_v$. Then, an aggregation function is applied

$$\mathbf{h}^S = aggr(\{\mathbf{h}_v^{(i)} | v \in V, \ 1 \leq i \leq d\}), \tag{14.33}$$

where $aggr(\cdot)$ is the aggregator function. Note that the aggregation may depend on all the hidden representations computed by the different GC layers and not just the last one. $\mathbf{h}^S$ is the fixed-size graph-level representation. Subsequently, the *readout*$(\cdot)$ function (usually implemented by a multilayer perceptron) applies some nonlinear transformation on $\mathbf{h}^S$. Finally, an output layer (e.g., the *LogSoftMax* for a classification problem) is applied.

14.7.1. *Aggregation Function and Readout*

As we highlighted above, the GC can be used to perform either graph classification or node classification. Therefore, the main additional component required by graph classification GNNs is the aggregator function. An effective and efficient graph-level representation should be, as much as possible, invariant to different isomorphic representations of the input graph, thus letting the learning procedure to focus only on the property prediction task, with no need to worry about the way the graph in the input is represented. The simplest aggregation operators adopted in the literature are linear, namely the average and the sum of vertex representations. This kind of operators have been used in many GNN models. For instance, NN4G [15] (described in Section 14.3.2) computes, for each graph, the average graph vertex representation for each hidden layer, and concatenates them. Other approaches consider only the last graph convolution layer to compute such an average [37]. A more complex approach exploits multilayer perceptrons to transform node representations before a sum aggregator is applied [19].

In the last few years, several more complex (nonlinear) techniques to perform aggregation have been proposed. One of these is *SortPooling* [31], which is a nonlinear pooling operator, used in conjunction with concatenation to obtain an aggregation operator. The idea is to select a predetermined number of vertex embeddings using a sorting function, and to concatenate them, obtaining a graph-level representation of fixed size. Note, however, that this representation ignores some of the nodes of the graph, thus losing potentially important information.

In many cases, using such simple aggregators inevitably results in a loss of information due to the mix of numerical values they introduce. A much better approach, from a conceptual point of view, would be to consider all the representations of nodes of a graph as a (multi)set, and the aggregation function to learn as a function defined on these (multi)sets. To face this setting, the DeepSets [52] network has been recently proposed. The idea is to design neural networks that take sets as the input. A DeepSet maps the elements of the input set in a high-dimensional space via a learned $\phi(\cdot)$ function, usually implemented as a multilayer perceptron. It then aggregates node representations by summing them, and finally it applies the readout, i.e., the $\rho(\cdot)$ function (another MLP), to map the graph-level representation to the output of the task at hand. Formally, a DeepSets network can be defined as follows:

$$sf(X) = \rho\left(\sum_{x_i \in X} \phi(x_i)\right), \tag{14.34}$$

for some $\rho(\cdot)$ and $\phi(\cdot)$ functions, if X is countable. Navarin et al. [53] proposed a graph aggregation scheme based on DeepSets implementing the $\phi(\cdot)$ function as a multilayer perceptron. An interesting property of this approach is that it has been proven that any function $sf(X)$ over a set X satisfying the following two properties:

(1) variable number of elements in the input, i.e., each input is a set $X = \{x_1, \ldots, x_m\}$ with x_i belonging to some set $\mathcal{X}$ (typically a vectorial space) and $M > 0$;
(2) permutation invariance;

is decomposable in the form of Eq. (14.34).

Moreover, under some assumptions, DeepSets are universal approximators of functions over countable sets, or uncountable sets with a fixed size. Therefore, they are potentially very expressive from a functional point of view.

Recently, Pasa et al. [54] proposed to extend this approach by implementing $\phi(\cdot)$ by exploiting self-organizing maps (SOMs) to map the node representations in the space defined by the activations of the SOM neurons. The resulting representation embeds the information about the similarity between the various inputs. In fact, similar input structures will be mapped in similar output representations (i.e., node embeddings). Using a fully unsupervised mapping for the $\phi(\cdot)$ function may lead to the loss of task-related information. To avoid this issue, the proposed method makes the $\phi(\cdot)$ mapping supervised by stacking, after the SOM, a graph convolution layer that can be trained via supervised learning, allowing to better incorporate topological information in the mapping.

14.7.2. *Graph Pooling*

Pooling operators have been defined and used in convolutional neural networks (CNNs) for image processing. Their aim is to improve the performance of the network by introducing some degree of local invariance into transformations of the image, such as scale, translation, or rotation transformations. Replicating these operators in the context of graphs turns out to be very complex for different reasons. First, in the GNN setting—compared to standard CNNs—graphs contain no natural notion of spatial locality because of the complex topological structure. Moreover, unlike image data, in the graph context the number and degree of nodes are not fixed, thus making it even more complex to define a general graph pooling operator. In order to address these issues, different types of graph pooling operators have been proposed in the last two years. In general, graph pooling operators are defined so as to learn a clustering of nodes that allows to uncover the hierarchical topology given by the underlying sub-graphs. In a GNN architecture, the graph pooling operators can be inserted after one or more GC layers.

One example of the first proposed graph pooling operators is DiffPool [55]. DiffPool computes a node clustering by learning a cluster assignment matrix $S^{(l)}$ over the node embedding computed after l GC layers. Let us denote the adjacency matrix at the l-th layer as $A^{(l)}$ and the node embedding matrix as $Z^{(l)}$. DiffPool computes $A^{(l+1)}$, $X^{(l+1)}$, which are, respectively, the new adjacency matrix and the new matrix of embeddings for each of the nodes/clusters in the graph. $X^{(l+1)}$ is computed by aggregating the nodes embeddings $Z^{(l)}$ according to the cluster assignments $S^{(l)}$, generating embeddings for each of the clusters:

$$X^{(l+1)} = S^{(l)^\top} Z^{(l)}.$$

Similarly, the new adjacency matrix $A^{(l+1)}$ represents the connections between clusters, and is computed as

$$A^{(l+1)} = S^{(l)^\top} A^{(l)} S^{(l)}.$$

The main limitation of DiffPool is the computation of the soft clustering assignments, since during the early phases of training, a dense assignment matrix must be stored in memory. Asymptotically, this incurs a quadratic storage complexity over the number of graph vertices, making the application of DiffPool in large graphs unfeasible.

To face this complexity issue, a sparse version of graph pooling has been proposed [56], where a differentiable graph coarsening method is used to reduce the size of the graph in an adaptive manner within a graph neural network pipeline.

The sparsity of this method is achieved by applying a node dropping policy, that basically drops a fixed number of nodes from the original graph. The nodes to drop are selected based on a *projection score* computed for each node. This method allows to reduce the memory storage complexity, which becomes linear in the number of edges and nodes of the graph.

Another recently proposed graph pooling method is MinCutPool [57]. The method is based on the *k-way normalized minCUT* problem, which that is the task of partitioning V in k disjoint subsets by removing the minimum number of edges. The idea is to learn the parameters in a MinCutPool layer by minimizing the minCUT objective, which can be jointly optimized with a task-specific loss. The method, similarly to DiffPool, uses a cluster assignment matrix. This matrix is computed by solving a relaxed continuous formulation of the minCUT optimization problem that can be solved in polynomial time and guarantees a near-optimal solution.

14.8. Experimental Comparison

In this section, we revise some of the most interesting results obtained by GNN models in different tasks. First, we outline the main applications of GNNs and the dataset commonly used as benchmarks to evaluate the strengths and the weaknesses of the models. Then, we discuss a selection of the results obtained by models that achieved notable results.

14.8.1. *Applications and Benchmark Datasets*

Graph structured data are ubiquitous in nature; therefore, there are a wide number of possible real-world applications of graph neural networks. However, it is important to take into account that in the past some problems were usually modeled using flat or sequential representations, instead of using graphs. This is due to the fact that for some tasks involving graph structured data, considering the topological information is not crucial, and using a simpler model may bring benefits in terms of performance. In this section, we list and discuss the most interesting tasks on which GNNs have been successfully applied in the last few years.

One of the most prominent areas in which GNNs have been applied with success is Cheminformatics. In fact, many chemical compound datasets are often used to benchmark new models. In Cheminformatics, different tasks can be considered. In general, the input is the molecular structure, while the output varies based on the specific task. The majority of tasks in benchmark datasets model graph classification or regression problems. An example is the quantitative structure–property relationship (QSPR) analysis, where the aim is to predict one or more chemical properties (e.g., toxicity, solubility) of the input chemical compound. Other tasks in this field include finding structural similarities among compounds, drug side-effect identification, and drug discovery. The datasets related to these applications, commonly used as benchmarks, are MUTAG [58], PTC [59], NCI1 [60], PROTEINS [61], D&D [62], and ENZYMES [61]. The first two datasets contain chemical compounds represented by their molecular graphs, where each node is labeled with an atom type, and the edges represent bonds between them. MUTAG contains aromatic and hetero-aromatic nitro compounds, and the task is to predict their mutagenic effect on a bacterium. PTC contains chemical compounds and the task is to predict their carcinogenicity for male rats. In NCI1, the graphs represent anti-cancer screens for cell lung cancer. The last three datasets, PROTEINS, D&D, and ENZYMES, contain graphs that represent proteins. Each node corresponds to an amino acid, and an edge connects two of them if they are less than 6Å apart. In particular, ENZYMES, unlike the other reported datasets (that model binary classification problems), allows testing the models on multiclass classification over six classes.

Another interesting field where GNNs have achieved good results is social network analysis. A social network is modeled as a graph where nodes represent users, and edges the relationships between them (e.g., friendship, co-authorship). Usually, the tasks on social graphs regard node or graph classification. For what concerns node classification, three major datasets in the literature are usually employed to assess the performances of GNNs: Cora [63], Citeseer [64], and PubMed [65]. Each dataset is represented as a single graph. Nodes represent documents, and node features are sparse bag-of-words feature vectors. Specifically, the task requires us to classify the research topics of papers. Each node represents a scientific publication described by a 0/1-valued word vector indicating the absence/presence of the corresponding word from a dictionary. For what concerns graph classification on social datasets, the most popular social benchmarks are COLLAB, IMDB-BINARY (IMDB-B), IMDB-MULTI (IMDB-M), REDDIT-BINARY, and REDDIT-MULTI [66]. In COLLAB, each graph represents a collaboration network of the corresponding researcher with other researchers from three fields of physics. The task consists in predicting the physics field the researcher belongs to. IMDB-B and IMDB-M are composed of graphs derived from actors/actresses who have acted in different movies on IMDB, together with the movie genre information. Each graph has a target that represents the movie genre. IMDB-B models a binary classification task, while IMDB-M contains graphs that belong to three different classes. Unlike the bioinformatics datasets, the nodes contained in the social datasets do not have any associated label. REDDIT-BINARY and REDDIT-MULTI contain graphs that represent online discussion threads where nodes represent users, and an edge represents the fact that one of the two users responded to the comment of the other user. In REDDIT-BINARY, four popular subreddits are considered. Two of them are question/answer-based subreddits, while the other two are discussion-based subreddits. A graph is labeled according to whether it belongs to a question/answer-based community or a discussion-based community. By contrast, in REDDIT-MULTI, there are five subreddits involved and the graphs are labeled with their corresponding subreddits.

14.8.2. *Experimental Setup and Validation Process*

In the last few years, many new graph neural network models have been proposed. However, despite the theoretical advancements reached by the latest contributions in the field, comparing the results of the various proposed methods turns out to be hard. Indeed, many different methods (not all correct) to perform validation, and thus select the model's hyper-parameters, were used. In a recently published paper [67], the authors highlighted and discussed the importance of the validation strategy, especially when dealing with graph neural networks. Moreover, they experimentally proved that the experimental settings of many papers are ambiguous or not reproducible. Another important issue is related to the correct usage of data splits for model selection versus model assessment. A fair method to evaluate a model requires two distinct phases: model selection on the validation set, and model assessment on the test set. Unfortunately, in many works, in particular, in graph classification, some of the hyper-parameter are selected by considering the best results directly on the test set, clearly an incorrect procedure. This is also due to the fact that some datasets have a limited number of samples, in particular in validation, and thus a hyper-parameter selection performed using the validation set is extremely unstable. However, performing model selection and model assessment in an incorrect way could lead to overly optimistic and biased estimates of the true predictive performance of a model. Another aspect that should be considered comparing two or more models is related to the amount of information used in input and output encoding. In fact, it is common practice in the literature to augment node descriptors with structural features. For example, some models add the degree (and some clustering coefficients) to each node feature vector [55], or add a one-hot representation of node degrees [49]. Obviously, this encoding difference makes it even harder to compare the experimental results published in the literature. Good experimental practices suggest that all models should be consistently compared using the same input representations, and using the same validation strategy. For this reason, the results reported in the following section are limited to models that have been evaluated using the same, fair methodology.

14.8.3. *Experimental Results*

In this section, we report and discuss the most meaningful results obtained by some of the models discussed in the previous sections. Table 14.1 reports the results on classification tasks over bioinformatics benchmark datasets, while in

Table 14.1:   Accuracy comparison among several state-of-the-art models on graph classification tasks

Model\Dataset	PTC	NCI1	PROTEINS	D&D	ENZYMES
PSCN [32]	60.00 ±4.82	76.34 ±1.68	75.00 ±2.51	76.27 ±2.64	—
FGCNN [53]	58.82 ±1.80	81.50 ±0.39	74.57 ±0.80	77.47 ±0.86	— —
SOM-GCNN [54]	62.24 ±1.7	83.30 ±0.45	75.22 ±0.61	78.10 ±0.60	50.01 ±2.9
DGCNN [67]	— —	76.4 ±1.7	72.9 ±3.5	76.6 ±4.3	38.9 ±5.7
GIN [67]	— —	80.0 ±1.4	73.3 ±4.0	75.3 ±2.9	59.6 ±4.5
DIFFPOOL [67]	— —	76.9 ±1.9	73.7 ±3.5	75.0 ±3.5	59.5 ±5.6
GraphSAGE [67]	— —	76.0 ±1.8	73.0 ±4.5	72.9 ±2.0	58.2 ±6.0

Table 14.2:   Accuracy comparison among several state-of-the-art models on graph classification tasks considering social network datasets

Model\Dataset	COLLAB	IMDB-B	IMDB-M	RED.-B	RED.-5K
PSCN [32]	72.60 ±2.15	71.00 ±2.29	45.23 ±2.84	86.30 ±1.58	49.10 ±0.70
DGCNN [67]	57.4 ±1.9	53.3 ±5.0	38.6 ±2.2	72.1 ±7.8	35.1 ±1.4
GIN [67]	75.9 ±1.9	66.8 ±3.9	42.2 ±4.6	87.0 ±4.4	53.8 ±5.9
DIFFPOOL [67]	67.7 ±1.9	68.3 ±6.1	45.1 ±3.2	76.6 ±2.4	34.6 ±2.0
GraphSAGE [67]	71.6 ±1.5	69.9 ±4.6	47.2 ±3.6	86.1 ±2.0	49.9 ±1.7

Table 14.2 we report the results on classification tasks over social network datasets. Finally, Table 14.3 reports the most interesting results in the literature for what concerns the task of node classification. The results reported in the tables show that there isn't a method that obtains the best performance on all the considered

Table 14.3: Accuracy comparison among several state-of-the-art models on nodes classification tasks considering social network datasets

Model\Dataset	Citeseer	Cora	PubMed
Cheby [68]	70.2 ±1.0	81.4 ±0.7	78.4 ±0.4
GCN [68]	71.1 ±0.7	81.5 ±0.6	79.0 ±0.6
GAT [68]	70.8 ±0.5	83.1 ±0.4	78.5 ±0.3
SGC [68]	71.3 ±0.2	81.7 ±0.1	78.9 ±0.1
ARMA [68]	72.3 ±1.1	82.8 ±0.6	78.8 ±0.3
LGC [21]	72.9 ±0.3	85.0 ±0.3	80.2 ±0.4
APPNP [68]	71.8 ±0.5	83.3 ±0.5	80.1 ±0.2
GCNII [26]	73.4	85.5	80.3

datasets/tasks. This behavior suggests that each of the considered datasets and tasks stress different aspects of the graph convolution operators. For what concerns graph classification and bioinformatics datasets, the best results are obtained by the SOM-GCNN in all datasets except ENZYMES, where GIN, obtains the best result. A very similar accuracy is achieved by DIFFPOOL. These results emphasize the importance of using an expressive aggregation and readout methodology. Indeed SOM-GCNN, GIN, and DIFFPOOL introduce novel expressive aggregation methodologies. The social network results in Table 14.2 show that even in these datasets, GIN obtains very interesting performances since it obtains the best results in three datasets: COLLAB, and two versions of REDDIT (binary classification and multiclass). These datasets have a significantly higher number of edges and nodes per graph than the two IMDB datasets, where PSCN obtains a better accuracy. In node classification tasks results (Table 14.3), the GCNII shows the best performances in all datasets. In Cora, the accuracy obtained by GCNII is very close to the one obtained by LGC. In Citeseer, GCNII performs 1% better than LGC, which achieved the second highest result. In PubMed, the accuracy values of GCNII, LGC, and APPNP are very close; indeed the performances of the three methods are less than one standard deviation apart.

14.9. Open-Source Libraries

The growth in popularity of GNN models poses new challenges for the existing computing libraries and frameworks aimed at developing DNN models. In fact, the particular representations of the nodes and of the diffusion operators make it necessary to handle the sparsity of GNN operations efficiently in widespread GPU hardware. Moreover, considering the enormous size of some graphs (e.g., social networks datasets) it became crucial to implement the possibility of scaling the computations to large-scale graphs and multiple GPUs. For these reasons, some new libraries that extend and adapt the functionality of widely adopted DNN frameworks, such as PyTorch [69] and TensorFlow [70], have been recently developed. These libraries provide high-level interfaces and methods to implement and develop multiple GNN variants. In the following section, we review three commonly adopted libraries that are built on the top of PyTorch and TensorFlow to develop GNN models: PyTorch Geometrics, Deep Graph Library, and Spektral.

14.9.1. *Pytorch-Geometric*

PyTorch Geometric (PyG) [68] is a widespread library that is built upon PyTorch. PyG includes various methods for deep learning on graphs and other irregular structures, from a variety of published papers. The library allows to easily develop GNN architectures thanks to an interface that implements message passing. This interface presents methods to define the message, update the node embeddings, and perform neighborhood aggregation and combination. Moreover, multiple pooling operations are provided. For what concerns the data management, the library implements a mini-batch loader working either for many small graphs, or when the input is a single giant graph. Finally, the library implements loaders and management functions for the most common benchmark datasets.

PyG exploits dedicated GPU scatter and gather kernels to handle sparsity, instead of using sparse matrix multiplication kernels. The scatters allow to operate on all edges and nodes in parallel, thus significantly accelerating the GNN processing.

14.9.2. *Deep Graph Library*

Deep Graph Library (DGL) [71] is a framework-agnostic library. In fact, it can use PyTorch, TensorFlow, or MXNet [72] as backends. Similarly to PyG, DGL provides a message passing interface. The interface exposes three main methods: the message function to define the message; the reduce function that allows each node to access the received messages and perform aggregation; and the update function that operates on the aggregation results. This function is typically used to combine the aggregation with the original features of a node and to compute the updated node embedding.

To improve the performance in graph processing, DGL adopts advanced optimization techniques such as kernel fusion, multithread and multiprocess acceleration, and automatic sparse format tuning. In particular, it leverages on specialized kernels for GPUs or TPUs that allow to improve the parallelization of matrix multiplications between both dense and sparse matrices. The adopted parallelization scheme is chosen by the library using heuristics that consider multiple factors including the input graph. Thanks to these optimizations, compared to other popular GNN frameworks, DGL shows better performance both in terms of computational time demand and memory consumption.

14.9.3. *Spektral*

Very recently, a new library dubbed Spektral [73] has been introduced. The Spektral library is based on the Keras API and TensorFlow 2. The library provides the essential building blocks for creating graph neural networks. Moreover, it implements some of the most common GC layers as Keras layers. This allows to use them to build Keras models, and thus they inherit the most important features of Keras such as the training loop, callbacks, distributed training, and automatic support for GPUs and TPUs. At the time of writing, Spektral implements 15 different GCN layers, based on the message passing paradigm. Furthermore, the library provides several graph pooling layers and global graph pooling methods. Comparing Spektral with PyG and DGL, it is important to notice that Spektral is developed specifically for the TensorFlow ecosystem. In terms of computational performance, Spektral's implementation of GC layers is comparable to the one of PyG.

14.10. Conclusions and Open Problems

In this chapter, we introduced and discussed graph neural networks (GNNs). We firstly introduced the main building block of GNNs: the graph convolution (GC). We discussed how this component is exploited by graph neural networks to compute a (hopefully) sound and meaningful representation for graph nodes, and how GC operators evolved from the first definitions to the GC layers recently proposed in the literature. The experimental results obtained using GNNs show the benefits of using this type of model when dealing with structured data. Despite the good results obtained in several graph-based applications, there are several open problems and challenges. One of the main open problems is scalability. Several models that obtain very good results in benchmark datasets turn out to be not scalable to large-scale settings. Developing models capable of dealing with very large graphs is crucial, since several interesting tasks require dealing with huge amounts of data (e.g., social networks).

In addition, from a theoretical prospective, graph neural networks offer very interesting and challenging open problems. Indeed, the expressiveness of many graph neural networks is rather limited. As we discussed, recent works showed that GNNs are as powerful as the one-dimensional Weisfeiler–Lehman graph invariant test. Only recently, a few models that try to overcome this limit have been introduced. The encouraging results highlight that more research has to be carried out in this direction.

From the architectural point of view, GNNs belong to the deep learning framework, but most of the models in the literature use a very number amount of stacked convolutional layers. Going deep into the number of layers leads to some known issues such as the complex gradient propagation through the layers, and the over-smoothing problem [25]. Exploiting deeper models would allow obtaining richer representations of graph nodes to be obtained; therefore, finding a model that allows to develop deeper GNNs, could help to further improve the state-of-the-art performances.

References

[1] A. Sperduti, D. Majidi, and A. Starita, Extended Cascade-Correlation for syntactic and structural pattern recognition. In eds. P. Perner, P. S. Wang, and A. Rosenfeld, *Advances in Structural and Syntactical Pattern Recognition, 6th International Workshop, SSPR '96*, Leipzig, Germany, August 20–23, 1996, *Proceedings*, vol. 1121, *Lecture Notes in Computer Science*, pp. 90–99. Springer (1996). doi: 10.1007/3-540-61577-6_10. URL https://doi.org/10.1007/3-540-61577-6_10.

[2] A. Sperduti and A. Starita, Supervised neural networks for the classification of structures, *IEEE Trans. Neural Networks*, **8**(3), 714–735 (1997).

[3] M. M. Bronstein, J. Bruna, Y. Lecun, A. Szlam, and P. Vandergheynst, Geometric deep learning: going beyond Euclidean data, *IEEE Signal Process. Mag.*, **34**(4), 18–42 (2017). ISSN 10535888.

[4] P. Frasconi, M. Gori, and A. Sperduti, A general framework for adaptive processing of data structures, *IEEE Trans. Neural Networks*, **9**(5), 768–786 (1998). doi: 10.1109/72.712151. URL https://doi.org/10.1109/72.712151.

[5] M. Collins and N. Duffy, Convolution kernels for natural language. In *Proceedings of the Advances in Neural Information Processing Systems*, vol. 14, pp. 625–632 (2001).

[6] R. I. Kondor and J. Lafferty, Diffusion kernels on graphs and other discrete structures. In *ICML* (2002).

[7] N. Shervashidze, P. Schweitzer, E. J. van Leeuwen, K. Mehlhorn, and K. M. Borgwardt, Weisfeiler-Lehman graph kernels, *JMLR*, **12**, 2539–2561 (2011).

[8] G. Da San Martino, N. Navarin, and A. Sperduti, Ordered decompositional DAG kernels enhancements, *Neurocomputing*, **192**, 92–103 (2016).

[9] A. Feragen, N. Kasenburg, J. Petersen, M. de Bruijne, and K. M. Borgwardt, Scalable kernels for graphs with continuous attributes. In *Neural Information Processing Systems (NIPS) 2013*, pp. 216–224 (2013).

[10] G. Da San Martino, N. Navarin, and A. Sperduti, Tree-based kernel for graphs with continuous attributes, *IEEE Trans. Neural Networks Learn. Syst.*, **29**(7), 3270–3276 (2018). ISSN 2162-237X.

[11] G. Nikolentzos, G. Siglidis, and M. Vazirgiannis, Graph kernels: a survey, *CoRR*, **abs/1904.12218** (2019). URL http://arxiv.org/abs/1904.12218.

[12] N. M. Kriege, F. D. Johansson, and C. Morris, A survey on graph kernels, *Appl. Network Sci.,* **5**(1), 6 (2020). doi: 10.1007/s41109-019-0195-3. URL https://doi.org/10.1007/s41109-019-0195-3.

[13] A. Krizhevsky, I. Sutskever, and G. E. Hinton, ImageNet classification with deep convolutional neural networks. In eds. P. L. Bartlett, F. C. N. Pereira, C. J. C. Burges, L. Bottou, and K. Q. Weinberger, *Advances in Neural Information Processing Systems 25: 26th Annual Conference on Neural Information Processing Systems 2012. Proceedings of a meeting held December 3–6 (2012)*, Lake Tahoe, Nevada, United States, pp. 1106–1114 (2012). URL https://proceedings.neurips.cc/paper/2012/hash/c399862d3b9d6b76c8436e924a68c45b-Abstract.html.

[14] F. Scarselli, M. Gori, A. C. Ah Chung Tsoi, M. Hagenbuchner, and G. Monfardini, The graph neural network model, *IEEE Trans. Neural Networks*, **20**(1), 61–80 (2009).

[15] A. Micheli, Neural network for graphs: a contextual constructive approach, *IEEE Trans. Neural Networks*, **20**(3), 498–511 (2009).

[16] L. B. Almeida, A learning rule for asynchronous perceptrons with feedback in a combinatorial environment. In eds. M. Caudil and C. Butler, *Proceedings of the IEEE First International Conference on Neural Networks*, San Diego, CA, pp. 609–618 (1987).

[17] F. J. Pineda, Generalization of back-propagation to recurrent neural networks, *Phys. Rev. Lett.*, **59**(19), 2229–2232 (1987). ISSN 1079-7114. doi: 10.1103/PhysRevLett.59.2229. URL https://link.aps.org/doi/10.1103/PhysRevLett.59.2229.

[18] M. Defferrard, X. Bresson, and P. Vandergheynst, Convolutional neural networks on graphs with fast localized spectral filtering. In *Neural Information Processing Systems (NIPS)*, pp. 3844–3852 (2016).

[19] J. Gilmer, S. S. Schoenholz, P. F. Riley, O. Vinyals, and G. E. Dahl, Neural message passing for quantum chemistry. In *Proceedings of the 34th International Conference on Machine Learning*, pp. 1263–1272 (2017).

[20] D. I. Shuman, S. K. Narang, P. Frossard, A. Ortega, and P. Vandergheynst, The emerging field of signal processing on graphs: extending high-dimensional data analysis to networks and other irregular domains, *IEEE Signal Process. Mag.,* **30**(3), 83–98 (2013).

[21] N. Navarin, W. Erb, L. Pasa, and A. Sperduti, Linear graph convolutional networks. In *European Symposium on Artificial Neural Networks, Computational Intelligence and Machine Learning*, pp. 151–156 (2020).

[22] T. N. Kipf and M. Welling, Semi-supervised classification with graph convolutional networks. In *ICLR*, pp. 1–14 (2017).

[23] C. Morris, M. Ritzert, M. Fey, W. L. Hamilton, J. E. Lenssen, G. Rattan, and M. Grohe, Weisfeiler and Leman go neural: higher-order graph neural networks. In *Proceedings of the AAAI Conference on Artificial Intelligence*, vol. 33, pp. 4602–4609 (2019).

[24] J. Klicpera, A. Bojchevski, and S. Günnemann, Predict then propagate: graph neural networks meet personalized pagerank. In *7th International Conference on Learning Representations, ICLR 2019,* New Orleans, LA, USA, May 6–9 (2019). OpenReview.net (2019).

[25] K. Oono and T. Suzuki, Graph neural networks exponentially lose expressive power for node classification. In *ICLR* (2020).

[26] M. Chen, Z. Wei, Z. Huang, B. Ding, and Y. Li, Simple and deep graph convolutional networks. In *Proceedings of the 37th International Conference on Machine Learning, ICML 2020, 13–18 July 2020, Virtual Event*, vol. 119, *Proceedings of Machine Learning Research*, pp. 1725–1735. PMLR (2020). URL http://proceedings.mlr.press/v119/chen20v.html.

[27] P. Veličković, G. Cucurull, A. Casanova, A. Romero, P. Liò, and Y. Bengio, Graph attention networks. In *ICLR* (2018).

[28] D. Bahdanau, K. Cho, and Y. Bengio, Neural machine translation by jointly learning to align and translate. In eds. Y. Bengio and Y. LeCun, *3rd International Conference on Learning Representations, ICLR 2015,* San Diego, CA, USA, May 7–9, 2015, *Conference Track Proceedings* (2015). URL http://arxiv.org/abs/1409.0473.

[29] W. Hamilton, Z. Ying, and J. Leskovec, Inductive representation learning on large graphs. In *Proceedings of the Advances in Neural Information Processing Systems,* pp. 1024–1034 (2017).

[30] Y. Li, D. Tarlow, M. Brockschmidt, and R. Zemel, Gated graph sequence neural networks. In *ICLR* (2016).

[31] M. Zhang, Z. Cui, M. Neumann, and Y. Chen, An end-to-end deep learning architecture for graph classification. In *AAAI Conference on Artificial Intelligence* (2018).

[32] M. Niepert, M. Ahmed, and K. Kutzkov, Learning convolutional neural networks for graphs. In *International conference on machine learning,* pp. 2014–2023 (2016).

[33] N. Navarin, D. V. Tran, and A. Sperduti, Learning kernel-based embeddings in graph neural networks. In eds. G. D. Giacomo, A. Catalá, B. Dilkina, M. Milano, S. Barro, A. Bugarín, and J. Lang, *ECAI 2020 — 24th European Conference on Artificial Intelligence,* 29 August–8 September 2020, *Santiago de Compostela,* Spain, August 29–September 8, 2020 — *Including 10th Conference on Prestigious Applications of Artificial Intelligence (PAIS 2020),* vol. 325, *Frontiers in Artificial Intelligence and Applications,* pp. 1387–1394. IOS Press (2020). doi: 10.3233/FAIA200243. URL https://doi.org/10.3233/FAIA200243.

[34] N. Shervashidze, P. Schweitzer, E. J. v. Leeuwen, K. Mehlhorn, and K. M. Borgwardt, Weisfeiler-lehman graph kernels, *J. Mach. Learn. Res.,* **12,** 2539–2561 (2011).

[35] F. M. Bianchi, D. Grattarola, C. Alippi, and L. Livi, Graph neural networks with convolutional ARMA filters, *arXiv preprint* (2019).

[36] H. Pei, B. Wei, K. C.-C. Chang, Y. Lei, and B. Yang, Geom-GCN: ceometric graph convolutional networks. In *International Conference on Learning Representations* (2019).

[37] J. Atwood and D. Towsley, Diffusion-convolutional neural networks. In *Neural Information Processing Systems (NIPS),* pp. 1993–2001 (2016).

[38] D. V. Tran, N. Navarin, and A. Sperduti, On filter size in graph convolutional networks. In *2018 IEEE Symposium Series on Computational Intelligence (SSCI),* pp. 1534–1541. IEEE (2018).

[39] F. Wu, T. Zhang, A. H. de Souza, C. Fifty, T. Yu, and K. Q. Weinberger, Simplifying graph convolutional networks, *ICML* (2019).

[40] R. Liao, Z. Zhao, R. Urtasun, and R. S. Zemel, LanczosNet: multi-scale deep graph convolutional networks. In *7th International Conference on Learning Representations, ICLR 2019* (2019).

[41] T. Chen, S. Bian, and Y. Sun, Are powerful graph neural nets necessary? A dissection on graph classification, *arXiv preprint arXiv:1905.04579* (2019).

[42] S. Luan, M. Zhao, X.-W. Chang, and D. Precup, Break the ceiling: stronger multiscale deep graph convolutional networks. In *Proceedings of the Advances in Neural Information Processing Systems,* pp. 10945–10955 (2019).

[43] E. Rossi, F. Frasca, B. Chamberlain, D. Eynard, M. Bronstein, and F. Monti, Sign: scalable inception graph neural networks, *arXiv preprint arXiv:2004.11198* (2020).

[44] M. Liu, H. Gao, and S. Ji, Towards deeper graph neural networks. In *Proceedings of the 26th ACM SIGKDD International Conference on Knowledge Discovery & Data Mining,* pp. 338–348 (2020).

[45] M. S. Schlichtkrull, T. N. Kipf, P. Bloem, R. van den Berg, I. Titov, and M. Welling, Modeling relational data with graph convolutional networks. In eds. A. Gangemi, R. Navigli, M. Vidal, P. Hitzler, R. Troncy, L. Hollink, A. Tordai, and M. Alam, *The Semantic Web — 15th International Conference, ESWC 2018,* Heraklion, Crete, Greece, June 3–7, 2018, *Proceedings,* vol. 10843,

Lecture Notes in Computer Science, pp. 593–607. Springer (2018). doi: 10.1007/978-3-319-93417-4\38. URL https://doi.org/10.1007/978-3-319-93417-4_38.

[46] M. Simonovsky and N. Komodakis, Dynamic edge-conditioned filters in convolutional neural networks on graphs. In *CVPR* (2017).

[47] D. Duvenaud, D. Maclaurin, J. Aguilera-Iparraguirre, R. Gómez-Bombarelli, T. Hirzel, A. Aspuru-Guzik, and R. P. Adams, Convolutional networks on graphs for learning molecular fingerprints. In *Neural Information Processing Systems (NIPS)*, pp. 2215–2223, Montreal, Canada (2015).

[48] R. C. Read and D. G. Corneil, The graph isomorphism disease, *J. Graph Theory*, **1**(4), 339–363 (1977).

[49] K. Xu, W. Hu, J. Leskovec, and S. Jegelka, How powerful are graph neural networks? In *7th International Conference on Learning Representations, ICLR 2019*, New Orleans, LA, USA, May 6–9 (2019). OpenReview.net (2019). URL https://openreview.net/forum?id=ryGs6iA5Km.

[50] H. Maron, H. Ben-Hamu, H. Serviansky, and Y. Lipman, Provably powerful graph networks. In *Proceedings of the Advances in Neural Information Processing Systems*, vol. 32 (2019).

[51] C. Morris, G. Rattan, and P. Mutzel, Weisfeiler and Leman go sparse: towards scalable higher-order graph embeddings. In *NeurIPS* (2019).

[52] M. Zaheer, S. Kottur, and S. Ravanbhakhsh, Deep sets. In *Neural Information Processing Systems (NIPS)*, pp. 3391–3401 (2017).

[53] N. Navarin, D. V. Tran, and A. Sperduti, Universal readout for graph convolutional neural networks. In *International Joint Conference on Neural Networks, IJCNN 2019*, Budapest, Hungary, July 14–19, 2019, pp. 1–7. IEEE (2019). doi: 10.1109/IJCNN. 2019.8852103. URL https://doi.org/10.1109/IJCNN.2019.8852103.

[54] L. Pasa, N. Navarin, and A. Sperduti, Som-based aggregation for graph convolutional neural networks, *Neural Comput. Appl.*, 2020. URL https://doi.org/10.1007/s00521-020-05484-4.

[55] R. Ying, J. You, C. Morris, X. Ren, W. L. Hamilton, and J. Leskovec, Hierarchical graph representation learning with differentiable pooling. In *Neural Information Processing Systems (NIPS)* (2018).

[56] C. Cangea, Veličković, N. Jovanović T. Kipf, and P. Li'o, Towards Sparse Hierarchical Graph Classifiers. In *NIPS Relational Representation Learning Workshop* (2018).

[57] F. M. Bianchi, D. Grattarola, and C. Alippi, Spectral clustering with graph neural networks for graph pooling. In *International Conference on Machine Learning*, pp. 874–883. PMLR (2020).

[58] A. K. Debnath, R. L. Lopez de Compadre, G. Debnath, A. J. Shusterman, and C. Hansch, Structure-activity relationship of mutagenic aromatic and heteroaromatic nitro compounds. Correlation with molecular orbital energies and hydrophobicity, *J. Med. Chem.*, **34**(2), 786–797 (1991). ISSN 0022-2623.

[59] C. Helma, R. D. King, S. Kramer, and A. Srinivasan, The predictive toxicology challenge 2000–2001, *Bioinformatics*, **17**(1), 107–108 (2001).

[60] N. Wale, I. A. Watson, and G. Karypis, Comparison of descriptor spaces for chemical compound retrieval and classification, *Knowl. Inf. Syst.*, **14**(3), 347–375 (2008).

[61] K. M. Borgwardt, C. S. Ong, S. Schönauer, S. Vishwanathan, A. J. Smola, and H.-P. Kriegel, Protein function prediction via graph kernels, *Bioinformatics*, **21**(Suppl 1), 47–56 (2005).

[62] P. D. Dobson and A. J. Doig, Distinguishing enzyme structures from non-enzymes without alignments, *J. Mol. Biol.*, **330**(4), 771–783 (2003).

[63] A. K. McCallum, K. Nigam, J. Rennie, and K. Seymore, Automating the construction of internet portals with machine learning, *Inf. Retrieval*, **3**(2), 127–163 (2000). ISSN 13864564. doi: 10.1023/A:1009953814988.

[64] C. L. Giles, K. D. Bollacker, and S. Lawrence, CiteSeer: an automatic citation indexing system, *Proceedings of the ACM International Conference on Digital Libraries*, pp. 89–98 (1998).

[65] P. Sen, G. Namata, M. Bilgic, L. Getoor, B. Galligher, and T. Eliassi-Rad, Collective classification in network data, *AI Mag.*, **29**(3), 93–93 (2008).

[66] P. Yanardag and S. Vishwanathan, A structural smoothing framework for robust graph comparison, *Proceedings of the Advances in Neural Information Processing Systems,* **28**, 2134–2142 (2015).

[67] F. Errica, M. Podda, D. Bacciu, and A. Micheli, A fair comparison of graph neural networks for graph classification. In *International Conference on Learning Representations* (2020).

[68] M. Fey and J. E. Lenssen, Fast graph representation learning with PyTorch Geometric. In *ICLR 2019 Workshop on Representation Learning on Graphs and Manifolds* (2019).

[69] A. Paszke, S. Gross, F. Massa, A. Lerer, J. Bradbury, G. Chanan, T. Killeen, Z. Lin, N. Gimelshein, L. Antiga, A. Desmaison, A. Kopf, E. Yang, Z. DeVito, M. Raison, A. Tejani, S. Chilamkurthy, B. Steiner, L. Fang, J. Bai, and S. Chintala, PyTorch: an imperative style, high-performance deep learning library. In eds. H. Wallach, H. Larochelle, A. Beygelzimer, F. d'Alché-Buc, E. Fox, and R. Garnett, *Advances in Neural Information Processing Systems 32*, pp. 8024–8035. Curran Associates, Inc. (2019).

[70] M. Abadi, P. Barham, J. Chen, Z. Chen, A. Davis, J. Dean, M. Devin, S. Ghemawat, G. Irving, M. Isard, et al., Tensorflow: a system for large-scale machine learning. In *12th USENIX Symposium on Operating Systems Design and Implementation (OSDI 16)*, pp. 265–283 (2016).

[71] M. Wang, D. Zheng, Z. Ye, Q. Gan, M. Li, X. Song, J. Zhou, C. Ma, L. Yu, Y. Gai, T. Xiao, T. He, G. Karypis, J. Li, and Z. Zhang, Deep graph library: a graph-centric, highly-performant package for graph neural networks, *arXiv preprint arXiv:1909.01315* (2019).

[72] T. Chen, M. Li, Y. Li, M. Lin, N. Wang, M. Wang, T. Xiao, B. Xu, C. Zhang, and Z. Zhang, Mxnet: a flexible and efficient machine learning library for heterogeneous distributed systems, *arXiv preprint arXiv:1512.01274* (2015).

[73] D. Grattarola and C. Alippi, Graph neural networks in tensor flow and keras with spektral, *arXiv preprint arXiv:2006.12138* (2020).

Chapter 15

A Critical Appraisal on Deep Neural Networks: Bridge the Gap between Deep Learning and Neuroscience via XAI

Anna-Sophie Bartle[*,x], *Ziping Jiang*[*,¶], *Richard Jiang*[*,‖],
Ahmed Bouridane[†,**], *and Somaya Almaadeed*[‡,††]

LIRA Center, Lancaster University, Lancaster LA1 4YW, UK
[†]*Computer and Information Sciences, Northumbria University, NE1 8ST, UK*
[‡]*Computer Sciences, Qatar University, Doha, Qatar*
[x]*a.bartle1@lancaster.ac.uk*
[¶]*z.jiang7@lancaster.ac.uk*
[‖]*r.jiang2@lancaster.ac.uk*
[**]*ahmed.bouridane@northumbria.ac.uk*
[††]*S_alali@qu.edu.qa*

Starting in the early 1940s, artificial intelligence (AI) has come a long way, and today, AI is a powerful research area with many possibilities . Deep neural networks (DNNs) are part of AI and consist of several layers—the input layers, the so-called hidden layers, and the output layers. The input layers receive data; the data are then converted into computable variables (i.e., vectors) and are passed on to the hidden layers, where they are computed. Each data point (neuron) is connected to another data point within a different layer that passes information back and forth. Adjusting the weights and bias at each hidden layer (having several iterations between those layers), such a network maps the input to output, thereby generalizing (learning) its knowledge. At the end, the deep neural network should have enough input to predict results for specific tasks successfully. The history of DNNs or neural networks is, in general, closely related to neuroscience, as the motivation of AI is to teach human intelligence to a machine. Thus, it is possible to use the knowledge of the human brain to develop algorithms that can simulate the human brain. This is performed with DNNs. The brain is considered an electrical network that sets off electrical impulses. During this process, information is carried from one synapse to another, just like it is done within neural networks. However, AI systems should be used carefully, which means that the researcher should always be capable of understanding the system he or she created, which is an issue discussed within explainable AI and DNNs.

15.1. Introduction

Artificial intelligence (AI) is a widely used term in today's society. However, defining AI is not an easy task as it is a broad research area that includes various approaches and techniques and which is used within different research areas such as natural language processing (NLP), machine vision, multi-agent systems, and so on. AI can, nevertheless, be described as the intelligence of machines. Such intelligent systems are described as systems that "processes information in order to do something purposeful" and that are built by humans to make those systems think and act like human beings [1]. How human-like a system thinks and acts is tested using Alan Turing's so-called Turing test, which is a way to test machine intelligence; a system passes the test if a user of the system cannot tell whether he or she is interacting with a human or a computer [2]. Hence, the goal of AI is to construct systems that behave like a human, trying to implement human-like intelligence. Thus, throughout this chapter, artificial intelligence is understood as "the ability to do the right thing at the right moment by studying and developing computational artefacts that exhibit some facets of intelligent behavior" [1].

To understand current trends in AI, this chapter starts with a short summary of the history of AI and neural networks. It then continues with the introduction of deep neural networks, thereby explaining the term *deep learning*. Since DNNs make use of neuroscience, the third part of this chapter briefly discusses the interchangeable connections and possibilities between neuroscience and DNNs. The fourth section continues with the notion of explainable AI (XAI) and DNNs, demonstrating some of the difficulties such smart systems face. This is followed by a critical review on DNNs. The survey ends with a discussion on possible future trends of AI and tries to emphasize the main points of the chapter in a brief conclusion.

15.2. History of Artificial Intelligence and Neural Networks

Artificial intelligence is all about mechanically replicating the process of the human way of thinking and acting. The idea, like many other big discoveries, came from classical philosophers and is, as such, still a controversial topic in philosophy [3]. The history of artificial intelligence is structured into four seasons—spring, fall, summer, and winter [4]. The first real occurrence of AI dates back to the early 1940s, when the first robot was developed by Gregory Powell and Mike Donavan [4]. The two engineers tried to create a robot that was able to react to specific orders given by humans, thereby following the Three Laws of Robotics proposed by Isaac Asimov—to not harm a human being, to obey the given orders, and to not put its own existence at risk. At the same time, Alan Turing, one of the still most influential mathematicians in testing the intelligence of machines, created a machine that was able to decipher the Enigma code used by the German military in World War II, which was, until then, an impossible task. In 1950, Alan Turing published his still used and famous Turing test, which considers whether an artificial system can be called intelligent or not; as soon as an artificial system cannot be distinguished from a human, it can be considered intelligent.

The academic discipline of AI was founded in 1956, during the Dartmouth Summer Research Project on AI at the Dartmouth College, by Marvin Minsky and John McCarthy, marking the beginning of the AI spring. The season lasted 20 years, during which AI blossomed and was significantly successful. One of the most impressive works during that time was the development of the dialogue system ELIZA, which was written by Joseph Weizenbaum somewhere between 1964 and 1966; the system demonstrated the possibilities of artificial systems understanding natural language. In the 1970s, Marvin Minsky stated that in less than a decade, it would be possible to create artificial machines that are as intelligent as the average human being. However, due to the limited computing capacities of computers available during that time and because of using only basic algorithms, the success of AI stopped advancing, thereby losing important funding from big companies and governments, marking the beginning of the AI fall and winter, which lasted again for about two decades [4].

ELIZA demonstrates why early strategies and implementations of AI failed to replicate human intelligence within artificial systems. The system shows the lack of initiative and knowledge, since ELIZA has no real-world knowledge or common sense. Moreover, the dialogue systems lack memory capacity and struggle with adopting the correct grammar of a language. However, another approach was the introduction of artificial neural networks (ANNs) by Warren McCulloch and Walter Pitts in 1943 [5, 6], who defined the so-called threshold logic, which divides AI into two approaches—one focusing on biological processes and the other on neural Networks that eventually led to the implementation of finite-state automata. Moreover, the Hebbian learning theory, which was developed during the 1940s by Donald Hebb, also stated the possibility of creating ANNs. Such ANNs should be able to replicate the processes of neurons of the human brain since the brain itself is an electrical network that sets off electrical impulses, during which information is carried from one synapse to another. Frank Rosenblatt, moreover, showed that it was possible for perceptrons (a type of neural network) "to learn and make decisions" based on the input data [4]. In 1975, the backpropagation algorithm was introduced by Werbos. The algorithm implements a multi-layer network consisting of various hidden layers. In all the layers, the input data can be used for training, namely modifying the weights of the nodes that are interconnected with the other nodes of the network; each node represents some sort of input. During this "learning" process, errors made by such networks are exponentially reduced since they are distributed in parallel between all the nodes available in the network [4]. In 1997, AI celebrated a breakthrough with IBM's Deep Blue, a chess-playing program that was able to beat the world's best chess player, Gary Kasparov, using collections of rules that follow simple "if–then" principles. Such artificial systems can be implemented for logical-mathematical problems; however, they would fail in tasks involving the process of facial recognition [4]. In 2015, ANNs were reintroduced in the form of Google's DeepMind AlphaGo, which was developed by Google and which was able to beat the world's best Go player; Go is a board game that exceeds the number of possible moves in chess by far. As we can see, AI and ANNs have come a long way, with the above-mentioned details being only a brief summary of the history and development of AI and its corresponding ANNs.

15.3. Rise of Deep Neural Networks

Deep neural networks, or rather deep learning, have become popular over the last couple of years as they demonstrated one breakthrough after another—be it tasks in solving the difficulties of image recognition and automatic translation or in beating the world's champion in the board game Go. Our class definition for deep learning is that "it uses specialized algorithms to model and understand complex structures and relationships among data and datasets" using multiple layers [3]. The era of deep learning started with ImageNet, an image database created by Fei-Fei Li [7] in 2009. ImageNet set the milestone for image and facial recognition processes that are, for example, used to unlock smartphones. By 2010, many AI researchers tried to develop their deep learning system, trying to train the best and most accurate DNNs. In 2014, Ian Goodfellow created a deep learning neural network called the generative adversarial network (GAN), which aims to generate synthetic data. From the viewpoint of classification, the discriminative capability of the GAN became better at classifying input data by "learning" from its errors on synthetic data, thereby allowing the generator to adjust its weights and produce more realistic data to fool the discriminator [7, 8].

As we can see in Figure 15.1, simple neural networks do not look that different from DNNs as both consist of input, hidden, and output layers connected to one another. The input layers consist of input data such as words or pixels, which are converted into calculable variables (i.e., vectors), which are then passed on to one or more hidden layers that consist of so-called nodes (neurons) connected to one another via synapses. The various hidden layers draw information from the received data to produce a result via an output layer [3]. Whereas some researchers suggest that the difference between simple neural networks and deep neural networks is the increased number of hidden layers within DNNs (multi-layer networks), others suggest that there is no difference as both have neurons and synapses that are interconnected and share the same functionality—using weights and bias and an activation function to change and optimize the next layer's outcome [7].

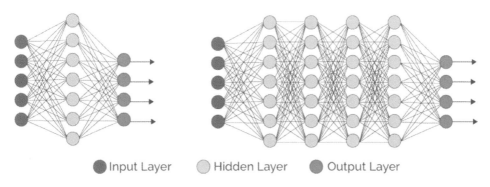

Figure 15.1:   Left: Simple neural network. Right: Deep neural network.

Deep learning networks need to iterate over large datasets (input) to create reliable solutions, as has been seen successfully in a wide range of applications [9–12]. The input data contain labels (supervised learning), which enable the network to classify the various input data points into various categories to which the input belongs. By adjusting and modifying the weights of the nodes (connections between the neurons) through backpropagation (generalizing the learning algorithm), it is able to reduce the error function, mapping more and more input data to the correct output layer, thereby producing more reliable output. Results of various studies have shown that the more the hidden layers available, the better the outcome is. The word *deep* comes from the many hidden layers used to produce better results. However, having too many hidden layers may lead to overgeneralizing the data, creating suboptimal solutions, since classifying overgeneralized input data into certain groups might not be explicitly clear [3].

Since we have seen a rapid and exponential growth of available data, training DNNs with huge amounts of data is possible. DNNs rely heavily on large datasets, on which they need training to provide reliable predictions and results. In this respect, humans are far better at learning rules and classifying certain objects into categories. This is because humans need only a few examples to understand the concept behind it. Therefore, deep learning can only help with problems for which a huge amount of data is available, but it should be avoided if this is not the case [3].

However, just like any other technique used in AI, deep learning has its limitations. DNNs can compute non-open problems. However, to solve problems with a hierarchical structure (such as embedded sentences), sentences with ambiguous meaning, or problems that require one to draw open-ended inferences, DNNs are rather useless because there are no straightforward solutions available. This is so because deep learning is "hermeneutic" [3] since DNNs are "being self-contained and isolated from other, potentially useful knowledge" [3], though there exists a large variety of combined methods, such as deep kernel methods, deep Gaussian processes, Bayesian drop-out techniques, etc. For straightforward problems, DNNs are capable of learning the connections between input and output layers. Nevertheless, DNNs offer a great opportunity to solve certain problems and to make some things easier and more efficient (e.g., facial recognition to unlock one's smartphone).

15.4. Neuroscience and Deep Neural Networks

The rise of deep neural networks dates back to the 1940s, during which time it was found that the brain sends electrical impulses from synapse to synapse, thereby transferring and computing information received from one node to the other to produce a result. Since then, ANNs and DNNs have been built and developed, often using insights and findings of the field of neuroscience to further develop already existing algorithms. Therefore, it might be possible to improve and further develop DNNs by better understanding the biological human brain (be it from humans or other living beings, e.g., animals and plants) to create even better and more human-like intelligent systems. However, it is not only AI that can draw inferences from neuroscience, but also the other way around, since AI can be used to recognize and detect, for example, certain illnesses whose malformation would hardly be recognized as such [13].

Using neuroscience to develop and improve DNNs is an obvious assumption, since the main goal of AI is to teach artificial intelligent systems to act like and be as intelligent as humans. In AI, human intelligence, for example, was thought to consist of symbolic representations that need to be manipulated to produce a learning effect. However, the idea of reducing the brain and its functions in a symbolic representation was found to be too simple compared to the complex interactions necessary to solve certain tasks in the real world. Therefore, neural networks within AI research were developed, trying to implement algorithms to simulate the information processing that happens within such networks through dynamic and interconnected neurons. These neurons are then fine-tuned by adjusting the weights of the connected neurons between the layers and its parameters, thereby reducing the errors made by the system and maximizing the system's reliable outcome. Since the successful implementation of such networks showed promising results, especially in terms of simulating human behavior and intelligence, the research of the functionality of the human brain (neuroscience) was and is taken more and more into consideration—after all, the idea of such ANNs came from neuroscience, which provided first insights into the human brain [13]—making it possible in the first place to develop such deep learning systems and its underlying algorithms for AI.

Reinforcement learning, moreover, played an important role in the development of deep learning. Reinforcement learning is about maximizing the reward by learning how to act to get a positive result, thereby learning to avoid actions that lead to negative outcomes. This can be compared to the learning process within the human brain—correct learning trials lead to an increase in dopamine neuron activation, successfully pushing the learning process [14].

Another interesting and rather important aspect within the human brain is the memory capacity. Human intelligence has the ability to maintain information for quite some time, making it possible to further process such information at a later stage (as it is needed for embedded sentences, for example, in which the main clause is interrupted by a subordinate clause). However, over the years, AI systems have improved at maintaining and storing information thanks to the recurrent neural networks and long short-term memory (LSTM) networks that have been developed. Nevertheless, more research needs to be done to make such networks successfully solve rather complex tasks such as commonsense understanding—understanding the real world when interacting with a problem [13].

Thus, understanding the human brain could be a prerequisite to creating even better and more robust intelligent machines as it might provide and inspire new types of algorithms by understanding the functionality of the living brain. This can be done through "analysis, visualization, causal manipulation, and hypothesis-driven experiments" within neuroscience [13].

The expansion of interest from AI to neuroscience might be as useful as the impact neuroscience has on AI, with slightly different approaches and perspectives. AI, for example, uses various algorithms and architectures to imitate the human brain, so as to reproduce the underlying calculations the brain does when processing information. Therefore, AI might give useful insights into the working processes of the brain, thereby connecting the computational level—the purpose of the computational process—with the algorithmic level, which includes the processes and computations that are necessary. AI not only provides various possibilities to analyze data coming from functional magnetic resonance imaging (fMRI) and magnetoencephalography (MEG) but also helps to provide information on the computational and algorithmic processes underlying the information processes within the brain. Based on the information provided by AI, neuroscientists and psychologists could adapt their research field accordingly.

A close cooperation between both departments could, thus, benefit both parties—for AI could build better and more reliable intelligent systems by understanding the functions of the brain, whereas neuroscientists could learn more about the possible mechanisms underlying the brain to find new research approaches (e.g., treatment options for various illnesses). Neuroscientists, for example, found that the above-mentioned dopamine neuron activation during the learning process within the human brain resembles the algorithm found in temporal difference (TD) learning [15]. TD learning is a method used in reinforcement learning, which dynamically adjusts its learning "predictions to match later, more accurate, predictions" [15]. Therefore, a close cooperation might be beneficial for both research areas.

15.5. Explainable AI and DNNs

Due to the problem that AI systems become less and less interpretable even though they become more and more complicated, explainable AI (XAI) and DNNs represent a research initiative trying to draw attention to the need for intelligent machines to remain explainable—being able to describe the underlying mechanisms and algorithms of such artificial systems. This is an important task [16] as it would mean that scenes depicted in science-fiction movies, in which super-intelligent systems take over the world, could not happen as there is always enough knowledge and know-how on how to stop and limit possible errors of such artificial systems, rather than just having luck that the system was capable of creating such intelligent solutions.

Moreover, XAI wants to move beyond AI systems (e.g., DNNs) as such machines still need concrete training sets to succeed in one specific task. The problem is that there is still no way of making AI systems think in a contextual, abstract way; this, in turn, narrows down the usefulness of such machines as they can only be used for a narrowed specific task for which the system has the know-how as it is trained on such kinds of data; the system knows how to compute the data without having the ethical understanding of what the actual task is about. XAI, thus, tries to draw attention to the ethical problems AI systems cause by questioning whether those systems should be given such a huge responsibility as they lack important knowledge. Thus, XAI discusses whether developing AI systems should be stopped in order to avoid artificial systems from taking over the world [16, 17].

The problematic notion of not having sufficient knowledge and expertise to explain the underlying functions and computations of DNNs is demonstrated in Figure 15.2. Here we can see many techniques used within AI in relation to how well such techniques are explainable. The purple techniques (neural networks and deep learning) are the current trends and are implemented the most when building current AI systems. However, it seems that the higher the accuracy the approach obtains, the less explainable they are even though their performance increases. This means that it is unknown why the algorithm chooses one result over the other. Therefore, this not only causes ethical problems, as already mentioned above, but also limits the developmental possibilities that such systems could have if they

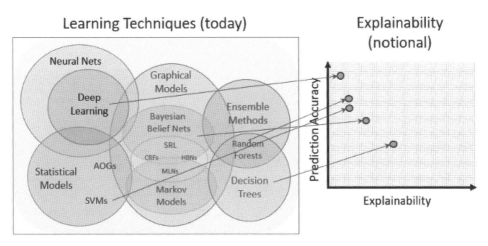

Figure 15.2: Techniques used in AI and the extent to which they are understood and can be explained (retrieved at [16]).

could be fully understood. Understanding is one of the most important steps for moving beyond and creating even better systems [16].

For various fields, AI is helpful and should be used, for example, in diagnosing medical conditions. However, the results given by intelligent machines should always be interpretable and explainable. Thus, for example, a doctor should not solely rely on the machine's diagnosis, but should also be able to ask questions to the machine, which in turn should be able to provide understandable answers. To achieve this, it is necessary for the machine to understand and explain its given results. Therefore, the system should be capable of processing abstract information, which still needs to be developed further in the future in order for humans to understand the underlying information processes within the system [17].

Moreover, one important aspect of XAI concerns the predictions made by AI systems and whether such predictions are reliable. The goal is to comprehend a system's underlying computational processes that are used to make such predictions to create algorithms that make even better and more reliable predictions. Therefore, we need to understand the rationale of such systems (similar to understanding animal behavior in order to react to their behavior). There are two ways for humans to understand the underlying processes of such AI systems, namely the deep approach and the black-box approach [17]. Within the deep approach, the researcher tries to understand the different blocks making up the system completely (e.g., looking at the parameters of perceptrons, trying to understand what activates and changes them, etc.) [17]; this, however, is hard to accomplish as it requires expert knowledge to draw generalizations out of such systems.

The other approach is called the black-box approach, in which the system is treated like a black box in which no knowledge about its contents is present. In the

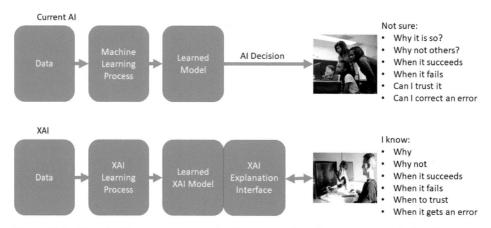

Figure 15.3: Today's AI systems raise loads of questions since they are not explainable. However, XAI tries to raise awareness that moving beyond the explainable is a risk that should be avoided by first trying to understand the implemented model and its actions before moving to even more complex tasks. First understanding systems will lead to even better systems and is a saver, as AI systems cannot take over the decision-making process since humans still understand what is going on.

approach, the researcher tries to understand the behavior of the system by playing around with and manipulating its input to interpret the framework by looking at the various outputs of the system [17]. Thus, with the acquired knowledge, machines can specifically be trained on how to do what they were already been doing, but now with the knowledge, comprehension, and intention of the programmer, which leads to even better and more robust systems as well as more security on such systems, as it is all about understanding what the system is doing before moving on to even more complex algorithms. Figure 15.3 captures the intentions of XAI very well.

15.6. Critical Review on Deep Neural Networks

Even though intelligent machines have exceeded human intelligence in solving some of the straightforward logical/mathematical problems such as the recently developed DNN, AlphaGo, which won against the world's champion in the board game Go, DNNs haven't reached the status of human intelligence in other areas such as natural language processing. DNNs, as already discussed, consist of several layers, and generally speaking, the more layers a DNN has, the harder it is to train [3, 18].

Moreover, systems such as self-driving cars and speech recognition play important roles in our daily life and will continue to grow in importance over the next couple of years [12]. Most users of such systems are often not interested in AI and ANN/DNN and, thus, are frequently not interested in knowing the underlying processes happening within such AI systems, since their focus mainly lies on the abilities and capabilities those systems offer. However, this section gives a brief summary of the different architectures that can be implemented within deep learning approaches and techniques. All architectures have in common that they are made up of "multi-layered artificial neural architectures that can learn complex, non-linear functional mappings, given sufficient computational resources and training data" [20]. Since it reads and computes a huge amount of data, it simplifies manual work as it is an automatic process to recognize patterns, giving more or less sufficient outcomes.

As already mentioned, DNNs consist of the input, hidden, and output layers, each consisting of interconnected, functional neurons that compute and carry information, making it possible to map input data to the output. The number of hidden layers is thereby important, since at each hidden layer, the neurons of the next layer are connected to the results, and predictions are made based on the outcome of the previous hidden layer. This is done by adjusting weights and bias, thus adapting certain learning rules that eventually capture some generalizations in the data. Within each hidden layer, the system learns more about the data and tries to find rules that can be generalized for a specific task the network needs to fulfill.

The input consists of training examples, e.g., words (of sentences) or pixels (of pictures), which are converted into vectors or certain types of embeddings and to whom synaptic weights are assigned. The dot product between each of the input vectors and its assigned weights are calculated and the results for each calculation are added. Depending on the dimensionality of each of the input vectors and weights, the output for each input [20] is an m-dimensional vector and the summation becomes "an m-dimensional hyperplane." The neural network "learns an approximation to the function that produced each of the outputs from its corresponding input" with the approximation being "the partition of the input space into samples that minimizes the error function between the output of the ANN given its training inputs and the training outputs" [20]—also known as universal approximation theorem.

The universal approximation theorem states that "any ... mapping between input and output vectors can be approximated to with arbitrary accuracy with an ANN provided that it has a sufficient number of neurons in a sufficient number of layers with a specific activation function" [20, 21]. Thus, all parts of an artificial neuron, including the activation and error function, are necessary to build a working network that is able to optimize the connections between input and output pairs, thereby minimizing the errors made by the system.

Nevertheless, especially a DNN's success lies in better performance with newer and more powerful GPU machines and its optimized regularization techniques that are getting better at avoiding overfitting of data, but still managing to find adaptive learning rates, which is not least because of the availability of large training datasets containing high-quality labels [20, 21].

Throughout the years, various deep learning architectures have been developed. The architectures can be distinguished from design; however, their advantages are not really comparable since most DNNs are chosen depending on their performance in specific tasks. Convolutional neural networks (CNNs), for example, are rather used for tasks concerning computer vision, whereas recurrent neural networks (RNN) are likely used for sequence and time series modeling tasks [20].

One of the most basic architectures of deep learning is the so-called deep feed-forward network in which only the connections between the neurons move forward in such a way that the connections move from the first hidden layer in one direction over all the hidden layers available within the network, capturing nonlinear relations of data [21]. Due to its simple implementation, it is an often-used architecture that uses backpropagation, thus first assigning random weights to the input data and throughout the training process, fine-tunes those weights, thereby reducing the system's error rate [20].

Unlike the feed-forward network moving in one direction, recurrent neural networks (RNNs) form a cycle during processing in which the subset of outputs of a given hidden layer becomes the input of the next hidden layer, thereby "forming a feedback loop" [21]. RNNs are, therefore, able to maintain some of the information received from the previous hidden models and are often used to develop networks that try to tackle practical problems such as speech recognition, or video classification, in which the video is analyzed on a frame-by-frame basis. Having a phrase of three words, the system would need three hidden layers, each layer analyzing and maintaining one of the words.

Long short-term memory (LSTM) is a specific type of RNN that was designed to maintain even more information, for which their long-range dependencies were developed more closely. As such, the input does not move from layer to layer, but from block to block, each block consisting of different layers—namely, the input, forget, and output blocks in which a logistic function keeps track of the information of the input data [21]. Hence, LSTM models are used within tasks such as part-of-speech tagging in NLP or speech recognition modeling.

Another kind of deep learning network is called restricted Boltzmann machine (RBM), which serves as a stochastic neural network. Due to its ability to learn from supervised as well as unsupervised data (labeled vs. unlabeled data), it is an often-used tool. The network was developed by Paul Smolensky in 1986; however, it became popular only in 2002, when the algorithm was reintroduced by Hinton [20]. RBMs are often used in feature learning, which enables systems to automatically classify data based on feature detection [20, 21].

Another popular and widely used deep network is the convolutional neural network (CNN), which contains convolutions and multi-layer perceptrons (usually consisting of three or more layers) calculating a result by using convolution operation on the input data and passing the outcome to the following layer [20]. By this additional calculation, it offers even deeper neural networks using only a few parameters (filters). However, CNNs are capable of successfully breaking down the characteristics of, e.g., images, and learning these representations throughout the different layers. Therefore, CNNs are often used in image and facial recognition processes as well as in NLP applications such as semantic parsing [21].

The last DNN mentioned here is called the sequence-to-sequence model, which consists of two different recurrent neural networks—namely, the encoder, encoding the input data, and the decoder, which is responsible to produce output by using the information provided by the encoder. It is a rather new model that still needs to be developed further, as it is used for difficult and highly complex tasks such as question-answering systems, machine translation, and chatbots [20, 21].

Even though there are many more DNNs that fulfill various influential tasks, this section just mentioned a few architectures to demonstrate some of the differences among such architectures and to provide various examples on how different implementations of such DNNs exist and what they are used for.

From the viewpoint of neuroscience, deep learning as the state-of-the-art AI technique has its roots in the emulation of the human brain. To make DNNs explainable, an ultimate goal is to find a way to match human intelligence and build a human-made "brain" or at least, at a functionally higher level, map the deep architectures to the layered information processing units in the brain. However, there are yet important differences between the features of current mainstream DNNs and the human brain. First, a human brain is more like an analogue circuit without the ability to store high-precision parameters. Secondly, neurons in the human brain are randomly interconnected instead of the carefully "handcrafted" architectures of the current mainstream DNNs. Such a randomly interconnected architecture [18, 19], known as Turing's type-B machine (unorganized machine), can lead to a generalized AI.

From the viewpoint of neuroscience, XAI can help bridge the gap between deep learning and neuroscience in a mutually beneficial way. On the one hand, XAI helps build an abstract DNN model that is more easily understood by humankind [22, 23]; on the other, XAI models [16, 17, 26] derived from DNNs can also help in understanding the mechanisms of the human brain [24–27].

15.7. Discussion and Conclusion

In this chapter, we came to the conclusion that human intelligence does not solely consist of logical/mathematical intelligence but also of "linguistic, spatial, musical kinaesthetic, interpersonal, intrapersonal, naturalist, and existential" intelligence [1]. Due to its multi-dimensionality, it is difficult to include all these abilities of a human brain into one single system; hence, most AI systems only include parts of the above-mentioned possible intelligence aspects, focusing on games such as chess or Go.

The history of AI goes back to the early 1940s, when AI was already a broadly discussed topic that was eventually implemented and converted into algorithms computable by computers. AI tries to replicate human intelligence by simulating the brain functions. However, implementing the human brain in some kind of artificial environment is no easy task; the human brain is too complex an organ to be understood simply by looking at it. It rather takes many years to capture only small fractions of the knowledge the brain has to offer and, thus, it will take even more years to discover more parts of the brain that have been hidden so far. Since the underlying computations of the brain can give insights about the functionality of the brain and the other way around, neuroscientists and researchers in AI should work together since both parties would benefit from such cooperation. However, future work should not solely focus on human intelligence. Rather, it should also focus on animals or plants since they also have powerful abilities that should somehow be captured. Thus, focusing solely on human intelligence might make us blind to understanding and creating new powerful intelligent systems [1].

Even though intelligent systems offer great possibilities, the research initiatives of explainable AI and DNNs warn against giving such intelligent systems too much power without even understanding the computational process underlying such newly developed systems. They argue that a system should first be understood before trying to develop even newer and better algorithms that would outperform the old algorithms. Not understanding the concepts could have a negative impact since such systems could develop in such a way—as described in science-fiction movies—that they would overpower the human world, with human beings having no power to stop them due to their inability to understand the system's underlying logic. Thus, before developing newer and better algorithms that are even less explainable than DNNs, older systems should be fully understood. This not only makes understanding the system easier and better but also enables the programmer to create even better and more human-like algorithms, since understanding processes of the brain can provide useful information.

Moreover, since machines are taking over the decision-making process in many daily situations, one should ask questions on what kind of suggestions such systems give. Intelligent machines still mostly lack the ability to process abstract information or anything that requires real-world knowledge. Thus, we should be careful in putting too much trust in such intelligent machines; rather, we should keep questioning the outcomes and predictions made by such systems. Furthermore, it is not only abstract information such systems are having difficulties computing, but also drawing inference from hierarchical structures (e.g., embedded sentences) or commonsense understanding. Future works could focus on how to handle such kinds of problems. Moreover, AI could be used to build algorithms that optimize the situations in daily life for small farmers, giving insights into current weather conditions, planting situations, the condition of their soil, and so on, thus making farming more attractive and profitable, even for small farmers. Moreover, because cultures become increasingly diverse, working on better translation services might support the inclusion process and cross-cultural communication, providing better chances, especially for younger immigrants, to receive education [1].

In conclusion, artificial intelligence and deep neural networks have come a long way and will most likely be a big topic in the coming years. AI offers great possibilities; however, such intelligent systems should always be used with caution, keeping in mind the consequences of using such systems. AI comes with a great deal of knowledge and can simplify certain things; however, understanding how such intelligent systems work, especially when losing control, can be a dangerous task.

References

[1] V. Dignum, *Responsible Artificial Intelligence: How to Develop and Use AI in a Responsible Way*, Springer Nature Switzerland (2019).
[2] A. M. Turing, Computing machinery and intelligence, *Mind*, **59**, pp. 433–460 (1950).
[3] G. Marcus, Deep learning: a critical appraisal, New York University, pp. 1–27 (2017).
[4] M. Haenlein and A. Kaplan, A brief history of artificial intelligence, *California Management Review*, **61**(4), pp. 5–15 (2019).
[5] Wikipedia, History of artificial intelligence, in Wikipedia, retrieved from https://en.wikipedia.org/wiki/History_of_artificial_intelligence.
[6] Wikipedia, History of artificial neural networks, in Wikipedia, retrieved from https://en.wikipedia.org/wiki/History_of_artificial_neural_networks.
[7] T. Greene, 2010–2019: the rise of deep learning, in the next web, (2020), https://thenextweb.com/artificialintelligence/2020/01/02/2010-2019-the-rise-of-deep-learning/, accessed 5th of January 2020.
[8] I. Goodfellow, J. Pouget-Abadie, M. Mirza, B. Xu, D. Warde-Farley, S. Ozair, A. Courville, and Y. Bengio, Generative adversarial nets, in *Advances in neural information processing systems*, pp. 2672–2680 (2014).
[9] C. Chiang, C. Barnes, P. Angelov, and R. Jiang, Deep learning based automated forest health diagnosis from aerial images, *IEEE Access* (2020).
[10] G. Storey, R. Jiang, A. Bouridane, and C. T. Li, 3DPalsyNet: a facial palsy grading and motion recognition framework using fully 3D convolutional neural networks, *IEEE Access* (2019).
[11] Z. Jiang, P. L. Chazot, M. E. Celebi, D. Crookes, and R. Jiang, Social behavioral phenotyping of drosophila with a 2D-3D hybrid CNN framework, *IEEE Access* (2019).
[12] G. Storey, A. Bouridane, and R. Jiang, Integrated deep model for face detection and landmark localisation from 'in the wild' images, *IEEE Access* (2018).
[13] D. Hassabis, D. Kumaran, C. Summerfield, and M. Botvinick, Neuroscience-inspired artificial intelligence, *Neuron*, **95**, pp. 145– 258 (2017).
[14] J. R. Hollerman and W. Schultz, Dopamine neurons report an error in the temporal prediction of reward during learning, *Nat.Neurosci.*, **1**(4), pp. 304-309 (1998).

[15] Wikipedia, Temporal difference learning, in Wikipedia—the Free Encyclopedia, retrieved from https://en.wikipedia.org/wiki/Temporal_difference_learning

[16] M. Lukianoff, Explainable artificial intelligence (XAI) is on DARPA's agenda—why you should pay attention, in towards data science, https://towardsdatascience.com/explainable-artificial-intelligence-xai-is-on-darpas-agenda-why-you-should-pay-attention-b63afcf284b5 (2019).

[17] J. Torres, Explainable AI: the next frontier in human-machine harmony, Towards Data Science, https://towardsdatascience.com/explainable-ai-the-next-frontier-in-human-machine-harmony-a3ba5b58a399 (2019).

[18] R. Jiang and D. Crookes, Shallow unorganized neural networks using smart neuron model for visual perception, *IEEE Access*, **7**, pp. 152701–152714 (2019).

[19] C. S. Webster, Alan Turing's unorganized machines and artificial neural networks: his remarkable early work and future possibilities. *Evol. Intell.*, **5**, pp. 35–43 (2012).

[20] S. Saptarshi, S. Basak, P. Saikia, S. Paul, V. Tsalavoutis, F. D. Atiah, V. Ravi, and R. A. Peters, A review of deep learning with special emphasis on architectures, applications and recent trends, *Knowledge-Based Syst.*, **194**, p. 105596 (2020).

[21] A. Shreshtha and A. Mahmood, Review of deep learning algorithms and architectures, *IEEE Access*, **7**, pp. 53040–53065 (2019).

[22] J. E. T. Taylor and G. W. Taylor, Artificial cognition: how experimental psychology can help generate explainable artificial intelligence, *Psychon. Bull. Rev.*, pp. 6276–6282 (2020).

[23] R. M. Byrne, Counterfactuals in explainable artificial intelligence (XAI): evidence from human reasoning, in *Proceedings of the Twenty-Eighth International Joint Conference on Artificial Intelligence (IJCAI-19)*, **1**, pp. 6276–6282 (2019).

[24] M.-A. T. Vu, T. Adalı, D. Ba, G. Buzsáki, D. Carlson, K. Heller, C. Liston, C. Rudin, V. Sohal, A. Widge, H. Mayberg, G. Sapiro, and K. A. Dzirasa, A shared vision for machine learning in neuroscience, *J. Neurosci.*, **18**, pp. 1601–1607 (2018).

[25] J. M. Fellous, G. Sapiro, A. Rossi, H. Mayberg, and M. Ferrante, Explainable artificial intelligence for neuroscience: behavioral neurostimulation, *Front. Neurosci.*, **13**, p. 1346 (2019).

[26] R. Evans and E. Grefenstette, Learning explanatory rules from noisy data, *J. Artif. Intell. Res.*, **2**, pp. 1–64 (2017).

[27] A. M. Zador, A critique of pure learning and what artificial neural networks can learn from animal brains, *Nat. Commun.*, **10**(3770), pp. 1–7 (2019).

Chapter 16

Ensemble Learning

Y. Liu and *Q. Zhao*[†]

School of Computer Science and Engineering
The University of Aizu
Aizu-Wakamatsu, Fukushima 965-8580, Japan
*yliu@u-aizu.ac.jp
[†]qf-zhao@u-aizu.ac.jp

An ensemble system adopts the divide-and-conquer strategy. Instead of using a single learning model to solve a given task, the ensemble system combines a set of learning models that learn to subdivide the task, and thereby solve it more efficiently. This chapter introduces ensemble learning in training a set of cooperative learning models from the view of bias–variance–covariance trade-off in supervised learning. Three types of ensemble learning methods are discussed based on how interactions are performed among the individual learning models in their learning. As an example of ensemble learning, negative correlation learning is described, and analyzed by estimating bias, variance, and covariance on a regression task with different noise conditions. Finally, ensemble systems with awareness are briefly introduced.

16.1. Bias–Variance Trade-Off in Supervised Learning

There are two components in a general supervised learning model. The first component is called a probability space $(\mathcal{E}, Pr)$ where each elementary event in the event set $\mathcal{E}$ associates with two random variables of the input pattern $\mathbf{x}$ and the desired output y. y is a scalar for simplicity in this chapter. $\mathbf{x}$ is a vector in R^p. All of the events in $\mathcal{E}$ follow the probability distribution Pr. The second component is a learning machine that can be implemented by a set of functions $F(\mathbf{x}, \mathbf{w})$, $\mathbf{w} \in W$, where W is a space of real-valued vectors.

Supervised learning is to search the function $F(\mathbf{x}, \mathbf{w})$ so that the expected squared error is minimized,

$$R(\mathbf{w}) = E[(F(\mathbf{x}, \mathbf{w}) - y)^2] \tag{16.1}$$

635

where E represents the expectation value over the probability space $(\mathcal{E}, Pr)$. Because the probability distribution Pr is normally unknown in practice, only a training set $D = \{(\mathbf{x}(1), y(1)), \cdots, (\mathbf{x}(N), y(N))\}$ is available where the data in the training set is supposed to follow the unknown probability distribution Pr. The expected squared error is therefore minimized on the training set D:

$$R(\mathbf{w}) = E_D[(F(\mathbf{x}, \mathbf{w}) - y)^2] \tag{16.2}$$

$$= \Sigma_{i=1}^{N} E\left[(F(\mathbf{x}(i), \mathbf{w}) - y(i))^2\right] \tag{16.3}$$

The learned function $F(\mathbf{x}, \mathbf{w})$ would depend on the training set D. The different training sets D might lead to different $F(\mathbf{x}, \mathbf{w})$, so that function $F(\mathbf{x}, \mathbf{w})$ is written as $F(\mathbf{x}, D)$ to show its explicit dependence on the training set D.

Suppose that all the training sets D of given size N would be available, from which N data points could be independently selected by following the probability distribution Pr. All the training sets D of given size N will form a new probability space $(\mathcal{E}^{(N)}, Pr^{(N)})$. Let E_D represent the expected squared error $E_D[(F(\mathbf{x}, D) - y)^2]$ over $(\mathcal{E}^{(N)}, Pr^{(N)})$ and E with no subscript denote the expectation over $(\mathcal{E}, Pr)$. With respect to the training set D, there is the following separation of the mean-squared error [1]:

$$
\begin{aligned}
E_D\left[(F(\mathbf{x}, D) - y)^2\right] &= E_D\left[F(\mathbf{x}, D)^2\right] - 2y E_D\left[F(\mathbf{x}, D)\right] + y^2 \\
&= (E_D\left[F(\mathbf{x}, D)\right] - y)^2 \\
&\quad + E_D\left[F(\mathbf{x}, D)^2\right] - (E_D\left[F(\mathbf{x}, D)\right])^2 \\
&= (E_D\left[F(\mathbf{x}, D)\right] - y)^2 + var_D(F(\mathbf{x}, D)) \quad (16.4)
\end{aligned}
$$

where the variance $var_D(F(\mathbf{x}, D))$ could be represented as

$$
\begin{aligned}
var_D(F(\mathbf{x}, D)) &= E_D[(F(\mathbf{x}, D) - E_D[F(\mathbf{x}, D)])^2] \\
&= E_D[F(\mathbf{x}, D)^2] - (E_D[F(\mathbf{x}, D)])^2 \quad (16.5)
\end{aligned}
$$

The term $(E_D\left[F(\mathbf{x}, D)\right] - y)^2$ in Eq. (16.4) shows the bias of the approximating function $F(\mathbf{x}, D)$, which measures how much the average function value at $\mathbf{x}$ deviates from y. The other term $var_D(F(\mathbf{x}, D))$ indicates the variance of the approximating function $F(\mathbf{x}, D)$, which displays the changes of the function values at $\mathbf{x}$ from one training set to another.

As Eq. (16.4) shows, the expected mean-square value includes two terms of bias and variance. If neither bias nor variance is negative, both of them for the approximating function $F(\mathbf{x}, D)$ should be small for achieving good performance.

On the one hand, the obtained function $F(\mathbf{x}, D)$ would not be able to capture some of the aspects of the data if it would be too simple. It might either overestimate or underestimate most of $(\mathbf{x}, y)$. Both cases would lead to large bias. On the other hand, if the function $F(\mathbf{x}, D)$ were too complex, it would be capable of implementing numerous solutions that are consistent with the training data. However, for data different from the training data, a wide range of values of $F(\mathbf{x}, D)$ might appear as the training set D varies so that its variance would become large. The complexity of $F(\mathbf{x}, D)$ for best matching all the data would be hard to determine if only a small set of data points would be available. In practice, there is usually a trade-off between bias and variance [1]. Decreasing bias by introducing more parameters often tends to increase variance. Optimization of reducing parameters for the smaller variance often tends to increase bias.

16.2. Bias–Variance–Covariance Trade-Off in Ensemble Learning

Rather than applying a single function $F(\mathbf{x}, D)$ on D, an ensemble system is to combine a set of $F_i(\mathbf{x}, D)$. One way of combination is to use their simple average as output:

$$F(\mathbf{x}, D) = \frac{1}{M} \Sigma_{i=1}^{M} F_i(\mathbf{x}, D) \tag{16.6}$$

where M is the number of individual approximating functions in the ensemble. The expected mean-squared error of the ensemble can be represented by individual function outputs:

$$E_D[(F(\mathbf{x}, D) - y)^2] = E_D\left[\left(\frac{1}{M} \Sigma_{i=1}^{M} F_i(\mathbf{x}, D) - y\right)^2\right] \tag{16.7}$$

Based on Eq. (16.4), the following decomposition can be driven:

$$E_D\left[\left(\frac{1}{M} \Sigma_{i=1}^{M} F_i(\mathbf{x}, D) - y\right)^2\right] = \left(E_D\left[\frac{1}{M} \Sigma_{i=1}^{M} F_i(\mathbf{x}, D)\right] - y\right)^2$$
$$+ var_D\left(\frac{1}{M} \Sigma_{i=1}^{M} F_i(\mathbf{x}, D)\right) \tag{16.8}$$

where the two terms on the right side of Eq. (16.8) are the bias and the variance of the ensemble, respectively. The second term of the ensemble variance may be further divided into two terms:

$$var_D \left(\frac{1}{M} \Sigma_{i=1}^{M} F_i(\mathbf{x}, D) \right)$$

$$= E_D \left[\left(\frac{1}{M} \Sigma_{i=1}^{M} F_i(\mathbf{x}, D) - E_D \left[\frac{1}{M} \Sigma_{i=1}^{M} F_i(\mathbf{x}, D) \right] \right)^2 \right]$$

$$= E_D \left[\frac{1}{M^2} \left(\Sigma_{i=1}^{M} (F_i(\mathbf{x}, D) - E_D[F_i(\mathbf{x}, D)]) \right)^2 \right]$$

$$= E_D \left[\frac{1}{M^2} (\Sigma_{i=1}^{M} (F_i(\mathbf{x}, D) - E_D[F_i(\mathbf{x}, D)]) \right.$$

$$\left. \times (\Sigma_{j=1}^{M} (F_j(\mathbf{x}, D) - E_D[F_j(\mathbf{x}, D)])) \right]$$

$$= E_D \left[\frac{1}{M^2} \Sigma_{i=1}^{M} (F_i(\mathbf{x}, D) - E_D[F_i(\mathbf{x}, D)])^2 \right]$$

$$+ E_D \left[\frac{1}{M^2} \Sigma_{i=1}^{M} \Sigma_{j=1, j \neq i}^{M} (F_i(\mathbf{x}, D) - E_D[F_i(\mathbf{x}, D)]) \right.$$

$$\left. \times (F_j(\mathbf{x}, D) - E_D[F_j(\mathbf{x}, D)]) \right] \qquad (16.9)$$

where the first one is the average of the variance of individual functions. The second is the average covariance among the different functions in the ensemble.

Corresponding to the bias–variance trade-off for a single function, there is a bias–variance–covariance trade-off among an ensemble. If all the individual functions F_i would be positively correlated greatly, there would be little reduction of the variance for the ensemble with such individual functions. If the individual functions F_i would be uncorrelated, the weighted average covariance among them would become zero while the variance of theirs could decay at $\frac{1}{M}$. Both experimental and theoretical results have suggested that when individual functions in an ensemble are unbiased, negatively correlated functions would lead to the most effective ensemble [2]. The ensemble would be less effective when its combined individual functions are uncorrelated. There might hardly be any gain by combining positively correlated functions in an ensemble.

16.3. Three Types of Ensemble Learning Methods

Based on how interactions are performed in learning, three types of ensemble learning methods are discussed for the learning models implemented by neural networks. It should be pointed out that these ensemble learning methods are also applicable to other learning models.

16.3.1. *Independent Ensemble Learning*

It is clear that there is no advantage of combining a set of identical neural networks for an ensemble learning system. The individual neural networks have to be different, and cooperative as well. Data sampling is a common approach to training individual neural networks to be different, in which cross-validation [3, 4] and bootstrapping [5] have been widely used.

Cross-validation is a method for estimating prediction error in its original form [6]. Cross-validation can be used for sampling data for training a set of networks by splitting the data into m roughly equal-sized sets, and training each network on the different sets independently. As indicated by Meir [7], for a small dataset with noise, such data splitting might help to reduce the correlation among the m trained neural networks more drastically than those trained on the whole data.

If a large number of individual neural networks should be trained, splitting the given data with no overlapping would lead each set of data to be too small to train a neural network. Therefore, data re-sampling such as bootstrap [5] would be helpful if available data samples are limited. Bootstrap was introduced for estimating the standard error of a statistic [5]. Breiman [8] applied the idea of bootstrap for bagging predictors. In bagging predictors, a training set containing N patterns is perturbed by sampling with replacement N times from the original dataset. The perturbed dataset may contain repeats. This procedure can be repeated to generate a number of different datasets with overlapping.

16.3.2. *Sequential Ensemble Learning*

It is uncertain how different the trained neural networks would be after independent ensemble learning when there is no interaction in their learning. Some neural networks by independent ensemble learning might still be positively correlated, and do little help in their combined ensemble system. Sequential ensemble learning trained a set of neural networks in a particular order by re-sampling the data based on what early trained neural networks had learned. Boosting is one example of sequential ensemble learning. Boosting algorithm was originally proposed by Schapire [9]. Schapire proved that it is theoretically possible to convert a weak learning algorithm that performs only slightly better than random guessing into one that achieves arbitrary accuracy. The proof presented by Schapire [9] is constructive. The construction uses filtering to modify the distribution of examples in such a way as to force the weak learning algorithm to focus on the harder-to-learn parts of the distribution.

Boosting trains a set of learning machines sequentially on the datasets that have been filtered by the previously trained learning machines [9]. The original boosting procedure is as follows [10]. The first machine is trained with N_1 patterns randomly chosen from the available training data. After the first machine has been trained, a second training set with N_1 patterns is randomly selected on which the first machine would have 50% error rate. That is, there are 50% of patterns in the training set, which will be misclassified by the first machine. Once the second machine is trained on the second training set, the third set of training patterns will be filtered through the first and second machines. Those patterns would be added into the third training set if the first two machines did not disagree with them. Such a data filtering process would be continued until a total of N_1 patterns are selected. Accordingly, the third machine will be trained on the third training set. During testing on the ensemble with these three trained machines, each new pattern will be classified using the following voting scheme. If the first two machines would agree on the new pattern, their answer would be taken as the output for the new pattern. Otherwise, the new pattern would be labeled by the third machine.

16.3.3. *Simultaneous Ensemble Learning*

Both the independent ensemble learning and sequential ensemble learning follow a two-stage design process of training individual neural networks first, and combining them thereafter. The direct interactions among the individual neural networks cannot be exploited until the integration stage. Feedback from the integration might not be fully used in training the existing individual neural networks in the ensemble or any newly added to the ensemble. In order to inject the feedback from the integration into learning each neural network, simultaneous ensemble learning trains a set of neural networks interactively. Negative correlation learning [11–13] and the mixtures-of-experts architectures [14, 15] are two examples of simultaneous ensemble learning.

The mixtures-of-experts architecture is to train multiple networks through competitive and associative learning [14, 15]. The mixtures-of-experts architecture applied the principle of divide and conquer for solving a complex problem by decomposing it into a set of simpler subproblems. It is assumed that the data can be adequately summarized by a collection of functions, where each of them can be defined over a local region of the input space. The mixtures-of-experts architecture adaptively partitions the input space into possibly overlapping regions, and allocates different networks to summarize the data located in different regions. The mixtures-of-experts architecture consists of two layers of networks, including a gating network and a number of expert networks. In the mixtures-of-experts architecture, all expert networks are allowed to look at the input, and make their best guess. The gating network uses the normalized exponential transformation to weight the outputs of the expert networks to provide an overall best guess. All the parameter adjustments in the expert networks and gating network are performed simultaneously. Although the mixtures-of-experts architecture can produce biased individual networks whose estimates are negatively correlated [16], it did not directly address the issue of the bias–variance–covariance trade-off.

16.4. Statistical Analysis of Negative Correlation Learning

16.4.1. *Negative Correlation Learning*

Given the training set $D = \{(\mathbf{x}(1), y(1)), \cdots, (\mathbf{x}(N), y(N))\}$, the output of an ensemble with M neural networks can be defined by a simple average among the outputs from all individual neural networks on the nth training pattern $\mathbf{x}(n)$:

$$F(n) = \frac{1}{M} \Sigma_{i=1}^{M} F_i(n) \tag{16.10}$$

where $F_i(n)$ is the output of neural network i on $\mathbf{x}(n)$. Negative correlation learning trains all individual neural networks in the ensemble simultaneously and interactively by introducing a correlation penalty term into the error function for each neural network [11–13]. The error function E_i of the ith neural network on the training set is given by

$$E_i = \frac{1}{N} \Sigma_{n=1}^{N} E_i(n)$$

$$= \frac{1}{N} \Sigma_{n=1}^{N} \left[\frac{1}{2} (F_i(n) - y(n))^2 + \lambda p_i(n) \right] \tag{16.11}$$

where $E_i(n)$ is the error function of neural network i at presentation of the nth training pattern. In the right side of Eq. (16.11), the first term is the mean-squared error of individual network i, while the second term p_i is a correlation penalty function. The purpose of minimizing p_i is to directly correlate each individual's error negatively with errors for the rest of the ensemble. The penalty function p_i can be chosen as

$$p_i(n) = (F_i(n) - F(n)) \Sigma_{j \neq i} (F_j(n) - F(n)). \tag{16.12}$$

The parameter λ is used to adjust the strength of the penalty.

The partial derivative of E_i with respect to the output of network i on the nth training pattern is

$$\frac{\partial E_i(n)}{\partial F_i(n)} = F_i(n) - y(n) + \lambda \frac{\partial p_i(n)}{\partial F_i(n)}$$

$$= F_i(n) - y(n) + \lambda \Sigma_{j \neq i} (F_j(n) - F(n))$$

$$= F_i(n) - y(n) + \lambda \Sigma_{j=1}^{M} (F_j(n) - F(n)) - \lambda(F_i(n) - F(n))$$

$$= F_i(n) - y(n) - \lambda(F_i(n) - F(n))$$

$$= (1 - \lambda)(F_i(n) - y(n)) + \lambda(F(n) - y(n)) \tag{16.13}$$

where the output of ensemble $F(n)$ is supposed to have a constant value with respect to $F_i(n)$. Backpropagation can be used for weight adjustments in the mode of pattern-by-pattern updating in negative correlation learning. Therefore, weight updating of all the individual networks can be performed simultaneously using Eq. (16.13) after the presentation of each training data. One complete presentation of the entire training set during the learning process is called an epoch.

From Eqs. (16.11), (16.12), and (16.13), it can be seen that negative correlation learning has the following learning characteristics:

(1) During the training process, all the individual neural networks interact with each other through their penalty terms in the error functions. Not only does each F_i minimize the difference between $F_i(n)$ and $y(n)$, but also the difference between $F_i(n)$ and $F(n)$.
(2) At $\lambda = 0.0$, no correlation penalty is enforced so that all the individual neural networks will be trained independently.
(3) At $\lambda = 1$, Eq. (16.13) becomes

$$\frac{\partial E_i(n)}{\partial F_i(n)} = F(n) - y(n) \tag{16.14}$$

The error of the ensemble for the nth training pattern can be represented as

$$E_{ensemble} = \frac{1}{2}(\frac{1}{M}\Sigma_{i=1}^{M} F_i(n) - y(n))^2 \tag{16.15}$$

The partial derivative of $E_{ensemble}$ with respect to F_i on the nth training pattern is

$$\frac{\partial E_{ensemble}}{\partial F_i(n)} = \frac{1}{M}\left(\frac{1}{M}\Sigma_{i=1}^{M} F_i(n) - y(n)\right)$$

$$= \frac{1}{M}(F(n) - y(n)) \tag{16.16}$$

Therefore, the following relation exists:

$$\frac{\partial E_i(n)}{\partial F_i(n)} = M \times \frac{\partial E_{ensemble}}{\partial F_i(n)} \tag{16.17}$$

It shows that minimization of the error function of the ensemble is achieved by minimizing the error functions of the individual networks. From this point of view, negative correlation learning provides a novel way to decompose the learning task of the ensemble into a number of subtasks for different individual networks [17–22].

16.4.2. *Simulation Setup*

The following regression task has been used to estimate the bias of mixture-of-experts architectures and the variance and covariance of experts' weighted outputs [16]:

$$f(\mathbf{x}) = \frac{1}{13}\left[10\sin(\pi x_1 x_2) + 20\left(x_3 - \frac{1}{2}\right)^2 + 10x_4 + 5x_5\right] - 1 \quad (16.18)$$

where $\mathbf{x} = [x_1, \ldots, x_5]$ is an input vector whose components lie between zero and one. The value of $f(\mathbf{x})$ lies in the interval $[-1, 1]$.

Twenty-five training sets, $(\mathbf{x}^{(k)}(l), y^{(k)}(l))$, $l = 1, \ldots, L$, $L = 500$, $k = 1, \ldots, K$, $K = 25$, were created at random. The reason for creating 25 training sets is that the same setting was used to analyze the mixture-of-experts [16]. Each set consisted of 500 input–output patterns in which the components of the input vectors were independently sampled from a uniform distribution over the interval $(0,1)$. In the noise-free condition, the target outputs were not corrupted by noise; in the small noise condition, the target outputs were created by adding noise sampled from a Gaussian distribution with a mean of zero and a variance of $\sigma^2 = 0.1$ to the function $f(\mathbf{x})$; in the large noise condition, the target outputs were created by adding noise sampled from a Gaussian distribution with a mean of zero and a variance of $\sigma^2 = 0.2$ to the function $f(\mathbf{x})$.

A testing set of 1024 input–output patterns, $(\mathbf{t}(n), d(n))$, $n = 1, \ldots, N$, $N = 1024$, was also generated. For this set, the components of the input vectors were independently sampled from a uniform distribution over the interval $(0,1)$, and the target outputs were not corrupted by noise in all three conditions.

The ensemble architecture used in negative correlation learning consists of eight 3-layer feedforward neural networks where each of them has one hidden layer with five hidden nodes. The hidden node in the hidden layer is defined by the logistic function:

$$\varphi(y) = \frac{1}{1 + \exp(-y)} \quad (16.19)$$

The output layer is defined as a linear combination of the outputs from the hidden nodes.

For each estimation of bias, variance, and covariance of an ensemble, 25 simulations were conducted. In each simulation, the ensemble was trained on a different training set from the same initial weights distributed inside a small range so that different simulations of an ensemble yielded different performances solely due to the use of different training sets. Such simulation setup follows the suggestions from Jacobs [16].

16.4.3. *Measurement of Bias, Variance, and Covariance*

The equations for measuring bias, variance, and covariance can be derived from Eqs. (16.8) and (16.9). The average outputs of the ensemble and the individual network i on the nth pattern in the testing set, $(\mathbf{t}(n), d(n))$, $n = 1, \ldots, N$, are denoted, respectively, by $\overline{F}(\mathbf{t}(n))$ and $\overline{F}_i(\mathbf{t}(n))$, which are given by

$$\overline{F}(\mathbf{t}(n)) = \frac{1}{K} \Sigma_{k=1}^K F^{(k)}(\mathbf{t}(n)) \tag{16.20}$$

and

$$\overline{F}_i(\mathbf{t}(n)) = \frac{1}{K} \Sigma_{k=1}^K F_i^{(k)}(\mathbf{t}(n)) \tag{16.21}$$

where $F^{(k)}(\mathbf{t}(n))$ and $F_i^{(k)}(\mathbf{t}(n))$ are the outputs of the ensemble and the individual network i on the nth pattern in the testing set from the kth simulation, respectively, and $K = 25$ is the number of simulations. The integrated bias E_{bias}, integrated variance E_{var}, and integrated covariance E_{cov} of the ensemble are defined by, respectively,

$$E_{bias} = \frac{1}{N} \Sigma_{n=1}^N \left(\overline{F}(\mathbf{t}(n)) - d(n) \right)^2 \tag{16.22}$$

and

$$E_{var} = \Sigma_{i=1}^M \frac{1}{N} \Sigma_{n=1}^N \frac{1}{K} \Sigma_{k=1}^K \frac{1}{M^2} \left(F_i^{(k)}(\mathbf{t}(n)) - \overline{F}_i(\mathbf{t}(n)) \right)^2 \tag{16.23}$$

and

$$E_{cov} = \Sigma_{i=1}^M \Sigma_{j=1, j \neq i}^M \frac{1}{N} \Sigma_{n=1}^N \frac{1}{K} \Sigma_{k=1}^K$$
$$\frac{1}{M^2} \left(F_i^{(k)}(\mathbf{t}(n)) - \overline{F}_i(\mathbf{t}(n)) \right) \left(F_j^{(k)}(\mathbf{t}(n)) - \overline{F}_j(\mathbf{t}(n)) \right) \tag{16.24}$$

We may also define the integrated mean-squared error (MSE) E_{mse} on the testing set as

$$E_{mse} = \frac{1}{N} \Sigma_{n=1}^N \frac{1}{K} \Sigma_{k=1}^K \left(F^{(k)}(\mathbf{t}(n)) - d(n) \right)^2 \tag{16.25}$$

The integrated mean-squared error E_{train} on the training set is given by

$$E_{train} = \frac{1}{L} \Sigma_{l=1}^L \frac{1}{K} \Sigma_{k=1}^K \left(F^{(k)}(\mathbf{x}^{(k)}(l)) - y^{(k)}(l) \right)^2 \tag{16.26}$$

It is clear that the following equality holds:

$$E_{mse} = E_{bias} + E_{var} + E_{cov} \tag{16.27}$$

16.4.4. *Measuring Bias, Variance, and Covariance for Different Strength Parameters*

This section to investigate the dependence of E_{bias}, E_{var}, and E_{cov} on the strength parameter λ in Eq. (16.11) for negative correlation learning.

16.4.4.1. *Results in the noise-free condition*

The results of negative correlation learning in the noise-free condition for the different values of λ at epoch 2000 are given in Table 16.1. The results suggest that both E_{bias} and E_{mse} appeared to decrease with increasing value of λ. It seems that E_{var} increased as the value of λ increased, and E_{cov} decreased as the value of λ increased.

It is interesting that negative correlation learning controls not only E_{var} and E_{cov}, but also the E_{bias} of the ensemble. Compared with independent training (i.e., $\lambda = 0.0$ in negative correlation learning), although negative correlation learning created larger variance, the sum of the variance and covariance in negative correlation learning was smaller because of the negative covariance.

At the same time, negative correlation learning reduced the bias of the ensemble significantly. In order to find out why E_{bias} decreased with increasing value of λ, the concept of capability of a trained ensemble is introduced. The capability of a trained ensemble is measured by its ability to produce correct input–output mapping on the training set used, specifically by its integrated mean-squared error E_{train} on the training set. The smaller E_{train} is, the larger capability the trained ensemble has. Table 16.1 shows the results of the error E_{train} for different λ values. It was observed that the smaller error E_{train} was obtained using the larger value of λ. It seemed that the value of strength parameter λ played a role in deciding the capability of the ensemble. Increasing the value of λ led to increasing the capability of the ensemble. When $\lambda = 0$, the capability of the ensemble trained was not big enough to produce correct input–output mapping, so the ensemble had a relatively larger E_{bias}. When $\lambda = 1$, the ensemble trained had the smallest E_{train} and the highest

Table 16.1: The results of negative correlation learning in the noise-free condition for different λ values at epoch 2000

λ	E_{bias}	E_{var}	E_{cov}	E_{mse}	E_{train}
0.0	1.31×10^{-3}	1.51×10^{-4}	1.40×10^{-4}	1.60×10^{-3}	1.25×10^{-3}
0.25	1.07×10^{-3}	1.78×10^{-4}	7.96×10^{-5}	1.33×10^{-3}	1.02×10^{-3}
0.50	8.67×10^{-4}	2.50×10^{-4}	-2.60×10^{-5}	1.09×10^{-3}	8.14×10^{-4}
0.75	5.21×10^{-4}	4.04×10^{-4}	-2.51×10^{-4}	6.74×10^{-4}	4.88×10^{-4}
1.0	9.11×10^{-5}	0.274853	-0.274746	1.98×10^{-4}	1.14×10^{-4}

capability of producing correct input–output mapping, so it had the smallest E_{bias}.

From Eq. (16.27), the integrated MSE consists of the sum of three terms: the integrated bias, variance, and covariance. Therefore, negative correlation learning provides a control of bias, variance, and covariance through the choice of λ value to achieve good performance. For this regression task with noise-free condition and the ensemble architecture used, it was observed that the bias–variance–covariance trade-off was optimal for $\lambda = 1.0$ in the sense of minimizing the MSE.

Figures 16.1–16.5 show the learning curves of E_{bias}, E_{var}, E_{cov}, E_{mse}, and E_{train} for negative correlation learning ($\lambda = 1.0$) and independent training (i.e., $\lambda = 0$ in negative correlation learning). For negative correlation learning, E_{bias}, E_{mse}, and E_{train} decreased very quickly at the early training stage and continued to reduce stably; E_{var} increased quickly at the early training stage and then reduced slightly while E_{cov} reduced quickly at early training stage and continued to reduce stably. It is important to note that the integrated covariance became negative during the training procedure in negative correlation learning. In general, negative correlation learning produced faster convergence in terms of minimizing the MSE.

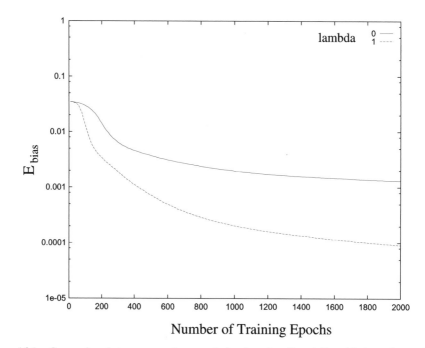

Figure 16.1: Comparison between negative correlation learning ($\lambda = 1.0$) and independent training (i.e., $\lambda = 0$ in negative correlation learning) on E_{bias}. The vertical axis is the value of E_{bias} and the horizontal axis is the number of training epochs.

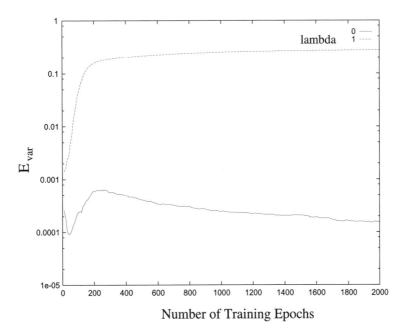

Figure 16.2: Comparison between negative correlation learning ($\lambda = 1.0$) and independent training (i.e., $\lambda = 0$ in negative correlation learning) on E_{var}. The vertical axis is the value of E_{var} and the horizontal axis is the number of training epochs.

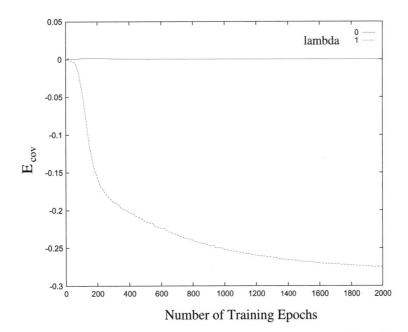

Figure 16.3: Comparison between negative correlation learning ($\lambda = 1.0$) and independent training (i.e., $\lambda = 0$ in negative correlation learning) on E_{cov}. The vertical axis is the value of E_{cov} and the horizontal axis is the number of training epochs.

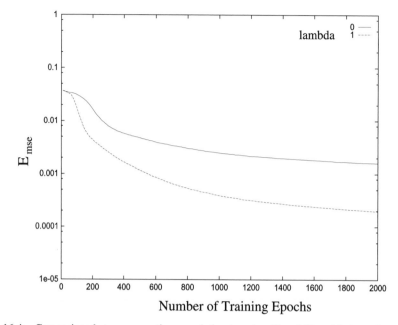

Figure 16.4: Comparison between negative correlation learning ($\lambda = 1.0$) and independent training (i.e., $\lambda = 0$ in negative correlation learning) on E_{mse}. The vertical axis is the value of E_{mse} and the horizontal axis is the number of training epochs.

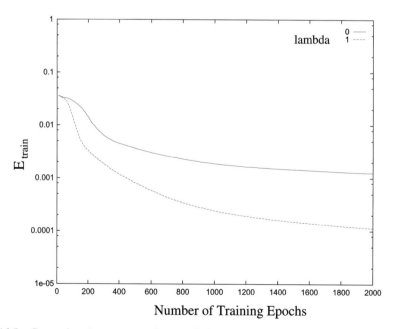

Figure 16.5: Comparison between negative correlation learning ($\lambda = 1.0$) and independent training (i.e., $\lambda = 0$ in negative correlation learning) on E_{train}. The vertical axis is the value of E_{train} and the horizontal axis is the number of training epochs.

16.4.4.2. *Results in the noise conditions*

Tables 16.2 and 16.3 compare the performance of negative correlation learning for different strength parameters in both small noise (variance $\sigma^2 = 0.1$) and large noise (variance $\sigma^2 = 0.2$) conditions. The results show that there were same trends for E_{bias}, E_{var}, and E_{cov} in both noise-free and noise conditions. That is, E_{bias} appeared to decrease with increasing value of λ. E_{var} seemed to increase as the value of λ increased, and E_{cov} seemed to decrease as the value of λ increased. However, E_{mse} appeared to decrease first and then increase with increasing value of λ.

In order to find out why E_{mse} showed different trends in noise-free and noise conditions, the integrated mean-squared error E_{train} on the training set is also shown in Tables 16.2 and 16.3. When $\lambda = 0$, the ensemble trained had a relatively large E_{train}. This indicated that the capability of the ensemble trained was not big enough to produce correct input–output mapping (i.e., it was underfitting) for this regression task. When $\lambda = 1$, the ensemble learned too many specific input–output relations (i.e., it was overfitting), and it might memorize the training data and therefore be less able to generalize between similar input–output patterns. Although the overfitting was not observed for the ensemble used in noise-free condition, too large capability of the ensemble would lead to overfitting for both noise-free and noise conditions because of the ill-posedness of any finite training set. Choosing a proper value of λ is important, and also problem dependent. For the noise conditions used for this

Table 16.2: The results of negative correlation learning in the small noise condition for different λ values at epoch 2000

λ	E_{bias}	E_{var}	E_{cov}	$E_{var} + E_{cov}$	E_{mse}	E_{train}
0.0	0.0046	0.0018	0.0074	0.0092	0.0138	0.0962
0.25	0.0041	0.0020	0.0068	0.0088	0.0129	0.0940
0.5	0.0038	0.0027	0.0059	0.0086	0.0124	0.0915
0.75	0.0029	0.0046	0.0051	0.0097	0.0126	0.0873
1.0	0.0023	0.2107	−0.1840	0.0267	0.0290	0.0778

Table 16.3: The results of negative correlation learning in the large noise condition for different λ values at epoch 2000

λ	E_{bias}	E_{var}	E_{cov}	$E_{var} + E_{cov}$	E_{mse}	E_{train}
0.0	0.0083	0.0031	0.0135	0.0166	0.0249	0.1895
0.25	0.0074	0.0035	0.0126	0.0161	0.0235	0.1863
0.5	0.0061	0.0048	0.0120	0.0168	0.0229	0.1813
0.75	0.0051	0.0087	0.0109	0.0196	0.0247	0.1721
1.0	0.0041	0.3270	−0.2679	0.0591	0.0632	0.1512

Table 16.4: Comparison between negative correlation learning (NCL) and the mixture-of-experts (ME) architecture

Noise condition	Method	E_{bias}	E_{var}	E_{cov}	E_{mse}
Small	NCL with $\lambda = 0.5$	0.004	0.003	0.006	0.012
	NCL with $\lambda = 1$	0.002	0.211	−0.184	0.029
	ME	0.008	0.030	−0.020	0.018
Large	NCL with $\lambda = 0.5$	0.006	0.005	0.012	0.023
	NCL with $\lambda = 1$	0.004	0.327	−0.268	0.063
	ME	0.013	0.065	−0.040	0.038

regression task and the ensemble architectured used, the bias–variance–covariance trade-off was optimal for $\lambda = 0.5$ among the tested values of λ in the sense of minimizing the MSE on the testing set.

16.4.4.3. *Comparisons with other work*

Table 16.4 compares the results of negative correlation learning with $\lambda = 0.5$ and $\lambda = 1$ to those produced by the mixture-of-experts architecture [16]. In the small noise case, the integrated MSE of the mixture-of-experts architecture was about 0.018, while the integrated MSE of negative correlation learning with $\lambda = 0.5$ was 0.012. The integrated MSE achieved by the mixture-of-experts architecture was about 0.038 in the large noise case, which is compared to 0.023 by negative correlation learning with $\lambda = 0.5$. Although both the mixture-of-experts architecture and negative correlation learning tend to create negatively correlated networks, negative correlation learning can achieve good performance by controlling bias, variance, and covariance through the choice of λ value.

16.4.5. *Correlations among the Individual Networks*

The section compares the correlations among the individual networks and the biases of the individual networks created by negative correlation learning and independent training, respectively. The correlation between network i and network j is given by

$$Cor(i, j) = \frac{\sum_{n=1}^{N} \sum_{k=1}^{K} \left(F_i^{(k)}(\mathbf{t}(n)) - \overline{F}_i(\mathbf{t}(n)) \right) \left(F_j^{(k)}(\mathbf{t}(n)) - \overline{F}_j(\mathbf{t}(n)) \right)}{\sqrt{\sum_{n=1}^{N} \sum_{k=1}^{K} \left(F_i^{(k)}(\mathbf{t}(n)) - \overline{F}_i(\mathbf{t}(n)) \right)^2 \sum_{n=1}^{N} \sum_{k=1}^{K} \left(F_j^{(k)}(\mathbf{t}(n)) - \overline{F}_j(\mathbf{t}(n)) \right)^2}}$$

(16.28)

and the bias of network i is given by

$$Bias(i) = \frac{1}{N} \frac{1}{K} \sum_{n=1}^{N} \sum_{k=1}^{K} \left(F_i^{(k)}(\mathbf{t}(n)) - d(n) \right)^2$$

(16.29)

where $F_i^{(k)}(\mathbf{t}(n))$ is the output of the network i on the nth pattern in the testing set, $(\mathbf{t}(n), d(n))$, $n = 1, \ldots, N$, from the kth simulation, $\overline{F}_i(\mathbf{t}(n))$ represents the average output of the network i on the nth pattern in the testing set.

16.4.5.1. *Results in the noise-free condition*

In order to observe the effect of the correlation penalty terms, Table 16.5 shows the correlations among the individual networks trained by independent training (i.e., $\lambda = 0$ in negative correlation learning) and negative correlation learning with $\lambda = 0.5$ and $\lambda = 1$ in the noise-free condition. There are $\binom{8}{2} = 28$ correlations among different pairs of networks. For negative correlation learning with $\lambda = 0.5$, 18 correlations among them had negative values. For negative correlation learning with $\lambda = 1$, the number of negative correlations increased to 20. The results suggest that negative correlation learning leads to negatively correlated networks. In contrast, for the independent training without the correlation penalty terms, 27 correlations were positive and only one was negative. Because every individual network learns the same task in the independent training, the correlations among them are generally positive. In negative correlation learning, each individual network learns different

Table 16.5: The correlations among the individual networks trained by negative correlation learning with different λ values in the noise-free condition

	$Cor(1, 2) = 0.042$	$Cor(1, 3) = -0.031$	$Cor(1, 4) = 0.129$	$Cor(1, 5) = 0.0289$
	$Cor(1, 6) = 0.251$	$Cor(1, 7) = 0.226$	$Cor(1, 8) = 0.213$	$Cor(2, 3) = 0.053$
	$Cor(2, 4) = 0.078$	$Cor(2, 5) = 0.043$	$Cor(2, 6) = 0.031$	$Cor(2, 7) = 0.046$
$\lambda = 0$	$Cor(2, 8) = 0.165$	$Cor(3, 4) = 0.233$	$Cor(3, 5) = 0.208$	$Cor(3, 6) = 0.151$
	$Cor(3, 7) = 0.065$	$Cor(3, 8) = 0.155$	$Cor(4, 5) = 0.087$	$Cor(4, 6) = 0.203$
	$Cor(4, 7) = 0.100$	$Cor(4, 8) = 0.104$	$Cor(5, 6) = 0.086$	$Cor(5, 7) = 0.199$
	$Cor(5, 8) = 0.222$	$Cor(6, 7) = 0.326$	$Cor(6, 8) = 0.126$	$Cor(7, 8) = 0.253$
	$Cor(1, 2) = -0.023$	$Cor(1, 3) = -0.070$	$Cor(1, 4) = 0.114$	$Cor(1, 5) = -0.049$
	$Cor(1, 6) = -0.002$	$Cor(1, 7) = -0.129$	$Cor(1, 8) = -0.078$	$Cor(2, 3) = 0.006$
	$Cor(2, 4) = -0.0004$	$Cor(2, 5) = -0.138$	$Cor(2, 6) = -0.071$	$Cor(2, 7) = -0.138$
$\lambda = 0.5$	$Cor(2, 8) = 0.042$	$Cor(3, 4) = -0.021$	$Cor(3, 5) = -0.062$	$Cor(3, 6) = -0.047$
	$Cor(3, 7) = -0.006$	$Cor(3, 8) = 0.0200$	$Cor(4, 5) = 0.052$	$Cor(4, 6) = -0.081$
	$Cor(4, 7) = 0.071$	$Cor(4, 8) = -0.140$	$Cor(5, 6) = 0.085$	$Cor(5, 7) = 0.157$
	$Cor(5, 8) = -0.091$	$Cor(6, 7) = 0.188$	$Cor(6, 8) = 0.018$	$Cor(7, 8) = -0.019$
	$Cor(1, 2) = -0.368$	$Cor(1, 3) = 0.221$	$Cor(1, 4) = -0.177$	$Cor(1, 5) = 0.038$
	$Cor(1, 6) = -0.383$	$Cor(1, 7) = 0.096$	$Cor(1, 8) = -0.288$	$Cor(2, 3) = -0.131$
	$Cor(2, 4) = -0.244$	$Cor(2, 5) = -0.161$	$Cor(2, 6) = -0.087$	$Cor(2, 7) = -0.364$
$\lambda = 1$	$Cor(2, 8) = -0.272$	$Cor(3, 4) = -0.203$	$Cor(3, 5) = -0.277$	$Cor(3, 6) = -0.335$
	$Cor(3, 7) = -0.248$	$Cor(3, 8) = -0.158$	$Cor(4, 5) = 0.068$	$Cor(4, 6) = -0.159$
	$Cor(4, 7) = -0.152$	$Cor(4, 8) = 0.053$	$Cor(5, 6) = -0.056$	$Cor(5, 7) = -0.039$
	$Cor(5, 8) = 0.122$	$Cor(6, 7) = -0.026$	$Cor(6, 8) = 0.078$	$Cor(7, 8) = 0.185$

Table 16.6: The biases among the individual networks trained by negative correlation learning with different λ values in the noise-free condition

$\lambda = 0$	$Bias(1) = 0.0024$	$Bias(2) = 0.0041$	$Bias(3) = 0.0032$	$Bias(4) = 0.0022$
	$Bias(5) = 0.0030$	$Bias(6) = 0.0025$	$Bias(7) = 0.0027$	$Bias(8) = 0.0020$
$\lambda = 0.5$	$Bias(1) = 0.0031$	$Bias(2) = 0.0045$	$Bias(3) = 0.0054$	$Bias(4) = 0.0020$
	$Bias(5) = 0.0040$	$Bias(6) = 0.0025$	$Bias(7) = 0.0031$	$Bias(8) = 0.0024$
$\lambda = 1$	$Bias(1) = 8.0774$	$Bias(2) = 12.1147$	$Bias(3) = 3.3489$	$Bias(4) = 5.5513$
	$Bias(5) = 1.0458$	$Bias(6) = 8.7573$	$Bias(7) = 2.3400$	$Bias(8) = 2.6317$

parts or aspects of the training data so that the problem of correlated errors can be removed or alleviated.

Table 16.6 shows the biases of the individual networks trained by independent training (i.e., $\lambda = 0.0$ in negative correlation learning) and negative correlation learning with $\lambda = 0.5$ and $\lambda = 1$. In independent training, all the individual networks are trained to implement the whole learning task. In contrast, different individual networks are trained to implement the subtasks of the whole learning task so that the individual networks created by negative correlation learning had larger bias values than those of the individual networks created by independent training. However, as shown in (16.17), the ensemble in negative correlation learning is trained to implement the whole learning task. This is the reason why the ensemble combined by these individual networks had smaller integrated bias, as shown in Tables 16.1, 16.2 and 16.3.

16.4.5.2. *Results in the noise conditions*

Tables 16.7 and 16.9 show the correlations among the individual networks trained by independent training (i.e., $\lambda = 0$ in negative correlation learning) and negative correlation learning with $\lambda = 0.5$ and $\lambda = 1$ in the small and large noise conditions. Tables 16.8 and 16.10 show the biases of these networks.

The values of the correlations among the individual networks had relatively larger positive values when λ was 0. They reduced to relatively smaller positive values when λ was increased to 0.5. Most of them became negative values when λ was further increased to 1. Overall, the results indicated that the neural networks trained by negative correlation learning tended to be negatively correlated neural networks in both the noise-free and noise conditions.

On the other hand, the biases of the individual networks trained by negative correlation learning were larger than those of the individual networks trained by independent training. Nevertheless, the ensembles created by negative correlation learning had smaller integrated biases.

Table 16.7: The correlations among the individual networks trained by negative correlation learning with different λ values in the small noise condition

	$Cor(1,2) = 0.685$	$Cor(1,3) = 0.593$	$Cor(1,4) = 0.703$	$Cor(1,5) = 0.655$
	$Cor(1,6) = 0.451$	$Cor(1,7) = 0.705$	$Cor(1,8) = 0.658$	$Cor(2,3) = 0.579$
	$Cor(2,4) = 0.568$	$Cor(2,5) = 0.645$	$Cor(2,6) = 0.462$	$Cor(2,7) = 0.694$
$\lambda = 0$	$Cor(2,8) = 0.737$	$Cor(3,4) = 0.708$	$Cor(3,5) = 0.560$	$Cor(3,6) = 0.498$
	$Cor(3,7) = 0.551$	$Cor(3,8) = 0.518$	$Cor(4,5) = 0.601$	$Cor(4,6) = 0.558$
	$Cor(4,7) = 0.599$	$Cor(4,8) = 0.571$	$Cor(5,6) = 0.425$	$Cor(5,7) = 0.731$
	$Cor(5,8) = 0.610$	$Cor(6,7) = 0.443$	$Cor(6,8) = 0.396$	$Cor(7,8) = 0.737$
	$Cor(1,2) = 0.385$	$Cor(1,3) = 0.356$	$Cor(1,4) = 0.280$	$Cor(1,5) = 0.351$
	$Cor(1,6) = 0.325$	$Cor(1,7) = 0.402$	$Cor(1,8) = 0.341$	$Cor(2,3) = 0.302$
	$Cor(2,4) = 0.289$	$Cor(2,5) = 0.355$	$Cor(2,6) = 0.188$	$Cor(2,7) = 0.304$
$\lambda = 0.5$	$Cor(2,8) = 0.392$	$Cor(3,4) = 0.404$	$Cor(3,5) = 0.294$	$Cor(3,6) = 0.255$
	$Cor(3,7) = 0.273$	$Cor(3,8) = 0.276$	$Cor(4,5) = 0.249$	$Cor(4,6) = 0.310$
	$Cor(4,7) = 0.287$	$Cor(4,8) = 0.263$	$Cor(5,6) = 0.276$	$Cor(5,7) = 0.351$
	$Cor(5,8) = 0.327$	$Cor(6,7) = 0.302$	$Cor(6,8) = 0.185$	$Cor(7,8) = 0.314$
	$Cor(1,2) = -0.141$	$Cor(1,3) = -0.136$	$Cor(1,4) = -0.177$	$Cor(1,5) = -0.172$
	$Cor(1,6) = -0.126$	$Cor(1,7) = -0.141$	$Cor(1,8) = -0.035$	$Cor(2,3) = -0.099$
	$Cor(2,4) = -0.162$	$Cor(2,5) = -0.148$	$Cor(2,6) = 0.047$	$Cor(2,7) = -0.126$
$\lambda = 1$	$Cor(2,8) = 0.038$	$Cor(3,4) = -0.227$	$Cor(3,5) = -0.128$	$Cor(3,6) = -0.037$
	$Cor(3,7) = -0.067$	$Cor(3,8) = -0.087$	$Cor(4,5) = -0.176$	$Cor(4,6) = -0.241$
	$Cor(4,7) = -0.081$	$Cor(4,8) = -0.037$	$Cor(5,6) = -0.031$	$Cor(5,7) = -0.084$
	$Cor(5,8) = -0.274$	$Cor(6,7) = -0.052$	$Cor(6,8) = 0.004$	$Cor(7,8) = -0.007$

Table 16.8: The biases among the individual networks trained by negative correlation learning with different λ values in the small noise condition

$\lambda = 0$	$Bias(1) = 0.0177$	$Bias(2) = 0.0170$	$Bias(3) = 0.0212$	$Bias(4) = 0.0193$
	$Bias(5) = 0.0185$	$Bias(6) = 0.0228$	$Bias(7) = 0.0183$	$Bias(8) = 0.0178$
$\lambda = 0.5$	$Bias(1) = 0.0249$	$Bias(2) = 0.0244$	$Bias(3) = 0.0287$	$Bias(4) = 0.0284$
	$Bias(5) = 0.0250$	$Bias(6) = 0.0274$	$Bias(7) = 0.0260$	$Bias(8) = 0.0264$
$\lambda = 1$	$Bias(1) = 2.7812$	$Bias(2) = 4.3145$	$Bias(3) = 2.0255$	$Bias(4) = 3.7067$
	$Bias(5) = 2.0343$	$Bias(6) = 1.2497$	$Bias(7) = 2.4406$	$Bias(8) = 1.2872$

16.4.6. *Measuring Bias, Variance, and Covariance for Different Ensemble Sizes*

This section investigates the dependence of E_{bias}, E_{var}, and E_{cov} on the ensemble size, i.e., the number of individual networks in the ensemble. The ensemble architectures used in negative correlation learning are composed of 4, 8, 16, and 32 individual networks, respectively. All individual networks have 5 hidden nodes.

Table 16.9: The correlations among the individual networks trained by negative correlation learning with different λ values in the large noise condition

	$Cor(1, 2) = 0.654$	$Cor(1, 3) = 0.615$	$Cor(1, 4) = 0.657$	$Cor(1, 5) = 0.735$
	$Cor(1, 6) = 0.512$	$Cor(1, 7) = 0.656$	$Cor(1, 8) = 0.584$	$Cor(2, 3) = 0.582$
	$Cor(2, 4) = 0.540$	$Cor(2, 5) = 0.647$	$Cor(2, 6) = 0.477$	$Cor(2, 7) = 0.706$
$\lambda = 0$	$Cor(2, 8) = 0.665$	$Cor(3, 4) = 0.714$	$Cor(3, 5) = 0.667$	$Cor(3, 6) = 0.492$
	$Cor(3, 7) = 0.639$	$Cor(3, 8) = 0.605$	$Cor(4, 5) = 0.626$	$Cor(4, 6) = 0.520$
	$Cor(4, 7) = 0.565$	$Cor(4, 8) = 0.577$	$Cor(5, 6) = 0.528$	$Cor(5, 7) = 0.737$
	$Cor(5, 8) = 0.622$	$Cor(6, 7) = 0.574$	$Cor(6, 8) = 0.446$	$Cor(7, 8) = 0.684$
	$Cor(1, 2) = 0.320$	$Cor(1, 3) = 0.376$	$Cor(1, 4) = 0.392$	$Cor(1, 5) = 0.342$
	$Cor(1, 6) = 0.239$	$Cor(1, 7) = 0.388$	$Cor(1, 8) = 0.329$	$Cor(2, 3) = 0.375$
	$Cor(2, 4) = 0.316$	$Cor(2, 5) = 0.327$	$Cor(2, 6) = 0.229$	$Cor(2, 7) = 0.244$
$\lambda = 0.5$	$Cor(2, 8) = 0.361$	$Cor(3, 4) = 0.431$	$Cor(3, 5) = 0.397$	$Cor(3, 6) = 0.290$
	$Cor(3, 7) = 0.311$	$Cor(3, 8) = 0.390$	$Cor(4, 5) = 0.288$	$Cor(4, 6) = 0.370$
	$Cor(4, 7) = 0.318$	$Cor(4, 8) = 0.297$	$Cor(5, 6) = 0.349$	$Cor(5, 7) = 0.346$
	$Cor(5, 8) = 0.351$	$Cor(6, 7) = 0.373$	$Cor(6, 8) = 0.240$	$Cor(7, 8) = 0.333$
	$Cor(1, 2) = -0.128$	$Cor(1, 3) = -0.197$	$Cor(1, 4) = -0.134$	$Cor(1, 5) = -0.149$
	$Cor(1, 6) = -0.188$	$Cor(1, 7) = -0.0002$	$Cor(1, 8) = -0.034$	$Cor(2, 3) = -0.114$
	$Cor(2, 4) = -0.186$	$Cor(2, 5) = -0.084$	$Cor(2, 6) = -0.080$	$Cor(2, 7) = -0.132$
$\lambda = 1$	$Cor(2, 8) = -0.082$	$Cor(3, 4) = -0.189$	$Cor(3, 5) = -0.198$	$Cor(3, 6) = -0.058$
	$Cor(3, 7) = -0.150$	$Cor(3, 8) = -0.054$	$Cor(4, 5) = -0.102$	$Cor(4, 6) = -0.028$
	$Cor(4, 7) = -0.132$	$Cor(4, 8) = -0.198$	$Cor(5, 6) = -0.041$	$Cor(5, 7) = 0.009$
	$Cor(5, 8) = -0.007$	$Cor(6, 7) = -0.051$	$Cor(6, 8) = -0.084$	$Cor(7, 8) = -0.030$

Table 16.10: The biases among the individual networks trained by negative correlation learning with different λ values in the large noise condition

$\lambda = 0$	$Bias(1) = 0.0325$	$Bias(2) = 0.0308$	$Bias(3) = 0.0360$	$Bias(4) = 0.0359$
	$Bias(5) = 0.0349$	$Bias(6) = 0.0361$	$Bias(7) = 0.0323$	$Bias(8) = 0.0343$
$\lambda = 0.5$	$Bias(1) = 0.0480$	$Bias(2) = 0.0495$	$Bias(3) = 0.0474$	$Bias(4) = 0.0472$
	$Bias(5) = 0.0468$	$Bias(6) = 0.0438$	$Bias(7) = 0.0421$	$Bias(8) = 0.0501$
$\lambda = 1$	$Bias(1) = 3.0875$	$Bias(2) = 5.2799$	$Bias(3) = 3.7562$	$Bias(4) = 4.9059$
	$Bias(5) = 2.590$	$Bias(6) = 2.0779$	$Bias(7) = 3.3165$	$Bias(8) = 2.1227$

The results of both negative correlation learning and independent learning are given in Figures 16.6–16.9 for the different ensemble sizes and different λ values in the noise-free condition at epoch 2000. For independent training (i.e., $\lambda = 0$), E_{train} did not change much when varying the ensemble size. It indicated that the ensembles with different sizes trained by independent training had similar capabilities. E_{bias} decreased slightly when the ensemble size M was increased from 4 to 16, and then increased slightly when M was changed to 32. E_{var} seemed to decay at $1/M$, while E_{cov} increased with increasing ensemble size M. It was observed that the ensembles

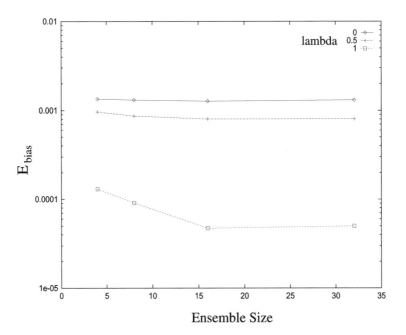

Figure 16.6: Comparison of negative correlation learning for the different ensemble sizes and different values of λ in the noise-free condition. The vertical axis is the value of E_{bias} on the testing set at epoch 2000 and the horizontal axis is the ensemble size.

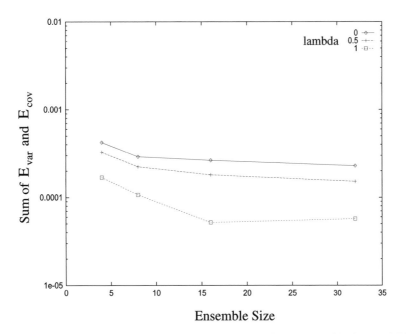

Figure 16.7: Comparison of negative correlation learning for different ensemble sizes and different values of λ in the noise-free condition. The vertical axis is the sum of E_{var} and E_{cov} on the testing set at epoch 2000 and the horizontal axis is the ensemble size.

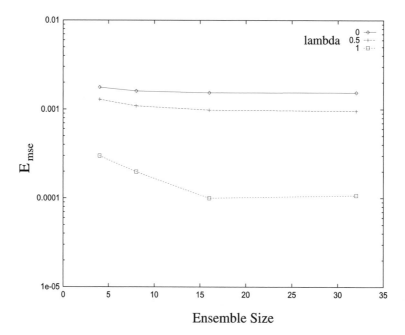

Figure 16.8: Comparison of negative correlation learning for different ensemble sizes and different values of λ in the noise-free condition. The vertical axis is the value of E_{mse} on the testing set at epoch 2000 and the horizontal axis is the ensemble size.

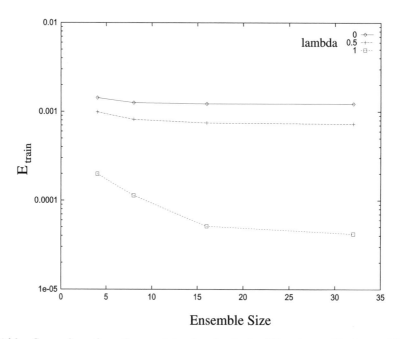

Figure 16.9: Comparison of negative correlation learning for the different ensemble sizes and different values of λ in the noise-free condition. The vertical axis is the value of E_{train} on the testing set at epoch 2000 and the horizontal axis is the ensemble size.

with 16 and 32 individual neural networks performed slightly better than the other two ensembles with four and eight individual networks.

For negative correlation learning with $\lambda = 0.5$, E_{bias} quickly dropped when M was increased from 4 to 16, and then increased slightly when M became 32. E_{var} appeared to decay approximately at $\frac{1}{M}$, while E_{cov} had negative values for $M = 4$ and $M = 8$, and increased to small positive values for $M = 16$ and $M = 32$. Both E_{mse} and E_{train} decreased with increasing ensemble size.

For negative correlation learning with $\lambda = 1$, smaller E_{bias} and larger E_{var} were obtained compared with those in negative correlation learning with $\lambda = 0.5$. Because of negative values of E_{cov}, the sum of E_{var} and E_{cov} was also smaller. It is apparent that for this regression task with noise-free condition and the same ensemble, negative correlation learning with $\lambda = 1$ performed better than negative correlation learning with $\lambda = 0.5$, and the latter performed better than independent training.

It needs to be noted that the capability of the ensemble trained by negative correlation learning was larger than that of the same ensemble trained by independent training. It is clear that negative correlation learning obtained much smaller E_{train} than that obtained by independent training. It is worth pointing out that larger ensemble size does not necessarily improve the performance of the ensemble. In fact, overfitting was observed for the ensemble with 32 individual networks trained by negative correlation learning with $\lambda = 1$.

16.5. Ensemble Learning with Awareness

Currently, learning systems have become large, heterogeneous, uncertain, and dynamic. They also need to match some conflict requirements, such as flexibility, performance, resource usage, and reliability. One key problem is how to dynamically resolve these requirements at run time when there exist dynamic and uncertain scenarios in the learning problems. For such learning problems, learning is not just a one-time optimization problem anymore. Instead, learning systems should be capable of dynamic management of different learning goals at run time. In this section, ideas of aware learning systems are introduced. It has been observed that learning systems could better manage trade-offs between goals at run time if they would be aware of their own state, behavior and performance [23, 24].

16.5.1. *Awareness System*

An awareness system consists of a number of aware units where each aware unit could be mathematically described as [23, 24]

$$\mathbf{y} = R_3(R_2(R_1(\mathbf{x}))), \tag{16.30}$$

where R_1 is a receptor, R_2 is a reactor, and R_3 is a relater. The input $\mathbf{x}$ and the output $\mathbf{y}$ are usually represented as real vectors. Each element of $\mathbf{x}$ can come from a physical sensor, a software sensor, or a lower level aware unit. Each element of $\mathbf{y}$ is a concept to be aware of or some information to be used by a higher level aware unit.

The function of the receptor R_1 is to receive data $\mathbf{x}$ from the environment and conduct the data preprocessing of filtering out irrelevant noises, enhancing the signals, and normalizing or standardizing the inputs. The input $\mathbf{x}$ from different kinds of sensors can therefore be treated in the same way after R_1. The function of the reactor R_2 is to react to the output of R_1, and extract or select important features. The function of the relater R_3 is to detect certain events, make proper decisions based on the features provided by R_2, and relate the detected events to other aware units.

An aware unit has two operation modes, working mode and learning mode. In the working mode, data flow forward from lower-level aware units to higher-level aware units. In the learning mode, data flow backward by sending feedback to the receptor through the relater and reactor. System parameters can therefore be adjusted based on the feedback.

When the contexts are complex and dynamically changing, the system must be able to learn and become more and more aware autonomously. An aware unit is certainly not enough to cope with such complex contexts although one aware unit itself can be used as an aware system. It is desirable to use an aware unit as a subsystem to form a larger ensemble system with other aware units.

16.5.2. *Three-Level Awareness*

The term "awareness computing" was originally used in the context of computer-supported cooperative work, ubiquitous computing, social network, and others [23, 24]. It has been considered by researchers as a process for acquiring and distributing context information related to what is happening, what happened, and what is going to happen in an environment under concern conditions.

Three levels of awareness could be introduced into a system. At the low level of awareness, the system has neither awareness nor decision. It just provides the context for the human users to be aware of any useful information contained in the context. Such a low level of awareness appears in most monitoring systems for traffic control, nuclear power plants, and public facilities. These systems could run smoothly at routine cooperative work. However, in emergent cases, human users might fail to detect possible dangers by lacking computing power in the human brain even if the background information were provided seamlessly.

At the middle level of awareness, a system can be aware of the importance or urgency of different context patterns so that critical information can be provided to the human user or some other systems in a more noticeable, comprehensible and/or visible way. The awareness ability of human users could be enhanced significantly on detecting some danger and seizing a chance. Many decision-supporting systems developed so far have such a level of awareness although their developers did not intend to build awareness in the systems at the beginning.

At the high level of awareness, a system is aware of the meaning of the context patterns and can make corresponding decisions for the user. These kinds of systems have been used in smart homes and smart offices, in which the server may be aware of human users' actions, locations, and behaviors and can provide suitable services based on different context patterns. The system is able to switch light on or off to keep the best lighting conditions in a smart office and provide software/hardware resources to meet the requirements of a user in cloud computing.

Even if these systems with certain levels of awareness are indeed smart, they are not intelligent. The events to be aware of are normally pre-defined in those smart systems. The decisions made are programmed by using some manually definable rules. For example, many context-aware systems developed from mobile computing are implemented by using some smart sensors connected to a server through a base station. Awareness could be automatically built through correlation maps between the input and the output. When the output can be derived directly from the input, it would be simple to find the correlation map. However, such a correlation map could be hard to build in the real world. In practice, there could be many unforeseen outputs that are not registered in the system. Therefore, the system should be able to detect possible new outputs. Meanwhile, the current input may be the factor for many outputs to occur. The system should be able to modify the correlation map dynamically so that the scope of possible outputs can be narrowed down after more information is acquired. It is a kind of dynamic optimization problem that could be solved effectively by evolutionary algorithms. A population of search agents could be defined to work together during a search. To speed up a search, the agents may share knowledge through imitation or by acquiring some appropriate knowledge [25]. It is expected that awareness systems would stimulate smart systems, and create real intelligence in the near future.

References

[1] S. Geman, E. Bienenstock, and E. Doursat, Neural networks and the bias/variance dilemma, *Neural Comput.*, **4**, 1–58 (1992).

[2] R. T. Clemen and R. L. Winkler, Limits for the precision and value of information from dependent sources, *Oper. Res.*, **33**, 427–442 (1985).

[3] A. Krogh and J. Vedelsby, Neural network ensembles, cross validation, and active learning. In eds. G. Tesauro, D. S. Touretzky, and T. K. Leen, *Advances in Neural Information Processing Systems 7*, pp. 231–238. The MIT Press (1995).

[4] E. A. Bender, *Mathematical Methods in Artificial Intelligence* (IEEE Computer Society Press, Los Alamitos, CA, 1996).

[5] B. Efron and R. J. Tibshirani, *An Introduction to the Bootstrap* (Chapman & Hall, 1993).

[6] M. Stone, Cross-validatory choice and assessment of statistical predictions, *J. R. Stat. Soc.*, **36**, 111–147 (1974).

[7] R. Meir, Bias, variance, and the combination of least squares estimators. In eds. G. Tesauro, D. S. Touretzky, and T. K. Leen, *Advances in Neural Information Processing Systems 7*, pp. 295–302. The MIT Press (1995).

[8] L. Breiman, Bagging predictors, *Mach. Learn.*, **24**, 123–140 (1996).

[9] R. E. Schapire, The strength of weak learnability, *Mach. Learn.*, **5**, 197–227 (1990).

[10] H. Drucker, C. Cortes, L. D. Jackel, Y. LeCun, and V. Vapnik, Boosting and other ensemble methods, *Neural Comput.*, **6**, 1289–1301 (1994).

[11] Y. Liu and X. Yao, Simultaneous training of negatively correlated neural networks in an ensemble, *IEEE Trans. Syst. Man Cybern. Part B: Cybern.*, **29**(6), 716–725 (1999).

[12] Y. Liu and X. Yao, Ensemble learning via negative correlation, *Neural Networks*, **12**(10), 1399–1404, 1999.

[13] Y. Liu, X. Yao, and T. Higuchi, Evolutionary ensembles with negative correlation learning, *IEEE Trans. Evol. Comput.*, **4**(4), 380–725 (2000).

[14] R. A. Jacobs, M. I. Jordan, S. J. Nowlan, and G. E. Hinton, Adaptive mixtures of local experts, *Neural Comput.*, **3**, 79–87 (1991).

[15] M. I. Jordan and R. A. Jacobs, Hierarchical mixtures-of-experts and the EM algorithm, *Neural Comput.*, **6**, 181–214 (1994).

[16] R. A. Jacobs, Bias/variance analyses of mixture-of-experts architectures, *Neural Comput.*, **9**, 369–383 (1997).

[17] Y. Liu and X. Yao, A cooperative ensemble learning system. In *Proc. of the 1998 IEEE International Joint Conference on Neural Networks (IJCNN'98)*, pp. 2202–2207. IEEE Press, Piscataway, NJ, USA (1998).

[18] Y. Liu and X. Yao, Towards designing neural network ensembles by evolution. In *Parallel Problem Solving from Nature—PPSN V: Proc. of the Fifth International Conference on Parallel Problem Solving from Nature*, vol. 1498, *Lecture Notes in Computer Science*, pp. 623–632. Springer-Verlag, Berlin (1998).

[19] Y. Liu, Awareness learning for balancing performance and diversity in neural network ensembles. In *Proc. of the International Conference on Natural Computation, Fuzzy Systems and Knowledge Discovery*, pp. 113–120. Springer, Cham (2019).

[20] Y. Liu, Learning targets for building cooperation awareness in ensemble learning. In *Proc. of 2018 9th International Conference on Awareness Science and Technology (iCAST)*, pp. 16–19. IEEE (2018).

[21] Y. Liu, Combining two negatively correlated learning signals in a committee machine. In *Proc. of 2018 IEEE International Conference on Signal Processing, Communications and Computing (ICSPCC)*, pp. 1–4. IEEE (2018).

[22] Y. Liu, Bidirectional negative correlation learning. In *Proc. of International Symposium on Intelligence Computation and Applications*, pp. 84–92. Springer, Singapore (2017).

[23] Q. Zhao, Reasoning with awareness and for awareness: realizing an aware system using an expert system, *IEEE Syst. Man Cybern. Mag.*, **3**(2), 35–38 (2017).

[24] Q. Zhao, Making aware systems interpretable. In *Proc. of 2016 International Conference on Machine Learning and Cybernetics (ICMLC)*, pp. 881–887. IEEE (2016).

[25] I. Chowdhury, K. Su, and Q. Zhao, MS-NET: modular selective network round robin based modular neural network architecture with limited redundancy, *Int. J. Mach. Learn. Cybern.*, **12**, 763–781 (2021). https://doi.org/10.1007/s13042-020-01201-8.

https://doi.org/10.1142/9789811247323_0017

Chapter 17

A Multistream Deep Rule-Based Ensemble System for Aerial Image Scene Classification

Xiaowei Gu[*,‡,¶] *and Plamen P. Angelov*[†,§]

*Department of Computer Science, Aberystwyth University
Aberystwyth, Ceredigion, SY23 3DB, UK
[†]*School of Computing and Communications, Lancaster University*
Bailrigg, Lancaster, LA1 4WA, UK
[‡]*xig4@aber.ac.uk*
[§]*p.angelov@lancaster.ac.uk*

Aerial scene classification is the key task for automated aerial image understanding and information extraction, but is highly challenging due to the great complexity and real-world uncertainties exhibited by such images. To perform precise aerial scene classification, in this research, a multistream deep rule-based ensemble system is proposed. The proposed ensemble system consists of three deep rule-based systems that are trained simultaneously on the same data. The three ensemble components employ ResNet50, DenseNet121, and InceptionV3 as their respective feature descriptors because of the state-of-the-art performances the three networks have demonstrated on aerial scene classification. The three networks are fine-tuned on aerial images to further enhance their discriminative and descriptive abilities. Thanks to its prototype-based nature, the proposed approach is able to self-organize a transparent ensemble predictive model with prototypes learned from training images and perform highly explainable joint decision-making on testing images with greater precision. Numerical examples based on both benchmark aerial image sets and satellite sensor images demonstrated the efficacy of the proposed approach, showing its great potential in solving real-world problems.

17.1. Introduction

Remotely sensed aerial images are data sources of great importance for Earth observation and are fundamental for a wide variety of real-world applications,

---

¶Corresponding author.

such as environmental monitoring and urban planning [1]. Rapid development of sensing techniques has led to a significant growth in the volumes of aerial images acquired over the past decade, enabling much detailed analysis of the Earth's surface. As a key task in aerial image understanding, the main aim of aerial scene classification is to automatically assign distinct land-use class labels to aerial images based on their semantic contents. However, it is widely recognized as a challenging task due to the huge volume, high intraclass diversity, low interclass variation, complex geometrical structures, and spatial patterns of these remotely sensed images. Recently, aerial scene classification has received lots of attention and is now a hotly researched topic in the fields of machine learning and remote sensing [2].

Deep neural network (DNN)-based approaches have gained huge popularity in the remote sensing community because of their impressive performance on many benchmark problems for aerial scene classification [3]. Thanks to the capability of automatically learning informative representations of raw input images with multiple levels of abstraction [4], DNNs are currently considered to be one of the state-of-the-art approaches in the remote sensing domain [5]. For example, F. Zhang et al. [6] proposed a gradient boosting random ensemble framework composed of multiple DNNs for aerial scene classification. Zhang et al. [7] introduced a multiscale dense network that utilizes multiscale information in the network structure for hyper-spectral remote sensing image classification. Zhang et al. [8] combined a convolutional neural network (CNN) and a capsule network into a new deep architecture, achieving competitive classification performance on public challenging benchmark remote sensing image datasets. Liu et al. [9] used a Siamese CNN model to learn discriminative feature representations from aerial images for scene classification. However, DNNs are widely known "black box" models with high system complexity, but lacking transparency. The training process is computationally expensive and requires huge amounts of labeled training data to construct a well-performing model. Their decision-making and reasoning processes are not explainable to humans. Most importantly, DNNs are fragile to real-world uncertainties as they can fail easily when handling data with unfamiliar patterns. These deficiencies hinder the performance of DNNs in real-world applications [10].

An alternative approach to making use of the powerful representation learning ability of DNNs is to directly use off-the-shelf pretrained DNNs as feature descriptors. Many works [11–13] have reported good performance on aerial scene classification using mainstream classifiers, i.e., k-nearest neighbor [14], support vector machine [15] and random forest [16], with high-level semantic features extracted from aerial images by DNNs pretrained on natural images such as ImageNet [17]. Popular pretrained DNNs for aerial scene classification include

VGGNet [18], InceptionNet [19, 20], ResNet [21], DenseNet [22], etc. Although this avoids the computationally expensive and time-consuming training process of DNNs, the issue of lacking explainability remains unsolved because the model transparency of mainstream classifiers is often very low on high-dimensional, complex problems such as image classification.

The deep rule-based (DRB) classifier [10, 23] is a recently introduced generic approach for image classification by integrating a zero-order prototype-based fuzzy rule-based system with a multilayer image-processing architecture. As an attractive alternative to DNNs, DRB has demonstrated great performance across a variety of image classification problems [24–26] and, at the same time, offers high-level model transparency and explainability thanks to its prototype-based nature. Despite its competitive results on aerial scene classification problems, it is observed that DRB sometimes misclassifies aerial images into wrong land-use categories due to the high intraclass diversity and low interclass variation. The main reason for this is because the pretrained DNNs employed by DRB were originally trained on natural images. Therefore, they fail to capture the most distinctive characteristics of different land-use categories from aerial images. To address this problem, one feasible solution is to tune the pretrained DNNs for aerial scene classification such that more descriptive high-level semantic features can be extracted from aerial images through DNN activation [27]. Furthermore, due to the highly complex nature of aerial images, a single fine-tuned DNN may not be able to provide better performance. Since different DNNs have their own strengths and weaknesses, a more promising approach is to employ multiple fine-DNNs together such that images of different land-use categories can be discriminated with great precision despite of the presence of intraclass diversity and interclass similarity.

Following this principle, in this chapter, a novel multistream deep rule-based ensemble (MSDRBE) system is proposed for aerial scene classification. The proposed framework consists of three DRB systems trained simultaneously. Each DRB system self-organizes a set of prototype-based IF...THEN rules from training images for classification in a fully autonomous, objective, and transparent manner. To ensure the diversity of ensemble components, the three DRB systems use ResNet50, DenseNet121, and InceptionV3 as their respective feature descriptors for feature extraction. The three employed DNNs are the state-of-the-art models for aerial scene classification, showing great performance. To further enhance their descriptive abilities, they have been fine-tuned on benchmark aerial imagery in advance. During decision-making, land-use categories of unlabeled aerial images are determined by the scores of confidence produced by the three DRB systems within the ensemble framework jointly. Numerical examples of benchmark aerial image datasets show that MSDRBE is able to achieve top performance on aerial scene classification, outperforming the state-of-the-art approaches.

17.2. Preliminaries

In this section, technical details of DRB are summarized to make this chapter self-contained [10, 23]. The general architecture of DRB is seen in Figure 17.1.

A standard DRB consists of the following four components [10, 23]:

(1) **Pre-processing module:** The main purposes of this module include: (i) preparing input images for feature extraction; and (ii) augmenting the input images to improve the generalization ability. Therefore, it is usually composed of several sub-layers with different functionalities, e.g., normalization, rotation, scaling, and segmentation.

(2) **Feature descriptor:** This component converts each image, **I**, to a more meaningful and descriptive feature vector, denoted as x

$$x \leftarrow \frac{F(\mathbf{I})}{||F(\mathbf{I})||};$$ (17.1)

where $F(\cdot)$ represents the feature extraction process; $|| \cdot ||$ is the L_2 norm.

DRB may employ different types of commonly used feature descriptors for feature extraction, depending on the nature of the problem. An ensemble of feature descriptors can further be considered for extracting more discriminative representations from images [28].

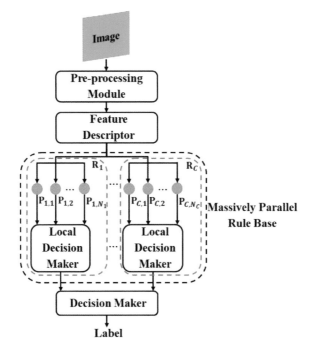

Figure 17.1: Architecture of DRB.

(3) **Massively parallel rule base:** This component is the "learning engine" of DRB, composed of C massively parallel IF...THEN fuzzy rules identified from training images through a self-organizing and human-interpretable manner. Each IF...THEN rule, denoted as $\mathbf{R}_n$ ($n = 1, 2, \ldots, C$), is identified from training images of a particular class separately, and is formulated as follows [23, 29]:

$$\mathbf{R}_n : IF\,(\mathbf{I} \sim P_{n,1})\ OR\ (\mathbf{I} \sim \mathbf{P}_{n,2})\ OR \cdots OR\ (\mathbf{I} \sim \mathbf{P}_{n,N_n})$$
$$THEN\ (\mathbf{I}\ belongs\ to\ class_n), \tag{17.2}$$

where C is the number of classes, $\mathbf{I}$ stands for a particular image, $\mathbf{P}_{n,j}$ is the jth prototype of the nth class, and N_n is the number of prototypes identified from images of the nth class.

(4) Decision maker:

This is the final component of DRB, which assigns class labels to unlabeled images based on their visual similarities to prototypes of different classes.

The system identification and validation processes of DRB are given by the next two subsections.

17.2.1. *Identification Process*

Since the massively parallel fuzzy rules of DRB are learned separately from labeled training images of different classes, only the identification process of the nth rule, $\mathbf{R}_n$, is presented here. The same principle can be applied to other massively parallel fuzzy rules within the system.

Identification process of $\mathbf{R}_n$ [10, 23]

Step 0. For each newly arrived training image of the nth class, denoted as $\mathbf{I}_{n,k}$, its feature vector $x_{n,k}$ is first extracted by the feature descriptor.

Step 1. If $\mathbf{I}_{n,k}$ is the very first observed image of the nth class, namely, $k = 1$, it initializes $\mathbf{R}_n$ with the global meta-parameters set by

$$N_n \leftarrow 1; \quad \boldsymbol{\mu}_n \leftarrow x_{n,k}, \tag{17.3}$$

where $x_{n,k}$ is the corresponding feature vector of $\mathbf{I}_{n,k}$; $\boldsymbol{\mu}_n$ denotes the global mean of feature vectors of observed labeled training images of the nth class. $\mathbf{I}_{n,k}$ itself becomes the first prototype of $\mathbf{R}_n$, denoted as $\mathbf{P}_{n,N_n}$, and the local parameters associated with $\mathbf{P}_{n,N_n}$ are initialized by

$$\mathbf{P}_{n,N_n} \leftarrow \mathbf{I}_{n,k}; \quad \boldsymbol{p}_{n,N_n} \leftarrow x_{n,k}; \quad S_{n,N_n} \leftarrow 1; \quad r_{n,N_n} \leftarrow r_o, \qquad (17.4)$$

where S_{n,N_n} is the number of images associated with $\mathbf{P}_{n,N_n}$; $\boldsymbol{p}_{n,N_n}$ is the feature vector of $\mathbf{P}_{n,N_n}$; r_{n,N_n} is the radius of the area of influence around $\mathbf{P}_{n,N_n}$; r_o is a small value, $r_o = \sqrt{2(1 - cos(\frac{\pi}{6}))}$ [23].

Then, $\mathbf{R}_n$ is initialized as follows:

$$\mathbf{R}_n : \quad IF \ (\mathbf{I} \sim \mathbf{P}_{n,N_n})$$

$$THEN \ (I \ belongs \ to \ class \ n), \qquad (17.5)$$

and the identification process returns back to **Step 0** for the next image.

If $\mathbf{I}_{n,k}$ is not the very first image, namely, $k > 1$, the global mean is updated by

$$\mu_n \leftarrow \frac{(k-1)\mu_n + x_{n,k}}{k}, \qquad (17.6)$$

and the process enters **Step 2**.

Step 2. Data density values at $\mathbf{I}_{n,k}$ and $\mathbf{P}_{n,j}$ $(j = 1, 2, \ldots, N_n)$ are calculated as follows [30].

$$D_n(\mathbf{Z}) = \frac{1}{1 + \frac{||z - \mu_n||^2}{1 - ||\mu_n||^2}}, \qquad (17.7)$$

where $\mathbf{Z} = \mathbf{I}_{n,k}, \mathbf{P}_{n,1}, \mathbf{P}_{n,2}, \ldots, \mathbf{P}_{n,N_n}$; $z = x_{n,k}, \boldsymbol{p}_{n,1}, \boldsymbol{p}_{n,2}, \ldots, \boldsymbol{p}_{n,N_n}$.

The nearest prototype, denoted as $\mathbf{P}_{n,j*}$, to $\mathbf{I}_{n,k}$ is identified based on the similarity in-between using the following equation:

$$j^* = \min_{j=1,2,\ldots,N_n} (||x_{n,k} - \boldsymbol{p}_{n,j}||). \qquad (17.8)$$

Then, the process enters **Step 3**.

Step 3. In this step, *Condition 1* is examined firstly to see whether $\mathbf{I}_{n,k}$ has the potential to become a new prototype:

$$Condition \ 1: If \ (D_n(\mathbf{I}_{n,k}) > \max_{j=1,2,\ldots,N_n} (D_n(\mathbf{P}_{n,j})))$$

$$Or \ (D_n(\mathbf{I}_{n,k}) < \min_{j=1,2,\ldots,N_n} (D_n(\mathbf{P}_{n,j}))) \qquad (17.9)$$

$$Or \ (||x_{n,k} - \boldsymbol{p}_{n,j*}|| > r_{n,j*})$$

$$Then \ (\mathbf{I}_{n,k} \ becomes \ a \ new \ prototype)$$

If *Condition 1* is satisfied, $\mathbf{I}_{n,k}$ is recognized as a new prototype ($N_n \leftarrow N_n + 1$) and added to $\mathbf{R}_n$ in the form of Eq. (17.2). Local meta-parameters of the new prototype are set by Eq. (17.4). Otherwise (if **Condition 1** is not met), $\mathbf{I}_{n,k}$ is used to update the meta-parameters of $\mathbf{P}_{n,j^*}$ as follows:

$$\mathbf{p}_{n,j^*} \leftarrow \frac{S_{n,j^*}\mathbf{p}_{n,j^*} + x_{n,k}}{S_{n,j^*}+1}; \quad S_{n,j^*} \leftarrow S_{n,j^*}+1;$$

$$r_{n,j^*} = \frac{1}{2}\sqrt{r_{n,j^*}^2 + (1 - \|\mathbf{p}_{n,j^*}\|^2)}.$$

$$(17.10)$$

Then, the identification process goes back to **Step 0** if new images are available.

17.2.2. *Validation Process*

During the validation process, given an unlabeled image, $\mathbf{I}$, each of the C massively parallel IF...THEN fuzzy rules within DRB will generate a score of confidence, denoted as $\lambda_n(\mathbf{I})$ $(n = 1, 2, \ldots, C)$. $\lambda_n(\mathbf{I})$ is calculated based on the visual similarity between $\mathbf{I}$ and prototypes identified from labeled training images of the corresponding class [10, 23].

$$\lambda_n(\mathbf{I}) = \max_{j=1,2,\ldots,N_n} (e^{-\|x-p_{n,j}\|^2}) \qquad (17.11)$$

Based on the obtained scores of confidence, $\lambda_1(\mathbf{I}), \lambda_2(\mathbf{I}), \ldots, \lambda_C(\mathbf{I})$ (C scores, in total), the class label of $\mathbf{I}$ is determined using the "winner takes all" principle [10, 23].

$$label \leftarrow class_{n^*}; \quad n^* = \arg\max_{n=1,2,\ldots,C} (\lambda_n(\mathbf{I})). \qquad (17.12)$$

17.3. The Proposed Framework

The architecture of the proposed MSDRBE framework is presented in Figure 17.2, where it can be observed that MSDRBE is composed of three DRB systems, namely, (i) DRB-R; (ii) DRB-D, and (iii) DRB-I.

The pre-processing modules employed by the three DRB systems have the exact same structure, which can be seen in Figure 17.3. As shown by this figure, each pre-processing module consists of the following three sub-layers:

(1) Re-scaling layer:
   This layer re-scales input images to the size of 248 × 248 pixels [31]. Note that the original spatial resolution of images may be changed due to re-scaling.
(2) Segmentation layer:
   This layer crops five sub-images with the same size of 224 × 224 pixels from the central area and four corners of each image for data augmentation [32].
(3) Flipping layer:
   This layer creates a mirror from each image segment by flipping it horizontally.

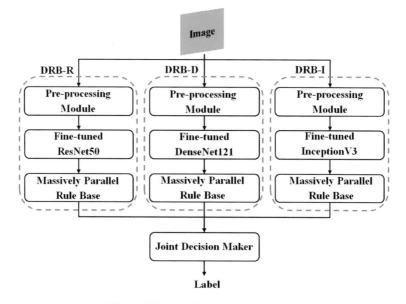

Figure 17.2:   Architecture of MSDRBE.

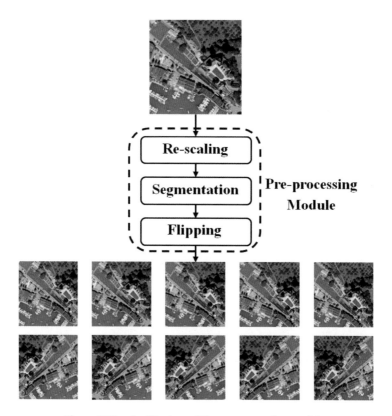

Figure 17.3:   Architecture of the pre-processing module.

Thus, a total of $M_o = 10$ new sub-images are created from each input image I by the pre-processing module. The segmentation and flipping layers effectively improve the generalization ability of DRB, allowing the system to capture more semantic information from the input images [28].

DRB-R, DRB-D, and DRB-I employ the fine-tuned ResNet50 [21], DenseNet121 [22] and InceptionV3 [20] as their respective high-level feature descriptors. MSDRBE employs the three DNNs for feature extraction because they have demonstrated the state-of-the-art performance on aerial scene classification with fewer parameters than alternative DNNs [33, 34]. For example, ResNet50 has 2.5 million parameters, DenseNet121 has only 0.8 million parameters, and InceptionV3 has 2.4 million parameters. Since each DNN has its own focus and can provide a unique view of the images, using the three DNNs together in the proposed MSDRBE can effectively enhance its capability of image understanding. Technical details of the three DNNs used by MSDRBE are summarized briefly as follows:

(1) ResNet50 [21]:
   This network is one of the widely used DNNs for object detection and classification and has 50 layers. It addresses the gradient degradation problem by reformulating the layers to learn a residual mapping, which correspondingly improves the network capacity and performance. Some researchers further suggest that ResNet50 is able to outperform other DNNs that are trained using the ImageNet datasets [17] on aerial scene classification [33].

(2) DenseNet121 [22]:
   This DNN is a variant of the popular DenseNet that uses dense connections to address the gradient degradation problem. As its name suggests, DenseNet121 has 121 layers. Each convolutional layer within the network is connected to all subsequent layers and, thus, each convolutional layer receives feature maps from all previous layers as inputs. The dense connections maximize the information flow passing between different layers, enabling DenseNet121 to achieve better performance with fewer parameters.

(3) InceptionV3 [20]:
   InceptionV3 is a popular DNN with 159 layers from the InceptionNet family. The design principle of InceptionNet is to increase both the depth and width of the network for performance improvement. Compared with its previous versions, namely, InceptionV1 and InceptionV2, InceptionV3 introduces the idea of factorization by decomposing large convolutions into smaller convolutions, which effectively reduces the number of parameters without decreasing the system efficacy. InceptionV3 offers the state-of-the-art performance on image classification and is widely used for transfer learning.

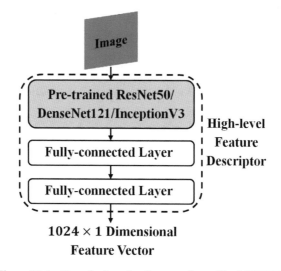

Figure 17.4: Transfer learning framework used by MSDRBE.

As mentioned in Section 17.1, the transfer learning technique is leveraged to fine-tune ResNet50, DenseNet121, and InceptionV3 to make them better fit for aerial scene classification. Transfer learning is an effective method to train a DNN using limited data without overfitting. The main aim of transfer learning is to utilize the previously learned knowledge to solve new problems better and faster [34, 35]. The diagram of the transfer learning framework used by MSDRBE is depicted in Figure 17.4 for illustration. In this research, the final softmax predicting layers of the three DNNs are replaced with two fully connected layers, each has 1024 rectified linear units (ReLUs), and the rest of the original networks are frozen to accelerate the fine-tuning process. Then, the modified DNNs are fine-tuned on an aerial scene classification problem [5]. The parameters layers are updated so that more discriminative high-level semantic features can be extracted from aerial images by the three DNNs.

During the system identification and learning processes of MSDRBE, the three fine-tuned high-level feature descriptors will summarize each input image into a 1024×1 dimensional discriminative representation based on the feature vectors extracted from the 10 sub-images produced by the pre-processing module.

$$x \leftarrow \frac{F(\mathbf{I})}{||F(\mathbf{I})||}; \quad F(\mathbf{I}) = \sum_{j=1}^{M_o} \mathrm{DN}(\mathbf{I}^{(j)}), \qquad (17.13)$$

where $\mathbf{I}^{(j)}$ represents the jth sub-image of $\mathbf{I}$; $\mathrm{DN}(\mathbf{I}^{(j)})$ represents the 1024×1 dimensional feature vector extracted from $\mathbf{I}^{(j)}$ by the high-level DNN-based feature descriptor, which can be either ResNet50, DenseNet121, or InceptionV3.

The identification process of each DRB within the proposed MSDRBE is conducted separately following the exact same process as described in Section 17.2.1. During the validation process, MSDRBE adopts the weighted voting mechanism for determining the class labels of unlabeled images.

For each unlabeled image, **I**, the three ensemble components of MSDRBE, namely, DRB-R, DRB-D, and DRB-I, produce three sets of scores of confidence using Eq. (17.11) (see Section 17.2.2). The three sets of scores of confidence (one set per ensemble component, C scores per set) are then collected by the joint decision maker and integrated to the overall scores of confidence as follows:

$$\hat{\lambda}_n(\mathbf{I}) = \frac{\lambda_n^R(\mathbf{I}) + \lambda_n^D(\mathbf{I}) + \lambda_n^I(\mathbf{I})}{3}, \qquad (17.14)$$

where $n = 1, 2, \ldots, C$; $\lambda_n^R(\mathbf{I})$, $\lambda_n^D(\mathbf{I})$, and $\lambda_n^I(\mathbf{I})$ are the scores of confidence produced by DRB-R, DRB-D, and DRB-I, respectively.

The class label of **I** is finally determined using the "winner takes all" principle

$$label \leftarrow class_{n^*}; \quad n^* = \arg\max_{n=1,2,\ldots,C} (\hat{\lambda}_n(\mathbf{I})). \qquad (17.15)$$

17.4. Numerical Experiments and Evaluation

In this section, numerical experiments on benchmark aerial scene classification problems are conducted for evaluating the performance of the proposed MSDRBE approach. The DRB and MSDRBE algorithms were developed on the MATLAB R2018a platform. Numerical experiments were conducted on a Windows 10 laptop with dual core i7 CPU with a clock rate of 2.60 GHz×2 and 16 GB RAM. The three high-level DNN-based feature descriptors employed by MSDRBE, namely, ResNet50, DenseNet121, and InceptionV3, were implemented using the Keras module from Tensorflow. The DNN fine-tuning was conducted on a Linux server with two NVIDIA GP100GL GPUs.

17.4.1. Dataset Description

The following four widely used benchmark datasets for aerial scene classification, namely, NWPU45 [5], UCMerced [36], WHU-RS19 [37], and RSSCN7 [38] were involved in the numerical experiments conducted in this research. Key information on the four datasets involved in this research is summarized in Table 17.1.

The NWPU45 dataset [5] was utilized for fine-tuning the three DNNs employed by MSDRBE, namely, ResNet50, DenseNet121, and InceptionV3. This dataset contains 31,500 aerial images of 45 different land-use categories, 700 images per category. All images have a uniform size of 256 × 256 pixels. The NWPU45 dataset is currently one of the largest datasets for aerial scene classification covering most

Table 17.1:   Key information of four aerial image sets

Dataset	Images	Categories	Images per category	Image size	Spatial resolution (m)
NWPU45	31,500	45	700	256×256	0.2~30
UCMerced	2100	21	100	256×256	0.3
WHU-RS19	950	19	50	600×600	up to 0.5
RSSCN7	2800	7	400	400×400	—

of the commonly seen land-use categories; thus, it is very suitable for fine-tuning the DNNs. Example images of this dataset are given in Figure 17.5.

To improve the generalization ability of the fine-tuned networks, each image of the NWPU45 dataset was re-scaled to the size of 248 × 248 pixels and five new images were cropped out from the central area and four corners of the original image. In this way, this dataset was augmented to five times larger. During the fine-tuning process, 80% of the images of the augmented dataset were randomly selected out to form the training set and the rest 20% were used as the validation set.

The performance of MSDRBE was evaluated on the UCMerced [36], WHU-RS19 [37], and RSSCN7 [38] datasets. The UCMerced dataset [36] consists of 21 land-use categories; each category has 100 images with the size of 256 × 256 pixels. The spatial resolution of the images is 0.3 m per pixel. The WHU-RS19 dataset [37] contains 950 aerial images with the size of 600 × 600 pixels. The 950 images are evenly distributed in 19 land-use categories. The spatial resolution is up to 0.5 m per pixel. The RSSCN7 dataset [38] has 2800 aerial images evenly distributed in seven land-used categories with the image size of 400 × 400 pixels. Images of each category are obtained at four different scales with 100 images per scale. Example images of the three datasets are illustrated in Figures 17.6–17.8, respectively.

During the experiments for performance evaluation, each dataset was randomly split into labeled training and unlabeled testing sets with two different ratios by following the commonly used experimental protocols [2]. For the UCMerced dataset, the splitting ratios between training images and testing images per category were set to 5:5 and 8:2. For the WHU-RS19 dataset, the splitting ratios were set to 4:6 and 6:4. The splitting ratios were set to 2:8 and 5:5 for the RSSCN7 dataset.

17.4.2. DNN Implementation

As described in Section 17.3, the pretrained ResNet50, DenseNet121, and Inception V3 are employed as the feature descriptors for the three ensemble component DRB systems of MSDRBE. To facilitate feature extraction, the final predicting layers of the three DNNs were replaced with two fully connected layers, each layer

Airplane

Airport

Baseball Diamond

Basketball Court

Beach

Bridge

Chaparral

Church

Circular Farmland

Cloud

Commercial area

Dense Residential

Desert

Forest

Freeway

Golf Course

Ground Track Field

Harbor

Industrial Area

Intersection

Island

Lake

Meadow

Medium Residential

Mobile Home Park

Mountain

Overpass

Palace

Parking Lot

Railway

Railway Station

Rectangular Farmland

River

Roundabout

Runway

Sea Ice

Ship

Snowberg

Sparse Residential

Stadium

Storage Tank

Tennis Court

Terrace

Therma Power Station

Wetland

Figure 17.5:   Example images of the NWPU45 dataset.

Figure 17.6:   Example images of the UCMerced dataset.

Figure 17.7:   Example images of WHU-RS19 dataset.

| Grass | Field | Industry | River and Lake | Forest |

| Residential | Parking |

Figure 17.8:   Example images of RSSCN7 dataset.

Table 17.2: Setting of data augmentation

Setting	Value
Horizontal flipping	True
Vertical flipping	True
Rotation range	22
Width shifting range	0.19
Height shifting range	0.18
Fill mode	nearest

consists of 1024 ReLUs with a dropout rate of 0.3, and the remaining parts of the DNNs are frozen. The input size of the three DNNs was adjusted to 224 × 224 pixels.

During the fine-tuning process, a 45-way softmax layer was added to the three networks (because the NWPU45 dataset has a total of 45 classes). Note that this softmax layer was removed after fine-tuning, and the 1024 × 1 dimensional activations from the second fully connected layer were used as the feature vectors of images. The adaptive moment estimation (Adam) algorithm [39] was used as the optimizer for updating the parameters of the final two fully connected layers of DNNs by minimizing the categorical cross-entropy loss function. The setting for data augmentation was listed in Table 17.2 [40]. The batch size was set to 10 and the learning rate was set as 10^{-5}. The three networks were fine-tuned for 25 epochs to avoid over-fitting, and the corresponding accuracy and loss during training and validation were shown in Figures 17.9–17.11, respectively. It can be observed from the three figures that both the training and validation accuracy of ResNet50, DenseNet121, and InceptionV3 all converged to nearly 100% after 25 training epochs, showing that the knowledge learned from ImageNet datasets [17] has been transferred successfully to the aerial scene classification tasks.

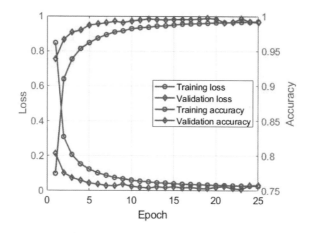

Figure 17.9: Accuracy and loss during fine-tuning of ResNet50.

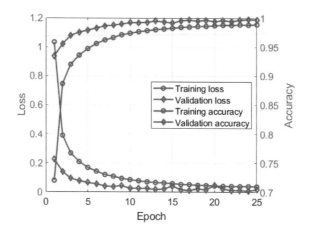

Figure 17.10: Accuracy and loss during fine-tuning of DenseNet121.

17.4.3. *Results and Comparison*

Experimental results obtained by using the proposed MSDRBE framework on the UCMerced dataset are reported in Table 17.3, where the average classification accuracy and the standard deviation after 25 Monte Carlo experiments are presented. To validate the effectiveness of the proposed ensemble framework, classification performances of DRB-R, DRB-D, and DRB-I are given in the same table. The state-of-the-art results of existing works are also presented in Table 17.3 as well for benchmark comparison.

Following the same protocol, the classification performance of MSDRBE, DRB-R, DRB-D, and DRB-I on the WHU-RS19 dataset under two different training–testing split ratios as mentioned at the beginning of this section are tabulated

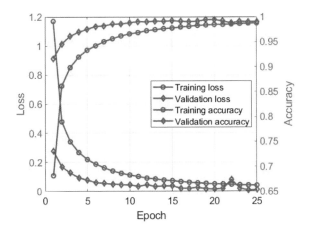

Figure 17.11: Accuracy and loss during fine-tuning of InceptionV3.

Table 17.3: Numerical results on UCMerced and comparison with the state-of-the-art

| Algorithm | Percentage of training images per category | |
	50%	80%
MSDRBE	**0.9718 ± 0.0046**	0.9791 ± 0.0062
DRB-R	0.9534 ± 0.0050	0.9635 ± 0.0073
DRB-D	0.9510 ± 0.0063	0.9620 ± 0.0092
DRB-I	0.9432 ± 0.0071	0.9503 ± 0.0078
GCLBP [41]	—	0.9000 ± 0.0210
MS-CLBP+FV [42]	—	0.9300 ± 0.0120
MTJSLRC [43]	—	0.9107 ± 0.0067
CaffeNet [2]	0.9396 ± 0.0067	0.9502 ± 0.0081
VGG-VD-16 [2]	0.9414 ± 0.0069	0.9521 ± 0.0120
GoogLeNet [2]	0.9270 ± 0.0060	0.9431 ± 0.0089
SalM3LBP-CLM [44]	0.9421 ± 0.0075	0.9575 ± 0.0080
SalM3LBP [44]	0.8997 ± 0.0085	0.9314 ± 0.0100
salCLM(eSIF) [44]	0.9293 ± 0.0092	0.9452 ± 0.0079
TEX-Net-LF [45]	0.9589 ± 0.0037	0.9662 ± 0.0049
VGG-16-CapsNet [8]	0.9533 ± 0.0018	0.9881 ± 0.0022
ARCNet-VGG [46]	0.9681 ± 0.0014	**0.9912 ± 0.0040**
SeRBIA [47]	0.9636 ± 0.0041	0.9786 ± 0.0099

in Table 17.4. In addition, the state-of-the-art approaches in the literature are also listed for comparison.

Similar to the previous two numerical examples in this subsection, the classification accuracy rates obtained by MSDRBE and its ensemble components, as well as the results obtained by the state-of-the-art approaches on the RSSCN7 dataset under two different experimental settings are reported in Table 17.5.

Table 17.4: Numerical results on WHU-RS19 and comparison with the state-of-the-art

| Algorithm | Percentage of training images per category | |
	40%	60%
MSDRBE	**0.9821 ± 0.0040**	0.9854 ± 0.0058
DRB-R	0.9540 ± 0.0059	0.9619 ± 0.0081
DRB-D	0.9594 ± 0.0047	0.9695 ± 0.0070
DRB-I	0.9490 ± 0.0060	0.9544 ± 0.0097
GCLBP [41]	—	0.9100 ± 0.0150
MS-CLBP+FV [42]	—	0.9432 ± 0.0120
MTJSLRC [43]	—	0.9174 ± 0.0114
CaffeNet [2]	0.9511 ± 0.0120	0.9624 ± 0.0056
VGG-VD-16 [2]	0.9544 ± 0.0060	0.9605 ± 0.0091
GoogLeNet [2]	0.9312 ± 0.0082	0.9471 ± 0.0133
SalM3LBP-CLM [44]	0.9535 ± 0.0076	0.9638 ± 0.0082
SalM3LBP [44]	0.8974 ± 0.0184	0.9258 ± 0.0089
salCLM(eSIF) [44]	0.9381 ± 0.0091	0.9592 ± 0.0095
TEX-Net-LF [45]	0.9761 ± 0.0036	0.9800 ± 0.0046
ARCNet-VGG [46]	0.9750 ± 0.0049	**0.9975 ± 0.0025**
SeRBIA [47]	0.9757 ± 0.0060	0.9802 ± 0.0054

Table 17.5: Numerical results on RSSCN7 and comparison with the state-of-the-art

| Algorithm | Percentage of training images per category | |
	20%	50%
MSDRBE	0.9132 ± 0.0052	0.9308 ± 0.0052
DRB-R	0.8828 ± 0.0058	0.9064 ± 0.0060
DRB-D	0.8624 ± 0.0051	0.8873 ± 0.0073
DRB-I	0.8515 ± 0.0080	0.8709 ± 0.0071
CaffeNet [2]	0.8557 ± 0.0095	0.8825 ± 0.0062
VGG-VD-16 [2]	0.8398 ± 0.0087	0.8718 ± 0.0094
GoogLeNet [2]	0.8255 ± 0.0111	0.8584 ± 0.0092
TEX-Net-LF [45]	0.8861 ± 0.0046	0.9125 ± 0.0058
SeRBIA [47]	**0.9485 ± 0.0037**	**0.9619 ± 0.0057**

17.4.4. *Discussion*

Tables 17.3–17.5 show that MSDRBE is able to outperform the state-of-the-art approaches across the three aerial scene classification problems. The classification accuracy rate obtained by MSDRBE on the UCMercet dataset is 97.18% if 50% of the images are used for training and 97.91% if 80% of images are used for training. MSDRBE achieves 98.21% and 98.54% classification accuracy on the WHU-RS19 dataset given 40% and 60% of images for training, respectively. For the RSSCN7 dataset, the classification accuracy rates of MSDRBE on the testing images are 91.32% and 93.08% under two different training–testing split ratios, respectively. The classification accuracy comparison between MSDRBE and its three ensemble components, namely, DRB-R, DRB-D, and DRB-I, further justifies the efficacy of the proposed ensemble framework.

However, it can be observed from the performance comparison that ARCNet-VGG [46] is able to achieve slightly higher classification accuracy than MSDRBE on the UCMerced dataset with 80% of images for training and the WHU-RS19 dataset with 60% of images for training, respectively. The main reason is that although both MSDRBE and ARCNet-VGG utilized the transfer learning technique, ARCNet-VGG directly used UCMerced and WHU-RS19 datasets for knowledge transferring. Meanwhile, MSDRBE used an alternative aerial image set, namely, NWPU45, for fine-tuning the DNNs and, then, its performance was evaluated on other datasets. In this way, MSDRBE actually performed knowledge transferring twice during the experiments. The first knowledge transferring happened during the fine-tuning process on the NWPU45 dataset and the second knowledge transferring happened during the feature extraction process on UCMerced, WHU-RS19, and RSSDN7 datasets. The significant variabilities in terms of the geometrical structures and spatial patterns exhibited by images of different aerial image sets inevitably have an adverse influence on the performance of MSDRBE. Nevertheless, since ARCNet-VGG was fine-tuned on UCMerced and WHU-RS19 datasets directly, it failed to achieve good performance when there were insufficient training images. Therefore, it was outperformed by MSDRBE in the other two cases.

SeRBIA was able to surpass MSDRBE on the RSSCN7 dataset thanks to its unique chunk-by-chunk semi-supervised learning mechanism. Despite that it uses only pre-trained VGGNet and AlexNet [48] for feature extraction, SeRBIA [47] is capable of self-learning from unlabeled images and self-expanding its knowledge base for more precise classification. On the other hand, MSDRBE managed to outperform SeRBIA on the UCMerced and WHU-RS19 datasets thanks to its highly discriminative features extracted by the three fine-tuned DNNs. Thus, one may conclude that MSDRBE can produce even better classification results if it adopts similar semi-supervised learning techniques as used by SeRBIA. Meanwhile, one could expect that SeRBIA will perform much better on aerial scene classification tasks if the fine-tuned DNNs are employed as its feature descriptors.

17.5. Applications to Large-Scale Satellite Sensor Images

In this section, numerical examples based on large-scale satellite sensor image are presented to demonstrate the applicability of MSDRBE in real-world scenarios, where a similar experimental protocol as used by SeRBIA [47] was considered.

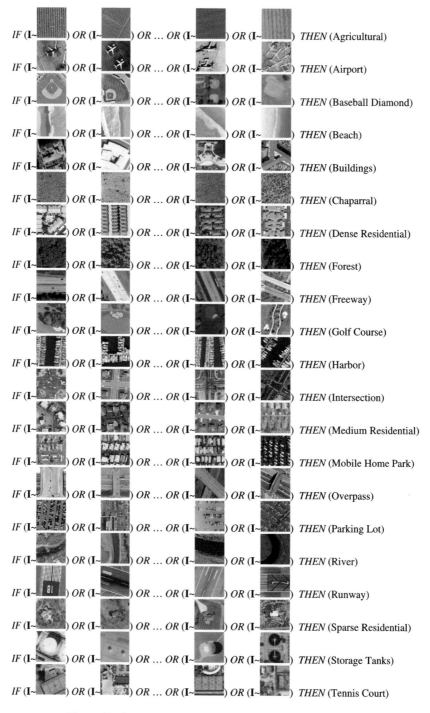

IF (**I**~   ) OR (**I**~   ) OR ... OR (**I**~   ) OR (**I**~   ) *THEN* (Agricultural)

IF (**I**~   ) OR (**I**~   ) OR ... OR (**I**~   ) OR (**I**~   ) *THEN* (Airport)

IF (**I**~   ) OR (**I**~   ) OR ... OR (**I**~   ) OR (**I**~   ) *THEN* (Baseball Diamond)

IF (**I**~   ) OR (**I**~   ) OR ... OR (**I**~   ) OR (**I**~   ) *THEN* (Beach)

IF (**I**~   ) OR (**I**~   ) OR ... OR (**I**~   ) OR (**I**~   ) *THEN* (Buildings)

IF (**I**~   ) OR (**I**~   ) OR ... OR (**I**~   ) OR (**I**~   ) *THEN* (Chaparral)

IF (**I**~   ) OR (**I**~   ) OR ... OR (**I**~   ) OR (**I**~   ) *THEN* (Dense Residential)

IF (**I**~   ) OR (**I**~   ) OR ... OR (**I**~   ) OR (**I**~   ) *THEN* (Forest)

IF (**I**~   ) OR (**I**~   ) OR ... OR (**I**~   ) OR (**I**~   ) *THEN* (Freeway)

IF (**I**~   ) OR (**I**~   ) OR ... OR (**I**~   ) OR (**I**~   ) *THEN* (Golf Course)

IF (**I**~   ) OR (**I**~   ) OR ... OR (**I**~   ) OR (**I**~   ) *THEN* (Harbor)

IF (**I**~   ) OR (**I**~   ) OR ... OR (**I**~   ) OR (**I**~   ) *THEN* (Intersection)

IF (**I**~   ) OR (**I**~   ) OR ... OR (**I**~   ) OR (**I**~   ) *THEN* (Medium Residential)

IF (**I**~   ) OR (**I**~   ) OR ... OR (**I**~   ) OR (**I**~   ) *THEN* (Mobile Home Park)

IF (**I**~   ) OR (**I**~   ) OR ... OR (**I**~   ) OR (**I**~   ) *THEN* (Overpass)

IF (**I**~   ) OR (**I**~   ) OR ... OR (**I**~   ) OR (**I**~   ) *THEN* (Parking Lot)

IF (**I**~   ) OR (**I**~   ) OR ... OR (**I**~   ) OR (**I**~   ) *THEN* (River)

IF (**I**~   ) OR (**I**~   ) OR ... OR (**I**~   ) OR (**I**~   ) *THEN* (Runway)

IF (**I**~   ) OR (**I**~   ) OR ... OR (**I**~   ) OR (**I**~   ) *THEN* (Sparse Residential)

IF (**I**~   ) OR (**I**~   ) OR ... OR (**I**~   ) OR (**I**~   ) *THEN* (Storage Tanks)

IF (**I**~   ) OR (**I**~   ) OR ... OR (**I**~   ) OR (**I**~   ) *THEN* (Tennis Court)

Figure 17.12:   Examples of massively parallel IF...THEN rules.

To perform automatic image analysis, the UCMerced dataset was used to prime MSDRBE at first. The UCMerced dataset contains 21 commonly seen land-use categories, in total, 2100 images with the same spatial resolution (0.3 m). This dataset is very suitable for training MSDRBE thanks to its relatively smaller image size, simpler structures, and less variety in terms of semantic contents within a single image. From images of this dataset, each ensemble component of MSDRBE self-organized 21 massively parallel IF...THEN rules. Examples of the IF...THEN rules identified by MSDRBE are given in Figure 17.12.

Twelve satellite sensor images of different areas of the UK were downloaded from Google Earth (Google Inc.) with spatial resolutions varying from 0.3 m to 30 m and the same image size of 600 × 800 pixels. The 12 images are given in Figures 17.13–17.24, where great variations in terms of the geometric structure and semantic contents can be observed from these images.

	A	B	C	D	E
1	Harbor: 100%	Harbor: 100%	Buildings: 43.6% DenseResidential: 28.7% SparseResidential: 27.7%	Intersection: 100%	DenseResidential: 54.3% Mobilehomepark: 45.7%
2	DenseResidential: 37.2% Mobilehomepark: 33.4% MediumResidential: 29.4%	DenseResidential: 50.9% Mobilehomepark: 49.1%	MediumResidential: 37.3% DenseResidential: 31.5% Intersection: 31.2%	Intersection: 42.6% StorageTank: 35% Buildings: 22.4%	MediumResidential: 38% DenseResidential: 35.5% Buildings: 26.5%
3	DenseResidential: 31.3% Mobilehomepark: 27.6% MediumResidential: 22.6% Intersection: 18.5%	Mobilehomepark: 26.2% ParkingLot: 21.2% Buildings: 19.9% DenseResidential: 17.2% Freeway: 15.5%	StorageTank: 57.6% SparseResidential: 42.4%	Buildings: 29% StorageTank: 19.6% Beach: 18.5% Freeway: 16.9% SparseResidential: 16%	StorageTank: 21.8% River: 21.6% Beach: 21% SparseResidential: 19.2% Buildings: 16.4%

Figure 17.13:   Classification result on satellite sensor image 1.

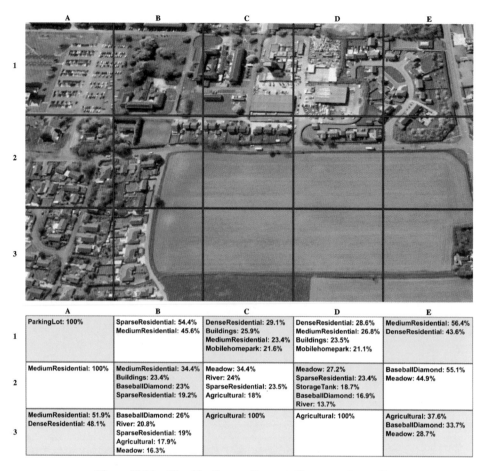

	A	B	C	D	E
1	ParkingLot: 100%	SparseResidential: 54.4% MediumResidential: 45.6%	DenseResidential: 29.1% Buildings: 25.9% MediumResidential: 23.4% Mobilehomepark: 21.6%	DenseResidential: 28.6% MediumResidential: 26.8% Buildings: 23.5% Mobilehomepark: 21.1%	MediumResidential: 56.4% DenseResidential: 43.6%
2	MediumResidential: 100%	MediumResidential: 34.4% Buildings: 23.4% BaseballDiamond: 23% SparseResidential: 19.2%	Meadow: 34.4% River: 24% SparseResidential: 23.5% Agricultural: 18%	Meadow: 27.2% SparseResidential: 23.4% StorageTank: 18.7% BaseballDiamond: 16.9% River: 13.7%	BaseballDiamond: 55.1% Meadow: 44.9%
3	MediumResidential: 51.9% DenseResidential: 48.1%	BaseballDiamond: 26% River: 20.8% SparseResidential: 19% Agricultural: 17.9% Meadow: 16.3%	Agricultural: 100%	Agricultural: 100%	Agricultural: 37.6% BaseballDiamond: 33.7% Meadow: 28.7%

Figure 17.14:   Classification result on satellite sensor image 2.

During the numerical examples, each satellite sensor image, denoted as **I**, was firstly segmented by a grid net with the grid size of 200×200 pixels into 3×4 non-overlapping sub-regions. Then, MSDRBE read these image segments one by one and produced a set of overall scores of confidence for each image segment, denoted as $\hat{\lambda}_1(\mathbf{I}_k), \hat{\lambda}_2(\mathbf{I}_k), \ldots, \hat{\lambda}_C(\mathbf{I}_k)$ using Eq. (17.14), where $C = 21$; $\mathbf{I}_k$ stands for the kth segment of **I**.

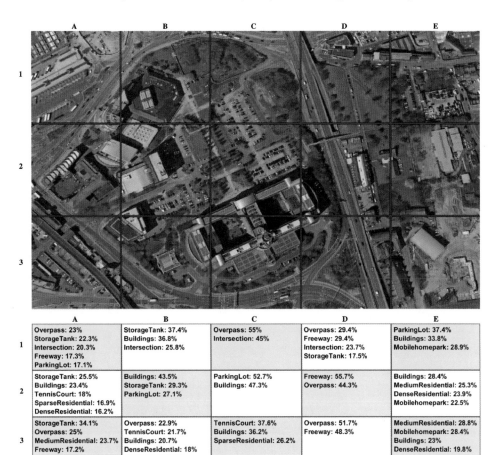

	A	B	C	D	E
1	Overpass: 23% StorageTank: 22.3% Intersection: 20.3% Freeway: 17.3% ParkingLot: 17.1%	StorageTank: 37.4% Buildings: 36.8% Intersection: 25.8%	Overpass: 55% Intersection: 45%	Overpass: 29.4% Freeway: 29.4% Intersection: 23.7% StorageTank: 17.5%	ParkingLot: 37.4% Buildings: 33.8% Mobilehomepark: 28.9%
2	StorageTank: 25.5% Buildings: 23.4% TennisCourt: 18% SparseResidential: 16.9% DenseResidential: 16.2%	Buildings: 43.5% StorageTank: 29.3% ParkingLot: 27.1%	ParkingLot: 52.7% Buildings: 47.3%	Freeway: 55.7% Overpass: 44.3%	Buildings: 28.4% MediumResidential: 25.3% DenseResidential: 23.9% Mobilehomepark: 22.5%
3	StorageTank: 34.1% Overpass: 25% MediumResidential: 23.7% Freeway: 17.2%	Overpass: 22.9% TennisCourt: 21.7% Buildings: 20.7% DenseResidential: 18% Intersection: 16.7%	TennisCourt: 37.6% Buildings: 36.2% SparseResidential: 26.2%	Overpass: 51.7% Freeway: 48.3%	MediumResidential: 28.8% Mobilehomepark: 28.4% Buildings: 23% DenseResidential: 19.8%

Figure 17.15:   Classification result on satellite sensor image 3.

By using *Condition 2*, the joint decision maker identified one or multiple land-use categories that share similar high-level semantic features with $\mathbf{I}_k$ [47]

$$Condition\ 2: If\ (\varphi \hat{\lambda}_n(\mathbf{I}_k) > \max_{j=1,2,...,C}(\hat{\lambda}_j(\mathbf{I}_k))),$$

(17.16)

$$Then\ (\mathbf{I}_k\ possesses\ semantic\ features\ of\ category\ y_n),$$

where $\varphi = 1.1$ in this research.

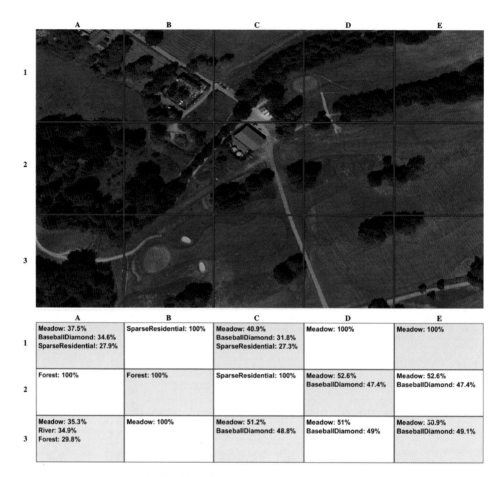

Figure 17.16:   Classification result on satellite sensor image 4.

Assuming that there were L_k land-use categories satisfying ***Condition 2***, denoted as $category_1^*, category_2^*, \ldots, category_{L_k}^*$, the respective likelihoods of the L_k most relevant land-use categories associated with $\mathbf{I}_k$ can be calculated as [47]

$$\ell_n^* = \frac{\tilde{\lambda}_n^*(\mathbf{I}_k)}{\sum_{j=1}^{L_k} \tilde{\lambda}_j^*(\mathbf{I}_k)}, \qquad (17.17)$$

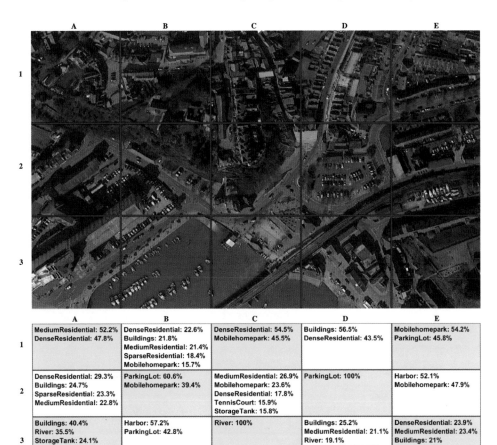

	A	B	C	D	E
1	MediumResidential: 52.2% DenseResidential: 47.8%	DenseResidential: 22.6% Buildings: 21.8% MediumResidential: 21.4% SparseResidential: 18.4% Mobilehomepark: 15.7%	DenseResidential: 54.5% Mobilehomepark: 45.5%	Buildings: 56.5% DenseResidential: 43.5%	Mobilehomepark: 54.2% ParkingLot: 45.8%
2	DenseResidential: 29.3% Buildings: 24.7% SparseResidential: 23.3% MediumResidential: 22.8%	ParkingLot: 60.6% Mobilehomepark: 39.4%	MediumResidential: 26.9% Mobilehomepark: 23.6% DenseResidential: 17.8% TennisCourt: 15.9% StorageTank: 15.8%	ParkingLot: 100%	Harbor: 52.1% Mobilehomepark: 47.9%
3	Buildings: 40.4% River: 35.5% StorageTank: 24.1%	Harbor: 57.2% ParkingLot: 42.8%	River: 100%	Buildings: 25.2% MediumResidential: 21.1% River: 19.1% SparseResidential: 18% DenseResidential: 16.6%	DenseResidential: 23.9% MediumResidential: 23.4% Buildings: 21% SparseResidential: 17.6% TennisCourt: 14%

Figure 17.17: Classification result on satellite sensor image 5.

where ℓ_n^* is the likelihood of $category_n^*$; $\tilde{\lambda}_n^*(\mathbf{I}_k)$ is the score of confidence corresponding to $category_n^*$ standardized by the mean v_k and standard deviation δ_k of the C overall scores of confidence calculated on $\mathbf{I}_k$ (namely, $\hat{\lambda}_1(\mathbf{I}_k)$, $\hat{\lambda}_2(\mathbf{I}_k)$, ..., $\hat{\lambda}_C(\mathbf{I}_k)$): $\tilde{\lambda}_n^*(\mathbf{I}_k) = \frac{\hat{\lambda}_n^*(\mathbf{I}_k) - v_k}{\delta_k}$. MSDRBE completed the analyzing process on I once all its image segments have been processed.

The analyzing results for the 12 satellite sensor images by MSDRBE are also presented in Figures 17.13–17.24 in the form of a 3 × 4 table with the background in white and yellow colors. In this research, the maximum value of L_k was set to be 5 for visual clarity [47].

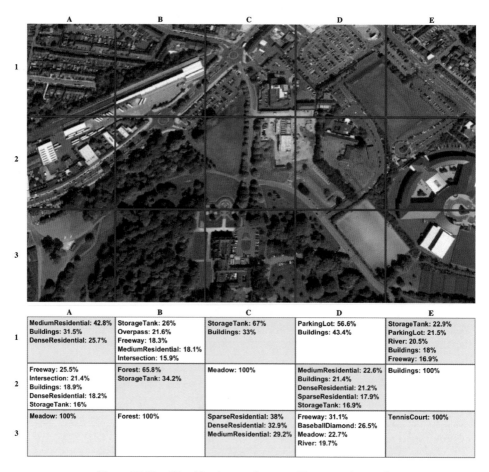

	A	B	C	D	E
1	MediumResidential: 42.8% Buildings: 31.5% DenseResidential: 25.7%	StorageTank: 26% Overpass: 21.6% Freeway: 18.3% MediumResidential: 18.1% Intersection: 15.9%	StorageTank: 67% Buildings: 33%	ParkingLot: 56.6% Buildings: 43.4%	StorageTank: 22.9% ParkingLot: 21.5% River: 20.5% Buildings: 18% Freeway: 16.9%
2	Freeway: 25.5% Intersection: 21.4% Buildings: 18.9% DenseResidential: 18.2% StorageTank: 16%	Forest: 65.8% StorageTank: 34.2%	Meadow: 100%	MediumResidential: 22.6% Buildings: 21.4% DenseResidential: 21.2% SparseResidential: 17.9% StorageTank: 16.9%	Buildings: 100%
3	Meadow: 100%	Forest: 100%	SparseResidential: 38% DenseResidential: 32.9% MediumResidential: 29.2%	Freeway: 31.1% BaseballDiamond: 26.5% Meadow: 22.7% River: 19.7%	TennisCourt: 100%

Figure 17.18:   Classification result on satellite sensor image 6.

From Figures 17.13–17.24 one can see that MSDRBE is able to classify the local regions of large-scale satellite images into one or multiple land-use categories in very high precision thanks to its ensemble structure and the fine-tuned DNN-based feature descriptors. In most cases, it can further accurately describe the respective likelihoods of the most relevant land-use categories associated with the sub-regions of these images. The results show the great potential of MSDRBE for analyzing large-scale satellite sensor images automatically.

However, it is also noticeable that MSDRBE made completely incorrect categorizations in some rare cases, such as the sub-region "A2" in image 12, where it should be "Mobile Home Park" instead of "Harbor." Due to the high similarity amongst high-level semantic features shared by different land-use categories, MSDRBE may

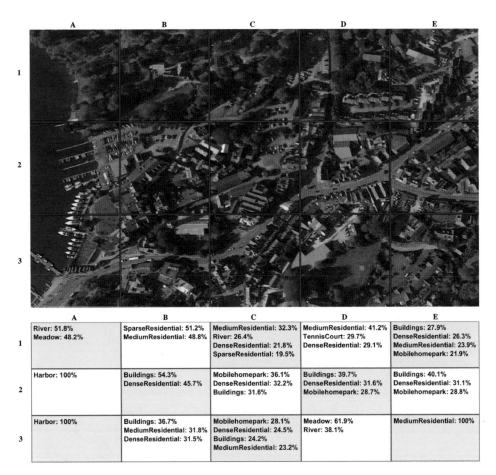

	A	B	C	D	E
1	River: 51.8% Meadow: 48.2%	SparseResidential: 51.2% MediumResidential: 48.8%	MediumResidential: 32.3% River: 26.4% DenseResidential: 21.8% SparseResidential: 19.5%	MediumResidential: 41.2% TennisCourt: 29.7% DenseResidential: 29.1%	Buildings: 27.9% DenseResidential: 26.3% MediumResidential: 23.9% Mobilehomepark: 21.9%
2	Harbor: 100%	Buildings: 54.3% DenseResidential: 45.7%	Mobilehomepark: 36.1% DenseResidential: 32.2% Buildings: 31.6%	Buildings: 39.7% DenseResidential: 31.6% Mobilehomepark: 28.7%	Buildings: 40.1% DenseResidential: 31.1% Mobilehomepark: 28.8%
3	Harbor: 100%	Buildings: 36.7% MediumResidential: 31.8% DenseResidential: 31.5%	Mobilehomepark: 28.1% DenseResidential: 24.5% Buildings: 24.2% MediumResidential: 23.2%	Meadow: 61.9% River: 38.1%	MediumResidential: 100%

Figure 17.19:   Classification result on satellite sensor image 7.

confuse land-use categories such as "Baseball Diamond" and "Meadow," "Storage Tank" and "Buildings," "Tennis Court" and "Buildings," "Mobile Home Park" and "Dense Residential." MSDRBE sometimes may also ignore other land-use categories if it categorizes a certain sub-region to "Intersection" despite that high-level semantic features of other land-use categories also appear in the same sub-region. This is due to the high similarity of high-level semantic features between images of land-use category "Intersection" and images of other categories such as "Dense Residential" and "Medium Residential." Nevertheless, such issues can be addressed successfully by making a preselection on benchmark datasets and removing the less representative images [47].

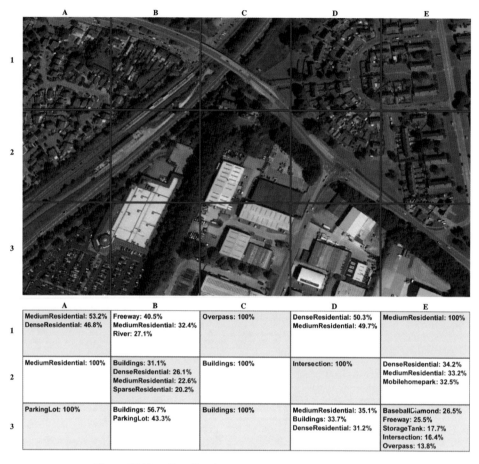

Figure 17.20:   Classification result on satellite sensor image 8.

17.6. Conclusion

In this research, a novel MSDRBE system is introduced for aerial scene classification. The proposed approach integrates three DRB systems to form an ensemble. Each DRB system employs a different DNN as its feature descriptor. However, instead of relying on the pretrained weights based on natural images, three DNNs used by MSDRBE are fine-tuned on aerial images to improve their capability to capture the more discriminative high-level semantic features from aerial images, allowing the DRB systems to self-organize a set of massively parallel IF...THEN rules composed of highly representative prototypes. A joint decision-making mechanism based on weighted voting is further adopted to maximize the prediction precision of the proposed approach. Numerical examples show the great performance of the proposed MSDRBE, surpassing the state-of-the-art approaches

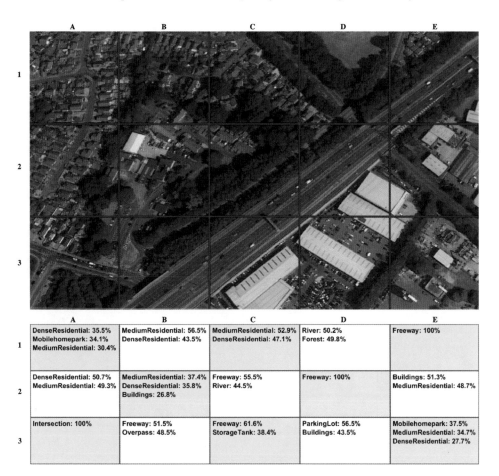

	A	B	C	D	E
1	DenseResidential: 35.5% Mobilehomepark: 34.1% MediumResidential: 30.4%	MediumResidential: 56.5% DenseResidential: 43.5%	MediumResidential: 52.9% DenseResidential: 47.1%	River: 50.2% Forest: 49.8%	Freeway: 100%
2	DenseResidential: 50.7% MediumResidential: 49.3%	MediumResidential: 37.4% DenseResidential: 35.8% Buildings: 26.8%	Freeway: 55.5% River: 44.5%	Freeway: 100%	Buildings: 51.3% MediumResidential: 48.7%
3	Intersection: 100%	Freeway: 51.5% Overpass: 48.5%	Freeway: 61.6% StorageTank: 38.4%	ParkingLot: 56.5% Buildings: 43.5%	Mobilehomepark: 37.5% MediumResidential: 34.7% DenseResidential: 27.7%

Figure 17.21:   Classification result on satellite sensor image 9.

on a variety of benchmark aerial scene classification problems. Applications to satellite sensor images further demonstrate the strong ability of MSDRBE in handling real-world uncertainties and solving real-world problems.

As for future work, there are several considerations. Firstly, a semi-supervised learning mechanism could be introduced to MSDRBE, enabling it to autonomously learn from unlabeled images and self-expand its knowledge base for more precise predictions. Secondly, a high-quality, large-scale aerial image set composed of images with different levels of scale, illumination, and resolution covering most of commonly seen land-use categories needs to be constructed in order to train a more effective MSDRBE for satellite sensor image analysis. Lastly, more creative joint decision-making mechanisms could be developed to further enhance the prediction precision, for example, by giving different weights to different ensemble components based on their classification accuracy rates on training images.

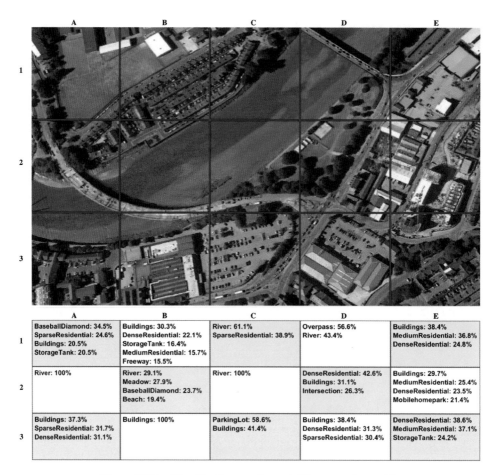

	A	B	C	D	E
1	BaseballDiamond: 34.5% SparseResidential: 24.6% Buildings: 20.5% StorageTank: 20.5%	Buildings: 30.3% DenseResidential: 22.1% StorageTank: 16.4% MediumResidential: 15.7% Freeway: 15.5%	River: 61.1% SparseResidential: 38.9%	Overpass: 56.6% River: 43.4%	Buildings: 38.4% MediumResidential: 36.8% DenseResidential: 24.8%
2	River: 100%	River: 29.1% Meadow: 27.9% BaseballDiamond: 23.7% Beach: 19.4%	River: 100%	DenseResidential: 42.6% Buildings: 31.1% Intersection: 26.3%	Buildings: 29.7% MediumResidential: 25.4% DenseResidential: 23.5% Mobilehomepark: 21.4%
3	Buildings: 37.3% SparseResidential: 31.7% DenseResidential: 31.1%	Buildings: 100%	ParkingLot: 58.6% Buildings: 41.4%	Buildings: 38.4% DenseResidential: 31.3% SparseResidential: 30.4%	DenseResidential: 38.6% MediumResidential: 37.1% StorageTank: 24.2%

Figure 17.22:   Classification result on satellite sensor image 10.

	A	B	C	D	E
1	Buildings: 57.1% DenseResidential: 42.9%	MediumResidential: 27.3% Mobilehomepark: 26.9% DenseResidential: 23% Buildings: 22.8%	DenseResidential: 28.4% SparseResidential: 26.6% Buildings: 25.8% MediumResidential: 19.2%	Forest: 52% River: 48%	MediumResidential: 27.6% Agricultural: 26.9% River: 26.6% Freeway: 18.9%
2	MediumResidential: 61.4% Freeway: 38.6%	Intersection: 52.2% Overpass: 47.8%	DenseResidential: 37.3% MediumResidential: 36.5% Buildings: 26.2%	Intersection: 100%	DenseResidential: 37.4% Mobilehomepark: 32.2% MediumResidential: 30.4%
3	Intersection: 100%	ParkingLot: 29.8% Mobilehomepark: 28.6% Buildings: 21% StorageTank: 20.6%	Mobilehomepark: 100%	Buildings: 55.2% DenseResidential: 44.8%	DenseResidential: 52.8% Mobilehomepark: 47.2%

Figure 17.23: Classification result on satellite sensor image 11.

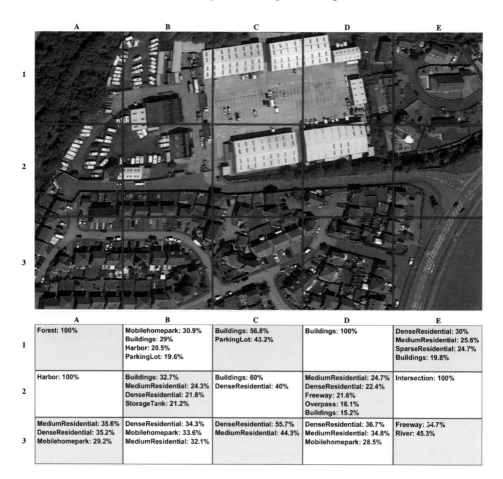

	A	B	C	D	E
1	Forest: 100%	Mobilehomepark: 30.9% Buildings: 29% Harbor: 20.5% ParkingLot: 19.6%	Buildings: 56.8% ParkingLot: 43.2%	Buildings: 100%	DenseResidential: 30% MediumResidential: 25.6% SparseResidential: 24.7% Buildings: 19.8%
2	Harbor: 100%	Buildings: 32.7% MediumResidential: 24.3% DenseResidential: 21.8% StorageTank: 21.2%	Buildings: 60% DenseResidential: 40%	MediumResidential: 24.7% DenseResidential: 22.4% Freeway: 21.6% Overpass: 16.1% Buildings: 15.2%	Intersection: 100%
3	MediumResidential: 35.6% DenseResidential: 35.2% Mobilehomepark: 29.2%	DenseResidential: 34.3% Mobilehomepark: 33.6% MediumResidential: 32.1%	DenseResidential: 55.7% MediumResidential: 44.3%	DenseResidential: 36.7% MediumResidential: 34.8% Mobilehomepark: 28.5%	Freeway: 54.7% River: 45.3%

Figure 17.24:   Classification result on satellite sensor image 12.

References

[1] D. Hou, Z. Miao, H. Xing, and H. Wu, Two novel benchmark datasets from ArcGIS and bing world imagery for remote sensing image retrieval, *Int. J. Remote Sens.*, **42**(1), 240–258 (2021). ISSN 0143–1161.

[2] G. Xia, J. Hu, F. Hu, B. Shi, X. Bai, Y. Zhong, and L. Zhang, Aid: a benchmark dataset for performance evaluation of aerial scene classification, *IEEE Trans. Geosci. Remote Sens.*, **55**(7), 3965–3981 (2017). ISSN 0196–2892.

[3] X. Zhu, D. Tuia, L. Mou, G. Xia, L. Zhang, F. Xu, and F. Fraundorfer, Deep learning in remote sensing: a comprehensive review and list of resources, *IEEE Geosci. Remote Sens. Mag.*, **5**(4), 8–36 (2017). ISSN 2473–2397.

[4] Y. Li, H. Zhang, X. Xue, Y. Jiang, and Q. Shen, Deep learning for remote sensing image classification: a survey, *WIREs Data Min. Knowl. Discov.*, **8**(6), e1264 (2018). ISSN 1942–4795.

[5] G. Cheng, J. Han, and X. Lu, Remote sensing image scene classification: benchmark and state of the art, *Proc. IEEE,* **105**(10), 1865–1883 (2017). ISSN 0018–9219.

[6] F. Zhang, B. Du, and L. Zhang, Scene classification via a gradient boosting random convolutional network framework, *IEEE Trans. Geosci. Remote Sens.*, **54**(3), 1793–1802 (2016). ISSN 0196–2892.

[7] C. Zhang, G. Li, and S. Du, Multi-scale dense networks for hyperspectral remote sensing image classification, *IEEE Trans. Geosci. Remote Sens.*, **57**(11), 9201–9222 (2019). ISSN 0196–2892.

[8] W. Zhang, P. Tang, and L. Zhao, Remote sensing image scene classification using CNN-CapsNet, *Remote Sens.*, **11**(5), 494 (2019). ISSN 2072–4292.

[9] X. Liu, Y. Zhou, J. Zhao, R. Yao, B. Liu, and Y. Zheng, Siamese convolutional neural networks for remote sensing scene classification, *IEEE Geosci. Remote Sens. Lett.*, **16**(8), 1200–1204 (2019). ISSN 1545–598X.

[10] X. Gu, P. P. Angelov, C. Zhang, and P. M. Atkinson, A massively parallel deep rule-based ensemble classifier for remote sensing scenes, *IEEE Geosci. Remote Sens. Lett.*, **15**(3), 345–349, 2018. ISSN 1545–598X.

[11] Q. Weng, Z. Mao, J. Lin, and W. Guo, Land-use classification via extreme learning classifier based on deep convolutional features, *IEEE Geosci. Remote Sens. Lett.*, **14**(5), 704–708 (2017). ISSN 1545–598X.

[12] G. Cheng, Z. Li, X. Yao, L. Guo, and Z. Wei, Remote sensing image scene classification using bag of convolutional features, *IEEE Geosci. Remote Sens. Lett.*, **14**(10), 1735–1739 (2017). ISSN 1545–598X.

[13] A. F. K. Guy, T. Akram, B. Laurent, S. Rameez, M. Mbom, and N. Muhammad, A deep heterogeneous feature fusion approach for automatic land-use classification, *Inf. Sci. (Ny),* **467**, 199–218 (2018). ISSN 0020–0255.

[14] N. S. Altman, An introduction to kernel and nearest-neighbor nonparametric regression, *Am. Stat.*, **46**(3), 175–185 (1992). ISSN 0003–1305.

[15] N. Cristianini and J. Shawe-Taylor, *An Introduction to Support Vector Machines and Other Kernel-Based Learning Methods* (Cambridge: Cambridge University Press, 2000).

[16] L. Breiman, Random forests, *Mach. Learn. Proc.*, **45**(1), 5–32 (2001). ISSN 2640–3498.

[17] O. Russakovsky, J. Deng, H. Su, J. Krause, S. Satheesh, S. Ma, Z. Huang, A. Karparg, A. Khosla, M. Bernstein, A. Berg, and F. Li, ImageNet large scale visual recognition challenge, *Int. J. Comput. Vis.*, **115**(3), 211–252 (2015). ISSN 0920–5691.

[18] K. Simonyan and A. Zissermann, Very deep convolutional networks for large-scale image recognition. In *International Conference on Learning Representations*, pp. 1–14, San Diego, USA (2015).

[19] C. Szegedy, W. Liu, Y. Jia, P. Sermanet, S. Reed, D. Anguelov, D. Erhan, V. Vanhoucke, A. Rabinovich, C. Hill, and A. Arbor, Going deeper with convolutions. In *IEEE conference on Computer Vision and Pattern Recognition*, pp. 1–9, Boston, USA (2015).

[20] C. Szegedy, V. Vanhoucke, S. Ioffe, J. Shlens, and Z. Wojna, Rethinking the inception architecture for computer vision. In *IEEE conference on Computer Vision and Pattern Recognition*, pp. 2818–2826, Las Vegas, USA (2016).

[21] K. He, X. Zhang, S. Ren, and J. Sun, Deep residual learning for image recognition. In *IEEE conference on Computer Vision and Pattern Recognition*, pp. 770–778, Las Vegas, USA (2016).

[22] G. Huang, Z. Liu, L. van der Maaten, and K. Q. Weinberger, Densely connected convolutional networks. In *IEEE conference on Computer Vision and Pattern Recognition*, pp. 4700–4708, Hawaii, USA (2017).

[23] P. P. Angelov and X. Gu, Deep rule-based classifier with human-level performance and characteristics, *Inf. Sci. (Ny)*, **463–464**, 196–213 (2018). ISSN 0020–0255.

[24] X. Gu and P. P. Angelov, A deep rule-based approach for satellite scene image analysis. In *IEEE International Conference on Systems, Man and Cybernetics*, pp. 2778–2783, Miyazaki, Japan (2018).

[25] D. C. R. Novitasari, D. Wahyuni, M. Munir, I. Hidayati, F. M. Amin, and K. Oktafianto, Automatic detection of breast cancer in mammographic image using the histogram oriented gradient (HOG) descriptor and deep rule based (DRB) classifier method. In *International Conference on Advanced Mechatronics, Intelligent Manufacture and Industrial Automation*, pp. 185–190, Batu-Malang, Indonesia (2018).

[26] A. B. Sargano, X. Gu, P. Angelov, and Z. Habib, Human action recognition using deep rule-based classifier, *Multimed. Tools Appl.*, **79**, 30653–30667 (2020). ISSN 1380–7501.

[27] R. P. de Lima and K. Marfurt, Convolutional neural network for remote-sensing scene classification: transfer learning analysis, *Remote Sens.*, **12**(1), 86 (2020). ISSN 2072–4292.

[28] X. Gu and P. Angelov, Deep rule-based aerial scene classifier using high-level ensemble feature descriptor. In *International Joint Conference on Neural Networks*, pp. 1–7, Budapest, Hungary (2019).

[29] X. Gu and P. P. Angelov, Self-organising fuzzy logic classifier, *Inf. Sci. (Ny)*, **447**, 36–51 (2018). ISSN 0020–0255.

[30] P. P. Angelov, X. Gu, and J. C. Principe, A generalized methodology for data analysis, *IEEE Trans. Cybern.*, **48**(10), 2981–2993 (2018). ISSN 2168–2267.

[31] M. I. Lakhal, H. Cevikalp, S. Escalera, and F. Ofli, Recurrent neural networks for remote sensing image classification, *IET Comput. Vis.*, **12**(7), 1040–1045 (2018). ISSN 1751–9632.

[32] F. Hu, G. Xia, J. Hu, and L. Zhang, Transferring deep convolutional neural networks for the scene classification of high-resolution remote sensing imagery, *Remote Sens.*, **7**(11), 14680–14707 (2015). ISSN 2072–4292.

[33] W. Li, Z. Wang, Y. Wang, J. Wu, J. Wang, Y. Jia, and G. Gui, Classification of high-spatial-resolution remote sensing scenes method using transfer learning and deep convolutional neural network, *IEEE J. Sel. Top. Appl. Earth Obs. Remote Sens.*, **13**, 1986–1995 (2020). ISSN 1939–1404.

[34] B. Cui, X. Chen, and Y. Lu, Semantic segmentation of remote sensing images using transfer learning and deep convolutional neural network with dense connection, *IEEE Access*, **8**, 116744–11675 (2020). ISSN 2169–3536.

[35] Z. Huang, Z. Pan, and B. Lei, Transfer learning with deep convolutional neural network for SAR target classification with limited labeled data, *Remote Sens.*, **9**(9), 1–21 (2017). ISSN 2072–4292.

[36] Y. Yang and S. Newsam, Bag-of-visual-words and spatial extensions for land-use classification. In *International Conference on Advances in Geographic Information Systems*, pp. 270–279, San Jose, USA (2010).

[37] G. Xia, W. Yang, J. Delon, Y. Gousseau, H. Sun, and H. Maitre, Structural high-resolution satellite image indexing. In *ISPRS, TC VII Symposium Part A: 100 Years ISPRS—Advancing Remote Sensing Science*, pp. 298–303, Vienna, Austria (2010).

[38] Q. Zou, L. Ni, T. Zhang, and Q. Wang, Deep learning based feature selection for remote sensing scene classification, *IEEE Geosci. Remote Sens. Lett.*, **12**(11), 2321–2325 (2015). ISSN 1545–598X.

[39] D. P. Kingma and J. L. Ba, Adam: a method for stochastic optimization. In *International Conference on Learning Representations*, pp. 1–15, San Diego, USA (2015).

[40] A. Bahri, S. G. Majelan, S. Mohammadi, M. Noori, and K. Mohammadi, Remote sensing image classification via improved cross-entropy loss and transfer learning strategy based on deep convolutional neural networks, *IEEE Geosci. Remote Sens. Lett.*, **17**(6), 1087–1091 (2020). ISSN 1545–598X.

[41] C. Chen, L. Zhou, J. Guo, W. Li, H. Su, and F. Guo, Gabor-filtering-based completed local binary patterns for land-use scene classification. In *IEEE international conference on Multimedia Big Data*, pp. 324–329, Beijing, China (2015).

[42] L. Huang, C. Chen, W. Li, and Q. Du, Remote sensing image scene classification using multi-scale completed local binary patterns and fisher vectors, *Remote Sens.*, **8**(6), 1–17 (2016). ISSN 2072–4292.

[43] K. Qi, W. Liu, C. Yang, Q. Guan, and H. Wu, Multi-task joint sparse and low-rank representation for the scene classification of high-resolution remote sensing image, *Remote Sens.*, **9**(1), 10 (2017). ISSN 2072–4292.

[44] X. Bian, C. Chen, L. Tian, and Q. Du, Fusing local and global features for high-resolution scene classification, *IEEE J. Sel. Top. Appl. Earth Obs. Remote Sens.*, **10**(6), 2889–2901 (2017). ISSN 1939–1404.

[45] R. M. Anwer, F. S. Khan, J. van de Weijer, M. Molinier, and J. Laaksonen, Binary patterns encoded convolutional neural networks for texture recognition and remote sensing scene classification, *ISPRS J. Photogramm. Remote Sens.*, **138**, 74–85 (2018). ISSN 0924–2716.

[46] Q. Wang, S. Member, S. Liu, and J. Chanussot, Scene classification with recurrent attention of VHR remote sensing images, *IEEE Trans. Geosci. Remote Sens.*, **57**(2), 1155–1167 (2019). ISSN 0196–2892.

[47] X. Gu, P. P. Angelov, C. Zhang, and P. M. Atkinson, A semi-supervised deep rule-based approach for complex satellite sensor image analysis, *IEEE Trans. Pattern Anal. Mach. Intell.* (2021). ISSN 0182–8828.

[48] A. Krizhevsky, I. Sutskever, and G. E. Hinton, ImageNet classification with deep convolutional neural networks. In *Proceedings of the Advances in Neural Information Processing Systems*, pp. 1097–1105, Lake Tahoe, USA (2012).

Part IV

Intelligent Control

Chapter 18

Fuzzy Model-Based Control: Predictive and Adaptive Approach

Igor Škrjanc* and Sašo Blažič†

Faculty of Electrical Engineering, University of Ljubljana
Tržaška 25, 1000 Ljubljana, Slovenia
*igor.skrjanc@fe.uni-lj.si
†saso.blazic@fe.uni-lj.si

This chapter deals with fuzzy model-based control. It focuses on two approaches that are presented and discussed, namely a predictive and an adaptive one. Both are based on the Takagi–Sugeno model form, which possesses the property of universal approximation of an arbitrary smooth nonlinear function and can be therefore used as a proper model to predict the future behavior of the plant. Despite many successful implementations of Mamdani fuzzy model-based approaches, it soon became clear that these approaches lack systematic ways to analyze the control system stability, performance, robustness, and the systematic way of tuning the controller parameters to adjust the performance. On the other hand, Takagi–Sugeno fuzzy models enable a more compact description of the nonlinear system, rigorous treatment of stability, and robustness. Perhaps the most important feature of Takagi–Sugeno models is the ability that they can be easily adapted to the different linear control algorithms to cope with the demanding nonlinear control problems.

18.1. Introduction

In this chapter, we face the problem of controlling a nonlinear plant. Classical linear approaches try to treat a plant as linear, and a linear controller is designed to meet the control objectives. Unfortunately, such an approach results in an acceptable control performance only if the nonlinearity is not too strong. The previous statement is far from being rigorous in the definitions of "acceptable" and "strong." However, the fact is that by increasing the control performance requirements, the problems with the nonlinearity also become much more apparent. So, there is a clear need to cope with the control of nonlinear plants.

The problem of control of nonlinear plants has received a great deal of attention in the past. A natural solution is to use a nonlinear controller that tries to "cancel" the nonlinearity in some sense or at least it increases the performance of the controlled system over a wide operating range with respect to the performance of an "optimal" linear controller. Since a controller is just a nonlinear dynamic system that maps controller inputs to controller actions, we need to somehow describe this nonlinear mapping and implement it into the controlled system. In the case of a finite-dimensional system, one possibility is to represent a controller in the state–space form where four nonlinear mappings are needed: state-to-state mapping, input-to-state mapping, state-to-output mapping, and direct input-to-output mapping. The Stone–Weierstrass theorem guarantees that all these mappings can be approximated by basis functions arbitrary well. Immense approximators of nonlinear functions have been proposed in the literature to solve the problem of nonlinear-system control. Some of the most popular ones are piecewise linear functions, fuzzy models, artificial neural networks, splines, wavelets, etc.

In this chapter, we put our focus on fuzzy controllers. Several excellent books exist that cover various aspects of fuzzy control [1–4]. Following a seminal paper of Zadeh [5] that introduced fuzzy set theory, the fuzzy logic approach was soon introduced into controllers [6]. In these early ages of fuzzy control, the controller was usually designed using Zadeh's notion of linguistic variables and fuzzy algorithms. It was often claimed that the approach with linguistic variables, linguistic values, and linguistic rules is "parameterless," and therefore the controllers are extremely easy to tune based on the expert knowledge that is easily transformable into the rule database. Many successful applications of fuzzy controllers have shown their ability to control nonlinear plants. But it soon became clear that the Mamdani fuzzy model control approach lacks systematic ways to analyze control system stability, performance, and robustness.

The Takagi–Sugeno fuzzy model [7] enables more compact description of the fuzzy system. Moreover, it enables rigorous treating of stability and robustness in the form of linear matrix inequalities [3]. Several control algorithms originally developed for linear systems can be adapted in a way that it is possible to combine them with the Takagi–Sugeno fuzzy models. Thus, the number of control approaches based on a Takagi–Sugeno model proposed in the literature in the past three decades is huge. In this chapter, we will show how to design predictive and adaptive controllers for certain classes of nonlinear systems where the plant model is given in the form of a Takagi–Sugeno fuzzy model. The proposed algorithms are not developed in an ad hoc manner, but having the stability of the overall system in mind. This is why the stability analysis of the algorithms complements the algorithms themselves.

18.2. Takagi–Sugeno Fuzzy Model

A typical fuzzy model [7] is given in the form of rules.

$$\mathbf{R}_j : \text{ if } x_{p1} \text{ is } \mathbf{A}_{1,k_1} \text{ and } x_{p2} \text{ is } \mathbf{A}_{2,k_2} \text{ and } \ldots \text{ and } x_{pq} \text{ is } \mathbf{A}_{q,k_q} \text{ then } y = \phi_j(\mathbf{x})$$

$$j = 1, \ldots, m$$

$$k_1 = 1, \ldots, f_1 \quad k_2 = 1, \ldots, f_2 \quad \ldots \quad k_q = 1, \ldots, f_q$$

$$(18.1)$$

The q-element vector $\mathbf{x}_p^T = [x_{p1}, \ldots, x_{pq}]$ denotes the input or variables in premise, and variable y is the output of the model. With each variable in premise x_{pi} ($i = 1, \ldots, q$), f_i fuzzy sets $(\mathbf{A}_{i,1}, \ldots, \mathbf{A}_{i,f_i})$ are connected, and each fuzzy set $\mathbf{A}_{i,k_i}$ ($k_i = 1, \ldots, f_i$) is associated with a real-valued function $\mu_{A_{i,k_i}}(x_{pi}) : \mathbb{R} \to [0, 1]$, that produces membership grade of the variable x_{pi} with respect to the fuzzy set $\mathbf{A}_{i,k_i}$. To make the list of fuzzy rules complete, all possible variations of fuzzy sets are given in Eq. (18.1), yielding the number of fuzzy rules $m = f_1 \times f_2 \times \cdots \times f_q$. The variables x_{pi} are not the only inputs of the fuzzy system. Implicitly, the n-element vector $\mathbf{x}^T = [x_1, \ldots, x_n]$ also represents the input to the system. It is usually referred to as the consequence vector. The functions $\phi_j(\cdot)$ can be arbitrary and smooth functions in general, although linear or affine functions are usually used.

The system in Eq. (18.1) can be described in closed form if the intersection of fuzzy sets is previously defined. The generalized form of the intersection is the so-called *triangular norm* (T-norm). In our case, the latter was chosen as algebraic product yielding the output of the fuzzy system:

$$\hat{y} = \frac{\sum_{k_1=1}^{f_1} \sum_{k_2=1}^{f_2} \cdots \sum_{k_q=1}^{f_q} \mu_{A_{1,k_1}}(x_{p1}) \mu_{A_{2,k_2}}(x_{p2}) \cdots \mu_{A_{q,k_q}}(x_{pq}) \phi_j(\mathbf{x})}{\sum_{k_1=1}^{f_1} \sum_{k_2=1}^{f_2} \cdots \sum_{k_q=1}^{f_q} \mu_{A_{1,k_1}}(x_{p1}) \mu_{A_{2,k_2}}(x_{p2}) \cdots \mu_{A_{q,k_q}}(x_{pq})} \quad (18.2)$$

It has to be noted that a slight abuse of notation is used in Eq. (18.2) since j is not explicitly defined as running index. From Eq. (18.1), it is evident that each j corresponds to the specific variation of indexes k_i, $i = 1, \ldots, q$.

To simplify Eq. (18.2), a partition of unity is considered, where functions $\beta_j(\mathbf{x}_p)$ defined by

$$\beta_j(\mathbf{x}_p) = \frac{\mu_{A_{1,k_1}}(x_{p1}) \mu_{A_{2,k_2}}(x_{p2}) \cdots \mu_{A_{q,k_q}}(x_{pq})}{\sum_{k_1=1}^{f_1} \sum_{k_2=1}^{f_2} \cdots \sum_{k_q=1}^{f_q} \mu_{A_{1,k_1}}(x_{p1}) \mu_{A_{2,k_2}}(x_{p2}) \cdots \mu_{A_{q,k_q}}(x_{pq})},$$

$$j = 1, \ldots, m$$

$$(18.3)$$

give information about the fulfillment of the respective fuzzy rule in the normalized form. It is obvious that $\sum_{j=1}^{m} \beta_j(\mathbf{x}_p) = 1$ irrespective of $\mathbf{x}_p$, as long as the denominator of $\beta_j(\mathbf{x}_p)$ is not equal to zero (that can be easily prevented by stretching the membership functions over the whole potential area of $\mathbf{x}_p$). Combining Eq. (18.2) and (18.3) and changing summation over k_i by summation over j, we arrive to the following equation:

$$\hat{y} = \sum_{j=1}^{m} \beta_j(\mathbf{x}_p)\phi_j(\mathbf{x}). \tag{18.4}$$

The class of fuzzy models have the form of linear models; this refers to $\{\beta^j\}$ as a set of basis functions. The use of membership functions in input space with overlapping receptive fields provides interpolation and extrapolation.

Very often, the output value is defined as a linear combination of consequence states

$$\phi_j(\mathbf{x}) = \boldsymbol{\theta}_j^T \mathbf{x}, \quad j = 1, \ldots, m, \quad \boldsymbol{\theta}_j^T = [\theta_{j1}, \ldots, \theta_{jn}] \tag{18.5}$$

If Takagi–Sugeno model of the 0-th order is chosen, $\phi_j(\mathbf{x}) = \theta_{j0}$, and in the case of the first order model, the consequent is $\phi_j(\mathbf{x}) = \theta_{j0} + \boldsymbol{\theta}_j^T \mathbf{x}$. Both cases can be treated by the model in Eq. (18.5) by adding 1 to the vector $\mathbf{x}$ and augmenting vector $\boldsymbol{\theta}$ with θ_{j0}. To simplify the notation, only the model in Eq. (18.5) will be treated in the rest of the chapter. If the matrix of the coefficients for the whole set of rules is written as $\boldsymbol{\Theta}^T = [\boldsymbol{\theta}_1, \ldots, \boldsymbol{\theta}_m]$ and the vector of membership values as $\boldsymbol{\beta}^T(\mathbf{x}_p) = [\beta^1(\mathbf{x}_p), \ldots, \beta^m(\mathbf{x}_p)]$, then Eq. (18.4) can be rewritten in the matrix form as

$$\hat{y} = \boldsymbol{\beta}^T(\mathbf{x}_p)\boldsymbol{\Theta}\mathbf{x}. \tag{18.6}$$

The fuzzy model in the form given in Eq. (18.6) is referred to as the affine Takagi–Sugeno model and can be used to approximate any arbitrary function that maps the compact set $\mathbf{C} \subset \mathbb{R}^d$ (d is the dimension of the input space) to $\mathbb{R}$ with any desired degree of accuracy [8–10]. The generality can be proven by Stone–Weierstrass theorem [11] which indicates that any continuous function can be approximated by fuzzy basis function expansion [12].

When identifying the fuzzy model, there are several parameters that can be tuned. One possibility is to only identify the parameters in the rule consequents and let the antecedent-part parameters untouched. If the position of the membership functions is good (the input space of interest is completely covered and the density of membership functions is higher where nonlinearity is stronger), then a good model can be obtained by only identifying the consequents. The price for this is to introduce any existing prior knowledge in the design of the membership functions. If, however, we do not know anything about the controlled system, we can use some evolving systems techniques where the process of identification changes not only the consequent parameters but also the antecedent parameters [13–17].

18.3. Fuzzy Model-Based Predictive Control

The fundamental methods that are essentially based on the principal of predictive control are generalized predictive control [18], model algorithmic control [19], and predictive functional control [20], Dynamic matrix control [21], extended prediction self-adaptive control [22], and extended horizon adaptive control [23]. All these methods have been developed for linear process models. The principle is based on the process model output prediction and calculation of control signal that brings the output of the process to the reference trajectory in a way to minimize the difference between the reference and the output signal in a certain interval, between two prediction horizons, or to minimize the difference in a certain horizon, called coincidence horizon. The control signal can be found by means of optimization or it can be calculated using the explicit control law formula [24, 25].

The nature of processes is inherently nonlinear and this implies the use of nonlinear approaches in predictive control schemes. Here, we can distinguish between two main group of approaches: the first group is based on the nonlinear mathematical models of the process in any form and convex optimization [26], while the second group relies on approximation of nonlinear process dynamics with nonlinear approximators such as neural networks [10, 27], piecewise-linear models [28], Volterra and Wiener models [29], multimodels and multivariables [30, 31], and fuzzy models [32, 33]. The advantage of the latter approaches is the possibility of stating the control law in the explicit analytical form.

In some highly nonlinear cases, the use of nonlinear model-based predictive control can be easily justified. By introducing the nonlinear model into predictive control problem, the complexity increases significantly. In [24, 25], an overview of different nonlinear predictive control approaches is given.

When applying the model-based predictive control with Takagi–Sugeno fuzzy model, it is always important how to choose fuzzy sets and corresponding membership functions. Many existing clustering techniques can be used in the identification phase to make this task easier. There exist many fuzzy model-based predictive algorithms [34–36] that put significant stress on the algorithm that properly arranges membership functions.

The basic idea of model-based predictive control is to predict the future behavior of the process over a certain horizon using the dynamic model and obtaining the control actions to minimize a certain criterion. Traditionally, the control problem is formally stated as an optimization problem, where the goal is to obtain control actions on a relatively short control horizon by optimizing the behavior of the controlled system in a larger prediction horizon. One of the main properties of most predictive controllers is that they utilize the so-called receding horizon approach. This means that even though the control signal is obtained on a larger interval in the current point of time, only the first sample is used while the whole optimization routine is repeated in each sampling instant.

The model-based predictive control relies heavily on the prediction model quality. When the plant is nonlinear, the model is also nonlinear. As it is very well-known, fuzzy model possesses the property of universal approximation of an arbitrary and smooth nonlinear function and can be used as a prediction model of a nonlinear plant. Many approaches originally developed for the control of linear systems can be adapted to include a fuzzy model-based predictor. In this chapter, fuzzy model is incorporated into the predictive functional control (PFC) approach. This combination provides the means of controlling nonlinear systems. Since no explicit optimization is used, the approach is very suitable for the implementation on an industrial hardware. The fuzzy model-based predictive control (FMBPC) algorithm is presented in the state–space form [37]. The approach is an extension of predictive functional algorithm [20] to the nonlinear systems. This approach was successfully used in many different practical implementations [38–40]. The proposed algorithm easily copes with phase nonminimal and time-delayed dynamics. The approach can be combined by a clustering technique to obtain the FMBPC algorithm where membership functions are not fixed a priori but this is not intention of this work.

18.3.1. *The Development of the Control Algorithm*

In the case of FMBPC, the prediction of the plant output is given by its fuzzy model in the state–space domain. This is why the approach in the proposed form is limited to the open-loop stable plants. By introducing some modifications the algorithm can be made applicable also for the unstable plants.

The problem of delays in the plant is circumvented by constructing an auxiliary variable that serves as the output of the plant if there were no delay present. The so-called *undelayed* model of the plant will be introduced for that purpose. It is obtained by "removing" delays from the original ("delayed") model and converting it to the state–space description:

$$\mathbf{x}_m^0(k+1) = \bar{\mathbf{A}}_m \mathbf{x}_m^0(k) + \bar{\mathbf{B}}_m \mathbf{u}(k) + \bar{\mathbf{R}}_m$$
$$y_m^0(k) = \bar{\mathbf{C}}_m \mathbf{x}_m^0(k), \tag{18.7}$$

where $y_m^0(k)$ models the "undelayed" output of the plant.

The behavior of the closed-loop system is defined by the reference trajectory that is given in the form of the reference model. The control goal is to determine the future control action so that the predicted output value coincides with the reference trajectory. The time difference between the coincidence point and the current time is called a coincidence horizon. It is denoted by H. The prediction is calculated under the assumption of constant future manipulated variables $(u(k) = u(k + 1) = \ldots = u(k + H - 1))$, i.e., the mean level control assumption is used. The H-step before the prediction of the "undelayed" plant output is then obtained from (18.7):

$$y_m^0(k + H) = \bar{\mathbf{C}}_m \left(\bar{\mathbf{A}}_m^H \mathbf{x}_m^0(k) + \left(\bar{\mathbf{A}}_m^H - \mathbf{I} \right) \left(\bar{\mathbf{A}}_m - \mathbf{I} \right)^{-1} \left(\bar{\mathbf{B}}_m u(k) + \bar{\mathbf{R}}_m \right) \right). \quad (18.8)$$

The reference model is given by the first-order difference equation

$$y_r(k + 1) = a_r y_r(k) + b_r w(k), \quad (18.9)$$

where w stands for the reference signal. The reference model parameters should be chosen so that the reference model gain is unity. This is accomplished by fulfilling the following equation:

$$(1 - a_r)^{-1} b_r = 1 \quad (18.10)$$

The main goal of the proposed algorithm is to find the control law that enables the reference trajectory tracking of the "undelayed" plant output $y_p^0(k)$. In each time instant, the control signal is calculated so that the output is forced to reach the reference trajectory after H time samples $(y_p^0(k + H) = y_r(k + H))$. The idea of FMBPC is introduced through the equivalence of the objective increment vector Δ_p and the model output increment vector Δ_m:

$$\Delta_p = \Delta_m \quad (18.11)$$

The former is defined as the difference between the predicted reference signal $y_r(k + H)$ and the actual output of the "undelayed" plant $y_p^0(k)$:

$$\Delta_p = y_r(k + H) - y_p^0(k). \quad (18.12)$$

The variable $y_p^0(k)$ cannot be measured directly. Rather, it will be estimated by using the available signals:

$$y_p^0(k) = y_p(k) - y_m(k) + y_m^0(k). \quad (18.13)$$

It can be seen that the delay in the plant is compensated by the difference between the outputs of the "undelayed" and the "delayed" model. When the perfect model of the plant is available, the first two terms on the right-hand side of Eq. (18.13) cancel and the result is actually the output of the "undelayed" plant model. If this is not the case, only the approximation is obtained. The model output increment vector Δ_m is defined by the following formula:

$$\Delta_m = y_m^0(k + H) - y_m^0(k). \tag{18.14}$$

The following is obtained from Eq. (18.11) by using Eq. (18.12) and (18.14), and introducing Eq. (18.8):

$$u(k) = g_0^{-1}\left((y_r(k + H) - y_p^0(k) + y_m^0(k)) - \bar{C}_m\bar{A}_m^H x_m^0(k)\right.$$
$$\left. - \bar{C}_m\left(\bar{A}_m^H - I\right)\left(\bar{A}_m - I\right)^{-1}\bar{R}_m\right), \tag{18.15}$$

where g_0 stands for

$$g_0 = \bar{C}_m\left(\bar{A}_m^H - I\right)\left(\bar{A}_m - I\right)^{-1}\bar{B}_m. \tag{18.16}$$

The control law of FMBPC in analytical form is finally obtained by introducing Eq. (18.13) into Eq. (18.15):

$$u(k) = g_0^{-1}\left((y_r(k + H) - y_p(k) + y_m(k)) - \bar{C}_m\bar{A}_m^H x_m^0(k)\right.$$
$$\left. - \bar{C}_m\left(\bar{A}_m^H - I\right)\left(\bar{A}_m - I\right)^{-1}\bar{R}_m\right). \tag{18.17}$$

In the following section, it will be shown that the realizability of the control law Eq. (18.17) relies heavily on the relation between the coincidence horizon H and the relative degree of the plant ρ. In the case of discrete-time systems, the relative degree is directly related to the pure time delay of the system transfer function. If the system is described in the state–space form, any form can be used in general, but the analysis is much simplified in the case of certain canonical descriptions. If the system is described in controllable canonical form in each fuzzy domain, then too matrices $\bar{A}_m, \bar{B}_m$, and $\bar{C}_m$ of the fuzzy model in Eq. (18.36) take the controllable canonical form:

$$\bar{A}_m = \begin{bmatrix} 0 & 1 & 0 & \cdots & 0 \\ 0 & 0 & 1 & \cdots & 0 \\ \vdots & \vdots & \vdots & \ddots & \vdots \\ 0 & 0 & 0 & \cdots & 1 \\ -\bar{a}_n & -\bar{a}_{n-1} & -\bar{a}_{n-2} & \cdots & -\bar{a}_1 \end{bmatrix}, \quad \bar{B}_m = \begin{bmatrix} 0 \\ 0 \\ \vdots \\ 0 \\ 1 \end{bmatrix},$$

$$\tag{18.18}$$

$$\bar{C}_m = \begin{bmatrix} \bar{b}_n & \cdots & \bar{b}_\rho & 0 & \cdots & 0 \end{bmatrix}, \quad \bar{R}_m = \begin{bmatrix} 0 \\ 0 \\ \vdots \\ 0 \\ \bar{r} \end{bmatrix}$$

where $\bar{a}_j = \sum_{i=1}^{m} \beta_i a_{j_i}$, $j = 1, \ldots, n$, $\bar{b}_j = \sum_{i=1}^{m} \beta_i b_{j_i}$, $j = \rho, \ldots, n$, and $\bar{r} = \sum_{i=1}^{m} \beta_i (r_i/b_i)$, $j = 1, \ldots, n$, and where the parameters a_{j_i}, b_{j_i}, and r_i are state–space model parameters defined as in Eq. (18.33). Note that the state–space system with matrices from Eq. (18.18) has a relative degree ρ that is reflected in the form of matrix $\bar{\mathbf{C}}_m$ – last ($\rho - 1$) elements are equal to 0 while $\bar{b}_\rho \neq 0$.

Prop 1. If the coincidence horizon H is lower than the plant relative degree ρ ($H < \rho$), then the control law as in Eq. (18.17) is not applicable.

Proof. By taking into account the form of matrices in Eq. (18.18), it can easily be seen that

$$\left(\bar{\mathbf{A}}_m^H - \mathbf{I}\right) \left(\bar{\mathbf{A}}_m - \mathbf{I}\right)^{-1} \bar{\mathbf{B}}_m = \begin{bmatrix} 0 \\ \vdots \\ 0 \\ 1 \\ \bullet \\ \vdots \\ \bullet \end{bmatrix}, \tag{18.19}$$

i.e., the first ($n - H$) elements of the vector are zeros, then there is the element 1, followed by ($H - 1$) arbitrary elements. It then follows from Eq. (18.16) and (18.19) that $g_0 = 0$ if $\rho > H$, and consequently the control law cannot be implemented. $\square$

The closed-loop system analysis makes sense only in the case of non-singular control law. Consequently, the choice of H is confined to the interval $[\rho, \infty)$.

18.3.2. *Stability Analysis*

The stability analysis of the proposed predictive control can be performed using an approach of linear matrix inequalities (LMI) proposed in [27] and [41] or it can be done assuming the frozen-time theory [42, 43] which discusses the relation between the nonlinear dynamical system and the associated linear time-varying system.

In our stability study, we have assumed that the frozen-time system given in Eq. (18.36) is a perfect model of the plant, i.e., $y_p(k) = y_m(k)$ for each k. Next, it is assumed that there is no external input to the closed-loop system ($w = 0$) – an assumption often made when analyzing stability of the closed-loop system. Even if there is external signal, it is important that it is bounded. This is assured by selecting a stable reference model, i.e., $|a_r| < 1$. The results of the stability analysis are also qualitatively the same if the system operates in the presence of bounded disturbances and noise.

Note that the last term in the parentheses of the control law in Eq. (18.17) is equal to $g_0\bar{r}$. This is obtained using Eq. (18.16) and (18.18). Taking this into account and considering the above assumptions the control law in Eq. (18.17) can be simplified to

$$u(k) = g_0^{-1}\left(-\bar{\mathbf{C}}_m\bar{\mathbf{A}}_m^H\mathbf{x}_m^0(k)\right) - \bar{r}. \tag{18.20}$$

Inserting the simplified control law in Eq. (18.20) into the model of the "undelayed" plant Eq. (18.7) we obtain

$$\mathbf{x}_m(k+1) = \left(\bar{\mathbf{A}}_m - \bar{\mathbf{B}}_m g_0^{-1}\bar{\mathbf{C}}_m\bar{\mathbf{A}}_m^H\right)\mathbf{x}_m^0(k). \tag{18.21}$$

The closed-loop state transition matrix is defined as

$$\mathbf{A}_c = \bar{\mathbf{A}}_m - \bar{\mathbf{B}}_m g_0^{-1}\bar{\mathbf{C}}_m\bar{\mathbf{A}}_m^H \tag{18.22}$$

If the system is in the controllable canonical form, the second term on the right-hand side of Eq. (18.22) has non-zero elements only in the last row of the matrix, and consequently, $\mathbf{A}_c$ is also in the Frobenius form. The interesting form of the matrix is obtained in the case $H = \rho$. If $H = \rho$, it can easily be shown that $g_0 = \bar{b}_\rho$ and that $\mathbf{A}_c$ takes the following form:

$$\mathbf{A}_c = \begin{bmatrix} 0 & 1 & 0 & 0 & \cdots & 0 \\ 0 & 0 & 1 & 0 & \cdots & 0 \\ 0 & 0 & 0 & 1 & \cdots & 0 \\ \vdots & \vdots & \vdots & \cdots & \ddots & \vdots \\ 0 & 0 & 0 & 0 & \cdots & 1 \\ 0 & \cdots & 0 & -\frac{\bar{b}_n}{\bar{b}_\rho} & \cdots & -\frac{\bar{b}_{\rho+1}}{\bar{b}_\rho} \end{bmatrix}. \tag{18.23}$$

The corresponding characteristic equation of the system is

$$z^\rho\left(z^{n-\rho} + \frac{\bar{b}_{\rho+1}}{\bar{b}_\rho}z^{n-\rho-1} + \frac{\bar{b}_{\rho+2}}{\bar{b}_\rho}z^{n-\rho-2} + \ldots + \frac{\bar{b}_{n-1}}{\bar{b}_\rho}z + \frac{\bar{b}_n}{\bar{b}_\rho}\right) = 0. \tag{18.24}$$

The solutions of this equation are closed-loop system poles: ρ poles lie in the origin of the z-plane, while the other $(n - \rho)$ poles lie in the roots of the polynomial $\bar{b}_\rho z^{n-\rho} + \bar{b}_{\rho+1}z^{n-\rho-1} + \ldots + \bar{b}_{n-1}z + \bar{b}_n$. These results can be summarized in the following proposition:

Prop 2. When the coincidence horizon is equal to the relative degree of the model ($H = \rho$), then $(n - \rho)$ closed-loop poles tend to open-loop plant zeros, while the rest (ρ) of the poles go to the origin of z-plane.

The proposition states that the closed-loop system is stable for $H = \rho$ if the plant is minimum phase. When this is not the case, the closed-loop system would become unstable if H is chosen to be equal to ρ. In such a case, the coincidence horizon should be larger.

The next proposition deals with the choice of a very large coincidence horizon.

Prop 3. When the coincidence horizon tends to infinity ($H \to \infty$) and the open-loop plant is stable, the closed-loop system poles tend to open-loop plant poles.

Proof. The proposition can be proven easily. In the case of stable plants, $\mathbf{A}_m$ is a Hurwitz matrix that always satisfies

$$\lim_{H \to \infty} \mathbf{A}_m^H = 0. \tag{18.25}$$

Combining Eqs. (18.22) and (18.25) we arrive at the final result

$$\lim_{H \to \infty} \mathbf{A}_c = \mathbf{A}_m \tag{18.26}$$

$\square$

The three propositions provide some design guidelines for choosing the coincidence horizon H. If $H < \rho$, the control law is singular and thus not applicable. If $H = \rho$, the closed-loop poles go to open-loop zeros, i.e., high-gain controller is being used. If H is very large, the closed-loop poles go to open-loop poles, i.e., low-gain controller is being used and the system is almost open-loop. If the plant is stable, the closed-loop system can be made stable by choosing coincidence horizon large enough.

18.3.3. *Practical Example: Continuous Stirred-Tank Reactor*

The simulated continuous stirred-tank reactor (CSTR) process consists of an irreversible, exothermic reaction, $A \to B$, in a constant volume reactor cooled by a single coolant stream, which can be modeled by the following equation [44]:

$$\dot{C}_A^0 = \frac{q}{V} \left[C_{A0} - C_A^0 \right] - k_0 C_A^0 \exp \left(\frac{-E}{RT} \right) \tag{18.27}$$

$$\dot{T} = \frac{q}{V} (T_0 - T) - \frac{k_0 \Delta H}{\rho C_p} C_A^0 \exp \left(\frac{-E}{RT} \right) + \frac{\rho_c C_{pc}}{\rho C_p V} q_c$$
$$\times \left[1 - \exp \left(-\frac{hA}{q_c \rho_c C_{pc}} \right) \right] (T_{c0} - T) \tag{18.28}$$

The actual concentration C_A^0 is measured with a time delay $t_d = 0.5 \, \text{min}$ is

$$C_A(t) = C_A^0(t - t_d). \tag{18.29}$$

The objective is to control the concentration of A (C_A) by manipulating the coolant flow rate q_c. This model is a modified version of the first tank of a two-tank CSTR example from [45]. In the original model, the time delay was zero.

Table 18.1: Nominal CSTR parameter values

Physical quantity	Symbol	Value
Measured product concentration	C_A	0.1 mol/l
Reactor temperature	T	438.54 K
Coolant flow rate	q_c	103.41 l min^{-1}
Process flow rate	q	100 l min^{-1}
Feed concentration	C_{A0}	1 mol/l
Feed temperature	T_0	350 K
Inlet coolant temperature	T_{c0}	350 K
CSTR volume	V	100 l
Heat transfer term	hA	7×10^5 cal min^{-1} K^{-1}
Reaction rate constant	k_0	7.2×10^{10} min^{-1}
Activation energy term	E/R	1×10^4 K
Heat of reaction	ΔH	-2×10^5 cal mol
Liquid densities	ρ, ρ_c	1×10^3 g/l
Specific heats	C_p, C_{pc}	1 cal g^{-1} K^{-1}

The symbol q_c represents the coolant flow rate (manipulated variable) and the other symbols represent constant parameters whose values are defined in Table 18.1. The process dynamics are nonlinear due to the Arrhenius rate expression that describes the dependence of the reaction rate constant on the temperature (T). This is why the CSTR exhibits some operational and control problems. The reactor presents multiplicity behavior with respect to the coolant flow rate q_c, i.e., if the coolant flow rate $q_c \in$ (11.1 l/min, 119.7 l/min), there are three equilibrium concentrations C_A. Stable equilibrium points are obtained in the following cases:

- $q_c > 11.1$ l/min $\Rightarrow$ stable equilibrium point 0.92 mol/$l < C_A < 1$ mol/l, and
- $q_c < 111.8$ l/min $\Rightarrow$ stable equilibrium point $C_A < 0.14$ mol/l (the point where $q_c \approx 111.8$ l/min is a Hopf bifurcation point).

If $q_c \in$ (11.1 l/min, 119.7 l/min), there is also at least one unstable point for the measured product concentration C_A. From the above facts, one can see that the CSTR exhibits quite complex dynamics. In our application, we are interested in the operation in the stable operating point given by $q_c = 103.41$ l min^{-1} and $C_A = 0.1$ mol/l.

18.3.3.1. *Fuzzy identification of the continuous stirred-tank reactor*

From the description of the plant, it can be seen that there are two variables available for measurement — measured product concentration C_A and reactor temperature T. For the purpose of control it is certainly beneficial to make use of both, although it is not necessary to feed reactor temperature if one wants to control product concentration. In our case, the simple discrete compensator was added to the measured reactor temperature output

$$\Delta q_{c_{ff}} = K_{ff} \left[T(k) - T(k-1) \right], \tag{18.30}$$

where K_{ff} was chosen to be 3, while the sampling time $T_s = 0.1$ min. The above compensator is a sort of the D-controller that does not affect the equilibrium points of the system (the static curve remains the same), but it does to some extent affect their stability. In our case, the Hopf bifurcation point moved from $(q_c, C_A) = (111.8 \, \text{l/min}, 0.14 \, \text{mol/l})$ to $(q_c, C_A) = (116.2 \, \text{l/min}, 0.179 \, \text{mol/l})$. This means that the stability interval for the product concentration C_A expanded from $(0, 0.14 \, \text{mol/l})$ to $(0, 0.179 \, \text{mol/l})$. The proposed FMBPC will be tested on the compensated plant, so we need fuzzy model of the compensated plant.

The plant was identified in a form of discrete second order model with the premise defined as $\mathbf{x}_p^T = [C_A(k)]$ and the consequence vector as $\mathbf{x}^T = \left[C_A(k), C_A(k-1), q_c(k-T_{D_m}), 1 \right]$. The functions $\phi_j(\cdot)$ can be arbitrary and smooth functions in general, although linear or affine functions are usually used. Due to strong nonlinearity, the structure with six rules and equidistantly shaped Gaussian membership functions was chosen. The normalized membership functions are shown in Figure 18.1.

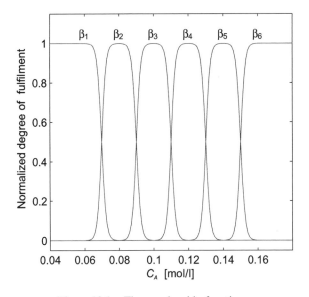

Figure 18.1: The membership functions.

The structure of the fuzzy model is the following:

$$\mathbf{R}_j : \text{ if } C_A(k) \text{ is } \mathbf{A}_j \text{ then } C_A(k+1)$$

$$= -a_{1j}C_A(k) - a_{2j}C_A(k-1)$$

$$+ b_{1j}q_c(k - T_{D_m}) + r_j \quad j = 1, \ldots, 6 \tag{18.31}$$

The parameters of the fuzzy form in Eq. (18.31) have been estimated using least square algorithm, where the data have been preprocessed using QR factorization [46]. The estimated parameters can be written as vectors $\mathbf{a}_1^T = [a_{11}, \ldots, a_{16}]$, $\mathbf{a}_2^T = [a_{21}, \ldots, a_{26}]$, $\mathbf{b}_1^T = [b_{11}, \ldots, b_{16}]$, and $\mathbf{r}_1^T = [r_{11}, \ldots, r_{16}]$. The estimated parameters in the case of CSTR are as follows:

$$\mathbf{a}_1^T = [-1.3462, -1.4506, -1.5681, -1.7114, -1.8111, -1.9157]$$

$$\mathbf{a}_2^T = [0.4298, 0.5262, 0.6437, 0.7689, 0.8592, 0.9485]$$

$$\mathbf{b}_1^T = [1.8124, 2.1795, 2.7762, 2.6703, 2.8716, 2.8500] \cdot 10^{-4}$$

$$\mathbf{r}_1^T = [-1.1089, -1.5115, -2.1101, -2.1917, -2.5270, -2.7301] \cdot 10^{-2}$$

$$\tag{18.32}$$

and $T_{D_m} = 5$.

After estimation of parameters, the TS fuzzy model Eq. (18.31) was transformed into the state–space form to simplify the procedure of obtaining the control law:

$$\mathbf{x}_m(k+1) = \sum_i \beta_i(\mathbf{x}_p(k)) \left(\mathbf{A}_{m_i}\mathbf{x}_m(k) + \mathbf{B}_{m_i}u(k - T_{D_m}) + \mathbf{R}_{m_i} \right) \tag{18.33}$$

$$y_m(k) = \sum_i \beta_i(\mathbf{x}_p(k))\mathbf{C}_m\mathbf{x}_m(k) \tag{18.34}$$

$$\mathbf{A}_{m_i} = \begin{bmatrix} 0 & 1 \\ -a_{2_i} & -a_{1_i} \end{bmatrix}$$

$$\mathbf{B}_{m_i} = \begin{bmatrix} 0 \\ 1 \end{bmatrix} \quad \mathbf{C}_m = \begin{bmatrix} b_{1_i} & 0 \end{bmatrix} \quad \mathbf{R}_{m_i} = \begin{bmatrix} 0 \\ r_i/b_i \end{bmatrix}, \tag{18.35}$$

where the process measured output concentration C_A is denoted by y_m and the input flow q_c by u.

The frozen-time theory [42,43] enables the relation between the nonlinear dynamical system and the associated linear time-varying system. The theory establishes the following fuzzy model:

$$\mathbf{x}_m(k+1) = \bar{\mathbf{A}}_m\mathbf{x}_m(k) + \bar{\mathbf{B}}_mu(k - T_{D_m}) + \bar{\mathbf{R}}_m$$

$$y_m(k) = \bar{\mathbf{C}}_m\mathbf{x}_m(k),$$

$$(18.36)$$

where

$$\bar{\mathbf{A}}_m = \sum_i \beta_i(\mathbf{x}_p(k))\mathbf{A}_{m_i}$$

$$\bar{\mathbf{B}}_m = \sum_i \beta_i(\mathbf{x}_p(k))\mathbf{B}_{m_i}$$

$$(18.37)$$

$$\bar{\mathbf{C}}_m = \sum_i \beta_i(\mathbf{x}_p(k))\mathbf{C}_{m_i}$$

$$\bar{\mathbf{R}}_m = \sum_i \beta_i(\mathbf{x}_p(k))\mathbf{R}_{m_i}$$

18.3.3.2. *Simulation results*

The reference tracking ability and disturbance rejection capability of the FMBPC control algorithm were tested experimentally on a simulated CSTR plant. The FMBPC was compared to the conventional PI controller.

In the first experiment, the control system was tested for tracking the reference signal that changed the operating point from nominal ($C_A = 0.1$ mol/l) to larger concentration values and back, and then to smaller concentration values and back. The proposed FMBPC used the following design parameters: $H = 9$ and $a_r = 0.96$. The parameters of the PI controller were obtained by minimizing the following criterion:

$$C_{PI} = \sum_{k=0}^{400}(y_r(k) - y_{PI}(k))^2,\qquad(18.38)$$

where $y_r(k)$ is the reference model output depicted in Figure 18.2, and $y_{PI}(k)$ is the controlled output in the case of PI control. This means that the parameters of the PI controller were minimized to obtain the best tracking of the reference model output for the case treated in the first experiment. The optimal parameters were $K_P = 64.6454\,\mathrm{l}^2\,\mathrm{mol}^{-1}\,\mathrm{min}^{-1}$ and $T_i = 0.6721$ min. Figure 18.2 also shows manipulated and controlled variables for the two approaches. In the lower part of the figure, the set-point is depicted with the dashed line, the reference model output with the magenta dotted line, the FMBPC response with the blue thick solid line and the PI response with the red thin solid line. The upper part of the figure represents the two control signals. The performance criteria obtained in the experiment are the

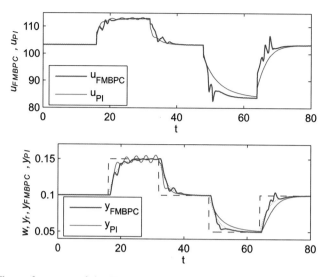

Figure 18.2: The performance of the FMBPC and the PI control in the case of reference trajectory tracking.

following:

$$C_{PI} = \sum_{k=0}^{400} (y_r(k) - y_{PI}(k))^2 = 0.0165 \tag{18.39}$$

$$C_{FMBPC} = \sum_{k=0}^{400} (y_r(k) - y_{FMBPC}(k))^2 = 0.0061. \tag{18.40}$$

The disturbance rejection performance was tested with the same controllers that were set to the same design parameters as in the first experiment. In the simulation experiment, the step-like positive input disturbance of 3 l/min appeared and disappeared later. After some time, the step-like negative input disturbance of -3 l/min appeared and disappeared later. The results of the experiment are shown in Figure 18.3 where the signals are depicted by the same line types as in Figure 18.2. Similar performance criteria can be calculated as in the case of reference tracking

$$C_{PI} = \sum_{k=0}^{400} (y_r(k) - y_{PI}(k))^2 = 0.0076 \tag{18.41}$$

$$C_{FMBPC} = \sum_{k=0}^{400} (y_r(k) - y_{FMBPC}(k))^2 = 0.0036 \tag{18.42}$$

The simulation results have shown that better performance criteria are obtained in the case of the FMBPC control in both control modes: the trajectory tracking

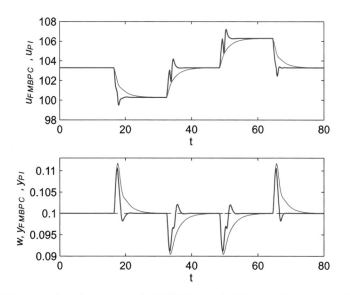

Figure 18.3:   The control performance of the FMBPC and the PI control in the case of disturbance rejection.

mode and the disturbance rejection mode. This is obvious because the PI controller assumes linear process dynamics, while the FMBPC controller takes into account the plant nonlinearity through the fuzzy model of the plant. The proposed approach is very easy to implement and provides a high control performance.

18.4. Direct Fuzzy Model Reference Adaptive Control

We have already established that the fuzzy controllers are capable of controlling nonlinear plants. If the model of the plant is not only nonlinear but also unknown or poorly known, the solution becomes considerably more difficult. Nevertheless, several approaches exist to solve the problem. One possibility is to apply adaptive control. Adaptive control schemes for linear systems do not produce good results, although adaptive parameters try to track the "true" local linear parameters of the current operating point that is conducted with some lag after each operating-point change. To overcome this problem, adaptive control was extended in the 1980s and 1990s to time-varying and nonlinear plants [47].

It is also possible to introduce some sort of adaptation into the fuzzy controller. The first attempts at constructing a fuzzy adaptive controller can be traced back to [48], where the so-called linguistic self-organizing controllers were introduced. Many approaches were later presented where a fuzzy model of the plant was constructed online, followed by control parameters adjustment [49]. The main drawback of these schemes was that their stability was not treated rigorously.

The universal approximation theorem [50] provided a theoretical background for new fuzzy direct and indirect adaptive controllers [50–52] whose stability was proven using the Lyapunov theory.

Robust adaptive control was proposed to overcome the problem of disturbances and unmodeled dynamics [53]. Similar solutions have also been used in adaptive fuzzy and neural controllers, i.e., projection [54], dead zone [55], leakage [56], adaptive fuzzy backstepping control [57], etc., have been included in the adaptive law to prevent instability due to reconstruction error.

The control of a practically very important class of plants is treated in this section that, in our opinion, occur quite often in process industries. The class of plants consists of nonlinear systems of arbitrary order but where the control law is based on the first-order nonlinear approximation. The dynamics not included in the first-order approximation are referred to as parasitic dynamics. The parasitic dynamics are treated explicitly in the development of the adaptive law to prevent the modeling error to grow unbounded. The class of plant also includes bounded disturbances.

The choice of simple nominal model results in very simple control and adaptive laws. The control law is similar to the one proposed by [58, 59] but an extra term is added in this work where an adaptive law with leakage is presented [60]. It will be shown that the proposed adaptive law is a natural way to cope with parasitic dynamics. The boundedness of estimated parameters, the tracking error, and all the signals in the system will be proved, if the leakage parameter σ' satisfies certain conditions. This means that the proposed adaptive law ensures the global stability of the system. A very important property of the proposed approach is that it can be used in the consequent part of Takagi–Sugeno-based control. The approach enables easy implementation in the control systems with evolving antecedent parts [13–17]. This combination results in a high-performance and robust control of nonlinear and slow time-varying systems [61–64].

18.4.1. *The Class of Nonlinear Plants*

Our goal is to design control for a class of plants that include nonlinear time-invariant systems, where the model behaves similarly to a first-order system at low frequencies (the frequency response is not defined for nonlinear systems, so frequencies are meant here in a broader sense). If the plant were the first-order system (without parasitic dynamics), it could be described by a fuzzy model in the form of if-then rules:

$$\textbf{if } z_1 \textbf{ is } A_{i_a} \textbf{ and } z_2 \textbf{ is } B_{i_b}, \textbf{ then } \dot{y}_p = -a_i y_p + b_i u + c_i$$

$$i_a = 1, \ldots, n_a \quad i_b = 1, \ldots, n_b \quad i = 1, \ldots, k, \tag{18.43}$$

where u and y_p are the input and the output of the plant, respectively, A_{i_a} and B_{i_b} are fuzzy membership functions, and a_i, b_i, and c_i are the plant parameters in the ith domain. Note the c_i term in the consequent. Such an additive term is obtained if a nonlinear system is linearized in an operating point. This additive term changes by changing the operating point. The term c_i is new compared to the model used in [58, 59]. The antecedent variables that define the domain in which the system is currently situated are denoted by z_1 and z_2 (actually, there can be only one such variable or there can also be more of them, but this does not affect the approach described here). There are n_a and n_b membership functions for the first and the second antecedent variables, respectively. The product $k = n_a \times n_b$ defines the number of fuzzy rules. The membership functions have to cover the whole operating area of the system. The output of the Takagi–Sugeno model is then given by the following equation:

$$\dot{y}_p = \frac{\sum_{i=1}^{k} \left[\beta_i^0(\mathbf{x}_p)(-a_i y_p + b_i u + c_i)\right]}{\sum_{i=1}^{k} \beta_i^0(\mathbf{x}_p)}, \tag{18.44}$$

where $\mathbf{x}_p$ represents the vector of antecedent variables z_i (in the case of fuzzy model given by Eq. (18.43), $\mathbf{x}_p = [z_1 \, z_2]^T$). The degree of fulfillment $\beta_i^0(\mathbf{x}_p)$ is obtained using the T-norm, which in this case is a simple algebraic product of membership functions:

$$\beta_i^0(\mathbf{x}_p) = T(\mu_{A_{i_a}}(z_1), \mu_{B_{i_b}}(z_2)) = \mu_{A_{i_a}}(z_1) \cdot \mu_{B_{i_b}}(z_2), \tag{18.45}$$

where $\mu_{A_{i_a}}(z_1)$ and $\mu_{B_{i_b}}(z_2)$ stand for degrees of fulfillment of the corresponding fuzzy rule. The degrees of fulfillment for the whole set of fuzzy rules can be written in a compact form as

$$\boldsymbol{\beta}^0 = \begin{bmatrix} \beta_1^0 & \beta_2^0 & \cdots & \beta_k^0 \end{bmatrix}^T \in \mathbb{R}^k, \tag{18.46}$$

or in a more convenient, normalized form

$$\boldsymbol{\beta} = \frac{\boldsymbol{\beta}^0}{\sum_{i=1}^{k} \beta_i^0} \in \mathbb{R}^k. \tag{18.47}$$

Due to Eq. (18.44) and (18.47), the first-order plant can be modeled in fuzzy form as

$$\dot{y}_p = -(\boldsymbol{\beta}^T \mathbf{a})y_p + (\boldsymbol{\beta}^T \mathbf{b})u + (\boldsymbol{\beta}^T \mathbf{c}). \tag{18.48}$$

where $\mathbf{a} = \begin{bmatrix} a_1 \, a_2 \ldots a_k \end{bmatrix}^T$, $\mathbf{b} = \begin{bmatrix} b_1 \, b_2 \cdots b_k \end{bmatrix}^T$, and $\mathbf{c} = \begin{bmatrix} c_1 \, c_2 \ldots c_k \end{bmatrix}^T$ are vectors of unknown plant parameters in respective domains ($\mathbf{a}, \mathbf{b}, \mathbf{c} \in \mathbb{R}^k$).

To assume that the controlled system is of the first order is a quite big generalization. Parasitic dynamics and disturbances are therefore included in the model of the plant. The fuzzy model of the first order is generalized by adding stable factor plant perturbations and disturbances, which results in the following model [58]:

$$\dot{y}_p(t) = -(\boldsymbol{\beta}^T(t)\mathbf{a})y_p(t) + (\boldsymbol{\beta}^T(t)\mathbf{b})u(t) + (\boldsymbol{\beta}^T\mathbf{c})$$
$$- \Delta_y(p)y_p(t) + \Delta_u(p)u(t) + d(t), \tag{18.49}$$

where p is a differential operator d/dt, $\Delta_y(p)$ and $\Delta_u(p)$ are stable strictly proper linear operators, while d is a bounded signal due to disturbances [58].

Equation (18.49) represents the class of plants to be controlled by the approach proposed in the following sections. The control is designed based on the model given by Eq. (18.48), while the robustness properties of the algorithm prevent the instability due to parasitic dynamics and disturbances.

18.4.2. The proposed fuzzy adaptive control algorithm

A fuzzy model reference adaptive control is proposed to achieve tracking control for the class of plants described in the previous section. The control goal is that the plant output follows the output y_m of the reference model. The latter is defined by a first order linear system $G_m(p)$:

$$y_m(t) = G_m(p)w(t) = \frac{b_m}{p + a_m}w(t), \tag{18.50}$$

where $w(t)$ is the reference signal while b_m and a_m are the constants that define desired behavior of the closed system. The tracking error

$$\varepsilon(t) = y_p(t) - y_m(t) \tag{18.51}$$

therefore represents some measure of the control quality. To solve the control problem, simple control and adaptive laws are proposed in the following subsections.

18.4.2.1. Control law

The control law is very similar to the one proposed by [58] and [59]:

$$u(t) = \left(\boldsymbol{\beta}^T(t)\hat{\mathbf{f}}(t)\right)w(t) - \left(\boldsymbol{\beta}^T(t)\hat{\mathbf{q}}(t)\right)y_p(t) + \left(\boldsymbol{\beta}^T(t)\hat{\mathbf{r}}(t)\right), \tag{18.52}$$

where $\hat{\mathbf{f}}(t) \in \mathbb{R}^k$, $\hat{\mathbf{q}}(t) \in \mathbb{R}^k$, and $\hat{\mathbf{r}}(t) \in \mathbb{R}^k$ are the control gain vectors to be determined by the adaptive law. This control law is obtained by generalizing the model reference adaptive control algorithm for the first-order linear plant to the fuzzy case. The control law also includes the third term that is new compared to the one in [59]. It is used to compensate the $(\boldsymbol{\beta}^T\mathbf{c})$ term in Eq. (18.49).

18.4.2.2. Adaptive law

The adaptive law proposed in this chapter is based on the adaptive law from [58]. The e_1-modification was used in the leakage term in [58]. An alternative approach was proposed in [59]. Here, we follow the basic idea from [59] while also adding a new adaptive law for $\hat{r}_i$:

$$\dot{\hat{f}}_i = -\gamma_{fi} b_{sign} \varepsilon w \beta_i - \gamma_{fi} \sigma' w^2 \beta_i^2 (\hat{f}_i - \hat{f}_i^*) \quad i = 1, 2, \ldots k$$

$$\dot{\hat{q}}_i = \gamma_{qi} b_{sign} \varepsilon y_p \beta_i - \gamma_{qi} \sigma' y_p^2 \beta_i^2 (\hat{q}_i - \hat{q}_i^*) \quad i = 1, 2, \ldots k \quad , \tag{18.53}$$

$$\dot{\hat{r}}_i = -\gamma_{ri} b_{sign} \varepsilon \beta_i - \gamma_{ri} \sigma' \beta_i^2 (\hat{r}_i - \hat{r}_i^*) \quad i = 1, 2, \ldots k$$

where γ_{fi}, γ_{qi}, and γ_{ri} are positive scalars referred to as adaptive gains, $\sigma' > 0$ is the parameter of the leakage term, $\hat{f}_i^*$, $\hat{q}_i^*$, and $\hat{r}_i^*$ are the a priori estimates of the control gains $\hat{f}_i$, $\hat{q}_i$, and $\hat{r}_i$ respectively, and b_{sign} is defined as follows:

$$b_{sign} = \begin{cases} 1 & b_1 > 0, b_2 > 0, \ldots b_k > 0 \\ -1 & b_1 < 0, b_2 < 0, \ldots b_k < 0 \end{cases}. \tag{18.54}$$

If the signs of all elements in vector **b** are not the same, the plant is not controllable for some β ($\beta^T \mathbf{b}$ is equal to 0 for this β) and any control signal does not have an effect.

It is possible to rewrite the adaptive law Eq. (18.53) in the compact form if the control gain vectors $\hat{\mathbf{f}}$, $\hat{\mathbf{q}}$, and $\hat{\mathbf{r}}$ are defined as

$$\hat{\mathbf{f}}^T = \begin{bmatrix} \hat{f}_1 & \hat{f}_2 & \cdots & \hat{f}_k \end{bmatrix}$$

$$\hat{\mathbf{q}}^T = \begin{bmatrix} \hat{q}_1 & \hat{q}_2 & \cdots & \hat{q}_k \end{bmatrix} \tag{18.55}$$

$$\hat{\mathbf{r}}^T = \begin{bmatrix} \hat{r}_1 & \hat{r}_2 & \cdots & \hat{r}_k \end{bmatrix}$$

Then the adaptive law Eq. (18.53) takes the following form:

$$\dot{\hat{\mathbf{f}}} = -\Gamma_f b_{sign} \varepsilon w \beta - \Gamma_f \sigma' w^2 \operatorname{diag}(\beta) \operatorname{diag}(\beta)(\hat{\mathbf{f}} - \hat{\mathbf{f}}^*)$$

$$\dot{\hat{\mathbf{q}}} = \Gamma_q b_{sign} \varepsilon y_p \beta - \Gamma_q \sigma' y_p^2 \operatorname{diag}(\beta) \operatorname{diag}(\beta)(\hat{\mathbf{q}} - \hat{\mathbf{q}}^*) \quad , \tag{18.56}$$

$$\dot{\hat{\mathbf{r}}} = -\Gamma_r b_{sign} \varepsilon \beta - \Gamma_r \sigma' \operatorname{diag}(\beta) \operatorname{diag}(\beta)(\hat{\mathbf{r}} - \hat{\mathbf{r}}^*)$$

where $\Gamma_f \in \mathbb{R}^{k \times k}$, $\Gamma_q \in \mathbb{R}^{k \times k}$, and $\Gamma_r \in \mathbb{R}^{k \times k}$ are positive definite matrices, $\operatorname{diag}(\mathbf{x}) \in \mathbb{R}^{k \times k}$ is a diagonal matrix with the elements of vector **x** on the main diagonal, while $\hat{\mathbf{f}}^* \in \mathbb{R}^k$, $\hat{\mathbf{q}}^* \in \mathbb{R}^k$, and $\hat{\mathbf{r}}^* \in \mathbb{R}^k$ are the a priori estimates of the control gain vectors.

18.4.2.3. *The sketch of the stability proof*

The reference model in Eq. (18.50) can be rewritten in the following form:

$$\dot{y}_m = -a_m y_m + b_m w. \tag{18.57}$$

By subtracting Eq. (18.57) from Eq. (18.49), the following tracking-error model is obtained:

$$\dot{\varepsilon} = -a_m \varepsilon + \left[(\boldsymbol{\beta}^T \mathbf{b})(\boldsymbol{\beta}^T \hat{\mathbf{f}}) - b_m \right] w - \left[(\boldsymbol{\beta}^T \mathbf{b})(\boldsymbol{\beta}^T \hat{\mathbf{q}}) + (\boldsymbol{\beta}^T \mathbf{a}) - a_m \right] y_p +$$
$$+ \left[(\boldsymbol{\beta}^T \mathbf{b})(\boldsymbol{\beta}^T \hat{\mathbf{r}}) + (\boldsymbol{\beta}^T \mathbf{c}) \right] + \Delta_u(p)u - \Delta_y(p)y_p + d \tag{18.58}$$

Now we assume that there exist constant control parameters $\mathbf{f}^*$, $\mathbf{q}^*$, and $\mathbf{r}^*$ that stabilize the closed-loop system. This is a mild assumption and it is always fulfilled unless the unmodeled dynamics are unacceptably high. These parameters are only needed in the stability analysis and can be chosen to make the "difference" between the closed-loop system and the reference model smaller in some sense (The definition of this "difference" is not important for the analysis.) The parameters $\mathbf{f}^*$, $\mathbf{q}^*$, and $\mathbf{r}^*$ are sometimes called the "true" parameters because they result in the perfect tracking in the absence of unmodeled dynamics and disturbances. The parameter errors are defined as

$$\tilde{\mathbf{f}} = \hat{\mathbf{f}} - \mathbf{f}^*$$
$$\tilde{\mathbf{q}} = \hat{\mathbf{q}} - \mathbf{q}^* \tag{18.59}$$
$$\tilde{\mathbf{r}} = \hat{\mathbf{r}} - \mathbf{r}^*$$

The expressions in the square brackets in Eq. (18.59) can be rewritten similarly as in [58]:

$$\left[(\boldsymbol{\beta}^T \mathbf{b})(\boldsymbol{\beta}^T \hat{\mathbf{f}}) - b_m \right] = b_{sign} \boldsymbol{\beta}^T \tilde{\mathbf{f}} + \eta_f = b_{sign} \sum_{i=1}^{k} \beta_i \tilde{f}_i + \eta_f$$

$$\left[(\boldsymbol{\beta}^T \mathbf{b})(\boldsymbol{\beta}^T \hat{\mathbf{q}}) + (\boldsymbol{\beta}^T \mathbf{a}) - a_m \right] = b_{sign} \boldsymbol{\beta}^T \tilde{\mathbf{q}} + \eta_q = b_{sign} \sum_{i=1}^{k} \beta_i \tilde{q}_i + \eta_q, \quad (18.60)$$

$$\left[(\boldsymbol{\beta}^T \mathbf{b})(\boldsymbol{\beta}^T \hat{\mathbf{r}}) + (\boldsymbol{\beta}^T \mathbf{c}) \right] = b_{sign} \boldsymbol{\beta}^T \tilde{\mathbf{r}} + \eta_r = b_{sign} \sum_{i=1}^{k} \beta_i \tilde{r}_i + \eta_r$$

where bounded residuals $\eta_f(t)$, $\eta_q(t)$, and $\eta_r(t)$ are introduced (the boundedness can be shown simply; see also [58]). The following Lyapunov function has been proposed for the proof of stability:

$$V = \tfrac{1}{2}\varepsilon^2 + \tfrac{1}{2}\sum_{i=1}^{k} \gamma_{fi}^{-1}\tilde{f}_i^2 + \tfrac{1}{2}\sum_{i=1}^{k} \gamma_{qi}^{-1}\tilde{q}_i^2 + \tfrac{1}{2}\sum_{i=1}^{k} \gamma_{ri}^{-1}\tilde{r}_i^2. \tag{18.61}$$

Calculating the derivative of the Lyapunov function along the solution of the system Eq. (18.58) and taking into account Eq. (18.60) and adaptive laws in Eq. (18.53) we obtain

$$\begin{aligned}
\dot{V} &= \varepsilon\dot{\varepsilon} + \sum_{i=1}^{k} \gamma_{fi}^{-1}\tilde{f}_i\dot{\hat{f}}_i + \sum_{i=1}^{k} \gamma_{qi}^{-1}\tilde{q}_i\dot{\hat{q}}_i + \sum_{i=1}^{k} \gamma_{ri}^{-1}\tilde{r}_i\dot{\hat{r}}_i \\
&= -a_m\varepsilon^2 + \eta_f w\varepsilon - \eta_q y_p\varepsilon + \eta_r\varepsilon + \varepsilon\Delta_u(p)u - \varepsilon\Delta_y(p)y_p + \varepsilon d \\
&\quad - \sum_{i=1}^{k} \sigma' w^2 \beta_i^2 (\hat{f}_i - f_i^*)\tilde{f}_i - \sum_{i=1}^{k} \sigma' y_p^2 \beta_i^2 (\hat{q}_i - \hat{q}_i^*)\tilde{q}_i \\
&\quad - \sum_{i=1}^{k} \sigma' \beta_i^2 (\hat{r}_i - \hat{r}_i^*)\tilde{r}_i.
\end{aligned} \tag{18.62}$$

In principle, the first term on the right-hand side of Eq. (18.62) is used to compensate for the next six terms while the last three terms prevent parameter drift. The terms from the second one to the seventh one are formed as a product between the tracking error $\varepsilon(t)$ and a combined error $E(t)$ defined as

$$E(t) = \eta_f(t)w(t) - \eta_q(t)y_p(t) + \eta_r(t) + \Delta_u(p)u(t) - \Delta_y(p)y_p(t) + d(t) \tag{18.63}$$

Equation (18.62) can be rewritten as

$$\begin{aligned}
\dot{V} &= -a_m \left(\varepsilon^2 - \frac{E\varepsilon}{a_m} \right) \\
&\quad - \sum_{i=1}^{k} \sigma' w^2 \beta_i^2 (\hat{f}_i - f_i^*)\tilde{f}_i - \sum_{i=1}^{k} \sigma' y_p^2 \beta_i^2 (\hat{q}_i - \hat{q}_i^*)\tilde{q}_i \\
&\quad - \sum_{i=1}^{k} \sigma' \beta_i^2 (\hat{r}_i - \hat{r}_i^*)\tilde{r}_i.
\end{aligned} \tag{18.64}$$

The first term on the right-hand side of Eq. (18.64) becomes negative, if $|\varepsilon| > \frac{|E|}{a_m}$. If the combined error were a priori bounded, the boundedness of the tracking error ε would be more or less proven. The problem lies in the fact that not only bounded signals $(w(t), \eta_f(t), \eta_q(t), \eta_r(t), d(t))$ are included in $E(t)$, but also are the ones whose boundedness is yet to be proven $(u(t), y_p(t))$. If the system becomes unstable, the plant output $y_p(t)$ becomes unbounded and, consequently, the same applies to the control input $u(t)$. If $y_p(t)$ is bounded, it is easy to see from the control law that $u(t)$ is also bounded. Unboundedness of $y_p(t)$ is prevented by leakage terms in the adaptive law. In the last three terms in Eq. (18.64) that are due to the leakage, there are three similar expressions. They have the following form:

$$(\hat{f}_i(t) - \hat{f}_i^*)\tilde{f}_i(t) = (\hat{f}_i(t) - \hat{f}_i^*)(\hat{f}_i(t) - f_i^*). \tag{18.65}$$

It is simple to see that this expression is positive if either $\hat{f}_i > \max\{\hat{f}_i^*, f_i^*\}$ or $\hat{f}_i < \min\{\hat{f}_i^*, f_i^*\}$. The same reasoning applies to $\hat{q}_i$ and $\hat{r}_i$. This means that the last three terms in Eq. (18.64) become negative if the estimated parameters are large (or small) enough. The novelty of the proposed adaptive law with respect to the one in [58] is in the quadratic terms with y_p and w in the leakage. These terms are used to help cancel the contribution of εE in Eq. (18.64):

$$\varepsilon E = \varepsilon \eta_f w - \varepsilon \eta_q y_p + \varepsilon \eta_r + \varepsilon \Delta_u(p)u - \varepsilon \Delta_y(p)y_p + \varepsilon d. \tag{18.66}$$

Since $\varepsilon(t)$ is the difference between $y_p(t)$ and $y_m(t)$ and the latter is bounded, $\varepsilon = O(y_p)$ when y_p tends to infinity. By analyzing the control law and taking into account stability of parasitic dynamics $\Delta_u(s)$ and $\Delta_y(s)$, the following can be concluded:

$$u = O(y_p), \Delta_u(p)u = O(y_p) \Rightarrow \varepsilon E = O(y_p^2). \tag{18.67}$$

The third term on the right-hand side of Eq. (18.64) is $-(\hat{q}_i - \hat{q}_i^*)\tilde{q}_i O(y_p^2)$, which means that the "gain" $(\hat{q}_i - \hat{q}_i^*)\tilde{q}_i$ with respect to y_p^2 of the negative contributions to $\dot{V}$ can always become greater (as a result of adaptation) than the fixed gain of quadratic terms with y_p in Eq. (18.66). The growth of the estimated parameters is also problematic because these parameters are control gains and high gains can induce instability in combination with parasitic dynamics. Consequently, σ' has to be large enough to prevent this type of instability. Note that the stabilization in the presence of parasitic dynamics is achieved without using an explicit dynamic normalization that was used in [58].

The stability analysis of a similar adaptive law for linear systems was treated in [65] where it was proven that all the signals in the system are bounded and the tracking error converges to a residual set whose size depends on the modeling error if the leakage parameter σ' chosen is large enough with respect to the norm of parasitic dynamics. In the approach proposed in this chapter, the "modeling error" is $E(t)$ from Eq. (18.63), and therefore the residual-set size depends on the size of the norm of the transfer functions $\|\Delta_u\|$ and $\|\Delta_y\|$, the size of the disturbance d, and the size of the bounded residuals $\eta_f(t)$, $\eta_q(t)$, and $\eta_r(t)$.

Only the adaptation of the consequent part of the fuzzy rules is treated in this chapter. The stability of the system is guaranteed for any (fixed) shape of the membership functions in the antecedent part. This means that this approach is very easy to combine with existing evolving approaches for the antecedent part. If the membership functions are slowly evolving, these changes introduce another term to $\dot{V}$ that can be shown not to be larger than $O(y_p^2)$. This means that the system stability is preserved by the robustness properties of the adaptive laws. If, however, fast changes in the membership functions occur, a rigorous stability analysis would have to be performed.

18.4.3. *Simulation Example: Three-Tank System*

A simulation example has been given that illustrates the proposed approach. A simulated plant was chosen since it is easier to make the same operating conditions than it would be when testing on a real plant. The simulated test plant consisted of three water tanks. The schematic representation of the plant is given in Figure 18.4. The control objective was to maintain the water level in the third tank by changing the inflow into the first tank.

When modeling the plant, it was assumed that the flow through the valve was proportional to the square root of the pressure difference on the valve. The mass conservation equations for the three tanks are

$$
\begin{aligned}
S_1\dot{h}_1 &= \phi_{in} - k_1 \operatorname{sign}(h_1 - h_2)\sqrt{|h_1 - h_2|} \\
S_2\dot{h}_2 &= k_1 \operatorname{sign}(h_1 - h_2)\sqrt{|h_1 - h_2|} - k_2 \operatorname{sign}(h_2 - h_3)\sqrt{|h_2 - h_3|}, \quad (18.68) \\
S_3\dot{h}_3 &= k_2 \operatorname{sign}(h_2 - h_3)\sqrt{|h_2 - h_3|} - k_3 \operatorname{sign}(h_3)\sqrt{|h_3|}
\end{aligned}
$$

where ϕ_{in} is the volume inflow into the first tank, h_1, h_2, and h_3 are the water levels in three tanks, S_1, S_2, and S_3 are areas of the tanks cross-sections, and k_1, k_2, and k_3 are coefficients of the valves. The following values were chosen for the parameters of the system:

$$
\begin{aligned}
S_1 &= S_2 = S_3 = 2 \cdot 10^{-2}\,\mathrm{m}^2 \\
k_1 &= k_2 = k_3 = 2 \cdot 10^{-4}\,\mathrm{m}^{5/2}\,\mathrm{s}^{-1}
\end{aligned}
\qquad (18.69)
$$

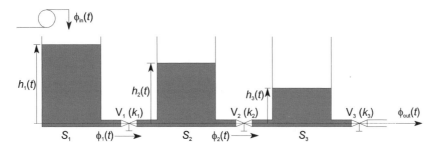

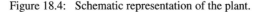

Figure 18.4:   Schematic representation of the plant.

The nominal value of inflow ϕ_{in} was set to $8 \cdot 10^{-5}$ m^3 s^{-1}, resulting in steady-state values 0.48 m, 0.32 m, and 0.16 m, for h_1, h_2, and h_3, respectively. In the following, u and y_p denote deviations of ϕ_{in} and h_3, respectively, from the operating point.

By analyzing the plant it can be seen that the plant is nonlinear. It has to be pointed out that the parasitic dynamics are also nonlinear, not just the dominant part as was assumed in deriving the control algorithm. This means that this example will also test the ability of the proposed control to cope with nonlinear parasitic dynamics. The coefficients of the linearized system in different operating points depend on u, h_1, h_2, and h_3 even though that only y_p will be used as an antecedent variable z_1, which is again a violation of the basic assumptions but still produces fairly good results.

The proposed control algorithm was compared to a classical model reference adaptive control (MRAC) with e_1-modification. Adaptive gains γ_{fi}, γ_{qi}, and γ_{ri} in the case of the proposed approach were the same as γ_f, γ_q, and γ_r, respectively, in the case of MRAC. A reference signal was chosen as a periodic piecewise constant function that covered quite a wide area around the operating point ($\pm 50\%$ of the nominal value). There were 11 triangular fuzzy membership functions (the fuzzification variable was y_p) used; these were distributed evenly across the interval $[-0.1, 0.1]$. As already mentioned, the evolving of the antecedent part was not done in this work. The control input signal u was saturated at the interval $[-8 \cdot 10^{-5}, 8 \cdot 10^{-5}]$. No prior knowledge of the estimated parameters was available to us, so the initial parameter estimates were 0 for all examples.

The design objective is that the output of the plant follows the output of the reference model $0.01/(s + 0.01)$. The reference signal was the same in all cases. It consisted of a periodic signal. The results of the experiment with the classical MRAC controller with e_1-modification are shown in Figure 18.5.

We used the following design parameters: $\gamma_f = 10^{-4}$, $\gamma_q = 2 \cdot 10^{-4}$, $\gamma_r = 10^{-6}$, $\sigma' = 0.1$. Figures 18.6 and 18.7 show the results of the proposed approach; the former shows a period of system responses after the adaptation has settled, and the latter depicts time plots of the estimated parameters. Since $\hat{\mathbf{f}}$, $\hat{\mathbf{q}}$, and $\hat{\mathbf{r}}$ are vectors, all elements of the vectors are depicted. Note that every change in the reference signal results in a sudden increase in tracking error ε (up to 0.01). This is due to the fact that zero tracking of the reference model with relative degree 1 is not possible if the plant has relative degree 3.

The experiments show that the performance of the proposed approach is better than the performance of the MRAC controller for linear plant which is expected due to nonlinearity of the plant. Very good results were obtained in the case of the proposed approach even though that the parasitic dynamics are nonlinear and linearized parameters depend not only on the antecedent variable y_p but also on

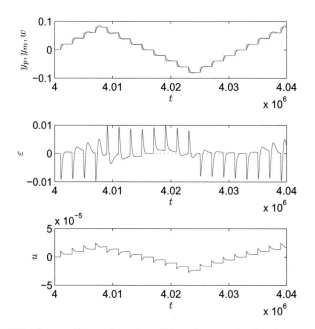

Figure 18.5: The MRAC controller — time plots of the reference signal and outputs of the plant and the reference model (upper figure), time plot of tracking error (middle figure), and time plot of the control signal (lower figure).

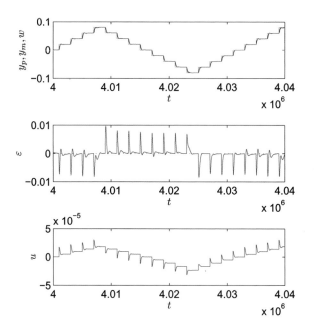

Figure 18.6: The proposed approach — time plots of the reference signal and outputs of the plant and the reference model (upper figure), time plot of tracking error (middle figure), and time plot of the control signal (lower figure).

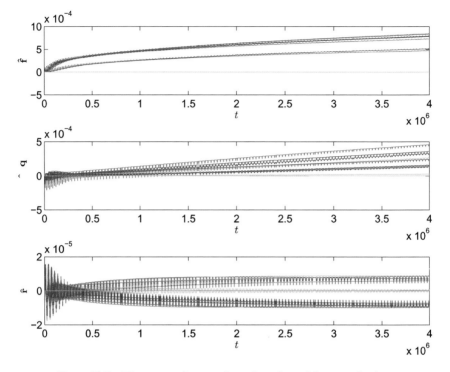

Figure 18.7:   The proposed approach — time plots of the control gains.

others. The spikes on ε in Figure 18.6 are consequences of the fact that the plant of relative degree 3 is forced to follow the reference model of relative degree 1. These spikes are inevitable no matter which controller is used.

The drawback of the proposed approach is relatively slow convergence since the parameters are only adapted when the corresponding membership is non-zero. This drawback can be overcome by using classical MRAC in the beginning when there are no parameter estimates or the estimates are bad. When the system approaches desired behavior the adaptation can switch to the proposed one by initializing all elements of vectors $\hat{\mathbf{f}}$, $\hat{\mathbf{q}}$, and $\hat{\mathbf{r}}$ with estimated scalar parameters from the classical MRAC.

18.5. Conclusion

This chapter presents two approaches to the control of nonlinear systems. We chose these two solutions because they are easy to tune and easy to implement on one hand, but they also guarantee the stability under some assumptions on the other. Both approaches also only deal with the rule consequents and are easy to extend to the variants with evolving antecedent part.

References

[1] W. Pedrycz, *Fuzzy Control and Fuzzy Systems* (Research Studies Press, 1993).

[2] K. Passino and S. Yurkovich, *Fuzzy Control* (Addison-Wesley, 1998).

[3] K. Tanaka and H. O. Wang, *Fuzzy Control Systems Design and Analysis: A Linear Matrix Inequality Approach* (John Wiley & Sons, Inc., New York, NY, USA, 2002).

[4] R. Babuska, *Fuzzy Modeling for Control* (Kluwer Academic Publishers, 1998).

[5] L. A. Zadeh, Outline of a new approach to the analysis of complex systems and decision processes, *IEEE Trans. Syst. Man Cybern.*, **SMC-3**(1), 28–44 (1973).

[6] E. Mamdani, Application of fuzzy algorithms for control of simple dynamic plant, *Proc. Inst. Electr. Eng.*, **121**(12), 1585–1588 (1974).

[7] T. Takagi and M. Sugeno, Fuzzy identification of systems and its applications to modelling and control, *IEEE Trans. Syst. Man Cybern.*, **15**, 116–132 (1985).

[8] B. Kosko, Fuzzy systems as universal approximators, *IEEE Trans. Comput.*, **43**(11), 1329–1333 (1994).

[9] H. G. Ying, Necessary conditions for some typical fuzzy systems as universal approximators, *Automatica*, **33**, 1333–1338 (1997).

[10] L.-X. Wang and J. M. Mendel, Fuzzy basis functions, universal approximation, and orthogonal least-squares learning, *IEEE Trans. Neural Networks*, **3**(5), 807–814 (1992).

[11] R. R. Goldberg, *Methods of Real Analysis* (John Wiley and Sons, 1976).

[12] C.-H. Lin, SISO nonlinear system identification using a fuzzy-neural hybrid system, *Int. J. Neural Syst.*, **8**(3), 325–337 (1997).

[13] P. Angelov, R. Buswell, J. A. Wright, and D. Loveday, Evolving rule-based control. In *EUNITE Symposium*, pp. 36–41, Tenerife, Spain (2001).

[14] P. Angelov and D. P. Filev, An approach to online identification of Takagi-Sugeno fuzzy models, *IEEE Syst Man Cybern. B: Cybern.*, **34**(1), 484–498 (2004).

[15] A. B. Cara, Z. Lendek, R. Babuska, H. Pomares, and I. Rojas, Online self-organizing adaptive fuzzy controller: application to a nonlinear servo system. In *Fuzzy Systems (FUZZ), 2010 IEEE International Conference on*, pp. 1–8 (2010). ISBN 1098-7584. doi: 10.1109/FUZZY.2010.5584027.

[16] P. Angelov, P. Sadeghi-Tehran, and R. Ramezani, An approach to automatic real-time novelty detection, object identification, and tracking in video streams based on recursive density estimation and evolving takagi-sugeno fuzzy systems, *Int. J. Intell. Syst.*, **26**(3), 189–205 (2011).

[17] P. Sadeghi-Tehran, A. B. Cara, P. Angelov, H. Pomares, I. Rojas, and A. Prieto, Self-evolving parameter-free rule-based controller. In *IEEE, Proc. 2012 World Congress on Computational Intelligence, WCCI-2012*, pp. 754–761. IEEE (2012). ISBN 978-1-4673-1489-3.

[18] D. W. Clarke, C. Mohtadi, and P. S. Tuffs, Generalized predictive control–part 1, part 2, *Automatica*, **24**, 137–160 (1987).

[19] J. Richalet, A. Rault, J. L. Testud, and J. Papon, Model predictive heuristic control: applications to industrial processes, *Automatica*, **14**, 413–428 (1978).

[20] J. Richalet, Industrial application of model based predictive control, *Automatica*, **29**(5), 1251–1274 (1993).

[21] C. R. Cutler and B. L. Ramaker, Dynamic matrix control — a computer control algorithm. In *Proceedings of the ACC*, San Francisco (1980).

[22] R. M. C. De Keyser, P. G. A. Van de Valde, and F. A. G. Dumortier, A comparative study of self-adaptive long-range predictive control methods, *Automatica*, **24**(2), 149–163 (1988).

[23] B. E. Ydstie, Extended horizon adaptive control. In *IFAC World Congress* (1985).

[24] B. W. Bequette, Nonlinear control of chemical processes: a review, *Ind. Eng. Chem. Res.*, **30**, 1391–1413 (1991).

[25] M. A. Henson, Nonlinear model predictive control: current status and future directions, *Comput. Chem. Eng.*, **23**, 187–202 (1998).

[26] J. L. Figueroa, Piecewise linear models in model predictive control, *Lat. Am. Appl. Res.*, **31**(4), 309–315 (2001).

[27] H. O. Wang, K. Tanaka, and M. F. Griffin, An approach to fuzzy control of nonlinear systems: stability and design issues, *IEEE Trans. Fuzzy Syst.*, **4**(1), 14–23 (1996).

[28] M. S. Padin and J. L. Figueroa, Use of CPWL approximations in the design of a numerical nonlinear regulator, *IEEE Trans. Autom. Control*, **45**(6), 1175–1180 (2000).

[29] F. J. Doyle, T. A. Ogunnaike, and R. K. Pearson, Nonlinear model-based control using second-order volterra models, *Automatica*, **31**, 697–714 (1995).

[30] N. Li, S. Li, and Y. Xi, Multi-model predictive control based on the Takagi-Sugeno fuzzy models: a case study, *Inf. Sci. Inf. Comput. Sci.*, **165**(3–4), 247–263 (2004).

[31] J. A. Roubos, S. Mollov, R. Babuska, and H. B. Verbruggen, Fuzzy model-based predictive control using Takagi-Sugeno models, *Int. J. Approximate Reasoning*, **22**(1–2), 3–30 (1999).

[32] J. Abonyi, L. Nagy, and F. Szeifert, Fuzzy model-based predictive control by instantaneous linearization, *Fuzzy Sets Syst.*, **120**(1), 109–122 (2001).

[33] I. Škrjanc and D. Matko, Predictive functional control based on fuzzy model for heat-exchanger pilot plant, *IEEE Trans. Fuzzy Syst.*, **8**(6), 705–712 (2000).

[34] D. Andone and A. Hossu, Predictive control based on fuzzy model for steam generator. In *Proceedings of the IEEE International Conference on Fuzzy Systems*, pp. 1245–1250 (2004).

[35] J.-H. Kim and U.-Y. Huh, Fuzzy model based predictive control. In *Proceedings of the IEEE International Conference on Fuzzy Systems*, pp. 405–409 (1998).

[36] H.-R. Sun, P. Han, and S.-M. Jiao, A predictive control strategy based on fuzzy system. In *Proceedings of the 2004 IEEE International Conference on Information Reuse and Integration*, pp. 549–552 (2004).

[37] S. Blažič and I. Škrjanc, Design and stability analysis of fuzzy model-based predictive control–a case study, *J. Intell. Rob. Syst.*, **49**(3), 279–292 (2007).

[38] D. Dovžan and I. Škrjanc, Control of mineral wool thickness using predictive functional control, *Rob. Comput. Integr. Manuf.*, **28**(3), 344–350 (2012).

[39] I. Škrjanc and G. Klančar, A comparison of continuous and discrete tracking-error model-based predictive control for mobile robots, *Rob. Auton. Syst.*, **87**, 177–187 (2017).

[40] R. Baždarić, D. Vončina, and I. Škrjanc, Comparison of novel approaches to the predictive control of a DC-DC boost converter, based on heuristics, *Energies*, **11**(12), 3300 (2018).

[41] K. Tanaka, T. Ikeda, and H. O. Wang, Robust stabilization of a class of uncertain nonlinear systems via fuzzy control: quadratic stabilizability, h$^\infty$ control theory, and linear matrix inequalities, *IEEE Trans. Fuzzy Syst.*, **4**(1), 1–13 (1996).

[42] D. J. Leith and W. E. Leithead, Gain-scheduled and nonlinear systems: dynamics analysis by velocity-based linearization families, *Int. J. Control*, **70**(2), 289–317 (1998).

[43] D. J. Leith and W. E. Leithead, Analytical framework for blended model systems using local linear models, *Int. J. Control*, **72**(7–8), 605–619 (1999).

[44] J. D. Morningred, B. E. Paden, and D. A. Mellichamp, An adaptive nonlinear predictive controller, *Chem. Eng. Sci.*, **47**, 755–762 (1992).

[45] M. A. Henson and D. E. Seborg, Input-output linearization of general processes, *AIChE J.*, **36**, 1753 (1990).

[46] T. K. Moon and W. C. Stirling, *Mathematical Methods and Algorithms for Signal Processing* (Prentice Hall, 1999).

[47] M. Krstić, I. Kanellakopoulos, and P. Kokotović, *Nonlinear and Adaptive Control Design* (John Wiley and Sons, 1995).

[48] T. J. Procyk and E. H. Mamdani, A linguistic self-organizing process controller, *Automatica*, **15**, 15–30 (1979).

[49] J. R. Layne and K. M. Passino, Fuzzy model reference learning control for cargo ship steering, *IEEE Control Syst. Mag.*, **13**, 23–34 (1993).

[50] L. X. Wang and J. M. Mendel, Fuzzy basis functions, universal approximation, and orthogonal least-squares learning, *IEEE Trans. Neural Networks*, **3**, 807–881 (1992).

[51] Y. Tang, N. Zhang, and Y. Li, Stable fuzzy adaptive control for a class of nonlinear systems, *Fuzzy Sets Syst.*, **104**, 279–288 (1999).

[52] H. Pomares, I. Rojas, J. González, F. Rojas, M. Damas, and F. J. Fernández, A two-stage approach to self-learning direct fuzzy controllers, *Int. J. Approximate Reasoning*, **29**(3), 267–289 (2002). ISSN 0888-613X.

[53] P. A. Ioannou and J. Sun, *Robust Adaptive Control* (Prentice-Hall, 1996).

[54] S. Tong, T. Wang, and J. T. Tang, Fuzzy adaptive output tracking control of nonlinear systems, *Fuzzy Sets Syst.*, **111**, 169–182 (2000).

[55] K.-M. Koo, Stable adaptive fuzzy controller with time varying dead-zone, *Fuzzy Sets Syst.*, **121**, 161–168 (2001).

[56] S. Ge and J. Wang, Robust adaptive neural control for a class of perturbed strict feedback nonlinear systems, *IEEE Trans. Neural Networks*, **13**(6), 1409–1419 (2002).

[57] S. Tong and Y. Li, Adaptive fuzzy output feedback tracking backstepping control of strict-feedback nonlinear systems with unknown dead zones, *IEEE Trans. Fuzzy Syst.*, **20**(1), 168–180 (2012).

[58] S. Blažič, I. Škrjanc, and D. Matko, Globally stable direct fuzzy model reference adaptive control, *Fuzzy Sets Syst.*, **139**(1), 3–33 (2003).

[59] S. Blažič, I. Škrjanc, and D. Matko, A new fuzzy adaptive law with leakage. In *2012 IEEE Conference on Evolving and Adaptive Intelligent Systems (EAIS)*, pp. 47–50 (2012).

[60] S. Blažič, I. Škrjanc, and D. Matko, A robust fuzzy adaptive law for evolving control systems, *Evolving Syst.*, pp. 1–8 (2013). doi: 10.1007/s12530-013-9084-7.

[61] G. Andonovski, P. Angelov, S. Blažič, and I. Škrjanc, A practical implementation of robust evolving cloud-based controller with normalized data space for heat-exchanger plant, *Appl. Soft Comput.*, **48**, 29–38 (2016).

[62] G. Andonovski, A. Bayas, D. Saez, S. Blažič, and I. Škrjanc, Robust evolving cloud-based control for the distributed solar collector field. In *2016 IEEE International Conference on Fuzzy Systems (FUZZ-IEEE)*, pp. 1570–1577 (2016). doi: 10.1109/FUZZ-IEEE.2016.7737877.

[63] G. Andonovski, P. Angelov, S. Blažič, and I. Škrjanc, Robust evolving cloud-based controller (RECCo). In *2017 Evolving and Adaptive Intelligent Systems (EAIS)*, pp. 1–6 (2017).

[64] S. Blažič and A. Zdešar, An implementation of an evolving fuzzy controller. In *2017 Evolving and Adaptive Intelligent Systems (EAIS)*, pp. 1–7, 2017.

[65] S. Blažič, I. Škrjanc, and D. Matko, Adaptive law with a new leakage term, *IET Control Theory Appl.*, **4**(9), 1533–1542 (2010).

Chapter 19

Reinforcement Learning with Applications in Autonomous Control and Game Theory

Kyriakos G. Vamvoudakis*,§, *Frank L. Lewis*†,¶, *and Draguna Vrabie*‡,∥

*Daniel Guggenheim School of Aerospace Engineering
Georgia Institute of Technology, GA, 30332, USA
†University of Texas at Arlington Research Institute
University of Texas, Arlington, TX 76118, USA
‡Pacific Northwest National Laboratory, WA 99352, USA
§kyriakos@gatech.edu.
¶lewis@uta.edu
∥draguna.vrabie@pnnl.gov

This book chapter showcases how ideas from control systems engineering, game theory, and computational intelligence have been combined to obtain a new class of control and game-theoretic techniques. Since reinforcement learning involves modifying the control policy based on responses from an unknown environment, we have the initial feeling that it is closely related to adaptive control. Moreover, reinforcement learning methods allow learning of optimal and game-theoretic solutions relative to prescribed cost/payoff metrics by measuring data in real time along system trajectories; hence, it also has relations to optimal feedback control. This chapter is an exposition of the research results that clarify these relations.

19.1. Background

Adaptive control has been one of the most widespread techniques for feedback control of modern engineered systems since the 1960s. Its effective and reliable use in aerospace systems, the industrial process industry, vehicle control, communications, and elsewhere is firmly established. Optimal control is equally widespread since it enables the design of feedback controllers with the purpose of minimizing energy, fuel consumption, performance time, or other premium quantities.

Optimal controllers are normally designed offline by solving the Hamilton–Jacobi–Bellman (HJB) equations, for example, the Riccati equation, using the complete knowledge of the system dynamics. Optimal control policies for nonlinear systems can be obtained by solving nonlinear HJB equations that cannot usually be solved. By contrast, adaptive controllers learn online to control unknown systems using data measured in real time along the system trajectories. Adaptive controllers are generally not optimal in the sense of minimizing user-prescribed performance functions. Indirect adaptive controllers have been designed that use system identification techniques to first identify the system parameters, and then use the obtained model to solve optimal design equations [1]. It is shown that adaptive controllers may satisfy certain inverse optimality conditions [2]. The design of adaptive controllers that learn online, in real time, the solutions to user-prescribed optimal control problems can be studied by means of reinforcement learning (RL) and adaptive dynamic programming techniques, and forms the subject of this chapter, which is a condensation of two papers that appeared in the *IEEE Control Systems Magazine* [3, 4].

The real-time learning of optimal policies for unknown systems occurs in nature. The limits within which living organisms can survive are often quite narrow and the resources available to most species are meager. Therefore, most organisms occurring in nature act in an optimal fashion to conserve resources while achieving their goals. Living organisms learn by acting on their environment, observing and evaluating the resulting reward stimulus, and adjusting their actions accordingly to improve the reward.

Inspired by natural learning mechanisms, that is, those occurring in biological organisms including animals and humans, RL techniques for machine learning and artificial intelligence have been developed and used mainly in the computational intelligence community [5–9] for autonomy [10]. The purpose of this chapter is to give an exposition of the usefulness of RL techniques for designing feedback policies for engineered systems, where optimal actions may be driven by objectives such as minimum fuel, minimum energy, minimum risk, maximum reward, and so on. We specifically focus on a family of techniques known as approximate or adaptive dynamic programming (ADP) [11–16, 19]. We show that RL ideas can be used to design a family of adaptive control algorithms that converge in real time to optimal control solutions while using data measured along the system trajectories. Such techniques may be referred to as optimal adaptive control. The use of RL techniques provides optimal control solutions for linear or nonlinear systems using adaptive control techniques. In effect, RL methods allow the solution of HJB equations, or for linear quadratic design, the Riccati equation, online and without knowing the full system dynamics.

In machine learning, RL [5, 7, 8] refers to the set of optimization problems that involve an actor or an agent that interacts with its environment and modifies its actions, or control policies, based on stimuli received in response to its actions.

RL is based on evaluative information from the environment and could be called action-based learning.

RL implies a cause-and-effect relationship between actions and reward or punishment. It implies goal-directed behavior at least insofar as the agent has an understanding of reward versus lack of reward or punishment. The idea behind RL is that of modifying actions or behavior policy in order to reduce the prediction error between anticipated future rewards and actual performance as computed based on observed rewards. The RL algorithms are constructed on the idea that effective control decisions must be remembered, by means of a reinforcement signal, such that they become more likely to be used a second time. Although the idea originates from experimental animal learning, where it is observed that the dopamine neurotransmitter acts as a reinforcement informational signal that favors learning at the level of the neuron [20, 21], RL is strongly connected, from a theoretical point of view, with adaptive control and optimal control methods.

Although RL algorithms have been widely used to solve the optimal regulation problems, some research efforts considered solving the optimal tracking control problem for discrete-time [22] and continuous-time systems [24, 25]. Moreover, existing methods require exact knowledge of the system dynamics a priori while finding the feedforward part of the control input using the dynamic inversion concept. In order to attain the required knowledge of the system dynamics, in [24], a plant model was first identified and then an RL-based optimal tracking controller was synthesized using the identified model.

One class of RL methods is based on the actor-critic structure shown in Figure 19.1, where an actor component applies an action, or control policy, to the environment, and a critic component assesses the value of that action. Based on this assessment of the value, one of several schemes can then be used to modify or improve the action, or control policy, in the sense that the new policy yields a value that is improved relative to the previous value. The learning mechanism supported by the actor–critic structure implies two steps, namely, policy evaluation, executed by the critic, followed by policy improvement, performed by the actor. The policy evaluation step is performed by observing from the environment the results of applying current actions.

It is of interest to study RL systems that have an actor–critic structure wherein the critic assesses the value of current policies based on some sort of optimality criteria [7, 17, 19, 26]. It is worth noting that the actor–critic structure is similar to the one encountered in adaptive control. However, adaptive control schemes make use of system identification mechanisms to first obtain a model of the system dynamics and then use this model to guide adaptation of the parameters of the controller/actor. In contrast, in the optimal RL algorithm case the learning process is moved to a higher level, having no longer as object of interest the details of a

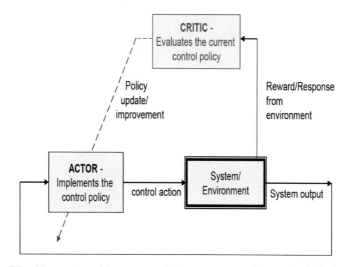

Figure 19.1:   RL with an actor-critic structure. This structure provides methods for learning optimal control solutions online based on data measured along the system trajectories.

system's dynamics, but a performance index that quantifies how close to optimality the closed loop control system operates. In this scheme, RL is a means of learning optimal behaviors by observing the real-time responses from the environment to non-optimal control policies. Two new research monographs on this subject are [27, 28].

The intention of this book chapter is to present the main ideas and algorithms of RL and approximate dynamic programming and to show how they are applied in the design of optimal adaptive feedback controllers. A few connections are also shown between RL and decision and control of systems distributed over communication graphs, including shortest path problems, relaxation methods, and cooperative control. In fact, we show that RL provides connections between optimal control, adaptive control, and cooperative control and decisions on finite graphs. This book chapter presents an expository development of ideas from RL and ADP and their applications in automatic control systems. Surveys of ADP are given in [29–41].

19.2. Markov Decision Processes and Stochasticity

A framework for studying RL is provided by Markov decision processes (MDP). In fact, dynamical decision problems can be cast into the framework of MDP. Included are feedback control systems for human engineered systems, feedback regulation mechanisms for population balance and survival of species [42], the balance of power between nations, decision-making in multi-player games, and economic mechanisms for the regulation of global financial markets. Therefore, we provide the development of MDP here.

Consider the MDP (X, U, P, R) where X is a set of states and U is a set of actions or controls. The transition probabilities $P : X \times U \times X \to [0, 1]$ give, for each state $x \in X$ and action $u \in U$, the conditional probability $P^u_{x,x'} = \Pr\{x'|x, u\}$ of transitioning to state $x' \in X$, given the MDP is in state x and takes action u. The cost function $R : X \times U \times X \to \mathbb{R}$ gives the expected immediate cost $R^u_{x,x'}$ paid after transition to state $x' \in X$, given the MDP starts in state $x \in X$ and takes action $u \in U$. The Markov property refers to the fact that transition probabilities $P^u_{x,x'}$ depend only on the current state x and not on the history of how the MDP attained that state.

The basic problem for MDP is to find a mapping $\pi : X \times U \to [0, 1]$ that gives for each state x and action u the conditional probability $\pi(x, u) = \Pr\{u|x\}$ of taking action u, given the MDP is in state x. Such a mapping is termed a closed-loop control or action strategy or policy. The strategy or policy is called stochastic or mixed if there is a non-zero probability of selecting more than one control when in state x. We can view mixed strategies as probability distribution vectors having as component i the probability of selecting the ith control action while in state $x \in X$. If the mapping $\pi : X \times U \to [0, 1]$ admits only one control with probability 1, then in every state x the mapping is called a deterministic policy. Then $\pi(x, u) = \Pr\{u|x\}$ corresponds to a function mapping states into controls $\mu(x) : X \to U$.

19.2.1. *Optimal Sequential Decision Problems*

Dynamical systems evolve causally through time. Therefore, we consider sequential decision problems and impose a discrete stage index k such that the MDP takes an action and changes states at non-negative integer stage values k. The stages may correspond to time or more generally to sequences of events. We refer to the stage value as the time. Denote state values and actions at time k by x_k, u_k. MDP evolves in discrete time. It is often desirable for human engineered systems to be optimal in terms of conserving resources such as cost, time, fuel, and energy. Thus, the notion of optimality should be captured in selecting control policies for MDP. Define therefore a stage cost at time k by $r_k \equiv r_k(x_k, u_k, x_{k+1})$. Then $R^u_{x,x'} = E\{r_k | x_k = x, u_k = u, x_{k+1} = x'\}$, with $E\{\cdot\}$ being the expected value operator. Define a performance index as the sum of future costs over the time interval $[k, k + T]$, $T > 0$,

$$J_{k,T} = \sum_{i=0}^{T} \gamma^i r_{k+1} \equiv \sum_{i=k}^{k+T} \gamma^{i-k} r_i, \tag{19.1}$$

where $0 \le \gamma < 1$ is a discount factor that reduces the weight of costs incurred further in the future.

Usage of MDP in the fields of computational intelligence and economics usually considers r_k as a reward incurred at time k, also known as utility and $J_{k,T}$ as a discounted return, also known as strategic reward. We refer instead to state costs and discounted future costs to be consistent with objectives in the control of dynamical systems. For convenience we call r_k the utility.

Consider that an agent selects a control policy $\pi_k(x_k, u_k)$ and uses it at each stage k of the MDP. We are primarily interested in stationary policies, where the conditional probabilities $\pi_k(x_k, u_k)$ are independent of k. Then $\pi_k(x, u) \equiv \pi(x, u) = \Pr\{u|x\}$, $\forall k$. Non-stationary deterministic policies have the form $\pi = \{\mu_0, \mu_1, \dots\}$, where each entry is a function $\mu_k(x) : X \to U; k = \{0, 1, \dots\}$. Stationary deterministic policies are independent of time so that $\pi = \{\mu, \mu, \dots\}$.

Select a fixed stationary policy $\pi(x, u) = \Pr\{u|x\}$. Then the "closed-loop" MDP reduces to a Markov chain with state space X. That is, the transition probabilities between states are fixed with no further freedom of choice of actions. The transition probabilities of this Markov chain are given by

$$p_{x,x'} \equiv P^{\pi}_{x,x'} = \sum_u \Pr\{x'|x, u\}\Pr\{u|x\} = \sum_u \pi(x, u) P^u_{x,x'}, \tag{19.2}$$

where the Chapman–Kolmogorov identity is used [46].

A Markov chain is ergodic if all the states are positive recurrent and aperiodic [46]. Under the assumption that the Markov chain corresponding to each policy, with transition probabilities given as in (19.2), is ergodic, it can be shown that every MDP has a stationary deterministic optimal policy [31, 47]. Then, for a given policy, there exists a stationary distribution $p_{\pi}(x)$ over X that gives the steady-state probability that the Markov chain is in state x.

The value of a policy is defined as the conditional expected value of future cost when starting in state x at time k and following the policy $\pi(x, u)$ thereafter,

$$V^{\pi}_k(x) = E_{\pi}\{J_{k,T}|x_k = x\} = E_{\pi}\left\{\sum_{i=k}^{k+T} \gamma^{i-k} r_i | x_k = x\right\}, \tag{19.3}$$

where $V^{\pi}(x)$ is known as the value function for policy $\pi(x, u)$.

The main objective of MDP is to determine a policy $\pi(x, u)$ to minimize the expected future cost,

$$\pi^{\star}(x, u) = \arg\min_{\pi} V^{\pi}_k(x) = \arg\min_{\pi} E_{\pi}\left\{\sum_{i=k}^{k+T} \gamma^{i-k} r_i | x_k = x\right\}. \tag{19.4}$$

This policy is termed as optimal policy, and the corresponding optimal value is given as,

$$V^{\star}_k(x) = \min_{\pi} V^{\pi}_k(x) = \min_{\pi} E_{\pi}\left\{\sum_{i=k}^{k+T} \gamma^{i-k} r_i | x_k = x\right\}. \tag{19.5}$$

In computational intelligence and economics, the interest is in utilities and rewards and the interest is in maximizing the expected performance index.

19.2.2. A Backward Recursion for the Value

By using the Chapman–Kolmogorov identity and the Markov property, we can write the value of policy $\pi(x, u)$ as,

$$V_k(x) = \sum_u \pi(x, u) \sum_{x'} P^u_{x,x'}[R^u_{x,x'} + \gamma V^\pi_{k+1}(x')]. \tag{19.6}$$

This equation provides a backwards recursion for the value at time k in terms of the value at time $k + 1$.

19.2.3. Dynamic Programming

The optimal cost can be written as

$$V^\star_k = \min_\pi V^\pi_k(x) = \min_\pi \sum_u \pi(x, u) \sum_{x'} P^u_{x,x'}[R^u_{x,x'} + \gamma V^\pi_{k+1}(x')]. \tag{19.7}$$

Bellman's optimality principle [32] states, "An optimal policy has the property that no matter what the previous control actions have been, the remaining controls constitute an optimal policy with regard to the state resulting from those previous controls." Therefore, we can write

$$V^\star_k = \min_\pi V^\pi_k(x) = \min_\pi \sum_u \pi(x, u) \sum_{x'} P^u_{x,x'}[R^u_{x,x'} + \gamma V^\star_{k+1}(x')]. \tag{19.8}$$

Suppose an arbitrary control u is now applied at time k and the optimal policy is applied from time $k + 1$ on. Then, Bellman's optimality principle says that the optimal control policy at time k is given by

$$\pi^\star(x, u) = \arg\min_\pi \sum_u \pi(x, u) \sum_{x'} P^u_{x,x'}[R^u_{x,x'} + \gamma V^\star_{k+1}(x')]. \tag{19.9}$$

Under the assumption that the Markov chain corresponding to each policy with transition probabilities given as in (19.2), is ergodic, every MDP has a stationary deterministic optimal policy. Then, we can equivalently minimize the conditional expectation over all actions u in state x. Therefore,

$$V_k^\star = \min_u \sum_{x'} P_{x,x'}^u [R_{x,x'}^u + \gamma V_{k+1}^\star(x')], \qquad (19.10)$$

$$u_k^\star = \arg\min_u \sum_{x'} P_{x,x'}^u [R_{x,x'}^u + \gamma V_{k+1}^\star(x')]. \qquad (19.11)$$

The backwards recursion (19.10) forms the basis for dynamic programming which gives offline methods for working backwards in time to determine optimal policies [5]. DP is an offline procedure [48] for finding the optimal value and optimal policies that requires knowledge of the complete system dynamics in the form of transition probabilities $P_{x,x'}^u = \Pr\{x'|x, u\}$ and expected costs, $R_{x,x'}^u = E\{r_k|x_k = x, u_k = u, x_{k+1} = x'\}$.

19.2.4. *Bellman Equation and Bellman Optimality Equation*

Dynamic programming is a backwards in time method for finding the optimal value and policy. By contrast, RL is concerned with finding optimal policies based on causal experience by executing sequential decisions that improve control actions based on the observed results of using a current policy. This procedure requires the derivation of methods for finding optimal values and optimal policies that can be executed forward in time. The key to this is the Bellman equation, which we now develop. References for this subsection include [7, 8, 19, 30]. To derive forward-in-time methods for finding optimal values and optimal policies, set now the time horizon T to $+\infty$ and define the infinite-horizon cost,

$$J_k = \sum_{i=0}^{\infty} \gamma^i r_{k+1} = \sum_{i=k}^{\infty} \gamma^{i-k} r_i. \qquad (19.12)$$

The associated infinite-horizon value function for *policy* $\pi(x, u)$ is,

$$V^\pi(x) = E_\pi\{\gamma^{i-k} r_i|x_k = x\}. \qquad (19.13)$$

By using (19.6) with $T = \infty$ it is seen that the value function for policy $\pi(x, u)$ satisfies the Bellman equation,

$$V^\pi(x) = \sum_u \pi(x, u) \sum_{x'} P_{x,x'}^u [R_{x,x'}^u + \gamma V^\pi(x')]. \qquad (19.14)$$

The key to deriving this equation is that the same value function appears on both sides, which is due to the fact that the infinite-horizon cost is used. Therefore, the Bellman equation (19.14) can be interpreted as a consistency equation that must be satisfied by the value function at each time stage. It expresses a relation between the current value of being in state x and the value of being in next state x' given that policy $\pi(x, u)$ is used. The solution to the Bellman equation is the value given by the infinite sum in (19.13).

The Bellman equation (19.14) is the starting point for developing a family of reinforcement learning algorithms for finding optimal policies by using causal experiences received stage-wise forward in time. The Bellman optimality equation (19.8) involves the minimum operator, and so does not contain any specific policy $\pi(x, u)$. Its solution relies on knowing the dynamics in the form of transition probabilities. By contrast, the form of the Bellman equation is simpler than that of the optimality equation and is easier to solve. The solution to the Bellman equation yields the value function of a specific policy $\pi(x, u)$. As such, the Bellman equation is well suited to the actor–critic method of RL shown in Figure 19.1. It is shown subsequently that the Bellman equation provides methods for implementing the critic in Figure 19.1, which is responsible for evaluating the performance of the specific current policy. Two key ingredients remain to be put in place. First, it is shown that methods known as policy iteration and value iteration use the Bellman equation to solve optimal control problems forward in time. Second, by approximating the value function in (19.14) by a parametric structure, these methods can be implemented online using standard adaptive control system identification algorithms such as recursive least-squares.

In the context of using the Bellman equation (19.14) for RL, $V^\pi(x)$ may be considered a predicted performance $\sum_u \pi(x, u) \sum_{x'} P^u_{x,x'} R^u_{x,x'}$, the observed one-step reward and $V^\pi(x')$ a current estimate of future behavior. Such notions can be capitalized on in the subsequent discussion of temporal different learning, which uses them to apply adaptive control algorithms that can learn optimal behavior online in real-time applications.

Given that the MDP is finite and has N states then the Bellman equation (19.14) is a system of N simultaneous linear equations for the value $V^\pi(x)$ of being in each state x given the current policy $\pi(x, u)$.

The optimal value satisfies,

$$V^\star(x) = \min_\pi V^\pi(x) = \min_\pi \sum_u \pi(x, u) \sum_{x'} P^u_{x,x'} [R^u_{x,x'} + \gamma \, V^\pi(x)], \qquad (19.15)$$

while Bellman's optimality principle gives the Bellman optimality equation,

$$V^\star(x) = \min_\pi V^\pi(x) = \min_\pi \sum_u \pi(x, u) \sum_{x'} P^u_{x,x'} [R^u_{x,x'} + \gamma \, V^\star(x)]. \qquad (19.16)$$

Now under the assumption of ergodicity on the Markov chains corresponding to each action/policy, the Bellman optimality equation (19.16) can be written as,

$$V^\star(x) = \min_u \sum_{x'} P^u_{x,x'} [R^u_{x,x'} + \gamma \, V^\star(x')], \qquad (19.17)$$

which is known as the HJB equation in control systems. The optimal control is given by,

$$u^{\star} = \arg\min_{u} \sum_{x'} P_{x,x'}^{u}[R_{x,x'}^{u} + \gamma \, V^{\star}(x')]. \tag{19.18}$$

Equations (19.17) and (19.18) can be written in the context of the feedback control of dynamical systems. In the linear quadratic regulator (LQR) case, the Bellman equation (19.14) becomes a Lyapunov equation and the optimality equation (19.16) becomes the well-known algebraic Riccati equation.

We shall see, in the subsequent subsection, two different algorithmic methods to solve the Bellman equation (19.14).

19.2.5. *Policy Iteration and Value Iteration*

Given a current policy $\pi(x, u)$, its value (19.13) can be determined by solving (19.14). This procedure is known as policy evaluation. Moreover, given the value for some policy $\pi(x, u)$ we can always use it to find another policy that is at least no worse. This step is known as policy improvement. Specifically, suppose that $V^{\pi}(x)$ satisfies (19.14). Then define a new policy $\pi'(x, u)$ by

$$\pi'(x, u) = \arg\min_{\pi} \sum_{\pi'} P_{x,x'}^{u}[R_{x,x'}^{u} + \gamma \, V^{\pi}(x')] \tag{19.19}$$

and it can be shown that the value is monotonically decreasing [7, 31]. The policy (19.19) is said to be greedy with respect to the value function. In the special case that $V^{\pi'}(x) = V^{\pi}(x)$ in (19.19), the value and the policy satisfy Eq. (19.17) and (19.18). In computational intelligence, "greedy" refers to quantities determined by optimizing over short or one-step horizons, without regard to potential impacts far into the future. Now we will form the basis for the policy and value iteration algorithms in the form of two steps, a policy evaluation and a policy improvement step. The policy evaluation step can be written as

$$V^{\pi}(x) = \sum_{u} \pi(x, u) \sum_{\pi'} P_{x,x'}^{u}[R_{x,x'}^{u} + \gamma \, V^{\pi}(x')], \quad \forall x \in S \subseteq X, \tag{19.20}$$

and the policy improvement step as

$$\pi'(x, u) = \arg\min_{\pi} \sum_{\pi'} P_{x,x'}^{u}[R_{x,x'}^{u} + \gamma \, V^{\pi}(x')], \quad \forall x \in S \subseteq X. \tag{19.21}$$

Here, S is a suitably selected subspace of the state space, to be discussed later. We call an application of (19.20) followed by an application of (19.21) one step.

This terminology is in contrast to the decision time stage k defined above. At each step of such algorithms, we obtain a policy that is no worse than the previous policy. Therefore, it is not difficult to prove convergence under fairly mild conditions to the optimal value and optimal policy. Most such proofs are based on the Banach Fixed Point Theorem. Note that (19.17) is a fixed point equation for $V^\star(\cdot)$. Then the two equations (19.20) and (19.21) define an associated map that can be shown under mild conditions to be a contraction map [8, 31, 49] which converges to the solution of (19.17). A large family of algorithms is available that implement the policy evaluation and policy improvement procedures in different ways, or interleave them differently, or select subspace $S \subseteq X$ in different ways, to determine the optimal value and optimal policy. The relevance of this discussion for feedback control systems is that these two procedures can be implemented for dynamical systems online in real time by observing the data measured along the system trajectories. The result is a family of adaptive control algorithms that converge to optimal control solutions. Such algorithms are of the actor–critic class of RL systems, as shown in Figure 19.1. There, a critic agent evaluates the current control policy using methods based on (19.20). After this evaluation is completed, the action is updated by an actor agent based on (19.21).

One method of RL for using (19.20) and (19.21) to find the optimal value and policy is called policy iteration and is described next.

Algorithm 19.1: Policy Iteration

1: **procedure**
2:    Given an initial admissible policy π_0
3:    **while** $\| V^{\pi^{(j)}} - V^{\pi^{(j-1)}} \| \ge \epsilon_{ac}$ **do**
4:       Solve for the value $V_j(x)$ using Bellman's equation

$$V_j(x) = \sum_u \pi_j(x, u) \sum_{x'} P_{x,x'}^u [R_{x,x'}^u + \gamma V_j(x')], \forall x \in X$$

5:       Update the control policy $\pi_{(j+1)}$ using

$$\pi_{j+1}(x, u) = \arg \min_\pi \sum_{\pi'} P_{x,x'}^u [R_{x,x'}^u + \gamma V_j(x')], \forall x \in X$$

6:       $j := j + 1$
7:    **end while**
8: **end procedure**

In Algorithm 19.1, ϵ_{ac} is a small number used to terminate the algorithm when two consecutive value functions differ by less than ϵ_{ac}.

At each step j the policy iteration algorithm determines the solution of the Bellman equation to compute the value $V_j(x)$ of using the current policy $\pi_j(x, u)$.

This value corresponds to the infinite sum (19.13) for the current policy. Then the policy is improved. The steps are continued until there is no change in the value or the policy. Note that j is not the time or stage index k, but a policy iteration step iteration index. As detailed in the next sections, policy iteration can be implemented for dynamical systems online in real time by observing data measured along the system trajectories. Data for multiple times k are needed to solve the Bellman equation at each step j. The policy iteration algorithm must be suitably initialized to converge. The initial policy $\pi_0(x, u)$ and value V_0 must be selected so that $V_1 \leq V_0$. Then, for finite Markov chains with N states, policy iteration converges in a finite number of steps, less than or equal to N, because there are only a finite number of policies [31].

If the MDP is finite and has N states, then the policy evaluation equation is a system of N simultaneous linear equations, one for each state. Instead of directly solving the Bellman equation, it can be solved by an iterative policy evaluation procedure.

A second method for using (19.20) and (19.21) in RL is value iteration.

Algorithm 19.2: Value Iteration

1: **procedure**
2:     Given an initial policy π_0
3:     **while** $|| V^{\pi^j} - V^{\pi^{(j-1)}} || \geq \epsilon_{ac}$ **do**
4:       Solve for the value $V_j(x)$ using Bellman's equation

$$V_{j+1}(x) = \sum_u \pi_j(x, u) \sum_{x'} P_{x,x'}^u [R_{x,x'}^u + \gamma V_j(x')], \forall x \in S_j \subseteq X$$

5:       Update the policy π_{j+1} using

$$\pi_{j+1}(x, u) = \arg \min_\pi \sum_{\pi'} P_{x,x'}^u [R_{x,x'}^u + \gamma V_j(x')], \forall x \in S_j \subseteq X$$

6:       $j := j + 1$
7:     **end while**
8: **end procedure**

In Algorithm 19.2, ϵ_{ac} is a small number used to terminate the algorithm when two consecutive value functions differ by less than ϵ_{ac}.

In subsequent sections, we show how to implement value iteration for dynamical systems online in real time by observing data measured along the system trajectories. Data for multiple times k are needed to solve the Bellman equation for each step j. Standard value iteration takes the update set as $S_j = X$, for all j. That is, the value and policy are updated for all states simultaneously. Asynchronous value iteration methods perform the updates on only a subset of the states at each step. In the extreme case, updates can be performed on only one state at each step.

It is shown in [31] that standard value iteration, which has $S_j = X$, $\forall j$, converges for finite MDP for all initial conditions when the discount factor satisfies $0 < \gamma < 1$. When $S_j = X$, $\forall j$ and $\gamma = 1$ an absorbing state is added and a "properness" assumption is needed to guarantee convergence to the optimal value. When a single state is selected for value and policy updates at each step, the algorithm converges, for all choices of initial value, to the optimal cost and policy if each state is selected for update infinitely often. More universal algorithms result if value update is performed multiple times for different choices of S_j prior to a policy improvement. Then, it is required that the updates are performed infinitely, often for each state, and a monotonicity assumption must be satisfied by the initial starting value.

Considering (19.16) as a fixed point equation, value iteration is based on the associated iterative map, which can be shown under certain conditions to be a contraction map.

In contrast to policy iteration, which converges under certain conditions in a finite number of steps, value iteration usually takes an infinite number of steps to converge [31]. Consider finite MDP and consider the transition probability graph having probabilities (19.2) for the Markov chain corresponding to an optimal policy $\pi^*(x, u)$. If this graph is acyclic for some $\pi^*(x, u)$, then value iteration converges in at most N steps when initialized with a large value. Having in mind the dynamic programming equation (19.6) and examining the value iteration, value update $V_j(x')$ can be interpreted as an approximation or estimate for the future stage cost-to-go from the future state x'. Those algorithms wherein the future cost estimates are themselves costs or values for some policy are called roll-out algorithms in [31]. Such policies are forward looking and self-correcting. It is shown that these methods can be used to derive algorithms for receding horizon control [50]. MDP, policy iteration, and value iteration are closely tied to optimal and adaptive control.

19.2.6. *Generalized Policy Iteration*

In policy iteration the system of linear equations (see Algorithm 19.1) is completely solved at each step to compute the value (19.13) of using the current policy $\pi_j(x, u)$. This solution can be accomplished by running iterations of the policy evaluation step until convergence. By contrast, in value iteration one takes only one iteration in the value update step. Generalized policy iteration algorithms make several iterations in their value update step. Usually, policy iteration converges to the optimal value in fewer steps j since it does more work in solving equations at each step. On the other hand, value iteration is the easiest to implement as it only takes one iteration of a recursion. Generalized policy iteration provides a suitable compromise between computational complexity and convergence speed. Generalized policy iteration is a special case of the value iteration algorithm given above, where we select $S_j = X, \forall j$, and perform value update multiple times before each policy update.

19.2.7. Q-Learning

The conditional expected value in (19.10), at iteration k is

$$Q_k^\star(x, u) = \sum_{x'} P_{x,x'}^u [R_{x,x'}^u + \gamma V_{k+1}^\star(x')]$$

$$= E_\pi \{r_k + \gamma V_{k+1}^\star(x') | x_k = x, u_k = u\} \qquad (19.22)$$

and is known as optimal Q function [51, 52]. In other words, the Q function is equal to the expected return for taking an arbitrary action u at time k in state x and thereafter following an optimal policy. The Q function is a function of the current state x and the action u.

In terms of the Q function, the Bellman optimality equation has the particularly simple form,

$$V_k^\star(x) = \min_u Q_k^\star(x, u), \qquad (19.23)$$

and

$$u_k^\star = \arg\min_u Q_k^\star(x, u), \qquad (19.24)$$

Given some fixed policy $\pi(x, u)$, define the Q function for that policy as,

$$Q_k^\pi(x, u) = E_\pi \{r_k + \gamma V_{k+1}^\pi(x') | x_k = x, u_k = u\}$$

$$= \sum_{x'} P_{x,x'}^u [R_{x,x'}^u + \gamma V_{k+1}^\pi(x')] \qquad (19.25)$$

where this function is equal to the expected return for taking an arbitrary action u at time k in state x and thereafter following the existing policy $\pi(x, u)$.

Note that $V_k^\pi(x) = Q_k^\pi(x, \pi(x, u))$; hence (19.25) can be written as the backwards recursion in the Q function,

$$Q_k^\pi(x, u) = \sum_{x'} P_{x,x'}^u [R_{x,x'}^u + \gamma Q_{k+1}^\pi(x', \pi(x', u'))]. \qquad (19.26)$$

The Q function is a two-dimensional function of both the current state x and the action u. By contrast, the value function is a 1-dimensional function of the state. For finite MDP, the Q function can be stored as a 2D lookup table at each state/action pair. Note that direct minimization in (19.8) and (19.9) requires knowledge of the state transition probabilities, which correspond to the system dynamics, and costs. By contrast, the minimization in (19.23) and (19.24) requires knowledge only of the Q function and not of the system dynamics. The utility of the Q function is twofold.

First, it contains information about control actions in every state. As such, the best control in each state can be selected using (19.24) by knowing only the Q function. Second, the Q function can be estimated online in real time directly from date observed along the system trajectories, without knowing the system dynamics information, that is, the transition probabilities. Later, we shall see how this is accomplished. The infinite horizon Q function for a prescribed fixed policy is given by,

$$Q^\pi(x, u) = \sum_{x'} P^u_{x,x'}[R^u_{x,x'} + \gamma V^\pi(x')] \tag{19.27}$$

which also satisfies the Bellman equation. Note that for a fixed policy $\pi(x, u)$

$$V^\pi(x) = Q^\pi(x, \pi(x, u)), \tag{19.28}$$

whence according to (19.27) the Q function satisfies the Bellman equation,

$$Q^\pi(x, u) = \sum_{x'} P^u_{x,x'}[R^u_{x,x'} + \gamma Q^\pi(x', \pi(x', u'))]. \tag{19.29}$$

The Bellman optimality equation for the Q function is given by

$$Q^\star(x, u) = \sum_{x'} P^u_{x,x'}[R^u_{x,x'} + \gamma \min_{u'} Q^\star(x', u')]. \tag{19.30}$$

It is interesting to compare (19.17) and (19.30) where the minimum operator and the expected value operator are reversed.

The algorithms defined in the previous subsections, namely policy iteration and value iteration, are really easy to implement in terms of the Q function (19.25) as follows.

Algorithm 19.3: Policy Iteration Using Q Function

1: **procedure**
2:    Given an initial admissible policy π_0
3:    **while** $\| Q^{\pi^j} - Q^{\pi^{(j-1)}} \| \geq \epsilon_{ac}$ **do**
4:      Solve for $Q_j(x)$ using

$$Q_j(x) = \sum_u \pi_j(x, u) \sum_{x'} P^u_{x,x'}[R^u_{x,x'} + \gamma Q_j(x', \pi(x', u'))], \forall x \in X$$

5:      Update the policy π_{j+1} using

$$\pi_{j+1}(x, u) = \arg\min_\pi Q_j(x, u), \forall x \in X$$

6:      $j := j + 1$
7:    **end while**
8: **end procedure**

Algorithm 19.4: Value Iteration Using Q Function

1: **procedure**
2:   Given an initial policy π_0
3:   **while** $\| Q^{\pi^j} - Q^{\pi^{(j-1)}} \| \geq \epsilon_{ac}$ **do**
4:     Solve for the value $Q_j(x)$ using Bellman's equation

$$Q_{j+1}(x) = \sum_u \pi_j(x,u) \sum_{x'} P^u_{x,x'}[R^u_{x,x'} + \gamma Q_j(x', \pi(x',u'))], \forall x \in S_j \subseteq X$$

5:     Update the policy π_{j+1} using

$$\pi_{j+1}(x,u) = \arg \min_\pi Q_j(x,u), \forall x \in S_j \subseteq X$$

6:     $j := j+1$
7:   **end while**
8: **end procedure**

In Algorithms 19.3 and 19.4, ϵ_{ac} is a small number used to terminate the algorithm when two consecutive Q functions differ by less than ϵ_{ac}.

As we show, the utility of the Q function is that these algorithms can be implemented online in real time, without knowing the system dynamics, by measuring data along the system trajectories. They yield optimal adaptive control algorithms, that is, adaptive control algorithms that converge online to optimal control solutions.

19.3. Methods for Implementing Policy Iteration and Value Iteration

Different methods are available for performing the value and policy updates for policy iteration and value iteration [7, 8, 31]. The three main methods are exact computation, Monte Carlo methods, and temporal difference learning. The last two methods can be implemented without knowledge of the system dynamics. Temporal difference learning is the means by which optimal adaptive control algorithms can be derived for dynamical systems.

Policy iteration requires a solution at each step of the Bellman equation for the value update. For a finite MDP with N states, this is a set of linear equations in N unknowns, namely, the values of each state. Value iteration requires performing the one-step recursive update at each step for the value update. Both of these can be accomplished exactly if we know the transition probabilities $P^u_{x,x'}$ and costs $R^u_{x,x'}$ of the MDP, which corresponds to knowing full system dynamics information. Likewise the policy improvements can be explicitly computed if the dynamics are known.

Monte Carlo learning is based on the definition (19.13) for the value function, and uses repeated measurements of data to approximate the expected value.

The expected values are approximated by averaging repeated results along sample paths. An assumption on the ergodicity of the Markov chain with transition probabilities (19.2) for the given policy being evaluated is implicit. This assumption is suitable for episodic tasks, with experience divided into episodes [7], namely, processes that start in an initial state and run until termination, and are then restarted at a new initial state. For finite MDP, Monte Carlo methods converge to the true value function if all states are visited infinitely often. Therefore, in order to ensure accurate approximations of value functions, the episode sample paths must go through all the states $x \in X$ many times. This issue is called the problem of maintaining exploration. Several methods are available to ensure this, one of which is to use "exploring starts", in which every state has nonzero probability of being selected as the initial state of an episode. Monte Carlo techniques are useful for dynamic systems control because the episode sample paths can be interpreted as system trajectories beginning in a prescribed initial state. However, no updates to the value function estimate or the control policy are made until after an episode terminates. In fact, Monte Carlo learning methods are closely related to repetitive or iterative learning control [53]. They do not learn in real time along a trajectory, but learn as trajectories are repeated.

19.4. Temporal Difference Learning and Its Application to Feedback Control

It has now been shown that the temporal difference method [7] for solving the Bellman equations leads to a family of optimal adaptive controllers, that is, adaptive controllers that learn online the solutions to optimal control problems without knowing the full system dynamics. Temporal difference learning is true online RL, wherein control actions are improved in real time by estimating their value functions by observing data measured along the system trajectories.

Policy iteration requires a solution at each step of N linear equations. Value iteration requires performing a recursion at each step. Temporal difference RL methods are based on the Bellman equation without using any systems dynamics knowledge, but using data observed along a single trajectory of the system. Therefore, temporal difference learning is applicable for feedback control applications. Temporal difference updates the value at each time step as observations of data are made along a trajectory. Periodically, the new value is used to update the policy. Temporal difference methods are related to adaptive control in that they adjust values and actions online in real time along system trajectories. Temporal difference methods can be considered stochastic approximation techniques whereby the Bellman equation (19.14) is replaced by its evaluation along a single sample path of the MDP. Then, the Bellman equation becomes a deterministic equation that allows the definition of a temporal difference error. Equation (19.6) is used to write the Bellman equation (19.14) for the infinite-horizon value (19.13). An alternative form of the Bellman equation is

$$V^\pi(x_k) = E_\pi\{r_k|x_k\} + \gamma\, E_\pi\{V_\pi(x_{k+1})|x_k\} \tag{19.31}$$

which is the basis for temporal difference learning.

Temporal difference RL uses one sample path, namely the current system trajectory, to update the value. Then, (19.31) is replaced by the deterministic Bellman's equation

$$V^\pi(x_k) = r_k + \gamma\, V_\pi(x_{k+1}), \tag{19.32}$$

which holds for each observed data experience set (x_k, x_{k+1}, r_k) at each time step k. This dataset consists of the current state x_k, the observed cost r_k, and the next state x_{k+1}. Hence we can define the temporal difference error as,

$$e_k = -V^\pi(x_k) + r_k + \gamma\, V^\pi(x_{k+1}), \tag{19.33}$$

and the value estimate is updated to make the temporal difference error small.

In the context of temporal difference learning, the interpretation of the Bellman equation is shown in Figure 19.2, where $V^\pi(x_k)$ may be considered as a predicted performance or value, r_k as the observed one step reward, and $\gamma\, V^\pi(x_{k+1})$ as a current estimate of the future value. The Bellman equation can be interpreted as a consistency equation that holds if the current estimate for the predicted value

1. Apply control action

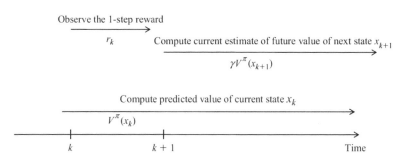

2. Update predicted value to satisfy the Bellman equation

$$V^\pi(x_k) = r_k + \gamma V^\pi(x_{k+1})$$

3. Improve control action

Figure 19.2: Temporal difference interpretation of the Bellman equation. The figure how the use of the Bellman equation captures the action, observation, evaluation, and improvement mechanisms of RL.

$V^\pi(x_k)$ is correct. Temporal difference methods update the predicted value estimate $\hat{V}^\pi(x_k)$ to make the temporal difference error small. The idea, based on stochastic approximation, is that if we use the deterministic version of Bellman's equation repeatedly in policy iteration or value iteration, then on average these algorithms converge toward the solution of the stochastic Bellman equation.

19.5. Optimal Adaptive Control for Discrete-Time Deterministic Systems

A family of optimal adaptive control algorithms can now be developed for dynamical systems. These algorithms determine the solutions to the Hamilton–Jacobi (HJ) design equations online in real time without knowing the system drift dynamics. In the LQR case, this means that they solve the Riccati equation online without knowing the system A matrix. Physical analysis of dynamical systems using Lagrangian mechanics or Hamiltonian mechanics produces system descriptions in terms of nonlinear ordinary differential equations. Discretization yields nonlinear difference equations. Most research in RL is conducted for systems that operate in discrete time [7, 26, 47]. Therefore, we cover discrete-time dynamical systems first and then continuous time systems.

Temporal difference learning is a stochastic approximation technique based on the deterministic Bellman's equation (19.32). Therefore, we lose little by considering deterministic systems here. Therefore, consider a class of discrete-time systems described by deterministic nonlinear dynamics in the affine state-space difference equation form,

$$x_{k+1} = f(x_k) + g(x_k)u_k, \quad k = 0, 1, \ldots \tag{19.34}$$

with state $x_k \in \mathbb{R}^n$ and control input $u_k \in \mathbb{R}^m$. We use this form because its analysis is convenient. The following development can be generalized to the sampled-data form $x_{k+1} = F(x_k, u_k)$.

A deterministic control policy is defined as a function from state space to control space $h(\cdot) : \mathbb{R}^n \to \mathbb{R}^m$. That is, for every state x_k, the policy defines a control action,

$$u_k = h(x_k), \tag{19.35}$$

which is a feedback controller.

The value function with a deterministic cost function can be written as

$$V^h(x_k) = \sum_{i=k}^{\infty} \gamma^{i-k} r(x_i, u_i) = \sum_{i=k}^{\infty} \gamma^{i-k}\left(Q(x_i) + u_i^{\mathrm{T}} R u_i\right), \tag{19.36}$$

where $0 < \gamma \le 1$ is a discount factor, $Q(x_k) \succ 0$, $R \succ 0$, and $u_k = h(x_k)$ is a prescribed feedback control policy. That is, the stage cost is,

$$r(x_k, u_k) = Q(x_k) + u_k^{\mathrm{T}} Q u_k \tag{19.37}$$

which is taken as quadratic in u_k to simplify the developments but can be any positive definite function of the control. We assume that the system is stabilizable on some set $\Omega \in \mathbb{R}^n$; that is, there exists a control policy $u_k = h(x_k)$ such that the closed-loop system $x_{k+1} = f(x_k) + g(x_k)h(x_k)$ is asymptotically stable on Ω.

For the deterministic value (19.36), the optimal value is given by Bellman's optimality equation,

$$V^{\star}(x_k) = \min_{h(\cdot)} \left(r(x_k, h(x_k)) + \gamma \, V^{\star}(x_{k+1}) \right), \tag{19.38}$$

which is just the discrete-time HJB equation. The optimal policy is then given as,

$$h^{\star}(x_k) = \arg \min_{h(\cdot)} \left(r(x_k, h(x_k)) + \gamma \, V^{\star}(x_{k+1}) \right). \tag{19.39}$$

In this setup, the deterministic Bellman's equation (19.32) is

$$V^h(x_k) = r(x_k, u_k) + \gamma \, V^h(x_{k+1}) = Q(x_k) + u_k^{\mathrm{T}} R u_k + \gamma \, V^h(x_{k+1}),$$
$$V^h(0) = 0, \tag{19.40}$$

which is a difference equation equivalent of the value (19.36). That is, instead of evaluating the infinite sum (19.36), the difference equation (19.40) can be solved with boundary condition $V(0) = 0$ to obtain the value of using a current policy $u_k = h(x_k)$.

The discrete-time Hamiltonian function can be defined as,

$$H(x_k, h(x_k), \Delta V_k) = r(x_k, h(x_k)) + \gamma \, V^h(x_{k+1}) - V^h(x_k), \tag{19.41}$$

where $\Delta V_k \equiv \gamma \, V^h(x_{k+1}) - V^h(x_k)$ is the forward difference operator. The Hamiltonian function captures the energy content along the trajectories of a system as reflected in the desired optimal performance. In fact, the Hamiltonian is the temporal difference error (19.33). The Bellman equation requires that the Hamiltonian be equal to zero for the value associated with a prescribed policy.

For the discrete-time linear quadratic regulator case, we have

$$x_{k+1} = Ax_k + Bu_k, \tag{19.42}$$

$$V^h(x_k) = \frac{1}{2} \sum_{i=k}^{\infty} \gamma^{i-k} \left(x_i^{\mathrm{T}} Q x_i + u_i^{\mathrm{T}} R u_i \right) \tag{19.43}$$

and the Bellman equation can be easily derived.

19.5.1. *Policy Iteration and Value Iteration for Discrete-Time Deterministic Dynamical Systems*

Two forms of RL can be used based on policy iteration and value iteration.

Algorithm 19.5: Policy Iteration Using Temporal Difference Learning

---

1: **procedure**
2:   Given an initial admissible policy $h_0(x_k)$
3:   **while** $|| V^{h^j} - V^{h^{(j-1)}} || \geq \epsilon_{ac}$ **do**
4:     Solve for $V_j(x_k)$ using

$$V_{j+1}(x_k) = r(x_k, h_j(x_k)) + \gamma V_{j+1}(x_{k+1})$$

5:     Update the policy h_{j+1} using

$$h_{j+1}(x_k) = -\frac{\gamma}{2} R^{-1} g^T(x_k) \nabla V_{j+1}(x_{k+1}),$$

6:     $j := j + 1$
7:   **end while**
8: **end procedure**

Algorithm 19.6: Value Iteration Using Temporal Difference Learning

---

1: **procedure**
2:   Given an initial policy $h_0(x_k)$
3:   **while** $|| V^{h^j} - V^{h^{(j-1)}} || \geq \epsilon_{ac}$ **do**
4:     Solve for $V_j(x_k)$ using

$$V_{j+1}(x_k) = r(x_k, h_j(x_k)) + \gamma V_j(x_{k+1})$$

5:     Update the policy h_{j+1} using

$$h_{j+1}(x_k) = -\frac{\gamma}{2} R^{-1} g^T(x_k) \nabla V_{j+1}(x_{k+1}),$$

6:     $j := j + 1$
7:   **end while**
8: **end procedure**

In Algorithms 19.5 and 19.6, ϵ_{ac} is a small number used to terminate the algorithm when two consecutive value functions differ by less than ϵ_{ac} and $\nabla V(x) = \frac{\partial V(x)}{\partial x}$. Note that in value iteration, we can select any initial control policy, not necessarily admissible or stabilizing. The policy iteration and value iteration algorithms just described are offline design methods that require knowledge of the discrete-time dynamics. By contrast, we next desire to determine online methods for implementing policy iteration and value iteration that do not require full dynamics information.

Policy iteration and value iteration can be implemented for finite MDP by storing and updating lookup tables. The key to implementing policy iteration and value iteration online for dynamical systems with infinite state and action spaces is to approximate the value function by a suitable approximator structure in terms of unknown parameters. Then, the unknown parameters are tuned online exactly as in system identification. This idea of value function approximation (VFA) is used by Werbos [26, 33] and is called approximate dynamic programming (ADP) or adaptive dynamic programming. The approach is used by Bertsekas and Tsitsiklis [31] and is called neuro-dynamic programming [8, 19, 31]. For nonlinear systems (19.34), the value function contains higher order nonlinearities. Then, we assume that the Bellman equation (19.40) has a local smooth solution [57]. Then, according to the Weierstrass higher-order approximation theorem, there exists a dense basis set $\phi_i(x)$ such that,

$$V(x) = W^{\mathrm{T}}\phi(x) + \epsilon_L(x) \tag{19.44}$$

where $\phi(x) = [\phi_1(x) \, \phi_2(x) \, \dots \, \phi_L(x)] : \mathbb{R}^n \to \mathbb{R}^L$ and $\epsilon_L(x)$ converges uniformly to zero as the basis sets $L \to \infty$. Note that in the LQR case, the weight vector consists of the elements of the symmetric Riccati matrix P. We are now in a position to present several adaptive control algorithms based on temporal difference RL that converge online to the optimal control solution.

Algorithm 19.7: Optimal Adaptive Control Using Policy Iteration

1: **procedure**
2:    Given an initial admissible policy $h_0(x_k)$
3:    **while** No convergence **do**
4:        Determine the least-squares solution W_{j+1} using

$$W_{j+1}^{\mathrm{T}}\left(\phi(x_k) - \gamma\,\phi(x_{k+1})\right) = r(x_k, h_j(x_k))$$

5:        Update the policy h_{j+1} using

$$h_{j+1}(x_k) = -\frac{\gamma}{2}R^{-1}g^{\mathrm{T}}(x_k)\nabla\phi^{\mathrm{T}}(x_{k+1})W_{j+1},$$

6:        $j := j + 1$
7:    **end while**
8: **end procedure**

Algorithm 19.8: Optimal Adaptive Control Using Value Iteration

1: **procedure**
2:    Given an initial policy $h_0(x_k)$
3:    **while** No convergence **do**
4:        Determine the least squares solution W_{j+1} using

$$W_{j+1}^{\mathrm{T}}\phi(x_k) = r(x_k, h_j(x_k)) + \gamma\,W_j^{\mathrm{T}}\phi(x_{k+1})$$

5:        Update the policy h_{j+1} using

$$h_{j+1}(x_k) = -\frac{\gamma}{2}R^{-1}g^{\mathrm{T}}(x_k)\nabla\phi^{\mathrm{T}}(x_{k+1})W_{j+1},$$

6:        $j := j + 1$
7:    **end while**
8: **end procedure**

19.5.2. *Introducing a Second "Actor" Neural Network*

Using value function approximation (VFA) allows standard system identification techniques to be used to find the value function parameters that approximately solve the Bellman equation. The approximator structure just described which is used for the approximation of the value function, is known as the critic neural network, as it determines the value of using the current policy. Using VFA, the policy iteration RL algorithm solves the Bellman equation during the value update portion of each iteration step j by observing only the dataset $(x_k, x_{k+1}, r(x_k, h_j(x_k)))$ each time along the system trajectory. In the case of value iteration, VFA is used to perform a value update.

The critic network solves the Bellman equation using the observed data without knowing the system dynamics. However, note that in the linear quadratic case (systems of the form $x_{k+1} = Ax_k + Bu_k$ with quadratic costs), the policy update is given by

$$K^{j+1} = -\left(B^{\mathsf{T}}P^{j+1}B + R\right)^{-1}B^{\mathsf{T}}P^{j+1}A, \tag{19.45}$$

which requires full knowledge of the dynamics.

This problem can be solved by introducing a second neural network for the control policy, known as the actor neural network [29, 33, 43]. Therefore, consider a parametric approximator structure for the control action

$$u_k = h(x_k) = U^{\mathsf{T}}\sigma(x_k) \tag{19.46}$$

with $\sigma(x) : \mathbb{R}^n \to \mathbb{R}^m$ being a vector of M activation functions and $U \in \mathbb{R}^{M \times m}$ being a matrix of weights or unknown parameters. Note that in the LQR case the basis set can be taken as the state vector. After convergence of the critic neural network parameters to W_{j+1} in policy iteration or value iteration, it is required to perform the policy update. To achieve this aim, we can use a gradient descent method for tuning the actor weights U, such as

$$U_{j+1}^{i+1} = U_{j+1}^i - \beta\sigma(x_k)\left(2R(U_{j+1}^i)^{\mathsf{T}}\sigma(x_k) + \gamma g^{\mathsf{T}}(x_k)\nabla\phi^{\mathsf{T}}(x_{k+1})W_{j+1}\right)^{\mathsf{T}}, \tag{19.47}$$

where $\beta \in \mathbb{R}^+$ is a tuning parameter. The tuning index i can be incremented with the time index k.

Note that the tuning of the actor neural network requires observations at each time k of the dataset x_k, x_{k+1}, that is, the current state and the next state. However, as per formulation (19.46), the actor neural network yields the control u_k at time k in terms of the state x_k at time k. The next state x_{k+1} is not needed in (19.46). Thus, after (19.47) converges, (19.46) is a legitimate feedback controller. Note also that, in the LQR case, the actor neural network (19.46) embodies the feedback gain computation (19.45). Equation (19.45) contains the state internal dynamics A, but (19.46) does not. Therefore, the A matrix is not needed to compute the feedback control.

The reason is that the actor neural network learns information about A in its weights, since x_k, x_{k+1} are used in its tuning. Finally, note that only the input function $g(\cdot)$ or, in the LQR case, the B matrix, is needed in (19.47) to tune the actor neural network. Thus, introducing a second actor neural network completely avoids the need for knowledge of the state drift dynamics $f(\cdot)$, or A in the LQR case.

19.6. Actor-Critic Structures for Optimal Adaptive Control

The implementation of RL using two neural networks, one as a critic and the other as an actor, yields the actor-critic RL structure shown in Figure 19.1. In this control system, the critic and the actor are tuned online using the observed data $(x_k, x_{k+1}, r(x_k, h_j(x_k)))$ along the system trajectory. The critic and the actor are tuned sequentially in both the policy iteration and the value iteration algorithms. That is, the weights of one neural network are held constant while the weights of the other are tuned until convergence. This procedure is repeated until both neural networks have converged. Thus, the controller learns the optimal controller online. This procedure amounts to an online adaptive optimal control system wherein the value function parameters are tuned online and the convergence is to the optimal value and control. The convergence of value iteration using two neural networks for the discrete-time nonlinear system (19.34) is proved in [43].

According to RL principles, the optimal adaptive control structure requires two loops, a critic and an actor, and operates at multiple timescales. A fast loop implements the control action inner loop, a slower timescale operates in the critic loop, and a third timescale operates to update the policy. Several actor-critic structures for optimal adaptive control have been proposed in [54–56].

19.6.1. Q-learning for Optimal Adaptive Control

It has just been shown how to implement an optimal adaptive controller using RL that only requires knowledge of the system input function $g(x_k)$. The Q learning RL method gives an adaptive control algorithm that converges online to the optimal control solution for completely unknown systems. That is, it solves the Bellman equation (19.40) and the HJB equation (19.38) online in real time by using data measured along the system trajectories, without any knowledge of the dynamics $f(x_k), g(x_k)$. Writing the Q function Bellman equation (19.29) along a sample path gives

$$Q^\pi(x_k, u_k) = r(x_k, u_k) + \gamma \, Q^\pi(x_{k+1}, h(x_{k+1})), \qquad (19.48)$$

which defines a temporal difference error,

$$e_k = -Q^\pi(x_k, u_k) + r(x_k, u_k) + \gamma \, Q^\pi(x_{k+1}, h(x_{k+1})). \qquad (19.49)$$

The Q function is updated using the algorithm,

$$Q_k(x_k, u_k) = Q_{k-1}(x_k, u_k) + \alpha_k[r(x_k, u_k)$$
$$+ \gamma \min_u Q_{k-1}(x_{k+1}, u_k) - Q_{k-1}(x_k, u_k)], \qquad (19.50)$$

with α_k being a tuning parameter. This algorithm is developed for finite MDP and the convergence proved by Watkins [51] using stochastic approximation (SA) methods. The Q learning algorithm (19.50) is similar to SA methods of adaptive control or parameter estimation used in control systems. Let us now derive methods for Q learning for dynamical systems that yield adaptive control algorithms that converge to optimal control solutions. Policy iteration and value iteration algorithms can be given using the Q function. A Q learning algorithm is easily developed for discrete-time dynamical systems using Q function approximation [9, 26, 33, 58]. Assume therefore that, for nonlinear systems, the Q function is parameterized as

$$Q(x, u) = W^T \phi(z), \qquad (19.51)$$

where $z_k \equiv [x_k^T \ u_k^T]^T$, W is the unknown parameter vector, and $\phi(z)$ is the basis set vector. Substituting the Q function approximation into the temporal difference error (19.49) yields

$$e_k = -W^T \phi(z_k) + r(x_k, u_k) + \gamma W^T \phi(z_{k+1}), \qquad (19.52)$$

on which either policy iteration or value iteration algorithms can be based. Considering the policy iteration algorithm defined before, the Q function evaluation step is

$$W_{j+1}^T (\phi(z_k) - \gamma \phi(z_{k+1})) = r(x_k, h_j(x_k)), \qquad (19.53)$$

and the policy improvement step is

$$h_{j+1}(x_k) = \arg \min_u (W_{j+1}^T \phi(x_k, u)), \quad \forall x \in X. \qquad (19.54)$$

Now, using value iteration, the Q learning is given by,

$$W_{j+1}^T \phi(z_k) = r(x_k, h_j(x_k)) + \gamma W_j^T \phi(z_{k+1}), \qquad (19.55)$$

and (19.54). Note that these equations do not require knowledge of the dynamics.

19.6.2. *Approximate Dynamic Programming Using Output Feedback*

The methods discussed above have relied on full state variable feedback. Little work has been done on the applications of RL for feedback control using output feedback. This corresponds to partially observable Markov processes. The design of an ADP controller that uses only the output feedback is given in [59].

19.7. Integral RL for Optimal Adaptive Control of Deterministic Continuous-Time Systems

RL is considerably more difficult for continuous-time systems [60] than for discrete-time systems, and fewer results are available. See [61] for the development of an offline policy iteration method for continuous-time systems. Using a method known as integral RL (IRL) [27–29, 44] allows the application of RL to formulate online optimal adaptive control methods for continuous-time systems. These methods find solutions to optimal HJ design equations and Riccati equations online in real time without knowing the system drift dynamics $f(x)$, or in the LQR case without knowing the A matrix.

Consider the continuous-time nonlinear dynamical system,

$$\dot{x} = f(x) + g(x)u, \quad t \geq 0, \tag{19.56}$$

where $x \in \mathbb{R}^n$ is the state, and $u \in \mathbb{R}^m$ is the control input. Also consider as $x = 0$ an equilibrium point, e.g., $f(0) = 0$ and $f(x) + g(x)u$ Lipschitz on a set $\Omega \subseteq \mathbb{R}^n$ that contains the origin. We assume that the system is stabilizable on Ω, that is, there exists a continuous control input function $u(t)$ such that the closed-loop system is asymptotically stable on Ω.

Define a performance measure or cost function that has the value associated with the feedback control policy $u = \mu(x)$ given by,

$$V^\mu(x(t)) = \int_t^\infty r(x(\tau), u(\tau)) \, d\tau, \tag{19.57}$$

where $r(x, u) = Q(x) + u^T R u$ is the utility function, $Q(x) \succeq 0, \forall x$ and $x = 0 \rightarrow Q(x) = 0$ and $R = R^T \succ 0$.

For the continuous-time LQR, we have,

$$\dot{x} = Ax + Bu, \tag{19.58}$$

$$V^\mu(x(t)) = \frac{1}{2} \int_t^\infty \left(x^T Q x + u^T R u\right) d\tau. \tag{19.59}$$

If the cost is smooth, then an infinitesimal equivalent to (19.57) can be found by Leibniz's formula, to be

$$0 = r(x, \mu(x)) + (\nabla V^\mu)^T (f(x) + g(x)\mu(x)), \quad V^\mu(0) = 0, \tag{19.60}$$

where ∇V^μ denotes the column gradient vector with respect to x.

This is the continuous-time Bellman equation. This equation is defined based on the continuous-time Hamiltonian function,

$$H(x, \mu(x), \nabla V^\mu) = r(x, \mu(x)) + (\nabla V^\mu)^T (f(x) + g(x)\mu(x)) \tag{19.61}$$

and the HJB equation is given by

$$0 = \min_{\mu} H(x, \mu(x), \nabla V^{\star}) \tag{19.62}$$

with an optimal control,

$$\mu^{\star} = \arg\min_{\mu} H(x, \mu(x), \nabla V^{\star}). \tag{19.63}$$

We now see the problem with continuous-time systems immediately. Comparing the continuous-time Hamiltonian (19.61) to the discrete-time Hamiltonian (19.41), it is seen that (19.61) contains the full system dynamics $f(x) + g(x)u$, while (19.41) does not. What this means is that the continuous-time Bellman equation (86) cannot be used as a basis for RL unless the full dynamics are known. RL methods based on (19.60) can be developed [49]. They have limited use for adaptive control purposes because the system dynamics must be known, state derivatives must be measured, or integration over an infinite horizon is required. In another approach, Euler's method can be used to discretize the continuous-time Bellman equation (19.60) (see [62]). Noting that

$$0 = r(x, \mu(x)) + (\nabla V^{\mu})^{\mathrm{T}}(f(x) + g(x)\mu(x)) = r(x, \mu(x)) + \dot{V}^{\mu}, \tag{19.64}$$

we use Euler's forward method to discretize this partial differential equation (PDE) in order to obtain,

$$
\begin{aligned}
0 &= r(x, \mu(x)) + \frac{V^{\mu}(x_{k+1}) - V^{\mu}(x_k)}{T} \\
&\equiv \frac{r_S(x_k, u_k)}{T} + \frac{V^{\mu}(x_{k+1}) - V^{\mu}(x_k)}{T},
\end{aligned}
\tag{19.65}
$$

where $T > 0$ is a sample period, i.e., $t = kT$ and $r_S(x_k, u_k) = Tr(x_k, u_k)$.

Now, note that the discretized continuous-time Bellman equation (19.65) has the same form as the discrete-time Bellman equation (19.40). Therefore, all the RL methods just described for discrete-time systems can be applied. However, this equation is an approximation only. An alternative exact method for continuous-time RL is given in [29, 44]. That method is termed integral RL (IRL). Note that the cost (19.57) can be written in the integral reinforcement form,

$$V^{\mu}(x(t)) = \int_{t}^{t+T} r(x(\tau), u(\tau))\mathrm{d}\tau + V^{\mu}(x(t + T)), \tag{19.66}$$

for some $T > 0$. This equation is exactly in the form of the discrete-time Bellman equation (19.40). According to Bellman's principle, the optimal value is given in terms of this construction as [5]

$$V^\star(x(t)) = \min_{\bar{u}(t:t+T)} \left(\int_t^{t+T} r(x(\tau), u(\tau)) d\tau + V^\star(x(t + T)) \right),$$

where $\bar{u}(t : t + T) = \{u(\tau) : t \leq \tau < t + T\}$ and the optimal control is given by,

$$\mu^\star(x(t)) = \arg \min_{\bar{u}(t:t+T)} \left(\int_t^{t+T} r(x(\tau), u(\tau)) d\tau + V^\star(x(t + T)) \right).$$

It is shown in [44] that the Bellman equation (19.60) is equivalent to the integral reinforcement form (19.66). That is, the positive definite solution of both is the value (19.57) of the policy $u = \mu(x)$. The integral reinforcement form (19.66) serves as a Bellman equation for continuous-time systems, and is a fixed point equation. Therefore, the temporal difference error for continuous-time systems can be defined as

$$e(t : t + T) = \int_t^\infty r(x(\tau), u(\tau)) d\tau + V^\mu(x(t + T)) - V^\mu(x(t)), \qquad (19.67)$$

which is an equation that does not involve the system dynamics. Now, it is easy to formulate policy iteration and value iteration for continuous-time systems. The following algorithms are termed integral RL for continuous-time systems [29], [44]. Both algorithms give optimal adaptive controllers for continuous-time systems, that is, adaptive control algorithms that converge to optimal control solutions.

Algorithm 19.9: IRL Optimal Adaptive Control Using Policy Iteration

---

1: **procedure**
2:　　Given an initial admissible policy $\mu_0(x)$
3:　　**while** $\| V^{\mu^j} - V^{\mu^{(j-1)}} \| \geq \epsilon_{ac}$ **do**
4:　　　　Solve for V_j using

$$V_{j+1}(x(t)) = \int_t^{t+T} r(x(s), \mu_j(x(s))) ds + V_{j+1}(x(t + T)), \quad V_{j+1}(0) = 0$$

5:　　　　Update the policy μ_{j+1} using

$$\mu_{j+1}(x_k) = -\frac{1}{2} R^{-1} g^T(x) \nabla V_{j+1},$$

6:　　　　$j := j + 1$
7:　　**end while**
8: **end procedure**

Algorithm 19.10: IRL Optimal Adaptive Control Using Value Iteration

---

1: **procedure**
2:    Given an initial policy $\mu_0(x)$
3:    **while** $\| V^{\mu^j} - V^{\mu^{(j-1)}} \| \geq \epsilon_{ac}$ **do**
4:       Solve for V_j using

$$V_{j+1}(x(t)) = \int_t^{t+T} r(x(s), \mu_j(x(s))) + V_j(x(t+T))$$

5:    Update the policy μ_{j+1} using

$$\mu_{j+1}(x) = -\frac{1}{2} R^{-1} g^T(x) \nabla V_{j+1},$$

6:       $j := j + 1$
7:    **end while**
8: **end procedure**

In Algorithms 19.9 and 19.10, ϵ_{ac} is a small number used to terminate the algorithm when two consecutive value functions differ by less than ϵ_{ac}; note that neither algorithm requires knowledge about the system drift dynamics function $f(x)$. That is, they work for partially unknown systems. Convergence of IRL policy iteration has been proved in [44]. An IRL algorithm for nonlinear systems has been proposed in [45].

19.7.1. *Online Implementation of IRL: A Hybrid Optimal Adaptive Controller*

Both of these IRL algorithms can be implemented online by RL techniques using value function approximation $V(x) = W^T \phi(x)$ in a critic approximator network. Using VFA in the policy iteration algorithm just defined yields

$$W_{j+1}^T[\phi(x(t)) - \phi(x(t+T))] = \int_t^\infty r(x(s), \mu_j(x(s))) ds. \tag{19.68}$$

Using VFA in the value iteration algorithm just defined yields

$$W_{j+1}^T \phi(x(t)) = \int_t^\infty r(x(s), \mu_j(x(s))) ds + W_j^T \phi(x(t+T))]. \tag{19.69}$$

Then, RLS or batch least-squares is used to update the value function parameters in these equations. On convergence of the value parameters, the action is updated.

IRL provides an optimal adaptive controller, that is, an adaptive controller that measures data along the system trajectories and converges to optimal control solutions. Note that only the system input coupling dynamics $g(x)$ is needed to implement these algorithms. The drift dynamics $f(x)$ is not needed. The implementation of IRL optimal adaptive control is shown in Figure 19.3. The time is incremented at each iteration by the period T. The RL time interval T need not be the same at each iteration. T can be changed depending on how long it takes to receive meaningful information from the observations and is not a sample period in the standard meaning. The measured data at each time increment are $(x(t), x(t + T), \rho(t : t + T))$ where

$$\rho(t : t + T) = \int_t^{t+T} r(x(\tau), u(\tau))d\tau, \tag{19.70}$$

is the integral reinforcement measured at each time interval. The integral reinforcement can be computed in real time by introducing an integrator $\dot{\rho} = r(x(t), u(t))$ as shown in Figure 19.3. That is, the integral reinforcement $\rho(t)$ is added as an extra continuous-time state. It functions as the memory or controller dynamics. The remainder of the controller is a sampled-data controller. Note that the control policy $\mu(t)$ is updated periodically after the critic weights have converged to the solution of (19.68) or (19.68). Therefore, the policy is piecewise constant in time. On the other hand, the control varies continuously with the state between each policy update. It is seen that IRL for continuous-time systems is in fact a hybrid continuous-time/discrete-time adaptive controller that converges to the optimal control solution in real time without knowing the drift dynamics $f(x)$. The optimal adaptive controller has multiple control loops and several timescales. The inner control action loop operates in continuous time. Data are sampled at intervals of length T. The critic network operates at a slower timescale depending on how long it takes to solve (19.68) or (19.68). Due to the fact that the policy update for continuous-time systems does not involve the drift dynamics $f(x)$, no actor neural network is needed in IRL. Only a critic neural network is needed for VFA.

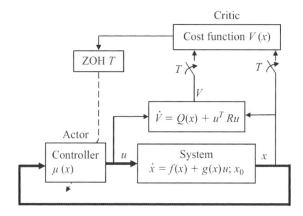

Figure 19.3: Hybrid optimal adaptive controller based on integral RL. It shows the two-timescale hybrid nature of the IRL controller. The integral reinforcement signal $\rho(t)$ is added as an extra state and functions as the memory of the controller. The Critic runs on a slow timescale and learns the value of using the current control policy. When the Critic converges, the Actor control policy is updated to obtain an improved value.

19.8. Synchronous Optimal Adaptive Control for Continuous-Time Systems

The IRL controller just given tunes the critic neural network to determine the value while holding the control policy fixed. Then, a policy update is performed. Now we develop an adaptive controller that has two neural networks, one for value function approximation and the other for control approximation. We could call these the critic neural network and actor neural network. The two neural networks are tuned simultaneously, that is, synchronously in time. This procedure is more nearly in line with accepted practice in adaptive control. Though this synchronous controller does require knowledge of the dynamics, it converges to the approximate local solutions of the HJB equation and the Bellman equation online, yet does not require explicitly solving either one. The HJB is usually impossible to solve for nonlinear systems, except for special cases.

Based on the continuous-time Hamiltonian (19.61) and the stationarity condition $0 = \frac{\partial H(x,u,\nabla V^{\mu})}{\partial u}$, a policy iteration algorithm for continuous-time systems could be written based on the policy evaluation step,

$$0 = H(x, \mu_j(x), \nabla V_{j+1}) \equiv r(x, \mu_j(x)) + (\nabla V_{j+1})^{\mathrm{T}}(f(x) + g(x)\mu_j(x)),$$

$$V_{j+1}(0) = 0 \tag{19.71}$$

and the policy improvement step

$$\mu_{j+1} = \arg\min_{\mu} H(x, \mu, \nabla V_{j+1}). \tag{19.72}$$

Unfortunately, (19.71) is a nonlinear partial differential equation and cannot usually be solved analytically. However, this policy iteration algorithm provides the structure needed to develop another adaptive control algorithm that can be implemented online using measured data along the trajectories and converges to the optimal control. Specifically, select a value function approximation (VFA), or critic neural network, structure as

$$V(x) = W_1^{\mathrm{T}}\phi(x) \tag{19.73}$$

and a control action approximation structure or actor neural network as,

$$u(x) = -\frac{1}{2}R^{-1}g^{\mathrm{T}}(x)\nabla\phi^{\mathrm{T}}W_2. \tag{19.74}$$

These approximators could be, for instance, two neural networks with unknown parameters or weights W_1, W_2 and $\phi(x)$ the basis set or activation functions of the first neural network. The structure of the second action neural network comes from the policy iteration algorithm. Then, tuning the neural network weights as

$$\dot{W}_1 = -\alpha_1 \frac{\sigma}{(\sigma^T \sigma + 1)^2} [\sigma^T W_1 + Q(x) + u^T R u],$$ (19.75)

and

$$\dot{W}_2 = -\alpha_2 \{(F_1 W_2 - \mathbf{1}^T \bar{\sigma}^T W_1) - \frac{1}{4} D(x) W_2 m^T(x) W_1\},$$ (19.76)

guarantees stability as well as convergence to the optimal value and control [63]. In these parameter estimation algorithms α_1, α_2 are positive tuning parameters, $F_1 \succ 0$ is a matrix picked appropriately to guarantee stability, and $\mathbf{1}$ is a row vector of ones with appropriate dimensions, $D(x) = \nabla\phi(x)g(x)R^{-1}g^T(x)\nabla\phi^T(x)$, $\sigma = \nabla\phi(f + gu)$, $\bar{\sigma} = \frac{\sigma}{\sigma^T\sigma+1}$, and $m(x) = \frac{\sigma}{(\sigma^T\sigma+1)^2}$. A persistence of excitation condition on $\bar{\sigma}(t)$ is needed to achieve convergence to the optimal value.

This synchronous policy iteration controller is an adaptive control algorithm that requires full knowledge of the system dynamics $f(x)$, $g(x)$, yet converges to the optimal control solution. That is, it solves, locally approximately, the HJB equation, which is usually intractable for nonlinear systems. In the continuous-time LQR case, it solves the ARE using data measured along the trajectories and knowledge of A, B. The utility of this algorithm is that it can approximately solve the HJB equation for nonlinear systems using data measured along the system trajectories in real time. The HJB is usually impossible to solve for nonlinear systems, except in some special cases.

The VFA tuning algorithm for W_1 is based on gradient descent, while the control action tuning algorithm is a form of backpropagation [33] that is, however, also tuned by the VFA weights W_1. This adaptive structure is similar to the actor–critic RL structure in Figure 19.1. However, in contrast to IRL, this algorithm is a continuous-time optimal adaptive controller with two parameter estimators tuned simultaneously, that is, synchronously and continuously in time. An algorithm that combines the advantages of the synchronous policy iteration algorithm and IRL has been proposed in [64]. The authors in [65] have proposed a model-free IRL algorithm, while the authors in [66] have used neural network-based identifiers for a model-free synchronous policy iteration.

19.9. Using RL for Multi-Player Nash, Stackelberg, and Graphical Games

Game theory provides an ideal environment to study multi-player decision and control problems, and offers a wide range of challenging and engaging problems. Game theory has been successful in modeling strategic behavior, where the outcome for each player depends on the actions of himself and all the other players.

Every player chooses a control to minimize, independently of the others, his own performance objective. Multi-player cooperative games rely on solving coupled HJ equations, which in the linear quadratic case reduce to coupled algebraic Riccati equations. RL techniques have been applied to design adaptive controllers that converge to the solutions of two-player zero-sum games in [28, 67], of multi-player non-zero-sum games in [68], of graphical games in [69–71], and of Stackelberg games in [72, 73]. In these cases, the adaptive control structure has multiple loops, with action networks and critic networks for each player. Below we provide a sketch on how to derive RL frameworks for zero- and non-zero-sum games. Graphical and Stackelberg games can be derived in a similar manner by following the appropriate citations.

19.9.1. *Zero-Sum Games*

Consider the nonlinear time-invariant system given by,

$$\dot{x}(t) = f(x(t)) + g(x(t))u(t) + k(x(t))d(t), \quad t \geq 0, \tag{19.77}$$

where $x \in \mathbb{R}^n$ is a measurable state vector, $u(t) \in \mathbb{R}^m$ is the control input, $d(t) \in \mathbb{R}^q$ is the adversarial input, $f(x) \in \mathbb{R}^n$, is the drift dynamics, $g(x) \in \mathbb{R}^{n \times m}$ is the input dynamics, and $k(x) \in \mathbb{R}^{n \times q}$ is the adversarial input dynamics. It is assumed that $f(0) = 0$ and $f(x) + g(x)u + k(x)d$ is locally Lipschitz and that the system is stabilizable.

The cost functional index to be optimized is defined as,

$$\mathcal{J}(x(0), u, d) = \int_0^\infty \left(r(x, u, d) \right) dt \equiv \int_0^\infty \left(Q(x) + u^{\mathrm{T}} R u - \gamma^2 \|d\|^2 \right) dt,$$

where $Q(x) \succeq 0$, $R = R^{\mathrm{T}} \succ 0$, and $\gamma \geq \gamma^\star \geq 0$, with $\gamma^\star$ being the smallest γ such that the system is stabilized. The value function with feedback control and adversarial policies can be defined as

$$V(x(t), u, d) = \int_t^\infty \left(r(x, u, d) \right) d\tau \equiv \int_t^\infty \left(Q(x) + u^{\mathrm{T}} R u - \gamma^2 \|d\|^2 \right) d\tau,$$

$$\forall x, u, d.$$

When the value is finite, a differential equivalent to this is the Bellman equation,

$$r(x, u, d) + \frac{\partial V}{\partial x}^{\mathrm{T}} \left(f(x) + g(x)u + k(x)d \right), \quad V(0) = 0,$$

and the Hamiltonian is given by

$$\mathcal{H}\left(x, u, d, \frac{\partial V}{\partial x}^{\mathrm{T}} \right) = r(x, u, d) + \frac{\partial V}{\partial x}^{\mathrm{T}} \left(f(x) + g(x)u + k(x)d \right).$$

Define the two-player zero-sum differential game as,

$$V^\star(x(0)) = \min_u \max_d \mathcal{J}(x(0), u, d),$$

subject to (19.77). It is worth noting that u is the minimizing player while d is the maximizing one.

To solve this zero-sum game, one needs to to solve the following HJ-Isaacs (HJI) equation,

$$r(x, u^\star, d^\star) + \frac{\partial V^{\star T}}{\partial x} \left(f(x) + g(x)u^\star + k(x)d^\star \right) = 0,$$

given a solution $V^\star \geq 0 : \mathbb{R}^n \to \mathbb{R}$ to this equation, one has

$$u^\star = -\frac{1}{2} R^{-1} g^T(x) \frac{\partial V^\star}{\partial x},$$

$$d^\star = \frac{1}{2\gamma^2} k^T(x) \frac{\partial V^\star}{\partial x}.$$

19.9.1.1. *Approximate solution*

Solving the HJI equation analytically is extremely difficult or even impossible. The following PI algorithm can be used to approximate the HJI solution by iterating on the Bellman equation. It terminates when two consecutive value functions do not differ (regarding a corresponding suitable norm error).

Algorithm 19.11: PI for Regulation in Zero-Sum Games ($\mathcal{H}_\infty$ Control)

1: **procedure**
2:     Given admissible policies $u^{(0)}$
3:     for $j = 0, 1, \ldots$ given u_j
4:     for $i = 0, 1, \ldots$ set $d^0 = 0$ to solve for the value $V_j^{(i)}(x)$ using Bellman's equation

$$Q(x) + \frac{\partial V_j^{i\,T}}{\partial x} \left(f(x) + g(x)u_j + k(x)d^i \right) + u_j^T R u_j - \gamma^2 \left\| d^2 \right\|^2 = 0, \ V_j^i(0) = 0,$$

$$d^{i+1} = \frac{1}{2\gamma^2} k^T(x) \frac{\partial V_j^i}{\partial x},$$

on convergence, set $V_{j+1}(x) = V_j^i(x)$
5:     Update the control policy u_{j+1} using

$$u_{j+1} = -\frac{1}{2} R^{-1} g^T(x) \frac{\partial V_{j+1}}{\partial x}.$$

6:     Go to 3
7: **end procedure**

The PI Algorithm 19.11 is an offline algorithm and requires complete knowledge of the system dynamics. In the following, it is desired to design an online PI algorithm that simultaneously updates the value function and policies and does not require knowledge of the internal dynamics.

19.9.1.2. *Approximate solution of zero-sum games using integral RL*

In [27,74], an equivalent formulation of the Bellman equation that does not involve the dynamics is found to be,

$$V(x(t - T)) = \int_{t-T}^{t} r(x(\tau), u(\tau), d(\tau)) d\tau + V(x(t)), \qquad (19.78)$$

for any time $t \geq 0$ and time interval $T > 0$. This equation is called the integral RL (IRL) Bellman equation.

It is assumed that there exist weights W_1 such that the value function $V^\star(x)$ is approximated as,

$$V^\star(x) = W_1^T \phi_1(x) + \epsilon(x), \quad \forall x,$$

where $\phi_1(x) : \mathbb{R}^n \to \mathbb{R}^N$ is the basis function vector, N is the number of basis functions, and $\epsilon(x)$ is the approximation error.

The optimal weights W_1 are not known and, as before, the current critic weights are used,

$$\hat{V}(x) = \hat{W}_c^T \phi_1(x), \quad \forall x, \qquad (19.79)$$

where $\hat{W}_c$ are the current estimated values of the ideal critic approximator weights W_1. Now, using (19.79) in (19.78), the approximate IRL equation is given as,

$$\Delta \phi_1(t)^T \hat{W}_c + \int_{t-T}^{T} \left(Q(x) + \hat{u}^T R \hat{u} - \gamma^2 \left\| \hat{d} \right\|^2 \right) d\tau = e_1,$$

where $\Delta \phi_1(t) = \phi_1(t) - \phi_1(t - T)$ and $e_1 \in \mathbb{R}^n$ is the approximation (residual) error after using current critic approximator weights and $\hat{u}, \hat{d}$ are given by,

$$\hat{u}(x) = -\frac{1}{2} R^{-1} g^T(x) \frac{\partial \phi_1}{\partial x}^T \hat{W}_u,$$

and

$$\hat{d}(x) = \frac{1}{2\gamma^2} k^T(x) \frac{\partial \phi_1}{\partial x}^T \hat{W}_d,$$

respectively, where $\hat{W}_u$ and $\hat{W}_d$ are the current estimated values of the optimal actor and disturbance policy weights, respectively.

Now it is desired to select $\hat{W}_c$ such that e_1 is minimized. Hence, after using a normalized gradient descent, one has

$$\dot{\hat{W}}_c = -\alpha \frac{\Delta\phi_1(t)}{\left(\Delta\phi_1(t)^{\mathrm{T}}\Delta\phi_1(t) + 1\right)^2}$$

$$\left(\Delta\phi_1(t)^{\mathrm{T}}\hat{W}_c + \int_{t-T}^{T} \left(Q(x) + \hat{u}^{\mathrm{T}}R\hat{u} - \gamma^2 \left\|\hat{d}\right\|^2\right)\mathrm{d}\tau\right),$$

The weights for the actor $\hat{W}_u$ need to be picked in order to guarantee closed-loop stability. Hence, one has

$$\dot{\hat{W}}_u = -\alpha_u \left((F_2\hat{W}_u - \mathbf{1}^{\mathrm{T}}T\Delta\phi_1(t)^{\mathrm{T}}\hat{W}_c) \right.$$

$$\left. - \frac{1}{4}\left(\frac{\partial\phi_1}{\partial x}g(x)R^{-1}g(x)^{\mathrm{T}}\frac{\partial\phi_1}{\partial x}^{\mathrm{T}}\right)\hat{W}_u\left(\frac{\Delta\phi_1(t)^{\mathrm{T}}}{\left(\Delta\phi_1(t)^{\mathrm{T}}\Delta\phi_1(t)\right) + 1}\right)^2\hat{W}_c\right),$$

where $\alpha_u \in \mathbb{R}^+$ is a tuning gain and $F_2 \succ 0$ is a user-defined positive definite matrix picked appropriately for stability. Similarly,

$$\dot{\hat{W}}_d = -\alpha_d \left((F_3\hat{W}_d - \mathbf{1}^{\mathrm{T}}T(\Delta\phi_1(t)^{\mathrm{T}}\hat{W}_c) \right.$$

$$\left. + \frac{1}{4\gamma^2}(\frac{\partial\phi_1}{\partial x}k(x)k(x)^{\mathrm{T}}\frac{\partial\phi_1}{\partial x}^{\mathrm{T}})\hat{W}_d\left(\frac{\Delta\phi_1(t)^{\mathrm{T}}}{\left(\Delta\phi_1(t)^{\mathrm{T}}\Delta\phi_1(t) + 1\right)^2}\right)^{\mathrm{T}}\hat{W}_c\right),$$

where $\alpha_d \in \mathbb{R}^+$ is a tuning gain and $F_3 \succ 0$ is a user-defined positive definite matrix picked appropriately for stability.

Please note that all derivations here are performed under the assumption that the value functions are smooth functions. If the smoothness assumption is not satisfied, then the theory of viscosity solutions can be used to solve the HJ equations.

A different approach than the integral RL algorithm is developed in [66] which uses a system identifier along with RL to avoid requiring the knowledge of the internal dynamics. The concurrent learning technique can also be employed to speed up the convergence of RL algorithms [75, 76].

19.9.2. *Non-Zero-Sum Nash Games*

This subsection considers N players playing a non-zero-sum dynamic game. The N agent/decision makers can be non-cooperative and can also cooperate in teams. Each of the agents has access to the full state of the system. In this section, non-cooperative solution concepts will be considered. RL is used to find the Nash equilibrium of non-cooperative games online in real time using measured data.

Consider the N-player nonlinear time-invariant differential game,

$$\dot{x}(t) = f(x(t)) + \sum_{j=1}^{N} g_j(x(t))u_j(t),$$

where $x \in \mathbb{R}^n$ is a measurable state vector, $u_j(t) \in \mathbb{R}^{m_j}$ are the control inputs, $f(x) \in \mathbb{R}^n$ is the drift dynamics and $g_j(x) \in \mathbb{R}^{n \times m_j}$ is the input dynamics. It is assumed that $f(0) = 0$ and $f(x) + \sum_{j=1}^{N} g_j(x)u_j$ is locally Lipschitz and that the system is stabilizable.

The cost functional associated with each player is given by,

$$\mathcal{J}_i(x(0), u_1, u_2, \dots, u_N) = \int_0^\infty \left(r_i(x, u_1, \dots, u_N) \right) dt$$

$$\equiv \int_0^\infty \left(Q_i(x) + \sum_{j=1}^{N} u_j^{\mathrm{T}} R_{ij} u_j \right) dt, \quad \forall i \in \mathcal{N},$$

where $Q_i(\cdot) \succeq 0$ is generally nonlinear and $R_{ii} \succ 0$, $\forall i \in \mathcal{N}$, $R_{ij} \succeq 0$, $\forall j \neq i \in \mathcal{N}$ are symmetric matrices and $\mathcal{N} := \{1, 2, \dots, N\}$.

The value can be defined as,

$$V_i(x, u_1, u_2, \dots, u_N) = \int_t^\infty \left(r_i(x, u_1, \dots, u_N) \right) d\tau, \quad \forall i \in \mathcal{N}, \forall x, u_1, u_2, \dots, u_N.$$

Differential equivalents to each value function are given by the following Bellman equation,

$$r_i(x, u_1, \dots, u_N) + \frac{\partial V_i}{\partial x}^{\mathrm{T}} \left(f(x) + \sum_{j=1}^{N} g_j(x)u_j \right) = 0, \quad V_i(0) = 0, \ \forall i \in \mathcal{N}.$$

The Hamiltonian functions is defined as

$$\mathcal{H}_i\left(x, u_1, \dots, u_N, \frac{\partial V_i}{\partial x}^{\mathrm{T}}\right) = r_i(x, u_1, \dots, u_N) + \frac{\partial V_i}{\partial x}^{\mathrm{T}} \left(f(x) + \sum_{j=1}^{N} g_j(x)u_j \right),$$

$\forall i \in \mathcal{N}.$

According to the stationarity conditions, the associated feedback control policies are given by,

$$u_i^\star = \arg\min_{u_i} \mathcal{H}_i\left(x, u_1, \dots, u_N, \frac{\partial V_i^\star}{\partial x}^{\mathrm{T}}\right) = -\frac{1}{2} R_{ii}^{-1} g_i^{\mathrm{T}}(x) \frac{\partial V_i}{\partial x}, \quad \forall i \in \mathcal{N}.$$

After substituting the feedback control policies into the Hamiltonian, one has the coupled HJ equations,

$$0 = Q_i(x) + \frac{1}{4} \sum_{j=1}^{N} \frac{\partial V_j}{\partial x}^{\mathrm{T}} g_j(x) R_{jj}^{-T} R_{ij} R_{jj}^{-1} g_j^{\mathrm{T}}(x) \frac{\partial V_j}{\partial x}$$

$$+ \frac{\partial V_i}{\partial x}^{\mathrm{T}} \left(f(x) - \frac{1}{2} \sum_{j=1}^{N} g_j(x) R_{jj}^{-1} g_j^{\mathrm{T}}(x) \frac{\partial V_j}{\partial x} \right), \quad \forall i \in \mathcal{N}. \qquad (19.80)$$

19.9.2.1. *Approximate solution for non-zero sum games*

A PI algorithm is now developed as follows by iterating on the Bellman equation to approximate the solution to the coupled HJ equations, where $\epsilon_{\mathrm{iac}} \forall i \in \mathcal{N}$. is a small number used to terminate the algorithm when two consecutive value functions differ by less than $\epsilon_{\mathrm{iac}}, \forall i \in \mathcal{N}$.

Algorithm 19.12: PI for Regulation in Non-Zero-Sum Games

1: **procedure**
2:     Given N-tuple of admissible policies $\mu_i^k(0)$, $\forall i \in \mathcal{N}$
3:     **while** $\|V_i^{\mu^{(k)}} - V_i^{\mu^{(k-1)}}\| \geq \epsilon_{\mathrm{iac}}$, $\forall i \in \mathcal{N}$ **do**
4:         Solve for the N-tuple of costs $V_i^k(x)$ using the coupled Bellman equations

$$Q_i(x) + \frac{\partial V_i^k}{\partial x}^{\mathrm{T}} (f(x) + \sum_{i=1}^{N} g_i(x)\mu_i^k) + \mu_i^{k^{\mathrm{T}}} R_{ii} \mu_i^k + \sum_{j=1}^{N} \mu_j^{k^{\mathrm{T}}} R_{ij} \mu_j^k = 0, \quad V^{\mu_i^k}(0) = 0.$$

5:         Update the N-tuple of control policies μ_i^{k+1}, $\forall i \in \mathcal{N}$ using

$$\mu_i^{k+1} = -\frac{1}{2} R_{ii}^{-1} g_i^{\mathrm{T}}(x) \frac{\partial V_i^k}{\partial x}^{\mathrm{T}},$$

6:     $k := k + 1$.
7:     **end while**
8: **end procedure**

19.9.2.2. *Approximate solution of non-zero sum games using integral RL*

It is obvious that (19.80) requires complete knowledge of the system dynamics. In [27], an equivalent formulation of the coupled IRL Bellman equation that does not involve the dynamics is given as,

$$V_i(x(t - T)) = \int_{t-T}^{t} r_i(x(\tau), u_1(\tau), \dots, u_N(\tau)) \mathrm{d}\tau + V_i(x(t)), \quad \forall i \in \mathcal{N},$$

for any time $t \geq 0$ and time interval $T > 0$.

Assume, as before, that there exist constant weights W_i and such that the value functions V_i^* are approximated on a compact set Ω as,

$$V_i^*(x) = W_i^{\mathrm{T}}\phi_i(x) + \epsilon_i(x), \quad \forall x, \ \forall i \in \mathcal{N},$$

where $\phi_i(x) : \mathbb{R}^n \to \mathbb{R}^{K_i}$, $\forall i \in \mathcal{N}$ are the basis function and basis set vectors, K_i, $\forall i \in \mathcal{N}$, is the number of basis functions, and $\epsilon_i(x)$ is the approximation error. From the approximation literature, the basis functions can be selected as sigmoids, tanh, polynomials, etc.

Assuming current weight estimates $\hat{W}_{ic}, \forall i \in \mathcal{N}$, the outputs of the critic are given by

$$\hat{V}_i(x) = \hat{W}_{ic}^{\mathrm{T}}\phi_i(x), \quad \forall x, \ i \in \mathcal{N}.$$

By using a procedure similar to that used for zero-sum games, the update laws can be rewritten as

$$\dot{W}_{ic} = -\alpha_i \frac{\Delta\phi_i(t)}{\left(\Delta\phi_i(t))^{\mathrm{T}}\Delta\phi_i(t) + 1\right)^2}$$

$$\left(\Delta\phi_i(t)^{\mathrm{T}}\hat{W}_{ic} + \int_{t-T}^{t}\left(Q_i(x) + \hat{u}_i^{\mathrm{T}}R_{ii}\hat{u}_i + \sum_{j=1}^{N}\hat{u}_j^{\mathrm{T}}R_{ij}\hat{u}_j\right)d\tau\right), \quad \forall i \in \mathcal{N},$$

and

$$\dot{\hat{W}}_{iu} = -\alpha_{iu}\left((F_i\hat{W}_{iu} - 1^{\mathrm{T}}\Delta\phi_i(t)^{\mathrm{T}}\hat{W}_{ic})\right.$$

$$-\frac{1}{4}\sum_{j=1}^{N}\left(\frac{\partial\phi_i}{\partial x}g_i(x)R_{ii}^{-T}R_{ij}R_{ii}^{-1}g_i(x)^{\mathrm{T}}\frac{\partial\phi_i}{\partial x}^{\mathrm{T}}\right)$$

$$\left.\hat{W}_{iu}\frac{\Delta\phi_i(t)^{\mathrm{T}}}{\left(\Delta\phi_i(t)^{\mathrm{T}}\Delta\phi_i(t) + 1\right)^2}\hat{W}_{jc}\right), \quad \forall i \in \mathcal{N},$$

respectively, with $\Delta\phi_i(t) := \phi_i(t) - \phi_i(t - T)$, and $F_i \succ 0$ is picked appropriately for stability.

A model-free learning algorithm for non-zero-sum Nash games has been investigated in [77]. System identification is used in [78] to avoid requiring the complete knowledge of the system dynamics.

19.10. Conclusion

This book chapter uses computational intelligence techniques to bring together adaptive control and optimal control. Adaptive controllers do not generally converge to optimal solutions, and optimal controllers are designed offline using full dynamics information by solving matrix design equations. The book chapter shows that methods from RL can be used to design new types of adaptive controllers that converge to optimal control and game-theoretic solutions online in real time by measuring data along the system trajectories. These are called optimal adaptive controllers, and they have multi-loop, multi-timescale structures that come from reinforcement learning methods of policy iteration and value iteration. These controllers learn the solutions to HJ design equations, such as the Riccati equation, online without knowing the full dynamical model of the system.

The readers are also directed to the works [34–39], and [40] for other RL-inspired control approaches.

Acknowledgements

This chapter is based upon the work supported by the NSF under grant numbers CPS-1851588, CPS-2038589, SATC-1801611, and S&AS-1849198, the ARO under grant number W911NF1910270, and the Minerva Research Initiative under grant number N00014-18-1-2160.

References

[1] K. J. Astrom, and B. Wittenmark, *Adaptive Control*, Addison-Wesley (1995).

[2] P. Ioannou and B. Fidan, *Adaptive Control Tutorial*, SIAM Press, Philadelphia (2006).

[3] F. L. Lewis, D. Vrabie, K. G. Vamvoudakis, RL and feedback control: using natural decision methods to design optimal adaptive controllers, *IEEE Control Syst. Mag.*, vol. 32, no. 6, pp. 76–105 (2012).

[4] K. G. Vamvoudakis, H. Modares, B. Kiumarsi, F. L. Lewis, Game theory-based control system algorithms with real-time RL, *IEEE Control Syst. Mag.*, vol. 37, no. 1, pp. 33–52 (2017).

[5] F. L. Lewis, D. Vrabie, and V. Syrmos, *Optimal Control*, 3rd edn., John Wiley, New York (2012).

[6] Z.-H. Li and M. Krstic, Optimal design of adaptive tracking controllers for nonlinear systems, *Automatica*, vol. 33, no. 8, pp. 1459–1473 (1997).

[7] R. S. Sutton and A. G. Barto, *RL: An Introduction*, MIT Press, Cambridge, Massachusetts (1998).

[8] W. B. Powell, *Approximate Dynamic Programming*, 2nd edn., Wiley, Hoboken (2011).

[9] P. J. Werbos, A menu of designs for RL over time, in *Neural Networks for Control*, eds. W. T. Miller, R. S. Sutton, P. J. Werbos, MIT Press, Cambridge, pp. 67–95 (1991).

[10] K. G. Vamvoudakis, P. J. Antsaklis, W. E. Dixon, J. P. Hespanha, F. L. Lewis, H. Modares, and B. Kiumarsi, Autonomy and machine intelligence in complex systems: a tutorial, *Proc. American Control Conference (ACC)*, pp. 5062–5079 (2015).

[11] F. L. Lewis, G. Lendaris, and D. Liu, Special issue on approximate dynamic programming and RL for feedback control, *IEEE Trans. Syst. Man Cybern. Part B*, vol. 38, no. 4 (2008).

[12] F. Y. Wang, H. Zhang, and D. Liu, Adaptive dynamic programming: an introduction, *IEEE Comput. Intell. Mag.*, pp. 39–47 (2009).

[13] S. N. Balakrishnan, J. Ding, and F. L. Lewis, Issues on stability of ADP feedback controllers for dynamical systems, *IEEE Trans. Syst. Man Cybern. Part B*, vol. 38, no. 4, pp. 913–917, special issue on ADP/RL, invited survey paper (2008).

[14] F. L. Lewis and D. Liu, *RL and Approximate Dynamic Programming for Feedback Control*, IEEE Press Series on Computational Intelligence (2013).

[15] J. Si, A. Barto, W. Powell, and D. Wunsch, *Handbook of Learning and Approximate Dynamic Programming*, IEEE Press, USA (2004).

[16] D. Prokhorov (ed.), *Computational Intelligence in Automotive Applications*, Springer (2008).

[17] X. Cao, *Stochastic Learning and Optimization*, Springer-Verlag, Berlin (2007).

[18] J. M. Mendel and R. W. MacLaren, RL control and pattern recognition systems, in *Adaptive, Learning, and Pattern Recognition Systems: Theory and Applications*, eds. J. M. Mendel and K. S. Fu, Academic Press, New York, pp. 287–318 (1970).

[19] L. Busoniu, R. Babuska, B. De Schutter, and D. Ernst, *RL and Dynamic Programming Using Function Approximators*, CRC Press, Boca Raton (2009).

[20] W. Schultz, Neural coding of basic reward terms of animal learning theory, game theory, microeconomics and behavioral ecology, *Curr. Opin. Neurobiol.*, vol. 14, pp. 139–147 (2004).

[21] K. Doya, H. Kimura, and M. Kawato, Neural mechanisms for learning and control, *IEEE Control Syst. Mag.*, pp. 42–54 (2001).

[22] H. Zhang, Q. Wei, and Y. Luo, A novel infinite-time optimal tracking control scheme for a class of discrete-time nonlinear systems via the greedy HDP iteration algorithm, *IEEE Trans. Syst. Man Cybern. Part B: Cybern.*, vol. 38, pp. 937–942 (2008).

[23] D. Wang, D. Liu, and Q. Wei, Finite-horizon neuro-optimal tracking control for a class of discrete-time nonlinear systems using adaptive dynamic programming approach, *Neurocomputing*, vol. 78, pp. 14–22 (2012).

[24] H. Zhang, L. Cui, X. Zhang, and X. Luo, Data-driven robust approximate optimal tracking control for unknown general nonlinear systems using adaptive dynamic programming method, *IEEE Trans. Neural Networks*, vol. 22, pp. 2226–2236 (2011).

[25] T. Dierks and S. Jagannathan, Optimal control of affine nonlinear continuous-time systems, *Proc. Am. Control Conf.*, pp. 1568–1573 (2010).

[26] P. J. Werbos, Approximate dynamic programming for real-time control and neural modeling, in *Handbook of Intelligent Control*, eds. D. A. White and D. A. Sofge, Van Nostrand Reinhold, New York (1992).

[27] D. Vrabie, K. G. Vamvoudakis, and F. L. Lewis, *Optimal Adaptive Control and Differential Games by RL Principles*, Control Engineering Series, IET Press (2012).

[28] H. Zhang, D. Liu, Y. Luo, and D. Wang, *Adaptive Dynamic Programming for Control: Algorithms and Stability*, Springer (2013).

[29] D. Vrabie and F. L. Lewis, Neural network approach to continuous-time direct adaptive optimal control for partially-unknown nonlinear systems, *Neural Networks*, vol. 22, no. 3, pp. 237–246 (2009).

[30] A. G. Barto, R. S. Sutton, and C. Anderson, Neuron-like adaptive elements that can solve difficult learning control problems, *IEEE Trans. Syst. Man Cybern.*, pp. 834–846 (1983).

[31] D. P. Bertsekas and J. N. Tsitsiklis, *Neuro-Dynamic Programming*, Athena Scientific, MA (1996).

[32] R. E. Bellman, *Dynamic Programming*, Princeton University Press, Princeton, NJ (1957).

[33] P. J. Werbos, Neural networks for control and system identification, *Proc. IEEE Conf. Decision and Control* (1989).

[34] B. Kiumarsi, K. G. Vamvoudakis, H. Modares, and F. L. Lewis, Optimal and autonomous control using RL: a survey, *IEEE Trans. Neural Networks Learn. Syst.*, vol. 29, no. 6, pp. 2042–2062 (2018).

[35] K. G. Vamvoudakis and N.-M. T. Kokolakis, *Synchronous RL-Based Control for Cognitive Autonomy*, Foundations and Trends in Systems and Control, vol. 8, no. 1–2, pp. 1–175 (2020).

[36] Z.-P. Jiang, T. Bian, and W. Gao, *Learning-Based Control: A Tutorial and Some Recent Results*, Foundations and Trends in Systems and Control, vol. 8, no. 3, pp. 176–284 (2020).

[37] R. Kamalapurkar, P. Walters, J. Rosenfeld, and W. Dixon, *RL for Optimal Feedback Control*, Springer (2018).

[38] D. Liu, Q. Wei, D. Wang, X. Yang, and H. Li, *Adaptive Dynamic Programming with Application in Optimal Control*, Springer (2017).

[39] K. G. Vamvoudakis, Y. Wan, F. L. Lewis, and D. Cansever (eds.), *Handbook of RL and Control*, to appear, Springer (2021).

[40] K. G. Vamvoudakis and S. Jagannathan (eds.), *Control of Complex Systems: Theory and Applications*, Elsevier (2016).

[41] Y. Jiang and Z.-P. Jiang, *Robust Adaptive Dynamic Programming*, John Wiley & Sons (2017).

[42] D. Prokhorov and D. Wunsch, Adaptive critic designs, *IEEE Trans. Neural Networks*, vol. 8, no. 5, pp. 997–1007 (1997).

[43] A. Al-Tamimi, F. L. Lewis, and M. Abu-Khalaf, Discrete-time nonlinear HJB solution using approximate dynamic programming: convergence proof, *IEEE Trans. Syst. Man Cybern. Part B*, vol. 38, no. 4, pp. 943–949, special issue on ADP/RL (2008).

[44] D. Vrabie, O. Pastravanu, M. Abu-Khalaf, and F. L. Lewis, Adaptive optimal control for continuous-time linear systems based on policy iteration, *Automatica*, vol. 45, pp. 477–484 (2009).

[45] D. Liu, X. Yang, and H. Li, Adaptive optimal control for a class of continuous-time affine nonlinear systems with unknown internal dynamics, *Neural Comput. Appl.*, vol. 23, pp. 1843–1850 (2013).

[46] A. Papoulis, *Probability, Random Variables and Stochastic Processes*, McGraw-Hill (2002).

[47] R. M. Wheeler and K. S. Narendra, Decentralized learning in finite Markov chains, *IEEE Trans. Automatic Control*, vol. 31, no. 6 (1986).

[48] R. A. Howard, *Dynamic Programming and Markov Processes*, MIT Press, Cambridge, MA (1960).

[49] P. Mehta and S. Meyn, Q-learning and Pontryagin's minimum principle, *Proc. IEEE Conf. Decision and Control*, pp. 3598–3605 (2009).

[50] H. Zhang, J. Huang, and F. L. Lewis, Algorithm and stability of ATC receding horizon control, *Proc. IEEE Symp. ADPRL*, Nashville, pp. 28–35 (2009).

[51] C. Watkins, Learning from delayed rewards, Ph.D. Thesis, Cambridge University, Cambridge, England (1989).

[52] C. J. C. H. Watkins and P. Dayan, Q-learning, *Mach. Learn.*, vol. 8, pp. 279–292 (1992).

[53] K. L. Moore, *Iterative Learning Control for Deterministic Systems*, Springer-Verlag, London (1993).

[54] S. Ferrari and R. F. Stengel, An adaptive critic global controller, *Proc. Am. Control Conf.*, pp. 2665–2670 (2002).

[55] D. Prokhorov, R. A. Santiago, and D. C. Wunsch II, Adaptive critic designs: a case study for neurocontrol, *Neural Networks*, vol. 8, no. 9, pp. 1367–1372 (1995).

[56] T. Hanselmann, L. Noakes, and A. Zaknich, Continuous-time adaptive critics, *IEEE Trans. Neural Networks*, vol. 18, no. 3, pp. 631–647 (2007).

[57] A. J. Van der Schaft, L2-gain analysis of nonlinear systems and nonlinear state feedback H8 control, *IEEE Trans. Automatic Control*, vol. 37, no. 6, pp. 770–784 (1992).

[58] S. Bradtke, B. Ydstie, and A. Barto, Adaptive linear quadratic control using policy iteration, *Proc. Am. Control Conf.*, Baltimore, pp. 3475–3479 (1994).

[59] F. L. Lewis and K. G. Vamvoudakis, RL for partially observable dynamic processes: adaptive dynamic programming using measured output data, *IEEE Trans. Syst. Man Cybern. Part B*, vol. 41, no. 1, pp. 14–25 (2011).

[60] K. Doya, RL in continuous time and space, *Neural Comput.*, vol. 12, pp. 219–245 (2000).

[61] M. Abu-Khalaf, F. L. Lewis, and J. Huang, Policy iterations on the Hamilton-Jacobi-Isaacs equation for state feedback control with input saturation, *IEEE Trans. Automatic Control*, vol. 51, no. 12, pp. 1989–1995 (2006).

[62] L. C. Baird, RL in continuous time: advantage updating, *Proc. Int. Conf. on Neural Networks*, Orlando, FL, pp. 2448–2453 (1994).

[63] K. G. Vamvoudakis and F. L. Lewis, Online actor-critic algorithm to solve the continuous-time infinite horizon optimal control problem, *Automatica*, vol. 46, no. 5, pp. 878–888 (2010).

[64] K. G. Vamvoudakis, D. Vrabie, and F. L. Lewis, Online learning algorithm for optimal control with integral RL, *Int. J. Robust Nonlinear Control*, vol. 24, no. 17, pp. 2686–2710 (2014).

[65] Y. Jiang and Z. P. Jiang, Computational adaptive optimal control for continuous-time linear systems with completely unknown dynamics, *Automatica*, vol. 48, pp. 2699–2704 (2012).

[66] S. Bhasin, R. Kamalapurkar, M. Johnson, K. G. Vamvoudakis, F. L. Lewis, and W. E. Dixon, A novel actor-critic-identifier architecture for approximate optimal control of uncertain nonlinear systems, *Automatica*, vol. 49, no. 1, pp. 82–92 (2013).

[67] D. Vrabie and F. L. Lewis, Adaptive dynamic programming for online solution of a zero-sum differential game, *J. Control Theory Appl.*, vol. 9, no. 3, pp. 353–360 (2011).

[68] K. G. Vamvoudakis and F. L. Lewis, Multi-player non-zero sum games: online adaptive learning solution of coupled Hamilton-Jacobi equations, *Automatica*, vol. 47, pp. 1556–1569 (2011).

[69] K. G. Vamvoudakis, F. L. Lewis, and G. R. Hudas, Multi-agent differential graphical games: online adaptive learning solution for synchronization with optimality, *Automatica*, vol. 48, no. 8, pp. 1598–1611 (2012).

[70] M. I. Abouheaf, F. L. Lewis, K. G. Vamvoudakis, S. Haesaert, and R. Babuska, Multi-agent discrete-time graphical games and RL solutions, *Automatica*, vol. 50, no. 12, pp. 3038–3053 (2014).

[71] K. G. Vamvoudakis and J. P. Hespanha, Cooperative Q-learning for rejection of persistent adversarial inputs in networked linear quadratic systems, *IEEE Trans. Autom. Control*, vol. 63, no. 4, pp. 1018–1031 (2018).

[72] K. G. Vamvoudakis, F. L. Lewis, M. Johnson, and W. E. Dixon, Online learning algorithm for stackelberg games in problems with hierarchy, *Proc. 51st IEEE Conf. on Decision and Control*, Maui, HI, pp. 1883–1889 (2012).

[73] K. G. Vamvoudakis, F. L. Lewis, and W. E. Dixon, Open-loop stackelberg learning solution for hierarchical control problems, *Int. J. Adapt. Control Signal Process.*, vol. 33, no. 2, pp. 285–299 (2019).

[74] K. G. Vamvoudakis, D. Vrabie, and F. L. Lewis, Online learning algorithm for zero-sum games with integral reinforcement learning, *J. Artif. Intell. Soft Comput. Res.*, vol. 1, no. 4, pp. 315–332 (2011).

[75] R. Kamalapurkar, P. Walters, and W. E. Dixon, Model-based RL for approximate optimal regulation, *Automatica*, vol. 64, pp. 94–104 (2016).

[76] R. Kamalapurkar, J. Klotz, and W. E. Dixon, Concurrent learning-based online approximate feedback Nash equilibrium solution of n-player nonzero-sum differential games, *IEEE/CAA J. Autom. Sin.*, vol. 1, no. 3, p. 239–247 (2014).

[77] K. G. Vamvoudakis, Non-zero sum Nash Q-learning for unknown deterministic continuous-time linear systems, *Automatica*, vol. 61, pp. 274–281 (2015).

[78] M. Johnson, R. Kamalapurkar, S. Bhasin, and W. E. Dixon, Approximate n-player nonzero-sum game solution for an uncertain continuous nonlinear system, *IEEE Trans. Neural Network Learn. Syst.*, vol. 26, no. 8, pp. 1645–1658 (2015).

Chapter 20

Nature-Inspired Optimal Tuning of Fuzzy Controllers

Radu-Emil Precup and Radu-Codrut David

Politehnica University of Timisoara,
Department of Automation and Applied Informatics,
Bd. V. Parvan 2, 300223 Timisoara, Romania
radu.precup@aut.upt.ro
davidradu@gmail.com

This chapter deals with the nature-inspired optimal tuning of fuzzy controllers. In the first part, the structures of low-cost proportional-integral (PI) and proportional-integral-derivative fuzzy controllers in their Mamdani and Takagi–Sugeno forms are discussed. In the second part, the operation principles of recent nature-inspired optimization algorithms are described, namely gray wolf optimizer (GWO), whale optimization algorithm (WOA), slime mold algorithm (SMA), hybrid particle swarm optimization–gravitational search algorithm (PSOGSA), and hybrid gray wolf optimizer–particle swarm optimization (GWOPSO) algorithm. Here, the information feedback model F1 in these algorithms, which leads to GWOF1, WOAF1, SMAF1, PSOGSAF1, and GWOPSOF1 algorithms, is introduced. In the third part, these nature-inspired algorithms are applied to the optimal tuning of Takagi–Sugeno PI-fuzzy controllers for nonlinear servo systems, minimizing the objective functions defined as the sum of times multiplied by absolute errors.

20.1. Introduction

As pointed out by Precup and David [1], the majority of fuzzy control applications uses fuzzy controllers (FCs) for direct feedback control or is placed at a lower level in hierarchical control system structures. However, fuzzy control can also be used at the supervisory level, for example, in adaptive control system structures [2]. Nowadays, fuzzy control is no longer used only to directly express the knowledge on the process or, in other words, to carry out model-free fuzzy control. A fuzzy controller can be tuned from a fuzzy model obtained in terms of system identification techniques, and thus it can be viewed in the framework of a model-based fuzzy control.

However, using as little information as possible on the process model and the systematic tuning based on the knowledge gained from experiments conducted on the real process belongs to the popular framework of data-driven control or model-free control. Some important techniques in this regard, focusing on the iterative experiment-based update of controller parameters, and exhibiting successful results, both classical and fresh ones, are iterative feedback tuning (IFT) [3, 4], model-free adaptive control (MFAC) [5, 6], simultaneous perturbation stochastic approximation [7, 8], correlation-based tuning [9, 10], frequency domain tuning [11, 12], iterative regression tuning [13], and adaptive online IFT [14]. Widely used non-iterative techniques are model-free control (MFC) [15, 16], virtual reference feedback tuning [17, 18], active disturbance rejection control (ADRC) [19, 20], data-driven predictive control [21, 22], unfalsified control [23, 24], data-driven inversion-based control [25, 26], and an approach that does not make an a priori assumption of the persistency of excitation on the system input, but it, however, studies equivalent conditions on the given data based on which different analysis and control problems can be solved [27].

The advantages of fuzzy control and data-driven or model-free control are merged in terms of the combination of these techniques. These combinations include H_∞ fuzzy control [28], fault-tolerant fuzzy control [29], parameterized data-driven fuzzy control [30], data-driven interpretable fuzzy control [31], MFC merged with fuzzy control [32, 33], MFAC merged with fuzzy control [34], ADRC mixed with fuzzy control [35, 36], fuzzy logic-based adaptive ADRC [37], and distending function-based data-driven arithmetic fuzzy control [38].

The following categories of FCs are most often used:

- Mamdani FCs, referred to also as linguistic FCs, with either fuzzy consequents, i.e., type-1 fuzzy systems [39] or singleton consequents, i.e., type-2 fuzzy systems. These FCs are usually used as direct closed-loop controllers.
- Takagi–Sugeno FCs, referred to also as type-3 fuzzy systems [39], with mainly affine consequents. These FCs are typically used as supervisory controllers.

As shown by Precup and David [1, 40], a systematic way to meet the performance specifications of fuzzy control systems is the optimal tuning of FCs in terms of optimization problems with variables represented by the parameters of FCs. Nature-inspired algorithms can solve these optimization problems to meet the performance specifications if they are expressed by adequately defined objective functions and constraints. The motivation for nature-inspired optimization algorithms in combination with fuzzy control and fuzzy modeling concerns their ability to cope with non-convex or non-differentiable objective functions due to controller structures and nonlinearities, and to process complexity, which can lead to multi-objective optimization problems.

A selection of latest and also representative nature-inspired algorithms applied to the optimal parameter tuning of FCs includes adaptive weight genetic algorithm (GA) for gear shifting [41], GA-based multi-objective optimization for electric vehicle powertrains [42], GA for hybrid power systems [43], engines [44], energy management in hybrid vehicles [45], wellhead back pressure [46], micro-unmanned helicopters [47], particle swarm optimization (PSO) algorithm with compensating coefficient of inertia weight factor for filter time constant adaptation in hybrid energy storage systems [48], set-based PSO algorithm with adaptive weights for optimal path planning of unmanned aerial vehicles [49], PSO algorithm for zinc production [50], inverted pendulums [51] and servo systems [40], hybrid PSO–artificial bee colony algorithm for frequency regulation in microgrids [52], imperialist competitive algorithm for human immunodeficiency [53], gray wolf optimizer (GWO) algorithms for sun-tracker systems [54] and servo systems [55], PSO, cuckoo search and differential evolution (DE) for gantry crane systems [56], whale optimization algorithm (WOA) for vibration control of steel structures [57] and servo systems [58, 59], grasshopper optimization algorithm for load frequency [60], DE for electro-hydraulic servo systems [20], gravitational search algorithm (GSA), charged system search (CSS) for servo systems [40], multiverse optimizer for fuzzy parameter tuning in structural motion systems [61], and slime mold algorithm (SMA) for servo systems [62].

This chapter is the second edition of an earlier work by Precup and David [1], which dealt with nature-inspired optimization of fuzzy controllers and fuzzy models. The current chapter focuses on nature-inspired optimization of fuzzy controllers and fuzzy models that are no more treated. The same optimization problems are considered; however, this chapter does not offer fuzzy controllers with a reduced process parametric sensitivity; the output sensitivity function is no more included in the objective function (equal to the sum of times multiplied by absolute errors), or, in other words, it can be considered that its weighting parameter in the objective function is zero. The same process is considered in both chapters, namely a family of nonlinear servo systems. The same controllers are also considered in both chapters, i.e., Takagi–Sugeno proportional-integral (PI)-fuzzy controllers. CSS algorithms were treated in the study conducted by Precup and David [1], while this chapter treats more recent algorithms, i.e., GWO, WOA, SMA, hybrid PSOGSA, and hybrid GWOPSO algorithm.

The current chapter exploits a recent and successful modification and also improvement of nature-inspired optimization algorithms characterized by a modification of their structure in terms of including information feedback models according to the general formulation given in an earlier study [63]. Six types of information feedback models are proposed by Wang and Tan [63], with individuals from previous iterations being selected in either a fixed or random manner and further used in the update process of the algorithms. The PSO and representative algorithms combined with information feedback models are discussed by Wang and Tan [63], the combination with NSGA-III is treated by Gu and Wang [64] and with multi-objective evolutionary algorithms based on decomposition by Zhang *et al.* [65]. The description of the introduction of the information feedback model F1 in these algorithms, which leads to GWOF1, WOAF1, and SMAF1, has already been presented by Precup *et al.* [62] but is connected to a different objective function and emphasized in this chapter, and the presentation of PSOGSAF1 and GWOPSOF1 algorithms is also included.

The next section gives insights into the design and tuning of Mamdani and Takagi–Sugeno FCs with dynamics focusing on PI-fuzzy controllers. Section 3 discusses the GWO, WOA, SMA, PSOGSA, and GWOPSO algorithm-based optimal tuning of FCs for nonlinear servo systems. Details on the introduction of the information feedback model F1 in nature-inspired optimization algorithms are also provided, which are aimed at the GWOF1, WOAF1, SMAF1, PSOGSAF1, and GWOPSOF1 algorithm-based optimal tuning of FCs for nonlinear servo systems. The conclusions are outlined in Section 4.

20.2. Structures and Design Methodology of Fuzzy Controllers

This chapter is expressed using the information given by Precup and David in an earlier study [1]. The FCs without dynamics offer nonlinear input–output static maps, which can be modified by the proper tuning of all parameters in the FC structure (the shapes and scaling factors of membership functions, the rule base, and the defuzzification method). The dynamics of integral and / or derivative type in the FC structure can be introduced on either the inputs or the outputs of the FC resulting in two versions of PI-fuzzy controllers [66]:

- the proportional-integral-fuzzy controller with integration of controller output (PI-FC-OI) and
- the proportional-integral-fuzzy controller with integration of controller input (PI-FC-II).

According to Sugeno and Kóczy [39, 67], both versions of PI-fuzzy controllers, with the structures given in Figure 20.1, are type-2 fuzzy systems.

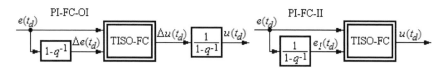

Figure 20.1: Structures of proportional-integral-fuzzy controllers [1].

As shown in Figure 20.1, the two PI-fuzzy controllers are built around the two inputs-single output fuzzy controller (TISO-FC), which is a nonlinear subsystem without dynamics. In addition, the input variables are also scheduling variables. The presentation is focused, as demonstrated by Precup and David [1], on PI-fuzzy controllers because they can be extended relatively easily to proportional-integral-derivative (PID)-fuzzy controllers and transformed in particular forms of proportional-derivative (PD)-fuzzy controllers. The structures presented in Figure 20.1 can also be transformed to be extended to two-degrees-of-freedom (2-DOF) fuzzy controllers, proposed in earlier studies by Precup and Preitl [68, 69] as fuzzy controllers with non-homogenous dynamics with respect to the input channels, and next developed in servo system and electrical drives applications [70, 71].

The dynamics are inserted in PI-FC-OI by the numerical differentiation of the control error $e(t_d)$, leading to the increment of control error $\Delta e(t_d) = e(t_d) - e(t_d - 1)$, and the numerical integration of the increment of control signal $\Delta u(t_d) = u(t_d) - u(t_d - 1)$, which gives the control signal $u(t_d)$. The variable t_d in Figure 20.1 is the current discrete time index, and q indicates the forward time shift operator. The dynamics is inserted in PI-FC-II by the numerical integration of $e(t_d)$ producing the integral of control error $e_I(t_d) = e_I(t_d - 1) + \Delta e(t_d)$. It is assumed that the nonlinear scaling factors of the input and output variables specific to TISO-FC are inserted in the controlled process.

As pointed out by Precup and David [1], the fuzzification in TISO-FC that belongs to PI-FC-OI is conducted in terms of the input (and also scheduling) and output membership functions illustrated in Figure 20.2 for Mamdani PI-fuzzy controllers. The fuzzification in TISO-FC, which belongs to PI-FC-II, is performed in terms of the same membership functions as those specific to PI-FC-OI, but the input variable $e_I(t_d)$ is used instead of $\Delta e(t_d)$, and the output variable $u(t_d)$ is used instead of $\Delta u(t_d)$. The relatively simple shapes of membership functions given in Figure 20.2, which is reflected in few parameters, contribute to ensuring the cost-effective implementation of FCs. Other distributions of membership

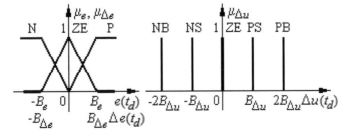

Figure 20.2: Input and output membership functions of Mamdani PI-fuzzy controllers with integration on controller output [1].

functions can modify the FC nonlinearities in a desired way. The Takagi–Sugeno PI-fuzzy controllers make use of only the input membership functions illustrated in Figure 20.2.

Both versions of the Mamdani PI-fuzzy controllers, namely PI-FC-OI and PI-FC-II, employ Mamdani's MAX-MIN compositional rule of inference assisted by the rule base exemplified as follows for PI-FC-OI [1]:

Rule 1: IF $e(t_d)$ IS N AND $\Delta e(t_d)$ IS P THEN $\Delta u(t_d)$ IS ZE,

Rule 2: IF $e(t_d)$ IS ZE AND $\Delta e(t_d)$ IS P THEN $\Delta u(t_d)$ IS PS,

Rule 3: IF $e(t_d)$ IS P AND $\Delta e(t_d)$ IS P THEN $\Delta u(t_d)$ IS PB,

Rule 4: IF $e(t_d)$ IS N AND $\Delta e(t_d)$ IS ZE THEN $\Delta u(t_d)$ IS NS,

Rule 5:IF $e(t_d)$ IS ZE AND $\Delta e(t_d)$ IS ZE THEN $\Delta u(t_d)$ IS ZE,

Rule 6: IF $e(t_d)$ IS P AND $\Delta e(t_d)$ IS ZE THEN $\Delta u(t_d)$ IS PS,

Rule 7: IF $e(t_d)$ IS N AND $\Delta e(t_d)$ IS N THEN $\Delta u(t_d)$ IS NB,

Rule 8: IF $e(t_d)$ IS ZE AND $\Delta e(t_d)$ IS N THEN $\Delta u(t_d)$ IS NS,

Rule 9: IF $e(t_d)$ IS P AND $\Delta e(t_d)$ IS N THEN $\Delta u(t_d)$ IS ZE, (20.1)

and the center of gravity method for singletons is used in the defuzzification module of the FCs. The inference engines of both versions of Takagi–Sugeno PI-fuzzy controllers are based on the SUM and PROD operators assisted by the rule base, which is exemplified here for PI-FC-OI [1]:

Rule 1: IF $e(t_d)$ IS N AND $\Delta e(t_d)$ IS P THEN $\Delta u(t_d) = K_P^1[\Delta e(t_d) + \mu^1 e(t_d)]$,

Rule 2: IF $e(t_d)$ IS ZE AND $\Delta e(t_d)$ IS P THEN $\Delta u(t_d) = K_P^2[\Delta e(t_d) + \mu^2 e(t_d)]$,

Rule 3: IF $e(t_d)$ IS P AND $\Delta e(t_d)$ IS P THEN $\Delta u(t_d) = K_P^3[\Delta e(t_d) + \mu^3 e(t_d)]$,

Rule 4: IF $e(t_d)$ IS N AND $\Delta e(t_d)$ IS ZE THEN $\Delta u(t_d) = K_P^4[\Delta e(t_d) + \mu^4 e(t_d)]$,

Rule 5: IF $e(t_d)$ IS ZE AND $\Delta e(t_d)$ IS ZE THEN $\Delta u(t_d) = K_P^5[\Delta e(t_d) + \mu^5 e(t_d)]$,

Rule 6: IF $e(t_d)$ IS P AND $\Delta e(t_d)$ IS ZE THEN $\Delta u(t_d) = K_P^6[\Delta e(t_d) + \mu^6 e(t_d)]$,

Rule 7: IF $e(t_d)$ IS N AND $\Delta e(t_d)$ IS N THEN $\Delta u(t_d) = K_P^7[\Delta e(t_d) + \mu^7 e(t_d)]$,

Rule 8: IF $e(t_d)$ IS ZE AND $\Delta e(t_d)$ IS N THEN $\Delta u(t_d) = K_P^8[\Delta e(t_d) + \mu^8 e(t_d)]$,

Rule 9: IF $e(t_d)$ IS P AND $\Delta e(t_d)$ IS N THEN $\Delta u(t_d) = K_P^9[\Delta e(t_d) + \mu^9 e(t_d)]$,

(20.2)

and the weighted average method is applied in the defuzzification module of the FCs.

Using the PI-fuzzy controller structures described above, the rule bases given in (20.1) and (20.2) make these controllers behave as bumpless interpolators between separately designed PI controllers. The maximum number of such controllers is nine, and the following conditions ensure the interpolation between only two separately designed PI controllers in case of Takagi–Sugeno PI-fuzzy controllers [1]:

$$K_P^1 = K_P^2 = K_P^4 = K_P^5 = K_P^6 = K_P^8 = K_P^9 = K_P,$$
$$K_P^3 = K_P^7 = \eta \, K_P,$$
$$\mu^1 = \mu^2 = \mu^3 = \mu^4 = \mu^5 = \mu^6 = \mu^7 = \mu^8 = \mu^9 = \mu. \tag{20.3}$$

The unified design methodology of the FCs described in this section consists of the following steps for Mamdani and Takagi–Sugeno PI-fuzzy controllers considered in their PI-FC-OI versions [1]:

Step 1. The continuous-time design of the linear PI controller with the transfer function $C(s)$

$$C(s) = \frac{k_c(1 + T_i s)}{s} = k_C \left(1 + \frac{1}{T_i s}\right), \quad k_C = k_c T_i \tag{20.4}$$

is performed, and it leads to the controller gain k_c (or k_C, depending on the expression of the PI controller transfer function) and integral time constant T_i.

Step 2. The sampling period T_s is set according to the requirements of quasi-continuous digital control. Tustin's method is then applied to discretize the continuous-time linear PI controller, and the recurrent equation of the incremental digital PI controller is

$$\Delta u(t_d) = K_P[\Delta e(t_d) + \mu e(t_d)], \tag{20.5}$$

where the expressions of the parameters that appear K_P and μ in Eqs. (20.3) and (20.5) are as demonstrated earlier by Precup and David [1]:

$$K_P = k_c \, (T_i - 0.5T_s), \quad \mu = \frac{T_s}{T_i - 0.5T_s}. \tag{20.6}$$

The parameter η, with typical values $0 < \eta < 1$, is introduced in Eq. (20.3) to alleviate the overshoot of the fuzzy control system when both inputs have the same sign. These PI-fuzzy controllers can also be applied to the control of non-minimum phase systems with right half-plane zeros, where such rule bases produce the alleviation of the downshoot as well.

Step 3. The modal equivalence principle [72] is applied to map the linear controller parameters onto the PI-fuzzy controller ones. The application of this principle to the Takagi–Sugeno PI-FC-OI results in the tuning condition

$$B_{\Delta e} = \mu B_e, \tag{20.7}$$

and the application to the Mamdani PI-FC-OI leads to the tuning conditions [1]

$$B_{\Delta e} = \mu B_e, \; B_{\Delta u} = K_P \mu B_e. \tag{20.8}$$

The tuning conditions for the Mamdani PI-FC-II are [66]

$$B_{\Delta e} = \frac{1}{\mu} B_e, \; B_{\Delta u} = K_P B_e, \tag{20.9}$$

and the tuning condition for the Takagi–Sugeno PI-FC-II is [1]

$$B_{\Delta e} = \frac{1}{\mu} B_e. \tag{20.10}$$

The value of the parameter B_e in Eqs. (20.7)–(20.10) must be set by the designer. This can be carried out according to the designer's experience, and the stability analysis of the fuzzy control system can be conducted in this regard. However, the systematic tuning of the parameter B_e will be presented as follows in terms of obtaining it after solving optimization problems, as this parameter will be one of the elements of the vector variables of the objective functions.

The PD-fuzzy controllers are designed using the methodology given above and dedicated to PI-fuzzy controllers. The design is carried out in terms of the PD-fuzzy controllers, which is actually the PI-FC-OI structure given in Figure 20.1 but with the output integrator dropped out.

The PID-fuzzy controller structure is presented in Figure 20.3, where the TISO-FC^{PD} block and the TISO-FC^{PI} block are identical to TISO-FC given in Figure 20.1, $u^{PD}(t_d)$ is the control signal of the PD controller, and $\Delta u^{PI}(t_d)$ is the increment of control signal calculated by the PI controller. The fuzzification uses the input membership functions exemplified in Figure 20.3 for the Takagi–Sugeno PID-fuzzy controller, with $g \in \{PI, PD\}$. Figure 20.3 also shows that this PID-fuzzy controller

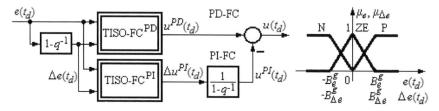

Figure 20.3:   Structure and input membership functions of Takagi–Sugeno PID-fuzzy controller [1].

structure consists of a parallel connection of two blocks, namely the proportional-derivative-fuzzy controller (PD-FC) and the proportional-integral-fuzzy controller (PI-FC).

Setting the sampling period T_s, Tustin's method leads to the discrete time PID controller with the following transfer function $C(q^{-1})$ and parameters [1]:

$$C(q^{-1}) = \frac{\rho_0 + \rho_1 q^{-1} + \rho_2 q^{-2}}{1 - q^{-1}},$$

$$\rho_0 = k_c \left(1 + \frac{T_d}{T_s}\right), \rho_1 = -k_c \left(1 + 2\frac{T_d}{T_s} - \frac{T_s}{T_i}\right), \rho_2 = k_c \frac{T_d}{T_s}. \tag{20.12}$$

The transfer function in (20.12) is expressed next as a parallel connection of discrete time PD and PI controllers with the superscripts PD and PI, respectively, associated to Figure 20.3 [1]

$$C(q^{-1}) = K_P^{PD}(1 - q^{-1} + \mu^{PD}) - \frac{K_P^{PI}(1 - q^{-1} + \mu^{PI})}{1 - q^{-1}},$$

$$K_P^{PD} = \rho_2, \mu^{PD} = -\frac{\rho_1}{\rho_2}, K_P^{PI} = \rho_2 - \rho_1 - \rho_0, \mu^{PI} = \frac{2\rho_2}{\rho_2 - \rho_1 - \rho_0}. \tag{20.13}$$

Therefore, the analogy of (20.13) and the transfer function associated to (20.5) fully justify carrying out the separate design of PI-FC and PD-FC outlined in Figure 20.3 in terms of the design methodology given above.

As pointed out by Precup and David [1], similar controller structures can be formulated in the framework of state feedback control systems. As Precup *et al.* pointed out [73], the general approach to deal with such fuzzy control systems makes use of Takagi–Sugeno–Kang fuzzy models of the process and carries out the stability analysis, producing linear matrix inequalities (LMIs) in terms of the parallel distributed compensation (PDC) approach. The PDC approach is important as it states that the dynamics of each local subsystem in the rule consequents of the Takagi–Sugeno–Kang fuzzy models of the process is controlled separately using the eigenvalue analysis [74, 75]. Recent results on LMI-based stability analysis include the relaxation of stability conditions producing fuzzy adaptive compensation control [76], nonlinear consequents [77], optimal filters with memory [78], application to chaotic systems [79], non-fragile control design [80], event-triggered control [81], indirect adaptive control [82], event-triggered fuzzy sliding mode control [83], the negative absolute eigenvalue approach [84], and the Lyapunov–Krasovskii functionals-based approach [85]. The effects of various parameters of the fuzzy models are discussed in relation with non-quadratic Lyapunov function-based approaches as the membership-function-dependent analysis [86, 87], non-quadratic stabilization of uncertain systems [88], piecewise continuous and smooth functions, piecewise continuous exact fuzzy models, general polynomial approaches [89, 90], sum-of-squares-based polynomial membership functions [91, 92], integral structure-based Lyapunov functions [93], the subspace-based improved sector nonlinearity approach [94], and interpolation function-based approaches [95]. Representative applications of different fuzzy control systems and algorithms include predictive functional control [96], evolving controllers [97, 98], robust adaptive fuzzy control [99], tensor product-based model transformation [100], signatures [101], and fuzzy-neural adaptive terminal iterative learning control [102]. Challenging processes subjected to fuzzy control are generally demonstrated by Precup *et al.* and Dzitac *et al.* [103, 104], and they also deal with gathering of robots [105], hybrid electric vehicles [106], vehicle navigation [107], traffic management [108], telemanipulation [109, 110], non-affine nonlinear systems [111], suspension systems [112], robotic motion control [113], machining processes [114], fault detection [115], turbojet engineers [116], and medical applications [117, 118].

The extensions of fuzzy controllers to type-2 fuzzy controllers prove additional performance improvement because of their extended flexibility, similar to 2-DOF fuzzy controllers. The tuning of type-2 fuzzy controllers is mainly based on optimization algorithms, and recent algorithms used in this purpose include the firefly algorithm [119], several algorithms in the framework of multi-objective optimization [120], chemical optimization [121], with a useful overview conducted by Castillo and Melin [122]. Significant real-world applications deal with virtual disk cloning [123], spacecraft and aerial robots [124, 125], quadrotors [126], unmanned aerial vehicles [127], induction motor drives [128], even-triggered control [129, 130], supervisory control [131], and networked control systems [132].

20.3. GWO, WOA, SMA, PSOGSA, and GWOPSO Algorithm-Based Optimal Tuning of Fuzzy Controllers for Nonlinear Servo Systems

This section is organized as follows: The recent nature-inspired optimization algorithms are first described. The optimization problem is next defined with a focus on the Takagi–Sugeno PI-fuzzy controller dedicated to the position control of a family of nonlinear servo systems, and the optimal tuning methodology is presented along with the mapping of nature-inspired optimization algorithms onto the optimization problem. The final subsection gives an example of validation on servo system lab equipment and real-time experimental results are included.

All algorithms presented in this section belong to the category of swarm intelligence algorithms in the general class of nature-inspired optimization algorithms. They make use of a total number of N agents, and each agent is assigned to a position vector $\mathbf{X}_i(k)$

$$\mathbf{X}_i(k) = [x_i^1(k)\ldots x_i^f(k)\ldots x_i^q(k)]^T \in D_s \subset \Re^q, i = 1\cdots N, \quad (20.14)$$

where [35] $x_i^f(k)$ is the position of ith agent in fth dimension, $f = 1\ldots q$, k is the index of the current iteration, $k = 1\ldots k_{\max}$, $k_{\max}$ is the maximum number of iterations, and T indicates matrix transposition. The expression of the search domain D_s is

$$D_s = [l^1, u^1] \times \cdots \times [l^f, u^f] \times \cdots \times [l^q, u^q] \subset \Re^q, \quad (20.15)$$

l^f are the lower bounds, u^f are the upper bounds, $f = 1\ldots q$, and

$$x_i^f(k) \in [l^f, u^f], i = 1\ldots N, f = 1\ldots q. \quad (20.16)$$

The significance of the agents will be different for each algorithm that is described in the next sub-sections. Another common feature of all algorithms that have been described as follows is that they are stopped after the maximum number of iterations $k_{\max}$ is reached.

20.3.1. *Gray Wolf Optimizer*

The agents in GWO algorithms are gray wolves. The operating mechanism of GWO starts with the random initialization of the population of agents that comprise the wolf pack [133] and continues with the exploration stage, which models the search for the prey. During this stage, the positions of the top three agents, namely the alpha (α), beta (β), and delta (δ) agents, dictate the search pattern; these first three best vector solutions obtained at each iteration are

$$\mathbf{X}^l(k) = x^{l1}(k) \quad \ldots \quad x^{lf}(k) \quad \ldots \quad x^{lq}(k)^T, l \in \{\alpha, \beta, \delta\}, \quad (20.17)$$

and they (namely $\mathbf{X}^\alpha(k)$, $\mathbf{X}^\beta(k)$, and $\mathbf{X}^\delta(k)$) are obtained in terms of

$$
\begin{aligned}
J_{a_j}(\mathbf{X}^\alpha(k)) &= \min_{i=1\ldots N}\{J(\mathbf{X}_i(k))|\mathbf{X}_i(k) \in D_s\}, \\
J_{a_j}(\mathbf{X}^\beta(k)) &= \min_{i=1\ldots N}\{J(\mathbf{X}_i(k))|\mathbf{X}_i(k) \in D_s\backslash\{\mathbf{X}^\alpha(k)\}\}, \\
J_{a_j}(\mathbf{X}^\delta(k)) &= \min_{i=1\ldots N}\{J(\mathbf{X}_i(k))|\mathbf{X}_i(k) \in D_s\backslash\{\mathbf{X}^\alpha(k), \mathbf{X}^\beta(k)\}\}, \\
J_{a_j}(\mathbf{X}^\alpha(k)) &< J_{a_j}(\mathbf{X}^\beta(k)) < J_{a_j}(\mathbf{X}^\delta(k)),
\end{aligned}
\quad (20.18)
$$

where $J : \Re^q \to \Re_+$ is the objective function in a minimization-type optimization problem.

The following search coefficients are defined:

$$a_l^f(k) = a(k)(2r_{1l}^f - 1),$$
$$c_l^f(k) = 2r_{2l}^f, l \in \{\alpha, \beta, \delta\},$$

(20.19)

where $r_{1l}^f \in [0, 1]$ and $r_{2l}^f \in [0, 1]$ are uniformly distributed random numbers, $f = 1 \dots q$, and the coefficients $a(k)$ are linearly decreased from 2 to 0 during the search process

$$a(k) = 2\left(1 - \frac{k-1}{k_{\max} - 1}\right), \quad f = 1 \dots q.$$

(20.20)

The approximate distances between the current solution and the alpha, beta, and delta solutions, i.e., $d_\alpha^{if}(k)$, $d_\beta^{if}(k)$, and $d_\delta^{if}(k)$, respectively, are [134]

$$d_l^{if}(k) = |c_l^f(k)x^{lf}(k) - x_i^f(k)|, \quad i = 1 \dots N, \ l \in \{\alpha, \beta, \delta\},$$

(20.21)

and the elements of the updated alpha, beta, and delta solutions are computed in terms of [134]

$$x^{lf}(k+1) = x^{lf}(k) - a_l^f(k)d_l^{if}(k), \quad f = 1 \dots q, \ i = 1 \dots N, \ l \in \{\alpha, \beta, \delta\},$$

(20.22)

and they lead to the updated expressions of the agents' positions obtained as the arithmetic mean of the updated alpha, beta, and delta agents [134]

$$x_i^f(k+1) = \frac{x^{\alpha f}(k+1) + x^{\beta f}(k+1) + x^{\delta f}(k+1)}{3}, \quad f = 1 \dots q, \ i = 1 \dots N.$$

(20.23)

with the following vector form of Eq. (20.23) [134]:

$$\mathbf{X}_i(k+1) = \frac{\mathbf{X}^\alpha(k+1) + \mathbf{X}^\beta(k+1) + \mathbf{X}^\delta(k+1)}{3}, \quad i = 1 \dots N.$$

(20.24)

20.3.2. Whale Optimization Algorithm

The agents in WOA are whales. The operating mechanism of WOA starts again with the random initialization of the population of agents that represent the set of whales [135]. A set of search-coefficient vectors $\mathbf{a}_i(k) \in \Re^q$ and $\mathbf{c}_i(k) \in \Re^q$ is introduced as follows at each iteration k in order to model the next stage of GWO, namely the prey encircling:

$$\mathbf{a}_i(k) = [a_i^1(k) \cdots a_i^f(k) \cdots a_i^q(k)]^T \in \mathfrak{R}^q,$$
$$\mathbf{c}_i(k) = [a_i^1(k) \cdots a_i^f(k) \cdots a_i^q(k)]^T \in \mathfrak{R}^q, i = 1 \cdots N, \tag{20.25}$$

and the elements of the coefficient vectors are defined as

$$a_i^f(k) = a(k)(2r_1^f - 1),$$
$$c_i^f(k) = 2r_2^f, \tag{20.26}$$

with the coefficients $a(k)$ linearly decreased from 2 to 0 during the search process according to (20.20), $r_1^f \in [0, 1]$ and $r_2^f \in [0, 1]$ are uniformly distributed numbers, $f = 1 \ldots q$.

Using the notation $\mathbf{X}_{best}(k)$ for the best agents' position vector in the population at iteration k, which fulfills

$$\mathbf{X}_{best}(k) = [x_{best}^1(k) \cdots x_{best}^f(k) \cdots a_{best}^q(k)]^T \in D_s \subset \mathfrak{R}^q,$$
$$J(\mathbf{X}_{best}(k)) = \min_{i=1 \cdots N} J(\mathbf{X}_i(k)), \tag{20.27}$$

the position update equation in WOA is [58, 59]

$$\mathbf{X}_i(k+1) = \begin{cases} \mathbf{X}_{best}(k) - \mathbf{f}_i(k), & \text{if C1,} \\ \mathbf{X}_{rand}(t) - \mathbf{g}_i(k), & \text{if C2,} \\ \mathbf{h}_i(k)e^{bl}\cos(2\pi l) + \mathbf{X}_{best}(k), & \text{otherwise,} \end{cases} \tag{20.28}$$

$$\text{C1}: p < 0.5 \text{ and } |a_i^f(k)| \leq 1 \forall f = 1 \cdots q,$$
$$\text{C2}: p < 0.5 \text{ and } |a_i^f(k)| > 1 \ \forall f = 1 \cdots q, \ i = 1 \cdots N,$$

where $p \in [0, 1]$ is a random number, the parameter $b = \text{const}$ defines the shape of the logarithmic spiral of whales' path, set to $b = 1$ for simplifying the shape, $l \in [-1, 1]$ is a uniformly distributed random number, *rand* is an arbitrary agent index, the associated position vector is $\mathbf{X}_{rand}(k)$

$$\mathbf{X}_{rand}(k) = [x_{rand}^1(k) \cdots x_{rand}^f(k) \cdots a_{rand}^q(k)]^T \in D_s \subset \mathfrak{R}^q, \tag{20.29}$$

and $\mathbf{f}_i(k), \mathbf{g}_i(k)$ are distance vectors with the expressions

$$\mathbf{f}_i(k) = [a_i^1|x_i^1(k) - x_{best}^1(k)| \cdots a_i^f|x_i^f(k) - x_{best}^f(k)|$$
$$\cdots a_i^q|x_i^q(k) - x_{best}^q(k)|]^T \in \mathfrak{R}^q,$$
$$\mathbf{g}_i(k) = [a_i^1|x_i^1(k) - x_{rand}^1(k)| \cdots a_i^f|x_i^f(k) - x_{rand}^f(k)|$$
$$\cdots a_i^q|x_i^q(k) - x_{rand}^q(k)|]^T \in \mathfrak{R}^q, \ i = 1 \cdots N. \tag{20.30}$$

20.3.3. *Slime Mold Algorithm*

The agents in SMA are elements of the slime mold. The operating mechanism of SMA starts with the random initialization of the population of agents that represent the slime mold [136]. Using the notation $S_i(k)$ for the fitness (i.e., the value of the objective function) of ith agent with the position vector $\mathbf{X}_i(k)$, the population is ranked in the ascending order of the fitness function values leading to two sets of position vectors, Set$_{FH}$, which is the ranked set of agents in the first half of the population, and Set$_{SH}$, which is the ranked set of agents in the second half of the population, in accordance with Precup *et al.* [62]

$$\{\mathbf{X}_1(k), \mathbf{X}_2(k), \ldots, \mathbf{X}_H(k), \mathbf{X}_{H+1}(k), \ldots, \mathbf{X}_N(k)\} = \text{Set}_{FH} \cup \text{Set}_{SH},$$

$$\text{Set}_{FH} = \{\mathbf{X}_1(k), \mathbf{X}_2(k), \ldots, \mathbf{X}_H(k)\},$$

$$\text{Set}_{SH} = \{\mathbf{X}_{H+1}(k), \ldots, \mathbf{X}_N(k)\}, \tag{20.31}$$

$$S_1(k) \leq S_2(k) \leq \cdots \leq S_H(k) \leq S_{H+1}(k) \leq \cdots \leq S_N(k),$$

where $H = \lfloor N/2 \rfloor$ is the integer part of $N/2$.

The vector $\mathbf{W}_i(k)$ of weights of slime mold consists of the elements (weights) $w_i^f(k)$, $f = 1 \cdots q$ [62]

$$\mathbf{W}_i(k) = [w_i^1(k) \ \cdots \ w_i^f(k) \ \cdots \ w_i^q(k)]^T, \ i = 1 \cdots N,$$

$$w_i^f(k) = \begin{cases} 1 + r_i^f \log(g_i(k)), & \text{if } \mathbf{X}_i(k) \in \text{Set}_{FH}, \\ 1 + r_i^f \log(g_i(k)), & \text{otherwise}, \end{cases} \tag{20.32}$$

$$g_i(k) = \frac{S_b(k) - S_i(k)}{S_b(k) - S_w(k) + \varepsilon} + 1, \quad i = 1 \cdots N, \ f = 1 \cdots q,$$

where log is the notation for the decimal logarithm, $r_i^f \in [0, 1]$ are random numbers, $\varepsilon = \text{const} > 0$ is relatively small to avoid zero denominator in Eq. (20.32), $S_b(k)$ and $S_w(k)$ are the best and worst fitness, respectively, obtained at the current iteration k in terms of Precup *et al.* [62]

$$S_b(k) = \min_{i=1\ldots N} S_i(k) = S_1(k),$$

$$S_w(k) = \max_{i=1\ldots N} S_i(k) = S_N(k). \tag{20.33}$$

The uniformly distributed random numbers v_a^f and v_b^f are next introduced:

$$v_a^f \in [-a, a], v_b^f \in [-b, b], f = 1 \cdots q,$$

$$a = \operatorname{arctanh}\left(1 - \frac{k}{k_{\max}}\right), \tag{20.34}$$

$$b = 1 - \frac{k}{k_{\max}}.$$

Using the notation $\mathbf{X}_b(k)$ for the best agent, representing the solution obtained so far (in all iterations until k), with the elements $x_b^f(k)$, $f = 1 \cdots q$ [62]

$$\mathbf{X}_b(k) = [x_b^1(k) \cdots x_b^f(k) \cdots x_b^q(k)]^T \in D_s \subset \Re^q, \tag{20.35}$$

and computing two agents, $\mathbf{X}_A(k)$ and $\mathbf{X}_B(k)$, which are randomly selected in the population (A and B are random integer indices, $A, B = 1...N$)

$$\mathbf{X}_A(k) = [x_A^1(k) \cdots x_A^f(k) \cdots x_A^q(k)]^T \in D_s \subset \Re^q,$$
$$\mathbf{X}_B(k) = [x_B^1(k) \cdots x_B^f(k) \cdots x_B^q(k)]^T \in D_s \subset \Re^q, \tag{20.36}$$

the position update equation is [136]

$$x_i^f(k+1) = \begin{cases} r^f(u^f - l^f) + l^f, & \text{if } r^f < z, \\ x_b^f(k) + v_a^f[w_i^f(k)x_A^f(k) - x_B^f(k)], & \text{if } r^f \geq z \text{ and } r_i^f < p_i, \ i = 1 \cdots N, \\ v_b^f x_i^f(k), & \text{otherwise,} \end{cases} \tag{20.37}$$

where $r^f \in [0, 1]$ are random numbers, $z \in [0, 0.1]$ is a constant parameter, the parameters p_i are computed in accordance with [136]

$$p_i = \tanh |S_i(k) - S_{\min}(k)|, \ i = 1 \cdots N, \tag{20.38}$$

and $S_{\min}(k)$ is the best fitness obtained so far (in all iterations until k)

$$S_{\min}(k) = \min_{i=1...N, \ k_b=0...k} S_i(k_b). \tag{20.39}$$

20.3.4. *Hybrid Particle Swarm Optimization–Gravitational Search Algorithm*

The hybridization of nature-inspired optimization algorithms is a solution to overcome certain shortcomings observed during the use of classical algorithms. The hybridization of PSO and GSA aims to obtain an improved search by combining the ability of social thinking specific to PSO and the local search capability of GSA.

The agents in PSOGSA are swarm particles with masses considered in the gravitational field. As shown by Precup and David [40], the operating mechanism of PSOGSA starts with the random initialization of the population of agents. The agent velocity vector $\mathbf{V}_i(k)$, where

$$\mathbf{V}_i(k) = [v_i^1(k) \cdots v_i^f(k) \cdots v_i^q(k)]^T \in \Re^q, \ i = 1 \cdots N, \tag{20.40}$$

is used to express and also explain the operating principle of PSOGSA. Let $\mathbf{P}_{g,Best}(k)$ be the best swarm position vector

$$\mathbf{P}_{g,Best}(k) = [p_g^1(k) \cdots p_g^f(k) \cdots p_g^q(k)]^T \in \Re^q, \tag{20.41}$$

which is updated in terms of [40]

$$\mathbf{P}_{g,Best}(k) = \mathbf{X}_i(k) \text{ if } J(\mathbf{X}_i(k)) < J(\mathbf{P}_{g,Best}(k)). \tag{20.42}$$

The velocity and position update equations are [40]

$$v_i^f(k+1) = \begin{cases} w(k)\, v_i^d(k) + c_1 r_1 [\mathbf{P}_{g,Best}(k) - x_i^f(k)] + c_2\, r_2 a_i^f(k) & \text{if } m_i(k) > 0, \\ w(k)\, v_i^f(k) + c_1 r_1 [\mathbf{P}_{g,Best}(k) - x_i^f(k)] & \text{otherwise,} \end{cases}$$

$$x_i^f(k+1) = x_i^f(k) + v_i^f(k+1), \ f = 1 \cdots q, \ i = 1 \cdots N, \tag{20.43}$$

where $r_1, r_2 \in [0, 1]$ are uniformly distributed random variables, $c_1, c_2 \geq 0$ are weighting factors; the parameter $w(k)$ is the inertia weight and $a_i^f(k)$ is the acceleration specific to GSA [137].

The parameter $w(k)$ specific to PSO is set in accordance with the recommendations given in the seminal papers on PSO [138, 139]. The following dependence expression of $w(k)$ is used in [40]:

$$w(k) = w_{max} - k \frac{w_{max} - w_{min}}{k_{max}}, \tag{20.44}$$

where upper w_{max} and lower w_{min} bounds are imposed to $w(k)$ to limit the particles movement in the search domain during the search process.

20.3.5. *Hybrid Gray Wolf Optimize–Particle Swarm Optimization*

The hybridization of GWO and PSO targets the improvement of the exploitation stage of GWO in terms of adding the ability of social thinking specific to PSO. The agents in GWOPSO are viewed as both gray wolves and swarm particles. As shown by David *et al.* [140], the operating mechanism of GWOPSO starts with the random initialization of the population of agents. As shown by David *et al.* [140], the approximate distances between the current solution and the alpha, beta, and delta solutions are modified with respect to (20.21), and the following relation is used:

$$d_i^{lf}(k) = |c_i^f(k)x^{lf}(k) - \omega_{PSO}x_i^f(k)|, \; i = 1 \cdots N, \; l \in \{\alpha, \beta, \delta\}, \; f = 1 \cdots q, \tag{20.45}$$

where the inertia weight ω_{PSO} specific to PSO is expressed as

$$\omega_{PSO} = 0.5(1 + r_\omega), \tag{20.46}$$

where $r_\omega \in [0, 1]$ is a uniformly distributed random variable.

The elements of the updated alpha, beta, and delta solutions are computed in terms of (20.22). However, the updated expressions of the agents' positions are no longer obtained as the arithmetic mean of the updated alpha, beta, and delta agents given in (20.23), and the following modified version of (20.23), derived from [140], is used:

$$x_i^f(k+1) = x_i^f(k) + \omega_{PSO}\{c_\alpha^f(k)r_\alpha[x^{\alpha f}(k+1) - x_i^f(k)]$$
$$+ c_\beta^f(k)r_\beta[x^{\beta f}(k+1) - x_i^f(k)] + c_\delta^f(k)r_\delta[x^{\delta f}(k+1) - x_i^f(k)]\}, \tag{20.47}$$
$$f = 1 \cdots q, i = 1 \cdots N,$$

where $r_\alpha, r_\beta, r_\delta \in [0, 1]$ are uniformly distributed random variables.

20.3.6. Nature-Inspired Optimization Algorithms with Information Feedback Model F1

Using the notation given in (20.14) for the position vector $\mathbf{X}_i(k)$ of ith agent at iteration k of a certain nature-inspired optimization algorithm without information feedback model (namely, the algorithms presented in the previous sub-sections), the notation $S_i(k)$ for its fitness, which is also equal to the objective function value J, and introducing the notation $\mathbf{Z}_i(k)$ for the position vector of ith agent at iteration k of the nature-inspired optimization algorithm with information feedback model F1 [62]

$$\mathbf{Z}_i(k) = [z_i^1(k) \cdots z_i^f(k) \cdots z_i^q(k)]^T \in D_s, \; i = 1 \cdots N, \tag{20.48}$$

where $z_i^f(k)$ is the position of ith agent in fth dimension, $f = 1 \cdots q$, the information feedback model F1 is characterized by the recurrent equation [63–65]

$$\mathbf{Z}_i(k+1) = \alpha_{F1}\mathbf{X}_i(k) + \beta_{F1}\mathbf{Z}_i(k). \tag{20.49}$$

The expressions of the weighting factors α_{F1} and β_{F1}, which satisfy

$$\alpha_{F1} + \beta_{F1} = 1, \tag{20.50}$$

are [63–65]

$$\alpha_{F1} = \frac{S_i(k)}{S_i(k) + S_i(k+1)},$$
$$\beta_{F1} = \frac{S_i(k+1)}{S_i(k) + S_i(k+1)}. \tag{20.51}$$

Equations (20.49)–(20.51) are integrated in GWO, WOAF1, SMA, PSOGSA, and GWOPSO algorithms, and they lead to GWOF1, WOAF1, SMAF1, PSOGSAF1, and GWOPSOF1 algorithms, respectively. Three out of these five algorithms are described in [62] and applied to the optimal tuning of fuzzy controllers.

20.3.7. *Problem Setting and Optimal Tuning Methodology*

The process is characterized by the following nonlinear continuous-time time-invariant single input-single output (SISO) state–space model, which defines a general class of nonlinear servo systems [1]:

$$m(t) = \begin{cases} -1, & \text{if } u(t) \leq -u_b, \\ \dfrac{u(t) + u_c}{u_b - u_c}, & \text{if } -u_b < u(t) < -u_c, \\ 0, & \text{if } -u_c \leq |u(t)| \leq u_a, \\ \dfrac{u(t) - u_a}{u_b - u_a}, & \text{if } u_a < u(t) < u_b, \\ 1, & \text{if } u(t) \geq u_b, \end{cases} \tag{20.52}$$

$$\dot{\mathbf{x}}_P(t) = \begin{bmatrix} 0 & 1 \\ 0 & -\dfrac{1}{T_\Sigma} \end{bmatrix} \mathbf{x}_P(t) + \begin{bmatrix} 0 \\ \dfrac{k_P}{T_\Sigma} \end{bmatrix} m(t) + \begin{bmatrix} 1 \\ 0 \end{bmatrix} d(t),$$

$$y(t) = [1 \quad 0]\mathbf{x}_P(t),$$

where k_P is the process gain, T_Σ is the small time constant, the control signal u is a pulse width modulated duty cycle, and m is the output of the saturation and dead zone static nonlinearity specific to the actuator. The dead zone and saturation nonlinearity is given in the first equation in (20.50), and it is characterized by the parameters u_a, u_b, and u_c, with $0 < u_a < u_b$ and $0 < u_c < u_b$. The state–space model in (20.50) includes the actuator and measuring element dynamics. The state vector $\mathbf{x}_P(t)$ is expressed as follows in (angular) position applications [1]:

$$\mathbf{x}_P(t) = [x_{P,1}(t) \quad x_{P,2}(t)]^T = [\alpha(t) \quad \omega(t)]^T, \tag{20.53}$$

where $\alpha(t)$ is the angular position, $\omega(t)$ is the angular speed, and the controlled output is $y(t) = x_{P,1}(t) = \alpha(t)$.

The nonlinearity in (20.52) is neglected in the following simplified model of the process expressed as the transfer function $P(s)$, defined in zero initial conditions, with u as input and y as output:

$$P(s) = \frac{k_{EP}}{s(1 + T_\Sigma s)}, \tag{20.54}$$

where the equivalent process gain k_{EP} is

$$k_{EP} = \begin{cases} \dfrac{k_P}{u_b - u_c}, & \text{if } -u_b < u(t) < -u_c, \\[3mm] \dfrac{k_P}{u_b - u_a}, & \text{if } u_a < u(t) < u_b. \end{cases} \tag{20.55}$$

The optimization problem that ensures the optimal tuning of FCs is

$$\rho^* = \arg \min_{\rho \in D_\rho} J(\rho),$$
$$(\rho) = \sum_{k=0}^{\infty} (k|e(k)|), \tag{20.56}$$

where J is the objective function, ρ is the vector variable of the objective function and also the parameter vector of the FC, ρ^* is the optimal value of the vector ρ, and D_ρ is the feasible domain of ρ. Precup and David [1] have recommended that the stability of the fuzzy control system should be taken into consideration when setting the domain D_ρ.

PI controllers with the transfer function given in (20.4) can deal with the processes modeled in (20.54). The extended symmetrical optimum (ESO) method [141, 142] is successfully employed to tune these controllers such that they guarantee a desired tradeoff to the performance specifications (i.e., maximum values of control system performance indices) imposed to the control system using a single tuning parameter, β, with the recommended values $1 < \beta < 20$. The diagrams presented in Figure 20.4 are useful to set the value of the tuning parameter β and, therefore, to achieve the tradeoff to the linear control system performance indices expressed as percent overshoot σ_1 [%], normalized settling time $\hat{t}_s = t_s/T_\Sigma$, normalized rise time $\hat{t}_r = t_r/T_\Sigma$, and phase margin Φ_m.

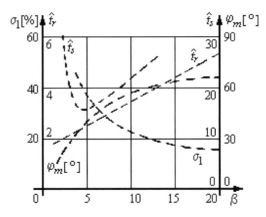

Figure 20.4:   Linear control system performance indices versus the parameter β specific to the ESO method for the step-type modification of the reference input [1].

The PI tuning conditions specific to the ESO method are [141, 142]

$$k_c = \frac{1}{\beta \sqrt{\beta} k_{EP} \, T_{\Sigma}^2}, \; T_i = \beta T_{\Sigma}, \; k_C = \frac{1}{\sqrt{\beta} k_{EP} T_{\Sigma}}. \qquad (20.57)$$

A simple version of set-point filter that ensures an improvement in the performance of the linear control system by canceling a zero in the closed-loop transfer function with respect to the reference input is [141, 142]

$$F(s) = \frac{1}{1 + \beta \, T_{\Sigma} s}. \qquad (20.58)$$

The PI-fuzzy controllers are tuned starting with the linear PI controllers such that to ensure the further improvement of the control system performance indices for the nonlinear process modeled in (20.52). As shown by Precup and David [1], the presentation and the results will be focused on the Takagi–Sugeno PI-FC-OI, but the presentation for the Mamdani PI-FC-OI and for both versions of PI-FC-II is straightforward.

The controller parameter vector, which will be determined by the optimal tuning methodology such that to solve the optimization problem defined in (20.56) is [1]

$$\rho = [\rho_1 \quad \rho_2 \quad \rho_3]^T = [\beta \quad B_e \quad \eta]^T, \qquad (20.59)$$

and the application of the optimal tuning methodology described as follows will give the optimal parameter vector ρ^* [1]

$$\rho^* = [\rho_1^* \quad \rho_2^* \quad \rho_3^*]^T = [\beta^* \quad B_e^* \quad \eta^*]^T. \qquad (20.60)$$

The optimization algorithms are mapped onto the optimization problem defined in (20.56) in terms of

$$q = 3,$$
$$D_s = D_\rho,$$
$$\mathbf{X}_i(k) = \rho, i = 1 \cdots N,$$
$$\mathbf{Z}_i(k) = \rho, i = 1 \cdots N,$$
$$S_i(k) = J, i = 1 \cdots N, \qquad (20.61)$$
$$\mathbf{X}_b(k_{\max}) = \rho^*,$$
$$\mathbf{X}_i(k_{\max}) = \rho^*,$$
$$\mathbf{X}_b(k_{\max}) = \rho^*,$$
$$\mathbf{Z}_b(k_{\max}) = \rho^*,$$

where $\mathbf{Z}_b$ in SMAF1 corresponds to $\mathbf{X}_b$ in SMA.

The optimal tuning methodology consists of the following steps:

Step 1. The sampling period T_s is set in accordance with the requirements of quasi-continuous digital control.

Step 2. The feasible domain D_ρ is set to include all constraints imposed to the elements of ρ.

Step 3. One of the nature-inspired optimization algorithms solves the optimization problem defined in (20.56) using (20.61), resulting in the optimal parameter vector ρ^* in (20.60) and three of the optimal parameters of the Takagi–Sugeno PI-fuzzy controller, namely β^*, B_e^* and η^*.

Step 4. The optimal parameter $B_{\Delta e}$ of the Takagi–Sugeno PI-fuzzy controller, with the notation $B_{\Delta e}^*$, results from (7), with the optimal parameters replaced in (6). The set-point filter with the transfer function defined in (20.58) is used in the fuzzy control system but with β^* instead of β.

20.3.8. *Application of Optimal Tuning Methodology*

The optimal tuning methodology is applied in this sub-section to a Takagi–Sugeno PI-FC-OI dedicated to the position control of a laboratory servo system in relation with the optimization problem defined in (20.56). The experimental set-up is illustrated in Figure 20.5. An optical encoder is used for the measurement of the angle and a tacho-generator for the measurement of the angular speed. The speed can also be estimated from the angle measurements. The PWM signals proportional with the control signal are produced by the actuator in the power interface. The main features of the experimental setup are [1] rated amplitude of 24 V, rated current of

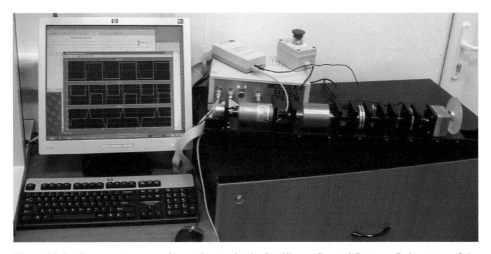

Figure 20.5: Servo system experimental setup in the Intelligent Control Systems Laboratory of the Politehnica University of Timisoara [1].

3.1 A, rated torque of 15 N cm, rated speed of 3000 rpm, and weight of inertial load of 2.03 kg. The values of the parameters of the process model given in (20.52) and (20.54), obtained by a least squares algorithm, are $u_a = 0.15$, $u_b = 1$, $u_c = 0.15$, $k_P = k_{EP} = 140$, and $T_\Sigma = 0.92$ s.

The sampling period was set to $T_s = 0.01$ s in step 1 of the optimal tuning methodology. The vector variable ρ belongs to the feasible domain (or the search domain) domain D_ρ set in step 2 as

$$D_\rho = \{\beta | 3 \leq \beta \leq 17\} \times \{B_e | 20 \leq B_e \leq 38\} \times \{\eta | 0.25 \leq \eta \leq 0.75\}. \quad (20.62)$$

The dynamic regimes considered in step 3 are characterized by the $r = 40$ rad step-type modification of the set-point and zero initial conditions. The upper limit of the sum in (20.56) was set to 2000 instead of ∞. This leads to the length of 20 s of the time horizon involved in the evaluation of the objective function by simulation or experiments conducted on the fuzzy control system.

The fixed parameters of the nature-inspired optimization algorithms applied in step 3 of the optimal tuning methodology are $z = 0.03$ and $\varepsilon = 0.001$ for SMA. The following are the parameters of PSOGA: an exponential decrease law of the gravitational constant was used, with the initial value $g_0 = 100$ and the exponent $\zeta = 8.5$, the parameter $\varepsilon = 10^{-4}$ that avoids possible divisions by zero in the GSA part, the weighting parameters $c_1 = c_2 = 0.3$ in the PSO part and the inertia weight parameters $w_{max} = 0.9$ and $w_{min} = 0.5$ to ensure a good balance between exploration and exploitation characteristics. The other algorithms do not work with fixed parameters. The same numbers of agents $N = 20$ and maximum number of iterations $k_{max} = 20$ were used for all algorithms in the comparison.

Table 20.1: Controller parameter and minimum objective function values after the application of the nature-inspired optimization algorithms.

	B_e^*	$B_{\Delta e}^*$	η^*	β^*	k_c^*	T_i^*	$J_{min} = J(\rho^*)$
GWO	21.1473	0.0447	0.6395	5.141	0.0034	4.7297	201,200.5
WOA	31.2222	0.0659	0.6673	5.1638	0.0034	4.7507	173,844.3
SMA	27.5679	0.0601	0.6315	5.1613	0.0034	4.7484	168,243.7
PSOGSA	34.9617	0.077	0.7367	4.03	0.0035	4.5507	192,835.4
GWOPSO	32.6942	0.0685	0.7219	5.1943	0.0034	4.7787	220,176.1
GWOF1	35.748	0.0753	0.6833	5.1647	0.0034	4.7515	163,129.8
WOAF1	35.6415	0.084	0.6192	4.773	0.0036	4.3912	168,119.9
SMAF1	37.9981	0.0809	0.7493	5.1112	0.0034	4.7023	155,117.2
PSOGSAF1	33.393	0.0701	0.6804	5.1903	0.0034	4.7751	170,003.3
GWOPSOF1	29.8815	0.0619	0.5706	5.3303	0.034	4.9039	214,907.6

Moreover, to ensure a fair comparison of the algorithms, to reduce the effects of random parameters in the algorithms, all results are given as average values taken for the best five runs of the algorithms.

The optimal controller parameters and the minimum objective function values are summarized in Table 20.1. The optimal parameter values of the linear part (i.e., the initial PI controller) are included as well.

Several conclusions can be drawn after the analysis of the results illustrated in Table 20.1. First, the values of the tuning parameters obtained after running the algorithms are close. Second, the best algorithm as far as the performance expressed as the smallest value of the minimum objective function concerned is SMAF1 followed by GWOF1. Third, as shown by Precup *et al.* [62], the introduction of the information feedback model F1 is beneficial generally as it leads to the reduction of the minimum value of the objective functions obtained by running all algorithms. Fourth, the hybridizations lead to performance improvement for PSOGSA but not for GWOPSO in the conditions of the application and objective function considered in this chapter.

Two typical fuzzy control system responses are presented in Figure 20.6 in terms of controlled output and control signal versus time considering the "average" controller after the first iteration of GWO (with the parameters $B_e = 33.2784$, $\eta = 0.5268$, and $B_{\Delta e} = 0.0676$), and the "average" controller after the application of 20 iterations of GWO (with the parameters given in the first row in Table 20.1). Figure 20.6 also highlights the improvement of the overshoot and settling time after the application of GWO. Both plots in Figure 20.6 also highlight the effects of the process nonlinearity in the initial and final part of the transients.

As specified by Precup and David [1], the comparison of nature-inspired optimization algorithms can be carried out by means of several performance indices.

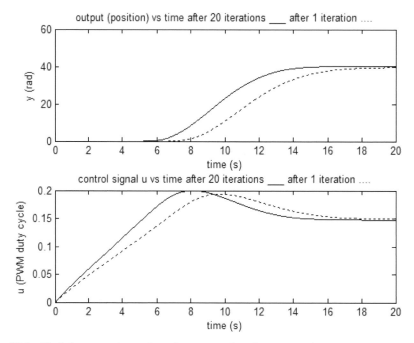

Figure 20.6: Real-time experimental results expressed as fuzzy control system responses y and u with after one iteration of GWO (dotted line) and 20 iterations of GWO (continuous line).

Three such indices are the convergence speed defined as the number of evaluations of the objective functions until finding their minimum values, the number of evaluations per iteration, and the standard deviation with respect to the average of the solutions. However, in all the cases the results of the comparisons of the performance indices should be presented, as performed in this section, in terms of average values for several runs of the algorithms to alleviate the impact of the random parameters specific to all nature-inspired optimization algorithms. The perspective of non-parametric statistical tests could also be provided [143–145]. Complexity analyses of the algorithms could be conducted as well.

20.4. Conclusions and Outlook

This chapter is a revised version of the one by Precup and David [1], and it presented aspects concerning the nature-inspired optimal tuning of fuzzy controllers. The presentation has been focused on Takagi–Sugeno and Mamdani PI-fuzzy controllers, and it shows that the presented design methodology and tuning methodology can be applied relatively easily to PD-fuzzy controllers and PID-fuzzy controllers.

Once the optimization problems are defined, the nature-inspired optimization algorithms can be applied to compute the optimal tuning of the parameters of fuzzy controllers. The chapter provides the exemplification of several such algorithms, namely GWO, WOA, SMA, hybrid PSOGSA, hybrid GWOPSO, and other algorithms, referred to as GWOF1, WOAF1, SMAF1, PSOGSAF1, and GWOPSOF1, obtained by the introduction of the information feedback model F1 in the former ones. The results can be extended with no major difficulties to other algorithms as CSS [1]. Other nature-inspired optimization algorithms are possible candidates for the optimal tuning of fuzzy controllers; such representative algorithms are population extremal optimization algorithms applied to continuous optimization and nonlinear controller optimal tuning problems [144–146], modified PSO applied to smart grids [147, 148], water cycle algorithms applied to resolve the traveling salesman problem [149], the bat algorithm applied to medical goods distribution [150], the differential evolution algorithm applied to fuzzy job-shop scheduling [151], NSGA-III with adaptive mutation applied to Big Data optimization [152], processing of crossover operations in NSGA-III for large-scale optimization [153], conflict monitoring optimization [154], and parallelized multiple swarm artificial bee colony algorithms for constrained optimization problems [155]. Other representative results are related to the optimal tuning of fuzzy control [156] and inclusion of fuzzy logic in nature-inspired optimization algorithms [157, 158], including their adaptation [159].

Summing up, we advise again — as shown by Precup and David [1] — the reduction of the number of parameters tuned by the nature-inspired optimization algorithms in order to have a reasonable dimension of the search space that will offer an efficient search for the optimal solution. The major shortcoming of nature-inspired optimization algorithms in optimal tuning of controllers is represented by the large number of evaluations of the objective functions. This can be solved by including gradient information that can be taken from data-driven approaches.

20.5. Acknowledgments

This work was supported by a grant from the Romanian Ministry of Education and Research, CNCS–UEFISCDI, project number PN-III-P4-ID-PCE-2020-0269, within PNCDI III.

References

[1] Precup, R.-E. and David, R.-C. (2016). Nature-inspired optimization of fuzzy controllers and fuzzy models. In Angelov, P. P. (ed.), *Handbook on Computational Intelligence*, Vol. 2: Evolutionary Computation, Hybrid Systems, and Applications. Singapore: World Scientific, pp. 697–729.

[2] Precup, R.-E. and Hellendoorn, H. (2011). A survey on industrial applications of fuzzy control. *Comput. Ind.*, **62**, pp. 213–226.

[3] Hjalmarsson, H. (2002). Iterative feedback tuning: an overview. *Int. J. Adapt. Control Signal Proc.*, **16**(5), pp. 373–395.

[4] Jung, H., Jeon, K., Kang, J.-G. and Oh, S. (2020). Iterative feedback tuning of cascade control of two-inertia system. *IEEE Control Syst. Lett.*, **5**(3), pp. 785–790.

[5] Hou, Z.-S. and Wang, Z. (2013). From model-based control to data-driven control: survey, classification and perspective. *Inf. Sci.*, **235**, pp. 3–35.

[6] Yu, W., Wang, R., Bu, X.-H. and Hou, Z.-S. (2020b). Model free adaptive control for a class of nonlinear systems with fading measurements. *J. Franklin Inst.*, **357**(12), pp. 7743–7760.

[7] Spall, J. C. and Cristion, J. A. (1998). Model-free control of nonlinear stochastic systems with discrete-time measurements. *IEEE Trans. Autom. Control*, **43**(9), pp. 1198–1210.

[8] Zamanipour, M. (2020). A novelty in Blahut-Arimoto type algorithms: optimal control over noisy communication channels. *IEEE Trans. Veh. Technol.*, **69**(6), pp. 6348–6358.

[9] Karimi, A., Miskovic, L. and Bonvin, D. (2004). Iterative correlation-based controller tuning. *Int. J. Adapt. Control Signal Proc.*, **18**(8), pp. 645–664.

[10] Sato, T., Kusakabe, T., Himi, K., Arakim N. and Konishi, Y. (2020). Ripple-free data-driven dual-rate controller using lifting technique: application to a physical rotation system. *IEEE Trans. Control Syst. Technol.*, doi: 10.1109/TCST.2020.2988613.

[11] Kammer, L. C., Bitmead, R. R. and Bartlett, P. L. (2000). Direct iterative tuning via spectral analysis. *Automatica*, **36**(9), pp. 1301–1307.

[12] da Silva Moreira, J., Acioli Júnior, G. and Rezende Barros, G. (2018). Time and frequency domain data-driven PID iterative tuning. *IFAC-PapersOnLine*, **51**(15), pp. 1056–1061.

[13] Halmevaara, K. and Hyötyniemi, H. (2006). Data-based parameter optimization of dynamic simulation models. In *Proc. 47th Conf. Simul. Model. (SIMS 2006)*. Helsinki, Finland, pp. 68–73.

[14] McDaid, A. J., Aw, K. C., Haemmerle, E. and Xie, S. Q. (2012). Control of IPMC actuators for microfluidics with adaptive "online" iterative feedback tuning. *IEEE/ASME Trans. Mechatron.*, **17**(4), pp. 789–797.

[15] Fliess, M. and Join, C. (2013). Model-free control. *Int. J. Control*, **86**(12), pp. 2228–2252.

[16] Fliess, M. and Join, C. (2020). Machine learning and control engineering: the model-free case. In *Proc. Fut. Technol. Conf. 2020 (FTC 2020)*. Vancouver, BC, Canada, pp. 1–20.

[17] Campi, M. C., Lecchini, A. and Savaresi, S. M. (2002). Virtual reference feedback tuning: a direct method for the design of feedback controllers. *Automatica*, **38**(8), pp. 1337–1346.

[18] Formentin, S., Campi, M. C., Caré, A. and Savaresi, S. M. (2019). Deterministic continuous-time Virtual Reference Feedback Tuning (VRFT) with application to PID design. *Syst. Control Lett.*, **127**, pp. 25–34.

[19] Gao, Z. (2006). Active disturbance rejection control: a paradigm shift in feedback control system design. In *Proc. 2006 Amer. Control Conf. (ACC 2006)*. Minneapolis, MN, USA, pp. 2399–2405.

[20] Roman, R.-C., Precup, R.-E. and Petriu, E. M. (2021). Hybrid data-driven fuzzy active disturbance rejection control for tower crane systems. *Eur. J. Control*, **58**, pp. 373–387.

[21] Kadali, R., Huang, B. and Rossiter, A. (2003). A data driven subspace approach to predictive controller design. *Control Eng. Pract.*, **11**(3), pp. 261–278.

[22] Lucchini, A., Formentin, S., Corno, M., Piga, D. and Savaresi, S. M. (2020). Torque vectoring for high-performance electric vehicles: a data-driven MPC approach. *IEEE Control Syst. Lett.*, **4**(3), pp. 725–730.

[23] Safonov, M. G. and Tsao, T.-C. (1997). The unfalsified control concept and learning. *IEEE Trans. Autom. Control*, **42**(6), pp. 843–847.

[24] Jiang, P., Cheng, Y.-Q., Wang, X.-N. and Feng, Z. (2016). Unfalsified visual servoing for simultaneous object recognition and pose tracking. *IEEE Trans. Cybern.*, **46**(12), pp. 3032–3046.

[25] Novara, C., Formentin, S., Savaresi, S. M. and Milanese, M. (2015). A data-driven approach to nonlinear braking control. In *Proc. 54th IEEE Conf. Dec. Control (IEEE CDC 2015)*. Osaka, Japan, pp. 1–6.

[26] Galluppi, O., Formentin, S., Novara, C. and Savaresi, S. M. (2019). Multivariable D2-IBC and application to vehicle stability control. *ASME J. Dyn. Syst. Meas. Control*, **141**(10), pp. 1–12.

[27] Van Waarde, H. J., Eising, J., Trentelman, H. L. and Camlibel, M. K. (2020). Data informativity: a new perspective on data-driven analysis and control. *IEEE Trans. Autom. Control*, **65**(11), pp. 4753–4768.

[28] Wu, H.-N., Wang, J.-W. and Li, H.-X. (2012). Design of distributed H_∞ fuzzy controllers with constraint for nonlinear hyperbolic PDE systems. *Automatica*, **48**(10), pp. 2535–2543.

[29] Simani, S., Alvisi, S. and Venturini, M. (2015). Data-driven design of a fault tolerant fuzzy controller for a simulated hydroelectric system. *IFAC-PapersOnLine*, **48**(21), pp. 1090–1095.

[30] Kamesh, R. and Rani, K. Y. (2016). Parameterized data-driven fuzzy model based optimal control of a semi-batch reactor. *ISA Trans.*, **64**, pp. 418–430.

[31] Juang, C.-F. and Chang, Y.-C. (2016). Data-driven interpretable fuzzy controller design through multi-objective genetic algorithm. In *Proc. 2016 IEEE Int. Conf. Syst. Man. Cybern. (SMC 2016)*. Budapest, Hungary, pp. 2403–2408.

[32] Roman, R.-C., Precup, R.-E. and David, R.-C. (2018). Second order intelligent proportional-integral fuzzy control of twin rotor aerodynamic systems. *Proc. Comput. Sci.*, **139**, pp. 372–380.

[33] Precup, R.-E., Roman, R.-C., Hedrea, E.-L., Petriu, E. M. and Bojan-Dragos, C.-A. (2021a). Data-driven model-free sliding mode and fuzzy control with experimental validation. *Int. J. Comput. Communic. Control*, **16**(1), 4076.

[34] Roman, R.-C., Precup, R.-E., Bojan-Dragos, C.-A. and Szedlak-Stinean, A.-I. (2019a). Combined model-free adaptive control with fuzzy component by virtual reference feedback tuning for tower crane systems. *Proc. Comput. Sci.*, **162**, pp. 267–274.

[35] Roman, R.-C., Precup, R.-E., Petriu, E. M. and Dragan, F. (2019b). Combination of data-driven active disturbance rejection and Takagi-Sugeno fuzzy control with experimental validation on tower crane systems. *Energies*, **12**(8), pp. 1–19.

[36] Roman, R.-C., Precup, R.-E. and Petriu, E. M. (2021). Hybrid data-driven fuzzy active disturbance rejection control for tower crane systems. *Eur. J. Control*, **58**, pp. 373–387.

[37] Touhami, M., Hazzab, A., Mokhtari, F. and Sicard, P. (2019). Active disturbance rejection controller with ADRC-fuzzy for MAS control. *Electr. Elecron. Autom. (EEA)*, **67**(2), pp. 89–97.

[38] Dombi, J. and Hussain, A. (2019). Data-driven arithmetic fuzzy control using the distending function. In Ahram, T., Taiar, R., Colson, S. and Choplin, A. (eds.), *IHIET: Human Interaction and Emerging Technologies*, Advances in Intelligent Systems and Computing, Vol. 1018. Cham: Springer, pp. 215–221.

[39] Sugeno, M. (1999). On stability of fuzzy systems expressed by fuzzy rules with singleton consequents. *IEEE Trans. Fuzzy Syst.*, **7**(2), pp. 201–224.

[40] Precup, R.-E. and David, R.-C. (2019). *Nature-Inspired Optimization Algorithms for Fuzzy Controlled Servo Systems*. Oxford: Butterworth-Heinemann, Elsevier.

[41] Eckert, J. J., Corrêa de Alkmin Silva, L., Dedini, F. G. and Corrêa, F. C. (2019a). Electric vehicle powertrain and fuzzy control multi-objective optimization, considering dual hybrid energy storage systems. *IEEE Trans. Veh. Technol.*, **69**(4), pp. 3773–3782.

[42] Eckert, J. J., Santiciolli, F. M., Yamashita, R. Y., Corrêa, F. C., Silva, L. C. A. and Dedini, F. G. (2019b). Fuzzy gear shifting control optimisation to improve vehicle performance, fuel consumption and engine emissions. *IET Control Theory Appl.*, **13**(16), pp. 2658–2669.

[43] Abadlia, I., Hassaine, L., Beddar, A., Abdoune, F. and Bengourina, M. R. (2020). Adaptive fuzzy control with an optimization by using genetic algorithms for grid connected a hybrid photovoltaic-hydrogen generation system. *Int. J. Hydr. Energy*, **45**(43), pp. 22589–22599.

[44] Masoumi, A. P., Tavakolpour-Saleh, A. R. and Rahideh, A. (2020). Applying a genetic-fuzzy control scheme to an active free piston Stirling engine: design and experiment. *Appl. Energy*, **268**, 115045.

[45] Fu, Z.-M., Zhu, L.-L., Tao, F.-Z., Si, P.-J. and Sun, L.-F. (2020). Optimization based energy management strategy for fuel cell/battery/ultracapacitor hybrid vehicle considering fuel economy and fuel cell lifespan. *Int. J. Hydr. Energy*, **45**(15), pp. 8875–8886.

[46] Liang, H.-B., Zou, J.-L., Zuo, K. and Khan, M. J. (2020). An improved genetic algorithm optimization fuzzy controller applied to the wellhead back pressure control system. *Mech. Syst. Signal Process.*, **142**, 106708.

[47] Hu, Y.-P., Yang, Y.-P., Li, S. and Zhou, Y.-M. (2020). Fuzzy controller design of micro-unmanned helicopter relying on improved genetic optimization algorithm. *Aerosp. Sci. Technol.*, **98**, 105685.

[48] Wu, T.-Z., Yu, W.-S. and Guo, L.-X. (2019). A study on use of hybrid energy storage system along with variable filter time constant to smooth DC power fluctuation in microgrid. *IEEE Access*, **7**, pp. 175377–175385.

[49] Wai, R.-J. and Prasetia, A. S. (2019). Adaptive neural network control and optimal path planning of UAV surveillance system with energy consumption prediction. *IEEE Access*, **7**, pp. 126137–126153.

[50] Xie, S.-W., Xie, Y.-F., Li, F.-B., Jiang, Z.-H. and Gui, W.-H. (2019). Hybrid fuzzy control for the goethite process in zinc production plant combining type-1 and type-2 fuzzy logics. *Neurocomputing*, **366**, pp. 170–177.

[51] Girgis, M. E. and Badr, R. I. (2021). Optimal fractional-order adaptive fuzzy control on inverted pendulum model. *Int. J. Dynam. Control*, **9**(1), pp. 288–298.

[52] Mohammadzadeh, A. and Kayacan, E. (2020). A novel fractional-order type-2 fuzzy control method for online frequency regulation in AC microgrid. *Eng. Appl. Artif. Intell.*, **90**, 103483.

[53] Reisi, N. A., Hadipour Lakmesari, S., Mahmoodabadi, M. J. and Hadipour, S. (2019). Optimum fuzzy control of human immunodeficiency virus type1 using an imperialist competitive algorithm. *Inf. Med. Unlocked*, **16**, 100241.

[54] Tripathi, S., Shrivastava A. and Jana, K. C. (2020). Self-tuning fuzzy controller for sun-tracker system using Gray Wolf Optimization (GWO) technique. *ISA Trans.*, **101**, pp. 50–59.

[55] Precup, R.-E., David, R.-C., Petriu, E. M., Szedlak-Stinean, A.-I. and Bojan-Dragos, C.-A. (2016). Grey wolf optimizer-based approach to the tuning of PI-fuzzy controllers with a reduced process parametric sensitivity. *IFAC-PapersOnLine*, **49**(5), pp. 55–60.

[56] Solihin, M. I., Chuan, C. Y. and Astuti, W. (2020). Optimization of fuzzy logic controller parameters using modern meta-heuristic algorithm for Gantry Crane System (GCS). *Mater. Today Proc.*, **29**, pp. 168–172.

[57] Azizi, M., Ejlali, R. G., Ghasemi, S. A. M. and Talatahari, S. (2019a). Upgraded whale optimization algorithm for fuzzy logic based vibration control of nonlinear steel structure. *Eng. Struct.*, **19**, pp. 53–70.

[58] David, R.-C., Precup, R.-E., Preitl, S., Petriu, E. M., Szedlak-Stinean A.-I. and Roman, R.-C. (2020a). Whale optimization algorithm-based tuning of low-cost fuzzy controllers with reduced parametric sensitivity. In *Proc. 28th Medit. Conf. Control Autom. (MED 2020)*. Saint-Raphael, France, pp. 440–445.

[59] David, R.-C., Precup, R.-E., Preitl, S., Szedlak-Stinean, A.-I., Roman, R.-C. and Petriu, E. M. (2020c). Design of low-cost fuzzy controllers with reduced parametric sensitivity based on whale optimization algorithm. In *Proc. 2020 IEEE Int. Conf. Fuzzy Syst. (FUZZ-IEEE 2020)*. Glasgow, UK, pp. 1–6.

[60] Nosratabadi, S. M., Bornapour, M. and Gharaei, M. A. (2019). Grasshopper optimization algorithm for optimal load frequency control considering predictive functional modified PID controller in restructured multi-resource multi-area power system with redox flow battery units. *Control Eng. Pract.*, **89**, pp. 204–227.

[61] Azizi, M., Ghasemi, S. A. M., Ejlali, R. G. and Talatahari, S. (2019b). Optimal tuning of fuzzy parameters for structural motion control using multiverse optimizer. *Struct. Des. Tall Spec. Build.*, **28**(13), e1652.

[62] Precup, R.-E., David, R.-C., Roman, R.-C., Petriu, E. M. and Szedlak-Stinean, A.-I. (2021b). Slime mould algorithm-based tuning of cost-effective fuzzy controllers for servo systems. *Int. J. Comput. Intell. Syst.*, **14**(1), pp. 1042–1052.

[63] Wang, G.-G. and Tan, Y. (2019). Improving metaheuristic algorithms with information feedback models. *IEEE Trans. Cybern.*, **49**(2), pp. 542–555.

[64] Gu, Z.-M. and Wang, G.-G. (2010). Improving NSGA-III algorithms with information feedback models for large-scale many-objective optimization. *Future Gener. Comput. Syst.*, **107**, pp. 49–69.

[65] Zhang, Y., Wang, G.-G., Li, K.-Q., Yeh, W.-C., Jian, M.-W. and Dong, J.-Y. (2020a). Enhancing MOEA/D with information feedback models for large-scale many-objective optimization. *Inf. Sci.*, **522**, pp. 1–16.

[66] Precup, R.-E. and Preitl, S. (1999a). *Fuzzy Controllers*. Timisoara: Editura Orizonturi Universitare.

[67] Kóczy, L. T. (1996). Fuzzy IF-THEN rulemodels and their transformation into one another. *IEEE Trans. Syst. Man Cybern. Part A: Syst. Humans*, **26**(5), pp. 621–637.

[68] Precup, R.-E. and Preitl, S. (1999b). Development of some fuzzy controllers with non-homogenous dynamics with respect to the input channels meant for a class of systems. In *Proc. 1999 Eur. Control Conf. (ECC 1999)*. Karlsruhe, Germany, pp. 61–66.

[69] Precup, R.-E. and Preitl, S. (2003). Development of fuzzy controllers with non-homogeneous dynamics for integral-type plants. *Electr. Eng.*, **85**(3), pp. 155–168.

[70] Precup, R.-E., Preitl, S., Petriu, E. M., Tar, J. K., Tomescu, M. L. and Pozna, C. (2009). Generic two-degree-of-freedom linear and fuzzy controllers for integral processes. *J. Franklin Inst.*, **346**(10), pp. 980–1003.

[71] Preitl, S., Stinean, A.-I., Precup, R.-E., Preitl, Z., Petriu, E. M., Dragos, C.-A. and Radac, M.-B. (2012). Controller design methods for driving systems based on extensions of symmetrical optimum method with DC and BLDC motor applications. *IFAC Proc. Vol.*, **45**(3), pp. 264–269.

[72] Galichet, S. and Foulloy, L. (1995). Fuzzy controllers: synthesis and equivalences. *IEEE Trans. Fuzzy Syst.*, **3**(2), pp. 140–148.

[73] Precup, R.-E., Preitl, S., Petriu, E. M., Roman, R.-C., Bojan-Dragos, C.-A., Hedrea, E.-L. and Szedlak-Stînean, A.-I. (2020a). A center manifold theory-based approach to the stability analysis of state feedback Takagi-Sugeno-Kang fuzzy control systems. *Facta Univ. Ser. Mech. Eng.*, **18**(2), pp. 189–204.

[74] Wang, H. O., Tanaka, K. and Griffin, M. F. (1996). An approach to fuzzy control of nonlinear systems: stability and design issues. *IEEE Trans. Fuzzy Syst.*, **4**(1), pp. 14–23.

[75] Tanaka, K. and Wang, H. O. (2001). *Fuzzy Control Systems Design and Analysis: A Linear Matrix Inequality Approach*. New York: John Wiley & Sons.

[76] Wang, Z.-H., Liu, Z., Chen, C. L. P. and Zhang, Y. (2019). Fuzzy adaptive compensation control of uncertain stochastic nonlinear systems with actuator failures and input hysteresis. *IEEE Trans. Cybern.*, **49**(1), pp. 2–13.

[77] Moodi, H., Farrokhi, M., Guerra, T.-M. and Lauber, J. (2019). On stabilization conditions for T-S systems with nonlinear consequent parts. *Int. J. Fuzzy Syst.*, **21**(1), pp. 84–94.

[78] Frezzatto, L., Lacerda, M. J., Oliveira, R. C. L. F. and Peres, P. L. D. (2019). H$_2$ and H$_\infty$ fuzzy filters with memory for Takagi-Sugeno discrete-time systems. *Fuzzy Sets Syst.*, **371**, pp. 78–95.

[79] Gunasekaran, N. and Joo, Y. H. (2019). Stochastic sampled-data controller for T-S fuzzy chaotic systems and its applications. *IET Control Theory Appl.*, **13**(12), pp. 1834–1843.

[80] Sakthivel, R., Mohanapriya, S., Kaviarasan, B., Ren, Y. and Anthoni, S. M. (2020). Non-fragile control design and state estimation for vehicle dynamics subject to input delay and actuator faults. *IET Control Theory Appl.*, **14**(1), pp. 134–144.

[81] Liu, D., Yang, G.-H. and Er, M. J. (2020). Event-triggered control for T-S fuzzy systems under asynchronous network communications. *IEEE Trans. Fuzzy Syst.*, **28**(2), pp. 390–399.

[82] Shamloo, N. F., Kalat, A. A. and Chisci, L. (2020). Indirect adaptive fuzzy control of nonlinear descriptor systems. *Eur. J. Control*, **51**, pp. 30–38.

[83] Jiang, B.-P., Karimi, H. R., Kao, Y.-G. and Gao, C.-C. (2020). Takagi-Sugeno model based event-triggered fuzzy sliding-mode control of networked control systems with semi-Markovian switchings. *IEEE Trans. Fuzzy Syst.*, **28**(4), pp. 673–683.

[84] Gandhi, R. V. and Adhyaru, D. M. (2020). Takagi-Sugeno fuzzy regulator design for nonlinear and unstable systems using negative absolute eigenvalue approach. *IEEE/CAA J. Autom. Sin.*, **7**(2), pp. 482–493.

[85] Xia, Y., Wang, J., Meng, B. and Chen, X.-Y. (2020). Further results on fuzzy sampled-data stabilization of chaotic nonlinear systems. *Appl. Math. Comput.*, **379**, 125225.

[86] Lam, H.-K. (2018). A review on stability analysis of continuous-time fuzzy-model-based control systems: from membership-function-independent to membership-function-dependent analysis. *Eng. Appl. Artif. Intell.*, **67**, pp. 390–408.

[87] Yang, X.-Z., Lam, H.-K. and Wu, L.-G. (2019). Membership-dependent stability conditions for type-1 and interval type-2 T-S fuzzy systems. *Fuzzy Sets Syst.*, **356**, pp. 44–62.

[88] Pang, B., Liu, X., Jin, Q. and Zhang, W. (2016). Exponentially stable guaranteed cost control for continuous and discrete-time Takagi-Sugeno fuzzy systems. *Neurocomputing*, **205**(1), pp. 210–221.

[89] Li, G.-L., Peng, C., Fei, M.-R. and Tian, Y.-C. (2020a). Local stability conditions for T-S fuzzy time-delay systems using a homogeneous polynomial approach. *Fuzzy Sets Syst.*, **385**, pp. 111–126.

[90] Xiao, B., Lam, H.-K., Yu, Y. and Li, Y.-D. (2020). Sampled-data output-feedback tracking control for interval type-2 polynomial fuzzy systems. *IEEE Trans. Fuzzy Syst.*, **28**(3), pp. 424–433.

[91] Yu, G.-R., Huang, Y.-C. and Cheng, C.-Y. (2018). Sum-of-squares-based robust H_∞ controller design for discrete-time polynomial fuzzy systems. *J. Franklin Inst.*, **355**(1), pp. 177–196.

[92] Zhao, Y.-X., He, Y.-X., Feng, Z.-G., Shi, P. and Du, X. (2019). Relaxed sum-of-squares based stabilization conditions for polynomial fuzzy-model-based control systems. *IEEE Trans. Fuzzy Syst.*, **27**(9), pp. 1767–1778.

[93] Yoneyama, J. (2017). New conditions for stability and stabilization of Takagi-Sugeno fuzzy systems. In *Proc. 2017 Asian Control Conf. (ASCC 2017)*. Gold Coast, Australia, pp. 2154–2159.

[94] Robles, R., Sala, A., Bernal, M. and González, T. (2017). Subspace-based Takagi-Sugeno modeling for improved LMI performance. *IEEE Trans. Fuzzy Syst.*, **25**(4), pp. 754–767.

[95] Meda-Campaña, J. A., Grande-Meza, A., de Jesús Rubio, J., Tapia-Herrera, R., Hernández-Cortés, T., Curtidor-López, A. V., Páramo-Carranza, L. A. and Cázares-Ramírez, I. O. (2018). Design of stabilizers and observers for a class of multivariable TS fuzzy models on the basis of new interpolation function. *IEEE Trans. Fuzzy Syst.*, **26**(5), pp. 2649–2662.

[96] Škrjanc, I. and Blažič, S. (2005). Predictive functional control based on fuzzy model: design and stability study. *J. Intell. Robot. Syst.*, **43**(2–4), pp. 283–299.

[97] Angelov, P., Škrjanc, I. and Blažič, S. (2013). Robust evolving cloud-based controller for a hydraulic plant. In *Proc. 2013 IEEE Conf. Evol. Adapt. Intell. Syst. (EAIS 2013)*. Singapore, pp. 1–8.

[98] Costa, B., Škrjanc, I., Blažič, S. and Angelov, P. (2013). A practical implementation of self-evolving cloud-based control of a pilot plant. In *Proc. 2013 IEEE Int. Conf. Cybern. (CYBCONF 2013)*. Lausanne, Switzerland, pp. 7–12.

[99] Blažič, S., Škrjanc, I. and Matko, D. (2014). A robust fuzzy adaptive law for evolving control systems. *Evol. Syst.*, **5**(1), pp. 3–10.

[100] Baranyi, P. (2004). TP model transformation as a way to LMI-based controller design. *IEEE Trans. Ind. Electron.*, **51**(2), pp. 387–400.

[101] Pozna, C. and Precup, R.-E. (2014). Applications of signatures to expert systems modeling. *Acta Polytech. Hung.*, **11**(2), pp. 21–39.

[102] Wang, Y.-C., Chien, C.-J., Chi, R.-H. and Hou, Z.-S. (2015). A fuzzy-neural adaptive terminal iterative learning control for fed-batch fermentation processes. *Int. J. Fuzzy Syst.*, **17**(3), pp. 423–433.

[103] Precup, R.-E., Angelov, P., Costa, B. S. J. and Sayed-Mouchaweh, M. (2015). An overview on fault diagnosis and nature-inspired optimal control of industrial process applications. *Comput. Ind.*, **74**, pp. 75–94.

[104] Dzitac, I., Filip, F. G. and Manolescu, M. J. (2017). Fuzzy logic is not fuzzy: World-renowned computer scientist Lotfi A. Zadeh. *Int. J. Comput. Commun. Control*, **12**(6), pp. 748–789.

[105] Bolla, K., Johanyák, Z. C., Kovács, T. and Fazekas, G. (2014). Local center of gravity based gathering algorithm for fat robots. In Kóczy, L. T., Pozna, C. R. and Kacprzyk, J. (eds.), *Issues and Challenges of Intelligent Systems and Computational Intelligence*, Studies in Computational Intelligence, Vol. 530. Cham, Heidelberg, New York, Dordrecht, London: Springer-Verlag, pp. 175–183.

[106] Johanyák, Z. C. (2015). A simple fuzzy logic based power control for a series hybrid electric vehicle. In *Proc. 9th IEEE Eur. Mod. Symp. Mat. Mod. Comput. Sim. (EMS 2015)*. Madrid, Spain, pp. 207–212.

[107] Vaščák, J. and Hvizdoš, J. (2016). Vehicle navigation by fuzzy cognitive maps using sonar and RFID technologies. In *Proc. IEEE 14th Int. Symp. Appl. Mach. Intell. Informat. (SAMI 2014)*. Herl'any, Slovakia, pp. 75–80.

[108] Vaščák, J., Hvizdoš, J. and Puheim, M. (2016). Agent-based cloud computing systems for traffic management. In *Proc. 2016 Int. Conf. Intell. Networks Collab. Syst. (INCoS 2016)*. Ostrava, Czech Republic, pp. 73–79.

[109] Ando, N., Korondi, P. and Hashimoto, H. (2004). Networked telemicromanipulation systems "Haptic Loupe". *IEEE Trans. Ind. Electron.*, **51**(6), pp. 1259–1271.

[110] Haidegger, T., Kovács, L., Precup, R.-E., Preitl, S., Benyó, B. and Benyó, Z. (2011). Cascade control for telerobotic systems serving space medicine. *IFAC Proc. Vol.*, **44**(1), pp. 3759–3764.

[111] Yu, Q.-X., Hou, Z.-S., Bu, X.-H. and Yu, Q.-F. (2020a), RBFNN-based data-driven predictive iterative learning control for nonaffine nonlinear systems. *IEEE Trans. Neural Networks Learn. Syst.*, **31**(4), pp. 1170–1182.

[112] Joelianto, E., Sutarto, H. Y., Airulla, D. G. and Zaky, M. (2010). Hybrid controller design based magneto-rheological damper lookup table for quarter car suspension. *Int. J. Artif. Intell.*, **18**(1), pp. 193–206.

[113] Aparanji, V. M., Wali, U. V. and Aparna, R. (2020). Multi-layer auto resonance network for robotic motion control. *Int. J. Artif. Intell.*, **18**(1), pp. 19–44.

[114] Haber, R. E. and Alique, J. R. (2004). Nonlinear internal model control using neural networks: an application for machining processes. *Neural Comput. Appl.*, **13**(1), pp. 47–55.

[115] Michail, K., Deliparaschos, K. M., Tzafestas, S. G. and Zolotas, A. C. (2016). AI-based actuator/sensor fault detection with low computational cost for industrial applications. *IEEE Trans. Control Syst. Technol.*, **24**(1), pp. 293–301.

[116] Andoga, R. and Fozo, L. (2017). Near magnetic field of a small turbojet engine. *Acta Phys. Pol. A*, **131**(4), pp. 1117–1119.

[117] Rotariu, C., Pasarica, A., Andruseac, G., Costinm H. and Nemescu, D. (2014). Automatic analysis of the fetal heart rate variability and uterine contractions. In *Proc. 8th Int. Conf. Exp. Electr. Power Eng. (EPE 2014)*. Iasi, Romania, pp. 1–6.

[118] Precup, R.-E., Teban, T.-A., Albu, A., Borlea, A.-B., Zamfirache, I. A. and Petriu, E. M. (2020b). Evolving fuzzy models for prosthetic hand myoelectric-based control. *IEEE Trans. Instrum. Meas.*, **69**(7), pp. 4625–4636.

[119] Lagunes, M. L., Castillo, O., Valdez, F., Soria, J. and Melin, P. (2018). Parameter optimization for membership functions of type-2 fuzzy controllers for autonomous mobile robots using the firefly algorithm. In *Proc. 2018 North Amer. Fuzzy Inform. Process. Soc. Ann. Conf. (NAFIPS 2018)*. Fortaleza, Brazil, pp. 569–579.

[120] Maldonado, Y., Castillo, O. and Melin, P. (2014). A multi-objective optimization of type-2 fuzzy control speed in FPGAs. *Appl. Soft Comput.*, **24**, pp. 1164–1174.

[121] Astudillo, L., Melin, P. and Castillo, O. (2013). Nature inspired chemical optimization to design a type-2 fuzzy controller for a mobile robot. In *Proc. Joint IFSA World Congr. NAFIPS Ann. Meet. (IFSA/NAFIPS 2013)*. Edmonton, AB, Canada, pp. 1423–1428.

[122] Castillo, O. and Melin, P. (2012). A review on the design and optimization of interval type-2 fuzzy controllers. *Appl. Soft Comput.*, **12**(4), pp. 1267–1278.

[123] Navarro, G., Umberger, D. K. and Manic, M. (2017). VD-IT2, Virtual disk cloning on disk arrays using a type-2 fuzzy controller. *IEEE Trans. Fuzzy Syst.*, **25**(6), pp. 1752–1764.

[124] Camci, E., Kripalani, D. R., Ma, L.-L., Kayacan, E. and Khanesar, M. A. (2018). An aerial robot for rice farm quality inspection with type-2 fuzzy neural networks tuned by particle swarm optimization-sliding mode control hybrid algorithm. *Swarm Evol. Comput.*, **41**, pp. 1–8.

[125] Sarabakha, A., Fu, C.-H. and Kayacan, E. (2019). Intuit before tuning: type-1 and type-2 fuzzy logic controllers. *Appl. Soft Comput.*, **81**, 105495.

[126] Kayacan, E., Sarabakha, A., Coupland, S., John, R. I. and Khanesar, M. A. (2018). Type-2 fuzzy elliptic membership functions for modeling uncertainty. *Eng. Appl. Artif. Intell.*, **70**, pp. 170–183.

[127] Sarabakha, A., Fu, C.-H., Kayacan, E. and Kumbasar, T. (2018). Type-2 fuzzy logic controllers made even simpler: from design to deployment for UAVs. *IEEE Trans. Ind. Electron.*, **65**(6), pp. 5069–5077.

[128] Venkataramana, N. N. and Singh, S. P. (2021). A novel interval type-2 fuzzy-based direct torque control of induction motor drive using five-level diode-clamped inverter. *IEEE Trans. Ind. Electron.*, **68**(1), pp. 149–159.

[129] Li, Z.-C., Yan, H.-C., Zhang, H., Lam, H.-K. and Wang, M. (2021). Aperiodic sampled-data-based control for interval type-2 fuzzy systems via refined adaptive event-triggered communication scheme. *IEEE Trans. Fuzzy Syst.*, **29**(2), pp. 310–321.

[130] Zhang, Z.-N., Su, S.-F. and Niu, Y.-G. (2020b). Dynamic event-triggered control for interval type-2 fuzzy systems under fading channel. *IEEE Trans. Cybern.*, doi: 10.1109/TCYB.2020.2996296.

[131] Shen, Q.-K., Shi, Y., Jia, R.-F. and Shi, P. (2021). Design on type-2 fuzzy-based distributed supervisory control with backlash-like hysteresis. *IEEE Trans. Fuzzy Syst.*, **29**(2), pp. 252–261.

[132] Du, Z.-B., Kao, Y.-G., Karimi, H. R. and Zhao, X.-D. (2020). Interval type-2 fuzzy sampled-data H_∞ control for nonlinear unreliable networked control systems. *IEEE Trans. Fuzzy Syst.*, **28**(7), pp. 1434–1448.

[133] Mirjalili, S., Mirjalili, S. M. and Lewis, A. (2014). Grey wolf optimizer. *Adv. Eng. Software*, **69**, pp. 46–61.

[134] Precup, R.-E., David, R.-C., Szedlak-Stinean, A.-I., Petriu E. M. and Dragan, F. (2017). An easily understandable grey wolf optimizer and its application to fuzzy controller tuning. *Algorithms*, 10(2), 68.

[135] Mirjalili, S. and Lewis, A. (2016). The whale optimization algorithm. *Adv. Eng. Software*, **95**, pp. 51–67.

[136] Li, S.-M., Chen, H.-L., Wang, M.-J., Heidari, A. A. and Mirjalili, S. (2020b). Slime mould algorithm: a new method for stochastic optimization. *Future Gener. Comput. Syst.*, **111**, pp. 300–323.

[137] Rashedi, E., Nezamabadi-pour, H. and Saryazdi, S. (2009). GSA: a gravitational search algorithm. *Inf. Sci.*, **179**(13), pp. 2232–2248.

[138] Kennedy, J. and Eberhart, R. C. (1995). A new optimizer using particle swarm theory. In *Proc. 6th Int. Symp. Micro Mach. Human Sci. (MHS'95)*. Nagoya, Japan, pp 39–43.

[139] Kennedy, J. and Eberhart, R. C. (1997). A discrete binary version of the particle swarm algorithm. In *Proc. 1997 IEEE Int. Conf. Syst. Man Cybern. (SMC'97)*. Orlando, FL, USA, vol. 5, pp. 4104–4108.

[140] David, R.-C., Precup, R.-E., Preitl, S., Roman, R.-C. and Petriu, E. M. (2020b). Fuzzy control systems with reduced parametric sensitivity design based on hybrid grey wolf optimizer-particle swarm optimization. In *Proc. 24th Int. Conf. Syst. Theory Control Comput. (ICSTCC 2020)*. Sinaia, Romania, pp. 66–71.

[141] Preitl, S. and Precup, R.-E. (1996). On the algorithmic design of a class of control systems based on providing the symmetry of open-loop Bode plots. *Buletinul Stiintific al U.P.T. Trans. Autom. Control Comput. Sci.*, **41**(55), pp. 47–55.

[142] Preitl, S. and Precup, R.-E. (1999). An extension of tuning relations after symmetrical optimum method for PI and PID controllers. *Automatica*, **35**, pp. 1731–1736.

[143] Derrac, J., García, S., Molina, D. and Herrera, F. (2011). A practical tutorial on the use of nonparametric statistical tests as a methodology for comparing evolutionary and swarm intelligence algorithms. *Swarm Evol. Comput.*, **1**(1), pp. 3–18.

[144] Li, L.-M., Lu, K.-D., Zeng, G.-Q., Wu, L. and Chen, M.-R. (2016). A novel real-coded population-based extremal optimization algorithm with polynomial mutation: a nonparametric statistical study on continuous optimization problems. *Neurocomputing*, **174**, pp. 577–587.

[145] Zeng, G.-Q., Xie, X.-Q., Chen, M.-R. and Weng, J. (2019). Adaptive population extremal optimization based PID neural network for multivariable nonlinear control systems. *Swarm Evol. Comput.*, **44**, pp. 320–334.

[146] Chen, M.-R., Zeng G.-Q. and Lu, K.-D. (2019). A many-objective population extremal optimization algorithm with an adaptive hybrid mutation operation. *Inf. Sci.*, **498**, pp. 62–90.

[147] Faria, P., Soares, J., Vale, Z., Morais, H. and Sousa, T. (2013). Modified particle swarm optimization applied to integrated demand response and DG resources scheduling. *IEEE Trans. Smart Grid*, **4**(1), pp. 606–616.

[148] Lu, K.-D., Zhou, W.-N., Zeng, G.-Q., and Zheng, Y.-Y. (2019). Constrained population extremal optimization-based robust load frequency control of multi-area interconnected power system. *Int. J. Electr. Power Ener. Syst.*, **105**, pp. 249–271.

[149] Osaba, E., Del Ser, J., Sadollah, A., Bilbao, M. N. and Camacho, D. (2018). A discrete water cycle algorithm for solving the symmetric and asymmetric traveling salesman problem. *Appl. Soft Comput.*, **71**, pp. 277–290.

[150] Osaba, E., Yang, X. S., Fister Jr, I., Del Ser, J., Lopez-Garcia, P. and Vazquez-Pardavila, A. J. (2019). A discrete and improved bat algorithm for solving a medical goods distribution problem with pharmacological waste collection. *Swarm Evol. Comput.*, **44**, pp. 273–286.

[151] Gao, D., Wang, G.-G. and Pedrycz, W. (2020). Solving fuzzy job-shop scheduling problem using DE algorithm improved by a selection mechanism. *IEEE Trans. Fuzzy Syst.*, **28**(12), pp. 3265–3275.

[152] Yi, J.-H., Deb, S., Dong, J.-Y., Alavi, J.-Y. and Wang, G.-G. (2020a). An improved NSGA-III algorithm with adaptive mutation operator for Big Data optimization problems. *Future Gener. Comput. Syst.*, **88**, pp. 571–585.

[153] Yi, J.-H., Xing, L.-N., Wang, G.-G., Dong, J.-Y., Vasilakos, A. V., Alavi, A. H. and Wang, L. (2020b). Behavior of crossover operators in NSGA-III for large-scale optimization problems. *Inf. Sci.*, **509**, pp. 470–487.

[154] Moattari, M. and Moradi, M. H. (2020). Conflict monitoring optimization heuristic inspired by brain fear and conflict systems. *Int. J. Artif. Intell.*, **18**(1), pp. 45–62.

[155] Subotic, M., Manasijevic, A. and Kupusinac, A. (2020). Parallelized Multiple Swarm Artificial Bee Colony (PMS-ABC) algorithm for constrained optimization problems. *Stud. Informat. Control*, **29**(1), pp. 77–86.

[156] Ochoa, P., Castillo, O. and Soria, J. (2020). Optimization of fuzzy controller design using a differential evolution algorithm with dynamic parameter adaptation based on type-1 and interval type-2 fuzzy systems. *Soft Comput.*, **24**(1), pp. 193–214.

[157] Rodríguez, L., Castillo, O., Soria, J., Melin, P., Valdez, F., Gonzalez, C. I., Martinez G. E. and Soto, J. (2017). A fuzzy hierarchical operator in the grey wolf optimizer algorithm. *Appl. Soft Comput.*, **57**, pp. 315–328.

[158] Castillo, O. and Amador-Angulo, L. (2018). A generalized type-2 fuzzy logic approach for dynamic parameter adaptation in bee colony optimization applied to fuzzy controller design. *Inf. Sci.*, **460–461**, pp. 476–496.

[159] Precup, R.-E., David, R.-C., Petriu, E. M., Preitl S. and Radac, M.-B. (2014). Novel adaptive charged system search algorithm for optimal tuning of fuzzy controllers. *Expert Syst. Appl.*, **41**(4), pp. 1168–1175.

Chapter 21

Indirect Self-evolving Fuzzy Control Approaches and Their Applications

Zhao-Xu Yang* and Hai-Jun Rong†

State Key Laboratory for Strength and Vibration of Mechanical Structures,
Shaanxi Key Laboratory of Environment and Control for Flight Vehicle,
School of Aerospace Engineering, Xi'an Jiaotong University,
Xi'an, 710049, P.R.China
*yangzhx@xjtu.edu.cn
†hjrong@mail.xjtu.edu.cn

21.1. Introduction

Intelligent control that takes inspiration from the autonomous learning, reasoning, and decision of living beings is very significant when a system has no help from prior knowledge, but remains under control. The classical approaches of intelligent control include, but are not be limited to, fuzzy inference systems (FIS), artificial neural networks (ANN), genetic algorithms (GA), particle swarm optimization (PSO), support vector machine (SVM), etc. Intelligent control systems, especially the novel *self-evolving fuzzy control systems* with structure evolution and parameter adjustment, have found great applications in engineering and industry.

21.1.1. *Self-evolving Fuzzy Model*

It is well known that fuzzy inference systems (FIS) can be used to closely approximate any nonlinear input–output mapping by means of a series of *if–then* rules [1]. In the design of FIS, there are two major tasks, viz., the structure identification and parameter adjustment. Structure identification determines the input–output space partition, antecedent and consequent variables of *if–then* rules, number of such rules, and initial positions of membership functions. The other task of parameter adjustment involves realizing the parameters for the fuzzy model structure determined in the previous step [2].

In most of the real applications, not all fuzzy rules contribute significantly to the system performance during the entire time period. A fuzzy rule may be active initially, but later it may contribute little to the system output. For this reason, the insignificant fuzzy rules have to be removed during learning to realize a compact fuzzy system structure. Using the ideas of adding and pruning hidden neurons to form a minimal RBF network in [3], a hierarchical online self-organizing learning algorithm for dynamic fuzzy neural networks (DFNN) has been proposed in [4]. Another online self-organizing fuzzy neural network (SOFNN) proposed by Leng et al. [5] also includes a pruning method. The pruning method utilizes the optimal brain surgeon (OBS) approach to determine the importance of each rule. However, in these two algorithms, the pruning criteria need all the past data received so far. Hence, they are not strictly sequential and further require increased memory for storing all the past data.

An online sequential learning algorithm using recursive least-square error (RLSE) was presented for a fixed fuzzy system structure [6]. It is referred to as an Online Sequential Fuzzy Extreme Learning Machine (OS-Fuzzy-ELM). In an OS-Fuzzy-ELM algorithm, the parameters of fuzzy membership functions are selected randomly and the consequent parameters of fuzzy rules are calculated analytically using least square error. For sequential learning, the consequent parameters are updated using RLSE and the training data can be presented one-by-one or chunk-by-chunk. The simulation results based on the function approximation and classification problems show that OS-Fuzzy-ELM produces better generalization performance with a smaller computation time. However, in the algorithm, the structure of the fuzzy system is determined before learning and once it is determined, it will never change according to the learning process.

To improve the performance of the above algorithms in the nonlinear learning problems, the difficulties described above need to be overcome. The self-evolving fuzzy models with both structure evolution and parameter adjustment are applied to reconstruct the nonlinear uncertainties. The structure evolution approach is presented to evolve the model structure and determine the initial values of the antecedent and consequent parameters in an incremental manner. Initially, the rule base of the self-evolving fuzzy model is empty and the rules are generated according to the structure learning algorithm with different criteria, which is designed for the automatic determination of rules that involve the recruiting and pruning of fuzzy rules. In this way, a compact rule base can be built. Thus, the self-evolving fuzzy control schemes yielded by the proposed fuzzy models are able to achieve a controller structure with an appropriate size during the approximation of nonlinear uncertainties. In the rest of this chapter, two typical self-evolving fuzzy models referred to as extended sequential adaptive fuzzy inference system (ESAFIS) [7] and meta-cognitive fuzzy inference system (McFIS) [8] with improvements in both accuracy and speed are described, which would be used to design the fuzzy controller.

21.1.2. *Self-Evolving Fuzzy Control System*

Adaptive identification and control of systems with uncertain time-varying parameters and unknown dynamics has been the focus of numerous studies. Among various adaptive control techniques, the feedback linearization method and the backstepping method are the effective control strategies and have been widely applied to uncertain nonlinear systems [9–11]. In the conventional control approaches, some a priori information about the nonlinear systems will be required. But the systems' nonlinear input–output relationship is generally hard to understand, thus their exact mathematical models are difficult to describe in an analytical form. To overcome the problem, some researchers [12] have turned to universal function approximators as a means of explicitly identifying complex nonlinear systems. Fuzzy models are powerful tools to account for the control of complex uncertain nonlinear systems without exact mathematical models. Therefore, they have been widely employed in the field of nonlinear system control [13].

A number of investigations have been performed for the fuzzy control of nonlinear systems based on the merger of fuzzy models and adaptive control techniques. With the fuzzy model structure, both linear and nonlinear parameterized models are achieved accordingly. In most control schemes [14–16], only consequent parameters of fuzzy rules are modified according to the rules obtained based on the Lyapunov function, while the antecedent fuzzy membership function parameters are assigned based on the designer's experience. It is obvious that as the fuzzy membership function parameters vary, differently shaped membership functions change simultaneously and display different shapes. This helps to seize fast-varying dynamics, alleviate approximation errors, and enhance control performance. Thus, some nonlinearly parameterized controllers are developed [17, 18] where both fuzzy membership function parameters and consequent parameters are updated. Although higher control performance can be achieved compared with the linear parameterized controllers, a large number of tunable parameters are required and also result in high computation complexity.

All the above-mentioned control methods address the issue of parameter adjustment of the fuzzy-neural model without considering structure learning. Nonlinear systems generally show dynamic changes due to nonstationary environments and external disturbances, which result in drifts and shifts of system states or new operating conditions and modes. From a practical point of view, there is no guarantee that a fixed controller structure has a satisfactory performance in online applications when the environment or the object of the controller changes. Thus, some fuzzy-neural models with self-adaptation capability have been developed so that model parameters and model structure are updated for rapidly adapting to a variety of unexpected dynamic changes. Besides in nonstationary environments, it is generally difficult to achieve a whole learning data with the uniform distribution that can cover all the system characteristics. In this case, dynamic learning is required to be able to identify useless data and delete them during the learning process.

Aircraft wing-rock motion and a thrust active magnetic bearing system, as application examples, suffer from inherent nonlinear uncertainties and fast time-varying characteristics. Considering these concerns, the main motivation of this work is to generate a self-adaptable controller structure and evolve it in the online mode. The controller can start with no pre-defined fuzzy rules, and does not need any offline pretraining or explicit model of the controlled system. The structure and parameters of the controller are adaptively adjusted according to the information extracted from nonstationary and uncertain data streams. To meet the goal, the self-evolving control approaches are proposed for uncertain nonlinear systems that are hard to formulate in mathematical forms due to nonstationary parameters and uncertainties. Recently, self-evolving fuzzy control approaches that combine the control technique with self-evolving fuzzy models have been employed to design the controllers for nonlinear systems with completely unknown functions. A key element in these fuzzy control approaches is that self-evolving fuzzy models are utilized to approximate the unknown dynamics exploiting the fact of being universal approximators.

21.2. Adaptive Fuzzy Control of Aircraft Wing-Rock Motion

Wing rock is a highly nonlinear aerodynamic phenomenon in which limits cycle roll oscillations are experienced by aircraft at high angles of attack [19]. Wing-rock motion is a concern because it may cause a loss of stability in the lateral/directional mode due to the large amplitudes and high frequencies of the rolling oscillations, thus degrading the maneuverability, tracking accuracy, and operational safety of high-performance fighters. To understand the underlying mechanism of wing-rock motion, some research has been conducted on the motion of slender delta wings, and several theoretical models that describe the nonlinear rolling motion have been developed using simple differential equations [20, 21]. During the past decades, many control techniques have been developed [22–25]. Based on the differential models, the control strategies used to suppress the wing-rock motion include nonlinear optimal feedback control [23], the adaptive control based on feedback linearization [24] and the robust H_∞ control [25]. Although these methods are successful in controlling wing-rock motion, a key assumption in these methods is that the system nonlinearities are known a priori, which is generally not applicable in the real world. The reason is that the aerodynamic parameters governing wing rock are inadequately understood and thus an accurate mathematical model for the wing-rock motion cannot be obtained. These present significant difficulties to the controller design using conventional control techniques.

In the proposed adaptive fuzzy control scheme, the fuzzy controller is built by employing ESAFIS to approximate the nonlinear dynamics of wing-rock motion. However, different from the original ESAFIS algorithm where a recursive least-square error (RLSE) is used to adjust the consequent parameters, they are updated based on the stable adaptive laws derived from a Lyapunov function that is an effective way to guarantee the stability of the closed-loop system. Moreover, a sliding controller is incorporated into the fuzzy controller and activated to work with the fuzzy controller for offsetting the modeling errors of the ESAFIS.

21.2.1. *Problem Formulation*

The nonlinear wing-rock motion for an 80° slender delta wing developed by Nayfeh et al. [21] is considered in the study, whose dynamics is described by the following differential equation:

$$\ddot{\phi} = \left(\frac{\rho U_\infty^2 S b}{2 I_{xx}} \right) C_l - D\dot{\phi} + u, \tag{21.1}$$

where ϕ is the roll angle, ρ is the density of air, U_∞ is the freestream velocity, S is the wing reference area, b is the chord, I_{xx} is the mass moment of inertia, D is the damping coefficient and fixed as 0.0001, u is the control input, and C_l is the roll moment coefficient that is given by

$$C_l = a_1\phi + a_2\dot{\phi} + a_3\phi^3 + a_4\phi^2\dot{\phi} + a_5\phi\dot{\phi}^2. \tag{21.2}$$

The aerodynamic parameters a_1 to a_5 are nonlinear functions of the angle of attack α and are presented in Table 21.1.

Table 21.1: Coefficients of Rolling Moment with Angle of Attack α.

α	a_1	a_2	a_3	a_4	a_5
15.0	−0.01026	−0.02117	−0.14181	0.99735	−0.83478
21.5	−0.04207	−0.01456	0.04714	−0.18583	0.24234
22.5	−0.04681	0.01966	0.05671	−0.22691	0.59065
25.0	−0.05686	0.03254	0.07334	−0.35970	1.46810

Substituting Eq. (21.2) into Eq. (21.1), the wing-rock dynamics is then rewritten as

$$\ddot{\phi} + \omega^2\phi = \mu_1\dot{\phi} + b_1\dot{\phi}^3 + \mu_2\phi^2\dot{\phi} + b_2\phi\dot{\phi}^2 + u. \tag{21.3}$$

The coefficients in the above equation are given by the following relations:

$$\omega^2 = -Ca_1, \quad \mu_1 = Ca_2 - D, \quad \mu_2 = Ca_4, \quad b_1 = Ca_3, \quad b_2 = Ca_5, \tag{21.4}$$

where $C(= \frac{\rho U_\infty^2 Sb}{2I_{xx}})$ is a fixed constant and equal to 0.354.

The values of the coefficients in Eq. (21.3) could be obtained for any angle of attack according to any interpolation method. In [21], author have has pointed out that the observed onset angle where μ_1 is zero corresponds to the onset of wing rock at "19–20 deg". This can be verified by observing the properties of the open-loop system with $u = 0$. Figures 21.1(a) and (b) present the time process of the calculated roll angle and the roll rate given by Eq. (21.3) for $\alpha = 15°$.

By choosing state variables $x_1 = \phi$ and $x_2 = \dot{\phi}$, the state equations of the wing-rock dynamics will be

$$\begin{aligned} \dot{x}_1 &= x_2 \\ \dot{x}_2 &= f(x_1, x_2) + u, \end{aligned} \tag{21.5}$$

where $f(x_1, x_2) = -\omega^2\phi + \mu_1\dot{\phi} + b_1\dot{\phi}^3 + \mu_2\phi^2\dot{\phi} + b_2\phi\dot{\phi}^2$ is assumed to be a bounded real continuous nonlinear function.

Defining $\mathbf{x} = [x_1, x_2]$, Eq. (21.5) can be further written in the following state–space form:

$$\dot{\mathbf{x}} = \mathbf{A}\mathbf{x} + \mathbf{b}f(\mathbf{x}) + \mathbf{b}u, \tag{21.6}$$

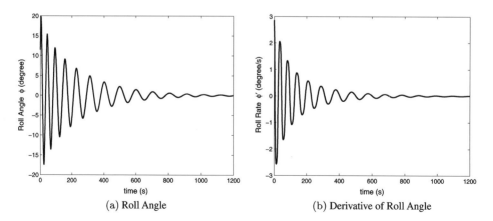

(a) Roll Angle (b) Derivative of Roll Angle

Figure 21.1: The time process of roll angle and its derivative for $\alpha = 15°$.

where

$$\mathbf{A} = \begin{bmatrix} 0 & 1 \\ 0 & 0 \end{bmatrix}, \quad \mathbf{b} = \begin{bmatrix} 0 \\ 1 \end{bmatrix}. \tag{21.7}$$

Define the output tracking error $e = \phi_d - \phi$, the reference output vector $\phi_d = [\phi_d, \dot{\phi}_d]^T$ and the tracking error vector $\mathbf{e} = [e, \dot{e}]^T = [e_1, e_2]^T$. The control law u is designed such that the state $\phi = [\phi, \dot{\phi}]^T$ can track the desired command $\phi_d = [\phi_d, \dot{\phi}_d]^T$ as closely as possible.

According to the feedback linearization method [26] and the dynamics system given by Eq. (21.6), the desired control input u^* can be obtained as follows:

$$u^* = \ddot{\phi}_d - f(\mathbf{x}) + k_1 \dot{e} + k_2 e, \tag{21.8}$$

where k_1 and k_2 are real numbers. By substituting Eq. (21.8) with Eq. (21.6), the following equation is obtained:

$$\ddot{e} + k_1 \dot{e} + k_2 e = 0, \tag{21.9}$$

By properly choosing k_1 and k_2, all the roots of the polynomial $s^2 + k_1 s + k_2 = 0$ are in the open left half-plane, which implies that the tracking error will converge to zero. Equation (21.9) also shows that the tracking of the reference command is asymptotically achieved from any initial conditions, i.e., $\lim_{t \to \infty} |\mathbf{e}| = 0$.

However, if the motion dynamics $f(\mathbf{x})$ is perturbed or unknown, it is difficult to implement this control law in practical applications. To circumvent this problem, an indirect adaptive fuzzy control strategy based on ESAFIS is designed. Before presenting the fuzzy control scheme, a brief description of ESAFIS is given in the following section.

21.2.2. *Extended Sequential Adaptive Fuzzy Inference System*

21.2.2.1. *Architecture of ESAFIS*

ESAFIS [7] is the extension version of the SAFIS [27] algorithm for improving its accuracy and speed. Different from SAFIS, ESAFIS can implement both the zero-order and first-order TS fuzzy models, which are commonly described as follows:

Rule k: If $(x_1$ is $A_{1k}) \cdots (x_{N_x}$ is $A_{N_x k})$, then $(\hat{y}_1$ is $a_{k1}) \cdots (\hat{y}_{N_y}$ is $a_{kN_y})$,

where A_{ik} $(i = 1, \ldots, N_x)$ denotes the fuzzy sets, namely, linguistic values associated with the ith input variable x_i in rule k, N_x is the dimension of the input vector $\mathbf{x}$ $(\mathbf{x} = [x_1, \ldots, x_{N_x}])$, N_h is the number of fuzzy rules, and N_y is the dimension of the output vector $\hat{\mathbf{y}}(\hat{\mathbf{y}} = [\hat{y}_1, \ldots, \hat{y}_{N_y}])$. In ESAFIS, the number of fuzzy rules N_h varies. Initially, there is no fuzzy rule and then during learning fuzzy rules are added and removed. For the zero-order TS fuzzy model, the consequence a_{kj} $(k = 1, 2, \ldots, N_h; \; j = 1, 2, \ldots, N_y)$ is a constant, while

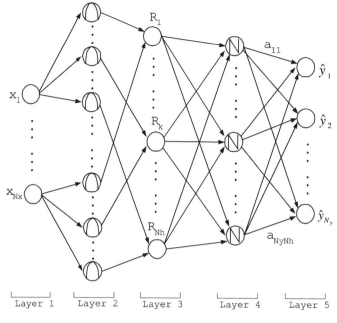

Figure 21.2: The structure of ESAFIS.

in the first-order TS fuzzy model, a linear combination of input variables, that is, $a_{kj} = q_{k0,j} + q_{k1,j}x_1 + \cdots + q_{kN_x,j}x_{N_x}$ is used as the consequence. A lot of research work has proved that the first-order TS fuzzy model possesses better performance in terms of system structure and learning ability than the zero-order TS fuzzy model [7, 28]. Thus, ESAFIS with the first-order TS fuzzy model is mainly studied here to construct the control law.

The structure of ESAFIS illustrated in Figure 21.2 consists of five layers to realize the above fuzzy rule model.

Layer 1: In layer 1, each node represents an input variable and directly transmits the input signal to layer 2.

Layer 2: In this layer, each node represents the membership value of each input variable. ESAFIS utilizes the function equivalence between an RBF network and an FIS. Thus, its antecedent part (if part) in fuzzy rules is achieved by Gaussian functions of the RBF network as used in many existing studies in the literature [29, 30]. The membership value of the fuzzy set $A_{ik}(x_i)$ for the ith input variable x_i in the kth Gaussian function is given by

$$A_{ik}(x_i) = \exp\left(-\frac{(x_i - \mu_{ik})^2}{\sigma_k^2}\right), \quad k = 1, 2, \ldots, N_h, \quad (21.10)$$

where N_h is the number of Gaussian functions, μ_{ik} is the center of the kth Gaussian function for the ith input variable, and σ_k is the width of the kth Gaussian function. In ESAFIS, the widths of all the input variables in the kth Gaussian function are the same.

Layer 3: Each node in this layer represents the "IF" part of if–then rules obtained by the sum–product composition and the total number of such rules is N_h. The firing strength (if part) of the kth rule is given by

$$R_k(\mathbf{x}) = \prod_{i=1}^{N_x} A_{ik}(x_i) = \exp\left(-\sum_{i=1}^{N_x} \frac{(x_i - \mu_{ik})^2}{\sigma_k^2}\right)$$

$$= \exp\left(-\frac{\|\mathbf{x} - \mu_k\|^2}{\sigma_k^2}\right). \tag{21.11}$$

Layer 4: The nodes in this layer are named normalized nodes, whose number is equal to the number of nodes in third layer. The kth normalized node is given by

$$\bar{R}_k = \frac{R_k(\mathbf{x})}{\sum_{k=1}^{N_h} R_k(\mathbf{x})}. \tag{21.12}$$

Layer 5: Each node in this layer corresponds to an output variable, which is given by the weighted sum of the output of each normalized rule. The system output is calculated as

$$\hat{\mathbf{y}} = \frac{\sum_{k=1}^{N_h} \mathbf{a}_k R_k(\mathbf{x})}{\sum_{k=1}^{N_h} R_k(\mathbf{x})}, \tag{21.13}$$

and the consequence is

$$\mathbf{a}_k = \mathbf{x}_e^T \mathbf{q}_k, \tag{21.14}$$

where $\mathbf{x}_e$ is the extended input vector by appending the input vector $\mathbf{x}$ with 1, that is, $[1, \mathbf{x}]^T$; $\mathbf{q}_k$ is the parameter matrix for the kth fuzzy rule and is given by

$$\mathbf{q}_k = \begin{bmatrix} q_{k0,1} & \cdots & q_{k0,N_y} \\ \vdots & \cdots & \vdots \\ q_{kN_x,1} & \cdots & q_{kN_x,N_y} \end{bmatrix}_{(N_x+1) \times N_y}. \tag{21.15}$$

The system output denoted by Eq. (21.13) can be rewritten as

$$\hat{\mathbf{y}} = \mathbf{HQ}, \tag{21.16}$$

where $\mathbf{Q}$ is the consequent parameter matrix existing in all N_h fuzzy rules and $\mathbf{H}$ is the vector representing the normalized firing strength of rules. The two parameters are given by

$$
\mathbf{Q} =
\begin{bmatrix}
q_{10,1} & \cdots & q_{10,N_y} \\
\vdots & \vdots & \vdots \\
q_{1N_x,1} & \cdots & q_{1N_x,N_y} \\
\vdots & \cdots & \vdots \\
q_{N_h0,1} & \cdots & q_{N_h0,N_y} \\
\vdots & \cdots & \vdots \\
q_{N_hN_x,1} & \cdots & q_{N_hN_x,N_y}
\end{bmatrix}_{N_h(N_x+1)\times N_y}
,
\tag{21.17}
$$

and

$$
\mathbf{H} = \left[\mathbf{x}_e^T \frac{R_1(\mathbf{x})}{\sum_{k=1}^{N_h} R_k(\mathbf{x})}, \ldots, \mathbf{x}_e^T \frac{R_{N_h}(\mathbf{x})}{\sum_{k=1}^{N_h} R_k(\mathbf{x})} \right]_{1 \times N_h(N_x+1)}.
\tag{21.18}
$$

21.2.3. *Learning Algorithm of ESAFIS*

The learning algorithm of ESAFIS involves the addition and removal of fuzzy rules online and the adjustment of the consequent parameters. To avoid the difficulty of knowing the input distribution as a priori knowledge in SAFIS, ESAFIS uses the concept of modified *influence* of a fuzzy rule to add and remove rules during learning. The modified *influence* represents a statistical contribution of the rule to the output using a certain limited number of samples. Suppose that the input observations are generated in a random distribution and arrive with the same sampling distribution; the modified *influence* $E_{\text{minf}}(k)$ can be estimated by using the recently received M training samples as long as the memory factor M is reasonably large. It is given by

$$
E_{\text{minf}}(k) = \sum_{l=n-M+1}^{n} \frac{\|\mathbf{x}_{le}^T \mathbf{q}_k\|}{M} \frac{R_k(\mathbf{x}_l)}{\sum_{k=1}^{N_h} R_k(\mathbf{x}_l)}.
\tag{21.19}
$$

The sequential learning process of ESAFIS is briefly summarized below. For details, see [7].

ESAFIS begins with no fuzzy rules. As the inputs $\mathbf{x}_n, \mathbf{y}_n$ (n is the time index) are received sequentially during learning, fuzzy rules are added or deleted based on the following two criteria, viz., the distance criterion and the modified *influence* of the newly added fuzzy rule $N_h + 1$,

$$
\begin{cases}
\|\mathbf{x}_n - \mu_{\text{nr}}\| > \epsilon_n \\
E_{\text{minf}}(N_h + 1) = \displaystyle\sum_{l=n-M+1}^{n} \frac{\|\mathbf{e}_n\|}{M} \frac{R_{N_h+1}(\mathbf{x}_l)}{\sum_{k=1}^{N_h+1} R_k(\mathbf{x}_l)} > e_g
\end{cases},
\tag{21.20}
$$

where ϵ_n, e_g are the thresholds to be selected appropriately, $\mathbf{x}_n$ is the latest input data, and μ_{nr} is the center of the fuzzy rule nearest to $\mathbf{x}_n$. e_g is the growing threshold and is chosen according to the desired learning accuracy. κ is an overlap factor that determines the overlap of fuzzy rules in the input space. $\mathbf{e}_n = \mathbf{y}_n - \hat{\mathbf{y}}_n$, where $\mathbf{y}_n$ is the true value and $\hat{\mathbf{y}}_n$ is the approximated value. ϵ_n is the distance threshold, which decays exponentially and is given as

$$\epsilon_n = \max \{\epsilon_{\max} \times \gamma^n, \epsilon_{\min}\}, \tag{21.21}$$

where $\epsilon_{\max}$ and $\epsilon_{\min}$ are the largest and the smallest length of interest and γ is the decay constant. The equation shows that initially it is the largest length of interest in the input space that allows fewer fuzzy rules to coarsely learn the system and then it decreases exponentially to the smallest length of interest in the input space that allows more fuzzy rules to finely learn the system.

When a new fuzzy rule $N_h + 1$ is added, its corresponding antecedent and consequent parameters are assigned as follows:

$$\begin{cases} q_{(N_h+1)0,j} = e_{nj}, & j = 1, 2, \ldots, N_y \\ q_{(N_h+1)i,j} = 0, & i = 1, 2, \ldots, N_x \\ \mu_{N_h+1} = \mathbf{x}_n \\ \sigma_{N_h+1} = \kappa \|\mathbf{x}_n - \mu_{nr}\| \end{cases}, \tag{21.22}$$

where e_{nj} is the jth element of the system output error vector $\mathbf{e}_n (= \mathbf{y}_n - \hat{\mathbf{y}}_n)$.

When there is no addition of a new rule, the consequent parameters of all existing rules ($\mathbf{Q}$) are modified based on an RLSE method. However, when this method is applied for controller design, problems such as the stability of the overall scheme and convergence of the approximation error arise. Thus, using the Lyapunov stability theory, stable parameter tuning laws instead of the RLSE method are derived for ESAFIS here that guarantee the stability of the overall system. This will be introduced in the following sections.

After parameter adjustment, the existing rules will change their influence on the system output and thus all rules need to be checked for possible pruning. If the *modified* influence of a rule is less than a certain pruning threshold e_p, the rule is insignificant to the output and should be removed. Given the pruning threshold e_p selected properly, the kth fuzzy rule will be removed by satisfying $E_{\min f}(k) < e_p$. When the kth rule needs to be removed from the existing fuzzy rules, the number of fuzzy rules will be reduced to $N_h - 1$ and all the parameters including the center μ_k, width σ_k, and consequence $\mathbf{q}_k$, related with this rule will be reduced from the related matrices to suit the reduced system.

The dynamical learning capability of ESAFIS can be used as the basis for learning in adaptive control. Generally, adaptive control approaches can be classified into two categories, namely, indirect and direct adaptive control schemes. In direct adaptive control, the control law u^* is approximated directly without explicitly attempting to determine the model of the dynamics $f(\mathbf{x})$. Unlike the direct adaptive control strategy, in the indirect control strategy, ESAFIS is used to identify the nonlinear motion dynamics $f(\mathbf{x})$ and then the fuzzy control law is implemented using the identified model. To fully depict the potential of ESAFIS in the design of the adaptive controller, in the following section, we focus on showing how to achieve stable indirect adaptive control for the wing-rock problem when ESAFIS is used as an online approximator.

21.2.4. *Design Procedure of Indirect Adaptive Fuzzy Control Scheme*

The proposed indirect adaptive fuzzy control scheme is illustrated in Figure 21.3, where two controllers are incorporated, viz, a fuzzy controller u_f and a sliding controller u_s. The fuzzy control term u_f is constructed using ESAFIS for learning the system dynamics $f(\mathbf{x})$ and is given as

$$u_f = \ddot{\phi}_d - \hat{f}(\mathbf{x}) + k_1\dot{e} + k_2e, \tag{21.23}$$

where $\hat{f}(\mathbf{x})$ is the approximated value from ESAFIS and is represented as

$$\hat{f}(\mathbf{x}) = \mathbf{HQ}_I. \tag{21.24}$$

According to the universal approximation theorem of fuzzy systems [31], there exists an optimal fuzzy system estimator to approximate the nonlinear dynamic

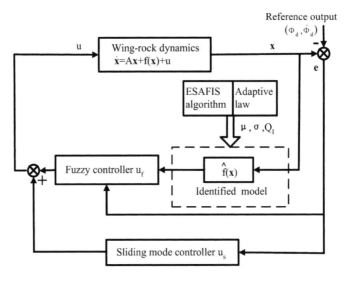

Figure 21.3:   The proposed indirect adaptive fuzzy control scheme.

function $f(x)$ in Eq. (21.6) such that

$$f(\mathbf{x}) = \mathbf{HQ}_I^* + \epsilon_I, \tag{21.25}$$

where ϵ_I is the approximation error and $\mathbf{Q}_I^*$ are the optimal parameters and is defined as follows:

$$\mathbf{Q}_I^* \overset{\Delta}{=} \mathrm{argmin} \left[\sup_{\mathbf{x} \in M_x} \| f(\mathbf{x}) - \hat{f}(\mathbf{x}) \| \right]. \tag{21.26}$$

where $\| \cdot \|$ represents the two-norm of a vector, and M_x is the predefined compact set of the input vector $\mathbf{x}$.

Using the approximation theory, the inherent approximation error ϵ_I can be reduced arbitrarily with the number of fuzzy rules increasing. In ESAFIS, the fuzzy system starts with no fuzzy rules. Fuzzy rules are dynamically recruited according to their significance to system performance and the complexity of the mapped system. Thus, it is reasonable to assume that ϵ_I is bounded by the constant $\bar{\epsilon}_I$, i.e., $|\epsilon_I| \leq \bar{\epsilon}_I$.

To compensate for approximation errors in representing the actual nonlinear dynamics by ESAFIS with ideal parameter values, a sliding mode controller u_s is used to augment the fuzzy controller above and thus the overall control law is considered as

$$u = u_f + u_s. \tag{21.27}$$

On the basis of Eqs. (21.23), (21.24), (21.25) and (21.27), the tracking error of Eq. (21.6) becomes

$$\dot{\mathbf{e}} = \Lambda \mathbf{e} + \mathbf{b}[\mathbf{H}\tilde{\mathbf{Q}}_I - \epsilon_I - u_s], \tag{21.28}$$

where $\tilde{\mathbf{Q}}_I (= \mathbf{Q}_I - \mathbf{Q}_I^*)$ is the parameter error with dimension $3N_h \times 1$ and $\mathbf{H}$ is the normalized firing strength with dimension $1 \times 3N_h$. Λ represents the 2×2 controllable canonical form matrix equaling

$$\Lambda = \begin{bmatrix} 0 & 1 \\ 0 & 0 \end{bmatrix} + \begin{bmatrix} 0 & 0 \\ -k_2 & -k_1 \end{bmatrix},$$
$$= \begin{bmatrix} 0 & 1 \\ -k_2 & -k_1 \end{bmatrix}. \tag{21.29}$$

During the modeling process of ESAFIS, the determination of fuzzy rules and antecedent parameters is based on its learning algorithm described above. Different from the RLSE method, the parameter $\mathbf{Q}_I$ is updated here using the following stable adaptive laws for satisfying the stability of the entire system.

Theorem 21.1. *Consider the wing-rock dynamics represented by Eq. (21.5). If the indirect fuzzy control law is designed as Eq. (21.23), the parameter update law* *and the sliding mode control law are designed as Eq. (21.30), the stability of the proposed indirect fuzzy control system can be assured.*

$$\dot{\mathbf{Q}}_I^T = -\eta_I \mathbf{e}^T \mathbf{PbH}$$
$$u_s = \bar{\varepsilon}_I \mathrm{sgn}(\mathbf{e}^T \mathbf{Pb}), \tag{21.30}$$

where

$$\mathrm{sgn}(\mathbf{e}^T \mathbf{Pb}) = \begin{cases} 1 & \mathbf{e}^T \mathbf{Pb} > 0 \\ -1 & \mathbf{e}^T \mathbf{Pb} < 0. \end{cases} \tag{21.31}$$

Proof. Consider the following Lyapunov function candidate;

$$V = \frac{1}{2}\mathbf{e}^T \mathbf{Pe} + \frac{1}{2\eta_I}\tilde{\mathbf{Q}}_I^T \tilde{\mathbf{Q}}_I, \tag{21.32}$$

where $\mathbf{P}$ is the symmetric and positive definite matrix; η_I is a positive constant that appears in the adaptation law and is referred to as the learning rate.

Using Eq. (21.28), the derivative of the Lyapunov function is given as

$$\dot{V} = \frac{1}{2}[\dot{\mathbf{e}}^T \mathbf{Pe} + \mathbf{e}^T \mathbf{P\dot{e}}] + \frac{1}{\eta_I}\dot{\tilde{\mathbf{Q}}}_I^T \tilde{\mathbf{Q}}_I$$

$$= \frac{1}{2}\mathbf{e}^T (\Lambda^T \mathbf{P} + \mathbf{P}\Lambda)\mathbf{e} + \left(\mathbf{e}^T \mathbf{PbH} + \frac{1}{\eta_I}\dot{\tilde{\mathbf{Q}}}_I^T\right)\tilde{\mathbf{Q}}_I - \mathbf{e}^T \mathbf{Pb}\epsilon_I - \mathbf{e}^T \mathbf{Pb}u_s$$

$$= -\frac{1}{2}\mathbf{e}^T \mathbf{Je} + \left(\mathbf{e}^T \mathbf{PbH} + \frac{1}{\eta_I}\dot{\tilde{\mathbf{Q}}}_I^T\right)\tilde{\mathbf{Q}}_I - \mathbf{e}^T \mathbf{Pb}\epsilon_I - \mathbf{e}^T \mathbf{Pb}u_s, \tag{21.33}$$

where $\mathbf{J} = -(\Lambda^T \mathbf{P} + \mathbf{P}\Lambda)$. $\mathbf{J}$ is a symmetric definite matrix and is selected by the user.

Based on Eq. (21.30), Eq. (21.33) becomes

$$\dot{V} = -\frac{1}{2}\mathbf{e}^T \mathbf{Je} - \mathbf{e}^T \mathbf{Pb}\epsilon_I - \mathbf{e}^T \mathbf{Pb}\bar{\varepsilon}_I \mathrm{sgn}(\mathbf{e}^T \mathbf{Pb}). \tag{21.34}$$

Equation (21.34) further satisfies the following condition:

$$\dot{V} \le -\frac{1}{2}\mathbf{e}^T \mathbf{Je} + |\mathbf{e}^T \mathbf{Pb}||\epsilon_I| - \mathbf{e}^T \mathbf{Pb}\bar{\varepsilon}_I \mathrm{sgn}(\mathbf{e}^T \mathbf{Pb}). \tag{21.35}$$

Since $|\mathbf{e}^T \mathbf{Pb}| = (\mathbf{e}^T \mathbf{Pb})\mathrm{sgn}(\mathbf{e}^T \mathbf{Pb})$, Eq. (21.35) becomes

$$\dot{V} \le -\frac{1}{2}\mathbf{e}^T \mathbf{Je} + |\mathbf{e}^T \mathbf{Pb}|(|\epsilon_I| - \bar{\varepsilon}_I). \tag{21.36}$$

Notice that

$$|\mathbf{e}^T \mathbf{Pb}|(|\epsilon_I| - \bar{\varepsilon}_I) \le 0. \tag{21.37}$$

So,

$$\dot{V} \leq -\frac{1}{2}\mathbf{e}^T\mathbf{J}\mathbf{e} \leq 0. \tag{21.38}$$

The above equation illustrates that $\dot{V}$ is negative semidefinite and thus the overall control scheme is guaranteed to be stable. Using Barbalat's lemma [32, 33], it can be seen that as $t \to \infty$, $\mathbf{e} \to 0$. Thus, the tracking error of the system will converge to zero. □

21.2.5. *Performance Evaluation*

In this section, the proposed indirect adaptive fuzzy control scheme is evaluated by controlling the wing-rock motion under $\alpha = 15°$. At the same time, the direct adaptive fuzzy control scheme using ESAFIS is considered for comparison. According to the guidelines described in [7, 27], the parameters existing in ESAFIS for the indirect and direct adaptive control schemes are commonly chosen as $\gamma = 0.99$, $\epsilon_{max} = 1.0$, $\epsilon_{min} = 0.1$, $\kappa = 5.0$, $e_g = 0.01$, $e_p = 0.001$, and $M = 40$. To stabilize the system, the coefficients in Eq. (21.9) are chosen as $k_1 = 2$ and $k_2 = 1$. Two initial simulation conditions, viz., small initial condition ($\phi(0) = 11.46$ degree, the $\dot{\phi}(0) = 2.865$ degree/s) and the large initial condition ($\phi(0) = 103.14$ degree, $\dot{\phi}(0) = 57.3$ degree/s), are used to investigate the effectiveness of the proposed control scheme. The reference trajectory vector is chosen as $(\phi_d, \dot{\phi}_d)^T = (0, 0)^T$. In addition, control schemes based on the RBF network [34] and the Takagi–Sugeno (TS) fuzzy system [35] are applied here to control the wing rock system for comparison.

The simulation results of the roll angle ϕ and the roll rate $\dot{\phi}$ from the indirect control schemes are illustrated in Figures 21.4 and 21.5, where the small and large

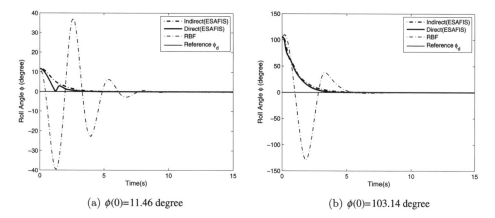

(a) $\phi(0)=11.46$ degree

(b) $\phi(0)=103.14$ degree

Figure 21.4: Roll angle for $\alpha = 15°$ under different initial states.

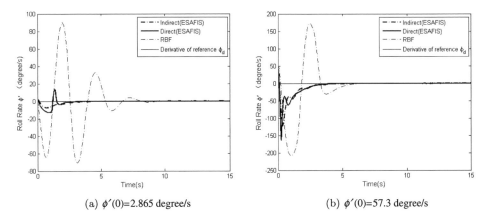

(a) $\phi'(0)=2.865$ degree/s   (b) $\phi'(0)=57.3$ degree/s

Figure 21.5: Roll rate for $\alpha = 15°$ under different initial states.

initial conditions are included. For comparison, the simulation results from the RBF network and the reference zero signals are also presented in the two figures. The results show that in the proposed adaptive fuzzy control scheme, the difference between the system output and the reference output is large at the beginning, but the system still remains stable and the system output asymptotically converges to the desired trajectory. The convergence time lasts about 5 sec whatever the initial condition is. This is much faster than that in the uncontrolled condition and also largely decreases the maneuverability burden caused by the undesired rolling motion. Compared with the RBF network, the proposed fuzzy control scheme achieves a faster error convergence speed and better transient results under the small and large initial conditions.

Besides, the simulation results from a similar work using the TS fuzzy system with a fixed system structure [35] are listed here for evaluating the performance of the proposed control scheme using ESAFIS. Figure 21.6 depicts the results of the roll angle and roll rate achieved in the indirect control scheme under the small initial condition. From the two figures, one can see that the TS fuzzy system obtains a faster converge speed than ESAFIS. However, ESAFIS has smaller roll rate errors during the initial learning process than the TS fuzzy system. Table 21.2 gives an overview of the comparison results from three algorithms based on the root mean square error (RMSE) between the reference and the actual values, as done in [30, 36, 37]. The E_ϕ and $E_{\dot{\phi}}$ shown in the table represent the RMSEs of roll angle and roll rate while E_{ave} is the average of both. It can be seen that the RMSEs of the ESAFIS are lower than those of RBF and the TS fuzzy system.

Using the ESAFIS learning algorithm, the fuzzy rules are generated automatically and their time evolution for small and large initial conditions over the whole learning process is depicted in Figures 21.7(a) and (b). One can clearly note that in

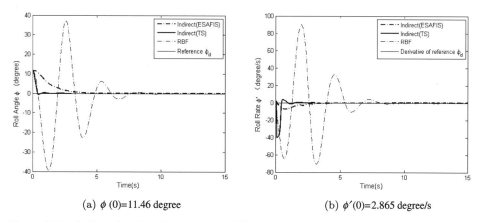

(a) $\phi(0)$=11.46 degree

(b) $\phi'(0)$=2.865 degree/s

Figure 21.6: Roll angle and roll rate for $\alpha = 15°$ under small initial states in the indirect control scheme.

Table 21.2: Comparison results with different algorithms for $\alpha = 15°$.

Algorithms	Small initial condition			Large initial condition		
	E_ϕ	$E_{\dot\phi}$	E_{ave}	E_ϕ	$E_{\dot\phi}$	E_{ave}
ESAFIS	2.85	1.90	2.38	21.27	20.48	20.88
TS	6.08	20.29	13.19	74.64	312.19	193.42
RBF	15.34	34.58	24.96	52.06	80.48	66.27

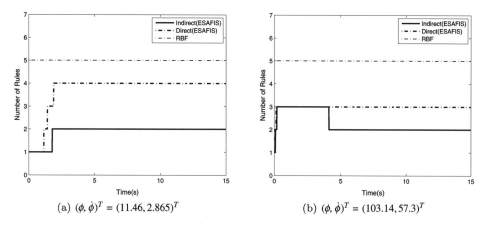

(a) $(\phi, \dot\phi)^T = (11.46, 2.865)^T$

(b) $(\phi, \dot\phi)^T = (103.14, 57.3)^T$

Figure 21.7: Number of rules/neurons for $\alpha = 15°$ under different initial states.

Table 21.3: Influence of number of rules on tracking performance for $\alpha = 15°$.

Parameter e_g	No. of Rules	E_ϕ	$E_{\dot\phi}$	E_{ave}
0.0001	3	2.85	1.90	2.38
0.001	3	2.85	1.90	2.38
0.01	2	2.85	1.90	2.38

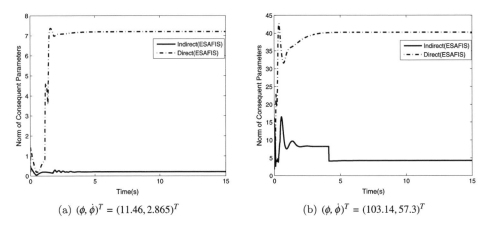

(a) $(\phi, \dot\phi)^T = (11.46, 2.865)^T$ (b) $(\phi, \dot\phi)^T = (103.14, 57.3)^T$

Figure 21.8: Norm of consequent parameters for $\alpha = 15°$ under different initial states.

this simulation study, the number of fuzzy rules required by ESAFIS is less than that of neurons required by RBF network and that of rules required by the TS fuzzy system. Thus, compared with the RBF network and the TS fuzzy system, ESAFIS produces a more compact system structure and also avoids the determination of fuzzy rules by trial-and-error before learning. To illustrate the influence of the number of rules on the tracking performance, some simulations are done under different numbers of rules obtained by varying the parameters. Table 21.3 gives the tracking RMSEs under different numbers of rules as the parameter e_g varies. From the table, it can be found that the number of rules has little variation although the parameter e_g changes in the range [0.01, 0.0001] and also the tracking performance almost remains the same with the number of rules changing. This implies that the proposed control schemes are robust to the number of rules and the design parameters. Figures 21.8(a) and (b) illustrate that the parameters $\mathbf{Q}_I$ and $\mathbf{Q}_D$ for small and large initial conditions are bounded throughout the control process. This guarantees the bounding of the control signals in the two initial conditions, which is depicted in Figure 21.9. The figure further shows that the control efforts for small and large initial conditions are smooth without high-frequency chattering phenomenon during the whole control process.

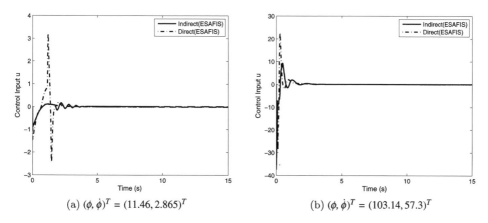

(a) $(\phi, \dot{\phi})^T = (11.46, 2.865)^T$ (b) $(\phi, \dot{\phi})^T = (103.14, 57.3)^T$

Figure 21.9: Control input u for $\alpha = 15°$ under different initial states.

21.3. Meta-cognitive Fuzzy-Neural Control of the Thrust Active Magnetic Bearing System

The thrust active magnetic bearing (TAMB) systems are capable of suspending and moving the rotor to the predefined positions functionally via the controlled electromagnetic force at high rotational speed without mechanical fiction. Thus, they are widely applied in many industrial applications, e.g., reaction wheels for artificial satellites, gas turbine engines, turbomolecular pumps, blood pumps, etc., Moreover, the TAMB system offers many practical and promising advantages, such as low noise, long service life, non-lubrication, low energy consumption, and light mechanical wear compared with the conventional ball bearing or sliding bearing.

In most real-world applications of the TAMB system, the controlled rotor should be positioned and moved precisely and functionally to deal with the different operation demands and environments. Since TAMBs are open-loop unstable systems, the design of an active control system constitutes an essential task for the position and tracking control of the rotor. In practice, the TAMB system suffers from inherent nonlinearities in electromechanical and motion dynamics [39], which have to be considered during the controller design process.

An indirect adaptive meta-cognitive fuzzy-neural control approach is proposed to control the rotor position of a nonlinear TAMB system with modeling uncertainties and external disturbances. In the current literature [14, 15, 17, 18, 40–42] the parameters existing in all the rules need to be adjusted and thus the size of the adjustable parameters is dependent on the number of input states and the fuzzy rules. In general, the number of fuzzy rules needs to be large enough to improve the approximation accuracy. In this case, a large online computation burden will be caused, resulting in a slow response time for real-time control applications. In the proposed meta-cognitive fuzzy-neural control approach, this problem can be alleviated by only adjusting the parameters of the rule nearest to the current input. The size of the adjustable parameters is independent of the size of the fuzzy rules and much lower than those of the existing work. Moreover, to guarantee the stability of the controlled system, projection-type adaptation laws for the parameters of the nearest rule are determined from the Lyapunov function. The zero convergence of tracking errors can be achieved according to the stability proof.

21.3.1. *Problem Formulation*

The considered TAMB system [43,44] is given by

$$\ddot{z}(t) = a(\mathbf{z}; t)\dot{z} + b(\mathbf{z}; t)z + g(\mathbf{z}; t)u(t) + d(\mathbf{z}; t), \tag{21.39}$$

where $a(\mathbf{z}; t) = -(c(t)/m)$, $b(\mathbf{z}; t) = Q_z(t)/m$, $g(\mathbf{z}; t) = Q_i(t)/m$, $d(\mathbf{z}; t) = f_{dz}(t)/m$, and $\mathbf{z} = [z\ \dot{z}]$, $f_{dz}(t)$ denotes system disturbances and is set as a combination of a small sinusoidal term $0.01\sin(2t) + 0.01$ and a random value in the range $[-0.001, 0.001]$. $u(t)$ represents the control current. m is the mass of the rotor, and z and $\dot{z}$ represent the axial position and velocity of the rotor, respectively. $c(t)$ is the friction coefficient, and $Q_z(t)$ and $Q_i(t)$ are the displacement and current stiffness parameters, respectively. These parameters are time-varying during real applications. With regard to simulation studies, they are assumed to suffer from the following perturbations:

$$c(t) = c_0 * (1 + 0.3\sin(2t)),$$

$$Q_z(t) = Q_{z0} * (1 + 0.2\sin(t)),$$

$$Q_i(t) = Q_{i0} * (1 + 0.3\cos(t)).$$

The TAMB is a typical second-order dynamic system that can be always represented as a general class of uncertain systems with order n

$$x^{(n)} = f(\mathbf{x}) + g(\mathbf{x})u + d(\mathbf{x}), \tag{21.40}$$

where u represents the control input. $\mathbf{x}(= [x, \dot{x}, \ldots, x^{(n-1)}]^T \in \Re^n)$ denotes the system state and is assumed to be measurable. $f(\mathbf{x})$ and $g(\mathbf{x})$ are assumed to be unknown and bounded real continuous functions. $d(\mathbf{x})$ represents the unknown but bounded modeling errors and external disturbances.

Let $x_1 = x$, $x_2 = \dot{x} = \dot{x}_1$, $x_3 = \ddot{x} = \dot{x}_2$, $\cdots$, and $x_n = x^{(n-1)} = \dot{x}_{(n-1)}$, then Eq. (21.40) becomes

$$\begin{cases} \dot{x}_i = x_{i+1}, \quad i = 1, 2, \ldots, n-1 \\ \dot{x}_n = f(\mathbf{x}) + g(\mathbf{x})u + d(\mathbf{x}) \end{cases} \tag{21.41}$$

where $\mathbf{x} = [x_1, x_2, \ldots, x_n]^T \in \Re^n$. Define the tracking error $\mathbf{e} = \mathbf{x} - \mathbf{x}_d$, the reference command $\mathbf{x}_d = [x_{1d}, x_{2d}, \ldots, x_{nd}]^T$, the tracking error vector $\mathbf{e} = [e_1, e_2, \ldots, e_n]^T$. The control objective of the proposed controller u is to force the state $\mathbf{x}$ to follow the specified desired trajectory $\mathbf{x}_d$ as closely as possible.

Assumption 1: The reference signals and their continuous first derivatives $\mathbf{x}_d, \dot{\mathbf{x}}_d$ are bounded and available.

Assumption 2: $g(\mathbf{x})$ is invertible for all $\mathbf{x} \in \Re^n$ and satisfies $g(\mathbf{x}) > \gamma_0$, with $\gamma_0 > 0$, $\gamma_0 \in \Re$.

   As pointed in [45], Assumption 2 is a strong restriction for many physical systems and is hard to hold in a whole space. The assumption can be relaxed to hold in a compact subset, as in [45]. The proposed control approach is applicable if Assumption 2 is satisfied only in a compact subset.

   The adaptive backstepping technique is introduced here for developing the nonlinear controller. Based on the backstepping technology, the control input u is constructed step-by-step based on a Lyapunov function for guaranteeing global stability. First, x_{2d} to x_{nd} are presented as fictitious control signals. Each $x_{(i+1)d}$ $(i = 1, 2, \ldots, n - 1)$ is designed with the purpose to reducing error $e_i = x_i - x_{id}$ in the previous design stage. The derivative of the error e_i in the ith step is equal to

$$\dot{e}_i = \dot{x}_i - \dot{x}_{id} = x_{i+1} - \dot{x}_{id} = x_{(i+1)d} + e_{i+1} - \dot{x}_{id}. \tag{21.42}$$

The virtual control $x_{(i+1)d}$ is defined as

$$x_{(i+1)d} = -k_i e_i + \dot{x}_{id} - e_{i-1}, \tag{21.43}$$

where k_i is a positive constant.

   After the fictitious controller x_{nd} is designed, the ideal controller u^* is designed to force the error $e_n = x_n - x_{nd}$ to be as small as possible. The ideal controller u^* is chosen as

$$u^* = g^{-1}(\mathbf{x})(-f(\mathbf{x}) - d(\mathbf{x}) - k_n e_n + \dot{x}_{nd} - e_{n-1}). \tag{21.44}$$

   A Lyapunov function $V_1 = \Sigma_{i=1}^{n} \frac{1}{2} e_i^2$ is defined and then according to Eqs. (21.42)–(21.44), the derivative of V_1 is

$$\dot{V}_1 = -\sum_{i=1}^{n} k_i e_i^2 \leq 0. \tag{21.45}$$

By properly choosing $k_i > 0$ $(i = 1, 2, \ldots, n)$, the stability of the system can be ensured and the tracking error will converge to zero. However, the exact mathematical models of $f(\mathbf{x})$, $g(\mathbf{x})$, and $d(\mathbf{x})$ are hard to achieve, which makes the ideal controller u^* in (21.44) unavailable. To solve the problem, an indirect meta-cognitive fuzzy-neural control u_f is built using the meta-cognitive fuzzy-neural model to approximate $f(\mathbf{x}) + d(\mathbf{x})(= f_d(\mathbf{x}))$ and $g(\mathbf{x})$ separately and is given as

$$u_f = \hat{g}^{-1}(\mathbf{x})[-\hat{f}_d(\mathbf{x}) - k_n e_n + \dot{x}_{nd} - e_{n-1}], \tag{21.46}$$

where $\hat{f}_d(\mathbf{x})$ and $\hat{g}(\mathbf{x})$ are the approximation models of the unknown nonlinear functions $f_d(\mathbf{x})$ and $g(\mathbf{x})$.

There exists the approximation errors in Eq. (21.46) when the meta-cognitive fuzzy-neural model is utilized to approximate $f_d(\mathbf{x})$ and $g(\mathbf{x})$. A sliding mode compensator u_s is applied here to offset the approximation errors. The whole actual control input is designed as

$$u = u_f + u_s. \tag{21.47}$$

According to the control law u in Eq. (21.47), the derivative of the error e_n without affecting the error $e_i (i = 1, 2, \ldots, n - 1)$ becomes

$$\dot{e}_n = f_d(\mathbf{x}) - \hat{f}_d(\mathbf{x}) + (g(\mathbf{x}) - \hat{g}(\mathbf{x}))u_f + g(\mathbf{x})u_s - k_n e_n - e_{n-1}. \tag{21.48}$$

In the following section, the proposed indirect meta-cognitive fuzzy-neural control approach is described in detail. Before this, the meta-cognitive fuzzy-neural model used to approximate the functions $f_d(\mathbf{x})$ and $g(\mathbf{x})$ is presented.

21.3.2. Meta-cognitive Fuzzy-Neural Model

21.3.2.1. Model structure

To design the controller u_f, the meta-cognitive fuzzy-neural model applies the following fuzzy rule to approximate $f_d(\mathbf{x})$ and $g(\mathbf{x})$:

Rule k : If x_1 is A_{1k} and $\cdots$ and x_n is A_{nk}, then $f_d(\mathbf{x})$ is a_{fk} and $g(\mathbf{x})$ is a_{gk}, where $A_{ik} (i = 1, \ldots, n)$ represents the fuzzy sets related to the ith input variable x_i in rule k, n is the input size, that is, $\mathbf{x}(\mathbf{x} = [x_1, \ldots, x_n]^T)$. The terms of $f_d(\mathbf{x})$ and $g(\mathbf{x})$ constitute the outputs of the fuzzy-neural model. The consequences a_{fk} and a_{gk} are constants.

A five-layer structure as depicted in Figure 21.10 is implemented to realize the fuzzy-neural model. The input layer represents the input states. The membership layer is used to calculate the membership value of each input variable from Gaussian functions. The rule layer illustrates the firing strength of the rules computed from the sum-product composition. The normalization layer is used to calculate the normalization values of the rules. The output layer represents the system outputs,

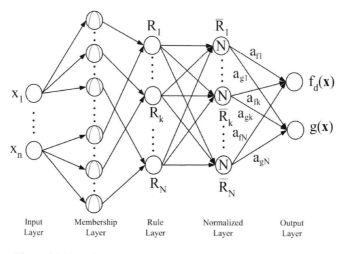

Figure 21.10: The structure of meta-cognitive fuzzy-neural model.

which is given with N rules as

$$f_d(\mathbf{x}) = \frac{\sum_{k=1}^{N} a_{fk} R_k(\mathbf{x})}{\sum_{k=1}^{N} R_k(\mathbf{x})} = \mathbf{a}_f \bar{\mathbf{R}}(\mathbf{x}), \qquad (21.49)$$

$$g(\mathbf{x}) = \frac{\sum_{k=1}^{N} a_{gk} R_k(\mathbf{x})}{\sum_{k=1}^{N} R_k(\mathbf{x})} = \mathbf{a}_g \bar{\mathbf{R}}(\mathbf{x}), \qquad (21.50)$$

where $\mathbf{a}_f = [a_{f1}, a_{f2}, \ldots, a_{fN}] \in \Re^{1 \times N}$, $\mathbf{a}_g = [a_{g1}, a_{g2}, \ldots, a_{gN}] \in \Re^{1 \times N}$, and $\bar{\mathbf{R}}(\mathbf{x}) = [R_1(\mathbf{x})/\Sigma_{k=1}^{N} R_k(\mathbf{x}), \ldots, R_N(\mathbf{x})/\Sigma_{k=1}^{N} R_k(\mathbf{x})]^T \in \Re^{N \times 1}$ are the normalization values of the rules. R_k is the firing strength of the kth rule and is given as

$$R_k(\mathbf{x}) = \prod_{i=1}^{n} A_{ik}(x_i) = \exp\left(-\sum_{i=1}^{n} \frac{(x_i - \mu_{ik})^2}{\sigma_k^2}\right)$$

$$= \exp\left(-\frac{\|\mathbf{x} - \mu_k\|^2}{\sigma_k^2}\right), \qquad (21.51)$$

where μ_k and σ_k are the center and width of the kth Gaussian membership function.

21.3.2.2. *Meta-cognitive learning mechanism*

The McFIS [8] carries out its sequential learning process by invoking the data deleting strategy, data learning strategy, and data reserving strategy. According to [8] in the data reserving strategy, data with lower knowledge will be kept for later learning but this is hard to realize in real-time controller design, where all the data are sampled sequentially and only one new observation is required anytime.

In our study, the knowledge of the reserved data is regarded as being similar to the existing data. Then, the reserved data are put in the deletion strategy for removing. Different from [8], two self-regulatory strategies, data learning and data deletion, are considered in our proposed meta-cognitive fuzzy-neural model and help perform the real-time control task efficiently. How the two strategies are implemented in the fuzzy-neural model is described below.

21.3.2.3. *Data learning strategy*

The data learning process of the meta-cognitive fuzzy-neural model involves online rule evolution and parameter update of the rule nearest to the current input data. It is noteworthy that evolution strategies of rules in the meta-cognitive fuzzy-neural model are the same as those of McFIS. But the way of parameter learning is different from [8] aiming to suit the real-time stable controller design. As in [8] the rules are determined incrementally according to the following conditions, $\|\mathbf{e}\| > E_a$ and $\psi < E_s$. ψ is the spherical potential and indicates the novelty of an input data $\mathbf{x}$, and is given as

$$\psi = \left| -\frac{2}{N} \sum_{k=1}^{N} R(\mathbf{x}, \mu_k) \right|. \tag{21.52}$$

E_s and E_a are the novelty and adding thresholds. E_a is self-regulated as

$$E_a = \delta E_a + (1 - \delta)\|\mathbf{e}\|, \tag{21.53}$$

where $\mathbf{e}$ depicts the tracking error. δ is the slope factor. The self-regulatory adding threshold E_a aims to capture the global knowledge initially and then fine-tunes the system at a later stage.

After adding a new fuzzy rule (the $(N+1)$th rule), its parameters are initialized as

$$\begin{aligned}
\mu_{N+1} &= \mathbf{x} \\
\sigma_{N+1} &= \kappa * \min_{\forall j} \|\mathbf{x} - \mu_k\|, \quad k = 1, \dots, N \\
a_{f,N+1} &= a_{g,N+1} = 0
\end{aligned} \tag{21.54}$$

where κ is the overlap parameter between the rule antecedents.

When $\|\mathbf{e}\| \geq E_l$, the rule parameters are modified. Similarly, the threshold, E_l, is self-regulated with tracking error as

$$E_l = \delta E_l + (1 - \delta)\|\mathbf{e}\|. \tag{21.55}$$

In the meta-cognitive fuzzy-neural model, the parameters of the nearest rule are modified according to the stable rules determined using the Lyapunov function in order to ensure the stability of the controlled system. This is described next.

During learning, the contribution of a rule to the output may become low. In this case, the insignificant rule should be removed from the rule base to avoid the overfitting. The kth rule contribution is given by

$$\beta_k = \bar{R}_k \max_i |e_i a_{fk} + e_i a_{gk}|, \quad i = 1, \ldots, n. \tag{21.56}$$

The kth rule is pruned if its contribution falls below a threshold value E_p for N_w consecutive inputs.

21.3.2.4. *Data deletion strategy*

If the data are not satisfied with the data learning strategy, they lack new knowledge to learn and are deleted without further learning. This avoids the over-learning of similar data and decreases the computational burden.

21.3.3. *Meta-cognitive Fuzzy-Neural Control Approach*

21.3.3.1. *System errors*

In the designed meta-cognitive fuzzy-neural controller u_f, the meta-cognitive fuzzy-neural model is used to reconstruct the functions $f_d(\mathbf{x})$ and $g(\mathbf{x})$. Based on the universal approximation property of a fuzzy-neural system, an optimal model exists to learn the terms $f_d(\mathbf{x})$ and $g(\mathbf{x})$ such that,

$$\begin{aligned} f_d(\mathbf{x}) &= \mathbf{a}_f^* \bar{\mathbf{R}}(\mathbf{x}; \mu^*, \sigma^*) + \varepsilon_f(\mathbf{x}), \\ g(\mathbf{x}) &= \mathbf{a}_g^* \bar{\mathbf{R}}(\mathbf{x}; \mu^*, \sigma^*) + \varepsilon_g(\mathbf{x}), \end{aligned} \tag{21.57}$$

where $\varepsilon_f(\mathbf{x})$ and $\varepsilon_g(\mathbf{x})$ represent approximation errors; $\mathbf{a}_f^*$, $\mathbf{a}_g^*$, μ^*, and σ^* are the optimal parameter vectors of $\mathbf{a}_f$, $\mathbf{a}_g$, μ, and σ, respectively.

To construct $f_d(\mathbf{x})$ and $g(\mathbf{x})$, the optimal values of $\mathbf{a}_f^*$, $\mathbf{a}_g^*$, μ^*, and σ^* need to be known but are unavailable. The online estimates $\hat{\mathbf{a}}_f$, $\hat{\mathbf{a}}_g$, $\hat{\mu}$, and $\hat{\sigma}$ are used to replace the optimal $\mathbf{a}_f^*$, $\mathbf{a}_g^*$, μ^*, and σ^*. Thus, the estimated functions $\hat{f}_d(\mathbf{x})$ and $\hat{g}(\mathbf{x})$ are used to approximate the unknown functions $f_d(\mathbf{x})$ and $g(\mathbf{x})$, which are given as

$$\begin{aligned} \hat{f}_d(\mathbf{x}) &= \hat{\mathbf{a}}_f \bar{\mathbf{R}}(\mathbf{x}; \hat{\mu}, \hat{\sigma}), \\ \hat{g}(\mathbf{x}) &= \hat{\mathbf{a}}_g \bar{\mathbf{R}}(\mathbf{x}; \hat{\mu}, \hat{\sigma}). \end{aligned} \tag{21.58}$$

Using the "winner rule" strategy [8], the optimal parameter vectors comprise two parts. One part represents optimal parameters of the active nearest rule, which are denoted as $a_{f,nr}^*$, $a_{g,nr}^*$, μ_{nr}^*, and σ_{nr}^*. The other part consists of the optimal parameters of fixed rules, which are denoted as a_{fs}^*, a_{gs}^*, μ_s^*, and σ_s^* ($1 \leq s \leq N$,

$s \neq nr$), thereby representing rules that have not been activated. Hence,

$$
\begin{aligned}
\mathbf{a}_f^* &= \begin{bmatrix} a_{f,nr}^* & \mathbf{a}_{fs}^* \end{bmatrix} \\
\mathbf{a}_g^* &= \begin{bmatrix} a_{g,nr}^* & \mathbf{a}_{gs}^* \end{bmatrix} \\
\bar{\mathbf{R}}(\mathbf{x}; \mu^*, \sigma^*) &= \begin{bmatrix} \bar{R}(\mathbf{x}; \mu_{nr}^*, \sigma_{nr}^*) \\ \bar{\mathbf{R}}(\mathbf{x}; \mu_s^*, \sigma_s^*) \end{bmatrix},
\end{aligned} \tag{21.59}
$$

where $\bar{R}(\mathbf{x}; \mu_{nr}^*, \sigma_{nr}^*)$ and $\bar{\mathbf{R}}(\mathbf{x}; \mu_s^*, \sigma_s^*)$ represent the normalized firing strengths of the active nearest rule and fixed rules, respectively. Similarly, the estimates $\hat{\mathbf{a}}_f$, $\hat{\mathbf{a}}_g$, $\hat{\mu}$, and $\hat{\sigma}$ are divided into $\hat{\mathbf{a}}_{f,nr}$, $\hat{\mathbf{a}}_{g,nr}$, $\hat{\mu}_{nr}$, $\hat{\sigma}_{nr}$, $\hat{\mathbf{a}}_{fs}$, $\hat{\mathbf{a}}_{gs}$, $\hat{\mu}_s$, and $\hat{\sigma}_s$.

The approximation errors between the actual functions and the estimated functions are given as

$$
\begin{aligned}
\epsilon_f(\mathbf{x}) = f_d(\mathbf{x}) - \hat{f}_d(\mathbf{x}) &= a_{f,nr}^* \bar{R}_{nr}(\mathbf{x}; \mu_{nr}^*, \sigma_{nr}^*) \\
&\quad - \hat{a}_{f,nr} \bar{R}_{nr}(\mathbf{x}; \hat{\mu}_{nr}, \hat{\sigma}_{nr}) + \varepsilon_f(\mathbf{x})
\end{aligned} \tag{21.60}
$$

$$
\begin{aligned}
\epsilon_g(\mathbf{x}) = g(\mathbf{x}) - \hat{g}(\mathbf{x}) &= a_{g,nr}^* \bar{R}_{nr}(\mathbf{x}; \mu_{nr}^*, \sigma_{nr}^*) \\
&\quad - \hat{a}_{g,nr} \bar{R}_{nr}(\mathbf{x}; \hat{\mu}_{nr}, \hat{\sigma}_{nr}) + \varepsilon_g(\mathbf{x})
\end{aligned} \tag{21.61}
$$

From Eq. (21.48), the approximation errors $(\epsilon_f(\mathbf{x}), \epsilon_g(\mathbf{x}))$ between the actual functions (f_d, g) and the estimated functions $(\hat{f}_d, \hat{g})$ need to be established to calculate the derivative of the error e_n. How they are accomplished are illustrated by the following theorem.

Theorem 1: The parameter estimation errors of the nearest rule are defined as

$$
\begin{aligned}
&\tilde{a}_{f,nr} = a_{f,nr}^* - \hat{a}_{f,nr}, \quad \tilde{a}_{g,nr} = a_{g,nr}^* - \hat{a}_{g,nr}, \quad \tilde{\mu}_{nr} = \mu_{nr}^* - \hat{\mu}_{nr}, \\
&\tilde{\sigma}_{nr} = \sigma_{nr}^* - \hat{\sigma}_{nr}.
\end{aligned} \tag{21.62}
$$

The function approximation errors $\epsilon_f(\mathbf{x})$ and $\epsilon_g(\mathbf{x})$ can be expressed as

$$
\begin{aligned}
\epsilon_f(\mathbf{x}) = \tilde{a}_{f,nr}\{\bar{R}_{nr}(\mathbf{x}; \hat{\mu}_{nr}, \hat{\sigma}_{nr}) &- \bar{R}'_{nr,\mu}(\mathbf{x}; \hat{\mu}_{nr}, \hat{\sigma}_{nr})\hat{\mu}_{nr} - \bar{R}'_{nr,\sigma}(\mathbf{x}; \hat{\mu}_{nr}, \hat{\sigma}_{nr})\hat{\sigma}_{nr}\} \\
&+ \hat{a}_{f,nr}\{\bar{R}'_{nr,\mu}(\mathbf{x}; \hat{\mu}_{nr}, \hat{\sigma}_{nr})\tilde{\mu}_{nr} + \bar{R}'_{nr,\sigma}(\mathbf{x}; \hat{\mu}_{nr}, \hat{\sigma}_{nr})\tilde{\sigma}_{nr}\} + d_f
\end{aligned} \tag{21.63}
$$

$$
\begin{aligned}
\epsilon_g(\mathbf{x}) = \tilde{a}_{g,nr}\{\bar{R}_{nr}(\mathbf{x}; \hat{\mu}_{nr}, \hat{\sigma}_{nr}) &- \bar{R}'_{nr,\mu}(\mathbf{x}; \hat{\mu}_{nr}, \hat{\sigma}_{nr})\hat{\mu}_{nr} - \bar{R}'_{nr,\sigma}(\mathbf{x}; \hat{\mu}_{nr}, \hat{\sigma}_{nr})\hat{\sigma}_{nr}\} \\
&+ \hat{a}_{g,nr}\{\bar{R}'_{nr,\mu}(\mathbf{x}; \hat{\mu}_{nr}, \hat{\sigma}_{nr})\tilde{\mu}_{nr} + \bar{R}'_{nr,\sigma}(\mathbf{x}; \hat{\mu}_{nr}, \hat{\sigma}_{nr})\tilde{\sigma}_{nr}\} + d_g
\end{aligned} \tag{21.64}
$$

where

$$
\bar{R}'_{nr,\mu}(\mathbf{x}; \hat{\mu}_{nr}, \hat{\sigma}_{nr}) = \frac{R_{nr} \sum_{s=1,s\neq nr}^{N} R_s}{\left(R_{nr} + \sum_{s=1,s\neq nr}^{N} R_s\right)^2} \frac{2(\mathbf{x} - \mu_{nr})^T}{\sigma_{nr}^2} \in R^{1 \times n}
$$

and

$$\bar{R}'_{nr,\sigma}(\mathbf{x}; \hat{\mu}_{nr}, \hat{\sigma}_{nr}) = \frac{R_{nr} \sum_{s=1, s\neq nr}^{N} R_s}{\left(R_{nr} + \sum_{s=1, s\neq nr}^{N} R_s\right)^2} \frac{2\|\mathbf{x} - \mu_{nr}\|^2}{\sigma_{nr}^3} \in R$$

are the derivatives of $\bar{R}_{nr}(\mathbf{x}; \mu_{nr}^*, \sigma_{nr}^*)$ with respect to μ_{nr}^* and σ_{nr}^* at $(\hat{\mu}_{nr}, \hat{\sigma}_{nr})$, respectively. d_f and d_g are the residual terms.

Proof. The derivation process of the approximation errors $\epsilon_f(\mathbf{x})$ and $\epsilon_g(\mathbf{x})$ in Eqs. (21.63)–(21.64) are similar and thus for simplicity, only how the approximation error $\epsilon_f(\mathbf{x})$ is achieved is described below. □

The approximation error $\epsilon_f(\mathbf{x})$ can be written as

$$\begin{aligned}
\epsilon_f(\mathbf{x}) &= a_{f,nr}^* \bar{R}_{nr}(\mathbf{x}; \mu_{nr}^*, \sigma_{nr}^*) - a_{f,nr}^* \bar{R}_{nr}(\mathbf{x}; \hat{\mu}_{nr}, \hat{\sigma}_{nr}) + a_{f,nr}^* \bar{R}_{nr}(\mathbf{x}; \hat{\mu}_{nr}, \hat{\sigma}_{nr}) \\
&\quad - \hat{a}_{f,nr} \bar{R}_{nr}(\mathbf{x}; \hat{\mu}_{nr}, \hat{\sigma}_{nr}) + \varepsilon_f(\mathbf{x}) \\
&= a_{f,nr}^* \tilde{\bar{R}}_{nr} + \tilde{a}_{nr} \hat{\bar{R}}_{nr} + \varepsilon_f(\mathbf{x}) \\
&= a_{f,nr}^* \tilde{\bar{R}}_{nr} - \hat{a}_{f,nr} \tilde{\bar{R}}_{nr} + \hat{a}_{f,nr} \tilde{\bar{R}}_{nr} + \tilde{a}_{f,nr} \hat{\bar{R}}_{nr} + \varepsilon_f(\mathbf{x}) \\
&= \tilde{a}_{f,nr} \tilde{\bar{R}}_{nr} + \hat{a}_{f,nr} \tilde{\bar{R}}_{nr} + \tilde{a}_{f,nr} \hat{\bar{R}}_{nr} + \varepsilon_f(\mathbf{x}),
\end{aligned} \tag{21.65}$$

where $\tilde{\bar{R}}_{nr} = \bar{R}_{nr}(\mathbf{x}; \mu_{nr}^*, \sigma_{nr}^*) - \bar{R}_{nr}(\mathbf{x}; \hat{\mu}_{nr}, \hat{\sigma}_{nr})$ and $\hat{\bar{R}}_{nr} = \bar{R}_{nr}(\mathbf{x}; \hat{\mu}_{nr}, \hat{\sigma}_{nr})$. In order to deal with $\tilde{\bar{R}}_{nr}$, Taylor's series expansion of $\bar{R}_{nr}(\mathbf{x}; \mu_{nr}^*, \sigma_{nr}^*)$ is taken about $\mu_{nr}^* = \hat{\mu}_{nr}$ and $\sigma_{nr}^* = \hat{\sigma}_{nr}$ such that

$$\begin{aligned}
\bar{R}_{nr}(\mathbf{x}; \mu_{nr}^*, \sigma_{nr}^*) &= \bar{R}_{nr}(\mathbf{x}; \hat{\mu}_{nr}, \hat{\sigma}_{nr}) + \bar{R}'_{nr,\mu}(\mathbf{x}; \hat{\mu}_{nr}, \hat{\sigma}_{nr})(\mu_{nr}^* - \hat{\mu}_{nr}) \\
&\quad + \bar{R}'_{nr,\sigma}(\mathbf{x}; \hat{\mu}_{nr}, \hat{\sigma}_{nr})(\sigma_{nr}^* - \hat{\sigma}_{nr}) + o(\mathbf{x}; \tilde{\mu}_{nr}, \tilde{\sigma}_{nr}),
\end{aligned} \tag{21.66}$$

where $o(\mathbf{x}; \tilde{\mu}_{nr}, \tilde{\sigma}_{nr})$ denotes the sum of high-order arguments in a Taylor's series expansion, and $\bar{R}'_{nr,\mu}(\mathbf{x}; \hat{\mu}_{nr}, \hat{\sigma}_{nr}) \in R^{1\times n}$ and $\bar{R}'_{nr,\sigma}(\mathbf{x}; \hat{\mu}_{nr}, \hat{\sigma}_{nr}) \in R$ are derivatives of $\bar{R}_{nr}(\mathbf{x}; \mu_{nr}^*, \sigma_{nr}^*)$ with respect to μ_{nr}^* and σ_{nr}^* at $(\hat{\mu}_{nr}, \hat{\sigma}_{nr})$. They are expressed as

$$\begin{aligned}
\bar{R}'_{nr,\mu}(\mathbf{x}; \hat{\mu}_{nr}, \hat{\sigma}_{nr}) &= \left. \frac{\partial \bar{R}_{nr}(\mathbf{x}; \mu_{nr}^*, \sigma_{nr}^*)}{\partial \mu_{nr}^*} \right|_{\substack{\mu_{nr}^* = \hat{\mu}_{nr} \\ \sigma_{nr}^* = \hat{\sigma}_{nr}}} \\
&= \frac{R_{nr} \sum_{s=1, s\neq nr}^{N} R_s}{\left(R_{nr} + \sum_{s=1, s\neq nr}^{N} R_s\right)^2} \frac{2(\mathbf{x} - \mu_{nr})^T}{\sigma_{nr}^2} \in R^{1\times n}
\end{aligned} \tag{21.67}$$

$$\bar{R}'_{nr,\sigma}(\mathbf{x};\hat{\mu}_{nr},\hat{\sigma}_{nr}) = \frac{\partial \bar{R}_{nr}(\mathbf{x};\mu^*_{nr},\sigma^*_{nr})}{\partial \sigma^*_{nr}}\Bigg|_{\substack{\mu^*_{nr}=\hat{\mu}_{nr}\\ \sigma^*_{nr}=\hat{\sigma}_{nr}}}$$

$$= \frac{R_{nr}\sum_{s=1,s\neq nr}^{N} R_s}{\left(R_{nr}+\sum_{s=1,s\neq nr}^{N} R_s\right)^2}\frac{2\|\mathbf{x}-\mu_{nr}\|^2}{\sigma^3_{nr}} \in R, \qquad (21.68)$$

Eq. (21.66) can then be expressed as

$$\tilde{\bar{R}}_{nr} = \bar{R}'_{nr,\mu}(\mathbf{x};\hat{\mu}_{nr},\hat{\sigma}_{nr})\tilde{\mu}_{nr} + \bar{R}'_{nr,\sigma}(\mathbf{x};\hat{\mu}_{nr},\hat{\sigma}_{nr})\tilde{\sigma}_{nr} + o(\mathbf{x};\tilde{\mu}_{nr},\tilde{\sigma}_{nr}) \quad (21.69)$$

Substituting Eq. (21.69) with Eq. (21.65) yields

$$\begin{aligned}
\epsilon_f(\mathbf{x}) = \tilde{a}_{f,nr}\{&\bar{R}'_{nr,\mu}(\mathbf{x};\hat{\mu}_{nr},\hat{\sigma}_{nr})\tilde{\mu}_{nr} \\
&+ \bar{R}'_{nr,\sigma}(\mathbf{x};\hat{\mu}_{nr},\hat{\sigma}_{nr})\tilde{\sigma}_{nr} + o(\mathbf{x};\tilde{\mu}_{nr},\tilde{\sigma}_{nr})\} \\
&+ \hat{a}_{f,nr}\{\bar{R}'_{nr,\mu}(\mathbf{x};\hat{\mu}_{nr},\hat{\sigma}_{nr})\tilde{\mu}_{nr} \\
&+ \bar{R}'_{nr,\sigma}(\mathbf{x};\hat{\mu}_{nr},\hat{\sigma}_{nr})\tilde{\sigma}_{nr} + o(\mathbf{x};\tilde{\mu}_{nr},\tilde{\sigma}_{nr})\} \\
&+ \tilde{a}_{f,nr}\bar{R}_{nr}(\mathbf{x};\hat{\mu}_{nr},\hat{\sigma}_{nr}) + \varepsilon_f(\mathbf{x}).
\end{aligned} \qquad (21.70)$$

According to the definition of $\tilde{\mu}_{nr}$, $\tilde{\sigma}_{nr}$, and $a^*_{f,nr}$, Eq. (21.70) is expressed as

$$\begin{aligned}
\epsilon_f(\mathbf{x}) &= \tilde{a}_{f,nr}\bar{R}'_{nr,\mu}(\mathbf{x};\hat{\mu}_{nr},\hat{\sigma}_{nr})(\mu^*_{nr}-\hat{\mu}_{nr}) + \tilde{a}_{f,nr}\bar{R}'_{nr,\sigma}(\mathbf{x};\hat{\mu}_{nr},\hat{\sigma}_{nr})(\sigma^*_{nr}-\hat{\sigma}_{nr}) \\
&\quad + \hat{a}_{f,nr}\bar{R}'_{nr,\mu}(\mathbf{x};\hat{\mu}_{nr},\hat{\sigma}_{nr})\tilde{\mu}_{nr} + \hat{a}_{f,nr}\bar{R}'_{nr,\sigma}(\mathbf{x};\hat{\mu}_{nr},\hat{\sigma}_{nr})\tilde{\sigma}_{nr} \\
&\quad + \tilde{a}_{f,nr}\bar{R}_{nr}(\mathbf{x};\hat{\mu}_{nr},\hat{\sigma}_{nr}) + a^*_{f,nr}o(\mathbf{x};\tilde{\mu}_{nr},\tilde{\sigma}_{nr}) + \varepsilon_f(\mathbf{x}) \\
&= \tilde{a}_{f,nr}\{\bar{R}_{nr}(\mathbf{x};\hat{\mu}_{nr},\hat{\sigma}_{nr}) - \bar{R}'_{nr,\mu}(\mathbf{x};\hat{\mu}_{nr},\hat{\sigma}_{nr})\hat{\mu}_{nr} - \bar{R}'_{nr,\sigma}(\mathbf{x};\hat{\mu}_{nr},\hat{\sigma}_{nr})\hat{\sigma}_{nr}\} \\
&\quad + \hat{a}_{f,nr}\{\bar{R}'_{nr,\mu}(\mathbf{x};\hat{\mu}_{nr},\hat{\sigma}_{nr})\tilde{\mu}_{nr} + \bar{R}'_{nr,\sigma}(\mathbf{x};\hat{\mu}_{nr},\hat{\sigma}_{nr})\tilde{\sigma}_{nr}\} + d_f, \qquad (21.71)
\end{aligned}$$

where

$$\begin{aligned}
d_f = \tilde{a}_{f,nr}\{&\bar{R}'_{nr,\mu}(\mathbf{x};\hat{\mu}_{nr},\hat{\sigma}_{nr})\mu^*_{nr} + \bar{R}'_{nr,\sigma}(\mathbf{x};\hat{\mu}_{nr},\hat{\sigma}_{nr})\sigma^*_{nr}\} \\
&+ a^*_{f,nr}o(\mathbf{x};\tilde{\mu}_{nr},\tilde{\sigma}_{nr}) + \varepsilon_f(\mathbf{x})
\end{aligned}$$

is the residual approximation error. The proof can be extended to the approximation error $\epsilon_g(\mathbf{x})$ (It is omitted here to save space.)

Based on Eqs. (21.42)–(21.43), (21.48), and (21.63)–(21.64), the system error dynamics equals

$$\dot{e}_i = -k_i e_i - e_{i-1} + e_{i+1}, \quad i = 1, 2, \ldots, n-1$$

$$\dot{e}_n = \tilde{a}_{f,nr}\left(\hat{\bar{R}}_{nr} - \hat{\bar{R}}'_{nr,\mu}\hat{\mu}_{nr} - \hat{\bar{R}}'_{nr,\sigma}\hat{\sigma}_{nr}\right) + \hat{a}_{f,nr}\left(\hat{\bar{R}}'_{nr,\mu}\tilde{\mu}_{nr} + \hat{\bar{R}}'_{nr,\sigma}\tilde{\sigma}_{nr}\right)$$

$$+ d_f + \left\{\tilde{a}_{g,nr}\left(\hat{\bar{R}}_{nr} - \hat{\bar{R}}'_{nr,\mu}\hat{\mu}_{nr} - \hat{\bar{R}}'_{nr,\sigma}\hat{\sigma}_{nr}\right)\right.$$

$$\left. + \hat{a}_{g,nr}\left(\hat{\bar{R}}'_{nr,\mu}\tilde{\mu}_{nr} + \hat{\bar{R}}'_{nr,\sigma}\tilde{\sigma}_{nr}\right) + d_g\right\}u_f + g(\mathbf{x})u_s - k_n e_n - e_{n-1}, \quad (21.72)$$

where $\hat{\bar{R}}'_{nr,\mu} = \bar{R}'_{nr,\mu}(\mathbf{x}; \hat{\mu}_{nr}, \hat{\sigma}_{nr})$ and $\hat{\bar{R}}'_{nr,\sigma} = \bar{R}'_{nr,\sigma}(\mathbf{x}; \hat{\mu}_{nr}, \hat{\sigma}_{nr})$. Now, our focus is on the error Eq. (21.72) and the determination of the adaptive laws for $\hat{a}_{f,nr}$, $\hat{a}_{g,nr}$, $\hat{\mu}_{nr}$, and $\hat{\sigma}_{nr}$ such that all signals remain bounded and $e_i (i = 1, 2, \ldots, n) = 0$.

21.3.3.2. *Controller structure and stability analysis*

Since the approximation errors d_f and d_g exist, the system stability cannot be confirmed. In this study, a sliding mode compensator u_s is constructed to handle the approximation errors so that system stability is guaranteed. This study assumes that the approximation errors d_f and d_g are bounded, i.e., $|d_f| \leq \bar{D}_f$ and $|d_g| \leq \bar{D}_g$. Actually, the error bounds, $\bar{D}_f$ and $\bar{D}_g$, are not easy to measure. Therefore, their estimated values $(\hat{D}_f, \hat{D}_g)$ are used to calculate the sliding mode compensator u_s and updated based on the bound estimation laws, which is given as

$$u_s = -\text{sgn}(e_n)\frac{\hat{D}_f + \hat{D}_g|u_f|}{\gamma_0}. \quad (21.73)$$

The parameters of the nearest rule $(\hat{a}_{f,nr}, \hat{a}_{g,nr}, \hat{\mu}_{nr}, \hat{\sigma}_{nr})$ are modified according to Eqs. (21.74)–(21.77) given as

$$\dot{\hat{a}}_{f,nr} = \begin{cases} 0 & \text{if } \hat{a}_{f,nr} \notin (B_f^{\min}, B_f^{\max}) \text{ and} \\ & e_n(\hat{\bar{R}}_{nr} - \hat{\bar{R}}'_{nr,\mu}\hat{\mu}_{nr} - \hat{\bar{R}}'_{nr,\sigma}\hat{\sigma}_{nr}) \\ & (\hat{a}_{f,nr} - \hat{a}^c_{f,nr}) > 0. \\ \gamma_f e_n(\hat{\bar{R}}_{nr} - \hat{\bar{R}}'_{nr,\mu}\hat{\mu}_{nr} \\ \quad -\hat{\bar{R}}'_{nr,\sigma}\hat{\sigma}_{nr}) & \text{otherwise.} \end{cases} \quad (21.74)$$

$$\dot{\hat{a}}_{g,nr} = \begin{cases} 0 & \text{if } \hat{a}_{g,nr} \notin (B_g^{\min}, B_g^{\max}) \text{ and} \\ & e_n(\hat{\bar{R}}_{nr} - \hat{\bar{R}}'_{nr,\mu}\hat{\mu}_{nr} - \hat{\bar{R}}'_{nr,\sigma}\hat{\sigma}_{nr}) \\ & u_f(\hat{a}_{g,nr} - \hat{a}^c_{g,nr}) > 0. \\ \gamma_g e_n(\hat{\bar{R}}_{nr} - \hat{\bar{R}}'_{nr,\mu}\hat{\mu}_{nr} \\ \quad -\hat{\bar{R}}'_{nr,\sigma}\hat{\sigma}_{nr})u_f & \text{otherwise.} \end{cases} \quad (21.75)$$

$$
\dot{\hat{\mu}}_{nr,j} =
\begin{cases}
0 & \begin{aligned} &\text{if } \hat{\mu}_{nr,j} \notin (B^{\min}_{\mu,j}, B^{\max}_{\mu,j}) \text{ and} \\ &e_n(\hat{a}_{f,nr} + \hat{a}_{g,nr} u_f)\hat{\bar{R}}'_{nr,\mu,j} \\ &(\hat{\mu}_{nr,j} - \hat{\mu}^c_{nr,j}) > 0, \\ &j = 1, 2, \ldots, n. \end{aligned} \\[2ex]
\dfrac{\gamma_\mu e_n(\hat{a}_{f,nr} + \hat{a}_{g,nr} u_f)}{\hat{\bar{R}}'_{nr,\mu,j}} & \text{otherwise.}
\end{cases}
\tag{21.76}
$$

$$
\dot{\hat{\sigma}}_{nr} =
\begin{cases}
0 & \begin{aligned} &\text{if } \hat{\sigma}_{nr} \notin (B^{\min}_\sigma, B^{\max}_\sigma) \text{ and} \\ &e_n(\hat{a}_{f,nr} + \hat{a}_{g,nr} u_f)\hat{\bar{R}}'_{nr,\sigma} \\ &(\hat{\sigma}_{nr} - \hat{\sigma}^c_{nr}) > 0. \end{aligned} \\[2ex]
\dfrac{\gamma_\sigma e_n(\hat{a}_{f,nr} + \hat{a}_{g,nr} u_f)}{\hat{\bar{R}}'_{nr,\sigma}} & \text{otherwise.}
\end{cases}
\tag{21.77}
$$

The error bounds $(\hat{D}_f, \hat{D}_g)$ are updated based on Eqs. (21.78)–(21.79), given as,

$$
\dot{\hat{D}}_f =
\begin{cases}
\gamma_{d_f}|e_n| & \text{if } \hat{D}_f \leq B_{df}. \\
0 & \text{otherwise.}
\end{cases}
\tag{21.78}
$$

$$
\dot{\hat{D}}_g =
\begin{cases}
\gamma_{d_g}|e_n| |u_f| & \text{if } \hat{D}_g \leq B_{dg}. \\
0 & \text{otherwise.}
\end{cases}
\tag{21.79}
$$

In these equations, γ_f, γ_g, γ_μ, γ_σ, γ_{df}, and γ_{dg} are the positive learning rates. In order to avoid the problem that the updated parameters may drift to infinity over time, the projection algorithm [46] is applied by limiting their lower and upper bounds $[B^{\min}_\Xi, B^{\max}_\Xi]$, $\Xi = \{f, g, \mu, \sigma\}$. $[B^{\min}_{\mu,j}, B^{\max}_{\mu,j}]$ is the jth element of the vector $[B^{\min}_\mu, B^{\max}_\mu]$. $\hat{a}^c_{f,nr} \in [B^{\min}_f, B^{\max}_f]$, $\hat{a}^c_{g,nr} \in [B^{\min}_g, B^{\max}_g]$, $\hat{\mu}^c_{nr,j} \in [B^{\min}_{\mu,j}, B^{\max}_{\mu,j}]$, and $\hat{\sigma}^c_{nr} \in [B^{\min}_\sigma, B^{\max}_\sigma]$ are any point in the acceptable range. $[0, B_{df}]$ and $[0, B_{dg}]$ are the error-bound ranges.

The following theorem shows the stability property of the proposed meta-cognitive fuzzy-neural control approach.

Theorem 2: Consider the system (Eq. (21.41)) with the fictitious control laws Eq. (21.43) and control law (21.47), where the meta-cognitive fuzzy-neural control u_f is given by Eq. (21.46), and the sliding mode compensator u_s is given by Eq. (21.73). If the adaptation laws of the fuzzy-neural model parameters and approximation error bounds are designed as in Eqs. (21.74)–(21.79), the convergence of the tracking errors and the stability of the proposed meta-cognitive fuzzy-neural control approach can be guaranteed.

Proof. Define a Lyapunov function candidate as

$$
V = \frac{1}{2}\sum_{i=1}^{n} e_i^2 + \frac{1}{2\gamma_f}\tilde{a}_{f,nr}^2 + \frac{1}{2\gamma_g}\tilde{a}_{g,nr}^2 + \frac{1}{2\gamma_\sigma}\tilde{\sigma}_{nr}^2
$$

$$
+ \frac{1}{2\gamma_\mu}\tilde{\mu}_{nr}^T\tilde{\mu}_{nr} + \frac{1}{2\gamma_{df}}\tilde{D}_f^2 + \frac{1}{2\gamma_{dg}}\tilde{D}_g^2 \tag{21.80}
$$

where $\tilde{D}_f = \bar{D}_f - \hat{D}_f$ and $\tilde{D}_g = \bar{D}_g - \hat{D}_g$. $\qquad\square$

Differentiating the Lyapunov function (Eq. (21.80)) and using Eq. (21.72) yields

$$
\dot{V} = \sum_{i=1}^{n} -k_i e_i^2 + e_n \tilde{a}_{f,nr}\left(\hat{\bar{R}}_{nr} - \hat{R}'_{nr,\mu}\hat{\mu}_{nr} - \hat{R}'_{nr,\sigma}\hat{\sigma}_{nr}\right)
$$

$$
+ e_n \tilde{a}_{g,nr}\left(\hat{\bar{R}}_{nr} - \hat{R}'_{nr,\mu}\hat{\mu}_{nr} - \hat{R}'_{nr,\sigma}\hat{\sigma}_{nr}\right) u_f + e_n(\hat{a}_{f,nr} + \hat{a}_{g,nr} u_f)\hat{R}'_{nr,\mu}\tilde{\mu}_{nr}
$$

$$
+ e_n(\hat{a}_{f,nr} + \hat{a}_{g,nr} u_f)\hat{R}'_{nr,\sigma}\tilde{\sigma}_{nr} + e_n d_f + e_n d_g u_f + e_n g(\mathbf{x}) u_s - \frac{1}{\gamma_f}\tilde{a}_{f,nr}\dot{\hat{a}}_{f,nr}
$$

$$
- \frac{1}{\gamma_g}\tilde{a}_{g,nr}\dot{\hat{a}}_{g,nr} - \frac{1}{\gamma_\sigma}\tilde{\sigma}_{nr}\dot{\hat{\sigma}}_{nr} - \frac{1}{\gamma_\mu}\dot{\hat{\mu}}_{nr}^T\tilde{\mu}_{nr} - \frac{1}{\gamma_{df}}\dot{\hat{D}}_f\tilde{D}_f - \frac{1}{\gamma_{dg}}\dot{\hat{D}}_g\tilde{D}_g,
$$

$$
\tag{21.81}
$$

where $\dot{\tilde{a}}_{f,nr} = -\dot{\hat{a}}_{f,nr}$, $\dot{\tilde{a}}_{g,nr} = -\dot{\hat{a}}_{g,nr}$, $\dot{\tilde{\sigma}}_{nr} = -\dot{\hat{\sigma}}_{nr}$, $\dot{\tilde{\mu}}_{nr} = -\dot{\hat{\mu}}_{f,nr}$, $\dot{\tilde{D}}_f = -\dot{\hat{D}}_f$, and $\dot{\tilde{D}}_g = -\dot{\hat{D}}_g$ are utilized.

Let

$$
V_f = e_n \tilde{a}_{f,nr}\left(\hat{\bar{R}}_{nr} - \hat{R}'_{nr,\mu}\hat{\mu}_{nr} - \hat{R}'_{nr,\sigma}\hat{\sigma}_{nr}\right) - \frac{1}{\gamma_f}\tilde{a}_{f,nr}\dot{\hat{a}}_{f,nr}
$$

$$
V_g = e_n \tilde{a}_{g,nr}\left(\hat{\bar{R}}_{nr} - \hat{R}'_{nr,\mu}\hat{\mu}_{nr} - \hat{R}'_{nr,\sigma}\hat{\sigma}_{nr}\right) u_f - \frac{1}{\gamma_g}\tilde{a}_{g,nr}\dot{\hat{a}}_{g,nr}
$$

$$
V_\mu = e_n(\hat{a}_{f,nr} + \hat{a}_{g,nr} u_f)\hat{R}'_{nr,\mu}\tilde{\mu}_{nr} - \frac{1}{\gamma_\mu}\dot{\hat{\mu}}_{nr}^T\tilde{\mu}_{nr}
$$

$$
= \sum_{j=1}^{n}\left[e_n(\hat{a}_{f,nr} + \hat{a}_{g,nr} u_f)\hat{R}'_{nr,\mu,j}\tilde{\mu}_{nr,j} - \frac{1}{\gamma_\mu}\dot{\hat{\mu}}_{nr,j}\tilde{\mu}_{nr,j} \right]
$$

$$
V_\sigma = e_n(\hat{a}_{f,nr} + \hat{a}_{g,nr} u_f)\hat{R}'_{nr,\sigma}\tilde{\sigma}_{nr} - \frac{1}{\gamma_\sigma}\tilde{\sigma}_{nr}\dot{\hat{\sigma}}_{nr}.
$$

Eq. (21.81) can be rewritten as

$$\dot{V} = \sum_{i=1}^{n} -k_i e_i^2 + V_f + V_g + V_\mu + V_\sigma + e_n d_f$$

$$+ e_n d_g u_f + e_n g(\mathbf{x}) u_s - \frac{1}{\gamma_{df}} \dot{\hat{D}}_f \tilde{D}_f - \frac{1}{\gamma_{dg}} \dot{\hat{D}}_g \tilde{D}_g. \tag{21.82}$$

When the adaptation law for the parameter $\hat{a}_{f,nr}$ is designed as Eq. (21.74) and the first condition is satisfied,

$$V_f = e_n \tilde{a}_{f,nr} \left(\hat{\bar{R}}_{nr} - \hat{\bar{R}}'_{nr,\mu} \hat{\mu}_{nr} - \hat{\bar{R}}'_{nr,\sigma} \hat{\sigma}_{nr} \right)$$

$$= -e_n \left(\hat{\bar{R}}_{nr} - \hat{\bar{R}}'_{nr,\mu} \hat{\mu}_{nr} - \hat{\bar{R}}'_{nr,\sigma} \hat{\sigma}_{nr} \right) (\hat{a}_{f,nr} - a^*_{f,nr}). \tag{21.83}$$

Since

$$a^*_{f,nr} \in (B_f^{\min}, B_f^{\max}), \quad \text{the condition } -e_n \left(\hat{\bar{R}}_{nr} - \hat{\bar{R}}'_{nr,\mu} \hat{\mu}_{nr} - \hat{\bar{R}}'_{nr,\sigma} \hat{\sigma}_{nr} \right)$$

$$(\hat{a}_{f,nr} - a^*_{f,nr}) < 0$$

holds. For the second condition of Eq. (21.74), $V_f = 0$. As a result, it can be concluded that $V_f \leq 0$.

If the adaptation laws for the parameters $\hat{a}_{g,nr}$, $\hat{\mu}_{nr,j}$, and $\hat{\sigma}_{nr}$ are designed as Eqs. (21.75)–(21.77), one can conclude that $V_g \leq 0$, $V_\mu \leq 0$, and $V_\sigma \leq 0$.

Consequently, with the design of u_s Eq. (21.73), Eq. (21.82) can be represented as,

$$\dot{V} = \sum_{i=1}^{n} -k_i e_i^2 + V_f + V_g + V_\mu + V_\sigma + e_n d_f$$

$$+ e_n d_g u_f - e_n g(\mathbf{x}) \operatorname{sgn}(e_n) \frac{\hat{D}_f + \hat{D}_g |u_f|}{\gamma_0} - \frac{1}{\gamma_{df}} \dot{\hat{D}}_f \tilde{D}_f - \frac{1}{\gamma_{dg}} \dot{\hat{D}}_g \tilde{D}_g$$

$$\leq \sum_{i=1}^{n} -k_i e_i^2 + |e_n||d_f| + |e_n||d_g||u_f| - e_n g(\mathbf{x}) \operatorname{sgn}(e_n) \frac{\hat{D}_f + \hat{D}_g |u_f|}{\gamma_0}$$

$$- \frac{1}{\gamma_{df}} \dot{\hat{D}}_f \tilde{D}_f - \frac{1}{\gamma_{dg}} \dot{\hat{D}}_g \tilde{D}_g. \tag{21.84}$$

Considering that $|d_f| \leq \bar{D}_f$ and $|d_g| \leq \bar{D}_g$ and with Assumption 2, Eq. (21.84) becomes

$$
\dot{V} \leq \sum_{i=1}^{n} -k_i e_i^2 + |e_n|\bar{D}_f + |e_n||u_f|\bar{D}_g - |e_n|(\hat{D}_f + \hat{D}_g|u_f|)
$$

$$
- \frac{1}{\gamma_{df}} \dot{\hat{D}}_f \tilde{D}_f - \frac{1}{\gamma_{dg}} \dot{\hat{D}}_g \tilde{D}_g
$$

$$
= \sum_{i=1}^{n} -k_i e_i^2 + |e_n|(\bar{D}_f - \hat{D}_f) + |e_n||u_f|(\bar{D}_g - \hat{D}_g)
$$

$$
- \frac{1}{\gamma_{df}} \dot{\hat{D}}_f \tilde{D}_f - \frac{1}{\gamma_{dg}} \dot{\hat{D}}_g \tilde{D}_g. \tag{21.85}
$$

Let

$$
V_{df} = |e_n|(\bar{D}_f - \hat{D}_f) - \frac{1}{\gamma_{df}} \dot{\hat{D}}_f \tilde{D}_f
$$

$$
V_{dg} = |e_n||u_f|(\bar{D}_g - \hat{D}_g) - \frac{1}{\gamma_{dg}} \dot{\hat{D}}_g \tilde{D}_g.
$$

When the adaptation law for the error-bound $\hat{D}_f$ is designed as Eq. (21.78) and the first condition is satisfied, $V_{df} = 0$. Using the second condition of Eq. (21.78) yields $V_{df} = |e_n|(\bar{D}_f - \hat{D}_f) \leq 0$ with $\hat{D}_f \geq B_{df} > \bar{D}_f$. Thus, it can be concluded that $V_{df} \leq 0$. Similarly, with the adaptation law (21.75) for the error bound $\hat{D}_g$, one can obtain $V_{dg} \leq 0$.

In this case, the derivative of V satisfies

$$
\dot{V} \leq \sum_{i=1}^{m} -k_i e_i^2 < 0. \tag{21.86}
$$

Equations (21.80) and (21.86) show that $V \geq 0$ and $\dot{V} \leq 0$, respectively. Thus,

$$
V(e_i(t), \tilde{a}_{f,nr}(t), \tilde{a}_{g,nr}(t), \tilde{\mu}_{nr}(t), \tilde{\sigma}_{nr}(t), \tilde{D}_f(t), \tilde{D}_g(t))
$$

$$
\leq V(e_i(0), \tilde{a}_{f,nr}(0), \tilde{a}_{g,nr}(0), \tilde{\mu}_{nr}(0), \tilde{\sigma}_{nr}(0), \tilde{D}_f(0), \tilde{D}_g(0)). \tag{21.87}
$$

This implies that $e_i(i = 1, 2, \ldots, n)$, $\tilde{a}_{f,nr}$, $\tilde{a}_{g,nr}$, $\tilde{\mu}_{nr}$, $\tilde{\sigma}_{nr}$, $\tilde{D}_f$, $\tilde{D}_g$ are bounded. Denoting function

$$
V_c(t) \equiv \sum_{i=1}^{n} k_i e_i^2
$$

$$
= -\dot{V}(e_i(t), \tilde{a}_{f,nr}(t), \tilde{a}_{g,nr}(t), \tilde{\mu}_{nr}(t), \tilde{\sigma}_{nr}(t), \tilde{D}_f(t), \tilde{D}_g(t)). \tag{21.88}
$$

Integrating (21.88) with respect to time can show that

$$\int_0^t V_c(\tau)d\tau$$

$$\leq V(e_i(0), \tilde{a}_{f,nr}(0), \tilde{a}_{g,nr}(0), \tilde{\mu}_{nr}(0), \tilde{\sigma}_{nr}(0), \tilde{D}_f(0), \tilde{D}_g(0))$$

$$-V(e_i(t), \tilde{a}_{f,nr}(t), \tilde{a}_{g,nr}(t), \tilde{\mu}_{nr}(t), \tilde{\sigma}_{nr}(t), \tilde{D}_f(t), \tilde{D}_g(t)), \quad (21.89)$$

Since $V(e_i(0), \tilde{a}_{f,nr}(0), \tilde{a}_{g,nr}(0), \tilde{\mu}_{nr}(0), \tilde{\sigma}_{nr}(0), \tilde{D}_f(0), \tilde{D}_g(0))$ is bounded and $V(e_i(t), \tilde{a}_{f,nr}(t), \tilde{a}_{g,nr}(t), \tilde{\mu}_{nr}(t), \tilde{\sigma}_{nr}(t), \tilde{D}_f(t), \tilde{D}_g(t))$ is nonincreasing and bounded, the following result can be obtained:

$$\lim_{t \to \infty} \int_0^t V_c(\tau)d\tau < \infty, \quad (21.90)$$

Since $\dot{V}_c(t)$ is bounded, it can be concluded that $\lim_{t \to \infty} V_c(t) = 0$ according to Barbalat's lemma [26], which implies that $e_i \to 0, i = 1, 2, \ldots, n$ as $t \to \infty$. Therefore, the proposed meta-cognitive fuzzy-neural control approach is asymptotically stable and the tracking errors of the system will converge to zero.

Remark: The synthesis associated with the overall architecture of the proposed meta-cognitive fuzzy-neural control approach is shown in Figure 21.11. The control input u is recursively constructed via the virtual control laws x_{2d} to x_{nd} and comprises two parts, viz., the sliding mode compensator u_s and the meta-cognitive fuzzy-neural control input u_f. u_s with the adaptive error-bound estimation laws is designed to attenuate the effects of the approximation error terms d_f and d_g. u_f is built using the meta-cognitive fuzzy-neural model to approximate the unknown functions $f_d(\mathbf{x})$ and $g(\mathbf{x})$. Different from the existing work [40–42], the proposed control method can perform both data deletion and data learning concurrently online. The data with similar information content are deleted and not employed to design the controller, which avoids over-learning and improves control performance. Data learning is capable of determining the system structure and modifying parameters simultaneously. All of the rules are automatically produced online and good initial values of all the rules are located, from which subsequent parameter tuning is implemented.

21.3.4. *Control Performance*

The desired trajectory is $z_d(t) = 0.005 \sin(5t)$ and the initial states are $(z, \dot{z}) = (-0.003, 0)^T$. The parameters of the TAMB system are set as $m = 7.35\,\text{kg}$, $c_0 = 3.5e - 4$, $Q_{i0} = 212.82 N/A$, and $Q_{z0} = -7.3e5\,N/m$. The parameters associated with the AMcFBC are selected as $E_a = 0.008$, $E_l = 0.002$, $\kappa = 0.8$, $E_s = 0.2$, $\gamma_\mu = \gamma_\sigma = \gamma_f = \gamma_g = 100$, and $\gamma_{df} = \gamma_{dg} = 0.02$.

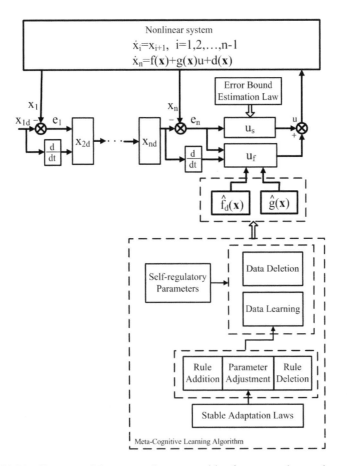

Figure 21.11: Structure of the proposed meta-cognitive fuzzy-neural control approach.

The simulation results of the TAMB control system using the proposed control approach are shown in Figure 21.12. For the sake of comparison, the results of the neural network control (NC) scheme with the fixed structure are included here. From the results, faster tracking responses are obtained by the proposed meta-cognitive fuzzy-neural controller since the meta-cognitive fuzzy-neural model can rapidly learn the system dynamics with the meta-cognitive learning capability. Figure 21.13(a) gives the spherical potential and the novelty threshold during the whole learning process. The tracking error (e) and the self-regulatory thresholds (E_a, E_l) related to the meta-cognitive learning mechanism are depicted in Figure 21.13(b). Figure 21.14(a) presents the rule evolution process of the proposed meta-cognitive fuzzy-neural controller, where a new rule is added to the model if $\psi < E_s$ and $e > E_a$. This occurs mainly during the initial learning process to rapidly learn the system dynamics and then insignificant rules are pruned after the meta-cognitive fuzzy-neural model captures the system dynamics. The local rules

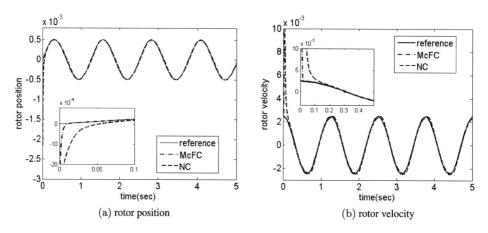

(a) rotor position

(b) rotor velocity

Figure 21.12:   Trajectories of the rotor position and velocity.

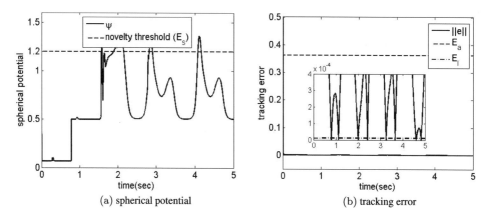

(a) spherical potential

(b) tracking error

Figure 21.13:   Spherical potential and tracking error with self-regulatory thresholds.

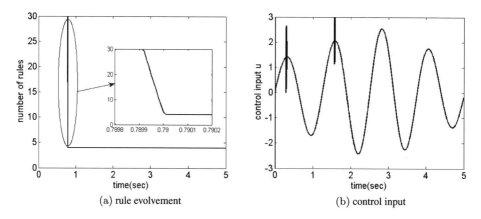

(a) rule evolvement

(b) control input

Figure 21.14:   Rule evolving process and control input.

pruning around 0.8 second are also shown in the figure for clear illustration. In this simulation study, the meta-cognitive fuzzy-neural controller generates a total of four fuzzy rules online as shown in Figure 21.14(a) while the NC requires eight hidden neurons determined by trial and error. When $e > E_l$ as shown in Figure 21.13(b), the data are used for updating the parameters of the nearest rule according to the stable adaptation laws Eq. (21.74)–(21.79). If the data are not satisfied with the adding and pruning of rules and the updating of parameters, they are removed from the learning process. Besides, from these results, one can infer that the proposed meta-cognitive fuzzy-neural control approach has the capability to adapt the structure of the fuzzy-neural system and its corresponding parameters in real time, even in a changing environment. Figure 21.14(b) depicts the control signal and shows the control inputs are bounded in the whole control phase based on the projection-type learning laws.

21.4. Conclusions

In this chapter, two kinds of indirect self-evolving fuzzy control systems utilizing ESAFIS and the meta-cognitive fuzzy-neural model are developed for the suppression of the wing-rock motion and rotor position control of a nonlinear TAMB system, respectively. The self-evolving fuzzy models are used to directly approximate the system dynamics and then the controller is constructed based on the approximation function. In the rule evolvement, the fuzzy rules are dynamically recruited and pruned such that a system structure of an appropriate size is autonomously achieved. When the learning criterion of parameter adjustment is satisfied, the parameters are updated via the projection-type update laws determined based on the Lyapunov function theory. This further guarantees the stability of the controlled system in the ultimate bounded sense. Simulation results demonstrate the feasibility and performance of the proposed controllers.

References

[1] Jang, J.-S. R., Sun, C.-T., and Mizutani, E. (1997). *Neuro-Fuzzy and Soft Computing: A Computational Approach to Learning and Machine Intelligence* (Prentice-Hall, Upper Saddle River, New Jersey).

[2] Mitra, S. and Hayashi, Y. (2000). Neuro-fuzzy rule generation: survey in soft computing framework, *IEEE Trans. Neural Networks*, **11**(3), pp. 748–768.

[3] Lu, Y., Sundararajan, N., and Saratchandran, P. (1997). A sequential learning scheme for function approximation using minimal radial basis function neural networks, *Neural Comput.*, **9**(2), pp. 461–478.

[4] Wu, S. and Er, M. J. (2000). Dynamic fuzzy neural networks-a novel approach to function approximation, *IEEE Trans. Syst. Man Cybern. Part B Cybern.*, **30**(2), pp. 358–364.

[5] Leng, G., McGinnity, T. M., and Prasad, G. (2005). An approach for on-line extraction of fuzzy rules using a self-organising fuzzy neural network, *Fuzzy Sets Syst.*, **150**(2), pp. 211–243.

[6] Rong, H.-J., Huang, G.-B., Sundararajan, N., and Saratchandran, P. (2009). Online sequential fuzzy extreme learning machine for function approximation and classification problems, *IEEE Trans. Syst. Man Cybern. Part B Cybern.*, **39**(4), pp. 1067–1072.

[7] Rong, H.-J., Sundararajan, N., Huang, G.-B., and Zhao, G.-S. (2011). Extended sequential adaptive fuzzy inference system for classification problems, *Evolving Syst.*, **2**, p. 7182.

[8] Subramanian, K. and Suresh, S. (2012). A meta-cognitive sequential learning algorithm for neuro-fuzzy inference system, *Appl. Soft Comput.*, **12**, pp. 3603–3614.

[9] Xu, B., Sun, F., Liu, H., and Ren, J. (2012). Adaptive Kriging controller design for hypersonic flight vehicle via back-stepping, *IET Control Theory Appl.*, **6**(4), pp. 487–497.

[10] Pashilkar, A. A., Sundararajan, N., and Saratchandran, P. (2006). Adaptive back-stepping neural controller for reconfigurable flight control systems, *IEEE Trans. Control Syst. Technol.*, **14**(3), pp. 553–561.

[11] van Soest, W. R., Chu, Q. P., and Mulder, J. A. (2006). Combined feedback linearization and constrained model predictive control for entry flight, *J. Guid. Control Dyn.*, **29**(2), pp. 427–434.

[12] Li, G., Wen, C., Zheng, W. X., and Chen, Y. (2011). Identification of a class of nonlinear autoregressive models with exogenous inputs based on kernel machines, *IEEE Trans. Signal Process.*, **59**(5), pp. 2146–2159.

[13] Takagi, T. and Sugeno, M. (1985). Fuzzy identification of systems and its applications to modelling and control, *IEEE Trans. Syst. Man Cybern.*, **SMC-15**(1), pp. 116–132.

[14] Zou, A.-M., Hou, Z.-G., and Tan, M. (2008). Adaptive control of a class of nonlinear pure-feedback systems using fuzzy backstepping approach, *IEEE Trans. Fuzzy Syst.*, **16**(4), pp. 886–897.

[15] Lin, F.-J., Shieh, P.-H., and Chou, P.-H. (2008). Robust adaptive backstepping motion control of linear ultrasonic motors using fuzzy neural network, *IEEE Trans. Fuzzy Syst.*, **16**(3), pp. 676–692.

[16] Wen, J. (2011). Adaptive fuzzy controller for a class of strict-feedback nonaffine nonlinear system, in *2011 9th IEEE International Conference on Control and Automation (ICCA)* (IEEE), pp. 1255–1260.

[17] Lin, C.-M. and Li, H.-Y. (2012). Tsk fuzzy CMAC-based robust adaptive backstepping control for uncertain nonlinear systems, *IEEE Trans. Fuzzy Syst.*, **20**(6), pp. 1147–1154.

[18] Chen, W., Jiao, L., Li, R. and Li, J. (2010). Adaptive backstepping fuzzy control for nonlinearly parameterized systems with periodic disturbances, *IEEE Trans. Fuzzy Syst.*, **18**(4), pp. 674–685.

[19] A. G. Sreenatha, V. Patki, M., and V. Joshi, S. (2000). Fuzzy logic control for wing-rock phenomenon, *Mech. Res. Commun.*, 27(3), pp. 359–364.

[20] Elzebda, J. M., Nayfeh, A. H., and Mook, D. T. (1989). Development of an analytical model of wing rock for slender delta wings, *J. Aircr.*, **26**(8), pp. 737–743.

[21] Nayfeh, A. H., Elzebda, J. M., and Mook, D. T. (1989). Analytical study of the subsonic wing-rock phenomenon for slender delta wings, *J. Aircr.*, **26**(9), pp. 805–809.

[22] Škrjanc, I. (2007). A decomposed-model predictive functional control approach to air-vehicle pitch-angle control, *J. Intell. Rob. Syst.*, **48**(1), pp. 115–127.

[23] Luo, J. and Lan, C. E. (1993). Control of wing-rock motion of slender delta wings, *J. Guid. Control Dyn.*, **16**(2), pp. 225–231.

[24] Monahemi, M. M. and Krstic, M. (1996). Control of wing rock motion using adaptive feedback linearization, *J. Guid. Control Dyn.*, **19**(4), pp. 905–912.

[25] Shue, S.-P., Agarwal, R. K., and Shi, P. (2000). Nonlinear H method for control of wing rock motions, *J. Guid. Control Dyn.*, **23**(1), pp. 60–68.

[26] Sundararajan, N., Saratchandran, P., and Yan, L. (2001). *Fully Tuned Radial Basis Function Neural Networks for Flight Control* (Boston: Kluwer academic publishers).

[27] Rong, H.-J., Sundararajan, N., Huang, G.-B., and Saratchandran, P. (2006). Sequential Adaptive Fuzzy Inference System (SAFIS) for nonlinear system identification and prediction, *Fuzzy Sets Syst.*, **157**(9), pp. 1260–1275.

[28] Wai, R.-J. and Yang, Z.-W. (2008). Adaptive fuzzy neural network control design via a T-S fuzzy model for a robot manipulator including actuator dynamics, *IEEE Trans. Syst. Man Cybern. Part B Cybern.*, **38**(5), pp. 1326–1346.

[29] de Jesús Rubio, J. (2009). Sofmls: online self-organizing fuzzy modified least-squares network, *IEEE Trans. Fuzzy Syst.*, 17(6), pp. 1296–1309.

[30] Lughofer, E. and Angelov, P. (2011). Handling drifts and shifts in on-line data streams with evolving fuzzy systems, *Appl. Soft Comput.*, **11**(2), pp. 2057–2068.

[31] Wang, L. (1994). *Adaptive Fuzzy Systems and Control: Design And Stability Analysis* (PTR Prentice Hall).

[32] Wang, L.-X. (1993). Stable adaptive fuzzy control of nonlinear systems, *IEEE Trans. Fuzzy Syst.*, **1**(2), pp. 146–155.

[33] Han, H., Su, C.-Y., and Stepanenko, Y. (2001). Adaptive control of a class of nonlinear systems with nonlinearly parameterized fuzzy approximators, *IEEE Trans. Fuzzy Syst.*, **9**(2), pp. 315–323.

[34] Singh, S. N., Yirn, W., and Wells, W. R. (1995). Direct adaptive and neural control of wing-rock motion of slender delta wings, *J. Guid. Control Dyn.*, **18**(1), pp. 25–30.

[35] Passino, K. M. (2005). *Biomimicry for Optimization, Control, and Automation* (Springer Science and Business Media).

[36] de Jesús Rubio, J., Vázquez, D. M., and Pacheco, J. (2010). Backpropagation to train an evolving radial basis function neural network, *Evolving Syst.*, 1(3), pp. 173–180.

[37] Lemos, A., Caminhas, W., and Gomide, F. (2011). Fuzzy evolving linear regression trees, *Evolving Syst.*, **2**(1), pp. 1–14.

[38] Lughofer, E., Bouchot, J.-L., and Shaker, A. (2011). On-line elimination of local redundancies in evolving fuzzy systems, *Evolving Syst.*, **2**(3), pp. 165–187.

[39] Ji, J., Hansen, C. H., and Zander, A. C. (2008). Nonlinear dynamics of magnetic bearing systems, *Int. J. Mater. Syst. Struct.*, **19**(12), pp. 1471–1491.

[40] Tong, S., Wang, T., Li, Y., and Chen, B. (2013). A combined backstepping and stochastic small-gain approach to robust adaptive fuzzy output feedback control, *IEEE Trans. Fuzzy Syst.*, **21**(2), pp. 314–327.

[41] Chang, Y.-H. and Chan, W.-S. (2014). Adaptive dynamic surface control for uncertain nonlinear systems with interval type-2 fuzzy neural networks, *IEEE Trans. Cybern.*, 44(2), pp. 293–304.

[42] Wen, J. and Jiang, C. (2011). Adaptive fuzzy controller for a class of strict-feedback nonaffine nonlinear systems, *J. Syst. Eng. Electron.*, **22**(6), pp. 967–974.

[43] Du, H., Zhang, N., Ji, J., and Gao, W. (2010). Robust fuzzy control of an active magnetic bearing subject to voltage saturation, *IEEE Trans. Control Syst. Technol.*, **18**(1), pp. 164–169.

[44] Lin, F.-J., Chen, S.-Y., and Huang, M.-S. (2010). Tracking control of thrust active magnetic bearing system via hermite polynomial-based recurrent neural network, *IET Electr. Power Appl.*, **4**(9), pp. 701–714.

[45] Ge, S. S., Hang, C. C., and Zhang, T. (1999). A direct adaptive controller for dynamic systems with a class of nonlinear parameterizations, *Automatica*, **35**, pp. 741–747.

[46] Spooner, J. T. and Passino, K. M. (1996). Stable adaptive control using fuzzy systems and neural networks, *IEEE Trans. Fuzzy Syst.*, **4**(3), pp. 339–359.

Part V

Evolutionary Computation

https://doi.org/10.1142/9789811247323_0022

Chapter 22

Evolutionary Computation: Historical View and Basic Concepts

Carlos A. Coello Coello*,ˣ, Carlos Segura†,¶, and Gara Miranda‡,∥

**Departamento de Computación (Evolutionary Computation Group),*
CINVESTAV-IPN México D.F., Mexico
†*Centro de Investigación en Matemáticas, Área Computación, Callejón Jalisco s/n,*
Mineral de Valenciana, Guanajuato, Mexico
‡*Dpto. Estadística, I. O. y Computación, Universidad de La Laguna,*
Santa Cruz de Tenerife, Spain
ˣ*carlos.coellocoello@cinvestav.mx*
¶*carlos.segura@cimat.mx*
∥*gmiranda@ull.edu.es*

22.1. Introduction

In most real-world problems, achieving optimal (or at least good) solutions results in saved resources, time, and expenses. These problems where optimal solutions are desired are known as *optimization problems*. In general, optimization algorithms search among the set of possible solutions (*search space*), evaluating the candidates—perhaps also analyzing their feasibility—and choosing from among them the final solution—or solutions—to the problem. Another perspective is that an optimization problem consists in finding the values of those variables that minimize/maximize the objective functions while satisfying any existing constraints. Optimization problems, involve *variables* that somehow define the search space. However, *constraints* are not mandatory: many unconstrained problems have been formulated and studied in the literature. In the case of the *objective function*, most optimization problems have been formulated on the basis of a single objective function. However, in many problems, it is actually necessary to optimize several different objectives at once [1]. Usually, such objectives are mutually competitive or conflicting, and values of variables that optimize one objective may be far from optimal for the others. Thus, in multi-objective optimization, there is no single and unique optimal solution, but rather a set of optimal solutions, none of them better than the others.

Optimization problems can be simple or complex depending on the number of objectives, the solution space, the number of decision variables, the constraints specified, etc. Some optimization problems that satisfy certain properties are relatively easy to solve [2]. However, many optimization problems are quite difficult to solve; in fact, many of them fit into the family of *NP-hard problems* [3]. Assuming that $P \neq NP$, there is no approach that guarantees that the optimal solution to these problems is achieved in polynomial time. In the same way, optimization algorithms can be very simple or complex depending on whether they are able to give exact or approximate solutions, whether they are less or more efficient, or even whether they need to be specifically designed for a particular problem or not. Moreover, algorithms can be also classified by the amount of completion time required in comparison to their input size. Some problems may have multiple related algorithms of differing complexity, while other problems might have no algorithms or, at least, no known efficient algorithms. Taking the above into account, when deciding which algorithmic technique to apply, much depends on the properties of the problem to be solved, but also on the expected results: the quality of the solution, the efficiency of the approach, the flexibility and generality of the method, etc.

Since many optimization algorithms have been proposed, with different purposes and from different perspectives, there is no single criterion that can be used to classify them. We can find different categories of algorithms in the literature, depending on the features related to their internal implementation, their general behavior scheme, the field of application, complexity, etc. For the purposes of this chapter, the classification presented in Figure 22.1 provides a meaningful starting point.

In general, most solution techniques involve some form of exploration of the set of feasible solutions. *Exact approaches* are usually based on an enumerative,

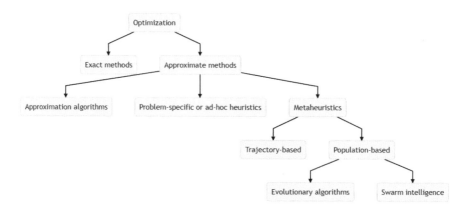

Figure 22.1: Classification of optimization methods.

exhaustive, or brute-force search that yields the optimal solution to the problem. However, in most problems dealing with real or large instances, the search space may be far too large, or there may not even exist a convenient way to enumerate it. In such situations, it is common to resort to some kind of *approximate method*. These approaches do not generally ensure optimal solutions, but some of them at least ensure a certain level of solution quality, e.g., *approximation algorithms*. *Ad hoc heuristics* are another kind of approximate method that incorporate information about the problem at hand in order to decide which candidate solution should be tested next or how the next candidate can be produced [4]. Since they are based on specific knowledge of the problem, such ad hoc methods have the drawback of being problem dependent. That is, a wide variety of heuristics can be specifically and successfully designed to optimize a given problem, but unfortunately, they cannot be directly extrapolated to another problem. The specific mechanisms or decisions that work well in one case may not work at all for related problems that share common features, e.g., problems belonging to the same family. As a result, such procedures are unable to adapt to particular problem instances or to extend to different problems. Restarting and randomization strategies, as well as combinations of simple heuristics, offer only partial and largely unsatisfactory answers to these issues [5].

Metaheuristics appear as a class of modern heuristics whose main goal is to address these open challenges [6, 7]. A metaheuristic is an approximate method for solving a very general class of problems. It combines objective functions and heuristics in an abstract and hopefully efficient way, usually without requiring a deep insight into their structure. Metaheuristics have been defined as master strategies to guide and modify other heuristics to produce solutions beyond those normally identified by ad hoc heuristics. Compared to exact search methods, metaheuristics are not able to ensure a systematic exploration of the entire solution space, so they cannot guarantee that optimal solutions will be achieved. Instead, with the aim of increasing efficiency, they seek to examine only the parts where "good" solutions may be found.

In most metaheuristics, a single solution, or a set of them, is maintained as active solutions and the search procedures are based on movements within the search space. New candidate solutions are built mainly in two ways: from scratch or as an evolution of current solutions. In many cases, these new candidate solutions are generated by means of a neighborhood definition, although different strategies are also used. At each process iteration, the metaheuristic evaluates different kinds of moves, some of which are selected to update the current solutions as determined by certain criteria (objective value, feasibility, statistical measures, etc.). Well-designed metaheuristics try to avoid being trapped in local optima or to repeatedly cycle through solutions that were already visited. It is also important to provide a reasonable assurance that the search does not overlook promising regions.

A wide variety of metaheuristics have been proposed in the literature [8]. In many cases, these criteria or combinations of moves are often performed stochastically by utilizing statistics obtained from samples from the search space, or based on a model of some natural phenomenon or physical process [9, 10]. Another interesting feature that arises when analyzing the internal operation of a metaheuristic involves the number of candidate solutions or states that are being managed at a time. *Trajectory-based metaheuristics* maintain a single current state at any given instant, which is replaced by a new one at each generation. In contrast, *population-based metaheuristics* maintain a current pool with several candidate states instead of a single current state.

As described before, in its search for better solutions and greater quality, research in the field of optimization has focused on the design of metaheuristics as general-purpose techniques to guide the construction of solutions, with the aim of improving the resulting quality. In recent decades, research in this field has led to the creation of new hybrid algorithms, combining different concepts from various fields such as genetics, biology, artificial intelligence, mathematics, physics, and neurology, among others [11]. In this context, evolutionary computation (EC) is a research area within computer science that studies the properties of a set of algorithms—usually called evolutionary algorithms (EAs)—that draw their inspiration from natural evolution. Initially, several algorithms intended to better understand the population dynamics present in evolution were designed [12]. Although the design of the EC schemes is based on drawing inspiration from natural evolution, a faithful modeling of biological processes is not usually incorporated. Since EAs are usually overly simplistic versions of their biological counterparts, using EAs to model population dynamics is not too widely accepted by the evolutionary biology community [13]. Instead, the advances achieved in recent decades have shown that the main strength of EC is that it can be successfully applied to numerous practical problems that appear in several areas such as process control, machine learning, and function optimization [14, 15]. For this reason, EC should be seen as a general and robust evolution-inspired framework devoted to problem-solving.

Although it is not easy to classify the kinds of problems that can be solved with EC, some taxonomies have been proposed. For instance, Everett distinguished between two main uses of EAs [16]: optimizing the performance of operating systems, and the testing and fitting of quantitative models. Another view was proposed by Eiben and Smith [17] by providing an analogy between problems and systems. In working systems, the three main components are: inputs, outputs, and the internal model connecting these two. They distinguished between three kinds of problems that can be solved with EC depending on which of the three components is unknown. In any case, the important fact is that EC has been successfully used in a huge number of applications such as numerical optimization, design of expert systems, training of neural networks, data mining, and many others. In general, EC might be potentially applied to any problem where we can identify a set of candidate solutions and a quality level associated with each of them.

This chapter is devoted to presenting the history and philosophy behind the use of EC, as well as introducing the reader to the design of EAs. In Section 22.2, a brief review of natural evolution theories is provided. In addition, some of the main concepts from the fields of evolution and genetics that have inspired developments in EC are introduced. Then, Section 22.3 presents the history and philosophy of the first EC approaches ever developed. Some of the latest developments, as well as the current unifying view of EC, are summarized in Section 22.4. Section 22.5 offers some observations on the design of EAs and describes some of the most popular components that have been used when tackling optimization problems with EC. Finally, some concluding remarks are given in Section 22.6.

22.2. The Fundamentals of Evolution

The term *evolution* is defined by the Oxford Dictionary as *the process by which different kinds of living organisms are thought to have developed and diversified from earlier forms during the history of the Earth.* A much more general definition of this term is *the gradual development of something, especially from a simple to a more complex form.* The word *evolution* originated from the Latin word *evolutio* which means unrolling, from the verb *evolvere.* Early meanings were related to physical movement, first recorded in describing a tactical "wheeling" maneuver in the realignment of troops or ships. Current senses stem from the notion of "opening out" and "unfolding," giving rise to a general sense of "development." The term appeared a couple of centuries before Darwin wrote *On the Origin of Species.* In fact, Darwin did not even use the word evolution in his book until the last line:

> There is grandeur in this view of life, with its several powers, having been originally breathed by the Creator into a few forms or into one; and that, whilst this planet has gone circling on according to the fixed law of gravity, from so simple a beginning endless forms most beautiful and most wonderful have been, and are being **evolved**.

22.2.1. *A Historical Review*

During the eighteenth century, a group of researchers, called naturalists, managed to gather a great deal of information on the flora and fauna in many different areas of our planet. In an attempt to organize and classify this remarkable amount of information, **Carl Linnaeus** (1707–1778) proposed a set of rules to assign genus and species labels to all known living beings. His taxonomy, called *System Naturae* [18], focused solely on the morphological properties of living beings to define the classification. Since this classification criterion was purely morphological, to Linnaeus the terms *species* identified distinct groups with no relation of origin. This perspective, called *fixity of species*, considered that each species was created as it was, and individuals did not experience changes over time. Linnaeus began his study believing this concept, but later rejected it after observing interbreeding between various species. Due to his extensive work in the field, he is considered the founding father of our current taxonomic system.

The accumulation of information provided by naturalists and the progress achieved in the taxonomies led to the adoption of new approaches, different from the fixity of species, and based on the fact that some species came from other species. This idea required defining a new classification that reflected the relationships among organisms. It was called *natural classification.* Although **Georges-Louis Leclerc**, Comte de Buffon (1707–1788), was the first to question Linnaeus's fixity of species, the first to propose a hypothesis on how one species could come from another was **Jean-Baptiste Pierre Antoine de Monet**, Chevalier de Lamarck (1744–1829). Lamarck, in his *Zoological Philosophy* [19], presented a systematic description for the evolution of living beings. For Lamarck, species develop as a result of their reaction and adaptation to the environment. These changes, therefore, must be gradual and will occur over long periods of time. Lamarck believed that certain organs are strengthened by the use that animals make of them, mainly due to the specific nature of their environment. Other organs, in contrast, are atrophied and eventually eliminated because they fall into disuse. For Lamarck, nature developed in the following way: circumstances create a need, that need creates habits, habits produce the changes resulting from the use or disuse of the organ and the means of nature are responsible for setting these modifications. Lamarck believed that these physiological changes acquired over the life of an organism could be transmitted to the offspring. This hypothesis is known as the *inheritance of acquired characteristics* and is also commonly referred to as Lamarckism. We can say, therefore, that Lamarck was the first to formulate a strictly evolutionary hypothesis, although the word "evolution" was at that time reserved for the development of the embryo, so his proposal was referred to as *transformism.* Despite Lamarck's hypothesis, there was no experimental evidence for the existence of mechanisms by which individuals could transmit the alleged improvements acquired over the course of their lives. In fact, Lamarckism is now considered an obsolete theory. The principles governing the transformation of the individual characteristics, which are now commonly accepted by science, were first established by Darwin and Wallace. The principles governing the transmission or inheritance of these characteristics were first established by Mendel.

In 1858, **Charles Robert Darwin** (1809–1882) and **Alfred Russel Wallace** (1823–1913) gave a presentation at the Linnean Society of London on a theory of the evolution of species by means of *natural selection* [20]. One year later, Darwin published *On the Origin of Species* [21], a work in which he provided a detailed explanation of his theory supported by numerous experiments and observations of nature. Darwin's theory—usually known as *Darwinism*—is based on a set of related ideas which try to explain different features of biological reality:

- Living beings are not static; they change continuously: some new organisms are created and some die out. This process of change is gradual, slow, and continuous, with no abrupt or discontinuous steps.
- Species diversify by adapting to different environments or ways of life, thus branching out. The implication of this phenomenon is that all species are somehow related—to varying degrees—and ultimately all species have a single origin in one common and a remote ancestor. That is, all living organisms can be traced back to a single and common origin of life.
- Natural selection is the key to the system. It is conceived as a result of two factors: the inherited natural variability of the individuals of a species, and the selection through survival in the struggle for life, i.e., the fittest individuals, who were born with favorable spontaneous modifications better suited to the environment, and are thus more likely to survive, reproduce and leave offspring with these advantages. This implies that each slight variation, if useful, is preserved.

Although Darwin knew that there should be a mechanism for transmitting these characteristics from the parents to offspring, he was unable to discover the transmission mechanism. It was **Gregor Johann Mendel** (1822–1884) who suggested a number of hypotheses that would set the basic underlying principles of heredity. Mendel's research [22] focused on plants (peas) and especially individual features, all unequivocally different from each other and having the peculiarity of not being expressed in a graduated form, i.e., the feature is only present or not present. This research led Mendel to three important conclusions:

- The inheritance of each trait is determined by "units" or "factors" that are passed on to descendants unchanged. These units are now called *genes*.
- An individual inherits one such unit from each parent for each trait.
- A trait may not show up in an individual but can still be passed on to the next generation. In this sense, the term *phenotype* refers to the set of physical or observable characteristics of an organism, while the term *genotype* refers to the individual's complete collection of genes. The difference between genotype and phenotype is that the genotype can be distinguished by looking at the deoxyribonucleic acid (DNA) of the cells and the phenotype can be established from observing the external appearance of an organism.

Mendel's laws laid the foundation of modern genetics and abolished the idea that characteristics are transmitted from parents to children through bodily fluids so that, once mixed, they cannot be separated, thus causing the offspring to have characteristics that will mix the characteristics of the parents. This theory is called *pangenesis* and is mainly based on observations such as how crossing plants with red flowers with plants with white flowers produces plants with pink flowers. Starting from Mendel's advances in genetics and the concept of natural selection, in the 1930s and 1940s the *modern evolutionary synthesis* was established [23–25]. Basically, this theory [26] served as a link between the unity of evolution ("the gene") and the mechanism of evolution ("the selection"), i.e., gradual changes and natural selection in populations are the primary mechanisms of evolution. According to this theory, genetic variation in populations arises mainly by chance through mutation (alteration or change in the genetic information—genotype—of a living being) and recombination (the mixing of the chromosomes produced at meiosis).

Finally, note that there are also theories that relate learning and evolution. This is the case of the Baldwin effect [27], which was proposed by **James Mark Baldwin**. This theory has also inspired some advances in EC.

22.2.2. *Main Concepts*

In the above description, some important definitions related to evolution and genetics were introduced. This section is devoted to describing some other terms that have been used in some popular books and papers on EC. A complete list of the terms contained in the papers on EC would be too extensive to be included. For this reason, we have selected the most broadly used terms:

- *DNA* (deoxyribonucleic acid): nucleic acid that consists of two long chains of nucleotides twisted into a double helix and joined by hydrogen bonds between the complementary bases adenine and thymine or cytosine and guanine. It is the main constituent of the chromosome and carries the genes as segments along its strands.
- *Chromosome*: structure within the nucleus of eukaryotic cells that bears the genetic material as a threadlike linear strand of DNA.
- *Gene*: as seen in the previous section, Mendel regarded "genes" as inherited factors that determine the external features of living beings. In modern genetics, a "gene" is defined as a sequence of DNA that occupies a specific location on a chromosome.
- *Diploid cell*: a cell that contains two sets of paired chromosomes. For example, humans have 2 sets of 23 chromosomes, for a total of 46 chromosomes. Exact replicas of diploid cells are generated through a process designed mitosis.

- *Haploid cell*: a cell that contains only one complete set of chromosomes. The genesis of a haploid cell can occur by the meiosis of diploid cells or by the mitosis of haploid cells. One haploid cell will merge with another haploid cell at fertilization, i.e., sperm and ova (also known as "gametes").
- *Locus*: the specific position of the chromosome where a gene or other DNA sequence is located.
- *Genetic linkage*: the tendency of genes that are located proximal to each other on a chromosome to be inherited together.
- *Alleles*: variant or alternative forms of a gene that are located at the same position —locus—on a chromosome.
- *Genotype*: genetic information of an organism. This information—contained in the chromosomes of the organism—may or may not be manifested or observed in the individual.
- *Phenotype*: a property observed in an organism, such as morphology, development, or behavior. It is the expression of the genotype in relation to a particular environment.
- *Epistasis*: the type of interaction between genes located at different loci on the same chromosome consisting of one gene masking or suppressing the expression of the other.

22.3. History of Evolutionary Computation

EC is a field of research with a fascinating but complex history. In its origins, several independent researchers proposed numerous approaches with the common feature of using natural evolution to inspire their implementations. Some of the developments were also inspired from other related fields such as artificial life [28] and other areas of artificial intelligence. EC had many independent beginnings, so different terms have been used to refer to concepts that are broadly similar. Given the similarities of the different schemes proposed, the term EC was invented in the early 1990s in an effort to unify the field of evolution-inspired algorithms [29].

Determining the merits of the various authors is not easy, which is why several different versions of the history of EC have been told [30]. In this section, we review the origins of EC, focusing on the most important milestones. Many of the bases of EC were developed in the 1960s and 1970s. During that period, three different popular schemes inspired by natural evolution were devised: evolutionary programming (EP), evolution strategies (ESs) and genetic algorithms (GAs). These schemes were inspired by the same ideas but some details, such as the nature of the representation and the operators applied, were different. In addition, there were several earlier attempts that highly influenced the advances in this area. Some of these proposals can be considered to be the first designed evolutionary algorithms

(EAs). In other cases, the schemes were substantially different from what is currently known as an EA. In any case, they are historically important because they had a significant impact on the subsequent studies carried out in the field. This section reviews the origins along with the three aforementioned types of EAs.

22.3.1. *Origins*

Wright and Cannon [31, 32] were probably the first researchers to influence the subsequent development of EC. They viewed natural evolution as a learning process where the genetic information of species is continuously changed through a trial-and-error mechanism. In this way, evolution can be regarded as a method whose aim is to maximize the adaptiveness of species to their environment. Wright went further and introduced the concept of fitness landscape to relate genotypes and fitness values. This concept has been extended and is widely used today to study the performance of EAs [33]. In addition, he developed one of the first studies where selection and mutation were linked, concluding that a proper balance between them is required to proceed successfully. These ideas were extended by Campbell [34]. He claimed that a blind-variation-and-selective-survival process is one of the main underlying principles of evolution, and hypothesized that "in all processes leading to expansions of knowledge, a blind-variation-and-selective-survival process is involved." This is one of the principles behind universal Darwinism, a proposal that extends the applicability of Darwin's theory to other areas beyond natural evolution.

Turing can also be considered another EC pioneer. In [35], Turing recognized a connection between machine learning and evolution. Specifically, Turing claimed that in order to develop an intelligent computer that passes the famous Turing test, a learning scheme based on evolution might be used. In this regard, the structure of the evolved machine is related to hereditary materials, changes made to the machine are related to mutations, and the use of an experimenter to evaluate the generated machines is related to natural selection. In addition, Turing had previously suggested that these kinds of methods might be used to train a set of networks that are akin to current neural networks [36]. Turing used the term "genetical search" to refer to these kinds of schemes. However, this paper was not published until 1968 [37] because his supervisor considered it a "schoolboy essay" [38]. By the time of its publication, other EAs had already appeared and the term "genetical search" was never adopted by the EC community.

Some important advances were made in the late 1950s and early 1960s, coinciding with the period in which electronic digital computers became more readily available. In this period, several analyses of the population dynamics appearing in evolution were carried out. A survey of the application of digital computers in this field was presented in [12]. Crosby identified three kinds of schemes:

- Methods based on studying the mathematical formulations that emerge in the deterministic analysis of population dynamics. These schemes usually assume an infinite population size and analyze the distributions of genes under different circumstances. An example of this type of scheme is the one developed by Lewontin [39], where the interactions between selection and linkage are analyzed.
- Approaches that simulate evolution but do not explicitly represent a population [40]. In these methods, the frequencies of the different potential genotypes are stored for each generation, resulting in a non-scalable scheme in terms of the number of genes. In addition, a faithful mathematical representation of the evolutionary system is required.
- Schemes that simulate evolution by explicitly maintaining a representation of the population. Fraser and some of his colleagues pioneered these kinds of methods and analyzed this approach in a set of papers published over the course of a decade [41,42]. The main conclusions drawn from these studies were gathered in their seminal book [43]. From its inception, this model was widely accepted, and several researchers soon adopted it [44,45]. In fact, even though there are several implementation details that differ from those used in current EAs, several authors regard the works of Fraser as representing the first invention of a GA [29]. As for the implementation details, the main difference with respect to GAs is that individuals are diploid instead of haploid. However, in our opinion, the key difference is not the implementation but the philosophy behind the use of the scheme. Fraser used its algorithms as a way to analyze population dynamics and not to solve problems, which is the typical current application of EAs.

There were other authors who proposed schemes resembling current EAs. Among them, the works of Friedman, Box, and Friedberg are particularly important and cited often. Friedman [46] hypothesized on the automatic design of control circuits by using a scheme inspired by natural evolution that was termed "selective feedback." His proposals were very different from current ones. For instance, there was no notion of population and/or generations. Moreover, Friedman did not implement his method, and some of his assumptions seem to be overly optimistic [30]. In any event, his research can be considered the first efforts in the field of evolvable hardware.

Box proposed a technique called "Evolutionary Operation" (EVOP) [47] to optimize the management processes of the chemical industry. His technique essentially used a single parent to generate multiple offspring by modifying a few production parameters at a time. Then, one individual was selected to survive to the next generation by considering certain statistical evidence. The system was not autonomous. Specifically, the variation and selection processes required human intervention, so it can be considered the first interactive EA.

The most important contribution of Friedberg et al. to the field of EC was their attempt to automatically generate computer programs using an evolutionary scheme [48, 49]. In the previous papers, Friedberg *et al.* did not identify any relationship between their proposal and natural evolution. However, in subsequent publications by his coauthors, such a relationship was explicitly identified [50]. In their first attempts, the aim was to automatically generate small programs with some simple functionalities that rely on a tailor-made instruction set. In order to direct the search to promising regions, problem-dependent information was considered by defining a variation scheme specifically tailored to the problem at hand. Even with this addition, their success was limited. Even so, some of the analyses they carried out were particularly important for the subsequent achievements in EC. Among their contributions, some of the most important are the following:

- The idea of dividing candidate solutions into classes is a precursor of the notions of *intrinsic parallelism* and *schema*, proposed years later by Holland [51].
- Several instruction sets were tested, showing, for the first time, the influence of genotype-to-phenotype mapping.
- A credit assignment algorithm was used to measure the influence of the single instructions. This idea is closely related to the work of Holland on GAs and classifier systems.

There are several more papers that did not elicit much attention when they were first published, but that proposed techniques very similar to others that were later reinvented. For instance, the work by Reed, Toombs and Barricelli [52] provides several innovations closely related to self-adaptation, crossover, and coevolution[1].

22.3.2. *Evolutionary Programming*

Evolutionary programming (EP) was devised by Fogel [53] while he was engaged in basic research on artificial intelligence for the National Science Foundation. At the time, most attempts to generate intelligent behavior used man as a model [54]. However, Fogel realized that since evolution had been able to create humans and other intelligent creatures, a model mimicking evolution might be successful. Note that, as previously described, some research into this topic had already been published by then. The basic ideas adopted by Fogel are similar: use variation and selection to evolve candidate solutions better adapted to the given goals. However, Fogel was not aware of the existing research and his proposals differed substantially

---

[1] Some preliminary work on coevolution was started in [57].

from them, meaning that his models can be considered a reinvention of evolution-based schemes.

Philosophically, the coding structures utilized in EP are an abstraction of the phenotype of different species [55]. As a result, the encoding of candidate solutions can be freely adapted to better support the requirements of the problems at hand. Since there is no sexual communication between different species, this view of candidate solutions also justifies the lack of recombination operators in EP. Thus, the non-application of recombination operators is due to a conceptual rather than a technical view. The lack of recombination, the freedom to adapt the encoding, and the use of a probabilistic survivor selection operator—not used in the initial versions of EP—might be considered the main features that distinguished EP from other EC paradigms [56].

In his first designs, Fogel reasoned that one of the main features that characterize intelligent behavior is the capacity to predict one's environment, coupled with a translation of said predictions into an adequate response so as to accomplish a given objective. A finite state transducer is a finite state machine (FSM) that allows a sequence of input symbols to be transformed into a sequence of output symbols. Depending on the states and given transitions, they can be used to model different situations and cause different transformations. Thus, Fogel viewed FSMs as a proper mechanism for dealing with the problem of generating intelligent behavior. In his initial experiments, the aim was to develop a FSM capable of predicting the behavior of an environment. The environment was considered to be a sequence of symbols belonging to a given input alphabet. The aim was to develop a FSM that, given the symbols previously generated by the environment, could predict the next symbol to emerge from the environment.

The initial EP proposal operates as follows. First, a population with N random FSMs is created. Then, each member of the population is mutated, creating as many offspring as parents. Five mutation modes are considered: add a state, delete a state, change the next state of a transition, change the output symbol of a transition, or change the initial state. Mutation operators are chosen randomly—other ways were also tested—and in some cases the offspring are subjected to more than one mutation. Finally, the offspring are evaluated and the best N FSMs are selected to survive. FSMs are evaluated in light of their capacity to correctly predict the next symbols in known sequences. Initially, the fitness is calculated by considering a small number of symbols, but as the evolution progresses, more symbols are attached to the training set.

In the first experiments carried out involving EP, different prediction tasks were tested: periodic sequences of numbers, sequences with noise, non-stationary environments, etc. Subsequently, more difficult tasks were considered. Among other applications, EP was used to tackle pattern recognition, classification, and control system design. All this research resulted in the publication of the first book on EC [58]. EP was also used to evolve strategies for gaming [59]. This work is particularly important because it is one of the first applications of coevolution.

It is also important to remark that in most of the initial studies on EP, the amount of computational results was not ample because of the limited computational power at the time of its inception. Most of these initial experiments were recapitulated and extended in a later period [60], providing a much deeper understanding of EP.

In the 1970s, most of the research into EP was conducted under the guidance of Dearholt. One of the main contributions of his work was the application of EP to practical problems. EP was applied to pattern recognition in regular expressions [61] and handwritten characters [62] and to classify different types of electrocardiograms [63]. These works incorporated several algorithmic novelties. Among them, the most influential were the use of several simultaneous mutation operators and the dynamic adaptation of the probabilities associated with the different mutation schemes.

Starting in the 1980s, EP diversified by using other arbitrary representations of candidate solutions in order to address different problems. The number of applications that have been addressed with EP is huge. In [60], EP was used to solve routing problems by considering a permutation-based encoding. In order to tackle the generation of computer programs, tree-based encoding was used in [64]. Real-valued vectors were used to deal with continuous optimization problems by [65] and to train neural networks by [66]. During this period, the feeling was that by designing problem-specific representations with operators specifically tailored to face a given problem, more efficient searches might be performed [54]. In fact, most EP practitioners defended that, by designing intelligent mutation schemes, the use of recombination operators might be avoided [64, 67].

Among the aforementioned topics, the application of EP to continuous optimization problems saw a large expansion in the 1990s. Over this period, great efforts were made to develop self-adaptive schemes. In self-adaptation, some of the parameters required by the algorithm are bound to each individual and evolved with the original variables. The variables of the problem are called *object parameters*, while those newly attached are called *strategy parameters*. Initial proposals adapted the scale factor of Gaussian mutation [68]. In more advanced variants of EP, several mutation operators are considered simultaneously [65]. Since self-adaptive schemes surpassed more traditional EP variants, self-adaptation was adopted by practitioners addressing problems where real encoding was not used, becoming a common mechanism in EP [69]. Self-adaptive EP for continuous optimization presents several similarities with ESs. One of the most important differences is that EP does not include recombination. In addition, some implementation details were also different in the first variants devised [17]. For instance, the order in which the object and strategy parameters were subjected to mutation was different in the two schemes, though these differences vanished over time. Moreover, it has been shown that there are cases where mutation alone can outperform schemes with recombination and vice versa [70]. There is also evidence that indicates that it is promising to adapt the parameters associated with crossover [71], which further stretches the barriers between EP and ESs. Since self-adaptation for continuous optimization was first proposed in ESs, the history of and advances in self-adaption for continuous optimization are presented in the section devoted to ESs.

22.3.3. *Evolution Strategies*

In the mid-1960s, three students at the Technical University of Berlin—Bienert, Schwefel and Rechenberg—were studying practical problems that arise in fluid mechanics and some related fields. Their desire was to build robots that could autonomously solve engineering problems [30]. They formulated these engineering tasks as optimization problems and developed autonomous machines that were automatically modified using certain rules. They also made some initial attempts at using traditional optimization schemes. However, since the problems were noisy and multimodal, their schemes failed to provide promising solutions. In order to avoid these drawbacks, they decided to apply mutation and selection methods analogous to natural evolution. Rechenberg published the first report on ESs by applying these ideas to minimize the total drag of a body in a wind tunnel [72]. Subsequently, other problems such as the design of pipes and efficient flashing nozzles were addressed [30].

Philosophically, the coding structures utilized in ESs are an abstraction of the phenotype of different individuals [55]. This is why the encoding of candidate solutions can be freely adapted to better support the requirements of the problems at hand. In addition, recombination among individuals is allowed in spite of not being implemented in the initial variants of ESs.

In the first problems tested, a set of quantitative discrete variables had to be adjusted. The initial proposal was very similar to the current (1+1)-ES and works as follows. First, a random solution is created and considered to be the current solution. Then, the current solution is mutated by slightly changing each variable. Specifically, mutation is implemented by emulating a Galton pin-board, so binomial distributions are used. The principle behind the design of this operator is to apply small mutations more frequently than large mutations, as is the case in nature. The current solution is replaced by the mutant only if the mutant solution is at least as good. This process is repeated until the stopping criterion is reached. Empirical evidence revealed the promising behavior of these kinds of schemes with respect to more traditional optimization methods.

In 1965, Schwefel first implemented an ES in a general computer [73]. In this case, ESs were mainly applied to continuous optimization. The most important contribution of the new variant was the incorporation of Gaussian mutation with zero mean, which is still the most typical distribution used nowadays. The mutation operator could be controlled by tuning the standard deviations—or step size—of the Gaussian distribution. Studies on the step size resulted in the first theoretical analyses of ESs.

As previously discussed, initial ES variants only kept a single solution at a time. However, in the late 1960s, the use of populations with several individuals was introduced. The first population-based scheme tested is now known as $(\mu+1)$-ES. This scheme uses a population with μ individuals. These individuals are used to create a new individual through recombination and mutation. Then, the best μ individuals from the $\mu+1$ individuals are selected to survive. This scheme resembles the steady state selection that was popularized much later in the field of GAs [74].

ESs were extended further to support any number of parents and offspring. In addition, two different selection schemes and a notation that is still in use were proposed. The first selection comprises the $(\mu+\lambda)$-ES. In this case, λ offspring are created from a population with μ individuals. Then, the best μ individuals from the union of parents and offspring are selected to survive. Schemes that consider the second kind of selection are known as (μ, λ)-ES. In this case, the best μ individuals from the λ offspring are selected to survive.

When ESs were first developed, the papers were written in German, meaning that they were accessible to a very small community. However, in 1981, Schwefel published the first book on ESs in English [75]. Since then, several researchers have adopted ESs and the number of studies in this area has grown enormously. Schwefel's book focuses on the use of ESs for continuous optimization, which is in fact the field where ESs have been more successful. In his book, Schwefel discusses, among other topics, the use of different kinds of recombinations and the adaptation of the Gaussian distributions adopted for mutation. Regarding recombination, some controversies and misunderstandings have appeared. The use of adaptive mutation is one of the distinguishing features of ESs, and the history of and advances in both topics are described herein. Most of the papers reviewed in this chapter involve continuous single-objective optimization problems. However, it is important to note that the application of ESs has not been limited to these kinds of problems. For instance, multi-objective [76], mixed-integer [77], and constrained problems [78] have also been addressed.

22.3.3.1. Recombination

Initially, four different recombination schemes were proposed by combining two different properties [75]. First, two choices were given for the number of parents taking part in creating an offspring: *bisexual* or *multisexual*. In bisexual recombination—also known as local— two parents are selected and they are used to recombine each parameter value. In the case of multisexual recombination— also known as global—different pairs of parents are selected for each parameter value. Thus, more than two individuals can potentially participate in the creation of each offspring. In addition, two different ways of combining two parameter values were proposed. In the *discrete* case, one of the values is selected randomly. In the *intermediary* case, the mean value of both parameters is calculated.

In the above recombination schemes, the number of parents taking part in each recombination cannot be specified. Rechenberg proposed a generalization that changed this restriction [79]. Specifically, a new parameter, ρ, is used to specify the number of parents taking part in the creation of each individual. The new schemes were called $(\mu/\rho, \lambda)$ and $(\mu/\rho+\lambda)$. Further extensions of the intermediary schemes were developed by weighting the contributions of the different individuals taking part in the recombination [80]. Different ways of assigning weights have been extensively tested. Previous schemes were not proper generalizations of the initial schemes, in the sense that the intermediary case calculates the mean of ρ individuals, and not the mean of two individuals selected from among a larger set, as was the case in the initial schemes. A more powerful generalization that allowed for both the original operators and those proposed by Rechenberg to be implemented was devised [81]. Thus, using the notation proposed in this last paper is preferable.

The situation became even more complicated because of a misinterpretation of the initial crossover schemes. In the survey presented in [82], the authors showed a formula indicating that in global recombination, one parent is chosen and held fixed while the other parent is randomly chosen anew for each component.[2] This new way of recombination was adopted by many authors over the following years, so when using global recombination, the exact definition must be carefully given.

22.3.3.2. *Adaptive mutation*

One of the main features that characterizes ESs is its mutation operator. In the case of continuous optimization, mutation is usually based on Gaussian distributions with zero mean. In most cases, individuals are disturbed by adding a random vector generated from a multivariate Gaussian distribution, i.e., the candidate solutions x_i are perturbed using Eq. (22.1). In this equation, C represents a covariance matrix.

$$x_i' = x_i + N_i(0, C) \tag{22.1}$$

---

[2]To the best of our knowledge, [82] was the first paper where this definition was given.

From the inception of ESs, it is clear that the features of C might have a significant effect on search performance. As a result, several methods that adapt C during the run have been developed. Many ES variants can be categorized into one of the following groups depending on how C is adapted [83]:

- Schemes where the surfaces of equal probability density are hyper-spheres. In these cases, the only free adaptive parameter is the global step size or standard deviation.
- Schemes where the surfaces of equal probability density are axis-parallel hyper-ellipsoids. In these cases, the most typical approach is to have as many free adaptive parameters as there are dimensions.
- Schemes where the surfaces of equal probability density are arbitrarily oriented hyper-ellipsoids. In these cases, any positive-definite matrix can be used, resulting in $(n^2 + n)/2$ free adaptive parameters.

The first adaptive ES considered the global step size as the only free parameter. These schemes originated from the studies presented in [84], which analyzed the convergence properties of ESs depending on the relative frequency of successful mutations. These analyses led to the first adaptive scheme [75], where the global step size is adjusted by an online procedure with the aim of producing successful mutations with a ratio equal to $1/5$. This rule is generally referred to as the "$\frac{1}{5}$ success rule of Rechenberg." However, this rule is not general so it does not work properly for many functions, which is why self-adaptive ESs were proposed. In the first of such variants, the only strategy parameter was the global step size, and this strategy parameter was subjected to variation using a log-normal distributed mutation.

In the case of schemes where the surfaces of equal probability are axis-parallel hyperellipsoids, a larger number of methods have been devised. A direct extension of previous methods considers the self-adaptation of n strategy parameters, where n is the number of dimensions of the optimization problem at hand. In such a case, each strategy parameter represents the variance in each dimension. Another popular ES variant is the *derandomized* scheme [85]. Ostermeier *et al.* realized that in the original self-adaptive ES, the interaction of the random elements can lead to a drop in performance. The scheme is based on reducing the number of random decisions made by ESs. Another interesting extension is termed *accumulation* [86]. In these variants, the adaptation is performed considering information extracted from the best mutations carried out during the whole run, and not only in the last generation. Note that these last variants favor adaptation instead of self-adaptation.

By adapting the whole covariance matrix, correlations can be induced among the mutations performed involving the different parameters, thus making ESs more suitable for dealing with non-separable functions. The first adaptive scheme where the whole matrix is adapted was presented in [75]. In this case, the coordinate system in which the step size control takes place, as well as the step sizes themselves, are self-adapted. In general, this method has not been very successful because it requires very large populations to operate properly. A very efficient and popular scheme is covariance matrix adaptation (cma-es) [83]. In this scheme, derandomization and accumulation are integrated in an adaptive scheme whose aim is to build covariance matrices that maximize the creation of mutation vectors that were successful in previous generations of the execution. This scheme is very complex and the practitioner must specify a large number of parameters. This has led to simpler schemes being devised. For instance, the covariance matrix self-adaptation scheme (cmsa) [87] reduces the number of parameters required by combining adaptation and self-adaptation. Many other not so popular schemes that are capable of adapting the whole covariance matrix have been devised. The reader is referred to [88] for a broader review of these kinds of schemes.

Finally, it is important to note that several schemes that favor some directions without adapting a full covariance matrix have been devised. For instance, in [89], the main descent direction is adapted. The main advantage of these kinds of schemes is the reduced complexity in terms of time and space. Since the time required for matrix computation is usually negligible in comparison to the function evaluation phase, these schemes have not been very popular. Still, they might be useful, especially for large-scale problems, where the cost of computing the matrices is much higher. In addition, several other adaptive and self-adaptive variants that do not fit into the previous categorization have been devised. For instance, some schemes that allow the use of Gaussian distributions with a non-zero mean have been proposed [90]. In addition, some methods not based on Gaussian mutation have been designed [91]. In this chapter, we have briefly described the fundamentals of different methods. The reader is referred to [88, 92, 93] for discussions of recent advances and implementation details for several ES variants.

22.3.4. *Genetic Algorithms*

Holland identified the relationship between the adaptation process that appears in natural evolution and optimization [51], and conjectured that it might have critical roles in several other fields, such as learning, control, and/or mathematics. He proposed an algorithmic framework inspired by these ideas, which was initially called the Genetic Plan and was subsequently renamed the Genetic Algorithm. GAs are based on progressively modifying a set of structures with the aim of adapting them to a given environment. The specific way of making these modifications is inspired by genetics and evolution. His initial aim was to formally study the phenomenon of adaptation. However, GAs were soon used as problem solvers. Specifically, GAs have been successfully applied to numerous applications, such as machine learning, control, and search and function optimization. A very popular use of GAs appeared in the development of *learning classifier systems*, which is an approach to machine learning based on the autonomous development of rule-based systems capable of generalization and inductive learning. The application of GAs as function optimizers was also soon analyzed [94], defining metrics, benchmark problems, and methodologies to perform comparisons. This is probably the field where GAs have been most extensively and successfully applied.

The evolutionary schemes devised by Holland are very similar to those previously designed by Bremermann [95] and Bledsoe [96]. In fact, "by 1962 there was nothing in Bremermann's algorithm that would distinguish it from what later became known as genetic algorithms" [97]. Moreover, they pioneered several ideas that were developed much later, such as the use of multisexual recombination, the use of real-encoding evolutionary approaches, and the adaptation of mutation rates. Moreover, since Bremermann's algorithm was very similar to the schemes described earlier by Fraser, some authors regard GAs as having been reinvented at least three times [29].

Philosophically, the coding structures utilized in GAs are an abstraction of the genotype of different individuals [55]. Specifically, each trial solution is usually coded as a vector, termed *chromosome*, and each element is denoted with the term *gene*. A candidate solution is created by assigning values to the genes. The set of values that can be assigned are termed *alleles*. In the first variants of GAs, there was an emphasis on using binary representations—although using other encodings is plausible—so even when continuous optimization problems were addressed, the preferred encoding was binary. Goldberg claimed that "GAs work with a coding of the parameter set, not the parameters themselves" [98], which is a distinguishing feature of GAs. This results in the requirement to define a mapping between genotype and phenotype.

The working principles of GAs are somewhat similar to those of EP and ESs. However, unlike other schemes, in most early forms of GAs, recombination was emphasized over mutation. The basic operation of one of the first GAs—denoted as canonical GA or simple GA—is as follows. First, a set of random candidate solutions is created. Then, the performance of each individual is evaluated and a *fitness value* is assigned to each individual. This fitness value is a measure of each individual's quality, and in the initial GA variants, it had to be a positive value. Based on the fitness values, a temporary population is created by applying *selection*. This selection process was also called *reproduction* in some of the first works on GAs [98]. The best-performing individuals are selected with larger probabilities and might be included several times in the temporary population. Finally, in order to create the population of the next generation, a set of variation operators is applied. The most popular operators are crossover and mutation, but other operators such as inversion, segregation, and translocation have also been proposed [98]. In most of the early research on GAs, more attention was paid to the crossover operator. The reason is that crossover was believed to be the major source of the power behind GAs, while the role of mutation was to prevent the loss of diversity [13]. This first variant was soon extended by Holland's students. Some of these extensions include the development of game-playing strategies, the use of diploid representations, and the use of adaptive parameters [99].

Among Holland's many contributions, the schema theorem was one of the most important. Holland developed the concepts of schemata and hyperplanes to explain the working principles of GAs. A schema is basically a template that allows grouping candidate solutions. In a problem where candidate solutions are represented with l genes, a schema consists of l symbols. Each symbol can be an allele of the corresponding gene or "*," which is the "don't care" symbol. Each schema designates the subset of candidate solutions in which the corresponding representations match every position in the schema that is different from "*." For instance, the candidate solutions "0 0 1 1" and "0 1 0 1" belong to the schema "0 * * 1." Note that the candidate solutions belonging to a schema form a hyperplane in the space of solutions. Holland introduced the concept of *intrinsic parallelism*—subsequently renamed as *implicit parallelism*—to describe the fact that the evaluation of a candidate solution provides valuable information on many different schemata. He hypothesized that GAs operate by better sampling schemata with larger mean fitness values.

The concept of schema was also used to justify the use of binary encoding. Specifically, Holland showed that by using binary encoding the number of schemata sampled in each evaluation can be maximized. However, the use of binary encoding was not extensively tested in his preliminary works, and its application has been a source of controversy. One of the first problems detected with the use of binary encoding is that, depending on the length of the vector, precision or efficiency might be sacrificed. It is not always easy to strike a proper balance, so dynamic parameter encoding methods have also been proposed [100]. Goldberg weakened the binary-encoding requirement by claiming that "the user should select the smallest alphabet that permits a natural expression of the problem" [98]. A strict interpretation of this means that the requirement for binary alphabets can be dropped [99]. In fact, several authors have been able to obtain better results by using representations different from the binary encoding, such as floating point representations. For instance, Michalewicz carried out an extensive comparison between binary and floating point representations [101]. He concluded that GAs operating with floating-point representations are faster and more consistent and provide a higher precision. Subsequently, Fogel and Ghozeil demonstrated that there are equivalences between any bijective representation [102]. Thus, for GAs with bijective representations, interactions that take place between the representation and other components are keys to their success.

Holland used the above concepts to develop the *schema theorem*, which provides lower bounds to the change in sampling rate for a single hyperplane from one generation to the next. For many years, the schema theorem was used to explain the working operation of GAs. However, several researchers have pointed out some weaknesses that call into question some of the implications of the theorem [103]. Some of the most well-known weaknesses pointed out by several researchers are the following. First, the schema theorem only provides lower bounds for the next generation and not for the whole run. Second, the schema theorem does not fully explain the behavior of GAs in problems that present large degrees of inconsistencies in terms of the bit values preferred [104]. Finally, considering the typical population sizes used by most practitioners, the number of samples belonging to high-order schemata—those with few "*"—is very low, so in these cases the theorem is not very accurate. In general, the controversies are not with the formulae, but with the implications that can be derived from them. The reader is referred to [105] for a more detailed discussion of this topic. Finally, we should note that other theoretical studies not based on the concept of schema have also been proposed to explain the behavior of GAs. In some cases, the model is simplified by assuming infinitely large population sizes [106]. In other cases, the Markov model has been used to analyze simple GAs with finite population sizes [107].

Due to the complexity of analyzing the mathematics behind GAs, there is a large amount of work focused on the practical use of GAs. For instance, the initial GA framework has been extended by considering several selection and variation operators. Regarding the former, note that, initially, selection was only used to choose the individuals that were subjected to variation. This operator is now known as *parent selection* or *mating selection* [17]. However, in most current GAs, a *survivor selection* or *environmental selection* is also carried out. The aim of this last selection—also called *replacement*—is to choose which individuals will survive to the next generation. In its most general form, survivor selection can operate on the union of parents and offspring. The number of selection operators defined in recent decades is very large, ranging from deterministic to stochastic schemes. Parent selection is usually carried out with stochastic operators. Some of the most well-known stochastic selectors are *fitness proportional selection*, *ranking selection*, and *tournament selection*. Alternatively, survivor selection is usually based on deterministic schemes. In the case of the survivor selection schemes, not only is the fitness used, but the age of individuals might also be considered. Some of the most-well known schemes are *age-based replacement* and *replace-worst*. Also of note is the fact that *elitism* is included in most current GAs. Elitist selectors ensure that the best individual from among parents and offspring is always selected to survive.

In these kinds of schemes, and under some assumptions, asymptotic convergence is ensured [108] and, in general, there is empirical evidence of its advantages. A topic closely related to replacement is the *steady state model* [74]. In the steady state model, after the creation of one or maybe a few offspring, the replacement phase is executed. Note that this model is closely related to the *generation gap* concept previously defined in [94]. The generation gap was introduced into GAs to permit overlapping populations.

In the same way, several crossover schemes have been proposed in the literature. The first GAs proposed by Holland operated with one-point crossover, whose operation is justified in light of the schema theorem. Specifically, Goldberg [98] claimed that in GAs with one-point crossover, short, low-order and highly fit schemata—which received the name of building blocks[3]—are sampled, recombined, and resampled to form strings of potentially higher fitness. However, this hypothesis has been very controversial. One of the basic features of one-point crossover is that bits from a single parent that are close together in the encoding are usually inherited together, i.e., it suffers from *positional bias*. This idea was borrowed in part from the biological concept of *coadapted alleles*. However, several authors have questioned the importance of this property [105]. In fact, Goldberg claimed that since many encoding decisions are arbitrary, it is not clear whether a GA operating in this way might obtain the desired improvements [98]. The inversion operator might in some way alleviate this problem by allowing the reordering of genes so that linkages between arbitrary positions can be created. Another popular attempt to identify linkages was carried out in the messy GA [110], which explicitly manipulates schemata and allows linking non-adjacent positions. More advanced linkage learning mechanisms have been depicted recently [111]. In addition, given the lack of a theory that fully justifies the use of one-point crossover, several different crossover operators, as well as alternative hypotheses to explain the effectiveness of crossover, have been proposed. Among these hypotheses, some of the widely accepted consider crossover as a macro-mutation or as an adaptive mutation [112]. Regarding alternative definitions of crossover operators, it has been shown empirically that depending on the problem, operators different from one-point crossover might be preferred. For instance, Syswerda showed the proper behavior of uniform crossover with a set of benchmark problems [113]. In the case of binary encoding, some of the most well-known crossover operators are the two-point crossover, multipoint crossover, segmented crossover, and uniform crossover [17]. Note that some multisexual crossover operators have also been provided. In fact,

---

[3]The term building block has also been used with slightly different definitions [109].

well before the popularization of GAs, Bremermann had proposed their use [30]. For other representations, a large set of crossover operators has been devised [17].

As mentioned earlier, several components and/or parameters in GAs have to be tuned. The first GA variants lacked procedures to automatically adapt these parameters and components. However, several adaptive GAs have also been proposed [114]. In these schemes, some of the parameters and/or components are adapted by using the feedback obtained during the search. In addition, most current GAs do not operate on binary strings, relying instead on encodings that fit naturally with the problem at hand. As a result, several variation operators specific to different chromosome representations have been defined. The reader is referred to [17] for a review of some of these operators.

22.4. A Unified View of Evolutionary Computation

The three main branches of EC—(EP, GAs, and ESs)—developed quite independently of each other over the course of about 25 years, during which several conferences and workshops devoted to specific types of EAs were held, such as the Evolutionary Programming Conference. However, in the early 1990s, it was clear to some researchers that these approaches have several similarities, and that findings in one kind of approach might also be useful for other types of EAs. Since these researchers considered that the topics covered by the conferences at the time period were too narrow, they decided to organize a workshop called "Parallel Problem Solving From Nature" that would accept papers on any type of EA, as well as papers based on other metaphors of nature. This resulted in a growth in the number of interactions and collaborations among practitioners of the various EC paradigms, and as a result, the different schemes began to merge naturally. This unification process continued at the *Fourth International Conference on Genetic Algorithms*, where the creators of EP, GAs, and ESs met. At this conference, the terms EC and EA were proposed and it was decided to use these terms as the common denominators of their approaches. Basically, an EA was defined as any approach toward solving problems that mimics evolutionary principles.[4] Similar efforts were undertaken at other conferences, such as in the *Evolutionary Programming Conference*. Finally, these unifying efforts resulted in the establishment in 1993 of the journal *Evolutionary Computation*, published by MIT Press. Furthermore, the original conferences were soon replaced by more general ones, such as the *Genetic and Evolutionary Computation Conference*[5] and the *IEEE Congress on Evolutionary*

---

[4]See http://ls11-www.cs.uni-dortmund.de/rudolph/ppsn
[5]The conference originally known as "International Conference on Genetic Algorithms" was renamed as "Genetic and Evolutionary Computation Conference" in 1999.

Computation. In addition, other journals specifically devoted to EC have appeared, such as the *IEEE Transactions on Evolutionary Computation*.

It is worth noting that since the different types of EAs were developed in an independent way, many ideas have been reinvented and explored more than once. In addition, there was no clear definition for each kind of scheme, so the boundaries between EC paradigms become blurred. Thus, for many contemporary EAs, it is very difficult and even unfair to claim that they belong to one or another type of EA. For instance, a scheme that adopts proportional parent selection, self-adaptation, and stochastic replacement merges ideas that were originally depicted in each of the initial types of EAs. For this reason, when combining ideas that were originated by practitioners of the different EC paradigms—which is very typical—, it is preferable to use the generic terms EC and EA.

In recent decades, several papers comparing the differences and similarities of the different types of EAs have appeared [115]. In addition, some authors have proposed unifying and general frameworks that allow for the implementation of any of these schemes [116, 117]. In fact, note that with a pseudocode as simple as the one shown in Algorithm 22.1, any of the original schemes can be implemented. Although this simple pseudocode does not fit with every contemporary EA, it does capture the main essence of EC by combining population, random variation, and selection. Two interesting books where the unifying view is used are: [17, 117].

The last two decades have seen an impressive growth in the number of EC practitioners. Thus, the amount of research that has been conducted in the area is huge. For instance, EAs have been applied to several kinds of optimization problems, such as constrained [118] and multi-objective [1, 119] optimization problems. Also, several efforts have been made to address the problem of premature convergence [120]. Studies conducted on this topic include the use of specific selection schemes such as fitness sharing [121], crowding schemes [94], restarting

---

Algorithm 22.1: Pseudocode of an Evolutionary Algorithm: A Unified View

---

1: **Initialization**: Generate an initial population with N individuals
2: **Evaluation**: Evaluate every individual in the population
3: **while** (not fulfilling the stopping criterion) **do**
4:    **Mating selection**: Select the parents to generate the offspring
5:    **Variation**: Apply variation operators to the mating pool to create a child population
6:    **Evaluation**: Evaluate the child population
7:    **Survivor selection**: Select individuals for the next generation
8: **end while**

---

mechanisms [122], and the application of multi-objective concepts to tackle single-objective problems [123]. Other highly active topics include the design of parallel EAs [124] and memetic algorithms [125]—related to Lamarck's hypothesis and the Baldwin effect, which were discussed earlier—which allows hybridizing EAs with more traditional optimization schemes. Note that for most of the topics that have been studied over the past decades, there were some preliminary works that were developed in the 1960s. For instance, the island-based model [126] was proposed in [127], while some preliminary works on hybrid models were presented as early as 1967 [128]. The aforementioned works represent only a very small cross-section of the topics that have been covered in recent years. It is beyond the scope of this chapter to present an extensive review of current research, so readers are referred to some of the latest papers published in some of the most popular conferences and journals in the field.

Interestingly, it is also remarkable that while considerable efforts have been made to unify the different EC paradigms, some new terms for referring to specific classes of EAs have also appeared in recent decades. However, in these last cases, their distinguishing features are clear, so there is no ambiguity in the use of such terms. For instance, Differential Evolution [129] is a special type of EA where the mutation is guided by the differences appearing in the current population. Another popular variant is Genetic Programming [130], which focuses on the evolution of computer programs.

Finally, we would like to state that while there has been considerable research into EC in the last decade, the number of topics that have yet to be addressed and further explored in the field is huge. Moreover, in recent years, there has been a remarkable increase in the number of proposals based on alternative nature-inspired phenomena [10]. In some cases, they have been merged with evolutionary schemes. Thus, similarly to the period where synergies were obtained by combining ideas that arose within different evolutionary paradigms, the interactions among practitioners of different nature-inspired algorithms might be beneficial for advancing this field.

22.5. Design of Evolutionary Algorithms

EC is a general framework that can be applied to a large number of practical applications. Among them, the use of EC to tackle optimization problems is probably the most popular one [17]. The generality of EC and the large number of different components that have been devised imply that when facing new problems, several design decisions must be made. These design decisions have an important impact on the overall performance [131], meaning that they must be made very carefully, and particularly, in order to draw proper conclusions, statistical comparisons are a crucial step in the design process [132]. Additionally, theoretical analyses support the proper design of EAs [133]. Thus, while EAs are usually referred to as general solvers, most successful EAs do not treat problems as black-box functions. Instead, information on the problem is used to alter the definition of the different components of the EA [134]. This section discusses some of the main decisions involved in the design of EAs and describes some of the most well-known components that have been used to handle optimization problems.

One of the first decisions to make when applying EAs is the way in which individuals are represented. The representation of a solution involves selecting a data structure to encode solutions [135] and, probably more importantly, a way to transform this encoding (genotype) into the phenotype [136]. Note that, in direct representations, there is no transformation between genotype and phenotype, whereas in cases where such a transformation is required, the representation is said to be indirect. Note that while in many cases a direct representation is effective, indirect representation allows for the introduction of problem-specific knowledge, the use of standard genetic operators and, in some cases, it facilitates the treatment of constraints, among other benefits. Several efforts to facilitate the process of designing, selecting, and comparing representations have been made. The recommendations provided by Goldberg [137], [138], [139] and [140] are interesting but too general, and in some cases there is a lack of theory behind these recommendations. A more formal framework is given by [136] that introduces some important features that should be taken into account, such as redundancy, scaling, and locality. The aim of this last framework is to reduce the black art behind the selection of proper representations. However, since analyses and recommendations are based on simplifications of EAs, there is usually a need to resort to trial-and-error mechanisms, which are combined with the analyses of these recommendations and features. Finally, it is important to note that the representation chosen influences other design decisions. For instance, variation operators are applied to the genotype, so its design depends on the representation.

In order to illustrate the representation process, let us consider a simple optimization problem such as the minimization of the function $f(x, y, z)$ (Eq. 22.2), where each variable is an integer number in the range $[0, 15]$.

$$f(x, y, z) = (x - 1)^2 + (y - 2)^2 + (z - 7)^2 - 2 \qquad (22.2)$$

Considering some of the first GAs designed, an alternative is to represent each number in base 2 with 4 binary digits. In such a case, individuals consist of a sequence of 12 binary digits or genes (based on the GAs nomenclature). Another possible choice—which is more widespread nowadays—is to use a gene for each variable, where each gene can have any value between 0 and 15. Figure 22.2 shows some candidate solutions considering both the binary and integer representations.

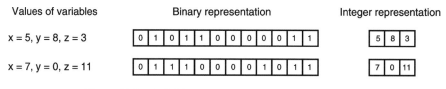

Figure 22.2: Individuals with binary and integer encoding.

Each cell represents a gene of the chromosome. Note that for this case, the base-2 encoding is an example of an indirect representation, whereas the second encoding is a direct representation. Another example of an indirect representation appeared at the *Second Edition of the Wind Farm Layout Optimization Competition* [141]. The purpose of this contest was to design optimizers to select the positions of turbines. Several of the top-ranked contestants noted that most high-quality solutions aligned several of the turbines in specific directions. Thus, instead of directly optimizing the positions, having problem-dependent information—relationship among directions and positions—can be used to design an indirect encoding, which focuses the search on promising regions of the search space. Consequently, instead of looking for thousands of positions, just a few parameters had to be optimized.

Another important component of EAs is the fitness function. The role of the fitness function is to assign a quality measure to each individual. Note that some problems might involve several requirements and objectives. In order to deal with these multiple aims, they might be combined into the fitness function to generate a global notion of quality. A taxonomy regarding typical kinds of requirements and methods to combine them is discussed in [142]. In simple EAs, the fitness function is used mainly in the selection stages. However, in more complex algorithms, such as memetic algorithms, other components also take the fitness function into account. The term *fitness function* is usually associated with maximization [17], but it has caused some controversy because in some papers minimization fitness functions are employed. Changing minimization into maximization or vice versa in the implementation of EAs is in many cases trivial, but when connecting selection operators and fitness functions, both components should agree in the optimization direction. Moreover, as discussed later, some selection operators make sense only when the fitness function is maximized and every candidate solution attains a positive fitness. Thus, when designing the fitness function, the way in which it will be used must be taken into account.

In order to illustrate the definition of a fitness function, let us consider an even simpler optimization problem, such as the minimization of the function $f(x)$ (Equation 22.3), where x is a real number in the range $(0, 15)$. In this case, a plausible fitness function for the minimization of $f(x)$ that guarantees that the fitness value of any candidate solution is positive is given by f_1 (Eq. 22.4). Note that 191 is larger than the maximum value of the function $f(x)$ in the range considered. Usually, this maximum value is not known, but any value greater than 191 might also be used if positive values are desired. However, depending on the other components—especially the selection operators—this specific constant might affect the performance of the optimization process. Alternatively, a fitness function that might produce negative values is given by the simpler function $f_2(x) = -f(x)$. In this last case, estimating the maximum value of the function is not a requirement. However, not every selection operator can be used with f_2.

$$f(x) = (x - 1)^2 - 5 \tag{22.3}$$

$$f_1(x) = -f(x) + 191 \tag{22.4}$$

Regarding the task of designing a fitness function, this is a straightforward process in some cases because it is just equal to (or a simple transformation of) the objective function. In these cases, the objective function is said to be self-sufficient [6]. For instance, in the case of the Traveling Salesman Problem, most effective optimizers just consider the minimization of the distance traveled, so the fitness function is viewed as the inverse of the distance. However, in other cases, this task is more complex. For instance, let us consider the Satisfiability Problem. In this case, each solution is mapped in the original problem to a 0 or 1 value, and the aim is to find a solution whose value is 1. Using only the binary value is not enough to guide the optimization process, so there is a need to define a more complex fitness function.

The definition of the fitness function heavily impacts the expected performance of EAs. The analysis of the fitness landscape is complex, especially for combinatorial optimization, but it is useful in identifying drawbacks of the proposed fitness function [143]. Recent advances such as local optima networks [144] facilitate the analyses, especially when dealing with high-dimensional problems. As an example, in the case of maximizing the nonlinearity of Boolean functions, the direct use of nonlinearity as the fitness function causes large plateaus that hinder the proper performance of EAs. Extending the fitness function by including additional information from the Walsh–Hadamard transform provides a better guide that results in improved performance [145, 146]. Finally, note that in some cases, the fitness function is adapted online once certain issues with the optimization process are detected [147].

An additional issue that might emerge with the design of fitness functions is that they might be too computationally expensive. This would result in just a few generations being evolved, with potentially poor results. Surrogate models can be used to alleviate this difficulty [148]. The main idea behind surrogate models is to approximate the fitness function with a more inexpensive process than the one initially designed. Different ways of building surrogate models have been proposed. Problem-dependent models rely on ad hoc knowledge of the problem and on the fact that in order to distinguish between very poor and high quality solutions, very accurate functions are not required. Thus, functions with different trade-offs between accuracy and computational cost might be designed and applied at different stages of the optimization process [149]. In contrast, problem-independent models usually rely on machine learning methods and other statistical procedures [150, 151]. Note that while the most typical use of surrogate models is to reduce the computational cost by providing inexpensive fitness functions, they have also been applied to redesign other components of an EA [148].

The selection operator is another important component that has a large impact on the overall performance of EAs [152]. One of the aims of selection is to focus the search on the most promising regions. Some of the first selectors designed made their decisions considering only the individuals' fitness values. However, other factors, such as age or diversity, are usually considered in state-of-the-art EAs [153]. Selection operators are applied in two different stages: parent selection and replacement. In both cases, stochastic and deterministic operators can be used, though the most popular choice is to apply stochastic operators in the parent selection stage and deterministic operators in the replacement phase [17].

A very popular stochastic selection operator is the *fitness proportional* operator. In the fitness proportional selection, the total fitness F is first calculated as the sum of the fitness values of the individuals in the current population. Then, the selection probability of an individual I_i (p_i) is calculated using Eq. (22.5), where fit represents the fitness function. In order to apply this selection scheme, the fitness function of every individual must be positive. Let us assume that we are using the fitness function given in Eq. (22.4) and that our current population consists of three individuals with $x = 2$, $x = 5$, and $x = 12$. Table 22.1 shows the fitness value and the selection probability associated with each individual. One of the weaknesses of this operator is that it is susceptible to function transposition, which means that its behavior changes if the fitness function of every individual is transposed by adding a constant value. This is illustrated in Figure 22.3. In this figure, a population

Table 22.1:   Fitness values and selection probabilities induced by the fitness proportional selection

Individual	Fitness	Selection Prob.
$x = 2$	195	0.43
$x = 5$	180	0.40
$x = 12$	75	0.17

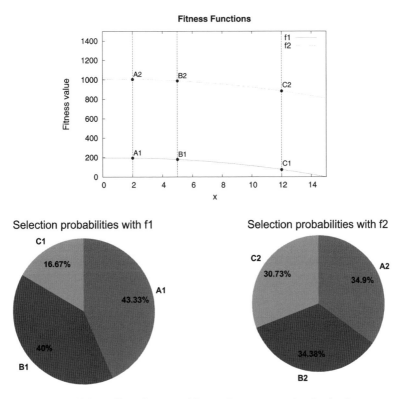

Figure 22.3: Effect of transposition on fitness proportional selection.

consisting of individuals A, B, and C is used. Two fitness functions are considered: the first one (f_1) is shown in Eq. (22.4), while the second one (f_2) is generated by replacing the value 191 in Eq. (22.4) with the value 1000. Figure 22.3 shows the fitness values of the different individuals, as well as the selection probabilities associated with the individuals when f_1 and f_2 are applied. Since the selection scheme is susceptible to function transposition, these probabilities differ, as can be seen in the pie charts. In addition, note that with f_2, the selection pressure is very low, i.e., all individuals are selected with very similar probabilities. The reason is that when the differences between the fitness values are small with respect to their absolute values, the selection pressure vanishes. This last effect is another of the known weaknesses that can affect fitness proportional selection.

$$p_i = \frac{fit(I_i)}{F} \qquad (22.5)$$

Another quite popular stochastic selection operator is the *tournament selection*. In this case, each time an individual must be selected, there is a competition between k randomly selected individuals, with the best one being chosen. Tournament selection has very different features than *fitness proportional* selection. For instance, it is invariant to transposition of the fitness function. However, this does not mean that it is superior to *fitness proportional* selection. For instance, when facing some fitness landscapes, *fitness proportional* selection can induce a larger focus on exploitation than *tournament selection*. Depending on the problem at hand, on the stopping criterion, and on the other components applied, this might be desired or counterproductive, so it is the task of the designer to analyze the interactions between the selectors and the fitness landscape.

The variation phase is another quite important component that is usually adapted to the problem at hand. Among the different operators, the crossover and mutation operators are the most popular, and a large number of different choices have been devised for each of them. For instance, [17] present several operators that can be applied with binary, integer, floating-point, and permutation representations. In order to better illustrate the working operation of crossover, two popular crossover operators that can be applied with binary, integer, and floating-point, representations are presented: the one-point and the uniform crossover. One-point crossover (Figure 22.4) operates by choosing a random gene, and then splitting both parents at this point and creating the two children by exchanging the tails. Alternatively, uniform crossover (Figure 22.5) works by treating each gene independently, and the parent associated with each gene is selected randomly. This might be implemented by generating a string with L random variables from a uniform distribution over $[0, 1]$, where L is the number of genes. In each position, if the value is below 0.5, the gene is inherited from the first parent; otherwise, it is inherited from the second parent. The second offspring is created using inverse mapping.

It is important to note that the crossover schemes discussed induce different linkages between the genes. For instance, in the one-point crossover, genes that are close in the chromosome are usually inherited together, while this is not the case in the uniform crossover. Depending on the meaning of each gene and on its position in the chromosome, introducing this kind of linkage might make sense or not. Thus, when selecting the crossover operator, the representation of the individuals must

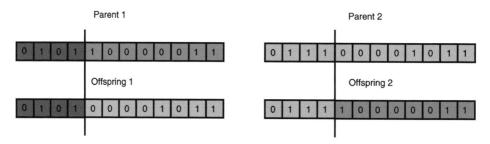

Figure 22.4:   Operation of one-point crossover.

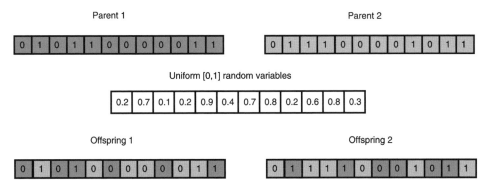

Figure 22.5: Operation of uniform crossover.

be taken into account. Finally, operators that try to learn a proper linkage between genes have been devised [111]. These kinds of operators have yielded significant benefits in several cases.

Note also that in many cases, problem-dependent crossover and mutation operators are designed. Properly designed crossover operators detect characteristics that are important for the problem and that are present in the parents. They then create offspring by combining these features. For instance, in the Graph Coloring Problem, the authors noted that the important feature is not the specific color assigned to each node, but the groups of nodes sharing the same color. Thus, ad hoc operators that inherit these kinds of features have been designed [154]. Additionally, ad hoc operators might establish a linkage between genes by considering problem-dependent knowledge. For instance, in the Frequency Assignment Problem, antennas that interact strongly with one another are inherited and/or mutated together with a larger probability than unrelated antennas [155]. Finally, in the case of crossover operators, it is also important to distinguish between the parent-centric and mean-centric operators because of the impact that this feature has on the dynamics of the population [156]. Properly designed operators that adapt this feature to the needs of the problem at hand have excelled [157].

Note that while we have discussed different components involved in the design of EAs independently, there are important interactions among them. Thus, regarding their performance, it is not possible to make categorical assertions. Depending on the components used, different balances between exploitation and exploration can be induced. It is therefore very important to recognize how to modify this balance, since it is one of the keys to success. In some cases, there is no explicit mechanism for managing the trade-off between exploration and exploitation. Note that due to the way EAs work, the diversity maintained in the population is one way to control this trade-off [158]. In fact, many authors regard the proper management of diversity as one of the cornerstones of proper performance [120]. Thus, several explicit strategies for managing diversity have been proposed [159]. In some ways, this can be viewed as another component of EAs, but it is not a completely independent component because it is highly coupled to some of the components already discussed. For instance, in [120], diversity management methods are classified as selection-based, population-based, crossover/mutation-based, fitness-based, and replacement-based, depending on the sort of component that is modified. Additionally, some implicit mechanisms that alter this degree, such as multi-objectivization, have been devised [123].

It is also important to note that for many problems, trajectory-based strategies are usually considered more powerful than EAs in terms of their intensification capabilities. As a result, several state-of-the-art optimizers are hybrids that incorporate trajectory-based strategies and/or other mechanisms to promote intensification [6, 160]. Thus, knowing the different ways of hybridizing algorithms is an important aspect of mastering the design of EAs.

Finally, given the difficulties in understanding and theoretically analyzing the interactions that appear in EAs, several components and parameterizations are typically tested during the design phase. By analyzing the performance of different components and the reasons for their good or poor performance, some alternative designs might be tested until a good enough scheme is obtained. Moreover, note that it is not just the components that have to be selected. A set of parameters must also be adapted to the problem at hand, and it is important that it is done systematically [114, 161]. In this regard, two kinds of methodologies have been devised [162]. *Parameter tuning* [163] can be thought of as searching for good parameters and components before the algorithm is executed, whereas *parameter control* strategies [164] alter the components and parameters during the run. This can be used, for instance, with the aim of applying an ensemble of variation operators whose probabilities and other internal parameters are changed during the optimization process [165, 166].

Table 22.2 summarizes some of the most important aspects to define when designing and running EAs. Note that in addition to all these aspects, we also have to consider the internal parameters associated with many of the operators mentioned above. We would like to remark that in the design of proper EAs, it is very important to ascertain the features and implications of using different components and parameter values and recognize the drawbacks that each of them can circumvent. This is because of the impossibility of testing every parameter and component combination, given how time-consuming and computationally insensitive this task is. Thus, designing efficient EAs for new problems is a complex task that requires knowledge in several areas that has been developed in recent decades through both experimental and theoretical studies. Generic tools for developing metaheuristics can facilitate this entire process [167–170].

Table 22.2:   Some aspects to consider when designing EAs

Component or aspect	Related decisions
Individual	Representation Evaluation (*fitness function*)
Population	Size Population sizing scheme Initialization
Evolution	Mutation operator Crossover operator Repair operator Intensification operator Probabilities for applying operators Parent selection Replacement scheme Diversity Management Strategy Hybridization
Stopping criterion	Number of evaluations of individuals Generations Time Given signs of stagnation A certain solution quality is achieved
Parameterization	Parameter control Parameter tuning

22.6. Concluding Remarks

EC is a very active area of research that studies the design and application of a set of algorithms that draw their inspiration from natural evolution. The first studies that influenced the development of EC date back to at least the 1930s. However, it was during the 1960s that the roots of EC were established. During the first stages of EC, several independent researchers devised different schemes that were applied to a diverse range of applications. Three different types of schemes were developed: EP, ESs, and GAs. Although each type of scheme had its own features, further developments made it clear that these schemes had a lot in common, so they began to merge in a natural way. In the 1990s, the terms EC and EA were proposed with the aim of unifying the terminology, and they were soon widely adopted by the community. In fact, it is now very difficult to claim that a given state-of-the-art EA belongs to any of the previous classes because they usually combine components from several types of schemes. The number of studies that have been carried out in the last decades is vast. These studies have yielded significant advances in EC; as a result, the number of problems that have been addressed with EAs has grown enormously.

One of the main handicaps of EC is that mastering EAs is a very complex task. One of the reasons is that despite the huge amount of research conducted in recent years, the discipline cannot yet be considered fully mature. For instance, we are still in a period where different researchers have opposing views with respect to several aspects of EAs, and, therefore, much more research is still required to fully understand EAs and the large number of different components that have been devised by various authors. Thus, designing EAs to tackle new problems is a complex task that involves trial-and-error processes and in-depth analyses in order to understand the interactions and implications of the different components proposed for the problem at hand. Fortunately, many tools that facilitate the use of EAs are now available and recent years have seen significant efforts made to facilitate the application of EAs. In the near future, we expect this area to grow even more as it continues to develop on its path to maturity.

Acknowledgments

The first author gratefully acknowledges financial support from CONACyT grant no. 2016-01-1920 (*Investigación en Fronteras de la Ciencia 2016*) and from a project from the 2018 SEP-Cinvestav Fund (application no. 4). The second author acknowledges the financial support from CONACyT through "Ciencia Básica" project no. 285599 and from the "Laboratorio de Supercómputo del Bajío" with project no. 300832. The third author acknowledges financial support from the Spanish Ministry of Economy, Industry and Competitiveness as part of the program "I+D+i Orientada a los Retos de la Sociedad" (contract number TIN2016-78410-R).

References

[1] Coello Coello, C. A., Lamont, G. B. and Van Veldhuizen, D. A. (2007). *Evolutionary Algorithms for Solving Multi-Objective Problems*, 2nd edn. (Springer, New York), ISBN 978-0-387-33254-3.

[2] Nocedal, J. and Wright, S. J. (2006). *Numerical Optimization*, 2nd edn. (Springer, New York, NY, USA).

[3] Brassard, G. and Bratley, P. (1996). *Fundamentals of Algorithms* (Prentice-Hall, New Jersey).

[4] Weise, T. (2008). *Global Optimization Algorithms: Theory and Application* (http://www.it-weise.de/).

[5] Glover, F. and Kochenberger, G. A. (eds.) (2003). *Handbook of Metaheuristics* (Kluver Academic Publishers), ISBN 1-4020-7263-5.

[6] Talbi, E.-G. (2009). *Metaheuristics: From Design to Implementation* (John Wiley & Sons), ISBN 978-0470278581.

[7] Gendreau, M. and Potvin, J.-Y. (eds.) (2019). *Handbook of Metaheuristics*, 3rd edn. (Springer, New York, NY, USA).

[8] Hussain, K., Salleh, M. N. M., Cheng, S. and Shi, Y. (2019). Metaheuristic research: a comprehensive survey, *Artif. Intell. Rev.*, **52**, pp. 2191–2233.

[9] Blum, C. and Roli, A. (2003). Metaheuristics in combinatorial optimization: overview and conceptual comparison, *ACM Comput. Surv.*, **35**(3), pp. 268–308.

[10] Del Ser, J., Osaba, E., Molina, D., Yang, X.-S., Salcedo-Sanz, S., Camacho, D., Das, S., Suganthan, P. N., Coello Coello, C. A. and Herrera, F. (2019). Bio-inspired computation: where we stand and what's next, *Swarm Evol. Comput.*, **48**, pp. 220–250.

[11] Molina, D., LaTorre, A. and Herrera, F. (2018). An insight into bio-inspired and evolutionary algorithms for global optimization: review, analysis, and lessons learnt over a decade of competitions, *Cognit. Comput.*, **10**, pp. 517–544.

[12] Crosby, J. L. (1967). Computers in the study of evolution, *Sci. Prog. Oxford*, **55**, pp. 279–292.

[13] Mitchell, M. (1998). *An Introduction to Genetic Algorithms* (MIT Press, Cambridge, MA, USA).

[14] Darwish, A., Hassanien, A. E. and Das, S. (2020). A survey of swarm and evolutionary computing approaches for deep learning, *Artif. Intell. Rev.*, **53**, pp. 1767–1812.

[15] Mirjalili, S., Faris, H. and Aljarah, I. (2020). *Evolutionary Machine Learning Techniques* (Springer).

[16] Everett, J. E. (2000). Model building, model testing and model fitting, in *The Practical Handbook of Genetic Algorithms: Applications*, 2nd edn. (CRC Press, Inc., Boca Raton, FL, USA), pp. 40–68.

[17] Eiben, A. E. and Smith, J. E. (2003). *Introduction to Evolutionary Computing*, Natural Computing Series (Springer).

[18] Linnaeus, C. (1735). *Systema naturae, sive regna tria naturae systematice proposita per secundum classes, ordines, genera, & species, cum characteribus, differentiis, synonymis, locis* (Theodorum Haak).

[19] de Monet de Lamarck, J. B. P. A. (1809). *Philosophie zoologique: ou Exposition des considérations relative à l'histoire naturelle des animaux* (Chez Dentu).

[20] Darwin, C. and Wallace, A. (1858). On the tendency of species to form varieties; and on the perpetuation of varieties and species by natural means of selection, *Zool. J. Linn. Soc.*, **3**, pp. 46–50.

[21] Darwin, C. (1859). *On the Origin of Species by Means of Natural Selection* (Murray), or the Preservation of Favored Races in the Struggle for Life.

[22] Mendel, G. (1865). Experiments in plant hibridization, in *Brünn Natural History Society*, pp. 3–47.

[23] Fisher, R. (1930). *The Genetical Theory of Natural Selection* (Oxford University Press), ISBN 0-19-850440-3.

[24] Wright, S. (1931). Evolution in mendelian populations, *Genetics*, **16**, pp. 97–159.

[25] Haldane, J. B. S. (1932). *The Causes of Evolution* (Longman, Green and Co.), ISBN 0-691-02442-1.

[26] Huxley, J. S. (1942). *Evolution: The Modern Synthesis* (Allen and Unwin).

[27] Baldwin, J. (1986). A new factor in evolution, *Am. Nat.*, **30**, pp. 441–451.

[28] Conrad, M. and Pattee, H. H. (1970). Evolution experiments with an artificial ecosystem, *J. Theor. Biol.*, **28**(3), pp. 393–409.

[29] Fogel, D. B. (1995). *Evolutionary Computation: Toward a New Philosophy of Machine Intelligence* (IEEE Press, Piscataway, NJ, USA).

[30] Fogel, D. B. (1998). *Evolutionary Computation: The Fossil Record* (Wiley-IEEE Press).

[31] Wright, S. (1932). The roles of mutation, inbreeding, crossbreeding and selection in evolution, in *VI International Congress of Genetics*, Vol. 1, pp. 356–366.

[32] Cannon, W. B. (1932). *The Wisdom of the Body* (W. W. Norton & Company, Inc.).

[33] Richter, H. (2014). Fitness landscapes: from evolutionary biology to evolutionary computation, in H. Richter and A. Engelbrecht (eds.), *Recent Advances in the Theory and Application of Fitness Landscapes, Emergence,Complexity and Computation*, Vol. 6 (Springer Berlin Heidelberg), pp. 3–31.

[34] Campbell, D. T. (1960). Blind variation and selective survival as a general strategy in knowledge-processes, in M. C. Yovits and S. Cameron (eds.), *Self-Organizing Systems*

(Pergamon Press, New York), pp. 205–231.

[35] Turing, A. M. (1950). Computing machinery and intelligence, *Mind*, **59**, pp. 433–460.

[36] Turing, A. M. (1948). Intelligent Machinery, Report, National Physical Laboratory, Teddington, UK.

[37] Evans, C. R. and Robertson, A. D. J. (eds.) (1968). *Cybernetics: Key Papers* (University Park Press, Baltimore, MD, USA).

[38] Burgin, M. and Eberbach, E. (2013). Recursively generated evolutionary turing machines and evolutionary automata, in X.-S. Yang (ed.), *Artificial Intelligence, Evolutionary Computing and Metaheuristics, Studies in Computational Intelligence*, Vol. 427 (Springer Berlin Heidelberg), pp. 201–230.

[39] Lewontin, R. C. (1964). The interaction of selection and linkage. I. General considerations; heterotic models, *Genetics*, **49**(1), pp. 49–67.

[40] Crosby, J. L. (1960). The use of electronic computation in the study of random fluctuations in rapidly evolving populations, *Philos. Trans. R. Soc. London, Ser. B*, **242**(697), pp. 550–572.

[41] Fraser, A. S. (1957). Simulation of genetic systems by automatic digital computers. I. Introduction, *Aust. J. Biol. Sci.*, **10**, pp. 484–491.

[42] Fraser, A. S. and Burnell, D. (1967). Simulation of genetic systems XII. Models of inversion polymorphism, *Genetics*, **57**, pp. 267–282.

[43] Fraser, A. S. and Burnell, D. (1970). *Computer Models in Genetics* (McGraw-Hill, NY).

[44] Gill, J. L. (1965). Effects of finite size on selection advance in simulated genetic populations, *Aust. J. Biol. Sci.*, **18**, pp. 599–617.

[45] Young, S. S. (1966). Computer simulation of directional selection in large populations. I. The programme, the additive and the dominance models, *Genetics*, **53**, pp. 189–205.

[46] Friedman, G. J. (1956). Selective feedback computers for engineering synthesis and nervous system analogy, Master's thesis, University of California, Los Angeles.

[47] Box, G. E. P. (1957). Evolutionary operation: a method for increasing industrial productivity, *Appl. Stat.*, **6**(2), pp. 81–101.

[48] Friedberg, R. M. (1958). A learning machine: part I, *IBM J. Res. Dev.*, **2**(1), pp. 2–13.

[49] Friedberg, R. M., Dunham, B. and North, J. H. (1959). A learning machine: part II, *IBM J. Res. Dev.*, **3**(3), pp. 282–287.

[50] Dunham, B., Fridshal, D., Fridshal, R. and North, J. H. (1963). Design by natural selection, *Synthese*, **15**(1), pp. 254–259.

[51] Holland, J. H. (1975). *Adaptation in Natural and Artificial Systems* (University of Michigan Press, Ann Arbor, MI, USA).

[52] Reed, J., Toombs, R. and Barricelli, N. A. (1967). Simulation of biological evolution and machine learning: I. Selection of self-reproducing numeric patterns by data processing machines, effects of hereditary control, mutation type and crossing, *J. Theor. Biol.*, **17**(3), pp. 319–342.

[53] Fogel, L. J. (1962). Autonomous automata, *Ind. Res.*, **4**, pp. 14–19.

[54] Fogel, L. J. (1999). *Intelligence through Simulated Evolution: Forty Years of Evolutionary Programming*, Wiley Series on Intelligent Systems (Wiley).

[55] Fogel, D. B. (1994). An introduction to simulated evolutionary optimization, *IEEE Trans. Neural Networks*, **5**(1), pp. 3–14.

[56] Fogel, D. B. and Chellapilla, K. (1998). Revisiting evolutionary programming, in *Proc. SPIE*, Vol. 3390, pp. 2–11.

[57] Barricelli, N. A. (1962). Numerical testing of evolution theories, *Acta Biotheor.*, **16**(1–2), pp. 69–98.

[58] Fogel, L. J., Owens, A. J. and Walsh, M. J. (1966). *Artificial Intelligence through Simulated Evolution* (John Wiley & Sons).

[59] Fogel, L. J. and Burgin, G. H. (1969). Competitive goal-seeking through evolutionary programming, Tech. Rep. Contract AF 19(628)-5927, Air Force Cambridge Research Labs.

[60] Fogel, L. J. and Fogel, D. B. (1986). Artificial intelligence through evolutionary programming, Tech. Rep. PO-9-X56-1102C-1, U.S. Army Research Institute, San Diego, CA.

[61] Lyle, M. (1972). An investigation into scoring techniques in evolutionary programming, Master's thesis, New Mexico State University, Las Cruces, New Mexico, USA.

[62] Cornett, F. N. (1972). An application of evolutionary programming to pattern recognition, Master's thesis, New Mexico State University, Las Cruces, New Mexico, USA.

[63] Dearholt, D. W. (1976). Some experiments on generalization using evolving automata, in *9th Hawaii Internation Conference on System Sciences* (Western Periodicals, Honolulu), pp. 131–133.

[64] Chellapilla, K. (1997). Evolving computer programs without subtree crossover, *IEEE Trans. Evol. Comput.*, **1**(3), pp. 209–216.

[65] Yao, X., Liu, Y. and Lin, G. (1999). Evolutionary programming made faster, *IEEE Trans. Evol. Comput.*, **3**(2), pp. 82–102.

[66] Porto, V. W. and Fogel, D. B. (1995). Alternative neural network training methods [active sonar processing], *IEEE Expert*, **10**(3), pp. 16–22.

[67] Fogel, D. B. and Atmar, J. W. (1990). Comparing genetic operators with gaussian mutations in simulated evolutionary processes using linear systems, *Biol. Cybern.*, **63**(2), pp. 111–114.

[68] Fogel, D. B., Fogel, L. J. and Atmar, J. W. (1991). Meta-evolutionary programming, in *Asilomar Conference in Signals Systems and Computers, 1991*, pp. 540–545.

[69] Fogel, L. J., Angeline, P. J. and Fogel, D. B. (1995). An evolutionary programming approach to self-adaptation on finite state machines, in *Annual Conference on Evolutionary Programming IV*, pp. 355–365.

[70] Richter, J. N., Wright, A. and Paxton, J. (2008). Ignoble trails—where crossover is provably harmful, in G. Rudolph, T. Jansen, S. Lucas, C. Poloni and N. Beume (eds.), *Parallel Problem Solving from Nature PPSN X, Lecture Notes in Computer Science*, Vol. 5199 (Springer Berlin Heidelberg), pp. 92–101.

[71] Jain, A. and Fogel, D. B. (2000). Case studies in applying fitness distributions in evolutionary algorithms. II. Comparing the improvements from crossover and Gaussian mutation on simple neural networks, in *2000 IEEE Symposium on Combinations of Evolutionary Computation and Neural Networks*, pp. 91–97.

[72] Rechenberg, I. (1965). Cybernetic solution path of an experimental problem, Tech. Rep. Library Translation 1122, Royal Air Force Establishment.

[73] Schwefel, H.-P. (1965). *Kybernetische Evolution als Strategie der experimentellen Forschung in der Strömungstechnik*, Dipl.-Ing. Thesis, Technical University of Berlin, Hermann Föttinger–Institute for Hydrodynamics.

[74] Whitley, D. and Kauth, J. (1988). *GENITOR: A Different Genetic Algorithm* (Colorado State University, Department of Computer Science).

[75] Schwefel, H.-P. (1981). *Numerical Optimization of Computer Models* (John Wiley & Sons, Inc., New York, NY, USA).

[76] Igel, C., Hansen, N. and Roth, S. (2007). Covariance Matrix adaptation for multi-objective optimization, *Evol. Comput.*, **15**(1), pp. 1–28.

[77] Li, R., Emmerich, M. T. M., Eggermont, J., Bäck, T., Schütz, M., Dijkstra, J. and Reiber, J. H. C. (2013). Mixed integer evolution strategies for parameter optimization, *Evol. Comput.*, **21**(1), pp. 29–64.

[78] Mezura-Montes, E. and Coello Coello, C. A. (2005). A simple multimembered evolution strategy to solve constrained optimization problems, *IEEE Trans. Evol. Comput.*, **9**(1), pp. 1–17.

[79] Rechenberg, I. (1978). Evolutionsstrategin, in B. Schneider and U. Ranft (eds.), *Simulations-methoden in der Medizin und Biologie* (Springer-Verlag, Berlin, Germany), pp. 83–114.

[80] Bäck, T. and Schwefel, H.-P. (1993). An overview of evolutionary algorithms for parameter optimization, *Evol. Comput.*, **1**(1), pp. 1–23.

[81] Eiben, A. E. and Bäck, T. (1997). Empirical investigation of multiparent recombination operators in evolution strategies, *Evol. Comput.*, **5**(3), pp. 347–365.

[82] Bäck, T., Hoffmeister, F. and Schwefel, H.-P. (1991). A survey of evolution strategies, in *Proceedings of the Fourth International Conference on Genetic Algorithms* (Morgan Kaufmann), pp. 2–9.

[83] Hansen, N. and Ostermeier, A. (2001). Completely derandomized self-adaptation in evolution strategies, *Evol. Comput.*, **9**(2), pp. 159–195.

[84] Rechenberg, I. (1973). *Evolutionsstrategie: Optimierung technischer Systeme nach Prinzipien der biologischen Evolution* (Frommann-Holzboog, Stuttgart).

[85] Ostermeier, A., Gawelczyk, A. and Hansen, N. (1994a). A derandomized approach to self-adaptation of evolution strategies, *Evol. Comput.*, **2**(4), pp. 369–380.

[86] Ostermeier, A., Gawelczyk, A. and Hansen, N. (1994b). Step-size adaptation based on non-local use of selection information, in Y. Davidor, H.-P. Schwefel and R. Manner (eds.), *Parallel Problem Solving from Nature PPSN III, Lecture Notes in Computer Science*, Vol. 866 (Springer Berlin Heidelberg), pp. 189–198.

[87] Beyer, H.-G. and Sendhoff, B. (2008). Covariance matrix adaptation revisited—the CMSA evolution strategy—, in G. Rudolph, T. Jansen, S. Lucas, C. Poloni and N. Beume (eds.), *Parallel Problem Solving from Nature—PPSN X, Lecture Notes in Computer Science*, Vol. 5199 (Springer Berlin Heidelberg), pp. 123–132.

[88] Rudolph, G. (2012). Evolutionary strategies, in G. Rozenberg, T. Bäck and J. Kok (eds.), *Handbook of Natural Computing* (Springer Berlin Heidelberg), pp. 673–698.

[89] Poland, J. and Zell, A. (2001). Main vector adaptation: a CMA variant with linear time and space complexity, in L. Spector, E. D. Goodman, A. Wu, W. B. Langdon, H.-M. Voigt, M. Gen, S. Sen, M. Dorigo, S. Pezeshk, M. H. Garzon and E. Burke (eds.), *Proceedings of the Genetic and Evolutionary Computation Conference (GECCO-2001)* (Morgan Kaufmann, San Francisco, California, USA), pp. 1050–1055.

[90] Ostermeier, A. (1992). An evolution strategy with momentum adaptation of the random number distribution, in R. Manner and B. Manderick (eds.), *Parallel Problem Solving from Nature 2, PPSN-II* (Elsevier, Brussels, Belgium), pp. 199–208.

[91] Yao, X. and Liu, Y. (1997). Fast evolution strategies, in P. Angeline, R. Reynolds, J. Mc-Donnell and R. Eberhart (eds.), *Evolutionary Programming VI, Lecture Notes in Computer Science*, Vol. 1213 (Springer Berlin Heidelberg), pp. 149–161.

[92] Bäck, T., Foussette, C. and Krause, P. (2013). *Contemporary Evolution Strategies*, Natural Computing Series (Springer).

[93] Li, Z., Lin, X., Zhang, Q. and Liu, H. (2020). Evolution strategies for continuous optimization: a survey of the state-of-the-art, *Swarm Evol. Comput.*, **56**, p. 100694.

[94] De Jong, K. A. (1975). An analysis of the behavior of a class of genetic adaptive systems., Ph.D. thesis, University of Michigan, Ann Arbor, Michigan, USA.

[95] Bremermann, H. J. (1962). Optimization through evolution and recombination, in M. C. Yovits, G. T. Jacobi and G. D. Golstine (eds.), *Proceedings of the Conference on Self-Organizing Systems* (Spartan Books, Washington, DC), pp. 93–106.

[96] Bledsoe, W. (1961). The use of biological concepts in the analytical study of "systems", Tech. Rep. Technical report of talk presented to ORSA-TIMS national meeting held in San Francisco, California, The University of Texas at Austin, USA.

[97] Fogel, D. B. and Anderson, R. W. (2000). Revisiting Bremermann's genetic algorithm. I. Simultaneous mutation of all parameters, in *2000 IEEE Congress on Evolutionary Computation*, Vol. 2, pp. 1204–1209.

[98] Goldberg, D. E. (1989). *Genetic Algorithms in Search, Optimization, and Machine Learning, Artificial Intelligence* (Addison-Wesley).

[99] Bäck, T., Fogel, D. B. and Michalewicz, Z. (1997). *Handbook of Evolutionary Computation*, 1st edn. (IOP Publishing Ltd., Bristol, UK).

[100] Schraudolph, N. and Belew, R. (1992). Dynamic Parameter Encoding for genetic algorithms, *Mach. Learn.*, **9**(1), pp. 9–21.

[101] Michalewicz, Z. (1994). *Genetic Algorithms + Data Structures = Evolution Programs* (Springer-Verlag New York, Inc., New York, NY, USA).

[102] Fogel, D. B. and Ghozeil, A. (1997). A note on representations and variation operators, *IEEE Trans. Evol. Comput.*, **1**(2), pp. 159–161.

[103] Altenberg, L. (1995). The Schema Theorem and Price's Theorem, in D. Whitley and M. D. Vose (eds.), *Foundations of Genetic Algorithms 3* (Morgan Kaufmann, San Francisco), pp. 23–49.

[104] Heckendorn, R. B., Whitley, D. and Rana, S. (1996). Nonlinearity, hyperplane ranking and the simple genetic algorithm, in R. K. Belew and M. D. Vose (eds.), *Foundations of Genetic Algorithms 4*, pp. 181–201.

[105] Whitley, D. and Sutton, A. (2012). Genetic algorithms: a survey of models and methods, in G. Rozenberg, T. Bäck and J. Kok (eds.), *Handbook of Natural Computing* (Springer Berlin Heidelberg), pp. 637–671.

[106] Vose, M. D. and Liepins, G. (1991). Punctuated equilibria in genetic search, *Complex Syst.*, **5**, pp. 31–44.

[107] Nix, A. and Vose, M. D. (1992). Modeling genetic algorithms with Markov chains, *Ann. Math. Artif. Intell.*, **5**(1), pp. 79–88.

[108] Eiben, A. E., Aarts, E. H. L. and Hee, K. M. (1991). Global convergence of genetic algorithms: a Markov chain analysis, in H.-P. Schwefel and R. Manner (eds.), *Parallel Problem Solving from Nature, Lecture Notes in Computer Science*, Vol. 496 (Springer Berlin Heidelberg), pp. 3–12.

[109] Radcliffe, N. J. (1997). Schema processing, in T. Bäck, D. B. Fogel and Z. Michalewicz (eds.), *Handbook of Evolutionary Computation* (Institute of Physics Publishing and Oxford University Press, Bristol, New York), pp. B2.5:1–10.

[110] Goldberg, D. E., Korb, B. and Deb, K. (1989). Messy genetic algorithms: motivation, analysis, and first results, *Complex Syst.*, **3**(5), pp. 493–530.

[111] Chen, Y. and Lim, M. H. (2008). *Linkage in Evolutionary Computation*, Studies in Computational Intelligence (Springer).

[112] Sivanandam, S. N. and Deepa, S. N. (2007). *Introduction to Genetic Algorithms* (Springer).

[113] Syswerda, G. (1989). Uniform Crossover in Genetic Algorithms, in *Proceedings of the 3rd International Conference on Genetic Algorithms* (Morgan Kaufmann Publishers Inc., San Francisco, CA, USA), pp. 2–9.

[114] Lobo, F. G., Lima, C. F. and Michalewicz, Z. (2007). *Parameter Setting in Evolutionary Algorithms*, 1st edn. (Springer Publishing Company, Incorporated).

[115] Bäck, T., Rudolph, G. and Schwefel, H.-P. (1993). Evolutionary programming and evolution strategies: similarities and differences, in D. B. Fogel and J. W. Atmar (eds.), *Second Annual Conference on Evolutionary Programming* (San Diego, CA), pp. 11–22.

[116] Bäck, T. (1996). *Evolutionary Algorithms in Theory and Practice: Evolution Strategies, Evolutionary Programming, Genetic Algorithms* (Oxford University Press, Oxford, UK).

[117] De Jong, K. A. (2006). *Evolutionary Computation: A Unified Approach* (MIT Press).

[118] Mezura-Montes, E. (2009). *Constraint-Handling in Evolutionary Optimization*, 1st edn. (Springer).

[119] Miguel Antonio, L. and Coello Coello, C. A. (2018). Coevolutionary multiobjective evolutionary algorithms: survey of the state-of-the-art, *IEEE Trans. Evol. Comput.*, **22**(6), pp. 851–865.

[120] Crepinšek, M., Liu, S.-H. and Mernik, M. (2013). Exploration and exploitation in evolutionary algorithms: a survey, *ACM Comput. Surv.*, **45**(3), pp. 35:1–35:33.

[121] Goldberg, D. E. and Richardson, J. (1987). Genetic algorithms with sharing for multimodal function optimization, in *Proceedings of the Second International Conference on Genetic Algorithms and their Application* (L. Erlbaum Associates Inc., Hillsdale, NJ, USA), pp. 41–49.

[122] Eshelman, L. (1991). The CHC adaptive search algorithm: how to have safe search when engaging in nontraditional genetic recombination, *Foundations of Genetic Algorithms*, pp. 265–283.

[123] Segura, C., Coello, C., Miranda, G. and León, C. (2016). Using multi-objective evolutionary algorithms for single-objective constrained and unconstrained optimization, *Ann. Oper. Res.*, **240**, pp. 217–250.

[124] Alba, E. (2005). *Parallel Metaheuristics: A New Class of Algorithms* (John Wiley & Sons, NJ, USA).

[125] Moscato, P. (1989). On evolution, search, optimization, genetic algorithms and martial arts: towards memetic algorithms, Tech. Rep. C3P Report 826, California Institute of Technology.

[126] Ma, H., Shen, S., Yu, M., Yang, Z., Fei, M. and Zhou, H. (2019). Multi-population techniques in nature inspired optimization algorithms: a comprehensive survey, *Swarm Evol. Comput.*, **44**, pp. 365–387.

[127] Bossert, W. (1967). Mathematical optimization: are there abstract limits on natural selection? in P. S. Moorehead and M. M. Kaplan (eds.), *Mathematical Challenges to the Neo-Darwinian Interpretation of Evolution* (The Wistar Institute Press, Philadelphia, PA), pp. 35–46.

[128] Kaufman, H. (1967). An experimental investigation of process identification by competitive evolution, *IEEE Trans. Syst. Sci. Cybern.*, **3**(1), pp. 11–16.

[129] Storn, R. and Price, K. (1995). Differential evolution: a simple and efficient adaptive scheme for global optimization over continuous spaces, Tech. rep., International Computer Science Institute, Berkeley, Tech. Rep. TR95012.

[130] Koza, J. R. (1990). Genetic programming: a paradigm for genetically breeding populations of computer programs to solve problems, Tech. rep., Stanford University, Stanford, California, USA.

[131] Rothlauf, F. (2011). *Design of Modern Heuristics: Principles and Application*, 1st edn. (Springer Publishing Company, Incorporated), ISBN 3540729615.

[132] Carrasco, J., Garca, S., Rueda, M., Das, S. and Herrera, F. (2020). Recent trends in the use of statistical tests for comparing swarm and evolutionary computing algorithms: practical guidelines and a critical review, *Swarm Evol. Comput.*, **54**, p. 100665.

[133] Doerr, B. and Neumann, F. (eds.) (2019). *Theory of Evolutionary Computation* (Springer International Publishing), ISBN 978-3-03-029413-7.

[134] Grefenstette, J. (1987). Incorporating problem specific knowledge into genetic algorithms, in L. Davis (ed.), *Genetic Algorithms and Simulated Annealing*, pp. 42–60.

[135] Ashlock, D., McGuinness, C. and Ashlock, W. (2012). Representation in evolutionary computation, in J. Liu, C. Alippi, B. Bouchon-Meunier, G. W. Greenwood and H. A. Abbass (eds.), *Advances in Computational Intelligence: IEEE World Congress on Computational Intelligence, WCCI 2012, Brisbane, Australia, June 10–15, 2012. Plenary/Invited Lectures* (Springer Berlin Heidelberg, Berlin, Heidelberg), ISBN 978-3-642-30687-7, pp. 77–97.

[136] Rothlauf, F. (2006). *Representations for Genetic and Evolutionary Algorithms* (Springer-Verlag, Berlin, Heidelberg), ISBN 354025059X.

[137] Goldberg, D. E. (1990). Real-coded genetic algorithms, virtual alphabets, and blocking, *Complex Syst.*, **5**, pp. 139–167.

[138] Radcliffe, N. J. (1992). Non-linear genetic representations, in R. Manner and B. Manderick (eds.), *Parallel Problem Solving from Nature 2, PPSN-II*, Brussels, Belgium, September 28–30, 1992 (Elsevier), pp. 261–270.

[139] Palmer, C. (1994). An approach to a problem in network design using genetic algorithms, unpublished PhD thesis, Polytechnic University, Troy, NY.

[140] Ronald, S. (1997). Robust encodings in genetic algorithms: a survey of encoding issues, in *Proceedings of 1997 IEEE International Conference on Evolutionary Computation (ICEC '97)*, pp. 43–48.

[141] Wilson, D., Rodrigues, S., Segura, C., Loshchilov, I., Hutter, F., Buenfil, G. L., Kheiri, A., Keedwell, E., Ocampo-Pineda, M., zcan, E., Pea, S. I. V., Goldman, B., Rionda, S. B., Hernndez-Aguirre, A., Veeramachaneni, K. and Cussat-Blanc, S. (2018). Evolutionary computation for wind farm layout optimization, *Renewable Energy*, **126**, pp. 681–691.

[142] Wilkerson, J. L. and Tauritz, D. R. (2011). A guide for fitness function design, in *Proceedings of the 13th Annual Conference Companion on Genetic and Evolutionary Computation, GECCO '11* (Association for Computing Machinery, New York, NY, USA), ISBN 9781450306904, p. 123124.

[143] Reeves, C. R. (2000). Fitness landscapes and evolutionary algorithms, in C. Fonlupt, J.-K. Hao, E. Lutton, M. Schoenauer and E. Ronald (eds.), *Artificial Evolution* (Springer Berlin Heidelberg, Berlin, Heidelberg), ISBN 978-3-540-44908-9, pp. 3–20.

[144] Adair, J., Ochoa, G. and Malan, K. M. (2019). Local optima networks for continuous fitness landscapes, in *Proceedings of the Genetic and Evolutionary Computation Conference Companion*, GECCO '19 (Association for Computing Machinery, New York, NY, USA), ISBN 9781450367486, p. 14071414.

[145] Clark, J. A., Jacob, J. L. and Stepney, S. (2004). Searching for cost functions, in *Proceedings of the 2004 Congress on Evolutionary Computation (IEEE Cat. No. 04TH8753)*, Vol. 2, pp. 1517–1524.

[146] López-López, I., Gómez, G. S., Segura, C., Oliva, D. and Rojas, O. (2020). Metaheuristics in the optimization of cryptographic Boolean functions, *Entropy*, **22**(9), pp. 1–25.

[147] Majig, M. and Fukushima, M. (2008). Adaptive fitness function for evolutionary algorithm and its applications, in *International Conference on Informatics Education and Research for Knowledge-Circulating Society (icks 2008)*, pp. 119–124.

[148] Shi, L. and Rasheed, K. (2010). A survey of fitness approximation methods applied in evolutionary algorithms, in Tenne Y. and Goh C. K. (eds.), *Computational Intelligence in Expensive Optimization Problems. Adaptation Learning and Optimization*, Vol. 2. (Springer Berlin Heidelberg, Berlin, Heidelberg), ISBN 978-3-642-10701-6, pp. 3–28.

[149] Jin, Y. (2011). Surrogate-assisted evolutionary computation: recent advances and future challenges, *Swarm Evol. Comput.*, **1**(2), pp. 61–70.

[150] Jin, Y. (2005). A comprehensive survey of fitness approximation in evolutionary computation, *Soft Comput.*, **9**(1), p. 312.

[151] Jin, Y., Wang, H., Chugh, T., Guo, D. and Miettinen, K. (2019). Data-driven evolutionary optimization: an overview and case studies, *IEEE Trans. Evol. Comput.*, **23**(3), pp. 442–458.

[152] Blickle, T. and Thiele, L. (1996). A comparison of selection schemes used in evolutionary algorithms, *Evol. Comput.*, **4**(4), pp. 361–394.

[153] Segura, C., Coello, C., Segredo, E., Miranda, G. and León, C. (2013). Improving the diversity preservation of multi-objective approaches used for single-objective optimization, in *2013 IEEE Congress on Evolutionary Computation (CEC)*, pp. 3198–3205.

[154] Galinier, P. and Hao, J.-K. (1999). Hybrid evolutionary algorithms for graph coloring, *J. Comb. Optim.*, **3**, pp. 379–397.

[155] Segura, C., Hernndez-Aguirre, A., Luna, F. and Alba, E. (2017). Improving diversity in evolutionary algorithms: new best solutions for frequency assignment, *IEEE Trans. Evol. Comput.*, **21**(4), pp. 539–553.

[156] Deb, K., Anand, A. and Joshi, D. (2002). A computationally efficient evolutionary algorithm for real-parameter optimization, *Evol. Comput.*, **10**(4), pp. 371–395.

[157] Jain, H. and Deb, K. (2011). Parent to mean-centric self-adaptation in sbx operator for real-parameter optimization, in B. K. Panigrahi, P. N. Suganthan, S. Das and S. C. Satapathy (eds.), *Swarm, Evolutionary, and Memetic Computing* (Springer Berlin Heidelberg, Berlin, Heidelberg), ISBN 978-3-642-27172-4, pp. 299–306.

[158] Arabas, J. and Opara, K. (2020). Population diversity of nonelitist evolutionary algorithms in the exploration phase, *IEEE Trans. Evol. Comput.*, **24**(6), pp. 1050–1062.

[159] Pandey, H. M., Chaudhary, A. and Mehrotra, D. (2014). A comparative review of approaches to prevent premature convergence in GA, *Appl. Soft Comput.*, **24**, pp. 1047–1077.

[160] Neri, F., Cotta, C. and Moscato, P. (2011). *Handbook of Memetic Algorithms* (Springer Publishing Company, Incorporated), ISBN 3642232469.

[161] López-Ibáñez, M., Dubois-Lacoste, J., Pérez Cáceres, L., Stützle, T. and Birattari, M. (2016). The irace package: iterated racing for automatic algorithm configuration, *Oper. Res. Perspect.*, **3**, pp. 43–58.

[162] Eiben, A. E., Hinterding, R. and Michalewicz, Z. (1999). Parameter control in evolutionary algorithms, *IEEE Trans. Evol. Comput.*, **3**(2), pp. 124–141.

[163] Huang, C., Li, Y. and Yao, X. (2020). A survey of automatic parameter tuning methods for metaheuristics, *IEEE Trans. Evol. Comput.*, **24**(2), pp. 201– 216.

[164] Gomes Pereira de Lacerda, M., de Araujo Pessoa, L. F., Buarque de Lima Neto, F., Ludermir, T. B. and Kuchen, H. (2021). A systematic literature review on general parameter control for evolutionary and swarm-based algorithms, *Swarm Evol. Comput.*, **60**, p. 100777.

[165] Mallipeddi, R., Suganthan, P., Pan, Q. and Tasgetiren, M. (2011). Differential evolution algorithm with ensemble of parameters and mutation strategies, *Appl. Soft Comput.*, **11**(2), pp. 1679–1696, the Impact of Soft Computing for the Progress of Artificial Intelligence.

[166] Wu, G., Mallipeddi, R. and Suganthan, P. N. (2019). Ensemble strategies for population-based optimization algorithms a survey, *Swarm Evol. Comput.*, **44**, pp. 695–711.

[167] Luke, S., Panait, L., Balan, G. and Et (2007). ECJ: a java-based evolutionary computation research system, http://cs.gmu.edu/_eclab/projects/ecj/.

[168] León, C., Miranda, G. and Segura, C. (2009). Metco: a parallel plugin-based framework for multi-objective optimization, *Int. J. Artif. Intell. Tools*, **18**(4), pp. 569–588.

[169] Liefooghe, A., Jourdan, L. and Talbi, E.-G. (2011). A software framework based on a conceptual unified model for evolutionary multiobjective optimization: paradiseomoeo, *Eur. J. Oper. Res.*, **209**(2), pp. 104–112.

[170] Durillo, J. J. and Nebro, A. J. (2011). jmetal: a java framework for multi-objective optimization, *Adv. Eng. Software*, **42**, pp. 760–771.

Chapter 23

An Empirical Study of Algorithmic Bias

Dipankar Dasgupta* and Sajib Sen†

Department of Computer Science,
University of Memphis, Memphis, USA
*ddasgupt@memphis.edu
†ssen4@memphis.edu

In all goal-oriented selection activities, the existence of a certain level of bias is unavoidable and may be desired for efficient AI-based decision support systems. However, a fair, independent comparison of all eligible entities is essential to alleviate explicit biasness in a competitive marketplace. For example, searching online for a good or a service, it is expected that the underlying algorithm will provide fair results by searching all available entities in the search category mentioned. However, a biased search can make a narrow or collaborative query, ignoring competitive outcomes, resulting in it costing the customers more or getting lower-quality products or services for the resources (money) they spend. This chapter describes algorithmic biases in different contexts with real-life case studies, examples, and scenarios; it provides best practices to detect and remove algorithmic bias.

23.1. Introduction

Because of the massive digitization of data and systems, decision-making processes are largely being driven by machines in private and public sectors. Recent advances in technologies such as artificial intelligence (AI), data science, etc., converting physical systems into an automated decision-making bot [1, 2]. Starting from suggestion of products to buy, movie recommendations, algorithms are also used in very high-stakes decisions such as loan application [3], dating [4], and hiring [5, 6]. The benefits of algorithmic decisions are undoubtedly very clear to humans [2]. Unlike a human, an algorithm or a machine does not get bored or tired [7–9] and works at a very high magnitude of different factors than humans [10–14]. On the contrary, like humans, decision supposed system is vulnerable to the different magnitude of biases that render into biased/unfair decisions [15, 16]. As technologies can also be used as an adversary to fool the system, AI is disrupting many areas of the economy. Not only that, as government sectors are embracing the automated system to improve their accuracy, AI has also been claimed to objectify democracy [1].

Although there are many definitions of bias/fairness by Dr. Narayanan [17], in the context of a decision support system, fairness is the absence of any collusion among different groups or any favoritism, prejudice based on inherent or derived characteristics of an individual or group. A catastrophic canonical example of a biased algorithm is the case of an automated software called COMPAS. The Correctional Offender Management Profiling for Alternative Sanctions (COMPAS) calculates or predicts the risk of a person recommitting another crime. Judges in the United States used the prediction of COMPAS to take a decision on whether to release an offender or keep him/her in prison. An investigation of that automated software discovered bias by providing higher risk to African Americans than to Caucasians with the same profile [18]. Similar but different impactful outcomes are also found in other areas of the automated system families. For example, artificial intelligence (AI)-based judges are found to be biased against darker-skinned contestants as beauty pageant winners [19], or facial recognition-based digital cameras overpredicts blinking for Asians [20]. These types of biases originated from neglected or inherent biases in data or model output.

Whether the bias generated from data can be removed by pre-processing, in-processing, and postprocessing [21] algorithm, tacit collusion from an algorithm is hard to detect. Biased technology can also turn users into newly minted economists. Take into consideration the controversial "price surge" case of ride-sharing service Uber [22]. On a New Year's Eve, their fare increases six to seven times than normal. On a quest for an explanation, Uber's own marketing recognizes its proprietary black-box (dynamic pricing) algorithm decision. They claimed that the market price automatically signals to increase prices to encourage more drivers to ensure the increased supply. On top of that, Uber's CEO also claimed that the company is not responsible for the price surge; it is the market that sets the price [23].

Seeing an automated intelligent system as a black-box created not only short-term effects like Uber's "price-surge" case but also brought serious consequences such as the COMPAS case. In this scenario, devising trust in a model's prediction as well as in the model is an important problem when the model has been deployed for decision making. The practice of using machine learning on blind faith should not be applied to terrorism detection or medical diagnosis [24]; also, the importance of human–machine responsibility needs to be considered, as the outcomes can be catastrophic. Involving an automated model/system in such an important real-life scenario needs to ensure trust. To convince a user to use and trust the deployed AI system, it is very important to ensure the two different (but interrelated) definitions of trust: (1) trusting a model's prediction and (2) trusting a model. Both definitions require that a user understand the model's behavior when it is deployed in the wild.

The explainability characteristics of an AI system is not only required from the consumer and developer perspectives but also helps law enforcers to validate the violation of antitrust law.

Our study offers a descriptive and normative study of algorithmic bias/collusion and its critically important implications in computational science, economics, and law. Our contributions are as follows:

(i) First, our explanation paints a descriptive and computationally explainable picture of the new change in commerce that is taking place by the algorithm-driven automated decision support system.

(ii) Second, taking that snapshot as a base, this article strives to identify the overall spectrum of consequences for consumer welfare and antitrust law.

(iii) Finally, this article provides a case study by using the explainable AI concept from literature to walk-through an automated decision support system and recommends best practices to overcome these issues.

A shorter version of our study was presented in COMPSAC 2020 workshop [25]. However, here we elaborated our study with more data, examples as well as a detailed explanation. We also provide additional case studies to support our arguments. Our study is divided as follows: Section 23.2 provides a classification of different bias, Section 23.3 gives examples of data biasness, and Section 23.4 illustrates algorithm bias/collusions with examples. Sections 23.5 and 23.6 detail categories of algorithmic bias, followed by the models to detect biasness in different case studies. The final section concludes with the outcome of our empirical study.

23.2. Classification of Bias

The definition of bias is different based on context and it can exist in many forms. Suresh and Guttag [26] pointed out different sources of bias in machine learning end-to-end projects. In [27], the authors provided a comprehensive list of biases starting from data origin, collection, and processing in a machine learning pipeline. In this chapter, different types of bias have been pointed out mainly based on the two above-mentioned research papers, along with other existing articles. After that, a circular relationship of these biases and different categorizations also provided a base for the chapter [28].

(1) **Historical Bias:** An example of historical bias can be an image search result of CEOs in 2018. The result shows more male CEOs than women, as only 5% of Fortune 500 CEOs were women in 2018. So, this type of bias is the already existing bias, and even through perfect sampling and feature selection this bias can integrate into the data generation process [26].

(2) **Representation Bias:** Bias generated from how people define and sample from a population and represent it [26]. ImageNet (shown in Figure 23.2 below) dataset bias towards Western countries is an example of representation bias.

(3) **Evaluation Bias:** This kind of bias happens when we choose an inappropriate and disproportionate benchmark to evaluate a model [26]. For example, choosing Audience and IJB-A as benchmarks for a facial recognition system will make the model evaluation biased, as these benchmarks are biased towards skin color and gender [29].

(4) **Aggregation Bias:** This type of bias originates when false inferences are drawn from a subgroup based on the observation of a different group, and consequently, the false conclusion affects the decision support system [26]. For example, a decision support system made on predicting diabetes patients can have aggregation bias because the main feature, HbA1c level, varies widely in diabetes patients across ethnicities and genders.

(5) **Population Bias:** Population bias arises when the dataset has different demographics, statistics, representatives, and user characteristics [27]. For example, a dataset of a social media platform may show that women are more prone to using Instagram, Facebook, whereas men use Twitter.

(6) **Behavioral Bias:** Bias based on different user behavior across different contexts, platforms, or datasets [27].

(7) **Content Production Bias:** When users generate content that differs structurally, lexically, semantically, and syntactically based on user characteristics, such as age or gender [27], content production bias aries.

(8) **Linking Bias:** When network attributes collected from user activities, interactions, or connections do not represent the true behavior of the users, this type of bias arises [27].

(9) **Temporal Bias:** This type of bias originates from the differences in user behaviors as well as the population over time [27].

(10) **Popularity Bias:** Popularity bias is one of the main biases for the recommendation system. Popular items tend to come first in search as well as in recommendations, which subsequently get reviewed by the user. However, this type of popularity can also be increased by fake reviews or social bots, which do not get checked.

(11) **Algorithmic Bias:** Algorithmic bias is when the bias is not present in the input data and is added purely by an algorithm [30].

(12) **Presentation Bias:** Bias generated based on how information is being presented [30]. For example, based on how contents is presented on the Web, the data generated from user clicks tend to get information that is biased toward content that is not presented well.

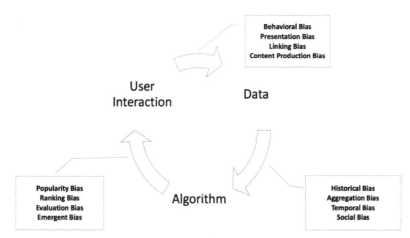

Figure 23.1:   Bias definitions in the data, algorithm, and user interaction feedback loop are placed on their most appropriate arrows [28].

(13) **Ranking Bias:** This type of bias is prevalent in the search engine optimization model. Ranking popular pages on the top results in the their getting viewed more than others, which creates the bias.

(14) **Social Bias:** When a model judgment gets affected by other people's actions or content, social bias arises.

(15) **Emergent Bias:** This type of bias can be found as an output of interaction with real users.

Dependency on data to make a machine learning model creates an existence of a feedback loop phenomenon, where the predicted outcome of a machine learning model affects future data that will be used for subsequent model training. As a result, the previously mentioned types of biases are intertwined with each other. Mehrabi et al. [28] categorize these definitions and types into three categories and represented them on the arrows of the machine learning model feedback loop (Figure 23.1).

23.3. Data Bias Examples

As mentioned in the previous section, there are multiple ways in which data can be biases. Among them, biases caused by unbalanced diversity and representation in data are more prevalent. Buolamwini and Gebru [29] showed that datasets such as IJB-A and Adience mainly contain light-skinned subjects. These datasets, which claim to be the benchmark for the facial recognition system, have 79.6% and 86.2% light-skinned subjects in IJB-A and Adience, respectively (Figure 23.3). Besides having unbalanced data, biases can also seep into the way we use and analyze the data. Buolamwini and Gebru [29] also showed that dividing data only by male and female is not enough. There are underlying biases against dark-skinned females if

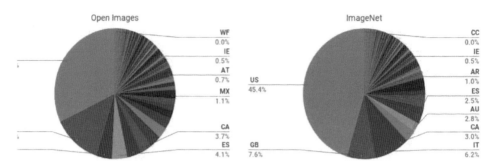

Figure 23.2: Fraction of each country, represented by their two-letter ISO codes, in Open Images and ImageNet image datasets. In both datasets, the US and Great Britain represent the top locations [31].

Figure 23.3: Geographical distribution representation for countries in the Open Images dataset. In their sample, almost one third of the data was US-based, and 60% of the data was from the six most represented countries across North America and Europe, [31].

we only consider data in two main groups. The authors suggested subdividing the data into four categories by gender (e.g., male and female) and by skin color (e.g., light and dark).

Chen et al. [32] pointed out the effects of data bias in medical fields where artificial intelligence systems are not treating all patients equally. This problem is not only in the medical field, skewed data toward a certain group, or unbalanced data but also in certain benchmark datasets—which subsequently create a bias toward downstream applications that are evaluated on these datasets. For example, the popular benchmark datasets ImageNet and Open Images have been found to contain representation bias and have been advised to incorporate geodiversity while creating such kinds of datasets [31].

23.4. Algorithmic Bias/Collusion Examples

Because of the blessings brought by big data and big analytics today, businesses (and governments) rely mostly on them. With the growth of technology as the cost of storing and analyzing data drops, companies are investing in "smart" and "self-learning" machines for faster prediction, planning, trade, and logistic support. Companies' interest also supported by the advances in artificial intelligence (AI). Naturally, these developments have many challenging ethical and legal questions to answer. With growth in the relationship between man and machine, the human's control—or lack of it—over machines and the accountability of machine activities have increased. Although these questions have long fascinated our interest, few would envision the day when these headways (and the ethical and legal hurdles boosted by them) would become an antitrust issue and lead to consumer discomfort.

Price fixing is illegal, and executives and companies, if found involved, are thrown into prison in the United States [33]. So, it made the news in 2015 when the U.S. Department of Justice (DOJ) charged a price-fixing cartel involved in selling posters through the Amazon marketplace. According to DOJ, David Topkins and his coconspirator agreed on using a specific pricing algorithm that collected their competitors' pricing information for specific posters sold online and then applied the sellers' pricing rules [34]. The goal of using the automated algorithm was to coordinate with the respective changes in the prices set by their competitors.

A skeptical reader might wonder: Can robo-sellers really raise prices? The simple and definitive answer is, they already have done so. In 2011, one could find a 20-year-old biology textbook on fruit flies for the surprising price of $23 million available on Amazon [35]. A reader may wonder how this is possible. This price was set by the interaction of two different sellers' algorithms. The algorithm of the first seller automatically set the price for their book at 1.27059 times that of the second seller's book. On the other hand, the second seller's algorithm set the price of their book at 0.9983 times that of the first book. As the two equations $x = 1.27059 * y$ and $y = 0.9983 * x$, cannot mitigate for positive numbers, the outcome of this interaction became an upward spiral, where each algorithm's price hike was responded to by the other algorithm's price hike and vice versa. This continuity resulted in both the books costing millions of dollars from April 8 to April 18, 2011 [35]. In simple thought, the fruit-fly textbook example seems to be a mistake caused by the product rather than a conscious anti-competitive intent. On the other hand, suspicion about Uber's algorithm for "price surge," mentioned earlier, signals to whether it had been designed to exploit the consumer. Such kinds of events echo calls for "algorithmic neutrality"—to prevent socially and economically harmful misuses. From the textbook example, we can strengthen our argument, whether their developers' intent or not, robo-sellers can automatically decide on pricing that eventually raises consumer price. In this case, price fixing played the role of algorithmic bias.

23.5. Algorithm Bias/Collusion Categories

Despite the unimaginable benefits of algorithms, there is a budding competition policy literature raising concerns about the potential of algorithmic bias leading to consumer harm. One of the main theories about harm talks about the possibilities of algorithm decisions leading to collusive outcomes, where consumers pay higher/unfair prices than in a competitive market. The following section discusses each of these theories of harm in turn.

23.5.1. *Messenger (The Classic Digital Cartel)*

This scenario is a digital equivalent of the smoke-filled room agreement. Here, algorithms are used intentionally to monitor, implement, and police cartels. In this category, humans agree to collude, and algorithms execute the collusion, acting as a messenger or intermediate medium for collusion (Figure 23.4).

An example of the "messenger" scenario is the CMA's Trod Ltd./GB eye Ltd. case, like David Topkins in the U.S., where two parties agreed on a classic horizontal price-fixing cartel using an algorithm. These two parties had an agreement of using automated repricing software to monitor and adjust their prices so that neither of them could undercut the other [37]. As there was a clear anti-competitive agreement between humans using the algorithm as the messenger, the law-enforcing agency CMA was able to establish the violation of antitrust law. From an economic perspective, companies are taking algorithms as a "messenger" to make explicitly collusive agreement for some of reasons:

(1) Two parties can easily detect and respond immediately to any deviations from the agreement.

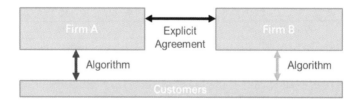

Figure 23.4: Explicit coordination implemented or facilitated by algorithms [36].

(2) The probability of accidental deviation is reduced.

(3) An algorithm ensures the reduction of agency slack.

From a practical perspective, users of algorithms used for competition (such as pricing algorithms) should be aware of sharing sensitive information about their algorithms, in public or with their competitors. This information would allow others to draw a conclusion about their algorithmic behavior or how the prices are/will be calculated. In other words, the algorithm may function as a "messenger" for competitively sensitive information.

23.5.2. *Hub-and-Spoke*

Unlike in the "messenger" scenario, the algorithm is not involved in explicit agreement/bias, but it is the use of the same algorithm by competitors that creates bias (possibly inadvertently) of fixing outcome/prices. As shown in Figure 23.5, if multiple competitors (such as firm A and firm B) use the same optimization algorithm (e.g., Algorithm X), this may lead the competitors to react in a similar way to external events (e.g., changes in demand, cost in a market). On top of that, if the competitors are somehow aware or able to infer that they are using the same optimization algorithm (Algorithm X), this may help an individual firm to interpret the competitor's market behavior, which will eventually come into implicit collusion as well as a biased environment. On a related spectrum of algorithmic biasness, individual firms might find themselves facing cartel allegations without having any intended involvement in a cartel. In this scenario, different individuals (the spokes) use the same third-party service provider's (the hub's) optimization algorithm to determine the outcome and intended reaction to market changes (shown in Figure 23.5). The recent Eturas case is an example of the hub-and-spoke agreement that exists in the online world. In the Eturas case, the administration of a Lithuanian online travel booking system sent an electronic notice to all its travel agents about a new technical restriction of putting a cap on the discount rate. According to

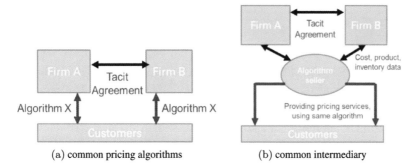

    (a) common pricing algorithms   (b) common intermediary

Figure 23.5: "Tacit" coordination [36].

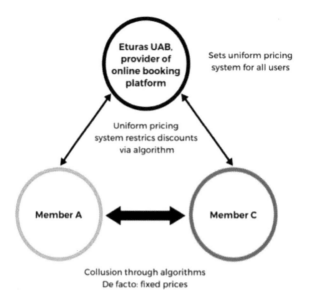

Figure 23.6:   Hub-and-spoke scenario of Eturas online booking platform with two agents [38].

the Court of Justice of the EU, travel agents who were aware of that notice and acted accordingly were presumed to have involved themselves in an online cartel agreement (see Figure 23.6). So, the example states that when individual firms sign up to using a platform's algorithm and are also aware of the fact that other competitors are also using the same algorithm, and that the platform's algorithm fixes prices to a certain level, it can be claimed that these firms have engaged in "hub-and-spoke" behavior.

Thus, when firms independently sign up to using a platform's algorithm, knowing that other competitors are using the same algorithm and that the algorithm fixes prices at a certain level, they can be held to have engaged in classic "hub-and-spoke" behavior, which eventually creates horizontal collusion.

Another exciting example of the "hub-and-spoke" scenario is when 700 petrol stations (25% of the Danish retail fuel market) in Rotterdam, the Netherlands, used advanced analytics software from a2i system to determine petrol prices (see Figure 23.7). Although in this scenario neither of the individuals with a2i were deemed to be involved in anti-competitive agreement, the group using the algorithm created a 5% (millions of euros) higher price margin than normal, as reported by the *Wall Street Journal* [39]. When multiple players or individuals use the same third-party algorithm or analytics, data points, and values, the likelihood of tacit alignment increases. Although a2i claims that their advance analytics helped companies to avoid price wars or eliminate them altogether, in fact, they had no intention of collusion, the unilateral use of a decision-making algorithm softened competition.

Price-Point

Artificial-intelligence software is being used by some gas stations to constantly adjust prices to maximize sales or margins. Here's how it works:

Step 1

Build a database of historical transactions to teach the software about market dynamics; add competitors' info.

Step 2

Connect software to live feeds of purchase data and other variables such as weather and traffic.

Step 3

Software compares live data to historical numbers to predict demand linked to prices.

Step 4

Owner sets strategy for each fuel at each station, including preferred balance between volume and margin and constraints such as minimum price.

Step 5

Algorithms determine price for each fuel and automatically adjust pumps throughout the day.

Step 6

Transactions in reaction to those prices fed back into system to generate new predictions and prices.

Source: WSJ analysis of a2i systems   THE WALL STREET JOURNAL.

Figure 23.7:   A example of gas stations changing prices using one third-party algorithm [39].

23.5.3. *Tacit Collusion on Steroids (Predictable Agent)*

This category mainly points out why computational speed along with market transparency has become a curse. Assume a market where all individuals or firms adopt their own optimization algorithm, access their rival's real-time algorithmic output (e.g., pricing information), and adjust their own algorithm within seconds or even in real time. This scenario eventually creates a perfect breeding ground for tacit collusion. One the one hand, market economy claims transparency in the market for a competition to exist among competitors, and on the other hand, transparency along with computational speed works against it. If a firm or individual increases their price (e.g., outcome from an optimization algorithm), their rival's system will respond in real time, which diminishes the risk of enough customers moving to the other sellers for that homogeneous product. This situation is also applicable when a firm decreases its price. So, ultimately, there is no competitive gain or incentive by offering a discount. Eventually, all competitors in the market reach a suitable "supra-competitive" equilibrium (i.e., a price which is higher than the price that would exist in a competitive environment). On top of that, monitoring a competitor's output/pricing and reacting based on that (i.e., conscious parallelism) is not unlawful by existing anti-competitive law, because of the absence of any form of explicit or trace of agreement (see Figures 23.8 and 23.9).

Conscious parallelism can be facilitated and stabilized to the extent (i) the rival's output is predictable, and (ii) through repeated action, competitors can decode each other's algorithmic output [40]. A relevant example of this is what happened to the textbook *The Making of a Fly* on the Amazon marketplace in 2011 [35]. A conscious parallelism concept (one algorithm reacts based on the output of another and vice versa) between two different sellers led the price of this textbook to rise from $106.23

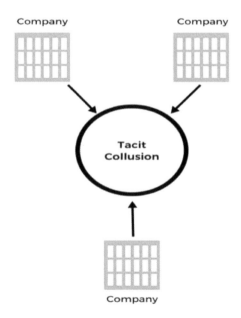

Figure 23.8: Use of pricing algorithms leading to tacit collusion [38].

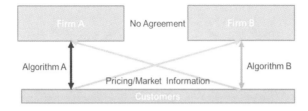

Figure 23.9: Tacit coordination without agreement between firm and algorithms but responding fast with the market change [36].

to $23 million. Although the example appeared to have a lack of "sanity checks" within the algorithms rather than any anti-competitive intent. However, this example demonstrates how algorithmic decision leads to the unintended outcome when there is no human intervention.

23.5.4. *Artificial Intelligence and Digital Eye*

This category discusses the situation when the exchange of information between algorithms is not a part of a human plan, but the developers/programmers have (unintentionally) overlooked the implementation of the required safeguards to prevent information exchange.

The important difference with the previous category (tacit collusion on steroid) is that this algorithm is not explicitly designed to tacitly collude, but it does so through its advanced self-learning capabilities. The similarity with the previous category is that like a "conscious parallelism" model, this model is also hard to detect by anti-competitive enforcement law. These algorithms not only maintain coordination but also generate this coordination by themselves. This category matches with self-learning AI models such as AlphaZero, which is used to beat a human chess master. Like others, the model follows the "Win-Continue Lose-Reverse" rule and adapts itself with the environment. Setting revenue as a goal, this model creates incremental change to the outcome (i.e., price). If the action increases revenue, then it continues in that direction; if not, then in the reverse direction. Making small changes, this model wants to learn the market demand and environment and requires very limited computation resources and data.

One real-life example can be Amazon's machine learning repricing algorithm [36]. Information collected by CMA [36] explains that their algorithmic simple re-pricer takes the seller's past pricing data, different competing firms' price data, and stock levels of the rivals to determine their optimum price. This algorithm also considers their rivals' publicly available pricing information and customer feedback. Whereas their simple re-pricers often offer the lowest price among competitors, their

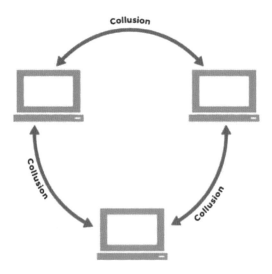

Figure 23.10:   Reinforcement/Automated learning between intelligent machine [38].

machine learning re-pricer optimize output by following specific goal "meeting sales target" or taking specific shares of "buy box" sales [36].

23.6. Software Agents for Collusion

Calvano et al. [41] provided an interesting experimental analysis where two software agents (Q-learning pricing algorithms) systematically learn to collude by themselves. The authors showed that although the collusion is partial, it is enforced by punishment if there any deviation. These two learning algorithms use trial-and-error strategies to learn by themselves, with no prior knowledge of the environment. They come into collusion by leaving no trace, without communicating with each other, and not having any instruction to collude. From the research, it is very apparent that software agents, in the absence of human intention, can create revenue for the owner by violating anti-competitive law.

Figure 23.11 shows how two different agents punish each other after a deviation at period 1. When agent 1 (red colored) lowers the price from 1.8 to 1.6 at period 1, its profit hikes to 1.2 (monopoly profit) and agent 2 comes into nash price. After period 1, agent 2 punishes itself and lowers the price too close to agent 1, which penalizes agent 1's profit. So, at period 2, both agent 1 and agent 2 come into temporary equilibrium and change each algorithm's behavior incrementally. From periods 2 to 9, both agents change their price by small incremental changes, and at period 10 they come into pre-shock situation again. Figure 23.11 above describes

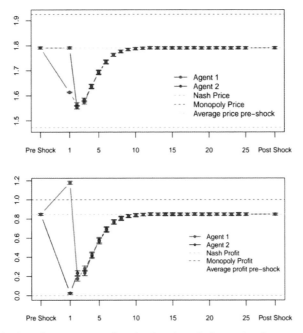

Figure 23.11: Price impulse response, prices (top) and profit (bottom), of two agents after deviation [41].

how software agents work even when there is a deviation in the market environment and eventually maintain supra-competitive profit and price level.

23.7. Model Explanation to Detect Untrustworthy Algorithm

By far, it is very clear that algorithms can be biased in different forms. Bias can be intentional, unintentional or a mix of both. Some algorithmic biases are detectable, and some are implicit. Some biases generate short-term benefits and harm, whereas some are for long-term consumer harm. As we can see with the pace of technological advancement, consumer welfare is getting compromised. To ensure consumer welfare and trust as well as to reduce anti-competitive intent, the idea of an algorithm as "black-box" needs to change. Human responsibility for algorithmic action as well as the human–machine relationship needs to be pointed out. Not only that, effective and understandable human interaction is important for machine learning systems to assess trust. We do not expect outcomes such as Uber's "price surge" when consumers are kept in the dark when explanations are expected. We want to trust systems where every action can be explained with reasons and facts. Emilio et al. [41] proposed several models to explain the "black-box" algorithm as a white box. Their approach is focused on mainly (i) trusting an algorithm's prediction, (ii) trusting the algorithm, and (iii) improving the model. In this chapter, we focus only on the local interpretable model-agnostic explanation (LIME) model to explain our algorithm. In a naïve explanation, LIME works as follows:

(A) Permute data (create fake dataset) based on each observation.
(B) Calculate distance (similarity score) between permutated data and observed observations.
(C) Make predictions on a new dataset using the "black-box" machine learned model.
(D) Choose m features from the permutated data that best describe the black-box algorithm.
(E) Fit a simple model to the permutated data with m features and similarity scores as weights.
(F) Feature weights from the simple model to provide an explanation for the complex "black-box" model's local behavior.

Examples shown in Figure 23.12 explain how explainability helps to trust a prediction as well as a model. For the sake of theoretical explanation, we need to define certain concepts and variables. Assume, $x \varepsilon R^d$ is the original representation of an instance (predicted output) being explained, where x denotes a binary vector $\{0, 1\}$. Let us assume that G is a potentially interpretable models such as decision tree, and $g \varepsilon G$ is an explainable model, where g acts over presence or absence of interpretable components. To explain $g \varepsilon G$, assume $\Omega(g)$ as a measure of complexity (as opposed to interpretability). For example, the length of a decision tree. Now, assume that the simple model being explained is denoted by f. In determining an instance, x belongs to the explained model, $f(x)$ denotes the probability, and $\pi_x(z)$ is defined as a proximity measure between perturbed instance z to x. We also define the unfaithfulness of g in approximating f in the locality defined by $\pi_x(z)$ by $L(f, g, \pi_x)$. To ensure the model's interpretability and local fidelity, we wish

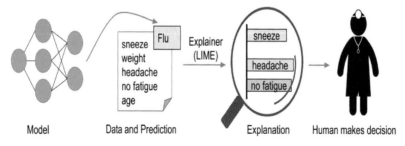

| Model | Data and Prediction | Explanation | Human makes decision |

Figure 23.12:   The LIME model explains the symptoms in the patient's history that led to the prediction of "flu". The model explains that sneezing and headache are contributing factors for the prediction, and no fatigue was used against it. This explanation helps the doctor to trust the model's prediction [42].

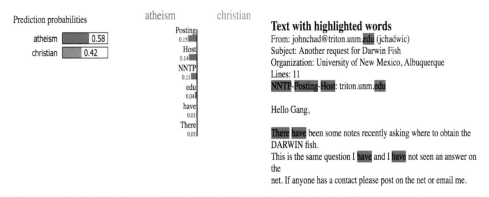

Figure 23.13: Explaining a prediction of classifiers to determine the class "Christianity" or "Atheism" based on text in documents. The bar chart shows the importance of the words that determine the prediction. and are highlighted in the document. Blue indicates "Atheism" and orange indicates "Christianity" [42].

to minimize $L(f, g, \pi_x)$, where complexity $\Omega(g)$ is maintained low enough to be interpretable.

$$\xi = argmin_{g \varepsilon G} L(f, g, \pi_x) + \Omega(g) \qquad (23.1)$$

From the theoretical explanation and the examples mentioned above, we wish to detect and reduce algorithmic bias by explaining the prediction (outcome) and improving the "black-box" algorithm from the programmers' point of view.

23.8. Case Study 1: Detecting Bias Using Explaining the Black Box

A simple search and optimization problem has been taken in this case to replicate the idea of a biased search or an optimized result. In this case study, we choose the popular standard Knuth Miles dataset (i.e., 128 representative U.S. cities with positions and populations) from the Stanford Graphbase database [43]. Each vertex in the graph is a city and each edge is an undirected path between two cities. We wanted to replicate an optimal route search algorithm (e.g., Google Maps algorithm) for the US highway road network, given the starting and ending points. For the sake of simplicity, in our experiment we filtered out edges that are more than 700 miles between cities. The goal of the algorithm is to provide the optimal (e.g., less traveled path) route to reach a destination. A sample search from San Jose, CA, to Tampa, FL, provided in Figure 23.14. This search result provides a route with a distance of 3049 miles. A similar search on a standard Google map provides a route with a distance of 2797 miles.

From a consumer's point of view, a consumer needs to be able to trust the algorithm's outcome as well as the algorithm we are proposing. To prove that the

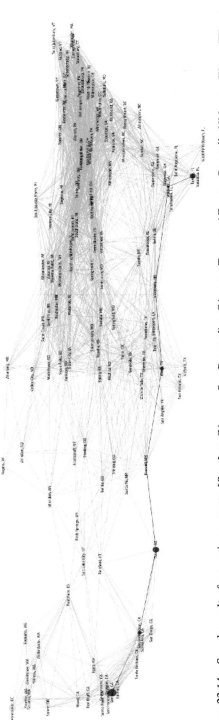

Figure 23.14: Search result of an optimum route [*San Jose CA => San Bernardino CA => Tucson, AZ => Roswell, NM => Waco, TX =>*
Vicksburg, MS => Valdosta, GA => Tampa, FL].

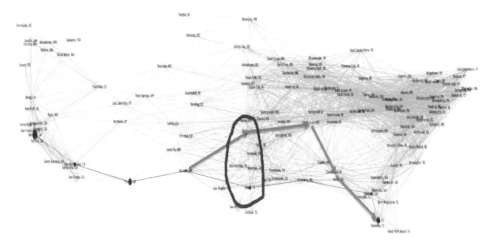

Figure 23.15: This figure shows how a biased and unbiased search result may vary. Unbiased search result: [*San Jose CA* => *San Bernardino CA* => *Tucson, AZ* => *Roswell, NM* => *Waco, TX* => *Vicksburg, MS* => *Valdosta, GA* => *Tampa, FL*]; Biased search result: [*San Jose, CA* => *San Bernardino, CA* => *Tucson, AZ* => *Roswell, NM* => *Wichita, MS* => *Saint Louis, MO* => *Tuscalosa, AL* => *Tampa, FL*].

LIME model works in this case, let us assume a biased search where the algorithm gets an incentive when it chooses some gas station in the map. In that case, the algorithm may provide a route (shown in Figure 23.15 as an orange line partial route), which turns out to be sub-optimal. This kind of prediction or outcome is harmful for the consumer but a gain for the algorithm as well as the one who owns it.

The search result shows a route from starting ("San Jose, CA") node to destination ("Tampa, FL") node, where each tuple indicates the neighboring node name and distance. To explain the algorithm's output using LIME model, let our optimization algorithm (g) be explainable. The measure of complexity $\Omega(g)$ for the explainable model g is choosing the best neighboring node starting from the start node to reach the optimum route to destination. In our case, $f(x)$ denotes the probability of x (optimal route) belonging to a certain class (i.e., optimum route class). We further use $\pi_x(z)$ as a proximity measure between an instance z (any node that is not a part of the optimum result) to x (nodes that are part of the optimum result) to define a locality around x. Finally, let $L(f, g, \pi_x)$ be a measure of how unfaithful g is in approximating f in the locality defined by π_x. So, to explain the model, we need to minimize $L(f, g, \pi_x)$ and $\Omega(g)$. In our case study, a user might ask why a certain node chose a certain neighboring node instead of choosing a random neighboring node. For example, from the starting node (San Jose, CA) the optimal result follows the next best node, "San Bernardino, CA," with 411 miles instead of choosing "San Francisco, CA," with 47 miles. An explanation for this result can be that in all probable data points (nodes) for the node "San Jose, CA," the probability of choosing "San Bernardino, CA," is high given that our destination of interest is the south-west. Even though the "San Francisco, CA" node is shorter in distance, it is in the opposite direction to our area of interest. A similar explanation goes for every chosen optimal node in our search result. Notice the case for the biased result: the "Roswell, NM" node chooses the "Wichita, KS" node instead of "Waco, TX". Even though this result is optimized by the "black-box" algorithm, an explanation for this result may provide the consumer an intuition of bias against the search result. For example, in our first explanation, we choose the optimum neighboring node that is towards south-west because our destination is in the south-west. So a selection optimized node in the south-west direction makes sense. The "Wichita, KS" node is more in the "north" direction than the "Waco, TX" node with respect to "Roswell, NM." So, if the algorithm's output can represent a couple of such examples, then the result will turn into a biased result for the consumer easily. With respect to theoretical explanation, the probability of choosing "Wichita, KS" by the "Roswell, NM" node is less than the "Waco, TX" node given the destination is "Tampa, FL."

23.9. Case Study 2: Detecting Bias Based on Node Coverage Rate

To demonstrate the implicit bias that exists in any algorithms (including AI-driven algorithms), we consider a coverage estimation problem. The idea is to show that with some parameter changes, the search (of N nodes) can be reduce n nodes (where $n < N$), producing sub-optimal results. Such reduction in search space, while beneficial from the business point of view, may be detrimental to customers. **Hypothetical Scenario**: To illustrate the concept mentioned above, we chose a popular problem for optimization called "0/1-knapsack" problem. The problem is defined below. Given a set of n items numbered from 1 to n, each with a weight w_i and a value v_i along with a maximum weight capacity W, the objective is to

$$Minimize \sum_{i=1}^{n} v_i x_i, \tag{23.2}$$

$$Subject\ to \sum_{i=1}^{n} w_i x_i \leq W, \tag{23.3}$$

where v_i is the value of item i, w_i is the weight of item i, and $x_i \varepsilon \{0, 1\}$.

Based on the above knapsack problem, we emulated an illustrative test case to demonstrate algorithmic biasness. Assume, that there are three objects $n = 3$, having associated values $= [4, 2, 10]$ and weights $= [8, 1, 4]$, where v_i and w_i represent the value and the weight for the ith object, respectively. Moreover, a bag having capacity $W = 10$ needs to fill up with the objects, keeping the object value as high as possible within the weight capacity. The ideal solution without any internal bias gives us a total gain of 12 by choosing items 2 and 3 (e.g., $2 + 10 = 12$). The same problem provides different results when we forcefully (or being biased) included the 1st item and whichever item comes after that in the result maintaining the constraint. That biased algorithm gave us a total gain of 6 by choosing items 1 and 2 (e.g., $4 + 2 = 6$). In both situations, none of the results exceeded the total capacity $W = 10$ but provided different outputs. This proves that an ideal algorithm can be biased as a programmer intends, and by this process some entity or object can get unfair advantages by giving incentive to the service provider. On the other hand, from the perspective of the user/service receiver, we believe that it is the ideal solution that can be achieved. This toy problem does not indicate any differences in node coverage between biased and unbiased algorithms, except a different gain. To extend the node coverage estimation problems, similar problems took into consideration the large dataset. In that case, instead of a deterministic algorithm, four metaheuristic algorithms were taken to replicate the idea of input data, "black-box" algorithm, and predictive output (i.e., optimal and non-optimal class).

Node coverage for biased and unbiased algorithm: Our hypothesis is that a biased algorithm will always have less node coverage than an unbiased one. To prove our hypothesis, we choose four different search and optimization metaheuristic algorithms such as the genetic algorithm, hill climbing with random walk, simulated annealing, and tabu search. We also choose a dataset by a randomly generated item's value and weight and a random threshold. This dataset is then used for four different algorithms (see Table 23.1).

1. **Genetic algorithm:** It is a metaheuristic algorithm that is generally used for search and optimization problems. This algorithm is biologically inspired by natural selection, crossover, and mutation. Some popular applications of the genetic algorithm in the field of artificial intelligence are given in [44, 46, 47].
2. **Hill climbing with random walk:** This is an iterative algorithm that starts with an arbitrary solution to a problem. For each next iteration, if there is a better solution, then an incremental change is made to the solution until no further improvement can be found.
3. **Simulated annealing:** It is also a metaheuristic algorithm used in search and optimization problems. This algorithm is used in a discrete search space. For problem space, where finding an approximate global optimum is more important than finding a local optimum, this algorithm is the best fit.
4. **Tabu search:** It is a special kind of metaheuristic algorithm used for search and optimization. This algorithm uses memory, which keeps track of visited solutions.

Table 23.1:   Sample Result of four algorithms run for 100 nodes dataset

Techniques	Nodes	Iter.	Avg Coverage	Optimal Coverage	Optimal Value/Gain
Genetic algorithm	100	200	57%	59%	15278
Hill climbing with random walk	100	200	55%	57%	17802
Simulated annealing	100	200	59%	60%	15485
Tabu search	100	200	47%	54%	17607

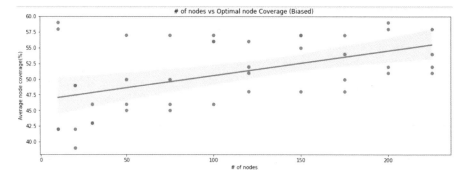

Figure 23.16: Regression plot of on the optimal node coverage of an unbiased algorithm with increasing number of nodes. Every datapoint on the y-axis represents values identified by each algorithm.

> If a potential solution can be found in the visited set for a short period of time, it is marked as tabu.

The parameter changes we were interested in are:

(1) Changing the number of nodes or data points for each of the four algorithms. For example, using different dataset with 50,100, or 200 nodes.
(2) Applying the same dataset for an output with a varying algorithm. For example, a dataset of 100 nodes was applied for the same result by four different algorithms.

Table 23.1 shows a sample result achieved with 100 nodes using the four algorithms separately. This same approach is then applied to a biased situation (same as a toy scenario concept) for each algorithm. From our result, we found that it is hard to determine whether an algorithm is biased or not by simply looking at its node coverage across different search spaces (see Figure 23.16 and Figure 23.17), but a comparison between the two result provides an approximate constant difference across different search spaces (see Figure 23.18).

From this case study, we can get an intuition that whether the "black-box" algorithm has been tested against any benchmark algorithm; then comparing the

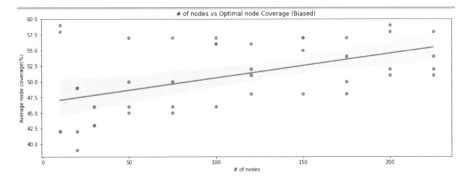

Figure 23.17: Regression plot of the optimal node coverage of a biased algorithm against an increasing number of nodes. Every datapoint on the y-axis represents values identified by each algorithm.

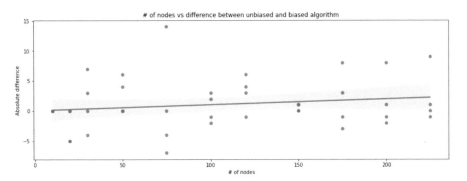

Figure 23.18: Differences in the coverage rate for biased and unbiased algorithm. The y-axis represents absolute node coverage rate difference with an increasing number of nodes on the x-axis.

result between these two algorithms across different search space, may reveal the biasness of the "black-box" algorithm or may simply raise the question of explanation of the result.

23.10. Engineers' and Researchers' Role in Mitigating Bias

Bias in AI-based systems can manifest from either data or algorithms and their parameter tunings. In particular, bias can be injected into framing the problem, collecting and preparing the data, and interpreting data and decision manipulation. While there is no defined solution to measure algorithms' fairness, some approaches can help detect and mitigate hidden algorithmic biases regardless of the data quality. According to the chief trust officer at a Vienna-based synthetic-data startup [47], tech companies need to be accountable for AI systems' decisions. It is also true that

AI provides an excellent opportunity for data scientists, businesses, and engineers to explore new application areas. He invites engineers to work hard to mitigate bias from datasets, from algorithms, and eventually from society. Now, it opens a new paradigm for engineers on how they should design their AI applications. It is to be noted that users of an AI system may unknowingly introduce bias based on how, where, and when they use it. Hence, developers need to take extra validation on their system design to mitigate such user bias.

There is no one-size-fits-all system to mitigate bias from AI, and it can be introduced at any point when learning the algorithm. However, according to ongoing research, the most promising and logical starting point is when the model parses data.

Researchers across different organizations are putting in effort to develop systems and algorithms to mitigate bias in AI. Toolkits like Aequitas measure bias in datasets; Themis-ml reduces tendency in data by using a bias mitigation algorithm. Researchers at IBM developed a standard interface for working professionals accommodating a complete toolkit called AI Fairness 360 to identify and mitigate bias in datasets and AI models. Some researchers also believe that watchdog systems to audit AI algorithms should be accommodated before deploying them into the real world because of the uncertainty of bias mitigation algorithms.

23.11. Conclusion

This empirical study highlighted the possible existence of algorithmic bias in search, optimization, and coverage problems with some real-world applications. From the examples and models reported in the literature, it is evident that algorithms, especially self-learning algorithms, can be made biased intentionally or unintentionally. In particular, based on catastrophic incidents caused by the "black-box" artificial intelligence algorithm, law enforcement is now holding developers responsible for their intelligent machines' decisions and actions. To have trust in intelligent systems or algorithms, cross-validation measures in detecting bias of different kinds are necessary. As a form of sanity check and preventive measures, software developers need to disclose algorithmic details such as explainable AI as a best practice. Considering the unparalleled benefits of AI and its possible misuse or abuse, regulations are essential for AI-based developers to take responsibility for their products [47]. Accordingly, proper guidelines and principles such as the Algorithmic Accountability Act [48] has been introduced for companies to audit their AI/ML systems for bias and discrimination and regulate the use of AI systems that are prone to be misused or bad for humanity. Mariya Gabriel, Europe's top official on the digital economy, said to companies using AI, "People need to be informed when they are in contact with an algorithm and not another human being. Any decision made by an algorithm must be verifiable and explained."

23.A.1. Appendix I

A search result from the starting ("San Jose, CA") node to the destination ("Tampa, FL") node, where each tuple indicates the neighboring node name and distance, is as follows,

"San Jose, CA" => [("San Francisco, CA," 47), ("Salinas, CA," 58), ("Stockton, CA," 80), ("Santa Rosa, CA," 102), ("Sacramento, CA," 127), ("Red Bluff, CA," 235), ("Reno, NV," 266), ("Santa Barbara, CA," 294), ("Weed, CA," 340), ("Santa Ana, CA," 395), ("San Bernardino, CA,' 411), ("San Diego, CA," 485), ("Salem, OR," 664)]

"San Bernardino, CA" => [("Santa Ana, CA," 54), ("San Diego, CA," 130), ("Santa Barbara, CA," 152), ("Salinas, CA," 374), ("Stockton, CA," 388), ("San Jose, CA," 411), ("Sacramento, CA," 435), ("San Francisco, CA," 450), ("Tucson, AZ," 460), ("Reno, NV," 470), ("Santa Rosa, CA," 505), ("Richfield, UT," 534), ("Red Bluff, CA," 566), ("Weed, CA," 671), ("Salt Lake City, UT," 681)]

"Tucson, AZ" => [("San Diego, CA," 423), ("San Bernardino, CA," 460), ("Roswell, NM," 469), ("Santa Ana, CA," 504), ("Santa Fe, NM," 523), ("Santa Barbara, CA," 607), ("Richfield, UT," 652)]

"Roswell, NM" => [("Santa Fe, NM," 196), ("San Angelo, TX," 320), ("Trinidad, CO," 323), ("Wichita Falls, TX," 389), ("Salida, CO," 423), ("Tucson, AZ," 469), ("Sherman, TX," 506), ("Waco, TX," 515), ("San Antonio, TX," 538), ("Seminole, OK," 539), ("Wichita, KS," 585), ("Tulsa, OK," 596), ("Sterling, CO," 601), ("Tyler, TX," 604), ("Salina, KS," 640), ("Victoria, TX," 651), ("Texarkana, TX," 666), ("Shreveport, LA," 691)]

"Waco, TX" => [("Tyler, TX," 134), ("Sherman, TX," 163), ("San Antonio, TX," 181), ("Wichita Falls, TX," 204), ("Victoria, TX," 223), ("San Angelo, TX," 228), ("Shreveport, LA," 233), ("Texarkana, TX," 270), ("Seminole, OK," 290), ("Tulsa, OK," 380), ("Vicksburg, MS," 419), ("Wichita, KS," 471), ("Roswell, NM," 515), ("Springfield, MO," 539), ("Salina, KS," 558), ("Topeka, KS," 612), ("Tupelo, MS," 620), ("Sedalia, MO," 640), ("Tuscaloosa, AL," 658), ("Saint Joseph, MO," 659), ("Trinidad, CO," 667), ("Selma, AL," 675), ("Santa Fe, NM," 681)]

"Vicksburg, MS" => [("Shreveport, LA," 186), ("Tupelo, MS," 230), ("Tuscaloosa, AL," 239), ("Texarkana, TX," 240), ("Selma, AL," 256), ("Tyler, TX," 285), ("Sherman, TX," 400), ("Waco, TX," 419), ("Springfield, MO," 460), ("Seminole, OK," 489), ("Tallahassee, FL," 496), ("Wichita Falls, TX," 511), ("Tulsa, OK," 522), ("Victoria, TX," 530), ("Saint Louis, MO," 530), ("Valdosta, GA," 542), ("Vincennes, IN," 556), ("Sedalia, MO," 575), ("San Antonio, TX,"

576), ("Swainsboro, GA," 579), ("Waycross, GA," 586), ("Terre Haute, IN," 614), ("Springfield, IL," 614), ("San Angelo, TX," 639), ("Savannah, GA," 669), ("Saint Joseph, MO," 687), ("Saint Augustine, FL," 690)]

"Valdosta, GA" => [("Waycross, GA," 63), ("Tallahassee, FL," 82), ("Saint Augustine, FL," 155), ("Swainsboro, GA," 168), ("Savannah, GA," 172), ("Tampa, FL," 233), ("Sarasota, FL," 286), ("Selma, AL," 302), ("Sumter, SC," 328), ("West Palm Beach, FL," 386), ("Tuscaloosa, AL," 387), ("Wilmington, NC," 449), ("Winston-Salem, NC," 476), ("Tupelo, MS," 483), ("Vicksburg, MS," 542), ("Rocky Mount, NC," 552), ("Roanoke, VA," 585), ("Williamson, WV," 655), ("Richmond, VA," 672), ("Staunton, VA," 673)]

References

[1] K. Ha, Why AI is a threat to democracy—and what we can do to stop it (2020). https://www.teo.chnologyreview.com/s/613010/why-ai-is-a-threat-to-democracyand-what-we-can-do-to-stop-it/.

[2] D. Dasgupta, Z. Akhtar, and S. Sen, Machine learning in cybersecurity: a comprehensive survey, *J. Def. Model. Simul.* (2020). doi: 10.1177/1548512920951275. URL https://doi.org/10.1177/1548512920951275.

[3] A. Mukerjee, R. Biswas, K. Deb, and A. P. Mathur, Multi–objective evolutionary algorithms for the risk–return trade–off in bank loan management, *Int. Trans. Oper. Res.*, **9**, 583–597 (2002).

[4] A. Webb, A love story: how I gamed online dating to meet my match, *Reviewing Data Driven Algorithmic Dating Sites* (2013).

[5] M. Bogen and A. Rieke, Help wanted: an examination of hiring algorithms, equity, and bias. Technical report, Upturn, Washington, DC (2018).

[6] L. Cohen, Z. C. Lipton, and Y. Mansour, Efficient candidate screening under multiple tests and implications for fairness, *CoRR*, **abs/1905.11361** (2019). URL http://arxiv.org/abs/1905.11361.

[7] S. Danziger, J. Levav, and L. Avnaim-Pesso, Extraneous factors in judicial decisions, *Proc. Natl. Acad. Sci.*, **108**, 6889–6892 (2011).

[8] A. O'Keeffe and M. McCarthy, *The Routledge Handbook of Corpus Linguistics* (2010).

[9] S. Sen, K. D. Gupta, and M. Manjurul Ahsan, Leveraging machine learning approach to setup software-defined network (SDN) controller rules during DDoS attack. In eds. M. S. Uddin and J. C. Bansal, *Proceedings of International Joint Conference on Computational Intelligence*, Springer, Singapore, pp. 49–60 (2020). ISBN 978-981-13-7564-4.

[10] N. Sadman, K. D. Gupta, A. Haque, S. Poudyal, and S. Sen, Detect review manipulation by leveraging reviewer historical stylometrics in amazon, yelp, facebook and google reviews. In *Proceedings of the 2020 The 6th International Conference on E-Business and Applications*, ICEBA 2020, New York, NY, USA, pp. 42–47 (2020). Association for Computing Machinery. ISBN 9781450377355. doi: 10.1145/3387263.3387272. URL https://doi.org/10.1145/3387263.3387272.

[11] M. M. Ahsan, K. D. Gupta, M. M. Islam, S. Sen, M. L. Rahman, and M. Shakhawat Hossain, Covid-19 symptoms detection based on nasnetmobile with explainable AI using various imaging modalities, *Mach. Learn. Knowl. Extr.*, **2**(4), 490–504 (2020). ISSN 2504-4990. doi: 10.3390/make2040027. URL http://dx.doi.org/10.3390/make2040027.

[12] N. Sadman, K. Datta Gupta, M. A. Haque, S. Sen, and S. Poudyal, Stylometry as a reliable method for fallback authentication. In *2020 17th International Conference on Electrical Engineering/Electronics, Computer, Telecommunications and Information Technology (ECTI-CON)*, pp. 660–664 (2020). doi: 10.1109/ECTI-CON49241.2020. 9158216.

[13] M. M. Ahsan, K. D. Gupta, M. M. Islam, S. Sen, M. L. Rahman, and M. Shakhawat Hossain, Covid-19 symptoms detection based on nasnetmobile with explainable AI using various imaging modalities, *Mach. Learn. Knowl. Extr.*, **2**(4), 490–504 (2020). ISSN 2504-4990. doi: 10.3390/make2040027. URL https://www.mdpi.com/2504-4990/2/4/27.

[14] Z. Akhtar, M. R. Mouree, and D. Dasgupta, Utility of deep learning features for facial attributes manipulation detection. In *2020 IEEE International Conference on Humanized Computing and Communication with Artificial Intelligence (HCCAI)*, pp. 55–60 (2020). doi: 10.1109/HCCAI49649.2020.00015.

[15] S. M. Julia Angwin, Jeff Larson and L. Kirchner, *Machine Bias: There's Software Used Across the Country to Predict Future Criminals. And It's Biased Against Blacks*, ProPublica (2016).

[16] A. Jain, Weapons of math destruction: how big data increases inequality and threatens democracy, *Bus. Econ.*, **52**, 123–125 (2017). doi: 10.1057/s11369-017-0027-3.

[17] A. Narayanan, Translation tutorial: 21 fairness definitions and their politics, *Presented at the Association Computing Machinery Conf. Fairness, Accountability, and Transparency*, New York, NY, USA (2018).

[18] J. Angwin, J. Larson, S. Mattu, and L. Kirchner, Machine bias (2016). URL https://www. propublica.org/article/machine-bias-risk-assessments-in-criminal-sentencing.

[19] S. Levin, A beauty contest was judged by AI and the robots didn't like dark skin (2016). URL https://www.theguardian.com/technology/2016/sep/08/artificial-intelligence-beauty- contest-doesnt-like-black-people.

[20] A. Rose, Are face-detection cameras racist? (2020). URL http://content.time.com/time/ business/article/0,8599,1954643,00.html.

[21] R. K. E. Bellamy, K. Dey, M. Hind, S. C. Hoffman, S. Houde, K. Kannan, P. Lohia, J. Martino, S. Mehta, A. Mojsilovic, S. Nagar, K. N. Ramamurthy, J. Richards, D. Saha, P. Sattigeri, M. Singh, K. R. Varshney, and Y. Zhang, AI fairness 360: an extensible toolkit for detecting, understanding, and mitigating unwanted algorithmic bias (2018).

[22] E. Posner, Why uber will—and should—be regulated, slate, Jan. 5, 2015 (endorsing arguments for regulation of surge pricing, Uber's term for raising prices at times of higher demand) (2015).

[23] M. Stoller, How Uber creates an algorithmic monopoly to extract rents (2004). https://www. nakedcapitalism.com/2014/04/matt-stoller-how-uber-creates-an-algorithmic-monopoly.html.

[24] R. Caruana, Y. Lou, J. Gehrke, P. Koch, M. Sturm, and N. Elhadad, Intelligible models for healthcare: predicting pneumonia risk and hospital 30-day readmission. In *Proceedings of the 21th ACM SIGKDD International Conference on Knowledge Discovery and Data Mining*, KDD '15, New York, NY, USA, pp. 1721–1730 (2015). Association for Computing Machinery. ISBN 9781450336642. doi: 10.1145/2783258.2788613. URL https://doi.org/ 10.1145/2783258.2788613.

[25] S. Sen, D. Dxasgupta, and K. D. Gupta, An empirical study on algorithmic bias. In *2020 IEEE 44th Annual Computers, Software, and Applications Conference (COMP-SAC)*, pp. 1189–1194 (2020). doi: 10.1109/COMPSAC48688.2020.00-95.

[26] H. Suresh and J. V. Guttag, A framework for understanding unintended consequences of machine learning, *CoRR*, **abs/1901.10002** (2019). URL http://arxiv.org/abs/1901.10002.

[27] A. Olteanu, C. Castillo, F. Diaz, and E. Kıcıman, Social data: biases, method-ological pitfalls, and ethical boundaries, *Front. Big Data*, **2**, 13 (2019). ISSN 2624-909X. doi: 10.3389/fdata.2019.00013. URL https://www.frontiersin.org/article/10. 3389/fdata.2019.00013.

[28] N. Mehrabi, F. Morstatter, N. Saxena, K. Lerman, and A. Galstyan, A survey on bias and fairness in machine learning (2019).

[29] J. Buolamwini and T. Gebru, Gender shades: intersectional accuracy disparities in commercial gender classification. In eds. S. A. Friedler and C. Wilson, *Proceedings of the 1st Conference on Fairness, Accountability and Transparency*, vol. 81, *Proceedings of Machine Learning Research*, New York, NY, USA, pp. 77–91 (2018). PMLR. URL http://proceedings.mlr.press/ v81/buolamwini18a.html.

[30] R. Baeza-Yates, Bias on the web, *Commun. ACM*, **61**(6), 54–61 (2018). ISSN 0001-0782. doi: 10.1145/3209581. URL https://doi.org/10.1145/3209581.

[31] S. Shankar, Y. Halpern, E. Breck, J. Atwood, J. Wilson, and D. Sculley, No classification without representation: assessing geodiversity issues in open data sets for the developing world (2017).

[32] I. Y. Chen, P. Szolovits, and M. Ghassemi, Can AI help reduce disparities in general medical and mental health care?, *AMA J. Ethics*, **21**(2), E167–179 (2019). ISSN 2376-6980. doi: 10.1001/amajethics.2019.167. URL https://doi.org/10.1001/amajethics.2019.167.

[33] US Dept of Justice, Criminal program update (US Dept of Justice, 2015). URL https://www.justice.gov/atr/division-update/2015/ criminal-program-update.

[34] US Dept of Justice, Former e-commerce executive charged with price fixing in the antitrust division's first online marketplace prosecution (2015).

[35] J. D. Sutter, Amazon seller lists book at $23,698,655.93—plus shipping (2011). URL http://www.cnn.com/2011/TECH/web/04/25/amazon.price.algorithm/index.html.

[36] CMA, Pricing algorithms (2018). URL https://www.icsa.org.uk/knowledge/governance-and-compliance/indepth/technical/pricing-algorithms.

[37] U Govt, *CMA* issues final decision in online cartel case (2016). URL https://www.gov.uk/government/news/cma-issues-final-decision-in-online-cartel-case.

[38] F. B. D. LLP, Pricing algorithms: the digital collusion scenarios (2017). URL https://www.freshfields.com/digital/.

[39] S. Schechner, Why do gas station prices constantly change? Blame the algorithm (2017). URL https://www.wsj.com/articles/why-do-gas-station-prices-constantly-change-blame-the-algorithm-1494262674.

[40] A. Ezrachi and M. E. Stucke, Algorithmic collusion: problems and counter measures (2017). URL https://one.oecd.org/document/DAF/COMP/WD(2017)25/en/pdf[https://perma.cc/53AY-V74Y.

[41] C. Emilio, C. Giacomo, D. Vincenzo, and P. Sergio, Artificial intelligence, algorithmic pricing and collusion (2018). URL https://ssrn.com/abstract=3304991orhttp://dx.doi.org/10.2139/ssrn.3304991.

[42] M. T. Ribeiro, S. Singh, and C. Guestrin, "Why should I trust you?": Explaining the predictions of any classifier (2016).

[43] D. E. Knuth, *The Stanford GraphBase: A Platform for Combinatorial Computing*, ACM Press (1993).

[44] K. Gupta and S. Sen, A genetic algorithm approach to regenerate image from a reduce scaled image using bit data count, *Broad Res. Artif. Intell. Neurosci.*, **9**(2), 34–44 (2018). ISSN 2067-3957. URL https://www.edusoft. ro/brain/index.php/brain/article/view/805.

[45] K. D. Gupta, D. Dasgupta, and S. Sen, Smart crowdsourcing based content review system (SCCRS): an approach to improve trustworthiness of online contents. In eds. X. Chen, A. Sen, W. W. Li, and M. T. Thai, *Computational Data and Social Networks*, Springer International Publishing, Cham, pp. 523–535 (2018). ISBN 978-3-030-04648-4.

[46] D. Dasgupta, AI vs. AI: viewpoints. Technical Report (No. CS-19-001), The University of Memphis, Memphis, TN (2019).

[47] J. Buolamwini and T. Gebru, Gender shades: intersectional accuracy disparities in commercial gender classification. In eds. S. A. Friedler and C. Wilson, *Proceedings of the 1st Conference on Fairness, Accountability and Transparency*, vol. 81, *Proceedings of Machine Learning Research*, New York, NY, USA, pp. 77–91 (2018). PMLR. URL http://proceedings.mlr.press/v81/buolamwini18a.html.

[48] K. Hao, Congress wants to protect you from biased algorithms, deepfakes, and other bad AI, MIT Technology Review (2019).

Chapter 24

Collective Intelligence: A Comprehensive Review of Metaheuristic Algorithms Inspired by Animals

Fevrier Valdez

Computer Science, Tijuana Institute of Technology,
Calzada Tecnologico S/N, Tijuana, 22450, BC, Mexico,
fevrier@tectijuana.mx

In this chapter, a survey on the optimization methods based on collective intelligence (CI) with animal behavior is described. The review presents some methods such as cuckoo search algorithm (CSA), particle swarm optimization (PSO), ant colony optimization (ACO), and bat algorithm (BA). We considered these algorithms because they are inspired by animal behavior and have been demonstrated to be useful for solving complex optimization problems in many applications. Moreover, the algorithms are inspired by CI. There are many other algorithms based on animal behavior but only the methods described above are considered, mainly because we have worked a lot with them and improved them using fuzzy logic to adapt parameters, thus managing to improve convergence, results, etc.

24.1. Introduction

The main motivation of this chapter is to review the methods based on CI and populations inspired by some animal species and their applications. CI is considered a specific computational process that provides a straightforward explanation for several social phenomena; it is the theory, design, application, and development of biologically motivated computational paradigms. Overall, the three areas of CI are neural networks [41], fuzzy systems [107], and evolutionary computation [104]. The most relevant contribution of this chapter is to review the importance of metaheuristics based on animals as motivation and see how the authors used these algorithms to solve complex optimization problems and achieve the best results compared with other traditional methods. We used a tool available at www.connectedpapers.com to calculate the relationship between the works. We also used the Web of Science Core Collection (WoS) to search the more recent works about these methods.

Optimization methods are commonly based on nature, biological evolution, animal species, and physical laws, and researchers often apply these methods to solve optimization problems, such as to improve important parameters in a control system; or in a neural network; to find the best architecture, in robotics, for example; to find the best route or to minimize the use of battery [110, 111]. These methods have been demonstrated to be better than traditional methods in complex problems. Some works can be reviewed in [1, 5, 42, 43, 52, 61, 98, 106, 113, 124].

This chapter is organized as follows: in Section 24.1 a brief introduction of collective intelligence is presented; in Section 24.2 the literature review and the methods analyzed in the chapter are presented; Section 24.3 shows the review and applications that have used these methods within computational intelligence; in Section 24.4 we describe the conclusions obtained after this review; and the references are presented at the end of the chapter.

24.2. Literature Review

Collective intelligence optimization methods have been widely used because they have demonstrated the ability to solve several complex optimization problems in many areas. The term "collective intelligence", has come into use [7–9, 12]. Swarm intelligence is the part of artificial intelligence that is based on the study of actions of individuals in various decentralized systems. This chapter describes some heuristic techniques based on animal behavior and populations throughout history that have been used by researchers as optimization methods to solve problems of everyday life and industry. This chapter provides a brief description of the metaheuristics CSA, PSO, ACO, and BA. In this section, Table 2.4 presents most popular optimization algorithms based on populations in chronological order.

24.2.1. *Cuckoo Search Algorithm*

The cuckoo optimization algorithm is based on the life of the bird called cuckoo [123]. The basis of this novel optimization algorithm is the specific breeding and egg laying behavior of this bird. Adult cuckoos and eggs are used in this modeling. Adult cuckoos lay eggs in other birds' habitats. Those eggs hatch and become mature cuckoos if they are not found and removed by host birds. The immigration of groups of cuckoos and the environmental specifications hopefully lead them to converge and reach the best place for reproduction and breeding. The objective function is in this

Table 24.1: Popular optimization algorithms inspired by populations in chronological order.

Year	Popular optimization algorithms based on populations
2020	Improved binary grey wolf optimizer
2020	Political optimizer [4]
2020	Chimp optimization algorithm [68]
2020	Black widow optimization algorithm [54]
2020	Coronavirus optimization algorithm [82]
2019	Improved spider monkey optimization [115]
2018	Monkey search algorithm [72]
2016	Whale optimization algorithm [86]
2016	Dolphin swarm algorithm [93]
2015	Ant lion optimizer [85]
2015	Lightning search algorithm [99]
2015	Artificial algae algorithm [109]
2012	Fruit fly optimization algorithm [90]
2012	Krill herd algorithm [45]
2010	Bat algorithm [126]
2010	Firefly algorithm [120]
2009	Cuckoo search [119]
2009	Biogeography-based optimization [101]
2009	Gravitational search algorithm [94]
2007	Intelligent water drops [59]
2006	Cat swarm optimization [19]
2006	Glow-worm [71]
2005	Artificial bee algorithm [64]
2005	Harmony search algorithm [49]
2005	Honey bee algorithm [105]
2002	Bacterial foraging algorithm [103]
2001	Bee colony optimization [80]
2002	Estimation of distribution algorithm [88]
1998	Shark search algorithm [57]
1992	Genetic programming [70]
1995	Particle swarm optimization [40]
1992	Ant colony optimization [24]
1989	Tabu search [50]
1979	Cultural algorithms [97]
1975	Genetic algorithms [58]
1966	Evolutionary programming [6]
1965	Evolution strategies [10]

best place. CSA was developed Yand and Deb [123]. CSA is a new, continuous, and overall conscious search based on the life of a cuckoo. Similar to other metaheuristic algorithms, CSA begins with a main population, a group of cuckoos. These cuckoos lay eggs in the habitat of other host birds. A random group of potential solutions is generated that represent the habitat in CSA [120, 121].

24.2.2. Ant Colony Optimization

One of the first behaviors studied by researchers was the ability of ants to find the shortest path between their nest and a food source. From these studies and observations followed the first algorithmic models of the foraging behavior of ants, as developed by Marco Dorigo [27,28]. Since then, research in the development of algorithms based on ants has been very popular, resulting in a large number of algorithms and applications. These algorithms that were developed as a result of studies on ant foraging behavior are referred to as instances of the ant colony optimization metaheuristic [30,31].

The ACO algorithm has been applied to the Traveling Salesman Problem (TSP) [27,28,30–32]. Given a set of cities and the distances between them, the TSP is the problem of finding the shortest possible path to visit every city exactly once. The possible path that visits every city exactly once can be represented by a complete weighted graph $G = (N, E)$, where N is the set of nodes representing the cities and E is the set of edges. Each edge is assigned a value d_{ij}, which is the distance between cities i and j. When applying the ACO algorithm to the TSP, a pheromone strength $\tau_{ij}(t)$ is associated with each edge (i, j), where $\tau_{ij}(t)$ is a numerical value that is modified during the execution of the algorithm and t is the iteration counter. Equation (24.1), shows the probabilistic rules of the ant k.

$$p_{ij}^k \frac{\left[\tau_{ij}\right]^\alpha \left[\eta_{ij}\right]^\beta}{\sum l \in \mathrm{N}_i^k \left[\tau_{ij}\right]^\alpha \left[\eta_{ij}\right]^\beta}, \text{ if } j \in N_i^k \qquad (24.1)$$

The ACO metaheuristic is inspired by the behavior of real ant colonies, which presented an interesting feature—how to find the shortest paths between the nest and food. On their way the ants deposit a substance called pheromone. This trail allows the ants to get back to their nest from the food source; it uses the evaporation of pheromone to avoid an unlimited increase of pheromone trails and allows the ants to forget bad decisions [33,35]. The probability of ant k going from node i to node j is the heuristic information, say, prior knowledge. It is the possible neighborhood of ant k when in the city i; it is the pheromone trail. α and β are parameters that determine the influence of the pheromone and prior knowledge, respectively (Eq. (24.1)).

24.2.3. Particle Swarm Optimization

Particle Swarm Optimization (PSO) is a population-based stochastic optimization technique developed by Eberhart and Kennedy in 1995, inspired by the social behavior of bird flocking or fish schooling.

   PSO has many processes similar to those that work with genetic algorithms. This algorithm initiates a swarm of random particles, where each of the contained particles could be a solution to the problem that is being worked on. These possible solutions are evaluated in each of the iterations that we have [66].

   PSO shares many similarities with evolutionary computation techniques such as Genetic Algorithms (GA) [17]. The system is initialized with a population of random solutions and searches for optima by updating generations. However, unlike GA, PSO has no evolution operators such as crossover and mutation. In PSO, the potential solutions, called particles, fly through the problem space by following the current optimum particles [2].

   Another reason that PSO is attractive is that there are few parameters to adjust. One version, with slight variations, works well in a wide variety of applications. Particle swarm optimization has been used for approaches that can be implemented across a wide range of applications, as well as for specific applications focused on a specific requirement.

24.2.4. *Bat Algorithm*

Bat algorithm is a bio-inspired algorithm developed by Yang [121], and it has been found to be very efficient. If we idealize some of the echolocation characteristics of microbats, we can develop various bat-inspired algorithms or bat algorithms. For simplicity, we now use the following approximate or idealized rules [118]:

1. All bats use echolocation to sense distance, and they also "know" the difference between food/prey and background barriers in some magical way.
2. Bats fly randomly with velocity $\mathbf{v_i}$ at position $\mathbf{x_i}$ with a fixed frequency $\mathbf{f}_{min}$, varying wavelength λ and loudness $\mathbf{A}_0$ to search for prey. They can automatically adjust the wavelength (or frequency) of their emitted pulses and adjust the rate of pulse emission r ε [0, 1], depending on the proximity of their target.
3. Although loudness can vary in many ways, we assume that it varies from a large (positive) $\mathbf{A}_0$ to a minimum constant value $\mathbf{A}_{min}$.

   For simplicity, the frequency $f \in [0, f_{max}]$, the new solutions $\mathbf{x_i}^t$, and velocity $\mathbf{v_i}^t$ at a specific time step t are represented by a random vector drawn from a uniform distribution [51].

24.3. Applications

In this chapter, we present review of the applications and relationship between the works of several authors. In this case, we describe only the works using each analyzed method. In particular, in this chapter, we study in detail only six algorithms based on collective intelligence, such as CSA, ACO, PSO, and BA algorithms. In this section, we present the connected papers using these methods and the most relevant applications found in recent years are presented.

24.3.1. *Cuckoo Search Review*

Using the site https://www.connectedpapers.com/, we can appreciate the detailed information about the relationship among published works around the world taking as reference the most important papers considered after an exhaustive review of the literature. The collected information can be useful to know which papers have been cited in the past years, the more relevant ones, the authors, etc. For example, the paper "Cuckoo search algorithm: a metaheuristic approach to solve structural optimization problems" [46] was considered for this study of CSA as the main work to calculate the relationship with the connected papers. Figure 24.1 shows the graph prepared using the software; we can observe that the obtained results are not necessarily works based on CSA. However, it is shown that the papers are linked with some topic about collective intelligence or similar works because the researchers have cited their works. The graph presents the papers that were most frequently cited. This usually means that they are important seminal works for this field and it would be a good idea to get familiar with them [14, 21–23, 47, 55, 56, 63, 74, 96].

Table 24.2 shows the information about the papers, authors, and citations to observe in detail the relationship among them.

In addition, the table shows applications of CSA in many areas with different methods. CSA has often been used to solve complex optimization problems. According to a search in the Web of Science (WoS) for "Cuckoo search applications," we found the following results. In total, 399 journal papers were found with the above-mentioned search words. However, we are presenting a brief description of only three papers, but the complete updated references can be found with the same query in WoS. Lin et al. [79] developed the dynamic risk assessment of food safety based on an improved hidden Markov model (HMM) integrating CSA (CS-HMM). CSA was used to conduct a global search to obtain the initial value of HMM, and then the Baum-Welch algorithm was used for modifying the initial value to obtain a trained risk assessment model. On the other hand, in [73] the cuckoo search and bee colony algorithm (CSBCA) methods were used for the optimization of test cases and generation of path convergence within minimal execution time. The performance of the proposed CSBCA was compared with the performance of existing methods such as PSO, CSA, bee colony algorithm (BCA), and firefly algorithm (FA). Finally, in [108], an improved CSA variant for constrained nonlinear optimization was proposed. Figure 24.2 shows the total number of papers by authors with at least three papers.

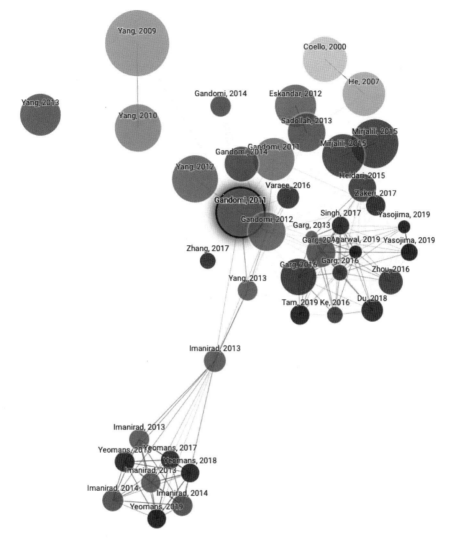

Figure 24.1: Papers associated with the original paper "Cuckoo search algorithm: a metaheuristic approach to solve structural optimization problems."

24.3.2. *Ant Colony Review*

In this section, we present the papers associated with ACO. The paper selected to make this analysis is "Ant colony optimization theory: a survey" [29]. In Figure 24.3, one can appreciate the full network with relationship works. Using the software, if we select a prior work, it will highlight all graph papers referencing it, and selecting a graph paper will highlight all referenced prior work. However, in this example, only the paper cited above is shown as the main work. Moreover, the tool allows making several searches. Each paper can be selected depending on our interests and

Table 24.2:　Prior works.

Paper	Last Author	Year	Citation	Graph Citation
Use of a self-adaptive penalty approach for engineering optimization problems	Carlos A. Coello, Coello	2000	791	28
Solving engineering optimization problems with the simple constrained particle swarm optimizer	Carlos A. Coello, Coello	2008	251	28
An augmented Lagrange multiplier based method for mixed integer discrete continuous optimization and its applications to mechanical design	S. N., Kramer	1994	476	26
Constraint-handling in genetic algorithms through the use of dominance-based tournament selection	Efrén, Mezura	2002	586	23
An effective co-evolutionary particle swarm optimization for constrained engineering design problems	Ling, Wang	2007	668	23
A new meta-heuristic algorithm for continuous engineering optimization: harmony search theory and practice	Zong Woo, Geem	2005	1444	23
Mixed variable structural optimization using Firefly Algorithm	Amir Hossein	2011	576	23
An improved particle swarm optimizer for mechanical design optimization problems	Q. H., Wu	2004	311	22
Society and civilization: an optimization algorithm based on the simulation of social behavior	Kim-Meow, Liew	2003	369	22
Gaussian quantum-behaved particle swarm optimization approaches for constrained engineering design problems	Leandro dos Santos	2010	256	21

the network is automatically built from the selected work. With this, it is possible to analyze in detail the relationship that exists between similar works. Table 24.3 shows the prior works with the analyzed paper mentioned earlier. We can appreciate the information of citations and authors [13, 15, 25, 26, 34, 36, 37, 44, 81, 102].

All applications with the ACO method using computational intelligence have been included. ACO using fuzzy systems is often used in parameter tuning to find the most important parameter of the methods. In addition, in the Web of science (WoS). we made a query with the topic "ACO with fuzzy logic" and found the following results. In total, 50 journal works were found with the search described above. However, a brief description of only the first three papers has been presented here, but the complete updated references can be found with the same search in WoS. In [11], a holistic optimization approach for inverted cart–pendulum control tuning,

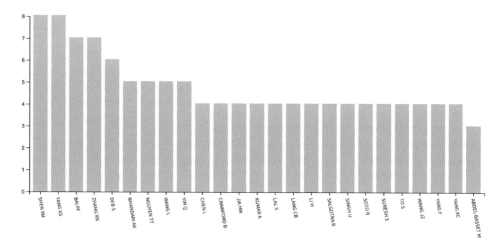

Figure 24.2:   CSA applications by authors.

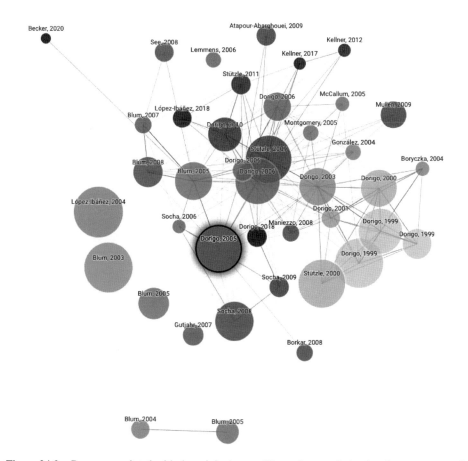

Figure 24.3:   Papers associated with the original paper "Ant colony optimization theory: a survey."

Table 24.3:   Prior works.

Ant system: optimization by a colony of cooperating agents	Alberto, Colorni	1996	10307	40
Ant colony system: a cooperative learning approach to the traveling salesman problem	Luca Maria, Gambardella	1997	7121	36
MACS-VRPTW: a multiple ant colony system for vehicle routing problems with time windows	Giovanni, Agazzi	1999	792	31
Optimization, learning and natural algorithms	Marco, Dorigo	1992	3373	31
Exact and approximate nondeterministic tree-search procedures for the quadratic assignment problem	Vittorio, Maniezzo	1999	337	30
MAX-MIN ant system	Holger H., Hoos	2000	2484	29
1 Positive feedback as a search strategy	Alberto, Colorni	1991	751	29
Ants can colour graphs	Alain, Hertz	1997	564	28
A new rank based version of the ant system: a computational study	Christine, Strauss	1997	888	28
AntNet: distributed stigmergetic control for communications networks	Marco, Dorigo	1998	1753	27

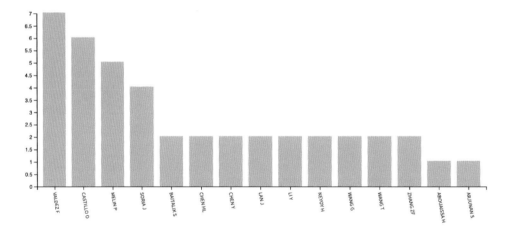

Figure 24.4:   ACO with fuzzy logic categorized by authors.

with a simplified ant colony optimization method with a constrained Nelder–Mead algorithm (ACO-NM), was proposed. On the other hand, in [18], an improved ACO algorithm optimized fuzzy PID controller for load frequency control in multi-area interconnected power systems was proposed. Finally, in [126], an improved ACO to design an A2-C1 type fuzzy logic system was developed. Figure 24.4 shows the number of publications by authors with at least one work.

In addition, in Figure 24.5 the results obtained by countries are shown, where it can be seen that India and China have the major number of publications with the query described above.

Other recent applications made with ACO can be seen in [53, 60, 83, 127].

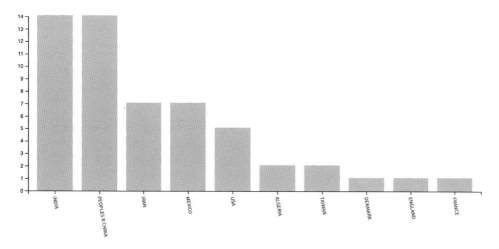

Figure 24.5: ACO with fuzzy logic categorized by countries.

24.3.3. *PSO Review*

As for the methods described earlier, we used the site https://www.connectedpapers.com/ to observe detailed information about the relationship among published works around the world taking as reference the most important papers considered after making an exhaustive review of the literature. The collected information can be useful to know which papers have been cited in the last years and which are more relevant, including the authors, etc. For example, the paper "Particle swarm optimization: an overview" [92] was considered for this study with PSO as the main work to review the relationship with the connected papers. Figure 24.6 shows the graph after use the software above earlier. The graph shows which papers are linked with some topics about collective intelligence or similar works because the researchers have cited their works using these references. The graph represents the papers that were most commonly cited. This usually means that they are important seminal works for this field and it would be a good idea to get familiar with them [20, 38, 39, 65, 67, 77, 84, 95, 100, 114]. Table 24.4 shows the relevant information about the connected papers shown in Figure 24.6.

In this part, the applications of the PSO algorithm in computational intelligence are presented. While searching the topic "PSO with neural networks" in WoS, the results showed 2360 publications related to this query. However, only three papers are described, but the updated references can be found using the same query in WoS.

In [62], A Novel PSO-Based Optimized Lightweight Convolution Neural Network for Movements Recognizing from Multichannel Surface Electromyogram was proposed. In [91], the authors proposed a work for prediction of clad characteristics using ANN and combined PSO-ANN algorithms in the laser metal deposition process. Finally, in [116], a PSO-GA based hybrid with

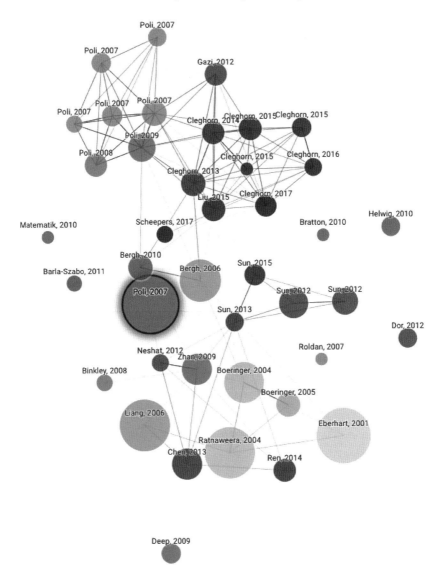

Figure 24.6: Papers connected with the original paper "Particle swarm optimization: an overview".

Adam Optimization for ANN training with application in Medical Diagnosis was developed.

Other works on PSO applied to neural networks, math functions, and control can be found reviewed in [3, 76, 78, 112]. In Figure 24.7, the results obtained by authors with at least 14 papers querying in WoS with the topic used in this part.

Table 24.4: Prior works on PSO.

Title	Last author	Year	Citations	Graph citations
A modified particle swarm optimizer	Russell C., Eberhart	1998	9129	38
The particle swarm—explosion, stability, and convergence in a multidimensional complex space	James, Kennedy	2002	7426	35
The fully informed particle swarm: simpler, maybe better	José, Neves	2004	1517	35
Population structure and particle swarm performance	Rui, Mendes	2002	1520	35
A cooperative approach to particle swarm optimization	Andries Petrus, Engelbrecht	2004	1764	31
Small worlds and mega-minds: effects of neighborhood topology on particle swarm performance	James, Kennedy	1999	1065	31
A new optimizer using particle swarm theory	James, Kennedy	1995	12238	31
Comprehensive learning particle swarm optimizer for global optimization of multimodal functions	S., Baskar	2006	2583	30
Self-organizing hierarchical particle swarm optimizer with time-varying acceleration coefficients	Harry C., Watson	2004	2391	30
Comparing inertia weights and constriction factors in particle swarm optimization	Yuhui, Shi	2000	2668	26

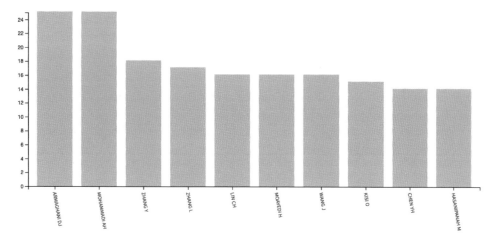

Figure 24.7: PSO with neural networks categorized by authors.

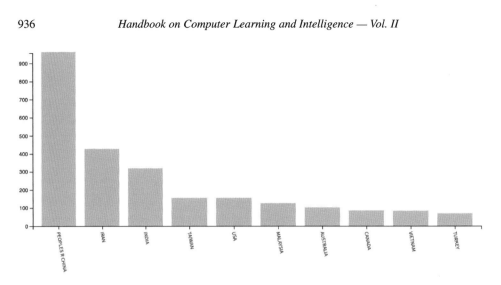

Figure 24.8:   PSO with neural networks categorized by countries.

Figure 24.8 shows the results obtained by countries, where it can be seen that China has the major number of publications related to the query described above.

24.3.4. *BA Review*

Like the other algorithms reviewed, we selected a popular article to observe the important connections between them and the network that was built after querying using the tool described earlier. The collected information can be useful to review which papers have been cited in the recent years, the ones that are more relevant, the authors, etc. For example, the paper "Bat algorithm: a novel approach for global engineering optimization" [125] was considered for this study with BA as the work to review the relationship with related papers. Figure 24.9 shows the graph obtained using the software described. The graph shows which papers are linked with some topics about collective intelligence or similar works because the researchers cited these references in their work. The graph represents the papers that were most commonly cited [20, 38, 39, 65, 67, 77, 84, 95, 100, 114].

Table 24.5 represents information about the graph presented in this section. We can observe that the first paper has 791 citations [16, 22, 23, 47, 55, 56, 69, 75, 96, 117].

We made a search in WoS, similar to the other methods analyzed in this chapter, with the topic "BA with fuzzy logic"; however, we found only 19 papers on this method, maybe because not many authors have tried to combine or apply these two techniques. Here, only three recent papers are presented but the other papers can

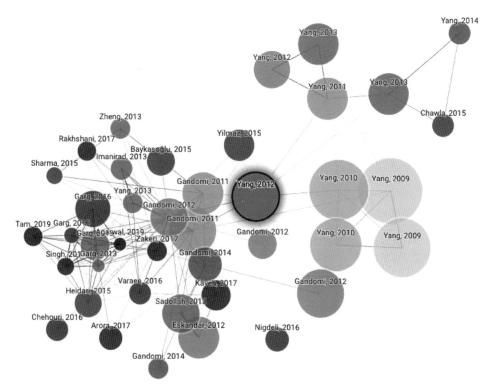

Figure 24.9: Papers connected with the original paper "Bat algorithm: a novel approach for global engineering optimization."

be reviewed in WoS. In addition, other works where this algorithm was used are cited.

In [48], an implementation of a novel hybrid BAT-fuzzy controller-based MPPT for a grid-connected PV battery system was made. In addition, in [89], a comparative study of the type-2 fuzzy particle swarm, bee colony, and bat algorithms in optimization of fuzzy controllers was presented. Finally, in [87], the smart bat algorithm for wireless sensor network deployment in a 3D environment was proposed.

Other recent applications of BA can be found in [69, 122]. Figure 24.10 shows the results obtained by authors with at least one paper by raising the query in WoS with the topic used in this part.

Finally, Figure 24.11 shows the results obtained, categorized by countries, where it can be seen that China has the maximum number of publications related to the query described above.

Table 24.5:   Prior works on BA.

Title	Last author	Year	Citations	Graph citations
Use of a self-adaptive penalty approach for engineering optimization problems	Carlos A. Coello, Coello	2000	791	26
Society and civilization: an optimization algorithm based on the simulation of social behavior	Kim-Meow, Liew	2003	369	23
A new meta-heuristic algorithm for continuous engineering optimization: harmony search theory and practice	Zong Woo, Geem	2005	1444	22
An improved particle swarm optimizer for mechanical design optimization problems	Q. H., Wu	2004	311	21
Nature-inspired metaheuristic algorithms	Xin-She, Yang	2008	3112	21
An augmented Lagrange multiplier based method for mixed integer discrete continuous optimization and its applications to mechanical design	S. N., Kramer	1994	476	21
Solving engineering optimization problems with the simple constrained particle swarm optimizer	Carlos A. Coello, Coello	2008	251	21
An effective co-evolutionary particle swarm optimization for constrained engineering design problems	Ling, Wang	2007	668	21
Mixed variable structural optimization using firefly algorithm	Amir Hossein, Alavi	2011	576	19
Constraint-handling in genetic algorithms through the use of dominance-based tournament selection	Efrén, Mezura-Montes	2002	586	19

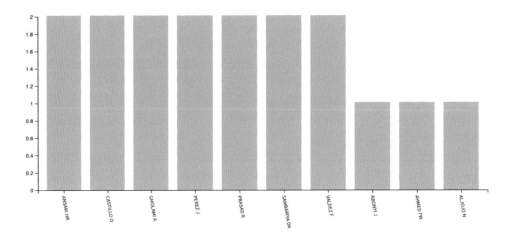

Figure 24.10:   BA with fuzzy logic categorized by authors.

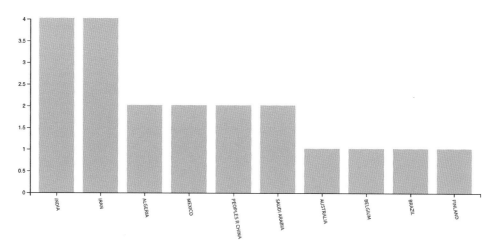

Figure 24.11: BA with fuzzy logic categorized by authors.

24.4. Conclusions

In this chapter, after conducting an exhaustive study of the different optimization methods inspired by collective intelligence, we can observe in detail the importance of these algorithms, and we can appreciate the activities developed by animals adapted to computational systems for solving complex problems in the real world. These algorithms are capable of improving the performance of many applications by combining different methods, which are usually required in many complex problems. For example, ant colony optimization is a metaheuristic motivated by the foraging behavior of ants. It represents a general algorithmic framework that can be applied to various optimization problems in management, engineering, and control. ACO takes inspiration from the behavior of various ant species to find the shortest path. PSO, inspired by the social behavior of bird flocking or fish schooling, is capable of solving many complex optimization problems. Finally, BA, the more recent method, is inspired by the behavior of the micro bats. It is capable of achieving positive results. In this chapter, we only analyzed the most relevant methods proposed in recent years; however, there are other works with other algorithms where the researchers can find similar algorithms. Therefore, in this chapter, we focused on the methods based on collective intelligence inspired by animal behavior. Recently, many researchers have been applying these techniques to solve complex applications and obtain better results than with traditional methods. In addition, it can be highlighted in this chapter that the optimization algorithms used with computational intelligence can be used to improve the results in many applications. Collective intelligence is nowadays used by researchers to achieve the best results in algorithms. The networks built with the most relevant works are used to make calculations, giving us a general panorama of the researchers applying these methods in the world.

Acknowledgment

We would like to express our gratitude to CONACYT, Tecnologico Nacional de Mexico/Tijuana Institute of Technology, for the facilities and resources granted for the development of this research.

References

[1] Abdel-Basset, M., L. A. Shawky (2019). Flower pollination algorithm: a comprehensive review. *Artif. Intell. Rev.,* **52**(4):2533–2557.

[2] Angeline, P. J. (1998). Using selection to improve particle swarm optimization. In *Proceedings 1998 IEEE World Congress on Computational Intelligence*, pp. 84–89.

[3] Argha, R., D. Diptam, C. Kaustav (2013). Training artificial neural network using particle swarm optimization algorithm. *Int. J. Adv. Res. Comput. Sci. Software Eng.*, **3**(3):430–434.

[4] Askari, Q., I. Younas, M. Saeed (2020). Political optimizer: a novel socio-inspired meta-heuristic for global optimization. *Knowledge-Based Syst.*, **195**:105709.

[5] Askarzadeh, A., E. Rashedi (2017). Harmony search algorithm.

[6] Bäck, T., G. Rudolph, H. P. Schwefel (1997). Evolutionary programming and evolution strategies: similarities and differences. In *Proceedings of the Second Annual Conference on Evolutionary Programming*, pp. 11–22.

[7] Beni, G. (1988). The concept of cellular robotic system. In *Proceedings of the 1988 IEEE International Symposium on Intelligent Control*, pp. 57–62. IEEE Computer Society Press.

[8] Beni, G., S. Hackwood (1992). Stationary waves in cyclic swarms. In *Proceedings of the 1992 International Symposium on Intelligent Control*, pp. 234–242. IEEE Computer Society Press.

[9] Beni, G., J. Wang (1989). Swarm intelligence. In *Proceedings of the Seventh Annual Meeting of the Robotics Society of Japan*, pp. 425–428. RSJ Press.

[10] Beyer, H. G., H. P. Schwefel (2002). Evolution strategies: a comprehensive introduction. *Nat. Comput.*, **1**:3–52.

[11] Blondin, M. J., P. M. Pardalos (2020). A holistic optimization approach for inverted cart-pendulum control tuning. *Soft Comput.*, **24**(6):4343–4359.

[12] Bonabeau, E., M. Dorigo, G. Theraulaz (1997). *Swarm Intelligence*. Oxford University Press.

[13] Bullnheimer, B., R. Hartl, C. Strauss (1997). A new rank based version of the ant system: a computational study. Working Paper No. 1, SFB Adaptive Information Systems and Modelling in Economics and Management Science, Vienna, to appear in CEJOR.

[14] Cagnina, L. C., S. Esquivel, C. Coello (2008). Solving engineering optimization problems with the simple constrained particle swarm optimizer. *Informatica (Slovenia)*, **32**:319–326.

[15] Caro, G. D., M. Dorigo (1998). AntNet: distributed stigmergetic control for communications networks. *arXiv abs/1105.5449.*

[16] Carreon-Ortiz, H., Valdez, F (2022). A new mycorrhized tree optimization nature-inspired algorithm. *Soft Comput*, **26**:4797–4817. https://doi.org/10.1007/s00500-022-06865-8.

[17] Castillo, O., P. Melin (2002). Hybrid intelligent systems for time series prediction using neural networks, fuzzy logic, and fractal theory. *IEEE Trans. Neural Networks*, **13**(6):1395–1408.

[18] Chen, G., Z. Li, Z. Zhang, S. Li (2020). An improved ACO algorithm optimized fuzzy PID controller for load frequency control in multi area interconnected power systems. *IEEE Access*, **8**:6429–6447.

[19] Chu, S. C., P. W. Tsai, J. S. Pan (2006). Cat swarm optimization. In *Proceedings of the 9th pacific Rim International Conference on Artificial Intelligence, LNAI 4099*, Guilin, pp. 854–858.

[20] Clerc, M., J. Kennedy (2002). The particle swarm—explosion, stability, and convergence in a multidimensional complex space. *IEEE Trans. Evol. Comput.*, **6**:58–73.

[21] Coelho, L. (2010). Gaussian quantum-behaved particle swarm optimization approaches for constrained engineering design problems. *Expert Syst. Appl.*, **37**:1676–1683.

[22] Coello, C. (2000). Use of a self-adaptive penalty approach for engineering optimization problems. *Comput. Ind.*, **41**:113–127.

[23] Coello, C., E. Mezura-Montes (2002). Constraint-handling in genetic algorithms through the use of dominance-based tournament selection. *Adv. Eng. Inf.*, **16**:193–203.

[24] Colorni, A., M. Dorigo, V. Maniezzo (1992). Distributed optimization by ant colonies. In Bourgine, F. V. P., ed., *Proceedings of the First European Conference on Artificial Life*, pp. 134–142. MIT Press.

[25] Costa, D., A. Hertz (1997). Ants can colour graphs. *J. Oper. Res. Soc.*, **48**:295–305.

[26] Dorigo, M. (1992). Optimization, learning and natural algorithms. Ph.D. Thesis, Politecnico di Milano, Italy.

[27] Dorigo, M. (1994). Learning by probabilistic Boolean networks. In *Proceedings of the IEEE International Conference on Neural Networks*, pp. 887–891.

[28] Dorigo, M., M. Birattari, T. Stützle (1992). Ant colony optimization. In *IEEE Computational Intelligence Magazine*, pp. 28–39.

[29] Dorigo, M., C. Blum (2005). Ant colony optimization theory: a survey. *Theor. Comput. Sci.*, **344**(2):243–278.

[30] Dorigo, M., E. Bonabeau, G. Theraulaz (2000). Ant algorithms and stigmergy. *Future Gener. Comput. Syst.*, **16**(8):851–871.

[31] Dorigo, M., G. D. Caro (1999a). Ant colony optimization: a new meta-heuristic. In *Proceedings of the IEEE Congress on Evolutionary Computation*, vol. 2, pp. 1470–1477.

[32] Dorigo, M., G. D. Caro (1999b). The ant colony optimization meta-heuristic. In *New Ideas in Optimization*, pp. 11–32.

[33] Dorigo, M., L. Gambardella (1996). A study of some properties of ant-Q. In *Proceedings of the Fourth International Conference on Parallel Problem Solving from Nature*, pp. 656–665.

[34] Dorigo, M., L. Gambardella (1997a). Ant colony system: a cooperative learning approach to the traveling salesman problem. *IEEE Trans. Evol. Comput.*, **1**:53–66.

[35] Dorigo, M., L. M. Gambardella (1997b). Ant colonies for the travelling salesman problem. *Biosystems*, **43**(2):73–81.

[36] Dorigo, M., V. Maniezzo, A. Colorni (1991). Positive feedback as a search strategy. Technical Report, No. 91-016, Politecnico di Milano, Milano.

[37] Dorigo, M., V. Maniezzo, A. Colorni (1996). Ant system: optimization by a colony of cooperating agents. *IEEE Trans. Syst. Man Cybern. Part B: Cybern.*, **26**(1):29–41.

[38] Eberhart, R., J. Kennedy (1995a). A new optimizer using particle swarm theory. In *Proceedings of the Sixth International Symposium on Micro Machine and Human Science (MHS'95)*, pp. 39–43.

[39] Eberhart, R., Y. Shi (2000). Comparing inertia weights and constriction factors in particle swarm optimization. In *Proceedings of the 2000 Congress on Evolutionary Computation. CEC00 (Cat. No.00TH8512)*, vol. 1, pp. 84–88.

[40] Eberhart, R., C. Kennedy (1995b). A new optimizer using particle swarm theory. In *Proc. Sixth Int. Symposium on Micro Machine and Human Science*, pp. 33–43.

[41] Feng, J., Y. Chai, C. Xu (2021). A novel neural network to nonlinear complex-variable constrained nonconvex optimization. *J. Franklin Inst.*, **358**(8):4435–4457.

[42] Fister, I., X. S. Yang, J. Brest, I. Fister (2013). Modified firefly algorithm using quaternion representation. *Expert Syst. Appl.*, **40**(18):7220–7230.

[43] Gallo, C., V. Capozzi (2019). A simulated annealing algorithm for scheduling problems. *J. Appl. Math. Phys.*, **7**:2579–2594.

[44] Gambardella, L., E. Taillard, G. Agazzi (1999). MACS-VRPTW: a multiple ant colony system for vehicle routing problems with time windows. In D. Corne, M. Dorigo and F. Glover, eds., *New Ideas in Optimization*, McGraw-Hill, London, UK, pp. 63–76.

[45] Gandomi, A., A. Alavi (2012). Krill herd: a new bio-inspired optimization algorithm. *Commun. Nonlinear Sci. Numer. Simul.*, **17**:4831–4845.

[46] Gandomi, A., X. S. Yang, A. Alavi (2013). Cuckoo search algorithm: a metaheuristic approach to solve structural optimization problems. *Eng. Comput.*, **29**:245–245.

[47] Gandomi, A. H., X. Yang, A. H. Alavi (2011). Mixed variable structural optimization using Firefly Algorithm. *Comput. Struct.*, **89**:2325–2336.

[48] Ge, X., F. Ahmed, A. Rezvani, N. Aljojo, S. Samad, et al. (2020). Implementation of a novel hybrid BAT-Fuzzy controller based MPPT for grid-connected PV-battery system. *Control Eng. Pract.*, **98**:104380.

[49] Geem, Z. W. (2008). Novel derivative of harmony search algorithm for discrete design variables. *Appl. Math. Comput.*, **199**(1):223–230.

[50] Glover, F. (1989). Tabu search—part I. *ORSA J. Comput.*, **1**(3):190–206.

[51] Goel, N., D. Gupta, S. Goel (2013). Performance of Firefly and Bat Algorithm for unconstrained optimization problems. *Int. J. Adv. Res. Comput. Sci. Software Eng.*, **3**(5):1405–1409.

[52] Greco, R., I. Vanzi (2019). New few parameters differential evolution algorithm with application to structural identification. *J. Traffic Transp. Eng. (Engl. Ed.)*, **6**(1):1–14.

[53] Hajewski, J., S. Oliveira, D. Stewart, L. Weiler (2020). gBeam-ACO: a greedy and faster variant of Beam-ACO. In *Proceedings of the 2020 Genetic and Evolutionary Computation Conference Companion (GECCO '20)*, pp. 1434–1440.

[54] Hayyolalam, V., A. A. P. Kazem (2020). Black widow optimization algorithm: a novel meta-heuristic approach for solving engineering optimization problems. *Eng. Appl. Artif. Intell.*, **87**:103249.

[55] He, Q., L. Wang (2007). An effective co-evolutionary particle swarm optimization for constrained engineering design problems. *Eng. Appl. Artif. Intell.*, **20**:89–99.

[56] He, S., E. Prempain, Q. Wu (2004). An improved particle swarm optimizer for mechanical design optimization problems. *Eng. Optim.*, **36**:585–605.

[57] Hersovici, M., M. Jacovi, Y. S. Maarek, D. Pelleg, M. Shtalhaim, et al. (1998). The shark-search algorithm. An application: tailored Web site mapping. *Computer Networks and ISDN Systems*, **30**(1):317–326.

[58] Holland, J. H. (1975). *Adaptation in Natural and Artificial Systems: An Introductory Analysis with Applications to Biology, Control, and Artificial Intelligence*. University of Michigan Press, Ann Arbor, MI.

[59] Hosseini, H. S. (2009). The intelligent water drops algorithm: a nature-inspired swarm-based optimization algorithm. *Int. J. Bio-Inspir. Comput.*, **1**(1/2):71.

[60] Huang, Z. M., W. Neng Chen, Q. Li, X. N. Luo, H. Q. Yuan, et al. (2020). Ant colony evacuation planner: an ant colony system with incremental flow assignment for multipath crowd evacuation. *IEEE Trans. Cybern.*, doi: 10.1109/TCYB.2020.3013271.

[61] Joshi, A. S., O. Kulkarni, G. M. Kakandikar, V. M. Nandedkar (2017). Cuckoo search optimization: a review. *Mater. Today: Proc.*, **4**(8):7262–7269.

[62] Kan, X., D. Yang, L. Cao, H. Shu, Y. Li, et al. (2020). A novel PSO-based optimized lightweight convolution neural network for movements recognizing from multichannel surface electromyogram. *Complexity*, **2020**:1–15.

[63] Kannan, B., S. Kramer (1994). An augmented Lagrange multiplier based method for mixed integer discrete continuous optimization and its applications to mechanical design. *J. Mech. Des.*, **116**:405–411.

[64] Karaboga, D. (2005). An idea based on honey bee swarm for numerical optimization, Technical Report—TR06, Erciyes University.

[65] Kennedy, J. (1999). Small worlds and mega-minds: effects of neighborhood topology on particle swarm performance. In *Proceedings of the 1999 Congress on Evolutionary Computation-CEC99 (Cat. No. 99TH8406)*, vol. 3, pp. 1931–1938.

[66] Kennedy, J., R. C. Eberhart (1995). Particle swarm optimization. In *Proceedings of IEEE International Conference on Neural Networks*, pp. 1942–1948.

[67] Kennedy, J., R. Mendes (2002). Population structure and particle swarm performance. In *Proceedings of the 2002 Congress on Evolutionary Computation. CEC'02 (Cat. No.02TH8600)* vol. 2, pp. 1671–1676.

[68] Khishe, M., M. R. Mosavi (2020). Chimp optimization algorithm. *Expert Syst. Appl.*, **149**:113338.

[69] Kotwal, A., R. Bharti, M. Pandya, H. Jhaveri, R. Mangrulkar (2021). Application of BAT algorithm for detecting malignant brain tumors. In Dey, N., Rajinikanth, V. (eds.) *Applications of BAT Algorithm and its Variants*. Springer Tracts in Nature-Inspired Computing. Springer, Singapore, pp. 119–132.

[70] Koza, J. (1994). Genetic programming as a means for programming computers by natural selection. *Stat. Comput.*, **4**(2):87–112.

[71] Krishnanand, K. N., D. Ghose (2006). Glowworm swarm based optimization algorithm for multimodal functions with collective robotics applications. *Multiagent Grid Syst.*, **2**(3):209–222.

[72] Kuliev, E., V. Kureichik (2018). Monkey search algorithm for ECE components partitioning. *J. Phys.: Conf. Ser.*, **1015**:042026.

[73] Lakshminarayana, P., T. Sureshkumar (2020). Automatic generation and optimization of test case using hybrid cuckoo search and bee colony algorithm. *J. Intell. Syst.*, **30**:59–72.

[74] Lee, K., Z. W. Geem (2005a). A new meta-heuristic algorithm for continuous engineering optimization: harmony search theory and practice. *Comput. Methods Appl. Mech. Eng.*, **194**:3902–3933.

[75] Lee, K., Z. W. Geem (2005b). A new meta-heuristic algorithm for continuous engineering optimization: harmony search theory and practice. *Comput. Methods Appl. Mech. Eng.*, **194**:3902–3933.

[76] Li, C., T. Wu (2011). Adaptive fuzzy approach to function approximation with PSO and RLSE. *Expert Syst. Appl.*, **38**:13266–13273.

[77] Liang, J., A. Qin, P. Suganthan, S. Baskar (2006). Comprehensive learning particle swarm optimizer for global optimization of multimodal functions. *IEEE Trans. Evol. Comput.*, **10**: 281–295.

[78] Lima, N. F. D., T. B. Ludermir (2011). Frankenstein PSO applied to neural network weights and architectures. *Evolutionary Computation (CEC)*, 2452–2456.

[79] Lin, X., J. Li, Y. Han, Z. Geng, S. Cui, et al. (2021). Dynamic risk assessment of food safety based on an improved hidden Markov model integrating cuckoo search algorithm: a sterilized milk study. *J. Food Process Eng.*, **n/a**(**n/a**):e13630.

[80] Lučćić, P., D. Teodorović (2001). Bee system: modeling combinatorial optimization transportation engineering problems by swarm intelligence. In *Preprints of the RISTAN IV Triennial Symposium on Transportation Analysis*, Sao Miguel, pp. 441–445.

[81] Maniezzo, V. (1999). Exact and approximate nondeterministic tree-search procedures for the quadratic assignment problem. *Informs J. Comput.*, **11**:358–369.

[82] Martínez-Álvarez, F., G. Asencio-Cortés, J. F. Torres, D. Gutiérrez-Avilés, L. Melgar-García, et al. (2020). Coronavirus optimization algorithm: a bioinspired metaheuristic based on the COVID-19 propagation model. *Big Data*, **8**(4):308–322.

[83] Mazinan, A., F. Sagharichiha (2015). A novel hybrid PSO-ACO approach with its application to SPP. *Evolving Systems*, **6**:293–302.

[84] Mendes, R., J. Kennedy, J. Neves (2004). The fully informed particle swarm: simpler, maybe better. *IEEE Trans. Evol. Comput.*, **8**:204–210.

[85] Mirjalili, S. (2015). The ant lion optimizer. *Adv. Eng. Software*, **83**:80–98.

[86] Mirjalili, S., A. Lewis (2016). The whale optimization algorithm. *Adv. Eng. Software*, **95**:51–67.

[87] Ng, C. K., C. H. Wu, W. H. Ip, K. Yung (2018). A smart bat algorithm for wireless sensor network deployment in 3-D environment. *IEEE Commun. Lett.*, 22(10):2120–2123.

[88] Ocenasek, J., J. Schwarz (2002). Estimation of distribution algorithm for mixed continuous-discrete optimization problems. In *2nd Euro-International Symposium on Computational Intelligence*, pp. 227–232.

[89] Olivas, F., G. A. Angulo, J. Perez, C. Camilo, F. Valdez, et al. (2017). Comparative study of type-2 fuzzy particle swarm, bee colony and bat algorithms in optimization of fuzzy controllers. *Algorithms*, **10**:101.

[90] Pan, W. T. (2012). A new fruit fly optimization algorithm: taking the financial distress model as an example. *Knowledge-Based Syst.*, **26**:69–74.

[91] Pant, P., D. Chatterjee (2020). Prediction of clad characteristics using ANN and combined PSO-ANN algorithms in laser metal deposition process. *Surf. Interfaces*, **21**:1–10.

[92] Poli, R., J. Kennedy, T. Blackwell (2007). Particle swarm optimization: an overview. *Swarm Intell.*, **1**.

[93] Qi Wu, T., M. Yao, J. Hua Yang (2016). Dolphin swarm algorithm. *Front. Inf. Technol. Electron. Eng.*, **17**:717–729.

[94] Rashedi, E., H. Nezamabadi-Pour, S. Saryazdi (2009). GSA: a gravitational search algorithm. *Inf. Sci.*, **179**(13):2232–2248.

[95] Ratnaweera, A., S. Halgamuge, H. Watson (2004). Self-organizing hierarchical particle swarm optimizer with time-varying acceleration coefficients. *IEEE Trans. Evol. Comput.*, **8**:240–255.

[96] Ray, T., K. Liew (2003). Society and civilization: an optimization algorithm based on the simulation of social behavior. *IEEE Trans. Evol. Comput.*, **7**:386–396.

[97] Reynolds, R. G. (1994). An introduction to cultural algorithms. In *Proceedings of the 3rd Annual Conference on Evolutionary Programming*, pp. 131–139.

[98] Rodrigues, D., L. Pereira, R. Nakamura, K. Costa, X. Yang, et al. (2013). João Paulo Papa, A wrapper approach for feature selection based on Bat Algorithm and Optimum-Path Forest. *Expert Syst. Appl.*, **41**:2250–2258.

[99] Shareef, H., A. A. Ibrahim, A. H. Mutlag (2015). Lightning search algorithm. *Appl. Soft Comput.*, **36**:315–333.

[100] Shi, Y., R. Eberhart (1998). A modified particle swarm optimizer. In *IEEE International Conference on Evolutionary Computation Proceedings. IEEE World Congress on Computational Intelligence (Cat. No.98TH8360)*, pp. 69–73.

[101] Simon, D. (2009). Biogeography-based optimization. evolutionary computation. *IEEE Trans. Evol. Comput.*, **12**:702–713.

[102] Stützle, T., H. Hoos (2000). MAX-MIN ant system. *Future Gener. Comput. Syst.*, **16**:889–914.

[103] Tang, W. J., Q. H. Wu, J. R. Saunders (2006). Bacterial foraging algorithm for dynamic environments. In *IEEE International Conference on Evolutionary Computation*, pp. 1324–1330.

[104] Telikani, A., A. H. Gandomi, A. Shahbahrami (2020). A survey of evolutionary computation for association rule mining. *Inf. Sci.*, **524**:318–352.

[105] Teodorovic, M. Dell'orco (2005).

[106] Teodorović, D. (2009). Bee colony optimization (BCO). In Lim, C. P., L. C. Jain, S. Dehuri, eds., *Innovations in Swarm Intelligence*, Springer Berlin Heidelberg, pp. 39–60.

[107] Trivedi, A., P. K. Gurrala (2021). Fuzzy logic based expert system for prediction of tensile strength in Fused Filament Fabrication (FFF) process. *Mater. Today: Proc.*, **44**:1344–1349.

[108] Tsipianitis, A., Y. Tsompanakis (2020). Improved Cuckoo Search algorithmic variants for constrained nonlinear optimization. *Adv. Eng. Software*, **149**.

[109] Uymaz, S. A., G. Tezel, E. Yel (2015). Artificial algae algorithm (AAA) for nonlinear global optimization. *Appl. Soft Comput.*, **31**:153–171.

[110] Valdez, F. (2016). Swarm intelligence: an introduction, history and applications. In *Handbook on Computational Intelligence*, pp. 587–606.

[111] Valdez, F. (2020). A review of optimization swarm intelligence-inspired algorithms with type-2 fuzzy logic parameter adaptation. *Soft Comput.*, **24**(1):215–226.

[112] Valdez, F., P. Melin, O. Castillo (2010). Evolutionary method combining Particle Swarm Optimisation and Genetic Algorithms using fuzzy logic for parameter adaptation and aggregation: the case neural network optimisation for face recognition. *Int. J. Artif. Intell. Soft Comput.*, **2**(1/2):77–102.

[113] Valdez, F., P. Melin, O. Castillo, O. Montiel (2008). A new evolutionary method with a hybrid approach combining particle swarm optimization and genetic algorithms using fuzzy logic for decision making. *Appl. Soft Comput.*, **11**(2):2625–2632.

[114] van den Bergh, F., A. Engelbrecht (2004). A cooperative approach to particle swarm optimization. *IEEE Trans. Evol. Comput.*, **8**:225–239.

[115] Wang, Z., J. Mumtaz, L. Zhang, L. Yue (2019). Application of an improved spider monkey optimization algorithm for component assignment problem in PCB assembly. *Procedia CIRP*, **83**:266–271.

[116] Yadav, R., A. Anubhav (2020). PSO-GA based hybrid with adam optimization for ANN training with application in medical diagnosis. *Cognit. Syst. Res.*, **64**:191–199.

[117] Yang, X. S. (2008). *Nature-Inspired Metaheuristic Algorithms*. Luniver Press.

[118] Yang, X. S. (2010a). A new metaheuristic bat-inspired algorithm. In *Nature Inspired Cooperative Strategies for Optimization*, eds. J. R. Gonzalez et al., Studies in Computational Intelligence, vol. 284, Springer, pp. 65–74.

[119] Yang, X., S. Deb (2009). Cuckoo search via Lévy flights. In *World Congress on Nature Biologically Inspired Computing (NaBIC)*, pp. 210–214.

[120] Yang, X. S. (2010b). *Nature-Inspired Metaheuristic Algorithms*, 2nd edn. Luniver Press.

[121] Yang, X. S. (2014). *Nature-Inspired Optimization Algorithms*. Elsevier Oxford.

[122] Yang, X. S. (2019). *Multiobjective Bat Algorithm (MOBA)*.

[123] Yang, X. S., S. Deb (2010a). Cuckoo search via Lévy flights. In *2009 World Congress on Nature & Biologically Inspired Computing (NaBIC)*, pp. 210–214.

[124] Yang, X. S., S. Deb (2010b). Eagle strategy using Lévy walk and firefly algorithms for stochastic optimization. In *Studies in Computational Intelligence*, vol. 284, pp. 101–111.

[125] Yang, X. S., A. Gandomi (2012). Bat algorithm: a novel approach for global engineering optimization. *Eng. Comput.*, **29**:464–483.

[126] Zhang, Z., T. Wang, Y. Chen, J. Lan (2019). Design of type-2 fuzzy logic systems based on improved ant colony optimization. *Int. J. Control Autom. Syst.*, **17**:536–544.

[127] Zhao, H. (2020). Optimal path planning for robot based on ant colony algorithm. In *2020 International Wireless Communications and Mobile Computing (IWCMC)*, pp. 671–675.

Chapter 25

Fuzzy Dynamic Parameter Adaptation for Gray Wolf Optimization of Modular Granular Neural Networks Applied to Human Recognition Using the Iris Biometric Measure

Patricia Melin*, Daniela Sánchez†, and Oscar Castillo‡

*Tijuana Institute of Technology,
Calzada Tecnologico, s/n, CP 22379, Tijuana, Mexico
*pmelin@tectijuana.mx
†daniela.sanchez@tectijuana.edu.mx
‡ocastillo@tectijuana.mx*

In this chapter, a gray wolf optimizer with dynamic parameter adaptation based on fuzzy theory for modular granular neural network (MGNN) has been proposed. These architectures have several parameters, such as the number of sub-granules, the percentage of data for the training phase, the learning algorithm, the goal error, the number of hidden layers and their number of neurons, and the optimization that seeks to find them. The effectiveness of this optimization with its fuzzy dynamic parameters adaptation is proved using a database of iris biometric measures. The advantage of the proposed fuzzy dynamic parameters adaptation is focused on determining the gray wolf optimizer parameters depending on the population behavior, i.e., depending on current results, the parameters are adjusted to improve results. Human recognition is an important area that can offer security to areas or information, especially if biometric measurements are used; for this reason, the method was applied to human recognition using a benchmark database with very good results.

25.1. Introduction

In this chapter, an approach for fuzzy dynamic adaptation of parameters for a gray wolf optimizer (GWO) applied to modular granular neural networks (MGNN) is proposed. The goal of the proposed adjustment of parameters applied to a gray wolf optimizer is to modify its parameters during its execution, i.e., the parameters are not fixed in the execution, allowing that depending on population behavior, their values can be again established each iteration [1, 2]. To prove the advantages of the proposed method, modular granular neural networks are applied to a benchmark iris database [3–5]. The use of a human recognition problem represents an important challenge [6] because the use of biometric measures in recent years has offered a greater guarantee of security in data, areas, or systems [7, 8]; for this reason, the selection of techniques used to perform this task must be very careful [9]. Among the most used techniques to perform human recognition, intelligent techniques can be found, such as artificial neural networks [10], fuzzy logic [11, 12], computer vision [13], and machine learning [14], among others.

Among the improvements made to conventional artificial neural networks, we can find ensemble neural networks (ENNs) [15, 16] and modular neural networks (MNNs) [17]. These kinds of neural networks are multiple artificial neural networks. In the case of ENNs, each neural network learns the same information or task, and for the MNNs, the information or task is divided into parts, and each part is learned by a neural network (module). On the other hand, in [18], a mixture of modular neural networks with granular computing (GrC) [19, 20] was proposed, where the granulation of information into subsets of different sizes was presented.

It is important to mention that artificial neural networks architectures can be designed by optimization techniques, such as genetic algorithm (GA) [21, 22], ant colony optimization (ACO) [23], particle swarm optimization (PSO) [24], bat algorithm [25], and fireworks algorithm (FA) [26] just to mention a few. When two or more intelligence techniques are combined, the resulting system is called a hybrid intelligent system [18, 27]; this kind of system has been widely applied with excellent results [28, 29].

In this chapter, a hybrid intelligent system is proposed where modular neural networks, granular computing, fuzzy logic, and a gray wolf optimizer are combined to improve recognition rates using iris biometric measures.

This chapter is organized as follows. The proposed hybrid optimization is described in Section 25.2. The results obtained by the proposed method are presented in Section 25.3. Statistical comparisons by hypothesis testing are presented in Section 25.4. Finally, conclusions and future lines of research are outlined in Section 25.5.

25.2. Proposed Method

The proposed fuzzy dynamic adaptation and its application are described in this section; this hybrid intelligence system builds modular neural networks with a granular approach, fuzzy logic, and a gray wolf optimizer.

25.2.1. *General Architecture of the Proposed Method*

The proposed hybrid intelligence system uses modular granular neural networks to achieve human recognition based on the iris biometric measure; this artificial neural network was proposed in [18]. In this work, a variant of the gray wolf optimizer with a fuzzy dynamic adaptation is proposed to perform the optimization of this kind of artificial neural network. In addition, a comparison with a GWO without fuzzy dynamic parameters adaptation is performed to know if the fuzzy inference system allows for improved results. The main objective of this hybrid optimization is to allow an adjustment of the optimization parameters to find optimal modular granular neural networks architectures.

The main task of the optimization techniques is to find the number of sub-granules (modules) and the respective neural architecture. In Figure 25.1, the granulation process is illustrated, where a whole granule represents a database. It can be divided into "m" sub-granules, where each sub-granule can be different in size; applied to human recognition, this implies images of a different number of persons. In this work, the gray wolf optimizer with a fuzzy dynamic adaptation performs the optimization of the granulation and the architecture of the modular granular neural networks.

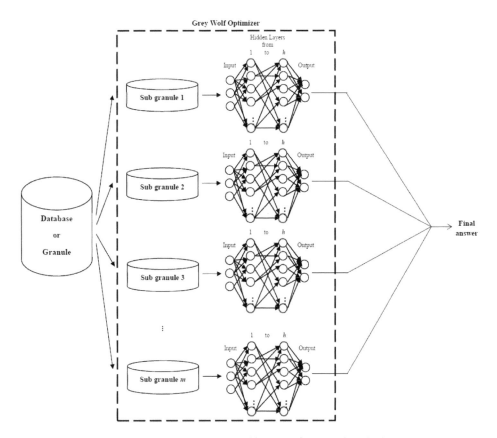

Figure 25.1: The general architecture of proposed method.

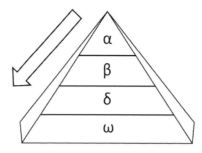

Figure 25.2:   The hierarchy of a gray wolf optimizer.

25.2.1.1. *Description of the gray wolf optimizer*

The gray wolf optimizer uses as its main paradigm the hunting behavior of gray wolves as proposed in [30]. In each pack of wolves, there are between 5 and 12 wolves, where each wolf has a place in the hierarchy. The leaders and who make important decisions is the group called alphas [31, 32]. In Figure 25.2, the hierarchy is illustrated.

As mentioned, this algorithm is based on the hunting behavior of gray wolves, but it is important to specify all those aspects and processes on which this algorithm is based. These aspects and processes and their mathematical model are mentioned below.

- **Social hierarchy:** The best solution is called alpha (α), the second-best solution is called beta (β), the third-best solution is called delta (δ), and the other wolves are called and considered as omega solutions (ω).
- **Encircling prey:** An important process during a hunt is when gray wolves encircle the prey. This process can be represented by the following expressions:

$$\vec{D} = |\vec{C} \cdot \vec{X}_p(t) - \vec{X}(t)|, \tag{25.1}$$

$$\vec{X}(t+1) = \vec{X}_p(t) - \vec{A} \cdot \vec{D}, \tag{25.2}$$

where $\vec{A}$ and $\vec{C}$ are coefficient vectors, $\vec{X}_p$ is the prey position vector, $\vec{X}$ is the position vector of a gray wolf, and t is the current iteration. The vector $\vec{A}$ and $\vec{C}$ are calculated by the following equations:

$$\vec{A} = 2\vec{a} \cdot \vec{r}_1 - \vec{a}, \tag{25.3}$$

$$\vec{C} = 2 \cdot \vec{r}_2, \tag{25.4}$$

where $\vec{r}_1$ and $\vec{r}_2$ are random vectors with values in 0 and 1 and $\vec{a}$ is a vector with components that linearly decreased from 2 to 0 during each iteration.

- **Hunting:** As alpha, beta, and delta solutions are the best solutions, these solutions know where the prey is; therefore, their positions allow the rest of the solutions to

```
Initialize the grey wolf population Xᵢ (i = 1, 2, ... , n)
Initialize a, A, and C
Calculate the fitness of each search agent
Xα = the best search agent
Xβ = the second best search agent
Xδ = the third best search agent
        while ( t < Max number of iterations)
                for each search agent
                        Update the position of the current search
        agent
        end for
        Update a, A, and C
        Calculate the fitness of all search agents
        Update Xα, Xβ, and Xδ
        t = t + 1
    end while
return Xα
```

Figure 25.3: The pseudocode of the original gray wolf optimizer.

update their positions based on them. This process is represented by the following equations:

$$\vec{D}_\alpha = |\vec{C}_1 \cdot \vec{X}_\alpha - \vec{X}|, \ \vec{D}_\beta = |\vec{C}_2 \cdot \vec{X}_\beta - \vec{X}|, \ \vec{D}_\delta = |\vec{C}_3 \cdot \vec{X}_\delta - \vec{X}| \quad (25.5)$$

$$\vec{X}_1 = \vec{X}_\alpha - \vec{A}_1 \cdot (\vec{D}_\alpha), \ \vec{X}_2 = \vec{X}_\beta - \vec{A}_2 \cdot (\vec{D}_\beta), \ \vec{X}_3 = \vec{X}_\delta - \vec{A}_3 \cdot (\vec{D}_\delta), \quad (25.6)$$

$$\vec{X}(t + 1) = \frac{\vec{X}_1 + \vec{X}_2 + \vec{X}_3}{3}. \quad (25.7)$$

- **Attacking prey:** This process consists of exploitation. Here $\vec{a}$ decreases from 2 to 0 during each iteration, and the $\vec{A}$ vector contains random numbers in an interval $[-a, a]$. This allows a search agent to update its next position. This position can be any position between its current position and the prey.
- **Search for prey:** This process consists of exploration. This process allows having divergence in the population. This algorithm represents it using $\vec{A}$. To avoid local optima problems and to favor exploration, a $\vec{C}$ vector with values in an interval $[0, 2]$ is used.

In Figure 25.3, the pseudocode of the original gray wolf optimizer is illustrated.

25.2.1.1.1. Description of the gray wolf optimizer with fuzzy dynamic parameter adaptation

The fuzzy dynamic parameter adaptation has been proposed to other optimization techniques and applied to artificial neural networks [1, 2]. In this work, a fuzzy inference system is proposed to adjust GWO parameters. The fuzzy inference system has two inputs variables and three outputs variables. All the variables use three

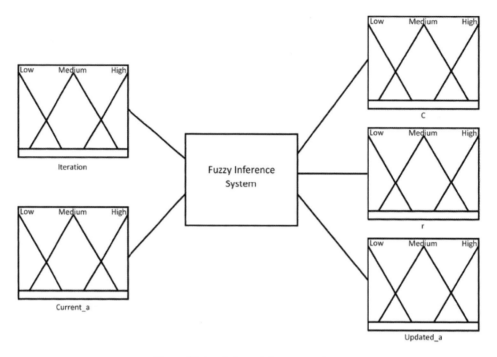

Figure 25.4:   A fuzzy inference system.

triangular functions, and their linguistic values are "Low," "Medium," and "High." Figure 25.4 illustrates the structure of the fuzzy inference system.

The inputs variables are:

- **Iteration:** Internally, a variable was added in the algorithm. This variable saves how many iterations the objective function remains without changing its value. This variable is restarted when its value arrives at 5.
- **Actual_a:** This input variable gets the current value of a used in the GWO.

The outputs variables are:

- **C:** As previously shown in Eq. (25.4), to calculate $\vec{C}$, a $\vec{r_2}$ is necessary. With this fuzzy variable, C is directly determined. This value is the same for all the $\vec{C}$ vector.
- **Updated_a** and **r:** As it is previously shown in Eq. (25.3), to calculate $\vec{A}$, a $\vec{a}$ and $\vec{r_1}$ are necessary. With these fuzzy variables, a and r are directly determined. These values are the same for all the $\vec{a}$ and $\vec{r}$ vectors.

The fuzzy IF–THEN rules used in the fuzzy systems are summarized in Figure 25.5. The range of each variable is shown in Table 25.1.

1. If (Iteration is Low) and (Actual_a is Low) then (C is High)(r is High)(Update_a is High)
2. If (Iteration is Low) and (Actual_a is Medium) then (C is Low)(r is Low)(Update_a is Low)
3. If (Iteration is Low) and (Actual_a is High) then (C is Low)(r is Low)(Update_a is Low)
4. If (Iteration is Medium) and (Actual_a is Low) then (C is High)(r is High)(Update_a is High)
5. If (Iteration is Medium) and (Actual_a is Medium) then (C is Medium)(r is Medium)(Update_a is Medium)
6. If (Iteration is Medium) and (Actual_a is High) then (C is Low)(r is Low)(Update_a is Low)
7. If (Iteration is High) and (Actual_a is Low) then (C is High)(r is High)(Update_a is High)
8. If (Iteration is High) and (Actual_a is Medium) then (C is Low)(r is Low)(Update_a is Low)
9. If (Iteration is High) and (Actual_a is High) then (C is Low)(r is Low)(Update_a is Low)

Figure 25.5:   Fuzzy rules of the fuzzy systems.

Table 25.1:   Ranges of variables

Variable	Range
Iteration	1 to 5
Actual_a	0 to 2
C	0 to 2
r	0 to 1
Updated_a	0 to 2

25.2.1.1.2. Description of the gray wolf optimizer for MGNN

The gray wolf optimizer aims at optimizing modular granular neural network architectures. The parameters that are subject to optimization are the number of sub-granules (modules), the percentage of data for the training phase, the learning algorithm, the goal error, the number of hidden layers, and the number of neurons of each hidden layer.

To determinate the total number of dimensions for each search agent, Eq. (25.8) is used, where each parameter to be optimized is represented by a dimension:

$$Dimensions = 2 + (3 * m) + (m * h), \qquad (25.8)$$

where m is the maximum number of sub-granules and h is the maximum number of hidden layers per module. The objective function is the following expression:

$$f = \sum_{i=1}^{m} \left(\left(\sum_{j=1}^{n_m} X_j \right) / n_m \right), \qquad (25.9)$$

where m is the total number of sub-granules (modules), X_j is 0 if the module provides the correct result and 1 if not, and n_m is the total number of data/images used for the testing phase in the respective module.

Table 25.2:   Values for search space

Parameters of MNNs	Minimum	Maximum
Modules (m)	1	10
Percentage of data for training	20	80
Error goal	0.000001	0.001
Learning algorithm	1	3
Hidden layers (h)	1	10
Neurons for each hidden layer	20	400

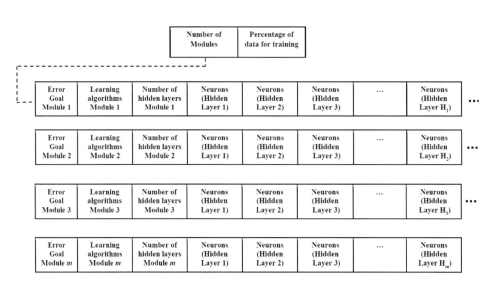

Figure 25.6:   A structure of each search agent.

25.2.2. *Proposed Method Applied to Human Recognition*

In [33], a gray wolf optimizer for MGNNs architectures was proposed but without a fuzzy dynamic parameter adaptation. To have a fair comparison, in this work, 10 search agents and maximum 30 iterations are used as in [33]. The minimum and maximum values used to limit the search space are summarized in Table 25.2. The gray wolf optimizer has two stopping conditions: when the maximum number of iterations is achieved or when the best solution has an error value equal to zero. In Figure 25.6, the structure of each search agent is illustrated, and in Figure 25.7, the diagram of the proposed method is presented.

For the MGNNs learning phase, the optimization technique can be selected from one of the following options:

1. Gradient descent with scaled conjugate gradient (SCG)
2. Gradient descent with adaptive learning and momentum (GDX)
3. Gradient descent with adaptive learning (GDA)

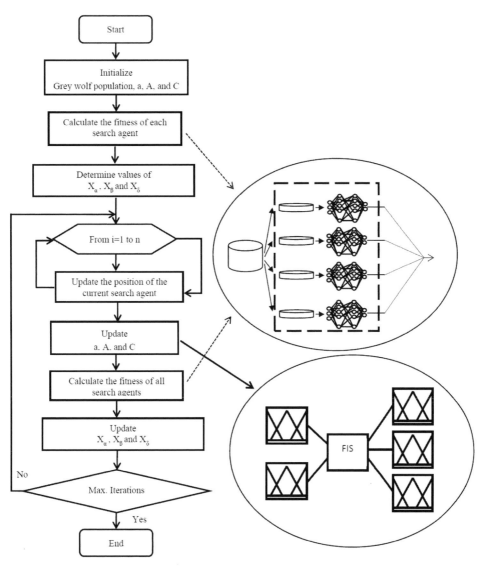

Figure 25.7: A Diagram of the proposed method.

25.2.2.1. *Data selection, database, and pre-processing*

The description of the database, data selection, and the pre-processing applied are presented below.

25.2.2.1.1. Data selection

In [18], a method to select images for each neural network phase (training and testing) was proposed. The optimization technique in each possible solution (search agent)

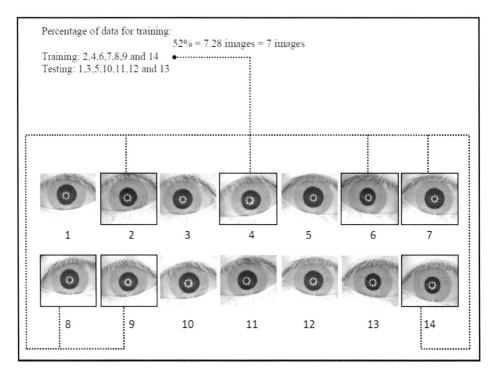

Figure 25.8: An example of images selection for training and testing phase.

has a percentage of data. This percentage is converted to a number of images, and images for each phase are selected randomly. In Figure 25.8, an example for the iris database is illustrated. In this case, a person has 14 images: 7 of them are for the training phase and 7 for the testing phase.

25.2.2.1.2. Database

The iris database was collected and presented by the Institute of Automation of the Chinese Academy of Sciences (CASIA) [34]. Each image has a dimension of 320 x 280, JPEG format. The database was formed with information from 77 persons, where each person has 14 images. Figure 25.9 illustrates a sample of the images of the iris database.

25.2.2.1.3. Pre-processing

In [35], L. Masek and P. Kovesi developed the pre-processing for the iris database. This pre-processing performed to each image is to obtain coordinates and radius of iris and pupil for performing a cut in iris. The image is resized to 21 × 21 pixels. In Figure 25.10, the pre-processing is shown.

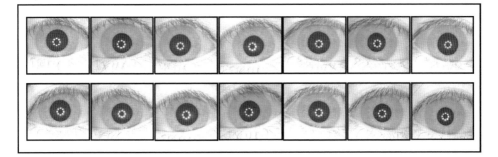

Figure 25.9: Sample of Iris database.

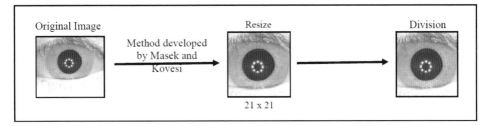

Figure 25.10: Sample pre-processing for Iris database.

25.3. Experimental Results

In this section, the results achieved by the proposed method applied to human recognition using iris as a biometric measure are shown. The main comparison of the proposed method is against a gray wolf optimizer without a fuzzy dynamic adaptation. In [33], the optimization of MGNN architectures was performed. In [36], an optimization is performed, but an automatic division of the images is performed, and each division is learned by a submodule. In both works, the GWO used up to 80% of images for the training phase. In this work, that test is replicated (test #1), and other using up to 50% of data for the training phase (test #2) is performed. A total of 20 runs were executed for each test to perform comparisons.

25.3.1. *Results Using up to 80% of Data for Training*

In this test, the proposed hybrid optimization can use up to 80% of the data for the training phase. In Table 25.3, the best five results with the proposed optimization are shown.

The behavior of run #8 is illustrated in Figure 25.11, where the best, the average, and the worst results of each iteration are presented. In Figure 25.12, alpha (first-best solution), beta (second-best solution), and delta (third-best solution) behaviors of

Table 25.3: The best five results (Test #1)

Run	Images		Num. hidden layers and Num. of neurons	Persons per module	Rec. Rate %	Error
	Training	Testing				
1	75% (1,3,4,5, 6,7,8,9,10,11 and 14)	25% (2,12, and 13)	5(232,31,20,25,31)	Module #1(1 to 11)	99.57	0.0043
			5(207,62,81,86,59)	Module #2(12 to 17)		
			5(200,70,145,180,190)	Module #3(18 to 23)		
			5(199,69,54,209,82)	Module #4(24 to 33)		
			5(58,163,210,126,214)	Module #5(34 to 46)		
			5(231,54,52,155,47)	Module #6(47 to 56)		
			5(41,141,182,224,202)	Module #7(57 to 63)		
			5(188,153,200,150,221)	Module #8(64 to 72)		
			3(247,100,69)	Module #9(73 to 77)		
8	77% (1,2,3,4,5,6,8,9,11,13 and 14)	23% (7,10, and 12)	5(228,146,214,163,228)	Module #1(1 to 12)	100	0
			5(196,114,113,210,96)	Module #2(13 to 18)		
			5(123,170,89,65,117)	Module #3(19 to 32)		
			5(180,143,200,223,203)	Module #4(33 to 39)		
			5(218,225,197,99,249)	Module #5(40 to 41)		
			5(142,111,250,49,221)	Module #6(42 to 44)		
			5(125,190,207,117,225)	Module #7(45 to 53)		
			5(155,160,164,53,194)	Module #8(54 to 59)		
			5(165,150,133,218,97)	Module #9(60 to 65)		
			5(89,91,164,54,168)	Module #10(66 to 77)		

			:			
10	76% (1,2,3,4,5,6,8,9, 11,13, and 14)	24% (7,10, and 12)	5(156,171,24,147,182)	Module #1(1 to 3)	99.57	0.0043
			4(127,151,48,48)	Module #2(4 to 14)		
			5(111,146,207,245,188)	Module #3(15 to 31)		
			5(156,242,45,211,154)	Module #4(32 to 40)		
			5(161,191,65,108,81)	Module #5(41 to 56)		
			5(126,186,70,140,45)	Module #6(57 to 62)		
			5(162,76,161,96,202)	Module #7(63 to 74)		
			5(157,94,217,188,225)	Module #8(75 to 77)		
13	75% (1,2,3,4,5,6,8,9, 11,13, and 14)	25% (7,10, and 12)	4(119,39,131,242)	Module #1(1 to 8)	99.57	0.0043
			4(44,173,119,71)	Module #2(9 to 14)		
			4(43,215,49,218)	Module #3(15 to 17)		
			5(30,179,96,145,234)	Module #4(18 to 26)		
			4(87,210,139,114)	Module #5(27 to 28)		
			4(35,115,27,240)	Module #6(29 to 37)		
			5(153,84,180,128,181)	Module #7(38 to 47)		
			4(63,61,40,123)	Module #8(48 to 62)		
			5(29,57,214,119)	Module #9(63 to 67)		
			1(148)	Module #10(68 to 77)		

(*Continued*)

Table 25.3: *(Continued)*

Run	Images		Num. hidden layers and Num. of neurons	Persons per module	Rec. Rate %	Error
	Training	Testing				
17	77% (1,2,3,5,6,7,8,9, 10,12, and 14)	23% (4,11, and 13)	5(202,140,211,137,156)	Module #1(1 to 4)	100	0
			5(167,179,239,73,108)	Module #2(5 to 9)		
			5(163,195,65,142,193)	Module #3(10 to 13)		
			5(236,189,153,109,152)	Module #4(14 to 15)		
			5(225,71,124,148,148)	Module #4(16 to 25)		
			5(32,172,113,138,198)	Module #6(26 to 33)		
			5(199,150,166,164,79)	Module #7(34 to 47)		
			5(180,148,112,162,79)	Module #8(48 to 58)		
			5(176,199,84,157,195)	Module #9(59 to 72)		
			5(228,223,231,219,224)	Module #10(73 to 77)		

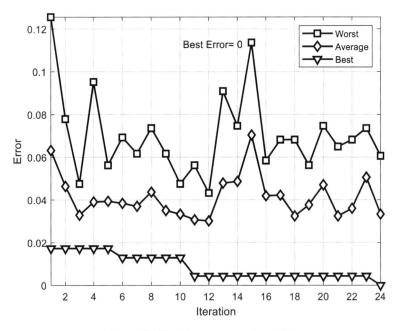

Figure 25.11: Convergence of run #8.

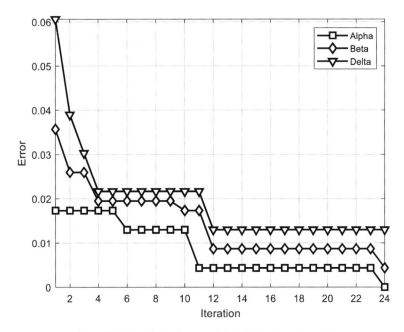

Figure 25.12: Alpha, beta, and delta behavior of run #8.

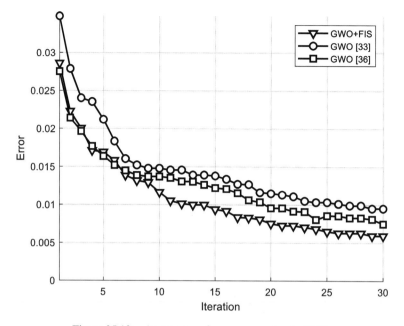

Figure 25.13:　An average of convergence (up to 80%).

Table 25.4:　Comparison of Results (Test #1)

Method	Best	Average	Worst
GWO [33]	100%	99.04%	97.84%
	0	0.0096	0.0216
GWO [36]	100%	99.31%	98.70%
	0	0.0069	0.0130
GWO + FIS	100%	99.40%	99.13%
	0	0.0060	0.0087

run #8 are presented. In Figure 25.13, the average convergence of 20 runs obtained by the GWO presented in [33, 36], and the proposed hybrid optimization are shown.

In Table 25.4, a comparison of results among [33, 36], and the proposed method is shown.

25.3.2. *Results Using up to 50% of Data for Training*

In this test, the proposed hybrid optimization can use up to 50% of data for the training phase. In Table 25.4, the best five results with the proposed optimization are shown.

The behavior of run #6 is shown in Figure 25.14, where the best, the average, and the worst result of each iteration are shown. In Figure 25.15, alpha (first-best

Table 25.5:   The best 5 results (Test #2)

Run	Images		Num. Hidden layers and Num. of neurons	Persons per module	Rec. Rate %	Error
	Training	Testing				
2	47% (1,3,5, 6,9,11, and 13)	53% (2,4,6,7, 8,10,12, and 14)	4(82,197,188,186)	Module #1(1 to 5)	97.40	0.0260
			5(184,111,88,77,191)	Module #2(6 to 15)		
			5(28,153,120,69,105)	Module #3(16 to 23)		
			4(188,142,159,123)	Module #4(24 to 30)		
			5(144,195,65,172,192)	Module #5(31 to 33)		
			2(169,175)	Module #6(34 to 35)		
			5(174,124,172,161,25)	Module #7(36 to 49)		
			3(124,171,73)	Module #8(50 to 53)		
			3(141,148,172)	Module #9(54 to 63)		
			4(48,197,161,83)	Module #10(64 to 77)		
4	48% (1,3,4, 5,6,9, and 13)	52% (2,7,8,10,11,12, and 14)	5(150,146,154,186,147)	Module #1(1 to 6)	97.40	0.0260
			5(147,146,86,111,154)	Module #2(7 to 10)		
			5(108,134,21,168,130)	Module #3(11 to 18)		
			5(142,96,196,181,71)	Module #4(19 to 23)		
			5(93,59,127,141,139)	Module #5(24 to 36)		
			5(69,160,150,97,161)	Module #6(37 to 48)		
			5(108,180,159,150,20)	Module #7(49 to 62)		
			5(129,147,135,37,199)	Module #8(63 to 64)		
			5(115,157,157,161,191)	Module #9(65 to 74)		
			5(92,144,197,176,179)	Module #10(75 to 77)		

(Continued)

Table 25.5: (Continued)

| Run | Images | | Num. Hidden layers and Num. of neurons | Persons per module | Rec. Rate % | Error |
	Training	Testing				
6	49% (1,2,3, 5,6,8, and 9)	51% (4,7,10, 11,12,13, and 14)	5(179,144,127,200,157)	Module #1(1 to 6)	97.77	0.0223
			5(150,100,186,82,157)	Module #2(7 to 14)		
			5(161,186,169,29,65)	Module #3(15 to 24)		
			5(182,138,154,150,180)	Module #4(25 to 41)		
			4(162,159,23,147)	Module #5(42 to 44)		
			5(170,182,98,99,63)	Module #6(45 to 52)		
			5(124,95,143,155,128)	Module #7(53 to 58)		
			5(163,149,59,183,170)	Module #8(59 to 62)		
			5(113,195,150,101,190)	Module #9(63 to 73)		
			5(182,179,193,194,52)	Module #10(74 to 77)		
9	43% (2,3,4,5,6, and 13)	57% (1,7,8,9, 10,11,12, and 14)	5(155,188,175,170,105)	Module #1(1 to 16)	97.40	0.0260
			5(165,160,194,147,26)	Module #2(17 to 26)		
			5(132,72,24,166,61)	Module #3(27 to 38)		
			5(133,29,153,40,32)	Module #4(39 to 46)		
			5(154,57,194,89,142)	Module #5(47 to 48)		
			5(198,166,177,58,82)	Module #6(49 to 52)		
			5(158,92,127,196,170)	Module #7(53 to 60)		
			5(175,178,120,29,157)	Module #8(61 to 71)		
			5(139,164,193,162,139)	Module #9(72 to 77)		

16	50% (2,3,4, 5,6,9, and 13)	52% (1,7,8,10,11,12, and 14)	⋮		97.59%	0.0241
			5(179,199,61,163,136)	Module #1 (1 to 11)		
			5(181,153,157,168,189)	Module #2(12 to 16)		
			5(171,190,174,100,43)	Module #3(17 to 22)		
			5(32,177,146,178,90)	Module #4(23 to 25)		
			5(144,149,151,170,178)	Module #5(26 to 41)		
			5(161,171,176,52,51)	Module #6(42 to 54)		
			5(155,174,108,185,127)	Module #7(55 to 63)		
			5(180,165,150,172,160)	Module #8(64 to 72)		
			5(167,130,116,119,131)	Module #9(73 to 77)		

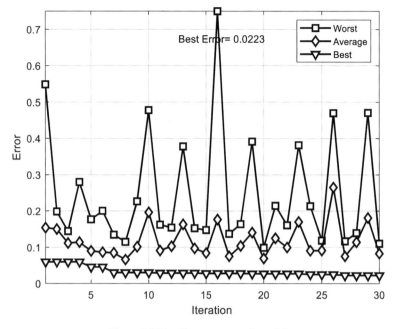

Figure 25.14:   Convergence of run #6.

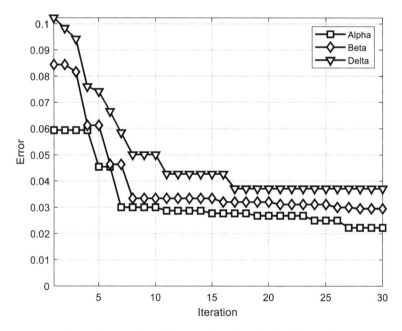

Figure 25.15:   Alpha, beta, and delta behavior of run #6.

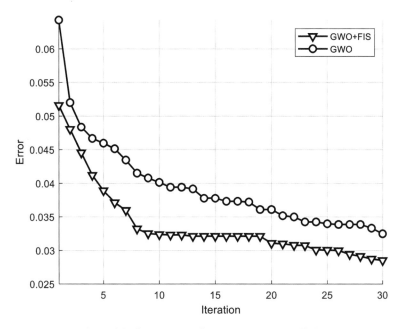

Figure 25.16: Average of convergence (up to 50%).

Table 25.6: Comparison of results (Test #2)

Method	Best	Average	Worst
GWO	97.59%	96.75%	95.82%
	0.0241	0.0325	0.0418
Proposed GWO	97.77%	97.16%	96.59%

solution), beta (second-best solution), and delta (third-best solution) behavior of run #6 are shown.

In Figure 25.16, the average convergence of 20 runs obtained by the GWO without fuzzy dynamic parameters adaptation and the proposed hybrid optimization are shown. The average convergence of the proposed method is better than the GWO without fuzzy dynamic parameters adaptation.

In Table 25.6, a comparison of results between the GWO without fuzzy dynamic parameters adaptation and the proposed hybrid optimization are shown. From the values in Table 25.6, we can say that better results are achieved by the proposed method; even the worst result is improved.

Table 25.7:   Values of test #1.

Method	N	Mean	Standard deviation	Error SD of the mean	Estimated difference	t value	p value	Degree of freedom
Melin P. [33]	20	99.036	0.478	0.11	−0.369	−2.98	0.0055	31
Proposed Method	20	99.405	0.280	0.063				
Sanchez D. [36]	20	99.307	0.407	0.097	−0.097	−0.88	0.384	33
Proposed Method	20	99.405	0.280	0.063				

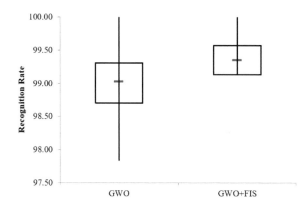

Figure 25.17:   Sample distribution (up to 80%, comparison #1).

25.4. Statistical Comparison of Results

To verify if the results achieved by the proposed method have been significantly improved, statistical t-tests are performed. In these t-tests, the previous recognition rates are used in the calculations.

25.4.1. *Statistical Comparison for Test #1*

In Table 25.7, the values obtained in the t-test among [33, 36], and the proposed optimization are shown, where t-values of 2.98 and 0.88 are obtained, respectively. This means that there is sufficient evidence to say that the proposed optimization improves results when compared with the method presented in [33]. In Figures 25.17 and 25.18, the distribution of the samples is illustrated.

25.4.2. *Statistical Comparison for Test #2*

In Table 25.8, the values obtained in the t-test between the proposed method and the GWO without a fuzzy dynamic parameter adaptation are shown, where the t value is 3.23. This means that there is sufficient evidence to say that the proposed

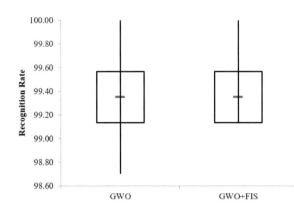

Figure 25.18:   Sample distribution (up to 80%, comparison #2).

Table 25.8:   Values of Test #2.

Method	N	Mean	Standard deviation	Error SD of the mean	Estimated difference	t value	p value	Degree of freedom
GWO	20	96.750	0.472	0.11	−0.413	−3.23	0.0027	34
Proposed Method	20	97.164	0.325	0.073				

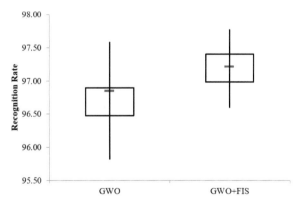

Figure 25.19:   Sample distribution (up to 50%).

optimization improved results. In Figure 25.19, the distribution of the samples is illustrated.

25.5. Conclusions

In this chapter, a fuzzy inference system to perform dynamic parameters adaptation applied to a gray wolf optimizer was proposed. To perform a comparison between the proposed optimization and a gray wolf optimizer without this adjustment, the human recognition was performed using the iris biometric measure. Both optimization techniques designed are modular granular neural networks architectures. This design consisted of the number of sub-granules, the percentage of data for the training phase, error goal, the learning algorithm, the number of hidden layers, and their respective number of neurons. The main objective is to minimize the error of recognition. The results show improvements when the proposed fuzzy inference system is used, but statistical comparisons were also performed, mainly with a previous work where a gray wolf optimizer was developed for MGNN optimization using the same general architecture. In conclusion, in general, the proposed hybrid optimization improved the recognition rates because it allowed for a change in parameters in each iteration depending on gray wolf population behavior. In future works, other parameters will be considered, and other fuzzy inference systems will be proposed to improve results, especially when less than 50% of the data for the training phase are used.

References

[1] B. González, F. Valdez, P. Melin and G. Prado-Arechiga, Fuzzy logic in the gravitational search algorithm enhanced using fuzzy logic with dynamic alpha parameter value adaptation for the optimization of modular neural networks in echocardiogram recognition, *Appl. Soft Comput.*, **37**, 245–254 (2015).

[2] D. Sánchez, P. Melin and O. Castillo, Particle swarm optimization with fuzzy dynamic parameters adaptation for modular granular neural networks, in J. Kacprzyk, E. Szmidt, S. Zadrożny, K. Atanassov and M. Krawczak (eds.), *Advances in Fuzzy Logic and Technology 2017. EUSFLAT 2017, IWIFSGN 2017. Advances in Intelligent Systems and Computing*, vol. 643, Springer, Cham, pp. 277–288 (2017).

[3] R. Abiyev and K. Altunkaya, Personal iris recognition using neural network, *Int. J. Secur. Appl.*, **2**, 41–50 (2008).

[4] M. De Marsico, A. Petrosino, and S. Ricciardi, Iris recognition through machine learning techniques: a survey, *Pattern Recognit. Lett.*, **82**(2), 106–115 (2016).

[5] A. M. Patil, D. S. Patil and P. Patil, Iris recognition using gray level co-occurrence matrix and Hausdorff dimension, *Int. J. Comput. Appl.*, **133**(8), 29–34 (2016).

[6] M. De Marsico, M. Nappi and H. Proença, *Human Recognition in Unconstrained Environments*, 1st edn., Academic Press (2017).

[7] S. Furnell and N. Clarke, Power to the people? The evolving recognition of human aspects of security, *Comput. Secur.*, **31**(8), 983–988 (2012).

[8] G. Schryen, G. Wagner and A. Schlegel, Development of two novel face-recognition CAPTCHAs: a security and usability study, *Comput. Secur.*, **60**, 95–116 (2016).

[9] M. Nixon, P. Correia, K. Nasrollahi, T. B. Moeslund, A. Hadid and M. Tistarelli, On soft biometrics, *Pattern Recognit. Lett.*, **68**(2), 218–230 (2015).

[10] J. Heaton, *Artificial Intelligence for Humans, Volume 3: Deep Learning and Neural Networks*, 1st edn., CreateSpace Independent Publishing Platform (2015).

[11] L. A. Zadeh, Some reflections on soft computing, granular computing and their roles in the conception, design and utilization of information/intelligent systems, *Soft Comput.*, **2**, 23–25 (1998).

[12] L. A. Zadeh and J. Kacprzyk, *Fuzzy Logic for the Management of Uncertainty*, 1st edn., Wiley-Interscience (1992).

[13] R. Chellappa, The changing fortunes of pattern recognition and computer vision, *Image Vision Comput.*, **55**(1), 3–5 (2016).

[14] Z.-T. Liu, M. Wu, W.-H. Cao, J.-W. Mao, J.-P. Xu and G.-Z. Tan, Speech emotion recognition based on feature selection and extreme learning machine decision tree, *Neurocomputing*, **273**, 271–280 (2018).

[15] L. K. Hansen and P. Salomon, Neural network ensembles, *IEEE Trans. Pattern Anal. Mach. Intell.*, **12**, 993–1001 (1990).

[16] A. Sharkey, *Combining Artificial Neural Nets: Ensemble and Modular Multi-net Systems*, 1st edn., Springer (1999).

[17] F. Azamm, Biologically inspired modular neural networks, PhD thesis, Virginia Polytechnic Institute and State University, Blacksburg, Virginia, USA (2000).

[18] D. Sánchez and P. Melin, Optimization of modular granular neural networks using hierarchical genetic algorithms for human recognition using the ear biometric measure, *Eng. Appl. Artif. Intell.*, **27**, 41–56 (2014).

[19] A. Gacek, Granular modelling of signals: a framework of granular computing, *Inf. Sci.*, **221**, 1–11 (2013).

[20] C. Zhong, W. Pedrycz, D. Wang, L. Li and Z. Li, Granular data imputation: a framework of granular computing, *Appl. Soft Comput.*, **46**, 307–316 (2016).

[21] J. H. Holland, *Adaptation in Natural and Artificial Systems*, 1st edn., University of Michigan Press (1975).

[22] K. F. Man, K. S. Tang, and S. Kwong, *Genetic Algorithms: Concepts and Designs*, 2nd edn., Springer (1999).

[23] M. Dorigo, Optimization, learning and natural algorithms, PhD Thesis, Politecnico di Milano, Italy (1992).

[24] J. Kennedy and R. Eberhart, Particle swarm optimization, in *Proceedings of ICNN'95 — International Conference on Neural Networks*, Perth, WA, Australia, vol. 4, pp. 1942–1948 (1995).

[25] X.-S. Yang, Bat algorithm: literature review and applications, *Int. J. Bio-Inspired Comput.*, **5**(3), 141–149 (2013).

[26] Y. Tan, *Fireworks Algorithm: A Novel Swarm Intelligence Optimization*, 1st edn., Springer (2015).

[27] M. Farooq, Genetic algorithm technique in hybrid intelligent systems for pattern recognition, *Int. J. Innovative Res. Sci. Eng. Technol.*, **4**(4), 1891–1898 (2015).

[28] P. Melin, D. Sánchez and O. Castillo, Genetic optimization of modular neural networks with fuzzy response integration for human recognition, *Inf. Sci.*, **197**, 1–19 (2012).

[29] G. Villarrubia, J. F. De Paz, P. Chamoso and F. De la Prieta., Artificial neural networks used in optimization problems, *Neurocomputing*, **272**, 10–16 (2018).

[30] S. Mirjalili, S. M. Mirjalili, and A. Lewis, Grey wolf optimizer, *Adv. Eng. Software*, **69**, 46–61 (2014).

[31] L. D. Mech, Alpha status, dominance, and division of labor in wolf packs, *Can. J. Zool.*, **77**, 1196–1203 (1999).

[32] C. Muro, R. Escobedo, L. Spector and R. Coppinger, Wolf-pack (Canis lupus) hunting strategies emerge from simple rules in computational simulations, *Behav. Processes*, **88**, 192–197 (2011).

[33] P. Melin and D. Sánchez, A grey wolf optimization algorithm for modular granular neural networks applied to iris recognition, in A. Abraham, P. K. Muhuri, A. K. Muda and N. Gandhi (eds.), *Advances in Intelligent Systems and Computing, 17th International Conference on Hybrid Intelligent Systems (HIS 2017)*, Delhi, India, Springer, pp. 282–293 (2017).

[34] Database of human iris. Institute of Automation of Chinese Academy of Sciences (CASIA) (2020). http://www.cbsr.ia.ac.cn/english/IrisDatabase.asp.

[35] L. Masek and P. Kovesi, MATLAB source code for a biometric identification system based on iris patterns, The School of Computer Science and Software Engineering, The University of Western Australia (2003).

[36] D. Sánchez, P. Melin and O. Castillo, A grey wolf optimizer for modular granular neural networks for human recognition, *Comput. Intell. Neurosci.*, **2017**, 1–26 (2017).

https://doi.org/10.1142/9789811247323_0026

Chapter 26

Evaluating Inter-task Similarity for Multifactorial Evolutionary Algorithm from Different Perspectives

Lei Zhou[*,¶]*, Liang Feng*[†,‖]*, Ming Jiang*[‡,**]*, and Kay Chen Tan*[§,††]

[*]*School of Computer Science and Engineering*
Nanyang Technological University, Singapore
[†]*College of Computer Science*
Chongqing University, China
[‡]*Department of Artificial Intelligence*
Xiamen University, China
[§]*Department of Computing*
Hong Kong Polytechnic University, Hong Kong SAR
[¶]*lei.zhou@ntu.edu.sg*
[‖]*liangf@cqu.edu.cn*
[**]*minjiang@xmu.edu.cn*
[††]*kctan@polyu.edu.hk*

The multifactorial evolutionary algorithm (MFEA) is a recently proposed method toward evolutionary multitasking. In contrast to the traditional single-task evolutionary search, MFEA conducts evolutionary search on multiple tasks simultaneously. It aims to improve convergence characteristics across multiple optimization problems at once by seamlessly transferring knowledge among them. For evolutionary multitasking, the similarity between tasks has great impact on the performance of MFEA. However, in the literature, only a few works have been conducted to provide deeper insights into the measure of task relationship in MFEA. In this chapter, we present a study of similarity measures between tasks for MFEA from three different viewpoints, i.e., the distance between best solutions, the fitness rank correlation, and the fitness landscape analysis. Furthermore, 21 multitasking problem sets are developed to investigate and analyze the effectiveness of the three similarity measures with MFEA for evolutionary multitasking.

26.1. Introduction

Taking inspiration from Darwin's evolution theory, evolutionary algorithms (EAs) have been proposed in the literature and have achieved great success in solving complex optimization problems, e.g., nonlinear, multimodal, and discrete NP-hard problems [1, 2]. By imitating the behavior of biological evolution, such as reproduction and natural selection, EAs are capable of preserving useful information from elite individuals and maintaining the balance between exploration and exploitation, which directs optimization toward promising areas of the problem search space [3]. EAs have been demonstrated to provide near-optimal, if not optimal, solutions to many real-world optimization problems, including vehicle routing [4, 5], aircraft engine design [6], image processing [7, 8], etc. However, as most of the existing EAs work in a single-task mode, the similarity between problems, which could enhance the evolutionary search process, is ignored in the present EA design.

Recently, in contrast to traditional EAs, the multifactorial evolutionary algorithm (MFEA) has been proposed with the aim of evolutionary multitask algorithm design, which solves multiple optimization problems (tasks) concurrently [9]. With the introduction of a unified representation for different tasks, MFEA is capable of exploiting the latent synergies between distinct (but possibly similar) optimization problems. In [9–11], MFEA has demonstrated superior search performances over the traditional single-task EA in terms of solution quality and convergence speed on a set of continuous, discrete, and the mixtures of continuous and combinatorial tasks.

In spite of the success obtained by MFEA, it is worth noting here that the performance of MFEA is greatly affected by the similarity between tasks [12]. Specifically, similar tasks can often enhance the problem solving on all the tasks, while dissimilar problems may deteriorate the optimization performance on one or all the tasks due to the negative transfer across tasks. It is thus desirable that the inter-task relationship should be identified before the execution of evolutionary multitasking, so that similar tasks can be grouped and solved via MFEA. In the literature, there are a few works that have proposed to study the task similarity for MFEA. In particular, in [13], the authors presented several illustrative examples to show how the synergy of tasks may affect the optimization performance. Further, a synergy metric ξ is proposed to measure the correlation between the objective functions, which is then used to predict the performance of MFEA. Particularly, when $\xi > 0$, an improved optimization performance is expected. However, as the calculation of ξ requires information of global optimal solution and function gradients, it is unpractical in real-world applications, where the global optimum is usually unknown and the gradients cannot be calculated. On the other hand, in [12], Spearman's rank correlation coefficient (SRCC) is employed as a measure for task similarity evaluation. In contrast to the synergy metric, it only requires the function objective values of a set of randomly sampled solutions. Therefore, this method can be applied to broader optimization problems. In this study, to verify the similarity metric, nine multitasking sets are divided into three categories with respect to task similarity based on the predefined thresholds of SRCC, which are denoted as *high similarity* (HS), *medium similarity* (MS), and *low similarity* (LS). The obtained empirical results with MFEA on these multitasking sets generally agree with the similarity categories of the benchmarks. However, as the number of multitasking sets investigated in [12] is small, the generalization capability of Spearman's rank correlation coefficient needs to be further confirmed.

In the field of statistics and machine learning, a variety of methods have been introduced to evaluate the task relationship from different views [14–16]. In contrast, in the literature, the study of task similarity for multitasking in optimization has received far less attention. Keeping this in mind, in this chapter, we embark on a study to measure the similarity between tasks for MFEA from three different views, i.e., the distance between best solutions, the fitness rank correlation, and the fitness landscape analysis. Particularly, we adopt the maximum mean discrepancy (MMD) to approximate the distance between best solutions, Spearman's rank correlation coefficient (SRCC) to measure the fitness rank correlation as in [12], and fitness distance correlation (FDC) to analyze the fitness landscape similarity across tasks. Further, we develop new multitasking benchmarks, which contain 21 multitasking problem sets, to investigate and analyze the effectiveness of the three similarity measures with MFEA for evolutionary multitasking.

The rest of this chapter is organized as follows. A brief introduction of evolutionary multitasking and the multifactorial evolutionary algorithm is given in Section 26.2. Section 26.3 gives the motivation behind the three views as well as the detailed methods of the similarity measures for MFEA in evolutionary multitasking. Section 26.4 contains empirical studies on the 21 newly developed multitasking sets to investigate the effectiveness of the three similarity measures. Lastly, the concluding remarks of this chapter and potential directions for future research are discussed in Section 26.5.

26.2. Preliminaries

In this section, the concept of evolutionary multitasking is introduced, which is followed by a brief review of the related works. Next, the details of the multifactorial evolutionary algorithm are presented.

26.2.1. *Evolutionary Multitasking*

In contrast to traditional EAs that solve one problem in a single run, evolutionary multitasking aims to tackle multiple optimization tasks simultaneously by exploiting the synergies between distinct tasks to enhance the optimization perfor-mance. Given K minimization tasks $\{f_1, f_2, \ldots, f_K\}$, the objective of evolutionary multitasking is to find $\{\mathbf{x_1}, \mathbf{x_2}, \ldots, \mathbf{x_K}\} = \text{argmin}\{f_1(\mathbf{x}), f_2(\mathbf{x}), \ldots, f_K(\mathbf{x})\}$ at the same time.

Since the precursory evolutionary multitask algorithm MFEA was first pro-posed in [9], it has witnessed an explosive growth of research efforts devoted to evolutionary multitasking. In particular, a plethora of strategies were proposed to enhance the performance of MFEA, such as decision variables manipulation [17, 18], search space alignment [19, 20], resource allocation [21, 22], and the control of knowledge transfer frequency [23], etc. Further, Feng et al. [24] diversified the family of MFEA with multifactorial particle swarm optimization (MFPSO) and multifactorial differential evolution (MFDE). Gupta et al. [25] extended MFEA to handle multi-objective optimization problems. Liaw et al. [26], Tang et al. [27], and Chen et al. [28] considered the simultaneous optimization of more than three tasks, which is also known as evolutionary many tasking. Feng et al. [29] proposed an explicit multitask framework in which knowledge is explicitly exchanged between tasks in the form of solutions. Besides the algorithm design, evolutionary multitasking has also been successfully applied to a wide range of real-world problems, such as machine learning [30, 31], operational research [32, 33], and engineering design [34, 35].

26.2.2. *The Multifactorial Evolutionary Algorithm*

The multifactorial evolutionary algorithm (MFEA) is proposed as an implementation of the evolutionary multitasking paradigm [9]. Particularly, in MFEA, tasks are encoded in a unified search space and translated into a task-specific solution with respect to each of the tasks when evaluated. To compare the individual solutions in a multitasking environment, the following properties for each individual are defined in MFEA.

— *Factorial Cost:* The factorial cost f_p of an individual p denotes its fitness or objective value on a particular task T_i. For K tasks, there will be a vector with length K, in which each dimension gives the fitness of p on the corresponding task.

— *Factorial Rank:* The factorial rank r_p simply denotes the index of individual p in the list of population members sorted in ascending order with respect to their factorial costs on one task.

— *Scalar Fitness:* The scalar fitness φ_p of an individual p is defined based on its best rank over all tasks, which is given by $\varphi_p = \dfrac{1}{\min_{j \in \{1, \ldots, K\}} r_p^j}$. Scalar fitness is used to select the solutions for survival in the next generation.

— *Skill Factor:* The skill factor τ_p of individual p denotes the task, amongst all tasks in *MFO*, on which p is most effective, i.e., $\tau_p = argmin\{r_p^j\}$, where $j \in \{1, \ldots, K\}$.

The pseudocode of MFEA is presented in Algorithm 26.1. The MFEA first initializes a population of N individuals and evaluates each of them on all tasks (lines 1–2). Then, the *skill factor* and *scalar fitness* are calculated for each individual in the population (line 3). Next, an offspring population is generated in each generation by *assortative mating* and evaluated via *vertical cultural transmission* (lines 5–6). Particularly, the *assortative mating* procedure conducts genetic operators, i.e., crossover and mutation, on selected parents where individuals with different *skill factors* are mated with a predefined probability. The *vertical cultural transmission* evaluates the offspring on specific tasks based on the *skill factor* of their parents. Finally, the *scalar fitness* and *skill factor* of individuals in both the parent and offspring populations are updated before the natural selection of solutions for the next generation (lines 7–8). The whole process continues until the stopping criteria are satisfied.

Algorithm 26.1: Pseudocode for MFEA.

1 Generate an initial population with N individuals.
2 Evaluate each individual on all the tasks.
3 Calculate *scalar fitness* and *skill factor* for each individual.
4 **While** *stopping criteria are not satisfied,* **do**
5   Apply *assortative mating* to generate an offspring population.
6   Evaluate offspring individuals via *vertical cultural transmission*.
7   Update the *scalar fitness* and *skill factor* of individuals in the parent and offspring populations.
8   Select the fittest N individuals to survive for the next generation.

26.3. Measuring the Similarity between Tasks for MFEA from Different Views

In this section, to explore the similarity measure of tasks for enhanced evolutionary multitasking, we present a study to investigate the task similarity from three different views. One is from the distance between best solutions, one is from the fitness rank correlation of sampled solutions, and the last is based on the fitness distance correlation. In particular, for evaluating task similarity based on fitness rank correlation, we employ the Spearman's rank correlation coefficient used in

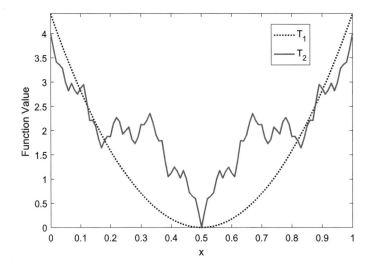

Figure 26.1: The function graph of two functions that have a common global optimum.

[12]. For the other two, we propose two new similarity metrics based on the best solution discrepancy and fitness landscape analysis, respectively.

26.3.1. *Similarity Measure Based on Distance between Best Solutions*

As discussed in [9], the key idea behind evolutionary multitasking is the sharing of useful traits across optimization tasks along the search process. If a high-quality solution found in one task happens to be the good solution of another, the sharing of this solution will enhance the corresponding optimization process significantly. For example, as illustrated in Figure 26.1, task T_1 and T_2 have a common global optimum. T_1 has a smooth landscape and is easy to solve, while T_2 contains lots of local optima. In this case, if the global optimum of T_1 has been found and transferred to T_2, T_2 will be solved directly for free. Taking this cue, an intuitive way of measuring the similarity between tasks for MFEA is based on the distance or discrepancy between the best solution of each task.

In practice, the optimum of a given task of interest is usually unknown beforehand, it is thus hard to obtain the corresponding distance or similarity between tasks directly. In this chapter, we propose to approximate the distance between tasks with maximum mean discrepancy(MMD) of the best sampled solutions of each task. MMD is a widely used statistical measure for comparing distributions in a Reproducing Kernel Hilbert Space (RKHS). It estimates the distance between two distributions with the distance between their corresponding means in the RKHS [16].

In particular, the pseudocode for the similarity measure with MMD is outlined in Algorithm 26.2. Given two tasks T_1 and T_2 with dimensions D_1 and D_2, two sets of solutions S_1 and S_2 of size n with dimension $D_{max}=\max(D_1, D_2)$ are uniformly and independently sampled in the unified search space. Next, the fitness vectors F_1 and F_2 are assigned to S_1 and S_2 based on the evaluation on T_1 and T_2, respectively. Further, the first m best solutions, denoted as Sb_1 and Sb_2, are selected from S_1 and S_2 accordingly to calculate the MMD[1], which is as follows:

$$MMD = \left\| \frac{1}{m} \sum_{i=1}^{m} g(Sb_1^i) - \frac{1}{m} \sum_{i=1}^{m} g(Sb_2^i) \right\|^2, \tag{26.1}$$

where $\| \cdot \|$ denotes the Euclidean norm, and $g(s)$ extracts the first $D_{min}=\min(D_1, D_2)$ dimensions of a solution s. A smaller MMD value implies that the distributions are more similar to each other.

Algorithm 26.2: Pseudocode for calculating the similarity measure with MMD.

Input : Two tasks T_1 and T_2.

Output: MMD value.

1 Uniformly and independently sample two sets of solutions S_1 and S_2 from the unified search space.

2 Evaluate S_1 and S_2 on T_1 and T_2, respectively.

3 Preserve the first m best solutions Sb_1 and Sb_2 from S_1 and S_2, respectively.

4 Calculate the MMD value using Eq. (26.1).

26.3.2. *Similarity Measure Based on Fitness Rank Correlation*

According to [12], the fitness rank correlation estimates the degree of similarity between two rankings of a single set of solutions according to their fitness values on two different tasks. In contrast to the measure in Section 26.3.1, which only focuses on the best solutions, the fitness rank correlation provides a similarity measure based on all the sampled solutions. The rationale behind it is that if the solutions that perform well on one task are also good on the other, the improvement on one task is likely to be beneficial to the other. Therefore, it is expected that MFEA could be effective on two tasks with a high positive fitness rank correlation. The calculation of the fitness rank correlation is based on Spearman's rank correlation coefficient (SRCC) used in [12].

The pseudocode for of the similarity measure with SRCC is presented in Algorithm 26.3. Given two tasks T_1 and T_2, n solutions are uniformly and independently sampled from the unified search space. By evaluating these n solutions

---

[1]In this study, linear mapping is considered in the calculation of MMD.

on T_1 and T_2, respectively, the corresponding rank vectors $\mathbf{r}_1$ and $\mathbf{r}_2$ can be achieved based on the obtained fitness values. The SRCC value is then calculated as follows:

$$SRCC = \frac{cov(\mathbf{r}_1, \mathbf{r}_2)}{\sigma(\mathbf{r}_1)\sigma(\mathbf{r}_2)}, \qquad (26.2)$$

where cov and σ denotes the covariance and standard deviation, respectively. Note that a higher value of SRCC indicates a more similar relationship between tasks.

Algorithm 26.3: Pseudocode for calculating the similarity measure with SRCC.

Input : Two tasks T_1 and T_2.
Output: SRCC value.
1 Uniformly and independently sample n solutions $\mathbf{S}$ from the unified search space.
2 Evaluate $\mathbf{S}$ on T_1 and T_2, respectively.
3 Obtain the rank vector $\mathbf{r}_1$ and $\mathbf{r}_2$ by ranking the solutions with respect to their fitness on T_1 and T_2, respectively.
4 Calculate the SRCC value using Eq. (26.2).

26.3.3. *Similarity Measure Based on Fitness Landscape Analysis*

Fitness landscape analysis (FLA) gives a systematic manner to analyze the property of a function's search space [36]. It thus provides us the possibility of measuring the similarity between tasks from the view of tasks' landscapes. To illustrate, Figure 26.2 gives a multitasking example of two tasks. In this figure, the blue and red curves represent task T_1 and T_2, respectively, that are going to be solved by MFEA simultaneously. The global optima of T_1 and T_2 are located at C and D, respectively. Assume the optimizations of both tasks start at point A. It is straightforward to see that task T_1 is able to find the global optimum at point C quickly, while task T_2 may get stuck at the local optimum A. However, if proper guidance can be derived based on the landscape analysis of T_1 and T_2, and the solution of T_1 at point C is transferred to T_2, it will direct the search of T_2 toward the corresponding global optimum at point D.

In the literature, the fitness distance correlation (FDC) is one of the commonly used measures for fitness landscape analysis, which was proposed by Terry Jones and Stephanie Forrest to predict the performance of GA on functions with known global minima (or maxima) [37]. It is based on the evaluation of how the solutions' fitness values are correlated with their distances to the global optimum. However, the original FDC evaluates the fitness-distance correlation of the same task, which is not able to measure the cross-task correlation required in the case of MFEA. Keeping

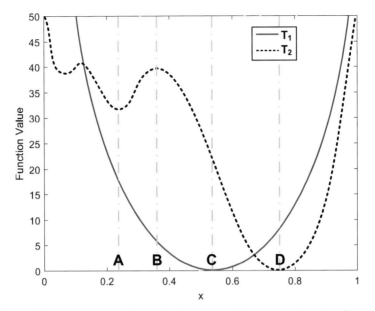

Figure 26.2: An illustrative example for similarity measure between tasks based on fitness landscape analysis.

this in mind, we propose a variant of FDC, called cross-task FDC (CTFDC), for the similarity measure of tasks in evolutionary multitasking.

Algorithm 26.4: Pseudocode for calculating the similarity measure with CTFDC.

Input : Two tasks T_1 and T_2.
Output: CTFDC value.
1 Randomly sample n solutions **S** from the unified search space.
2 Obtain the fitness vector $\mathbf{f}_1$ and $\mathbf{f}_2$ by Evaluate **S** on T_1 and T_2, respectively.
3 Get the best solutions s_1 of T_1 and s_2 of T_2.
4 For each solution s_i, calculate the distance between s_i and $s_1(s_2)$ to form the distance vector $\mathbf{d}_1(\mathbf{d}_2)$.
5 Calculate the CTFDC value using Eq. (26.3).

In particular, to calculate cross-task FDC, as depicted in Algorithm 26.4, we first uniformly and independently sample n solutions from the search space and evaluate them on tasks T_1 and T_2, respectively, to obtain the n dimensional fitness vectors $\mathbf{f}_1$ and $\mathbf{f}_2$. Then, the solution with best fitness value of each task, denoted as s_1 and s_2, is considered as the "global optimum" for the two tasks, respectively. Further, we obtain the distance vectors $\mathbf{d}_1$ and $\mathbf{d}_2$ by computing the Euclidean distance between the corresponding best solution (i.e., s_1 and s_2) and the other sampled solutions in each of the two tasks. Finally, CTFDC can be calculated as follows:

$$CTFDC_{T_1 \to T_2} = \frac{1/n \sum_{i=1}^{n} (\mathbf{f}_1^i - \bar{\mathbf{f}}_1)(\mathbf{d}_2^i - \bar{\mathbf{d}}_2)}{\sigma(\mathbf{f}_1)\sigma(\mathbf{d}_2)}, \tag{26.3}$$

where $\bar{\mathbf{f}}_1$ and $\bar{\mathbf{d}}_2$, $\sigma(\mathbf{f}_1)$ and $\sigma(\mathbf{d}_2)$ are the means and standard deviations of $\mathbf{f}_1$ and $\mathbf{d}_2$, respectively. Note that by replacing $\mathbf{f}_1^i$, $\mathbf{d}_2^i$, $\bar{\mathbf{f}}_1$, $\bar{\mathbf{d}}_2$, $\mathbf{f}_1$, and $\mathbf{d}_2$ with $\mathbf{f}_2^i$, $\mathbf{d}_1^i$, $\bar{\mathbf{f}}_2$, $\bar{\mathbf{d}}_1$, $\mathbf{f}_2$, and $\mathbf{d}_1$ in Eq. (26.3), respectively, we can obtain $CTFDC_{T_2 \to T_1}$ accordingly. As the covariance between fitness and distance is calculated across tasks, the proposed CTFDC can thus be considered as the fitness landscape analysis across tasks, which serves as the task similarity measure in the present study for MFEA. Note that a high CTFDC value indicates that the solutions that result in fitness improvement of T_1 (or T_2) have a high probability to bias the search of T_2 (or T_1) toward promising areas accordingly.

26.4. Experimental Results

To evaluate the effectiveness of the three similarity measures, an empirical study on the newly developed multitasking benchmarks, which contains 21 multitasking sets, is presented in this section.

26.4.1. *Experiment Configuration*

To investigate the similarity between different tasks, according to [12], seven functions (i.e., "Griewank," "Rastrigin," "Ackley," "Schwefel," "Sphere," "Rosenbrock," and "Weierstrass") are used as the individual tasks to be solved. The properties of these functions are summarized in Table 26.1. Further, refer to [12], when paired for multitasking, each function is rotated by a randomly generated $D \times D$ orthogonal matrix $\mathbf{M}$, where D denotes the dimension of the function.

Next, with the seven individual functions, we develop the new multitasking benchmarks by considering all the possible combinations of the functions, which

Table 26.1: Summary of properties of the individual functions

Function	Dimension	Search Space	Global Optimum
Griewank	$D = 50$	$[-100, 100]^D$	$[0, ..., 0]^D$
Rastrigin	$D = 50$	$[-50, 50]^D$	$[0, ..., 0]^D$
Ackley	$D = 50$	$[-50, 50]^D$	$[0, ..., 0]^D$
Schwefel	$D = 50$	$[-500, 500]^D$	$[420.9687, ..., 420.9687]^D$
Sphere	$D = 50$	$[-100, 100]^D$	$[0, ..., 0]^D$
Rosenbrock	$D = 50$	$[-50, 50]^D$	$[0, ..., 0]^D$
Weierstrass	$D = 25$	$[-0.5, 0.5]^D$	$[0, ..., 0]^D$

Table 26.2: Summary of the 21 multitasking problem sets

Multitasking Sets	Task Combination	Multitasking Sets	Task Combination	Multitasking Sets	Task Combination
P1	Griewank+Rastrigin	P2	Griewank+Ackley	P3	Griewank+Schwefel
P4	Griewank+Sphere	P5	Griewank+Rosenbrock	P6	Griewank+Weierstrass
P7	Rastrigin+Ackley	P8	Rastrigin+Schwefel	P9	Rastrigin+Sphere
P10	Rastrigin+Rosenbrock	P11	Rastrigin+Weierstrass	P12	Ackley+Schwefel
P13	Ackley+Sphere	P14	Ackley+Rosenbrock	P15	Ackley+Weierstrass
P16	Schwefel+Sphere	P17	Schwefel+Rosenbrock	P18	Schwefel+Weierstrass
P19	Sphere+Rosenbrock	P20	Sphere+Weierstrass	P21	Rosenbrock+Weierstrass

are summarized in Table 26.2. To evaluate the effectiveness of the three different similarity measures between tasks, a comparison between MFEA and the single-task evolutionary algorithm (SEA), which shares the same reproduction operator with MFEA, is performed on all the developed benchmarks. The configuration of parameters and search operators are configured according to [12] for fair comparison, which are detailed below:

(1) Population size: $N = 30$.
(2) Generation for each task: $G = 500$.
(3) Evolutionary operators:

- Crossover: *Simulated binary crossover* (SBX).
- Mutation: *Polynomial mutation.*

(4) Probability in assortative mating: $rmp = 0.3$.
(5) Independent run times: $R = 20$.
(6) The number of sampled solutions in MMD, SRCC, and CDFDC: $n = 1,000,000$.
(7) The number of best solutions selected in MMD: $m = 100$.

Lastly, as the calculation of the three similarity measures is based on uniformly and independently sampled solutions in the variable space, we consider the mean value of 10 independent calculation results for MMD, SRCC, and CTFDC in this study.

26.4.2. *Experimental Results and Analysis*

Table 26.3 summarizes the performance obtained by the MFEA and SEA on the 21 newly developed multitasking sets over 20 independent runs. In the table, column "True Performance" gives the comparison obtained by MFEA over SEA, while column "Predicted Performance" gives the predicted performance of MFEA indicated by the corresponding similarity measure. In particular, "1" denotes MFEA

Table 26.3: Results of the true performance obtained by MFEA over SEA, and the predicted performance of MFEA based on task similarity, on the 21 multitasking sets

Multitasking Sets	True Performance	Predicted Performance			Multitasking Sets	True Performance	Predicted Performance		
		MMD	SRCC	CTFDC			MMD	SRCC	CTFDC
P1	1	1	1	1	P2	1	1	1	1
P3	1	−1	−1	1	P4	1	1	1	1
P5	1	1	1	1	P6	1	1	1	1
P7	1	1	1	1	P8	1	−1	−1	1
P9	1	1	1	1	P10	1	1	1	1
P11	1	1	1	1	P12	−1	−1	−1	−1
P13	1	1	1	1	P14	1	1	1	1
P15	−1	1	−1	−1	P16	1	−1	−1	1
P17	1	−1	−1	1	P18	−1	−1	−1	−1
P19	1	1	1	1	P20	1	1	1	1
P21	1	1	1	1	Error rate	–	23.8%	19.0%	0%

obtained superior performance in terms of solution quality or convergence speed over SEA on both of the tasks, while "−1" indicates the deteriorated performance is achieved by MFEA against SEA on at least one task. It can be seen from the table that on 18 out of 21 multitasking sets, MFEA achieved superior performance over the single-task SEA, which again confirms the efficacy of the evolutionary multitasking as discussed in [9]. On the other hand, we observe deteriorated performance on three multitasking sets, i.e., $P12$, $P15$, and $P18$. This highlighted the importance of the study of task relationships for enhanced evolutionary multitasking performance. As depicted in Figure 26.3, where the averaged convergence traces of six representative multitasking sets are presented, enhanced problem-solving performance can be observed on "Weierstrass" when it is paired with"Rosenbrock" in multitasking (see Figure 26.3(f)). However, the search process gets trapped in local optimum when it is solved together with another function, i.e., "Schwefel" in Figure 26.3(e).

　　　Further, the predicted performance is obtained based on the task similarity evaluated by the three similarity measures between tasks. In the following, we explain how these predictions are obtained based on the calculated task similarities, and analyze the effectiveness of each similarity measure accordingly.

26.4.2.1. Results and analysis on MMD

The results of the MMD values for the 21 multitasking sets are listed in Table 26.4. As can be observed, the MMD values are small (less than 0.3) on task pairs that have the same global optimum. However, the MMD values become larger (greater than 0.4) when the function "Schwefel" is paired in the multitasking sets. In this section, we consider tasks in the multitasking sets with MMD < 0.3 to be more

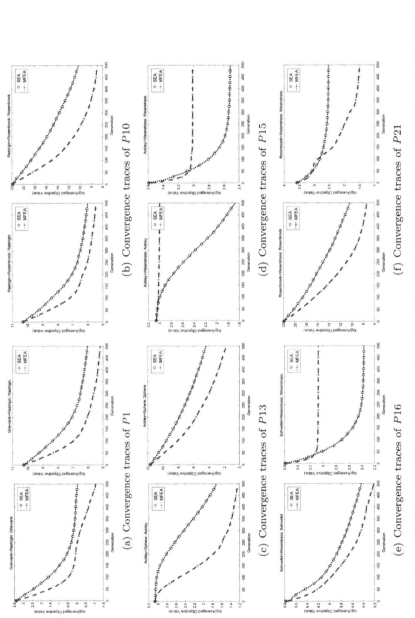

(a) Convergence traces of *P*1

(b) Convergence traces of *P*10

(c) Convergence traces of *P*13

(d) Convergence traces of *P*15

(e) Convergence traces of *P*16

(f) Convergence traces of *P*21

Figure 26.3:   Convergence traces of MFEA against SEA on 6 representative multitasking sets. *Y*-axis: Averaged fitness value in log scale; *X*-axis: Generation.

Table 26.4: The mean MMD values of 10 independent calculations on the 21 multitasking sets

Function	Griewank (T_2)	Rastrigin (T_2)	Ackley (T_2)	Schwefel (T_2)	Sphere (T_2)	Rosenbrock (T_2)	Weierstrass (T_2)
Griewank (T_1)	–	0.213	0.196	0.432	0.200	0.266	0.235
Rastrigin (T_1)	–	–	0.228	0.412	0.164	0.249	0.275
Ackley (T_1)	–	–	–	0.424	0.224	0.246	0.291
Schwefel (T_1)	–	–	–	–	0.405	0.417	0.400
Sphere (T_1)	–	–	–	–	–	0.238	0.222
Rosenbrock (T_1)	–	–	–	–	–	–	0.205
Weierstrass (T_1)	–	–	–	–	–	–	–

similar with each other and thus predict the corresponding MFEA performance as "1," otherwise, the corresponding prediction is "−1."

From Table 26.3, it can be observed that almost all multitasking sets with MMD values <0.3 have improved performance except set $P1$ (i.e., "Ackley+Weierstrass"). This confirmed the effectiveness of MMD as we discussed in Section 26.3.1 that if tasks have best solutions close to each other, enhanced problem-solving processes could be obtained via evolutionary multitasking. However, we also note that, on certain of the multitasking sets that possess MMD values greater than 0.3, improved performance has been obtained by MFEA over SEA. For example, on $P17$ that consists of functions "Schwefel" and "Rosenbrock," even though the global optimum of these two tasks are far away from each other, improved performance of MFEA has been observed on this set. On all the 21 benchmark sets, there are 5 incorrect predictions made by the MMD, and the predictions error rate is 23.8%.

In summary, although tasks sharing similar global optima can lead to enhanced search performance via multitasking, the tasks possess different global optima could also contain useful traits to help each other. Thus, only evaluating the task similarity based on best solutions is not appropriate.

26.4.2.2. Results and analysis on SRCC

Table 26.5 tabulates the results of the SRCC values for the 21 multitasking sets. According to [12], the multitasking sets are classified into three categories based on their SRCC values, i.e., *high similarity* (HS) with SRCC ≥ 0.8, *medium similarity* (MS) with $0.2 \leq$ SRCC < 0.8, and *low similarity* (LS) with SRCC < 0.2. In particular, the MFEA performance on the multitasking sets in HS and MS are predicted as "1," while the prediction on LS sets are "−1."

From the results obtained by MFEA in Table 26.3, we can observe that the predicted performance of SRCC agrees with the true performance of MFEA on all the HS and MS benchmark sets. However, on the LS benchmarks, where the

Table 26.5: The mean SRCC values of 10 independent calculations on the 21 multitasking sets

Function	Griewank (T_2)	Rastrigin (T_2)	Ackley (T_2)	Schwefel (T_2)	Sphere (T_2)	Rosenbrock (T_2)	Weierstrass (T_2)
Griewank (T_1)	–	1.000	0.222	−0.003	1.000	0.944	0.281
Rastrigin (T_1)	–	–	0.225	−0.005	1.000	0.943	0.281
Ackley (T_1)	–	–	–	0.001	0.230	0.213	0.072
Schwefel (T_1)	–	–	–	–	0.001	0.011	0.002
Sphere (T_1)	–	–	–	–	–	0.943	0.289
Rosenbrock (T_1)	–	–	–	–	–	–	0.275
Weierstrass (T_1)	–	–	–	–	–	–	–

Table 26.6: The mean CTFDC values of 10 independent calculations on the 21 multitasking sets

Function	Griewank (T_2)	Rastrigin (T_2)	Ackley (T_2)	Schwefel (T_2)	Sphere (T_2)	Rosenbrock (T_2)	Weierstrass (T_2)
Griewank (T_1)	–	0.558|0.558	0.549|0.099	0.550|0.046	0.558|0.558	0.565|0.515	0.550|0.120
Rastrigin (T_1)	–	–	0.549|0.098	0.542|0.135	0.543|0.543	0.572|0.528	0.545|0.119
Ackley (T_1)	–	–	–	0.112|0.041	0.116|0.548	0.109|0.504	0.116|0.127
Schwefel (T_1)	–	–	–	–	0.067|0.573	0.042|0.522	0.040|0.119
Sphere (T_1)	–	–	–	–	–	0.565|0.512	0.543|0.131
Rosenbrock (T_1)	–	–	–	–	–	–	0.556|0.135
Weierstrass (T_1)	–	–	–	–	–	–	–

performance is predicted as −1 by SRCC, four out of seven incorrect predictions can be observed, such as $P3$, $P8$, and $P16$. The prediction error of SRCC is thus 19%.

In summary, in contrast to the MMD measure, SRCC has a better task similarity measure between tasks; thus leading to improved prediction accuracy. However, it still cannot provide proper evaluation on the low-similarity multitasking sets.

26.4.2.3. *Results and analysis on CTFDC*

The results of the CTFDC values for the 21 multitasking sets are reported in Table 26.6. In the table, the two CTFDC values for each multitasking set represent $CTFDC_{T_1 \to T_2}$ and $CTFDC_{T_2 \to T_1}$, respectively. In this study, we consider a multitasking set consisting of similar tasks if one of the CTFDC values is greater than 0.3. Otherwise, the multitasking set is a dissimilar set. Accordingly, the predicted performance of the multitasking sets based on the CTFDC values are denoted by "1" and "−1" for the similar and dissimilar sets, respectively.

From the predicted and true performance of MFEA in Table 26.6, we can see that on all the 21 multitasking sets, the predicted performance based on CTFDC consistently agrees with the true performance. In particular, on sets such as *P3*, *P8*, and *P17*, etc., in which both the MMD and SRCC have incorrect predictions, the CTFDC provides the correct predictions.

  In summary, in contrast to MMD and SRCC, the CTFDC, which evaluates the task relationship based on the fitness landscape analysis, is able to provide a more reasonable measure of the similarity between tasks for evolutionary multitasking.

26.5. Conclusion

In this chapter, we presented a study of the similarity measures between tasks for MFEA from three different views, i.e., the distance between best solutions, the fitness rank correlation, and the fitness landscape analysis. In particular, we adopted the maximum mean discrepancy (MMD) to approximate the distance between best solutions, and Spearman's rank correlation coefficient (SRCC) to measure the fitness rank correlation as used in [12], and proposed a variant of fitness distance correlation (FDC) called cross-task FDC (CTFDC) to analyze the fitness landscape similarity across tasks. Moreover, to evaluate the effectiveness of the three similarity measures for MFEA, we developed 21 new multitasking benchmarks. The experimental results showed that the CTFDC-based similarity measure is more appropriate to be used as the similarity measure between tasks for evolutionary multitasking.

  For future works, we would like to test the CTFDC-based similarity measure on more different function pairs and conduct more comprehensive studies to explore how the CTFDC value is related to the performance of MFEA. Further, the similarity measures can also be used in the adaptive evolutionary multitasking algorithm design, which is able to adaptively select the tasks for multitasking toward enhanced problem-solving performance.

References

[1] Y. C. Lin, F. S. Wang, and K. S. Hwang, A hybrid method of evolutionary algorithms for mixed-integer nonlinear optimization problems. In *Proceedings of the 1999 IEEE Congress on Evolutionary Computation (CEC)*, vol. 3, pp. 2159–2166 (1999).
[2] O. Bräysy, W. Dullaert, and M. Gendreau, Evolutionary algorithms for the vehicle routing problem with time windows, *J. Heuristics*, **10**(6), 587–611 (2004).
[3] X. Yu and M. Gen, *Introduction to Evolutionary Algorithms* (Springer Science & Business Media, 2010).
[4] B. M. Baker and M. Ayechew, A genetic algorithm for the vehicle routing problem, *Comput. Oper. Res.*, **30**(5), 787–800 (2003).
[5] C. Prins, A simple and effective evolutionary algorithm for the vehicle routing problem, *Comput. Oper. Res.*, **31**(12), 1985–2002 (2004).
[6] L. Iuspa, F. Scaramuzzino, and P. Petrenga, Optimal design of an aircraft engine mount via bit-masking oriented genetic algorithms, *Adv. Eng. Software*, **34**(11–12), 707–720 (2003).
[7] Y. Wang, J. Wang, and H. Kang, Application of the genetic algorithm in image processing. In *Information, Computer and Application Engineering: Proceedings of the International*

Conference on Information Technology and Computer Application Engineering (ITCAE 2014), Hong Kong, China, 10–11 December 2014, p. 7. CRC Press (2015).

[8] M. Paulinas and A. Ušinskas, A survey of genetic algorithms applications for image enhancement and segmentation, *Inf. Technol. Control*, **36**(3) (2007).

[9] A. Gupta, Y. S. Ong, and L. Feng, Multifactorial evolution: toward evolutionary multitasking, *IEEE Trans. Evol. Comput.*, **20**(3), 343–357 (2016).

[10] A. Gupta, J. Mańdziuk, and Y. S. Ong, Evolutionary multitasking in bi-level optimization, *Complex Intell. Syst.*, **1**(1–4), 83–95 (2015).

[11] L. Zhou, L. Feng, J. Zhong, Y. S. Ong, Z. Zhu, and E. Sha, Evolutionary multitasking in combinatorial search spaces: a case study in capacitated vehicle routing problem. In *2016 IEEE Symposium Series on Computational Intelligence (SSCI)*, pp. 1–8 (2016).

[12] B. Da, Y. S. Ong, L. Feng, et al., Evolutionary multitasking for single-objective continuous optimization: benchmark problems, performance metric, and baseline results, *arXiv preprint arXiv:1706.03470* (2017).

[13] A. Gupta, Y. S. Ong, et al., Landscape synergy in evolutionary multitasking. In *2016 IEEE Congress on Evolutionary Computation (CEC)*, pp. 3076–3083 (2016).

[14] S. Bandaru, A. H. Ng, and K. Deb, Data mining methods for knowledge discovery in multi-objective optimization: part a — survey, *Expert Syst. Appl.*, **70**, 139–159 (2017).

[15] Y. Zhang and D. Y. Yeung, A regularization approach to learning task relationships in multitask learning, *ACM Trans. Knowl. Discovery Data*, **8**(3), 12 (2014).

[16] S. J. Pan, I. W. Tsang, et al., Domain adaptation via transfer component analysis, *IEEE Trans. Neural Networks*, **22**(2), 199–210 (2011).

[17] J. Ding, C. Yang, Y. Jin, and T. Chai, Generalized multitasking for evolutionary optimization of expensive problems, *IEEE Trans. Evol. Comput.*, **23**(1), 44–58 (2017).

[18] C. Yang, J. Ding, K. C. Tan, and Y. Jin, Two-stage assortative mating for multiobjective multifactorial evolutionary optimization. In *2017 IEEE 56th Annual Conference on Decision and Control (CDC)*, pp. 76–81 (2017).

[19] Z. Liang, H. Dong, C. Liu, W. Liang, and Z. Zhu, Evolutionary multitasking for multiobjective optimization with subspace alignment and adaptive differential evolution, *IEEE Trans. Cybern.* (2020). doi: 10.1109/TCYB.2020.2980888.

[20] Z. Tang, M. Gong, Y. Wu, W. Liu, and Y. Xie, Regularized evolutionary multi-task optimization: learning to intertask transfer in aligned subspace, *IEEE Trans. Evol. Comput.*, **25**(2), 262–276 (2020).

[21] Y. W. Wen and C. K. Ting, Parting ways and reallocating resources in evolutionary multitasking. In *2017 IEEE Congress on Evolutionary Computation (CEC)*, pp. 2404–2411 (2017).

[22] M. Gong, Z. Tang, H. Li, and J. Zhang, Evolutionary multitasking with dynamic resource allocating strategy, *IEEE Trans. Evol. Comput.*, **23**(5), 858–869 (2019).

[23] K. K. Bali, Y. S. Ong, A. Gupta, and P. S. Tan, Multifactorial evolutionary algorithm with online transfer parameter estimation: MFEA-II, *IEEE Trans. Evol. Comput.*, **24**(1), 69–83 (2019).

[24] L. Feng, W. Zhou, L. Zhou, S. Jiang, J. Zhong, B. Da, Z. Zhu, and Y. Wang, An empirical study of multifactorial PSO and multifactorial DE. In *2017 IEEE Congress on Evolutionary Computation (CEC)*, pp. 921–928 (2017).

[25] A. Gupta, Y. S. Ong, L. Feng, and K. C. Tan, Multiobjective multifactorial optimization in evolutionary multitasking, *IEEE Trans. Cybern.*, **47**(7), 1652–1665 (2016).

[26] R. T. Liaw and C. K. Ting, Evolutionary many-tasking based on biocoenosis through symbiosis: a framework and benchmark problems. In *2017 IEEE Congress on Evolutionary Computation (CEC)*, pp. 2266–2273 (2017).

[27] J. Tang, Y. Chen, Z. Deng, Y. Xiang, and C. P. Joy, A group-based approach to improve multifactorial evolutionary algorithm. In *IJCAI*, pp. 3870–3876 (2018).

[28] Y. Chen, J. Zhong, L. Feng, and J. Zhang, An adaptive archive-based evolutionary framework for many-task optimization, *IEEE Trans. Emerging Top. Comput. Intell.*, **4**(3), 369–384 (2019).

[29] L. Feng, L. Zhou, J. Zhong, A. Gupta, Y. S. Ong, K. C. Tan, and A. K. Qin, Evolutionary multitasking via explicit autoencoding, *IEEE Trans. Cybern.*, **49**(9), 3457–3470 (2018).

[30] B. Zhang, Training deep neural networks via multi-task optimisation. PhD thesis, Swinburne University of Technology Melbourne, Australia (2020).

[31] M. Dash and H. Liu, Feature selection for classification, *Intell. Data Anal.*, **1**(3), 131–156 (1997).

[32] L. Zhou, L. Feng, J. Zhong, Y. S. Ong, Z. Zhu, and E. Sha, Evolutionary multitasking in combinatorial search spaces: a case study in capacitated vehicle routing problem. In *2016 IEEE Symposium Series on Computational Intelligence (SSCI)*, pp. 1–8. IEEE (2016).

[33] K. K. Bali, A. Gupta, Y. S. Ong, and P. S. Tan, Cognizant multitasking in multiobjective multifactorial evolution: MO-MFEA-II, *IEEE Trans. Cybern.*, **51**(4), 1784–1796 (2020).

[34] A. Gupta, Y. S. Ong, L. Feng, and K. C. Tan, Multiobjective multifactorial optimization in evolutionary multitasking, *IEEE Trans. Cybern.*, **47**(7), 1652–1665 (2016).

[35] C. Yang, J. Ding, Y. Jin, C. Wang, and T. Chai, Multitasking multiobjective evolutionary operational indices optimization of beneficiation processes, *IEEE Trans. Autom. Sci. Eng.*, **16**(3), 1046–1057 (2018).

[36] E. Pitzer and M. Affenzeller, A comprehensive survey on fitness landscape analysis. In *Recent Advances in Intelligent Engineering Systems*, pp. 161–191, Springer (2012).

[37] T. Jones and S. Forrest, Fitness distance correlation as a measure of problem difficulty for genetic algorithms. In *International Conference on Genetic Algorithms*, pp. 184–192 (1995).

Index